UNDERSTANDING INTERRELIGIOUS RELATIONS

UNDERSTANDING INTERRELIGIOUS RELATIONS

EDITED BY

David Cheetham, Douglas Pratt,
and David Thomas

OXFORD
UNIVERSITY PRESS

OXFORD

UNIVERSITY PRESS

Great Clarendon Street, Oxford, OX2 6DP,
United Kingdom

Oxford University Press is a department of the University of Oxford.
It furthers the University's objective of excellence in research, scholarship,
and education by publishing worldwide. Oxford is a registered trade mark of
Oxford University Press in the UK and in certain other countries

First Edition published in 2013

Impression: 1

Published in the United States of America by Oxford University Press
198 Madison Avenue, New York, NY 10016, United States of America

British Library Cataloguing in Publication Data
Data available

Library of Congress Control Number: 2013938320

ISBN 978–0–19–964584–8 (hbk.)
978–0–19–964585–5 (pbk.)

As printed and bound by
CPI Group (UK) Ltd, Croydon, CR0 4YY

CONTENTS

LIST OF CONTRIBUTORS

Nicholas Adams is a lecturer in the School of Divinity, University of Edinburgh, UK

Mario I. Aguilar is Professor of Divinity and Director, Centre for the Study of Religion and Politics, University of St Andrews, UK

David Cheetham is a Senior Lecturer in the School of Philosophy, Theology and Religion, University of Birmingham, UK

Catherine Cornille is Professor of Comparative Theology at Boston College, Massachusetts, USA

Anna Halafoff is a Research Fellow at the Centre for Citizenship and Globalisation, Deakin University, Victoria, Australia

Elizabeth J. Harris is an Associate Professor in the Department of Theology, Philosophy and Religious Studies, Liverpool Hope University, UK

Ed Kessler MBE is the Founder Director, Woolf Institute, Cambridge and Fellow of St Edmunds College, Cambridge University, UK

Jeffery D. Long is Professor of Religion and Asian Studies, Elizabethtown College, Pennsylvania, USA

Marianne Moyaert is Professor of Comparative Theology and Interreligious Dialogue at the Free University of Amsterdam, and is concurrently a postdoctoral researcher in the Faculty of Theology, Catholic University of Leuven, Belgium

Peter C. Phan holds the Ignacio Ellacuria Chair of Catholic Social Thought, Theology Department, Georgetown University, Washington, DC, USA

Douglas Pratt is Professor of Religious Studies at the University of Waikato, New Zealand, and is Adjunct Professor of Theology and Interreligious Studies at the University of Bern, Switzerland

Perry Schmidt-Leukel is Professor of Religious Studies and Intercultural Theology at the University of Münster, Germany

Jonathan Y. Tan is a Senior Lecturer in the School of Theology, Australian Catholic University, Sydney NSW, Australia

David Thomas is Professor of Christianity and Islam and Nadir Dinshaw Professor of Inter Religious Relations, University of Birmingham, UK

David R. Vishanoff is an Associate Professor in the Religious Studies Program of the University of Oklahoma, Oklahoma, USA

Paul Weller is Professor of Inter-Religious Relations, University of Derby, and Visiting Fellow in the Oxford Centre for Christianity and Culture, Regent's Park College, University of Oxford, UK

Andrew Wingate OBE is a consultant, teacher, and theologian in interfaith relations, and was the founding Director of the St Philip's Centre, Leicester, UK

CHAPTER 1

Introduction

DAVID CHEETHAM, DOUGLAS PRATT,
AND DAVID THOMAS

The ways in which religious communities interact with one another, both historically and in the contemporary world, is now a major focus of scholarly research and teaching. Issues of interfaith engagement, inclusive of interreligious dialogue more specifically, and interreligious (or interfaith) relations more generally, together with issues pertaining to intra-religious engagement, attract widespread interest and concern among scholars and other specialists in religion, as well as also many others who have regard for the role of religion in today's world.[1] The focus of this book is very much on understanding the relations that obtain between religions. Within this field, dialogue is one area of relational engagement, so too conversion, the dynamics obtaining between majority and minority religious groups, the issue of belonging to more than one religion or faith tradition, cooperation, religion in the public domain, and the task of peace-building, to name but a few. And underlying all such issues is the question of how religions perceive, and so relate to, their 'others'. In a religiously plural world, how different religious communities get along with one another is not just an academic question; it is very much a focus of socio-political and wider community attention. The study of religions and religion in the twenty-first-century world must necessarily take account of relations *within* and *between* religions, whether this is approached from a theological, historical, political, or any other disciplinary perspective. Indeed, the increasing popularity of religious and

---

[1] Very often 'dialogue' and 'relations' terminologies are used interchangeably as if they are synonymous. So, too, variations on the 'between religions' (inter) terminology—as in compound (interreligious; interfaith), or hyphenated (inter-religious; inter-faith), or in some case paired (inter religious; inter faith). In this book we will mostly incline to the compound variants on the grounds that the sense of 'between' mostly refers to a general and wide range of conjunction. This orientation notwithstanding, for emphasis or where there is a focus on the point at which two or more religions meet, then hyphenated variants of the core terminology may be used. We disincline to the use of paired terms. Furthermore, the terms 'religion' and 'faith' name a multifaceted category of phenomena in each case and are not quite the same thing—on the one hand 'religion' is more a formal structure of ideas, behaviour, and texts; on the other 'faith' suggests a relatively amorphous sense of orientation, or broad system of ideas, identities, and values. This distinction is open to argument and finesse; for the most part we assume it is at least valid.

theological studies is symptomatic of this new awareness. And increasingly through the media the wider public is being exposed to issues and events that involve the interaction of one religion or religious community with another.

Interest in interreligious relations is undoubtedly growing, and so the aim of this volume is to provide a reference work of relevance to students and scholars, as well as to a wider public. It comprises two main parts. The first provides an introduction to, and expositions and critical discussions of, the ways in which 'the other' has been construed, addressed, and related to, in the major religious traditions. The second provides analyses of select key issues and debates in which interreligious relations are seen to be an integral constituent. It has thus been the intention of the editors to assemble an authoritative and scholarly work that discusses perspectives on the religious 'other', and on interreligious relations, that are typical of the different religious traditions; and to elicit substantial original chapters from a cross-section of emerging and established scholars on main debates and issues in the wider field of interreligious relations.

As has been often said, ours is an age of increased global religious diversity. Of course, in some parts of the world religious plurality has been the order of the day since time immemorial; in such situations, people have long been used to relating positively and pragmatically to their neighbours of other faiths. Interfaith harmony has had a long-standing pedigree. But equally clashes between religions, or religious groups, have also ebbed and flowed throughout human history, and in our day religion presents as a very pressing issue globally as well as regionally and locally—as seen in evidence of rising mutual anxieties if not outright antipathies between communities of Christians and Muslims. Contemporary flash-points of communal conflict with significant interreligious components are many and include such diverse settings as Thailand, Pakistan, Afghanistan, Syria, and Myanmar. And religions other than Islam and Christianity are also involved. In respect to many socio-political and cultural situations today, religion has a tendency to make things worse even as it can be a force to make things better. Ameliorating what makes things worse, and promoting whatever makes things better, is a challenge and task that not only confronts the religions and their leaders but also impacts upon, and is increasingly taken up by, governments that previously, from a secularist position, had resiled from even admitting religion within the body politic.

Interreligious dialogue and relations are not just warm fuzzy liberal sentiments; they constitute critical dimensions of inter-communal and international social realities and are increasingly—despite much obstinate avoidance by some religious folk, especially within Western secular societies—a necessary response to the widespread presence of diverse religions. More and more, local communities are religiously heterogeneous. And where this is a comparatively new phenomenon, a shift in perception and attitude must inevitably occur—either in the direction of openness towards, even empathetic interest in, the religious other; or else a withdrawal into an increasingly closed-off religious identity, often equated with fundamentalism and exclusivism, which at best politely tolerates, in practice simply ignores, and at worst actively abhors the religious other. In our day the extremists of one religion may—and at times very obviously do—reject outright the presence and validity of another religion, even variants of their own, as is amply demonstrated by some Islamic extremist groups in Nigeria, Pakistan, Afghanistan, and elsewhere.

Religious communities and scholars of religion engage with contemporary issues of inter-religious relations on many fronts and at many levels. Broadly speaking, the shift from regarding religions as objectively other, either the focus of scholarly investigation or the target of religious proselytization, was seeded in the late nineteenth century and came to flower during the twentieth. If the 1893 Parliament of World Religions in Chicago gives a definite date to the commencement of contemporary development in interreligious relations that contrasts with anything preceding, it was the shift within Christianity—which was then the world's predominant missionary religion—during the course of the twentieth century which gave rise not only to the phenomenon of interreligious dialogue but also to a radical rethink of that religion's stance towards the religious other that effectively brought interreligious relations out from the shadows. And those religions to which Christianity reached out a hand of dialogical détente, whilst varyingly cautious, and for good reason, for the most part responded in kind. The now virtually normalized situation of religious leaders, as well as interreligious enthusiasts, engaging in polite and friendly communications, sharing events, and even making common cause, is quite widespread.

At the same time, two consequential phenomena are now clearly present. On the one hand the situation of interreligious engagement of various sorts implies, requires, and can sometimes directly stimulate intra-religious dialogue. People within a religious tradition or family need to—and must—talk and relate among themselves about many things, but especially about what it means to be who they are within a religiously plural context. And it is happening. It is not only the Christian religion that has formalized this process in and through its ecumenical movement. Most world religions have today some form of world wide representative organization and gathering opportunity. And within many societies the emergence of awareness of the world religions as distinct spiritual and cultural traditions, and the consequent realization of the problems of relationship between them, have come to the fore. Arguably the pressing issue to arise out of a context of religious plurality is that of acknowledging 'the other' and the emergence of dialogue as a modality of relating to the other, both among internal variants (intra-religious dialogue) and between religions (interreligious dialogue). A number of scholars have identified and discussed allied issues and problems and have analysed and discussed prevailing current paradigms of understanding, commenting on their usefulness and limitations. This present volume reflects and dips into this heritage.

Our authors have brought to bear their unique and varied scholarly acumen to address the central question of 'otherness' in Part I, and the range of issues included in Part II. A multi-authored work inevitably reflects the different styles, expertise, and approaches of the authors involved. The editors have aimed for a measure of consistency and compatibility, but have not insisted that chapters, especially in Part I, are so blended that they are mirror images of each other. Indeed, such an approach would have resulted in an artificial imposition of similarity and sameness. The religions addressed in Part I have clearly different histories, approaches, and ways of thinking, doing, and being, and this is appropriately reflected by the different authorial treatment of them. Of course, not all religions are mentioned or attract the focus that some readers might have expected. In part this is simply a reflection of the limitations of space, as is the matter of the selection of issues in Part II. And their treatment reflects both the uniqueness of the respective subject matter and the rich diversity of academic perspective, expertise, and style of the authors. Indeed, it is these different authorial styles that provide the reader with varying examples of how the subject matter may be legitimately dealt with. Whilst attempting to be comprehensive and relevant, as well as focused on the key problematic of religions and their religious others, one book cannot hope to cover everything in this burgeoning field—each of our chapters could itself expand into a book! Rather it is the hope of the editors that this volume provides a substantial introduction and orientation to critical issues and perspectives pertaining to the quest to understand interreligious relations in the modern world.

Part I, following the introductory essay that provides a detailed rationale and introduction to the theme of religion and the religious other (Chapter 2), addresses this theme through the lenses of Hinduism, Buddhism, Christianity, and Islam which comprise the four major contemporary world religions, or religious 'sets' each with its own internal diversities; to which is added Judaism because of its significance in relation to Christianity and Islam and its place within current geo-political and interreligious contexts. All five religions register as having global impact, and feature prominently within contexts of interreligious engagement and allied discourse. Jeffery Long's broad survey of the vast spectrum of Hindu attitudes towards otherness (Chapter 3) reveals the luxuriant result of centuries of engagement and cross-fertilization of different traditions. He asks if Hinduism is identical with Brahmanism but suggests that this would be an unwarranted restriction of what is really 'a progressive universalism that aspires to include all otherness in a boundless unity'. When seeking to articulate Hindu identity, Long quotes an evocative image of an upside-down fig tree found in the fifteenth chapter of the *Bhagavad Gita*. He gives an account of a range of attitudes towards religious otherness that have occurred historically or exist simultaneously in the contemporary period: hatred and fear, philosophical engagement, generous inclusion, and an overarching homogeneity. He also contrasts the broad philosophical hospitality in Hindu thought (towards the wideness of religious expression and belief) with the cultural exclusivity that characterizes Indian society. These two 'trajectories'—exclusivist nationalism (for example, contemporary Hindutva) and inclusivist universalism—are held in tension. Despite the seeming contradiction between these two, Long proposes a causal relationship between them. Such is the ancient and enormous complexity of the Hindu traditions that the problem becomes one of identifying what constitutes otherness *per se*—what is *outside* of Hinduism in Indian culture? This is brought out by Long's telling quote from Sarvepalli Radhakrishnan who claimed that Hinduism 'is not a religion, but religion itself in its most universal and deepest significance'. Whilst Long eschews hasty assimilations between this universal perspective and modern liberal views in the West, we might observe that a perennial paradox of 'open' faith positions is that, while advocating a broad inclusiveness which seeks to embrace the varieties of religious expression, they also smother those same varieties.

Edward Kessler's review of Jewish approaches in Chapter 4 reminds us that the discourse of interreligious encounter is not just a philosophical or systematic concern. Kessler's starting point is geography and covenant. Religious others are understood in terms of their relationship to the land and by divine accommodation. Thus, there is a 'Jewish covenantal pluralism', where all people are described as being in relationship with God in different forms. When surveying the key aspects of Jewish relations with others, many of Kessler's items look like a familiar itinerary of notorious twentieth-century moments: the Holocaust; the Israeli–Palestinian conflict; tensions between Jew and Muslim. He also draws attention to the profound influence of Jewish thinkers such as Martin Buber and Emmanuel Levinas on twentieth-century thinking about 'the other'. Buber's influence extends far beyond the Jewish context, his 'I–Thou' construct becoming virtually a staple in the discussion about the meeting of people and faiths. Most distinctive have been his insights into the personal dimension of encounter, apart from the impersonal exchanges between 'religions' as institutions or bodies of systematic thought and practice (the *I–It*). That is, the meeting of *I–Thou* is a meeting of religious *people*, and this basic insight has had an important impact on subsequent thinking about how religions meet—less as institutions or doctrines; rather more as individual believers. Additionally, in terms of acute self-consciousness about the presence of otherness, the influence of Levinas cannot be underestimated: in the wake of the Holocaust the power of his voice is a forceful presence that has articulated an intense and uncompromising view of 'the other'. For Kessler, the other needs to be heard, and in a perceptive observation on Jewish thinking he makes the significant claim that a sympathetic relationship with the other should be seen as an indicator concerning a *legitimate* relationship with God.

In Chapter 5 Elizabeth Harris highlights the different aspects of Buddhist encounters with the religious other. Historically, much of this involved polemical engagement and contestation with Brahmanical philosophers following the Buddha's death. In some cases, Harris documents the ridiculing of the fallacies in other faiths (such as the belief in God or the soul). There is also an inclusivist stream in Buddhism that, typically, seeks to bring those others into the schema of the Buddhist tradition and/or appropriate the practices of those others. Because Buddhism emphasizes non-attachment to doctrine or the craving after absolutes, this allows attentiveness to efficacies in other practices which could be affirmed as provisional aids for spiritual progress, in accordance with the assumption that the Buddha's teaching is the key to ultimate liberation. Harris sums up her study of Buddhist attitudes towards the religious other by discerning a tension between the openness to effective practice in other religions and the desire to promote Buddhist teachings as superior. Indeed, both exclusivist and inclusivist teaching may be found in Buddhist texts. This is a vitally important observation that characterizes many inclusivist approaches that are illustrated in different contexts in the chapters of Part I.

Perry Schmidt-Leukel's extensive documentation of the relations between Christians and the religious other (Chapter 6) shows very clearly the sheer wealth of critical theological reflection that has been undertaken within a variety of Christian traditions about the religious other. Certainly, the great majority of the literature that addresses the issue of the religious other comes from Christian writers. This may suggest that concern about the presence of the religious other is something that is understood to have crucial implications for the claims of Christianity. Perhaps the stakes may not be so high in traditions that do not place such a great emphasis on the essential importance of particular revelation. In his comprehensive engagement with Christian postures towards otherness, Schmidt-Leukel considers the options presented by the classic typology in the theology of religions: exclusivism, inclusivism, and pluralism. In this and in other writings he is sceptical about the ability to be able to break free from this typology because he argues that the question it raises (what is the truth-relationship between the religions?) is unavoidable. Schmidt-Leukel advocates a pluralist model and argues that it is most able to promote a 'mutual fertilization' between religions. The future of Christianity is therefore caught up into a vision for the future of religion in general: an 'overarching human community' where the different religions are complementary.

Finally in Part I, David Thomas's account of Muslim approaches to the religious other (Chapter 7) tackles the canonical question about legitimate sources of authority. The canon is clear: the Qur'an and the Prophet are at the heart of Islam and steer the attitude of Muslims towards the religious other. He observes that no 'innovations' that are not directly connected to them can hope to achieve widespread acceptance. Nevertheless, as Thomas presents the Qur'anic and other material it becomes clear that there are both positive and negative attitudes in evidence. Early engagement with other faiths either evinces an ambivalent attitude towards them, or else other faiths are viewed as in some way simply 'deficient'. But this latter perspective is not a superior posture in any simplistic sense. This is clarified by a unique feature of Islam: it does not present itself as a faith that has been instituted *ex nihilo*. In this sense it enjoys a real, ontological continuity with the earlier Abrahamic traditions of Judaism and Christianity. Thus Thomas shows that, for al-Faruqi for instance, Islam is a 'reaffirmation' of the revelations contained in those two faiths. He also alerts us to the more open approaches evidenced in some Islamic thinking. For example, there is Mohammad Arkoun's idea of the complementary nature of religions, and also the recognition of an 'innate *religio naturalis*'. Nevertheless, notwithstanding such openness, Thomas points out that for Islam other faiths are measured according to their resemblance to, and affirmation of, the principle of *tawhid*. And this is a typically inclusivist strategy of recognizing one's own theology in the other.

The focus of Part I is thus very much on the main religious traditions which have not only a history of interreligious engagement of one sort or another, but also a substantial body of reflective and critical intellectual work addressing this very engagement. Other and more recent religions may give evidence of having joined the interfaith arena in recent times, perhaps even earlier, but have not yet produced a body of their own particular literature which can be referenced and quarried in respect of the aims of this book. This largely accounts for the exclusion of other religions or religious sects—such as Sikhism, Mormonism, and Baha'ism on the one hand, and Chinese religions on the other. However, such religions will not be ignored entirely; rather, their place may be found within the context of topics discussed in Part II.

The chapters of Part II comprise a series of substantial essays concerned with broad themes connected to interreligious relations. Focusing on examples from India and modern-day multi-religious England, and illustrated with anecdote and personal reminiscences, Chapter 8, by Andrew Wingate, traverses issues and examples pertaining to the vexed issue of conversion from one religion to another. Wingate delves into the twists and turns of conversion as a complex phenomenon that applies not just to individuals—as in the contemporary uncritical notion that religious identity is simply, and at best, a matter of individual 'choice'—but also families and whole communities, either in contexts of wholesale transfer or reorientation of religious identity and allegiance, or more widely in the problematic, even negative, response when an individual's new choice impacts upon the social group to which he or she belongs or, in some cases, formerly belonged. It is a commonplace that converts are most often highly enthusiastic about their new-found faith, or their changed identity, and are at times hostile to any relationship between their new religion and the one they have left; indeed they can embody a reactionary rejection of it, a stance that lends support to those hostile to interreligious détente of any sort. Alternatively, persons who have taken on a new or reoriented religious identity can at times be well placed as mediators between their new and their former religious communities. Conversion can have either a negative or a positive impact upon interreligious relations; as the saying goes, it all depends.

Marianne Moyaert's Chapter 9 gives an overview of the historical development of the contemporary phenomenon of interreligious dialogue. The significance of dialogue in the field of interreligious encounter is highlighted; it is very much a 'new' thing we are here dealing with. And this dialogue is no simple or unitary matter. Moyaert takes us into the meaning and dynamics of dialogue, discussing it from various perspectives and tackling a range of critical questions. Interreligious dialogue is engaged for a variety of reasons and within a multitude of contexts. Curiosity about an unknown 'other', a desire to learn about the other, to engage experientially as well as intellectually, and contexts of seeking collaboration for pragmatic purposes are among the rationales driving interreligious encounters and relations and so sparking various forms of intentional 'dialogue'. Critically, interreligious dialogue seeks at best to go beyond mere tolerance of a religious other and furthermore to challenge the appearance that negative perspectives and allied behaviours of intolerance, exclusion, and even religious violence are naturally predominant.

Chapter 10, by Peter Phan and Jonathan Tan, examines interreligious dynamics pertaining to relations between majority and minority groups. Beginning with a lively example of a Christian–Muslim encounter in the United States and opening up into an exploration of power relations, the authors traverse a number of key issues and problems, concluding with a ten-point proposal for shaping and promoting positive interreligious encounters between majority and minority communities beyond toleration *simpliciter*. They argue that toleration merely accentuates the domination of a majority group over minority groups; that is to say, the majority group has the power to control minority groups by either extending toleration or withholding toleration without any recourse by the minority groups. Of course, moving from reluctant tolerance to mutual trust is often easier said than done. Interreligious dialogue in the context of majority–minority relations is a uniquely delicate affair.

Douglas Pratt's Chapter 11 takes up the problematic and interconnected set of fundamentalism, exclusivism, and religious extremism on the basis that interreligious understanding needs to deal with the dark side of religion and *inter alia* the negative dimensions of interreligious encounters. Together and independently, fundamentalism, exclusivism, and extremism impact either directly or indirectly upon interreligious engagement. Whilst the term 'fundamentalism' arose in a uniquely Christian context, and even though the term does not always sit well in the various religious contexts to which it is often applied, its widespread use in contemporary discourse makes both it and the phenomenon to which it refers of great import and interest. Exclusivism names a predominant attitude and set of values descriptive of the history of much interreligious encounter. Religions, for the most part, have been mutually exclusive. Some still are; and many contain an exclusive element or tendency despite at the same time advocating positive interfaith relations. And both fundamentalism and exclusivism are at times directly linked to religious extremism. The nature of that link is explored by way of a typological paradigm that demonstrates a sequential and cumulative ideological development which highlights the nature of the link between religious fundamentalism and extremism.

The prospect of interfaith peace-building as the response to contexts of conflict in interreligious encounter is the subject of Chapter 12 by Anna Halafoff. Although many encounters between faiths can be constructive and dialogical, a large proportion is dissonant. Conflict comes in many forms: theological, political, cultural, militant, and so on. Grounded in empirical research, this chapter examines commitment of the interfaith movement to peace-building activities in order to illustrate that religions have long played, and continue to play, a role in conflict transformation. Acknowledging the challenge religion has posed to Enlightenment predictions of the decline of religious allegiance and influence in favour of the rise of a fully secular society, the chapter shows how the interfaith movement and its conflict-resolution and peace-building initiatives have expanded in Western societies as diverse cultural and religious groups have strengthened their social participation. The author concludes that despite, *and* ironically at times as a result of, the capacity of religions to incite both structural and direct violence, in fact religions have often played a peace-building role, and this is evidenced today by the increase in interfaith encounters and activities.

Chapter 13, by Nicholas Adams, explores interreligious engagement in the public sphere. One of the most pressing issues for multicultural societies is the negotiation of relations between religions in terms of their influence on, and interaction with, the state. What is the public voice of multiple religions in such societies? What kinds of dialogue or conflict between religions emerge in the context of the 'public square' and do such issues have an influence on the organization of societies and their governance? The author addresses eight challenges that face interreligious engagement in the public sphere. These include the interaction of religion, ethics, and politics, the matter of agenda appropriateness and of framing procedural and substantive issues, the relation between learning about religious life and the practical action that is required in the public sphere, whether in fact the goal of public engagement is to maximize agreement between parties, and the tension between a conception of service by a particular religious tradition to wider society as it stands and a conception of transforming that wider society and conforming it to the vision of a particular religious tradition.

Mario Aguilar's Chapter 14 examines the interconnections of dialogue, liberation, and justice. Liberation is an important theme within interreligious relations. However, it has many different dimensions and contexts. Religion can be utilized as an instrument of oppression as well as a source of freedom and tool of justice where liberation yields a common cause for interreligious cooperation. The author suggests that, for the twenty-first century, interreligious dialogue needs to focus on motifs of common humanity, including non-theistic traditions such as Buddhism, humanism, and atheism; common liberation of human beings from that which prevents full personal and communal dignity; and justice as a central component of all world religions which also connects religions with secular states that foster justice for all their members. The creation of just or unjust structures within a society is the responsibility of both the religious traditions and the non-religious communities. Aguilar engages, in effect, two case studies to address interreligious dialogue, liberation and justice. The first involves paying close attention to the teachings of the Roman Catholic Church's Second Vatican Council (1962–5) pertinent to dialogue, and with a focus on issues of conscience and human dignity. Attention then turns to dialogue for liberation, and the quest for justice, through the lens of Christian (Catholic) engagement with Buddhism. Thus through a twofold case study—developments in Roman Catholic Christian thought on the one hand, and Christian–Buddhist dialogical relationships on the other—the author argues that religions for the most part display a preference for justice, and this provides both a basis for fruitful dialogical interaction and a mandate for collaborative acts of liberation.

Chapter 15, by Catherine Cornille, explores the comparatively recent phenomenon of multiple religious belonging as both a by-product and a unique extension of interreligious dialogue. Indeed, multiple belonging has at times been regarded as a condition for interreligious dialogue truly to take place. And not all religious identities are clearly definable or distinct. Especially in the East, the notion of 'belonging' to more than one tradition is commonplace. Moreover, some key figures such as Aloysius Pieris (Christian-Buddhist) or Bede Griffiths (Christian-Hindu) have defined themselves in such terms. Profound dialogue with other religious traditions often leads to identification with some of their teachings and/or practices, and thus to some form of multiple belonging on the part of the dialogically engaged individual. The author offers a typology of multiple religious belonging and reflects on the relative import of such belonging for interreligious dialogue. Interreligious dialogue has been an area in which the boundaries of belonging have at times been challenged and stretched. Dialogue raises the question of the extent to which one may legitimately identify with elements from another religion and integrate those elements in to one's own tradition while still fully belonging to it.

Chapter 16 addresses the issue of boundaries and encounters. David Vishanoff asks if religious traditions should be considered as separate entities, each with clear doctrinal, communal, historical, and textual boundaries. Or might examples from the history of religions reveal more porous boundaries and mutual exchange in terms of cross-fertilization of beliefs, traditions, and even scriptures? The notion of interreligious encounter presupposes the existence of a boundary across which interaction takes place. Vishanoff explores why religions are so distinct from each other that interactions between their adherents constitute encounters, with all the sense of strangeness, adventure, and even danger that this evokes. Where there are boundaries, interactions become encounters. The chapter sets out to draw together various insights and case studies into a systematic account of this widespread though frequently elusive religious phenomenon, and raises salient questions pertaining to scholarly engagement with the topic.

The penultimate chapter, by Paul Weller, engages the subject of interreligious cooperation. In the context of a historical background and a discussion of select case studies, the author explores a range of questions and issues including the role and place of confidence-building; the question of who cooperates with whom and on what basis; and the possibilities and limitations connected with different organizational and structural forms for cooperation. The question of who initiates interreligious cooperation from within, across or beyond particular religions is also discussed, along with the range of aims and goals of such cooperation and the advantages and disadvantages of different forms of cooperation, together with the differences between interreligious cooperation organizations as such and initiatives set up for particular temporary purposes.

At the conclusion of a five-year 'Religion and Society' project undertaken in the UK, the director, Professor Linda Woodhead, offered an astute observation on the variable receptivity in academia to religion and its study: some hostilely reject it; others evince openness and appreciation.[2] And where a profound secular attitude predominates, 'it is not just that religion gets caricatured and demonised. It's that it gets left out of the picture altogether.' Of this dismissive secularism Woodhead comments: 'It's a crazily narrow-minded approach, which has to turn a blind eye to the luxuriantly variegated religiosity of most of the world, and ignore the past, including our own.' Yet secularity primarily means the allowance for, and affirmation of, diversity, including the presence of religion and, indeed, of religious diversity. A secular society as such need not be opposed to, or dismissive of, the presence of religion and religions. Religion today is richly diverse, ubiquitous, and persistent. The religious 'other' is also

---

[2] 'Restoring religion to the public square', *The Tablet*, 28 January 2012, 6–7.

today the religious neighbour. Yet fear of the 'other', of difference and diversity, is arguably the root problem besetting the contemporary context of religious plurality. A healthily secular society is accommodatingly pluralist; difference is not just 'tolerated' but embraced and valued. A healthy religious identity is likewise accommodating of diversity—not treating religious and other alterities as implicit threats or invalid irruptions.

The final chapter draws to a conclusion the undergirding theme of otherness and the overarching range of issues addressed, identifies some of the significant and emerging trends and issues, and reflects on the future of interreligious engagement and the continuing challenge to understand, as well as to act. It is the hope of the editors that the combination of a focus on the theme of the religious 'other' together with the selection of issues and concerns thrown up by the lived reality of interreligious relations will prove a stimulating and insightful entrée for the reader new to the field, and a useful contribution to wider scholarly discourse. Religion, and so relations between religions, is unavoidably part of our contemporary social landscape. Whether or not we are actively engaged, the quest to understand what is happening, and why, when religions and their communities intersect, is of wide import and relevance. And for today's religions and their peoples, it is arguably vital that the context and reality of interreligious engagements are deeply understood.

PART I

Religions and the Religious Other

CHAPTER 2

Religion and the Religious Other

DAVID CHEETHAM

If the chapters that follow largely concern the particular historical backgrounds and contexts that characterize specific religions, one of the tasks of this chapter must be to critically assess the validity of a more general viewpoint. Whilst the close accounts of the historical and religious contexts of the different religions, and the 'canonical' authorities (textual or otherwise) that govern their attitudes towards religious others, might be fairly straightforward to articulate, the possibility of *generalizations* and the meaningfulness of categories (such as 'religion') apart from such contexts and canons are perhaps harder to justify. From the perspective of the academic study of religion, the discussion about religions and the religious other is embedded in a broader debate about methodologies in theology and the study of religion and the dispute between modernist and post modernist accounts of the nature of religion(s) and how it is to be interpreted and compared. This is the question concerning the possibility of *theory*. More postmodern commentators would have been content with this section of the book to merely present the five religions and their relations with the religious other without any attempt to provide an overarching narrative or further comment. To go beyond this is to risk defining religion and otherness in universal or abstract terms. Given this, the suspicion is that the very idea of 'religion and the religious other' already betrays an assumption of universalizing principles behind the differences.

Yet, I shall attempt to argue that an account of the aspiration of religions to offer a universal or public rendering of their worldview means that talking about 'religion and the religious other' in a general sense itself owes just as much to religious desire to transcend finitude and temporality as it does to modern Western constructions of religion. I would also suggest that the possibility of being 'above' or 'outside' the historical-cultural expressions of religion is aligned to a basic commitment to a realist interpretation of religious language. In which case, a discussion of religions and the religious other is a concern that is an epiphenomenon of a perspective that seeks to point beyond language and offer a total interpretation of the human condition and the universe. However, in tension with this, even if the 'view from above' is a perspective that individual religions actually aspire to, there is another sense that the concrete meeting between religions and their religious others is more complex and rich than can be summed up by a single focal point or, in the evocative words of Richard Kearney, by an 'adamantine logos of pure correspondences'.[1]

Although this chapter seeks to accomplish a wide-ranging and comprehensive discussion, it is nevertheless constructed around two basic aspects and offers a critical engagement with each of them. The first concerns the possibility, or the 'very idea', of what might be called a 'de-contextualized perspective' on religion and there is an engagement with a number of authors, disciplines, and viewpoints: the academic study of religion as well as philosophical and religious viewpoints. The second aspect considers the question of 'the other' and, more specifically, the kinds of challenges that meeting 'the other' might present. In so doing, this section reviews some key thinkers in the debate, including Emmanuel Levinas. The chapter is concerned with both the general vision that underpins the very idea of 'religion and the religious other' and with the contextual and ethical complexities of meeting the other.

CONTEXT AND THEORY

One of the choices made by the editors of this volume was to offer accounts in Part I of interreligious engagement that could be properly exemplified in major religions. That is, rather than have an extensive range of chapters that deal with many more religious traditions—minor and major—it was decided to exhibit those major ones that had a long and complex history of engagement with religious others. The countervailing view would be to insist that one must be totally comprehensive, but although this undoubtedly would have produced an impressive breadth of coverage, it is possible that the themes of 'comparison' or 'dialogue' would have been imposed on some traditions artificially. This raises the question of the enforced agendas that demand that some exemplification be found of engagements and concerns—interfaith dialogue and exchange—that may never have taken place in any significant way in some traditions. In this connection, the Jewish philosopher, Peter Ochs, argues that comparison or dialogue should only be undertaken if the traditions have contexts that make it apposite. Failing that, he proposes the following: 'If no dialogue has in fact taken place, then two options are either to provide an environment for such a dialogue or to desist from comparison (without a dialogue, what is the reason for comparison?)'[2] Ochs's

---

[1] Richard Kearney, 'Introduction: Ricoeur's Philosophy of Translation', in Paul Ricoeur, *On Translation*, tr. Eileen Brennan (Abingdon and New York: Routledge, 2006), p. xvii.

[2] Peter Ochs, 'Comparative Religious Traditions', *Journal of the American Academy of Religion*, 74/1 (2006), 126.

argument is directed towards pedagogic contexts, but an interfaith movement with which he is most associated, Scriptural Reasoning, is a good example of deliberately generating an environment of encounter where a group of scholars from Abrahamic traditions meet and discover commonalities and differences through their open discussions of Abrahamic texts.[3] What is significant is that such encounters are not programmatic in that they do not presuppose agreement or commonality; rather, they may actually seek to improve the quality of disagreement. However, in the absence of this, Ochs believes that comparison should not be attempted. As such, he is prioritizing contextual actualities and experiences over the possibility of theoretical comparison.

The alternative to this view has been well articulated by the thoroughgoing modernist, Robert Segal, who thinks that Ochs's embargo ends up denying the role of the academic student of religion who wishes to gain a deeper understanding of religion through comparison. He complains: 'If I want to fathom Ghanian Methodists, why can I not compare them with any other group I choose? As long as I can identify similarities between Ghanian Methodists and adherents of religions of whom the Ghanians have never heard, why dare I not compare them?'[4] Segal's point is that the activity of trying to compare traditions which do not necessarily have a demonstrable history of engagement may help to discover something about those traditions; more specifically, it goes beyond a purely descriptive treatment of 'how' religions have engaged but addresses a broader question of 'why?'[5] It prompts a theoretical question about similarity and difference that may admittedly reflect what Segal calls an 'old comparativism' but which cannot be ruled out of a theoretical study of religions. Segal's point is academic—it is from the perspective of religious studies—but is it indicative of wider issues concerning how religions relate to each other outside of academic interests? So, does not the 'why' question resemble a *religious* interest also? Are not the comparisons undertaken by religious people an integral aspect of the quest for truth and inquisitiveness about other possible interpretations? This concerns the epistemological anxieties that are stirred by the presence of alternative (and potentially incompatible) truth-claims—something that Paul Griffiths characterizes as the *problem* of religious diversity, a problem for the believer.[6] In which case, for the believer to ignore the religious other, or to lack a comparative awareness, is to betray a lack of interest in bigger questions and the validity of one's own confession. This chapter is partly concerned with such broader enquiries, while the chapters that follow in this section present contextually rich instances of particular religions in interaction with religious others.

---

[3] See David Ford and C. C. Pecknold (eds), *The Promise of Scriptural Reasoning* (Oxford: Blackwell, 2006); also <http://www.scripturalreasoning.org>.

[4] Robert Segal, 'Response to Peter Ochs' "Comparative Religious Traditions"', *Journal of the American Academy of Religion*, 74/1 (2006), 131.

[5] Ochs, 'Comparative Religious Traditions', 130.

[6] See Paul Griffiths, *The Problem of Religious Diversity* (Oxford: Blackwell, 2001).

On the Very Idea[7]

The pluralistic vision of authors like Schmidt-Leukel in this volume would seem to be the most natural home for a topic like 'religion and the religious other'. Nevertheless, can the very idea be defended as a legitimate notion *apart* from the pluralistic agenda of liberal moderns? Much depends on what we are trying to achieve, what limits we set to the debate, and the usage of the term 'religion' in the academy and the world. In her chapter on Interreligious Dialogue within this volume, Marianne Moyaert supplies a skilful historical account of the rise of the concern for dialogue between faiths as something that reflected the modern ideals of equality, respect, and tolerance. Unlike some other writers who make much of the connection between the concept of religion and the intellectual politics of modernity, Moyaert's lucid account does not engage in the critique of modernity as an originating factor and her survey does not explicitly offer a critique of modern pluralistic theories either. She draws attention to the variety of influences that came together to bring about comparative religion and the dialogue between faith traditions. In addition to the impact of modern thinking, she highlights the influences of ecumenical dialogue, the experience and scholarship of Christian missionaries (many of whom were distinguished scholars of religion in universities), and the subsequent desire to reverse the colonial imperialism of the past.

These factors combined to compel critical reflection on the nature of religion and its multiple phenomena and how they might constructively relate. In an influential article which offers an analysis of the terms 'religion', 'religions', and 'religious',[8] the American scholar Jonathan Z. Smith argues that the sheer amount of new information and learning that occurred over the last century forced scholars to enquire about the meaning of religion: '[t]he question of religion arose in response to the explosion of data'.[9] Rather than be satisfied with the mere description or exhibition of the varieties of religious phenomena, Smith says that '[t]he urgent agendum was to bring order to this variety of species. Only an adequate taxonomy would convert a "natural history" of religion into a science.'[10]

Critics may well be suspicious of the search for an organizing principle that defines a single field and focus. The historical development of such an idea is not without interpretation or a hermeneutic of suspicion. In *The Meeting of Religions and the Trinity* (2000) and the more recent *Christianity and the World Religions* (2009), the Roman Catholic theologian, Gavin D'Costa, has remained steadfastly focused on advancing his criticism of the modernist tradition that he sees at the heart of liberal pluralism and in the drive to find universals in religion.

---

[7] The heading here is influenced by Donald Davidson's 'On the Very Idea of a Conceptual Scheme', *Proceedings and Addresses of the American Philosophical Association*, 47 (1973–4), 5–20. In this piece Davidson is concerned with the problems of translation and incommensurability.

[8] See 'Religion, Religions, Religious', in J. Z. Smith, *Relating Religion: Essays in the Study of Religion* (Chicago: University of Chicago Press, 2004), 179–96.

[9] Smith, *Relating Religion*, 18; see Michael Barnes, *Theology and the Dialogue of Religions* (Cambridge: Cambridge University Press, 2002), 6.

[10] Smith, *Relating Religion*, 187.

He undertakes historical detective work regarding the origins of the modern version of religion and argues that the category of religion has been invented and/or tamed by 'modernity's story':

> 'Religion' was an invention of the sixteenth century and deeply rooted in the work of the Cambridge Platonists, by the eighteenth century it was more a product of the European imagination than an encounter with an alternative form of power and discipline; and by the twentieth century 'religion' became a shadow of its pre-modern self precisely because it was allocated a private, not public, role in the political sphere; a role policed by modernity.[11]

D'Costa is not alone in this reading and he owes much of his thinking about modernity as a tradition to the work of Alasdair MacIntyre.[12] Further, talk of the 'policing' of religion by modernity shares affinities with the views of the British theologian and champion of Radical Orthodoxy, John Milbank.[13] Thus, Milbank argues that the very idea of dialogue between religions is predicated on an assumption of the natural reasonable religion that is a product of the secular modernist 'whose only possible outcome must be . . . a new hybridisation, yielding a new, and of course just as *particular*, elite religion for the votaries of dialogue themselves'.[14] Both D'Costa and Milbank claim that the move towards 'reasonable religion' comes with its own programme towards homogeneity; it is not a neutral concept but is a modernist tradition that privileges a Kantian notion of religion.

Paul Knitter defends liberal pluralism against the claim that it is a pawn of modernity or a Western imposition.[15] He contests the idea that pluralism is a Western construct and appeals to a common religious testimony that he argues is present in all religious traditions. Such testimony speaks about religious truth as 'universal truth', and most major religions advocate the idea that what is believed ought to be thought of as *publicly* rather than privately true.[16] Knitter is defending pluralism specifically, but it seems entirely possible to suggest that his defence could be used simply to acknowledge that the practice of generalization, and the appeal to universals, is something that characterizes religious *transcendent* vision. Milbank, who has expressed his opposition to liberalism, argues that the alleged need for a pluralist solution wrongly assumes that the encounter with the religious other is a new situation. On the contrary, 'every major religion is *already* the result of a confronting of the fact of religious differences and an attempt to subsume such differences . . . although the ways and degrees of

---

[11] Gavin D'Costa, *Christianity and World Religions: Disputed Questions in the Theology of Religions. An Introduction to the Theology of Religions* (Oxford: Wiley Blackwell, 2009), 58.

[12] e.g. see Alasdair MacIntyre, *After Virtue: A Study in Moral Theory*, 3rd edn (Notre Dame, Ind.: University of Notre Dame Press, 2007); *Whose Justice? Which Rationality?* (London: Duckworth, 1996).

[13] For Milbank's fullest development of this, see his *Theology and Social Theory: Beyond Secular Reason*, 2nd edn (Oxford: Blackwell, 2005).

[14] John Milbank, 'The End of Dialogue', in Gavin D'Costa (ed.), *Christian Uniqueness Reconsidered: The Myth of a Pluralistic Theology of Religions* (Maryknoll, NY: Orbis Books, 1990), 180.

[15] See Paul Knitter, 'Is the Pluralist Model a Western Imposition? A Response in Five Voices', in Paul Knitter (ed.), *The Myth of Religious Superiority: A Multi-Faith Exploration* (Maryknoll, NY: Orbis Books, 2005), 28–42.

[16] Knitter, 'Pluralist Model', 31–3.

constructing "universality" themselves vary enormously'.[17] Milbank's use of inverted commas around 'universality' indicates that he does not understand universality to be a neutral normativity, but a tradition-specific vision.

However, I would suggest that this still demonstrates that a universal vision, however traditionally framed, is an authentic aspect of religious epistemological ambitions or what might be described as a religious *stretching* that seeks to transcend the world and reach into eternity. Knitter's point is that if there is a desire to transcend contextual or historical concerns then this is not just something that is explainable in terms of a suspicious genealogical uncovering of universals in the Western intellectual tradition—but this is surely a valid observation apart from his pluralistic conclusion. Secondly, Knitter claims that theistic religions speak of the 'absolute mystery' about reality or God, and the mystics within different religions remind believers that there is an ultimate mystery about reality that can never be fully comprehended or encapsulated by their own traditions.[18] Whilst recognizing the importance of acknowledging differences as well as similarities, Knitter calls attention to 'shared aims' and 'common concerns'—such as fighting injustice, poverty, and oppression. His argument is that, despite the claims that pluralism is a product of Western modernism, the idea of universals and common purposes is something present in the religions themselves. In fact, the intuition that there is something deep to be shared and understood universally is an integral and fundamental part of *religious* truth.

Another pluralist, John Hick, argues in a similar fashion that many of the perceived commonalities and universals that pluralists are accused of forging from specifically Western liberal ideals are present in religious and philosophical traditions around the globe.[19] Whilst some critics of pluralism (e.g. D'Costa) will seek to engage in a genealogical investigation of its origins within Western modernism, Hick introduces his *An Interpretation of Religion* with a seemingly de-politicized agenda—his is 'a religious interpretation of religion' as opposed to a cultural, sociological, psychological, or anthropological interpretation.[20] In so doing, he seeks to engage with religion in its plurality from a non-reductionist perspective, one which takes the *object* of religious faith and practice seriously. Ironically, rather than Hick's pluralistic theory undermining the vitality of specific confessions, his pluralism is in fact intended to defend the *reality* of religious beliefs and experience despite the seeming contradictory truth-claims evident in different traditions. In this sense, his hypothesis is a response to the classic Humean claim that different religious experiences cancel each other out if they are used for their evidential value. So, against the conclusion that religious language cannot be fact-asserting due to the clashing plurality of many different claims, Hick's hypothesis is a defence of realism against anti-realist interpretations of religious beliefs.[21]

---

[17] Milbank, 'End of Dialogue', 180.
[18] Knitter, 'Pluralist Model', 33–6.
[19] e.g. see John Hick, *An Interpretation of Religion*, 2nd edn (Basingstoke and New York: Palgrave Macmillan, 2004), pp. xxxix–xli.
[20] Hick, *Interpretation*, 1.
[21] See also the discussion of realism and pluralism in Peter Byrne, *Prolegomena to Religious Pluralism: Reference and Realism in Religion* (London: Macmillan, 1995).

Nevertheless, in similar fashion to my observations on Knitter's defence of pluralism, I suggest that, although Hick closely connects his defence of a realist religious epistemology to his pluralistic hypothesis, his 'religious interpretation of religion' in its most basic form seems to be simply a matter of claiming that realism (as opposed to anti-realism) is a *proper* religious outlook. At its most fundamental level, then, advocating realism is simply to argue that religious language has a 'referent' outside of and independent of language and culture. Religious beliefs are not solely linguistic or cultural creations. Thus, if we return to the question expressed at the beginning of this section about the possibility of a general interest in 'religion and the religious other' apart from liberal pluralism, I would claim that this is possible if we consider the outward-look of religion, its aspirations to look beyond. However, this would be more consistent with a realist as opposed to an anti-realist interpretation of religious language. That is, whereas anti-realist conceptions of religious language are content to inhabit the narrative, humanly generated and culturally relative aspects of religious talk, the realist view looks for the validity of such talk *outside* of itself. If such reasoning is sound, then it suggests that the matter of 'religion and the religious other' as a general concern is something that can be categorized less as a species of modernity, and more as something deeply ingrained in the aspiration for objectivity or 'public' truth within religion itself and which has close affinities with a realist interpretation of religious language—*apart from a specifically pluralist vision.*

Hick's own account of 'world religion' emerges from an influential historical account of the evolution of religion in the work of Karl Jaspers that differentiates between pre-axial and post-axial orientations.[22] Pre-axial religions are primitive or localized religions that do not offer comprehensive accounts of the world and are therefore not unsettled by the presence of other religions. Pre-axial religion is concerned 'with the preservation of cosmic and social order'.[23] It is about sustaining vital patterns or seasons of nature and about upholding or underpinning the traditions of a particular community and region. Post-axial religion is concerned 'with the quest for salvation or liberation'.[24] Hick marks out the axial age as being from 800 to 200 BCE, a time when there is an enlargement of vision: 'man is no longer defined chiefly in terms of what tribe or clan he comes from or what particular god he serves but rather as a being capable of salvation'.[25] This particular account suits Hick's personal hypothesis about religion very much because his own common focal point within the diversity of religions is soteriological—all true religions share a purpose towards human transformation moving

---

[22] Karl Jaspers, *The Origin and Goal of History*, tr. Michael Bullock (New Haven: Yale University Press, 1953). Hick also cites several other sources, see in Hick, *Interpretation*, 35 n. 9.

[23] *Interpretation*, 22; John Milbank argues similarly: 'genuinely local religions (and of course relative isolation does not betoken primitiveness) may scarcely have had to confront the question of whether their beliefs and practices are relevant beyond the confines of their own society; this is presumably why they are so liable to conversion by or accommodating within the terms of a major religion, which is in part the result of such a confrontation.' Milbank, 'End of Dialogue', 180.

[24] Hick, *Interpretation*, 22.

[25] Robert Bellah, *Beyond Belief: Essays on Religion in a Post-Traditional World* (London and New York: Harper & Row, 1970), 33; cited in Hick, *Interpretation*, 30.

from self-centredness to reality-centredness. During the axial age, he suggests that 'all the major religious options, constituting the major possible ways of conceiving the ultimate were identified and established'.[26] If there is a weakness in this account it may not be located in the prima facie historical observation about a significant period of development of religions of 'global' scope, instead it is perhaps to be found in the underlying assumption that such scope is indicative of a common soteriological purpose—an alleged *axial* soteriology.[27] Scholars such as John Cobb[28] and S. Mark Heim[29] have challenged this assumption, arguing that religions have different goals and ends that are not necessarily reducible to a single purpose.

Advancing a more politically attentive account of 'world religion' from the perspective of the social sciences, Jonathan Z. Smith presents a distinction that resembles what Hick calls the axial and pre-axial religions, but for him it is a matter of proximity and power:

> It is impossible to escape the suspicion that a world religion is simply a religion like ours, and that it is, above all, a tradition that has achieved sufficient power and numbers to enter our history to form it, interact with it, or thwart it. We recognise both the unity within and the diversity among the world religions because they correspond to important geopolitical entities with which we must deal. All 'primitives' by way of contrast, may be lumped together, as may the 'minor religions,' because they do not confront our history in any direct fashion. From the point of view of power, they are invisible.[30]

Smith's suspicions follow investigations into the historical development of the study of religion in the academy and the use of classifications and distinctions made by scholars since the eighteenth century.[31] Nevertheless, even if the construct 'world religion' can be explained as a product of geo-political proximity, the comparative theologian Hugh Nicholson claims that it is above all a liberal *ideal*—an attempt to transcend particular politics and conflicts. In this sense, it does not so much represent a recognition of power with which one has to deal, rather it embodies a 'normative liberal ideal of a form of religion transcending the principle of political division and strife'.[32]

Tracing the origins of theological hegemonism, Nicholson also suggests that the oft-used typology (exclusivism, inclusivism, and pluralism) in the theology of religions is part of a liberal narrative that seeks to 'project a universal theological vision'. It does so by presenting

---

[26] Hick, *Interpretation*, 31.

[27] I would maintain that the force of this criticism is not dissipated by simply arguing that the axial religions contain genuine diversity and have phenomenologically different goals, because the very 'axial' *identification* is itself predicated on an alleged common intuition of cosmic optimism.

[28] See John Cobb, *Transforming Christianity and the World: A Way Beyond Absolutism and Relativism*, ed. Paul Knitter (Maryknoll, NY: Orbis Books, 1999).

[29] See S. Mark Heim, *Salvations: Truth and Difference in Religion* (Maryknoll, NY: Orbis Books, 1995).

[30] Smith, *Relating Religion*, 191–2.

[31] See also the account offered in Eric Sharpe, *Comparative Religion: A History*, 2nd edn (London: Duckworth, 1986).

[32] Hugh Nicholson, 'The New Comparative Theology and the Problem of Theological Hegemonism', in Francis Clooney (ed.), *The New Comparative Theology: Thinking Interreligiously in the 21st Century* (London: T & T Clark, 2010), 50.

the options in the typology as 'successive moments in a dialectic' towards overcoming exclusivism.[33] For Nicholson, part of the liberal strategy has been to address the issue of interreligious relations as a systematic problem rather than an historical or contextual one. Or rather, the options in the typology appear to be more concerned with overall meta-explanations of the presence of the religious other and how they fit into the universal landscape. Indeed, for Schmidt-Leukel, in this volume, the metaphysical and soteriological questions that the typology prioritizes are inescapable if one is engaged in theology of religions rather than merely comparative religion. In Nicholson's view, categories like 'world religion' are presented as distinct from other religious groups by virtue of the fact that they have 'transcended a particular cultural milieu'.[34] His dissection of the typology follows a now familiar line when it presents a genealogy of suspicion concerning the 'universal vision' of the liberal modern narrative. However, consistent with what has been suggested in the last few pages, it is not clear that projecting a universal theological vision should be identified solely with a liberal modern narrative.

Nevertheless, if we adopt Nicholson's view of 'world religion' as a de-politicized ideal, then we can see how this works in the context of the liberal state. 'World religion' becomes a close relative of the liberal values of equality, tolerance, and the reasonable society. Not only is 'world religion' a concept that functions as a universal category but it obtains its licence by legitimating the core values of the modern state.[35] The most obvious example of this is the powerfully influential political philosophy of John Rawls who envisages a liberal democratic state that only permits religious discourses to be part of the public square if they can be 'expressed in terms of political values'.[36] Although Rawls was not trying to impose a secular normativity, and in fact argued for an 'over-lapping consensus' of narratives, it is quite clear that secular liberal assumptions were seen as a guide for what can be included and what must be excluded from the public sphere. What is significant is that Rawls was keen to exclude the 'zeal to embody the whole truth'[37] that characterizes strong religious postures. Passionate commitment to a religious worldview could be permitted in the private sphere, but the public expression of these commitments had to be filtered by the expedient pragmatics of public reason. Thus, the success of Rawls's liberal society was based on the establishment of a democratic citizenship that did not claim to be a *comprehensive* system like a religious worldview and therefore allowed differences to exist together peacefully. The acceptable face of religion, and therefore its public voice, is accomplished by subjecting beliefs and narratives to a *reasonable distillation*.

---

[33] Nicholson, 'New Comparative Theology', 48.

[34] Nicholson, 'New Comparative Theology', 50.

[35] This is a point that underpins many of the complaints by critics of liberal pluralism like D'Costa, Milbank, and Kenneth Surin. See the latter's highly readable 'A "Politics of Speech": Religious Pluralism in the Age of McDonald's Hamburger', in D'Costa, *Christian Uniqueness Reconsidered*, 192–212.

[36] John Rawls, *The Law of Peoples with 'The Idea of Public Reason Revisited'* (Cambridge, Mass.: Harvard University Press, 1999), 142. See Christopher Insole's lucid defence of liberal politics (with reference to Rawls) in his *The Politics of Human Frailty: A Theological Defence of Political Liberalism* (Notre Dame, Ind.: University of Notre Dame Press, 2004).

[37] Rawls, *The Law of Peoples*, 132.

Notwithstanding the historical and geo-political dynamics that have influenced the tax-onomies of 'world religion' as a category, Jonathan Z. Smith clearly perceives a value in defining religion but the use of definition for him seems to be chiefly an *academic* tool. That is, he argues that 'religion' is not a 'native term'.[38] Rather, '[i]t is a second-order, generic concept that plays the same role in establishing a disciplinary horizon that a concept such as "language" plays in linguistics or "culture" plays in anthropology'.[39] Reinforcing this viewpoint, Robert Segal argues that generic theories of religion are not about finding an essence—on the contrary, the question of essence is a metaphysical issue—instead they are 'merely an empirical enterprise'.[40] Segal pours scorn on postmodern claims that theories of religion are merely Western hegemonies which peddle rationalist universals. He argues that theories make no claim to offer *sufficient* explanations of religion, rather, they are merely probabilistic. The presence of evidence that seems contrary to a theory is not an indication of the failure of the theory itself or, worse, that ignoring such material means that the 'master' theory has suppressed differences. It would be a facile criticism indeed that proposed that theories are useless simply because it was alleged that they depend on the denial of difference and complexity in favour of sameness *without exception*.[41] Segal argues that inconsistencies merely underline the 'provisional' nature of theories rather than undermining the usefulness of them altogether[42] and, furthermore, we might add that the acknowledgement of provisionality hardly seems to be an ingredient one would expect if theories were genuinely vehicles of conceptual oppression.

Nevertheless, matters become more complex when the theoretical activity of religious students and theologians of religions is employed to propose *solutions* to religious diversity. That is, the hope for peace between religions may have been presumptuously predicated on the discovery of comparative parities between religions by theologians and scholars of religion. This has recently been noted by Martin Kavka who suggests that religious studies, with its comparative method, seems to support the myth that one of its chief roles is to harmonize differences between religions with a view to the pedagogic effect such work has on students of religion: 'The rise of religious studies as a discipline is intertwined with the belief that this discipline itself could bring about peace through its acts of translation'.[43] It does not seem difficult to find examples of this in the academic history of the subject. Friedrich Heiler, in a visionary opening address to conference of historians of religion in 1958, claimed:

---

[38] Smith, *Relating Religion*, 193.

[39] Smith, *Relating Religion*, 194.

[40] Robert Segal, 'All Generalisations are Bad: Postmodernism on Theories', *Journal of the American Academy of Religion*, 74/1 (2006), 159.

[41] Critics of this can maintain that the theories impose their assumptions on the data and, in so doing, skew the interpretation. However, it seems impossible to avoid *conceptualization* altogether and the construction of models or frameworks of understanding is, arguably, unavoidable in order to advance beyond mere description.

[42] Smith, *Relating Religion*, 164.

[43] Martin Kavka, 'Translation', in Robert Orsi (ed.), *The Cambridge Companion to Religious Studies* (Cambridge: Cambridge University Press, 2012), 187.

One of the most important tasks of the science of religion is to bring to light this unity of all religions ... A new era will dawn upon mankind when the religions will rise to true tolerance and co-operation on behalf of mankind. To assist in preparing the way for this era is one of the finest hopes of the scientific study of religion.[44]

However, it is not clear that uncovering a unity between religions is the essential key to achieving tolerance and cooperation between religions. Thinking about relations between religions has become more complex and rich since Heiler uttered these words. Indeed, much of the literature in the past few decades that has explored approaches to interreligious dialogue has spoken just as vocally about the virtues of difference as it has about sameness in the meeting of religions. An indicative testimony to this is Catherine Cornille's recent influential text, *The Im-possibility of Inter religious Dialogue* (2008); the various sections contained within it provide a survey of the many approaches that have been explored—not just unity, but 'humility', 'commitment', 'interconnection', 'empathy', and 'hospitality'. However, this is not to suggest that the discovery of unity and comparative likenesses ceases to be a profitable task for religious studies or that theory does not have a place in its methodologies, rather it is to express doubt about any direct links between the academic practice of such a project in religious studies and promoting peace between religions. At least, since Heiler's speech, the study of religions and theology has become more complex and the relationship between the two disciplines a matter of intense debate.[45]

Returning to the very idea of 'religion and the religious other', if one is going to undertake the task of engaging with the general vision and scope then perhaps such an enterprise needs to inhabit the disciplines that reflect a more philosophical disposition? This is because the philosophical outlook seems to involve a kind of *de-contextualization*. Furthermore, the difference between the philosopher John Hick and the social scientist Jonathan Z. Smith is that the former prioritizes the *religious* problem of the presence of the 'same' rather than concentrating on the political or social problem. This is a feature that Smith is in fact fully aware of, as is clear from his treatment of the problem of otherness that we will see in a moment, though he understands it more as a contextual challenge. For Hick, a world (axial) religion is one that presents a comprehensive answer to universal questions of existence and meaning. In this sense, regardless of historical or geo-political proximity, there is a theological or *conceptual* proximity that causes difficulty and disrupts the universal claims of a particular faith tradition.

Speaking as a philosopher of religion, Christopher Insole highlights the importance in analytical philosophy of considering ideas in themselves apart from history and cultivating

---

[44] *Proceedings of the 9th International Congress for the History of Religions* (Tokyo: Maruzen, 1960), 19, 21; cited in Sharpe, *Comparative Religion*, 272.

[45] Some good anthologies include Maya Warrier and Simon Oliver (eds), *Theology and Religious Studies: An Exploration of Disciplinary Boundaries* (London: T&T Clark, 2008) and David Ford *et al.* (eds), *Fields of Faith: Theology and Religious Studies for the Twenty-First Century* (Cambridge: Cambridge University Press, 2012).

a 'studied and deliberate lack of interest in the complex discourses which constitute our various roles and identities in the world'.[46] That is, the practice of philosophy is to consider the merits of ideas and concepts apart from any historical or cultural recommendation or pedigree. This might suggest that considering 'religion and the religious other' as a generic decontextualized problem is something that concerns less the God of faith and more the 'god of the philosophers'. In which case, one of the more acute dilemmas from the perspective of religious faith is that a broader concern with the problem of the religious other leads to abstractions that move outside of specific traditions. In his critique of Hick's pluralism, Gavin D'Costa claims that the object of Hick's hypothesis, the Real, is such a transcategorial entity that it results in a 'transcendental agnosticism'.[47] Alternatively, George Pattison suggests that philosophy's 'intellectual eros' is 'analogous to the aspiration of religion' because the concept of God 'coincides with what fundamental philosophy seeks to uncover as the ever-intended but ever-unthought presupposition of thought'.[48] Thus, there emerges a peculiar dialectic between a sceptical questioning approach that forever engages in the critique of established ideas on the one hand, and a deep sense of the ultimate ('ever-intended but ever-unthought presupposition of thought') that drives the quest, on the other.

In summary, the very idea of 'religion and the religious other' can be addressed as an academic and a religious concern. It emerges from the comparative study of religion and the construction of theory, however for this reason it has been critiqued by scholars who draw attention to its liberal modern heritage—both political and philosophical—and the way it appears to favour a pluralistic perspective. Nevertheless, I have suggested that the discourse is more basically consistent with a realist interpretation of religious language and beliefs which, at least in the context of theistic traditions, imply that there are *external* reference points for religious claims. Thinking abstractly about 'religion and the religious other' is also wedded to the concept of 'world religion'. Alongside the more religious or philosophical readings of this that are possible, it might also be understood as a socio-political construct that reflects the power and proximity of certain traditions in relation to each other and their 'global' claims.

However, there is a limitation to the usefulness of a programme of abstracting ideas from contexts. Although it might resonate with both the academic interests of theorists of religion and, as we have said, a *realist* reading of religious beliefs, the actual practice may be richer and more complex. Indeed, the danger is that the pursuit of *focal* points may limit the range of engagements with otherness. That is, the face of the religious other may be more multifaceted than single conceptual or abstract focal points allow us to perceive.

---

[46]   Christopher Insole, 'Political Liberalism, Analytical Philosophy of Religion and the Forgetting of History', in Christopher Insole and Harriet Harris (eds), *Faith and Philosophical Analysis* (Aldershot: Ashgate 2005), 163.

[47]   Gavin D'Costa, 'John Hick and Religious Pluralism: Yet Another Revolution', in Harold Hewitt (ed.), *Problems in the Philosophy of Religion: Critical Studies of the Work of John Hick* (London: Macmillan, 1991), 7.

[48]   George Pattison, *A Short Course in Philosophy of Religion* (London: SCM Press, 2001), 119.

THE OTHER

In the opening sentences of a seminal work of the twentieth-century on the topic of 'the Other', the German philosopher Michael Theunissen wrote that '[f]ew questions have exerted so powerful a grip on the thought of this century than that of the "Other".'[49] One of the most influential interpretations of the meaning of otherness has come from a Jewish scholar who is mentioned in Edward Kessler's chapter in this section, Emmanuel Levinas. Although he fiercely articulates an intense sense of responsibility towards otherness, or its infinite demand, such an uncompromising attitude has not been the only dominant motif in Western thinking about the other. Following the gradual demise of a Cartesian emphasis on the rational subject—that which gains knowledge through thinking as an *individual-that-craves-certainty*—there is a post-Cartesian narrative that maintains that self-knowledge goes beyond the isolated individual and is achieved through a relationship with and interrogation by others. Moreover, although the presence of the other might create profound anxiety, this is by no means a negative experience. For example, Fred Dallmayr, tracing a genealogy through Hegel and Schelling, comments on the complexity of relations between 'I and Other' in Western thought, which he notes was 'not the relation of exclusivity, but one of mutual dependence', and that 'self-discovery presupposes the passage through otherness'.[50] That is, the presence of the other has been seen in much Western thinking as a constructive one—an aid to personal development through engagement—as well as something more unsettling and ethically demanding. In which case, Dallmayr thinks that otherness is not to be solely described in terms of alienation and he quotes Theodor Adorno's comment that fear of alienation 'would mostly cease if strangeness were no longer vilified'.

Dissatisfied with Heidegger's ontology of Being, Levinas insisted that ethics should be 'first philosophy', and that this is given the highest priority in philosophy. Such a priority is 'otherwise than being'[51]—the question of being is replaced by the infinite demand of the other. Constructing his own perspective on the dialogue between faiths in *Theology and the Dialogue of Religions* (2002), the Jesuit scholar Michael Barnes is deeply influenced by Levinas and, as a consequence, one of his primary questions in connection to the dialogue of religions is: 'How is the responsible subject to negotiate with the other without resorting to acts of subtle manipulation or more-or-less blatant violence?'[52] Here Barnes locates one of the primary anxieties in the theology of religions. This has also been well articulated by the Buddhist scholar Kristen Kiblinger in her critical reflections on inclusivism in the Buddhist tradition. She advocates an 'engaged inclusivism' which is

---

[49] Michael Theunissen, *The Other: Studies in the Social Ontology of Husserl, Heidegger, Sartre and Buber* (Cambridge, Mass.: MIT Press, 1984), 1.

[50] Fred Dallmayr, 'Introduction', in Theunissen, *The Other*, p. x.

[51] Emmanuel Levinas, *Otherwise than Being, or, Beyond Essence*, tr. Alphonso Lingis (The Hague: M. Nijhoff, 1981).

[52] Barnes, *Theology and Dialogue*, 27.

'less about acceptance than it is about sincere open consideration and the pursuit of accurate understanding'.[53] Put another way, properly ethical meetings with the religious other are about *giving way* to the auto-interpretation[54] offered by those others before any attempt is made to find continuities and affinities. For Barnes's Levinasian-inspired conscience, the theology of religions needs an 'adequate account of the vulnerability of the self in the face of the other'.[55]

'Vulnerability of self in the face of the other' is *one* distinctive attitude in the meeting of religions and it clearly resonates with ethical imperatives that are found at the heart of many religious traditions such as 'the Golden Rule'. However, if Levinas inspires a deep responsibility towards the other, especially in the post-Holocaust West, is his thinking appropriate for *active* (rather than passive) relationships between religions? In addressing this question, I want to be selective and focus the discussion on the ethics of meeting and the metaphysics of religious belief. The priority of Levinas is ethics rather than metaphysics or ontology, but it is possible that such a priority may obscure the religious vision that compels action towards the other. Because of the desire in his thought to avoid doing violence to the other, he appears to have produced a space of such *sacrality* that it is difficult to move. Additionally, it seems that there is a kind of pragmatic 'atheism' that occupies the centre of his ethical thought. Thus, Levinas thinks that the *Deus Absconditus* is a vital aspect of ethical life: 'The atheism of the metaphysician means, positively, that our relation with the metaphysical is an ethical behaviour and not theology'.[56] For Levinas, ethics is the true 'spiritual optics' and this means that '[e]verything that cannot be reduced to an interhuman relation represents not the superior form but the forever primitive form of religion'.[57] Perhaps most significant for our considerations is Levinas's suggestion of a divine withdrawal or hiddenness in order to allow the ethical to be formed and to flourish. Levinas uses language that implies that humanity achieves a form of *independent* authority: 'To hide one's face so as to demand the superhuman of man, to create a man who can approach God and speak of Him without always being in His debt—that is truly the mark of divine greatness!'[58]

In an excoriating critique of Levinas, the Orthodox theologian David Bentley Hart characterizes Levinas's contribution to twentieth-century ethics as one of 'absolutely unalloyed and hyperbolic intensity'.[59] In saying this, Hart is identifying Levinas's ethics with a type of agonistic nihilism. A similar characterization is offered by Gillian Rose, to whom Hart refers. For example, she notes that becoming 'the ethical [Levinas's] self is to be devastated,

[53]   Kristin Kiblinger, *Buddhist Inclusivism: Attitudes towards Religious Others* (Aldershot: Ashgate, 2005), 28.

[54]   This is a term employed by Gavin D'Costa. See *The Meeting of Religions and the Trinity* (Edinburgh: T&T Clark, 2000), 100.

[55]   Barnes, *Theology and Dialogue*, 23.

[56]   Emmanuel Levinas, *Totality and Infinity* (The Hague: M. Nijhoff, 1979), 78. See the discussion in Michael Purcell, *Levinas and Theology* (Cambridge: Cambridge University Press, 2006), 60–4.

[57]   Levinas, *Totality and Infinity*, 78, 79.

[58]   Emmanuel Levinas, *Difficult Freedom: Essays on Judaism*, tr. S. Hand (London: Athlone Press, 1990), 145.

[59]   David Bentley Hart, *The Beauty of the Infinite: The Aesthetics of Christian Truth* (Grand Rapids, Mich.: Eerdmans, 2003), 75.

traumatised . . . by the commandment to substitute *the other* for itself'.[60] Of specific interest to our concerns, Hart speculates that Levinas enjoys a position of influence in contemporary ethical thinking 'because [his work] appears apt to satisfy some commendable appetite in certain thinkers in this post-metaphysical age for *some* language of moral responsibility'.[61] This is a highly significant observation and it has important implications concerning the nature of encounter with otherness in a religious context and the particular *mood* that thinkers like Levinas promote. As we have seen, Levinas's prioritization of the ethical over a Heideggerian ontology means that his ethics seems to stem less from notions of divine command and more from an intense inter-human ethical commitment and infinite responsibility towards 'the Other' which, for Levinas, represents the deepest *sublime*.[62] Moreover, if Levinas's ethics is indeed a distinctively *post-metaphysical* offering, then does this make it oddly unsuited to the ethics set within the metaphysical frameworks that underpin the moral vision of many faiths? Not necessarily. For example, the advantage of Levinas's account is that it clears a space of opportunity for the human, and if the relationships between religious people of different traditions are removed from strongly held religious imperatives and metaphysics, then Levinas may actually be describing a mode of profound inter-human engagement that can be embraced more universally.[63] However, this also means that the explicitly religious or transcendent subject matter of religious faith (unless this is couched entirely in ethical terms) is not a crucial part of the meeting between religions. Arguably, meeting the religious other in a Levinasian sense appears to be an action which exists in parallel to overtly religious metaphysics and doctrinal confessions—it exists in our 'inter-human relations'. Although Levinas's autonomous ethic, with its masochistic self-renunciation, may indeed resonate with the self-emptying aspects found deep within many religious ethical practices, it is by no means certain that the meeting with the other can or should be determined by such austerity.

Such is the imperative in Levinas's thought to avoid reducing the other to the same and to affirm difference that critics, such as Paul Ricoeur, have asked if the face of the other can even be recognized. Levinas creates a sacred ground between same and the other, a pristine, sterilized no-man's land in which even any recognition of the other becomes an act of 'violence'. Thus, Barnes worries that the severity of Levinas's ethical politics ends up replacing the violence of imposing sameness with a 'violence which would paralyse the self'.[64] Furthermore, Rose suggests that to advocate such 'passivity beyond passivity'[65] as a response

---

[60] Gillian Rose, *Mourning Becomes the Law: Philosophy and Representation* (Cambridge: Cambridge University Press, 1996), 37.

[61] Rose, *Mourning*, 37.

[62] This is Hart's terminology and particular interpretation. See Hart's discussion of the ethical sublime, *The Beauty*, 75–93.

[63] I have a great deal of sympathy with the idea of 'human' spaces and I explore these in *Ways of Meeting and the Theology of Religions* (Aldershot: Ashgate, 2013), esp. ch. 3.

[64] Barnes, *Theology and Dialogue*, 70.

[65] See Rose, *Mourning*, 37.

to the other is in fact to have created a deceptive (because unreal) 'holy middle' between self and other. Rose's preference amounts to an appeal for the recognition of the 'broken middle'—that which is the untidy and often incongruent reality where ideas, persons, and communities are juxtaposed without any clear telos. She notes that some postmodern theologians, and she chooses Mark C. Taylor and John Milbank as examples, have sought to repair or 'mend' the middle and possess it in order to do so. In Taylor's case it is the advocacy of a 'nomadic' mode of being that is a denial of domination in public politics;[66] in Milbank's it is the creation of a 'holy sociology' that entails liberation from the secular. Critiquing such things, Rose claims that '[t]his rediscovery of the holy city, pagan, nomadic, Judaic, these mended middles over broken middle, at the end of the end of philosophy, may be witnessed as the postmodern convergent aspiration which, in effect, disqualifies the third, the middle, on which they would converge'.[67]

Rose's criticisms here provoke a question about the politics of the in-between. Do religions contain the narratives of space that permit the middle to be genuinely broken? Or is even this space to be invaded by their certainties? This raises a crucial issue for the meeting of religions—the *nature of the middle* and its significance. If there is to be a genuine relational sense of 'religion and the religious other' then there needs to be difference, perhaps an in-between, or at least a willingness to withdraw and allow the third space to exist—though by no means an uncluttered space. In addition, it is not obvious that such a space need be straightforwardly designated as the 'public sphere' in a Rawlsian sense—a sphere which is possibly laden more with political contingencies and pragmatism than with questions of truth. Philosophers of religious pluralism may see their chief task as defining a focal point—be it soteriological, ethical, mystical, and so on—around which religions can converge. However, there also needs to be the recognition of *private liminalities*. That is, apart from the dense articulations and demarcations by theologians or religious authorities, religious people meet religious others in day-to-day occurrences, moments, and events, some significant, others mundane. In the midst of the ambiguity of ordinariness, perhaps each finds a broken middle that they can inhabit.

Might we also say that disinterest or a 'passivity beyond passivity' is a dispiriting attitude for encountering the religious other? That is, if the meeting of religions is one of mutual self-renunciation or a 'holy middle' then there ceases to be a meeting at all. Moreover, encounters between religions and the religious other can involve a plethora of sights, sounds, rituals, practices, architectures, and cultural oddities. Finding an effective focal point or mode of connectivity with the religious other may be something that can involve the mutual recognition of the anodyne temporal phenomena of religions as much as dwelling on their ultimate concerns. Further, if engagement between religions and the religious other are to be *active* rather than passive then, rather than seeking a greater 'purity', there might be

---

[66] This is Rose's account of Taylor in *The Broken Middle*: Rose, *Mourning*, 284.
[67] Rose, *Mourning*, 284.

something more contingent and occasional. In his chapter, Jeffery Long's reference to the *Gita* and the overgrown fig tree creates a vivid image that evokes a *natural* sense of relation and development; meeting the other involves a complex negotiation that need not be predetermined.

The relationship between religions and their religious others is also something to be negotiated within a specific tradition. That is, there is the importance of *intra*-religious conversation in the meeting of religions. Ostensibly, this refers to conversations internal to a specific religious community or, perhaps, a kind of intra-textuality, but we might go further by claiming that this is a matter for the individual as well. In another important essay, Jonathan Z. Smith argues that 'otherness' is not a descriptive category but rather 'a political and linguistic project'.[68] Moreover, rather than thinking of the other as an ontological category, or an 'absolute state of being', Smith wants to accentuate the situational context that gives meaning to otherness: 'Something is other only in respect to something else.'[69] It is important to think of the 'proximate other'—both in the situational sense but also in terms of similarity. The real problem of the other, then, is not that he is something wholly alien, mysterious, or 'not like us', quite the contrary, it is when 'he is TOO-MUCH-LIKE-US, or when he claims to BE-US'. In which case, the urgency is not a matter of finding an appropriate location for the other but to 'situate ourselves'[70] in relation to that otherness. Again, Barnes seeks to move away from what he sees as rather monolithic debates in the theology of religions and reflect on the attitude and posture of the Christian self towards otherness. He writes: 'The crucial questions . . . are about what happens to Christian identity when the self encounters the other by crossing the threshold into another world.'[71] This is both a narrative that concerns the effect of the other on self-identity and, perhaps more profoundly, it betrays an inner dialogue of the *self with itself*—an internalized narrative. Such ideas are articulated by writers like Paul Ricoeur in his monumental *Oneself as Another*, and Maurice Merleau-Ponty in his *The Prose of the World*. The experience of the other is actually something that is found within my own self. For Ricoeur, the identity of the self is inextricably bound up in the presence of the other, selfhood and otherness are inseparable, and one may also be able to see the other as being like oneself. In a series of provocative insights, Merleau-Ponty writes:

> As I have said, we shall never understand how it is that another can appear to us; what is before us is an object. We must understand that the problem does not lie there but is to understand how I can make myself into two, how I can decenter myself. *The experience of the other is always that of a replica of myself, of a response to myself* . . . It is in the very depths of myself that this strange articulation with the other is fashioned. The mystery of the other is nothing but the mystery of myself . . . For the miracle of perception of another lies first of all

---

[68] Jonathan Z. Smith, 'What a Difference a Difference Makes', in Smith, *Relating Religion*, 275.
[69] Smith, 'What a Difference', 275.
[70] Smith, 'What a Difference', 275.
[71] Barnes, *Theology and Dialogue*, 23.

in that everything which qualifies as a being to my eyes does so only by coming, whether directly or not, within my range, by reckoning in my experience, entering my world.[72]

Even though Merleau-Ponty also stresses the other as external to the self, in the passage above he perceives that the encounter with the other is not merely a disruption that we apprehend outside of ourselves: it is not about exteriority *in toto*. Instead, having brought the other 'within my range', I manage to decentre myself and construct an experience of the other within myself. So, connecting this to our focus on 'religion and the religious other', the meeting with the religious other ought to be a profoundly *intra*-religious discussion; or even a matter for individual religious believers and their personal internalization of meetings with others. This does not involve reading the other as stranger or alien, or that which is somewhere distant geographically; but rather it involves self-recognition, empathy, sympathy, and perhaps a new sense of psychological proximity that makes the other 'understood' or, at least, brings the other more fully into view. However, here we have to balance, or at least acknowledge, two different imperatives: the need for an authentic reading of the other, *and* the need to cultivate positive attitudes of encounter with otherness. It is not clear that these two imperatives are complementary. If 'empathy' is about attempting to step inside or appropriate the experience of the other, then this may be difficult to reconcile with an equal imperative to uphold the autonomy or mystery of the other—to avoid hermeneutical violence by leaving the other pristine and *unread*.

UNIVERSAL VISIONS AND FINITE ENCOUNTERS

Elizabeth Harris's chapter on Buddhism in this section highlights a tension that seems to be held in common by many religions and their encounters with the religious other; this is a tension that is also indicated in other chapters—such as David Thomas's on Islam and Schmidt-Leukel's on Christianity. It relates to the possibility that the efficacy of the other's spiritual practices and observances might be acknowledged, admired, or even incorporated into their own religious tradition, but at the same time those practices are not understood on their own terms but are *subsumed* into the host narratives. Moreover, even if there is some form of mutual admiration or borrowing that occurs between traditions, we might ask how deep are such engagements with the religious other? Or, how influential are the teachings of one tradition when it comes to causing profound shifts in belief or even wholehearted adoption by the religious other? The British theologian, John Milbank, explains this with reference to the universality already present in *world* religions: 'The major religions are notoriously not

---

[72] Maurice Merleau-Ponty, *The Prose of the World*, ed. Claude Lefort, tr. John O-Neill (London: Heinemann, 1984), 135 (emphasis mine).

so susceptible to conversion, or accommodation, precisely because they already embody a more abstract, universal, and deterritorialized cultural framework…'[73] In the context of Buddhism, another scholar, Karl Schmeid, is sceptical concerning the influence of Christian belief on Buddhist teaching:

> They [Buddhists] tend to assume that even though Christianity may pose radical challenges to Buddhism in certain practical areas, it is quite inadequate when it comes to a philosophical understanding of reality. They expect to learn from Christian ethics and social involvement, from its active spirit and its methods of propagation, but such elements have nothing to do with the essence of religion as they see it, and there, at the core, Buddhism is unsurpassed.[74]

In the case of Buddhist–Christian relations the differences are perhaps even more acute when we consider the significant ontological differences (e.g. 'becoming' rather than 'being'). However, looking more broadly, this point highlights the *non-negotiable* aspects that are found in religions. What is precisely non-negotiable in some traditions is often difficult to pin down, and may actually be more culturally or historically determined and contingent than ontologically fixed.[75] Moreover, this is not allowed to be *rooted* in the other's own system in such a way that it would disrupt the core foundational beliefs of the host tradition—ultimately the core beliefs of a host tradition are not 'surpassed' by the other. Here there is simultaneously both a complementarity and competitiveness in the relationship. However, even this dilemma seems to assume some kind of parity between traditions in order for the other to be recognized and practices compared and absorbed. Thus a deeper question concerns *criteria*. How might the relationship between religions be classified? Whereas the authors of the subsequent chapters in this section might be able to cite authorities or canonical reference points for their pieces, the question is whether or not it is possible to do the same for what ostensibly looks like an abstract reflection on the essence of religion and the dynamics of relationships. Ellen Armour warns that '[t]he task of finding a conceptual vocabulary for religion that can cross cultures and contexts without falling prey to reductionism has proven an elusive task'.[76]

Reductionism may well be a consequence of trying to find commonality, but the practice of articulating an essence may actually be less offensive in this respect than *anodyne*. In this case, the danger is not so much the imposition of a homogeneity that irons out difference but

---

[73] Milbank, 'End of Dialogue', 180. As a variant on this, it could be suggested that the sheer wealth of experience, throughout long histories, means that explanations for the presence of the other are already fully established in the narrative of a major tradition. That is, it might not just be because of 'de-territorialization' or abstraction, but because of a long acquaintance with religious others that have set many *precedents*.

[74] Karl Schmied, 'Jesus in Recent Buddhist Writings Published in the West', in Perry Schmidt-Leukel *et al.* (eds), *Buddhist Perceptions of Jesus* (St Ottilien: EOS Verlag, 1999), 138.

[75] Or rather, the non-negotiable aspects of a tradition may have assumed their status due to historical factors leading to *ingrained* ideas and practices just as much as fundamental creeds and belief statements.

[76] Ellen Armour, 'Theology in Modernity's Wake', *Journal of the American Academy of Religion*, 74/1 (2006), 9.

more that such homogeneities turn out to be notoriously weak and content-less—they possess little power to iron out anything. This may be applicable to liberal theories of religion, but Jeffrey Long's discussion of Hinduism in this section of the book raises the question of a much more culturally ingrained form of homogeneity and essentialism. Radhakrishnan's view of Hinduism as 'religion itself' in its most basic and universal sense is hardly an anodyne feature in the political context of contemporary India. Moreover, it seems impossible to assess what religion is in its most *excellent* form. Whilst a more general enquiry might presume that it can draw on the range of examples evidenced in different faiths, the question remains as to *what* these examples illustrate.

In his discussion about the concept of a focal point, Frank Hoffman argues that the difficulty with finding a common focal point for religions is that it results in empty generalizations that have no real descriptive power. By using 'only *etic* categories…there will be "common ground" found in all religions but it will be so cliché ridden as to border on the vacuous'.[77] Nevertheless, such problems emerge when there is the search for a single focal point which is supposed to account for *all* the data. It is entirely possible to imagine that, just as the use of theory in the academic study of religion can serve to stake out provisional 'conceptual territories' in order to develop understanding, the actual encounter between religions may be facilitated by the acknowledgement of provisional or limited 'grounds' for meeting. Many of the most recent strategies in interreligious meeting have concentrated on distracting attention away from absolute concerns towards more limited contexts and objectives. So, for practitioners of comparative theology, the goal is to immerse oneself in an aspect of the other faith, perhaps a particular sacred text.[78] That is, concentrating on small localized areas and concerns rather than macro theological issues. Even less defined (deliberately so) are the surprising and improvised meetings between Abrahamic faiths created within the practice of Scriptural Reasoning which might indicate 'deep reasonings' that are not built upon fixed theological agreement or criteria but on friendships made from regular engagement and conversation.

Edward Kessler's chapter in this section reminds us of space and territory. In his case, geographical space denotes a covenantal relationship with different groups and the question of *territory* becomes another focal point for both encounter and conflict. Space is an opportunity for creative meeting. Spaces are important for the practice of Scriptural Reasoning where the idea of campus, house (with different places of worship in different religions: mosques, synagogues, temples), and tent (nomadic meeting ground) are differentiated. I have suggested elsewhere that the meanings that might be generated are created by the people that meet in these spaces whenever and wherever they happen. That is, through the frisson of encounter, engagement, friendship, commonality, or disagreement, *something*

---

[77] Frank Hoffman, 'The Concept of a Focal Point in Models for Inter-Religious Understanding', in James Kellenberger (ed.), *Inter-Religious Models and Criteria* (London: Macmillan, 1993), 174.

[78] See Francis Clooney, *Comparative Theology: Deep Learning across Religious Borders* (Oxford: Wiley-Blackwell, 2010).

emerges—apart from formal focal categories.[79] Additionally, what our discussion has suggested is that spaces are rarely pure. That is, they can be 'holy', 'broken', 'mended', or 'negotiated'.

I noted above Martin Kavka's observation that religious studies as an academic discipline was historically wedded to a sense of responsibility to *translate* religions for the sake of peace. Underpinning this was an assumption that uncovering a deeper unity between religious traditions was an important component in accomplishing mutual recognition. The work of French philosopher, Paul Ricoeur, has been described as a philosophy of translation. Ricoeur does not understand translation to be a mere act of linguistic facility. In the first essay in his *On Translation* (2006), he describes translation as 'work' that is deeply connected to an experience of gain and loss. There is a contrast between the urge to gain a 'perfect translation'—a gain in the sense that there would be no loss or sacrifice of meaning involved in either language in the process—and the acceptance that loss is inevitable because of 'the impassable difference of the peculiar and the foreign'.[80] The search for what Ricoeur calls a 'recaptured universality' is an attempt to 'abolish the memory of the foreign and maybe the love of one's own language, hating the mother tongue's provincialism'.[81] The inability to find an absolute translation produces a 'mourning', however in this very mourning is also to be found happiness when there is an acknowledgement of 'the difference between adequacy and equivalence, equivalence without adequacy'.[82] Instead of trying to gain the 'adamantine logos of pure correspondences',[83] there is 'linguistic hospitality...where the pleasure of dwelling in the other's language is balanced by the pleasure of receiving the foreign word at home, in one's own welcoming house'.[84] Underlying this is a sense of what might be called an intimacy with regard to seeing the other. That is, Ricoeur's mention of our own welcoming house points to an inner hospitality both in terms of the intra-textuality of communities and the personal worlds of individuals. In trying to locate this in the classic typology, perhaps Ricoeur's thoughts above are, conceptually, a relative of 'inclusivist' strategies that seek to view the other from *within* the scheme of one's own faith. He recognizes the sense of loss in trying—without possibility of success—to find the space for 'pure correspondences', but nonetheless describes an adventure in hospitality that is happy to settle for 'equivalence without adequacy'. The virtue of this is that, rather than deferring personal responsibility to the middle, so to speak, or imagining that the *real* ground for meeting the religious other is to be found in a third space, it forces us to review the resources for hospitality, basic character, and authenticity in our own traditions. In similar fashion, the postmodern sociologist, Zygmunt Bauman, suggested that a postmodern loss of ethical objectivity or certainty symbolized by rational ethical 'codes' ends up, ironically, compelling the need for moral responsibility and engagement.[85]

[79] See my *Ways of Meeting and the Theology of Religions*.
[80] Ricoeur, *On Translation*, 9.
[81] Ricoeur, *On Translation*, 9.
[82] Ricoeur, *On Translation*, 10.
[83] Kearney, 'Introduction: Ricoeur's Philosophy of Translation', p. xvii.
[84] Ricoeur, *On Translation*, 10.
[85] Zygmunt Bauman, *Life in Fragments* (Oxford: Blackwell, 1995), 34–7.

CONCLUSION

This chapter has wrestled with two aspects. The first aspect concerned the validity of 'religion and the religious other' as a general topic. Whilst recognizing the critics who are suspicious of the modern heritage of *religio*, it seems possible to propose that a more general interest emerges out of both a religious desire to transcend finitude and point beyond the temporal and contingent, as well as reflecting a more academic intellectual interest in theory and the philosophical practice of de-contextualization. From a religious perspective, I argued that speaking in general terms about religions and the religious other may simply emerge from a 'realist' view of religious language and expectations—and this is what gives licence to a discourse outside of (or 'above') culture. If this first aspect concerned the general vision of 'religion and the religious other', the second aspect sought to reflect on the practice of meeting the other. Here, the concrete actualities of engagement are more complex, demanding, and 'rich'. In fact, attempting to set up a pristine, neutral, or abstracted meeting space is problematic and potentially undesirable. Reflecting on the practice of meeting the other, one becomes wary of dealing with abstract *intensities* or, as Gillian Rose put it, 'holy middles'. Further, I suggested that if the meetings with 'others' are to be active rather than *sterilized* then, rather than seeking a greater purity in such meetings, we might settle for something more contingent and occasional. Paradoxically, even if the very idea of 'religions and the religious other' is inspired by a universal vision and outward-look, in our meetings we don't look for what Ricoeur called the 'perfect translation'. Our engagement with the concrete other ends up being a discourse of finitude where universal ideas or doctrines are often suspended or bracketed out.

FURTHER READING

Michael Barnes, *Theology and the Dialogue of Religions* (Cambridge: Cambridge University Press, 2002).

Willi Braun and Russell T. McCutcheon (eds), *Guide to the Study of Religion* (London: Continuum, 2011).

Peter Byrne, *Prolegomena to Religious Pluralism: Reference and Realism in Religion* (London: Macmillan, 1995).

Catherine Cornille, *The Im-Possibility of Interreligious Dialogue* (New York: Crossroad, 2008).

Patrik Fridlund, Lucie Kaennel, and Catherina Stenquist (eds), *Plural Voices: Intradisciplinary Perspectives on Interreligious Issues* (Leuven: Peeters, 2009).

Jonathan Z. Smith, *Relating Religion: Essays in the Study of Religion* (Chicago: University of Chicago Press, 2004).

Michael Theunissen, *The Other: Studies in the Social Ontology of Husserl, Heidegger, Sartre and Buber* (Cambridge, Mass.: MIT Press, 1984).

Hendrick Vroom, Henry Jansen, and Jerald Gort (eds), *Religions View Religions: Explorations in Pursuit of Understanding* (Amsterdam: Rodopi, 2005).

CHAPTER 3

Hinduism and the Religious Other

JEFFERY D. LONG

WHAT IS HINDUISM?

An historical review of Hindu relations with the religious other engages one with a variety of issues that have both theoretical and theological implications. What are the boundaries of Hinduism? Is it only the ideology of a localized, hereditary priesthood that has successfully suffused Indian civilization with its caste-based, fundamentally exclusionary social vision? Or is it a broader concept, with the word Hinduism being an unfortunate geographically and ethnically limiting term for a progressive universalism that aspires to include all otherness in a boundless unity, incorporating all religions and all philosophies—even modern science— into its vast vision of existence? Or is Hinduism something between these two opposite poles: a civilizational and cultural ethos that aspires to universality while it simultaneously affirms its deep rootedness in a specific geographic space and in a specific historical community? The aim of this chapter is not to resolve these questions. As phrased, they presuppose a singular essence of Hinduism whose nature can be definitively settled: that Hinduism *is* this or that. The reality is that the term Hinduism is used in many ways. The aim here is a sense of how those persons who are called Hindus have related to the religious other historically.

Hindu attitudes towards the religious other encompass a vast spectrum. On the one hand—and as with the members of other ancient, widespread religious communities—there are Hindus whose attitudes towards the religious other have been characterized primarily by fear and hatred, and who have sought to minimize their interactions with the other. There are also Hindus who have engaged with the other polemically, not out of hatred, but to advance ideas. On the other hand, there are Hindus who express an acceptance of the religious other so radical as to challenge the very notion of a singular tradition with set boundaries: who see all religions as alternative paths to the same ultimate goals to which Hindus aspire—in effect, as different forms of Hinduism. Views have also been expressed that see Hinduism as the highest, fullest, most comprehensive manifestation of the deep truths that all religions affirm. Finally, it must be noted that what is now called Hinduism is internally varied in such a way that the religious other towards whom all of these attitudes are directed is often a Hindu other. The object of one Hindu community's exclusion or acceptance can be another Hindu community. This is especially true the further back one goes in history. This last point is not insignificant or accidental but is, in part, an effect of how the term Hinduism has come to be defined and used in the past two centuries. For most of human history, the religion—or family of religions—which now goes by the name Hinduism was not called by this name, nor was there a singular community of persons who called themselves by the name Hindu. Rather, what existed—and, to some extent, what still exists—was a vast and complex network of sometimes overlapping and sometimes quite distinct traditions and communities to which the name Hindu is now collectively and retroactively applied, both by scholars of religion and by contemporary Hindu practitioners.[1]

A good image for the development of Hindu identity over time might be that of the upside-down fig tree found in the fifteenth chapter of the *Bhagavad Gītā*. 'There is an eternal fig tree, with its roots above and its branches below, and they say that the Vedic hymns are its leaves. Whoever knows this tree indeed knows the Vedas.'[2] The *Vedas* are a set of ancient texts regarded as sacred in what are now called Hindu traditions, and indeed it is the very fact that these traditions regard these texts in this way that constitutes them as Hindu. In its original context the tree image does not refer to the development of Hinduism through time but it may nevertheless be apt. Most religions develop 'branches' from the 'trunk' of the teaching of the original founder. Like the upside-down fig tree of the *Gītā*, Hinduism starts as many branches that coalesce into a trunk: the emergent Hindu identity. The traditions and systems of philosophy of the ancient and the classical periods become the rich, diverse inheritance of contemporary Hindus. Yesterday's religious 'other' becomes today's co-religionist. Branches merge to form a single trunk denoted by the novel term Hinduism. How did this coalescence occur? Why do some ancient and classical Indic traditions come to be regarded as Hindu? And why do others, such as Buddhism and Jainism, come to be defined as religiously other? The criterion that has become standard for defining a text, practice, or system of belief or worship as Hindu is its disposition towards the Vedas. If a tradition affirms the sanctity or authority of the Vedas it is seen as part of Hinduism. But if a tradition rejects Vedic authority, it is defined as *not* Hindu, and so as a religious other.

The definition of Hinduism with the Vedic family of religions is now dominant, both in scholarly discourse and among Hindus, with Buddhism and Jainism regarded as distinct and separate religious traditions, deserving of their own chapters in textbooks on the world's

---

[1] Cf. J. E. Llewellyn (ed.), *Defining Hinduism: A Reader* (New York: Routledge, 2005).
[2] *Bhagavad Gītā*, 15:1, tr. George Thompson (New York: North Point Press, 2008), 71.

religions, and often defined in opposition to Hinduism, due to their rejection of Vedic and Brahmanical authority and their criticisms of Vedic practices such as animal sacrifice and the exclusionary practices associated with the caste system. This definition of Hinduism is far from perfect, for it obscures the differences among the traditions it encompasses, as well as the similarities these traditions share with Buddhism and Jainism, which can be made to seem more *other* to ostensibly Hindu traditions than they truly are. For example, Buddhists and Jains share with Hindus a belief in a cycle of rebirth, a principle of action—or *karma*—that fuels this cycle, and the aspiration for *mokṣa*, or liberation from this cycle, as well as worshipping many of the same deities as Hindus, which take the form of guardians of the Buddhist or Jain *dharma*.[3] It is also the case that some Hindu traditions bear a greater resemblance to Buddhism and Jainism than they do to other Hindu traditions. One of the most contentious intra-Hindu debates is that between the non-dualist, Advaita form of Vedānta and more dualistic forms of Vedānta. It is not uncommon in the classical and medieval period for adherents of dualistic forms of Vedānta to attack Advaita Vedānta on the basis of its resemblances to Buddhism.[4]

Are there alternatives to the current definition? While the Hindu nationalist definition of Hinduism as encompassing all Indic religions allows the family of Indic traditions, with their shared assumptions, to fall under one term, it is rejected by at least some Jains, Sikhs, and Buddhists as imperialist. It would be like calling all Abrahamic religions forms of Islam or Judaism. Many contemporary Hindus believe a Hindu identity, essentially as understood today as the Vedic tradition, has always existed. The extensive polemical literature of the classical period, in which various systems of thought now regarded as Hindu debate one another as critically as they engage the beliefs of the Buddhists or the Jains, however, refutes this view. In reaction to this idea of Hinduism as eternal and changeless, another view has arisen which sees Hinduism as a wholly modern construct of orientalist scholarship in combination with the work of Hindus engaged in the project of nation-building and forging an identity out of ancient and classical Indic sources in opposition to Islam and Christianity.[5] But this view has been contested by scholars who have argued that it diminishes the role of Hindus in defining Hindu traditions, neglecting the degree to which indigenous trends towards a singular Hindu identity predate and engage with orientalist constructs.[6] For there is evidence that some measure of coalescence and synthesis of earlier traditions was occurring before the arrival of European scholars, who built on an identity construction process already under way, as in the

[3] See Jeffery D. Long, *A Vision for Hinduism: Beyond Hindu Nationalism* (London: I. B. Tauris, 2007), 34–5; and *Jainism: An Introduction* (London: I. B. Tauris, 2009), 23–7.

[4] The 16th-cent. Vedāntin, Vijñānabhikṣu, in fact regards Advaita as a *nāstika* system, and therefore, in today's terminology, as non-Hindu: a profoundly ironic fact, considering that mainstream modern constructions of Hinduism cast Advaita Vedānta as the pre-eminent Hindu school of thought. See Andrew J. Nicholson, *Unifying Hinduism: Philosophy and Identity in Indian Intellectual History* (New York: Columbia University Press, 2010), 119.

[5] See D. N. Jha, *Rethinking Hindu Identity* (London: Equinox, 2009); Sharada Sugirtharajah, *Imagining Hinduism: A Postcolonial Perspective* (London: Routledge, 2003); and Hermann Kulke and Gunther-Dietz Sontheimer (eds), *Hinduism Reconsidered* (New Delhi: Manohar, 2001).

[6] Cf. Brian K. Pennington, *Was Hinduism Invented? Britons, Indians, and the Colonial Construction of Religion* (New York: Oxford University Press, 2005).

work of the late medieval philosopher, Vijñānabhikṣu, who synthesized elements of the Sāṃkhya, Yoga, and Nyāya systems into his system of Vedānta, thus helping lay the foundation for the modern understanding of all of these schools of thought as parts of a shared, singular Hindu tradition. Although it is a relatively late development, it is also not a wholly modern one. Certainly orientalists and early Indian nationalists played a major role in constructing Hindu identity, but not in an historical vacuum, or with no basis in a prior indigenous discourse with a trajectory towards unifying previously disparate traditions. In addition to the historical argument, another criticism of the view that Hinduism is a wholly modern invention is that it tends to delegitimize the intellectual work of those Hindu thinkers of today who do perceive themselves as operating from within a singular tradition, casting them as mere 'Neo-Hindus', possessed of a sense of self that is somehow inauthentic due to its being based on a cultural construct—as if there were such a thing as a self that was *not* a cultural construct, or that a Hindu self is somehow less genuine than other selves.[7]

Hinduism and its Religious Others

Bearing in mind the inadequate and historically fraught nature of the term Hindu, and the fact that projecting this term onto the past is just that—a projection of unity onto what were at one time many diverse traditions—we now turn to a review of Hindu relations with the religious other.

Proto-Hinduism? A Mysterious, Compelling, and Peaceful Civilization

If one operates with the standard definition of Hinduism as the Vedic family of traditions and searches for relations between this family of traditions and its religious others, one presumably should look to the origins of this family of traditions—its roots (or in this case, its 'leaves') in earlier traditions. But when did the Vedic traditions originate? Scholarly consensus places the composition of the *Ṛg Veda*, the earliest extant Vedic text, between 1700 and 1500 BCE—though some Hindu scholars contest this, placing the *Ṛg Veda* at a much earlier point in time. Just prior to the standard date at which scholarly consensus places the composition of the *Ṛg Veda* was the advanced urban phase of the most ancient Indian civilization—the Indus Valley Civilization—which lasted from roughly 2600 to 1900 BCE. The Indus civilization as a whole, however, is even older than these dates suggest, for this civilization has antecedents in the Mehrgarh culture, which dates to roughly 7000 BCE. Some revisionist Hindu scholars, and others influenced by their arguments, claim that the *Ṛg Veda*

---

[7] The term 'Neo-Hindu' is generally attributed to Paul Hacker. See Wilhelm Halbfass, *Philology and Confrontation: Paul Hacker on Traditional and Modern Vedanta* (Albany, NY: SUNY, 1995).

dates from the period before the Indus Valley Civilization's advanced urban phase—between 7000 and 3000 BCE. These scholars argue, moreover, that the Indus civilization is itself the product of a Vedic culture.[8] While the weight of scholarly opinion is opposed to this view, adhering instead to the view that the *Ṛg Veda* was composed after the Indus civilization's advanced urban phase, and that the Indus civilization, moreover, represents a culture quite distinct from that revealed in the *Ṛg Veda*, it is certainly the case that ancient Vedic culture also shares some overlap with that of the civilization of the Indus Valley, such as a shared lunar calendar.[9] So even if it would be anachronistic to call the Indus Valley Civilization Hindu in anything like a modern sense—and to refer to it as Vedic would fly in the face of the weight of the evidence and scholarly reflection thereon—it might not be unreasonable to start our search for Hindu relations with the religious other with the Indus Valley Civilization: not as a Vedic culture, but a precursor of and contributor to at least one sub-current of that culture.

Our problem, though, is the fact that very little is known, beyond speculation on the meanings of archaeological artefacts, about the religion of the Indus Valley Civilization. Our current inability to read the Indus script creates a compelling aura of mystery around this advanced civilization, and also enables a good deal of speculative projection. What is known with some measure of reliability is that the Indus Valley had a very peaceful culture, with virtually no evidence of warfare or serious social strife for a period of roughly one thousand years—arguably the greatest achievement of this technically advanced, subtle, sophisticated civilization.[10] Was this because only one religion was practised in the Indus Valley, thus eliminating (or greatly reducing) the possibility of religious strife? It does seem clear that a shared ideology prevailed throughout the civilization, though the degree to which it could be characterized as religious remains unknown.

It is tempting to suggest, from a Hindu perspective, that the peaceful character of the Indus civilization is evidence of a theology of religious harmony, such as that promulgated in modern Hindu traditions, for instance the Vedānta movement of Sri Ramakrishna; or the ideal of equality of religions promoted by Mahātma Gandhi, which shall be examined below. At the same time, it might be equally tempting to suggest, from a 'new atheistic' perspective, that its peaceful nature is evidence that this culture was not religious at all, and so lacking in what has historically been one of humanity's major justifications for warfare. Just enough is known about this civilization to allow one's imagination to run wild with ideologically driven speculation, projecting contemporary biases onto this ancient culture.

---

[8] See Klaus K. Klostermaier, *A Survey of Hinduism*, 3rd edn (Albany, NY: SUNY, 2007), 17–29.

[9] Clear differences existed between the culture of the Indus Valley Civilization and that of the culture that composed the *Ṛg Veda* and, significantly, there is almost no evidence of warfare among diverse religious groups in the Indus Valley Civilization, whereas the *Ṛg Veda* depicts intense conflict between the group that composed its hymns and those who did not revere the gods and goddesses of the Vedic religion. See Wendy Doniger, *The Hindus: An Alternative History* (New York: Penguin, 2009), 86–102.

[10] Jane McIntosh, *A Peaceful Realm: The Rise and Fall of the Indus Civilization* (Boulder, Colo.: Westview Press, 2002).

The early Vedic period: Dāsas, Asuras, and Vrātyas

Turning now to the *Ṛg Veda*, a typology of religious self-identity and religious otherness can be found in the concepts of the *ārya*, or noble, and the *dāsa* or *dāsyu*. These concepts do not suggest a philosophy or theology of religious tolerance, but of aversion to the other; for the terms *dāsa* and *dāsyu* carry implications of the demonic, and of impiety. The *dāsas* are described as those who do not offer the ritual of sacrifice (*yajña*) to the Vedic deities (*devas*). This theme recurs later in the history of Hinduism, as the religious other continues to be characterized (and reviled) as the one who does not pay proper respect to the deities in the form of ritual offerings. During an earlier period in the history of the study of India, the division between *ārya* and *dāsa* was characterized as a racial conflict, fuelling speculation that the authors of the *Ṛg Veda* or their ancestors were light-skinned invaders who attacked a dark-skinned indigenous population. This interpretation has been rejected by many scholars in favour of the view that *ārya* and *dāsa* refer to cultural and ideological differences. The *dāsa*, again, is the reviled religious other who does not offer sacrifice to the deities.[11] The extent to which the warfare between *ārya* and *dāsa* depicted in the *Ṛg Veda* reflects actual, physical warfare or is a purely literary reflection of ideological differences internal to ancient Indian society is unknown. What is clear is that Indian society during the second millennium BCE was divided between those who practised sacrifice to Vedic deities and those who did not, and that those who practised such sacrifice—the *ārya*—regarded those who did not—the *dāsa*—as others towards whom they held an attitude of disapproval.

The distinction between *ārya* and *dāsa* is the earliest Vedic division between religious self and other, but it is not the only one. In the earliest hymns of the *Ṛg Veda*, two terms are used interchangeably to refer to the Vedic deities: the aforementioned *deva*, or 'shining one', and *asura*, or 'spirit'. In the *Avesta*, the literature of the Iranian branch of the Indo-Iranian religious culture, the word *asura*, or *ahura*, is retained and in the later Zoroastrian tradition that emerges from ancient Iranian religion the supreme deity is known by the name *Ahura Mazda*, or 'Wise Lord'. In the later Vedic literature, though, an *asura* comes to refer to a demonic being—the counterpart among the celestial beings of the *dāsa* or *dāsyu* in the human realm— and the *dāsa* is sometimes said to be a worshipper of *asuras*. The warfare between the good *devas* and demonic *asuras* becomes a major theme of later Hindu literature. However, in Zoroastrianism, the *daevas* become the demonic beings and Ahura Mazda the one true God. This transposition of terminology, with each group referring to the deities of the other as demons, and vice versa, is evidence of a very negative attitude towards the religious other. The practitioners of Avestan and Vedic religions see one another as worshipping the 'wrong' deities, the gods of the first group being the demons of the other, and vice versa. An analogy can be drawn with the metamorphosis of the Graeco-Roman nature deity, Pan, with his goat horns and hooves, into the classic Satan of European Christianity.

Apart from references to the *dāsas* as the opponents of Vedic culture and its deities and the transposition of the Vedic and Avestan terms for these two cultures' respective

---

[11]   See Burjor Avari, *India: The Ancient Past* (New York: Routledge, 2007), 61, 67–8.

deities and demons, the only other early Vedic reference to a religious other is to a myste-rious group known as the Vrātyas. With a name meaning 'one who has taken a vow', the Vrātyas were a sect of ascetics who engaged in practices akin to what would later be known as yoga. As described in the *Ṛg Veda* and the somewhat later *Atharva Veda*, they are regarded by Vedic authors with a blend of fear and reverence as persons on the margins of society in possession of paranormal abilities. Insinuations of their ferocity suggest that the Vrātyas may have been warrior monks akin to the later Nāth Yogīs of the medieval and modern periods.

The Vrātyas are a good early example of a group regarded as other by the mainstream Vedic tradition with which Hinduism would later be identified, but which would be regarded today as Hindu. They may constitute a link between contemporary Hindu sub-traditions such as that of the Nāth Yogīs and Śaivism and ancient non-Vedic traditions—including, possibly, that of the Indus Valley Civilization, with its depictions of a Śiva-like being sitting in what appears to be a yoga posture. They may also be genealogically related to ascetic groups that emerged in the middle of the first millennium before the Common Era—the late Vedic period—that include what are now known as the Buddhist and Jain communities.

The Śramaṇa Traditions: Buddhism and Jainism

The dominant religious other of the ancient and classical periods is Buddhism. A shared cri-tique of this 'other' comprises a unifying thread among the diverse traditions now called Hindu. Buddhism, emerging from the teaching of Siddhārtha Gautama in the fifth century BCE, became a very important religious, intellectual, and social presence throughout South Asia with the patronage of the Maurya emperor Aśoka in the third century BCE. The fortunes of this tradition rose and fell in various parts of the subcontinent over the course of the next millennium and a half as lay support was either granted or withheld from the *saṅgha*, the Buddhist monastic community, by kings and other wealthy persons. It was during this period that Buddhists also managed to transmit their tradition across Asia, making Buddhism, in effect, the first missionary religion as such. During the 1500 years of its ascendancy, Buddhism was seen as a major intellectual threat and competitor by the systems of thought now retroactively called Hindu—a threat so potent that Hindu intellectuals rehearsed anti-Buddhist arguments for centuries after actual Buddhist interlocutors were long gone from the subcontinent.

Another prominent religious other with which the ancient and classical Hindu sources engage is Jainism. A close relative of Buddhism, with which it is sometimes conflated—both in ancient and classical Hindu texts and in some early Indological writings—the Jain tradi-tion, in contrast with Buddhism, did not spread extensively outside India until the modern period. It did not die out in India, as Buddhism largely did, but rather survived as the tradition of an affluent, close-knit minority community. Furthermore, a religious other of the ancient and classical period that is widely denounced not only in texts now defined as Hindu, but in Buddhist and Jain sources as well, is the belief system known as Lokāyata or Cārvāka. The extent to which the adherents of this system can be seen as a *religious* other is debatable, however, and indeed depends upon one's definition of religion. The Lokāyatas were adherents of a materialistic metaphysic. They regarded all teachings about deities, an afterlife, or unseen worlds (in short, what many would today call *religion*) with deep suspicion—as clever attempts to dupe the gullible and the weak-minded.[12]

The emergence of Jainism and Buddhism, and the wider ascetic movement, known as the Śramaṇa movement, of which they formed a part, mark the next phase in the history of Hindu relations with the religious other. It is a phase characterized, on the one hand, by a strong rejection of certain features of the emergent Śramaṇa traditions in key Brahmanical texts, and on the other, by almost total assimilation of these same features on a popular level, as well as in later Brahmanical literature, such that contemporary Hinduism might be well be seen as a hybrid of Brahmanical and Śramaṇic religious thought and practice. How did the Śramaṇa movement emerge, and how did it come into contact with the Vedic tradition in such a way as to form its religious other? Between the composition of the early Vedic literature—around 1700 to 1500 BCE for the *Ṛg Veda* and up to about 900 BCE for the remaining early Vedic texts, the *Yajur*, *Sama*, and *Atharva Veda*—and the fifth century BCE there was a gradual expansion of Vedic religious culture from its point of origin in the north-western region of the subcontinent eastward and southward into the Ganges river valley.

Throughout these centuries of expansion, Vedic culture encountered other religious cultures in India, some of which it assimilated as part of the process that would eventually lead to the emergence of Hinduism as it is known today. When one speaks of the expansion of Vedic culture, one is not speaking of military conquest or invasion, though these were not altogether absent as Vedic tribal groups moved into the Ganges valley. One is speaking of social and cultural change, often occurring through the medium of peaceful (albeit spirited) debate and intellectual exchange. The Brahmin priesthood of the Vedic culture engaged in numerous dialogues with various other Indic religious ideologies, some of which it disputed and some of which it adopted. This was not a uniform process, as the Vedic culture and the Brahmin priesthood were not centralized, monolithic entities, any more than Hinduism is today. The eastern half of the Ganges valley was home to a religious culture distinct from the Vedic culture dominant in the north-west. This region, which Indologist Johannes Bronkhorst has dubbed 'Greater Magadha', configured its caste system differently than did the Brahmins of the Vedic

---

[12]   One does sometimes sees Lokāyata or Cārvāka thought described as 'Hindu materialism'. But adherents of this school of thought were most certainly seen as 'other' by adherents of the classical *āstika*, 'Hindu' systems of thought. See Debiprasad Chattopadhyaya, *Lokāyata: A Study in Ancient Indian Materialism* (New Delhi: People's Publishing House, 1959) and Amartya Sen, *The Argumentative Indian: Writings on Indian History, Culture, and Identity* (New York: Picador, 2006).

culture, giving pride of place to the *kṣatriya*, or Warrior caste, and placing very strong emphasis on the doctrines of *karma* and rebirth (which do not receive explicit mention in Vedic literature until the writing of the *Upaniṣads*, the earliest of which date from the time of interaction between the Vedic culture and the culture of Greater Magadha, the middle of the first millennium before the Common Era).[13] It could be argued that the Vedic traditions assimilated their ideas of *karma* and rebirth from the tradition of Greater Magadha.[14]

The point of greatest contention between the Vedic religious culture and the religious culture of Greater Magadha regarded the Vedic practice of ritual sacrifice to the *devas*, the aforementioned deities of the Vedic religion. There is evidence that the adherents of Greater Magadha's religious culture revered the same deities as the Brahmins. The adherents of the religious culture of Greater Magadha, however, objected to the ritual slaying and offering of animals as sacrifices for the deities, seeing violence as an evil action, productive of negative karmic effects. By inflicting harm on another being, one would be inviting similar harm on oneself, either in this life or in a future rebirth. Freedom from the cycle of rebirth required one to cease engaging in such harmful action. In place of the Brahmanical priest offering his sacrifices to the deities, the religious figure valorized in the religion of Greater Magadha was the ascetic who withdrew from all violence—and indeed, ultimately, from any action at all—in pursuit of a state of perfect freedom from action and its effects: *mokṣa*, or liberation, achieved through *nirvāṇa*, or absorption in the highest reality. The Brahmin, or *Brāhmaṇa*, is replaced by the *Śramaṇa*, or 'striver', who puts forth tremendous effort for the sake of enlightenment. The Brahmins, for their part, even while expressing ambivalence about the cruelty involved in animal sacrifice, believed it was necessary to upholding *ṛta*, or the order of the cosmos.

The opposition between the Brahmin and the Śramaṇa became a major dividing line between religious traditions in India from the middle of the first millennium BCE until the decline of Buddhism between the tenth and thirteenth centuries CE.[15] Both religious cultures soon spread beyond their respective points of origin in the north-western and north-eastern regions of India and established centres of influence throughout the subcontinent—temples, monasteries, and places of pilgrimage. The Brahmins constituted a *varṇa*, or caste—a hereditary priestly community—but this was compatible with considerable variety on the intellectual level, and a wide array of belief systems developed among them. These belief systems would emerge in the coming centuries as the *āstika* schools of thought, or *darśanas* as codified by later generations of Brahmanical scholars. Despite their many various differences—which, on some issues, were considerable—these systems of belief and practice were capable of

---

[13] Johannes Bronkhorst, *Greater Magadha: Studies in the Culture of Early India* (Leiden and Boston: Brill, 2007).

[14] Though a plausible case can also be made for the development of these ideas internally to the Vedic tradition as well, from the concept of the relationship between a ritual action (*karman*) and its desired effect or 'fruit' (*phala*). The two accounts need not be mutually exclusive, given the context of intellectual and cultural ferment of northern India during the 1st millennium BCE.

[15] See Wilhelm Halbfass, *India and Europe: An Essay in Understanding* (Albany, NY: SUNY, 1988), 14.

being perceived by later generations as being located, in some sense, in a shared Vedic religious culture.[16]

Similarly, the Śramaṇas were divided into many groups, each of which traced itself to a founding teacher regarded by its adherents as having reached *mokṣa*. The only two of these sects to survive to the present day are, of course, the Jains and the Buddhists. The Jains trace themselves to Mahāvīra (*c.*499–427 BCE), whom they regard as not the first, but only as the most recent in an ancient lineage of twenty-four enlightened masters known as *Tīrthaṅkaras*. Buddhism is, of course, traced to Siddhārtha Gautama, the Buddha (*c.*490–410 BCE), who is similarly regarded by Buddhists as only the most recent of the Buddhas, taking birth to show suffering beings the way to liberation from the cycle of rebirth. But other Śramaṇa groups existed in ancient and classical India as well, such as the Ājīvikas, who were established by a contemporary of Mahāvīra and the Buddha named Makkhali Gosāla. Like the Brahmins, the Śramaṇas, despite their various differences, possessed a shared ideology. What was this ideology? As already mentioned, the greatest difference between the Vedic ideology upheld by the Brahmins and the religious culture of Greater Magadha, from which the Śramaṇa movement emerged, was over the issue of animal sacrifice, which was upheld by the Brahmins as one of the requirements of Vedic ritual, but which was rejected by the Śramaṇas as a cruel, wicked practice, sure to bring bad *karma* to those who practised it.[17]

Significantly, the Brahmins and the Śramaṇas had differing views of the ordering of society, with the Brahmins being strong advocates of a division of the social order based on the relative purity of the occupations that persons pursued for their livelihood: a system of four main divisions of society known as the *varṇas*, each of which is further subdivided into hereditary, endogamous occupational groups known as *jātis*, to both of which the term *caste* is indiscriminately applied in the modern period. From a Brahmanical perspective, this social system was a reflection of *dharma*, the sacred order of the universe. The adherents of the Śramaṇa traditions did not oppose this division of society, in the sense of seeking to overturn the social order or replace it with an alternative; but they did not believe it had any particular sacrality, being merely a convenient, man-made way to divide labour, having no bearing upon the spiritual advancement or purity of the person. A member of any *varṇa* or *jāti*, male or female, could therefore become a Buddhist or Jain monk or nun and aspire to reach *mokṣa*. In religious terms, what mattered to the Buddhists and the Jains was not the parentage of the individual person, but the character of the person. According to one famous formulation that is attributed to the Buddha, 'It is by one's actions, and not by one's birth, that one becomes a

---

[16] The qualifier 'in some sense' is an important one, since one of the differences among these groups was the intensity of their commitment to the Vedas, with some, such as the Mīmāṃsakas, adhering quite closely to such doctrines as the eternal and non-man-made (*apauruṣeya*) nature of the Vedic texts, and others, such as the adherents of Sāṃkhya, being only nominally Vedic, in the sense that they did not explicitly reject the Vedas, but neither did the Vedas play a particularly strong role in their belief system or practice, so far as can be discerned from their texts.

[17] Growing discomfort with the practice of animal sacrifice, reflected even in Vedic texts, eventually led to the abandonment of sacrifice altogether by the mainstream Hindu tradition. See Doniger, *The Hindus* 115–16, and Avari, *India*, 96–8.

Brahmin.' The idea of Brahminhood itself is not being rejected so much as the connection between spiritual purity and birth. Indeed, many Brahmins joined the Śramaṇa movement.

Finally, because both birth–caste discrimination and animal sacrifice were upheld on the basis of the authority of the Vedas, the Śramaṇas rejected Vedic authority, as well as that of the Brahmins who claimed to uphold it. Just as the claim that the Śramaṇas 'reject caste' can be misconstrued as a far more radical claim than it is, the Śramaṇic rejection of the Vedas is not to be seen as a complete rejection of the entire content of this textual tradition; for, as has been mentioned, Buddhism and Jainism incorporate a host of shared beliefs, practices, and deities that are also to be found in the Vedas. What the Śramaṇas rejected was the notion that *any* set of texts or group of persons had absolute authority that had to be followed, even if following that authority led to behaviour that was clearly harmful or immoral, such as caste prejudice or the sacrifice of animals, or for that matter, anything that caused pain or harm— mental, emotional, or physical—to any living being.

In response to the challenge of the Śramaṇa traditions, one can trace two Brahmanical strategies through the Vedic and post-Vedic texts of the ancient and classical periods: that is, from the *Upaniṣads*, composed from the middle and into the latter half of the first millennium BCE, through the epic, legal, philosophical, and narrative literature of the first millennium CE. The first strategy, which has already been alluded to in various contexts, is opposition in the form of rhetorical as well as actual, institutional resistance to the Śramaṇa traditions as a dangerous and demonic religious other, to be refuted and rejected. As has been observed, it is a strategy that Brahmanical traditions also pursued with regard to one another, when there was disagreement on either ritual or philosophical issues, such as among the various schools of philosophy. One might be tempted to call this a 'conventional' response to the religious other, as it is commonly encountered in relations among the religious traditions of the world. The second strategy, though, is of a far more interesting nature, and would eventually come to define what is now widely regarded as a distinctively Hindu mode of interacting with the religious other: *inclusivism*. The first evidence of inclusivism in Brahmanical sources is in the *Upaniṣads*—late Vedic texts which incorporate many Śramaṇic views and critiques of Vedic traditions into their interpretation of reality. In the *Chāndogya Upaniṣad* especially, one finds criticisms of the notion that being a Brahmin by birth is a sufficient criterion for a life of holiness and worthiness for pursuing Vedic study.[18]

Throughout the *Upaniṣads*, one sees a critique of Vedic ritual to the extent that the fruits of such ritual—such as rebirth in heaven—are viewed by those who practise them as the ultimate good. The authors of the *Upaniṣads* are entirely at one with the Śramaṇas in seeing the ultimate good as release from the cycle of rebirth, and from the fruits of action. Also like the Śramaṇas, they see realizing this good as requiring a life of asceticism and renunciation. The 'Śramaṇization' of Hindu thought evidenced in the *Upaniṣads* is a trajectory that is

---

[18] See *Upaniṣads*, tr. Patrick Olivelle (New York: Oxford University Press, 1996).

continued in the Hindu epic literature of the early Common Era, such as in the *Bhagavad Gītā*, an Upaniṣad-style dialogue that is contained in the much larger *Mahābhārata*. The tone taken against adherents of the earlier Vedic ritual is striking, in words that could have been composed by a Buddhist or a Jain of the ancient or classical period.

> Some people please themselves by debating the Vedas. They recite the florid Vedic chants, but they have no insight, while ever saying that only the Vedas matter! In their hearts they are driven by desire and are eager for heaven. Their words promise rebirth as the fruit of their actions. Their talk is all about their elaborate rituals whose purpose is to gain pleasure and power. They are obsessed with pleasure and power! The words of the Vedas deprive them of good sense . . . The world of the Vedas is the natural world with its three conditions. Arjuna, live in the world that is beyond this one, free of its conditions and dualities . . . As useful as a water tank is when there is flooding in all directions, that is how useful all of the Vedas are for a Brahmin who has true insight.[19]

It is not that the efficacy of the Vedic ritual is denied. Such ritual does, indeed, according to the *Bhagavad Gītā* (and before it, the *Upaniṣads*), lead to the ends that its adherents promise. But these ends are not the ultimate end, from the perspective expressed here. Rebirth in the material world leads, as a Buddhist or Jain would say, to suffering. Even the attainment of one's desires is ultimately unsatisfactory, for the fruits of action are ephemeral. Freedom is the answer, achieved through renunciation of the fruits of action.

The division that results from the adoption by many Brahmins, such as the authors of the *Upaniṣads*, of a more Śramaṇic religious outlook, between these Brahmins and their more traditional brethren, who continued to uphold the ancient Vedic ritual, with its occasional acts of animal sacrifice, leads to the emergence of two distinct schools of Vedic interpretation: the earlier or *Pūrva Mīmāṃsā*, which can be identified with the older, more conservative school of Brahmanical thought, and the later, *Uttara Mīmāṃsā*, better known as Vedānta. It is not, however, only in the Vedānta tradition that a Śramaṇization of Hinduism can be seen. The *Dharma Śāstra*, or legal literature of the early classical period—roughly the end of the first millennium BCE and the beginning of the first millennium CE—displays, even in a conservative Brahmanical milieu, deep ambivalence about the act of animal sacrifice, incorporating endorsements of animal sacrifice alongside injunctions to avoid harming any living thing. By the end of the first millennium CE, due at least in part to reforms established by the Vedāntic teacher, or *ācārya*, Śaṅkara (788–820), animal sacrifice is all but abandoned in most Hindu communities, and the Śramaṇic dietary practice of vegetarianism becomes the standard for orthodox Brahmins. So widespread has vegetarianism and rejection of animal sacrifice become in contemporary Hinduism that scholarship which speaks of ancient Vedic animal sacrifice and non-vegetarian dietary practices is quite controversial, and rejected as a distortion of authentic Vedic practice.[20] One could almost argue that the inclusivist strategy of at least some Brahmins towards

---

[19]   *Bhagavad Gītā*, 2: 42–6 (tr. Thompson), 12–13.
[20]   See Jha, *Rethinking Hindu Identity,* 1–9, 48–61.

the Śramaṇic traditions has led, substantively, to a major transformation in the actual practice and self-understanding of the tradition. Hinduism is, in many ways, one could say, a Brahmanical container with Śramaṇic content: animal sacrifice is replaced by vegetarianism and the practice of caste coexists with a rejection of the idea of birth caste as having final religious significance. 'For, Arjuna, no matter how low their birth may be—whether they are women, or villagers, or low-caste slaves—those who rely on me all attain to the final goal.'[21]

The Śramaṇization of Hinduism can be illustrated by the transformation of one story in particular over the course of its repetition in various Hindu texts: the story of the Buddha *avatār*. In its first known occurrence, the story of the incarnation of the Hindu deity, Viṣṇu, as the Buddha, is a violently anti-Buddhist narrative. Invoking the ancient Vedic trope of the adherents of non-Vedic religions as *asuras*—or demonic beings characterized by their impious refusal to offer sacrifice to the deities (*devas*)—it is said that Viṣṇu appeared as the Buddha to delude the *asuras* into not performing Vedic ritual, thereby losing the powers it bestows.[22] In later Hindu texts, however, such as the *Gītā Govinda*, composed by the thirteenth-century poet, Jayadeva, and the *Devībhagavata Purāṇa*, it is said that Viṣṇu became incarnate as the Buddha 'in order to stop the slaughter of animals and to destroy the sacrifices of the wicked'.[23] As Doniger observes, 'For many centuries, Hindus worshiped as a Hindu god the image of the Buddha at the Mahabodhi temple in Bodh Gaya in Bihar (where the Buddha is said to have become enlightened, a major pilgrimage site for Buddhists).'[24]

It is tempting to conclude that the inclusion and actual assimilation of many elements of Śramaṇa traditions into Brahmanical religion—resulting, one could argue, in the emergence of what is now called Hinduism—was facilitated by the fact that, for all of their differences, the Brahmanical and Śramaṇa traditions shared much more than divided them, like the shared cosmology of *karma* and rebirth and the soteriological goal of liberation. Such a conclusion is inattentive to the extent to which this cosmology and this soteriological goal were also assimilated into the Vedic tradition from its encounter with the religious culture of Greater Magadha. Such an analysis also downplays the extent to which Hindus were able to assimilate, in a similar fashion in which they assimilated aspects of Buddhism and Jainism, elements of traditions with much more radically differing cosmological assumptions—namely, Islam and Christianity.

Islam, Sikhism, and Christianity

Leaving behind the classical period and entering the medieval phase of Indian history, around the thirteenth century, the next major religious other to confront Hindu traditions is Islam. This relative newcomer presents a different kind of challenge to Hindu thought from the

---

[21] *Bhagavad Gītā*, 9: 32. Kṛṣṇa's referring to those who 'rely on' him is also evidence of the emergent *bhakti*, or devotional, movement within Hinduism.

[22] See Doniger, *The Hindus*, 483.

[23] Doniger, *The Hindus*, 484.

[24] Doniger, *The Hindus*, 484.

religious others of the ancient and classical periods. If one sets aside Lokāyata materialism, which seems to have been widely rejected by all of other systems of thought,[25] the Buddhist and Jain other, again, share with most Hindu systems of thought a number of cosmological assumptions, such as the existence of the cycle of birth, death, and rebirth, or *saṃsāra*, and the principle of reciprocal action, or *karma*, which fuels this cycle, and the aspiration for liberation from this cycle, or *mokṣa*, as the ultimate soteriological aim, as well as sharing a number of deities, ritual observances, and even holidays.[26] Islam, however, includes a worldview more radically other to Hinduism than those of traditions like Buddhism and Jainism inasmuch as it affirms a strict monotheism, a single lifetime followed by divine judgement, a single eternal afterlife in either hell or paradise, and wholly aniconic forms of worship. Islam also constituted a major institutional challenge to Hinduism, with the overthrow of Hindu kings and the destruction of many Hindu institutions.

With the coming of European traders and missionaries in the early modern period, the next major religious other to Hinduism is Christianity, accompanied by forms of social, political, and economic organization and systems of philosophy truly different in their deep cosmological and metaphysical assumptions from those of Hinduism. Possibly even more dramatically than Islam, Christianity also constitutes an institutional challenge to Hinduism, particularly with the emergence of European colonial rule of India.[27] There is a danger, however, in overstating the 'otherness' of Muslims and Christians, to the degree that Indian Muslims and Christians, who have now lived for many centuries in a Hindu cultural milieu, share a good many assumptions and practices with Hindus that they do not share with their co-religionists from other parts of the world. Exaggerating the otherness of Indian Muslims and Christians is a very common trope of the Hindu nationalist movement, which shall be discussed in greater depth later, and which regards Muslims and Christians as adherents of 'foreign' religious traditions, disregarding the many ways in which Indian forms of Islam and Christianity have shaped and been shaped by Hindu thought and practice.[28] Its classic statement is Hindutva, or 'Hindu-ness', that differentiates non-Hindu Indians from Hindus on the basis of the fact that the former look to nations other than India as their *punya bhūmī*, or holy land, even though India is their *pitṛ bhūmī* or 'fatherland'. Thus, a Hindu is one for whom India is both *punya bhūmī* and *pitṛ bhūmī*.[29] In addition to rendering Indian Muslims and

[25] Although rejected by adherents of all the other systems of thought, the Lokāyata perspective may have been quite popular in terms of the numbers of its followers. Its name, meaning 'extended over the whole world', suggests this very possibility, as well as an additional rationale for the strong opposition it evoked.

[26] See Long, *Vision for Hinduism*, 34–5, and *Jainism*, 23–7.

[27] The arrival of European Christianity does not mark the first appearance of Christianity in India, for a small Christian community existed in the southern and western coastal regions of India for many centuries before the coming of the Europeans, as did small communities of Jews and Zoroastrians. None of these, however, presented the institutional or the conceptual challenge to Hindu traditions as those presented by Islam and European Christianity in the medieval and modern periods, respectively.

[28] See Peter Gottschalk, *Beyond Hindu and Muslim* (New York: Oxford University Press, 2005).

[29] See Vinayak Damodar Savarkar, *Hindutva* (New Delhi: Hindi Sahitya Sadan, 2003).

Christians second-class citizens in India, this formulation calls into question the idea of non-Indian Hindus, such as non-Indian adherents of Hindu movements in the West, although Hindu nationalists do embrace those non-Indians whom they see as 'fellow travellers'.[30]

The radically other nature of Islam and Christianity to Hinduism, contrasted here with the less radical otherness of Buddhism and Jainism to Hinduism, should be understood not in geographic or nationalistic terms, but in conceptual and doctrinal terms, inasmuch as these religions exhibit cosmological and ontological underpinnings very different from those of the Indic religions. But living religious communities, consisting of complex human persons, are defined by more than metaphysical views. A Japanese Buddhist may have less in common with an Indian Hindu than an Indian Muslim would, despite the similarities between their religious beliefs. Worldviews and traditions in the abstract underdetermine the total complex personhood of living human beings.

Early contacts between Muslims and Hindus were largely peaceful, occurring in a context of trade between travelling Arab merchants and Hindus in the coastal regions of India. Much more momentous, however—and strongly emphasized in Hindu nationalist accounts of history—were a series of invasions by Afghan, Turkish, and Mughal powers extending from the end of the first millennium of the Common Era to the fifteenth century. These invasions wrought great destruction upon Hindu and Jain institutions, such as temples and monasteries, and resulted in the complete destruction of Buddhism as an institutional presence in India. In combination with Hindu strategies of inclusivism, which increasingly rendered it into a form of Hinduism, Indian Buddhism had effectively ceased to exist by the thirteenth century. As the initial shock of invasion subsided, however, and Islam became a part of the Indian religious landscape, Hindus and Muslims began to respond in creative ways to one another. Before the coming of Islam, Hindu movements had arisen which emphasized devotion to a personal deity, or *bhakti*, as a path to liberation from rebirth—a view that is reflected in the *Bhagavad Gītā*. The adherents of Hindu devotional movements and the Sufis of Islam, especially, began to see the other traditions as potential repositories of deep spiritual wisdom, and of practices that each could appropriate for attaining greater nearness to the divine. Some Hindus started to adopt Sufi spiritual guides, or *pīrs*, as *gurus*, or teachers, and Muslims were similarly drawn to Hindu spiritual figures. Kabīr, for example, who lived from 1440 to 1518, is even today claimed by both Hindus and Muslims as a revered teacher of sacred wisdom.

This interreligious cooperation and cross-fertilization is remarkable given that it is hard to conceive of two religions more different from one another than Hinduism and Islam. Islam is emphatically monotheistic, regarding even the Christian Trinity as a deviation from the original monotheism taught by the prophet Jesus (as he is seen by Muslims). It is equally emphatically aniconic, associating images of the divine with the corrupt social order of pre-Islamic Arabia, in which a wealthy priesthood could determine who got to see the gods and who did not, charging exorbitant rates to devotees for a glimpse of their deities. The diversity of the

---

[30] See Long, *Vision for Hinduism*, 171–95.

forms of the divine in Hinduism and its celebration of imagery are seen even today by many Muslims as blasphemous—a holdover from a pagan era.

Similarly, Islam is generally insistent that there is one way to salvation: by obeying the injunctions of God as conveyed by God's messenger, the Prophet Muhammad. This is a stark contrast with the diversity of yogas, or spiritual paths and practices, and forms of the divine available as objects of devotion in Hindu traditions. Islam is an actively proselytizing tradition, while Hindu traditions typically are not. In the popular piety of medieval India, however, one sees both communities—Hindus and Muslims—shaking off the formal distinctions that their respective religious leaders would prefer to maintain between the two traditions. Rather than focusing upon their differences, however, Hindu and Muslim figures of this time emphasized a shared sense of the ubiquity of the divine presence and its availability to all who approach it with true devotion and a sincere and humble heart. Sufi saints began to incorporate the names of Hindu deities in their litanies of the many names of Allāh, and Hindu devotees began to chant verses from the Qur'an and to make pilgrimages to the tombs of Sufi saints. The sharing of one another's holy days and holy places remains a characteristic of Hindu and Islamic practice in many parts of South Asia even today.

This mutual accommodation was made possible by the presence in both traditions of movements that were uncomfortable with—and often rejected in strong terms—an emphasis on rigid formality, which was seen as interfering with the sincere and spontaneous quest of the devotee for the experience of the divine presence. Sufism—viewed in some quarters of the Islamic world with suspicion as a movement of dubious orthodoxy—found a highly receptive welcome in India. In Hinduism, popular devotion movements, which rejected Brahmanical formality and caste distinctions, were open to sincere devotion in any form— even forms that at first appeared to be foreign. Sufi and *bhakti* leaders saw in one another kindred spirits in search of an authentic experience as opposed to the dry formality of the 'official' exponents of their respective traditions. This process of popular mutual assimilation was eventually facilitated at the level of the state. The Mughal emperor, Akbar—a Muslim— who reigned from 1556 to 1605, formally adopted a policy of toleration toward all religions. Allowing his Hindu wife to build a temple to her deity in his palace, and even developing his own religion—a synthesis of all the religions of India that he knew—Akbar consistently ran afoul of exponents of Islamic orthodoxy in his imperial court. His policy of toleration both mirrored and accelerated what was already happening at the popular, village level between the Hindus and Muslims in his realm.

The *Sant*—'saint'—movement of this period consisted of figures with both Hindu and Islamic origins, such as the aforementioned Kabīr, who both claimed, and were claimed by, adherents of both religions seeing sincere devotion as having far greater importance than formal sectarian affiliation or religious identity. This movement culminated in the figure of Guru Nānak. In his famous teaching that 'there is no Hindu, there is no Muslim', Nānak captured the spirit of his era. Rather than unify the two traditions, however, Nānak's teaching led to the emergence of a third tradition—Sikhism—a religion distinct from both Hinduism and Islam while yet containing elements of both in its practices and doctrines. But there were also reactions against this widespread spirit of mutual synthesis and accommodation. The Mughal emperor Aurangzeb, reigning from 1658 to 1707, aggressively sought forcible conversion of both Hindus and Sikhs to Islam, returning to the earlier policy of destroying temples and torturing and slaughtering religious leaders who refused to convert. The memory of the wounds of this period still runs deeply enough (and is also deliberately cultivated by militant political leaders in both communities) to lead to a situation in which later leaders—including British colonial rulers and political parties in independent India and Pakistan—successfully exploited the worst fears of both communities for political gain. Yet such division and mutual suspicion occurs against the background of mutual respect and assimilation established in the era of the Sant movement. This environment of tolerance and pluralism is endangered by militancy and the hardening of negative attitudes on both sides—a militancy driven at least as much by the aspirations of Hindu and Islamic political groups as by what one might want to call authentically religious concerns.

Apart from the emergence of entirely new groups, such as the disciples of Kabīr and the Sikhs—how has Hindu inclusivism practised in relation to Islam had a concrete effect on Hindu belief and practice? If Hindu inclusivism towards the Buddhist and Jain traditions led to the abandonment by most Hindus of actual animal sacrifice and an emergent ethos of vegetarianism and non-violence, the Hindu inclusivist approach to Islam led to increased emphasis, in Hindu traditions, on the idea that the many deities of Hinduism are aspects of one, ultimately formless divine reality: a frequently encountered explanation given by Hindus today for the fact that Hindus have many deities. The very fact that contemporary Hindus are inclined to feel that the deities need to be explained at all is a mark of interaction with Islam. Though this idea can certainly be found in ancient Hindu texts—going all the way back to the *Ṛg Veda*, with its statement that 'Truth is one, though the wise speak of it in various ways'[31]—it receives greater emphasis in the medieval and modern periods. And in both the Sant movement and in Sikhism, one sees an emphasis on *nirguṇa bhakti*—that is, devotion to the divine without form. The *bhakti* movements of the first millennium were oriented towards specific forms or personae of the divine: to concrete deities with discrete personalities, such as Viṣṇu, Śiva, and Śakti (the Mother Goddess). The idea of *nirguṇa brahman*, or the divine without form, was chiefly the preserve of traditions such as Advaita Vedānta that perceived the divine reality as ultimately beyond form or personality: as an object of realization rather than of devotion. The Islamic idea of God as having no form, but as nevertheless a personal being, allows for devotion to a personal God beyond the concrete forms of the Hindu deities, and of which these deities can be seen as manifestations or aspects.

Popular expressions and influences on language, art, and literary and musical forms also show evidence of the hybrid Hindu–Islamic culture of the medieval period. A popular *bhajan*, or devotional song to the Hindu deity Rāma that is still sung in many Hindu temples, says,

---

[31] *Ṛg Veda*, 1: 164: 46c (my tr.).

'Īśvara Āllā tero nām', or 'Your name is Īśvara (the Lord, an old name for the divine in Hindu traditions) and Allāh, or God, (the predominant name for the divine in Islam)'. Christianity, like Islam, brought both theological and institutional challenges. Among the Hindu responses to this new religious other were, as might be expected, outright rejection of the 'foreign' tradition, as well as complete acceptance, on the part of those who converted to the new tradition and assimilated themselves to European culture. But as with Buddhism, Jainism, and Islam, the most distinctively Hindu responses were those of the reformers of the nineteenth and twentieth centuries who assimilated what they found to be true and beneficial in the Christian tradition, while rejecting whatever was incompatible with Hinduism.

A common response of modern Hindu thinkers to Christianity is to regard the figure of Jesus in a highly positive light, but then utilize him as a device for criticizing Christianity. The first modern Hindu author to write extensively about Jesus is widely seen as the founder of modern Hinduism, Ram Mohan Roy (1772–1833). Roy's best-known work on this topic, *The Precepts of Jesus*, is a Jeffersonian rewriting of the gospels that highlights Jesus' ethical teachings and omits references to such things as miracles and Jesus' divinity. The Unitarian flavour of this text is plainly evident—as is that of the reform organization that Roy established, the Brahmo Samaj. Equally evident is its polemical intent—to defend Hindu traditions against proselytizing by evangelical Christian missionaries by articulating a rationalistic and modern version of Hinduism based on Roy's interpretation of the *Upaniṣads*. Roy's work lays the foundation for later Hindu writing about Jesus. Keshub Chunder Sen devoted many of his lectures to a Hindu interpretation and appropriation of the life and teachings of Jesus.[32] Swami Prabhavananda, a twentieth-century monk of the Ramakrishna Order, wrote a commentary on the gospels titled *The Sermon on the Mount According to Vedanta*.[33] Paramahamsa Yogananda claimed to have had visionary encounters with Jesus, as did Ramakrishna; and the influence of the *Sermon on the Mount* on Mohandas K. Gandhi is well known. There is also a growing literature on the notion that Jesus visited India and studied yoga during the 'lost years' not described in the canonical gospels.[34]

The import of much of this literature is that the teachings of Jesus are not only fully compatible with Hinduism, but are far *more* compatible with Hinduism than Christianity, at least as it is generally understood by Christians. What is typically singled out as the error of orthodox Christianity, the point at which it parts company with the expansive, radical vision of its founder, is in its insistence upon faith in Jesus, meaning conversion to Christianity, as a necessary and sufficient condition for salvation. This contrasts with Hindu religious inclusivism, which is seen as more in keeping with Jesus' proclamation that God is love: God accepts the sincere devotee, in whatever form the devotee chooses to see God. This reflects the sensibility of the earlier Sant movement, as well as that of many Hindu texts.

---

[32] See Glyn Richards (ed.), *A Source-Book of Modern Hinduism* (London: Curzon Press, 1985), 30–8.

[33] Swami Prabhavananda, *The Sermon on the Mount According to Vedanta* (Hollywood, Calif.: Vedanta Press, 1964).

[34] See e.g. Swami Abhedananda, *Christ the Yogi* (Whitefish, Mont.: Kessinger Publishing, 2005).

Beyond the appropriation of Jesus, the imprint of Christianity on Hinduism due to the inclusivist strategy pursued by modern Hindu intellectuals includes not only what might be called properly Christian elements, but aspects of what might more broadly be called Western or European thought: a desire to explain Hinduism in 'scientific' terms, a reappropriation of aspects of Hindu traditions that emphasize active work to improve society, and the very idea of Hinduism as 'a religion'—a member of a species, alongside others.

Two Trajectories: Exclusivist Nationalism and Inclusivist Universalism

If one were to characterize Hindu relations with the religious other in terms of one common typology of theologies of religion—as exclusivist, inclusivist, or pluralist—one would say that exclusivism in a soteriological sense, according to which only Hindus (or a particular group of Hindus) have access to the truths one needs to possess in order to attain the ultimate aim of life, is exceedingly rare in Hindu traditions.[35] This is in contrast with both Christianity and Islam, in which soteriological exclusivist theologies of religion are more prominent, leading to the strong emphasis on proselytizing in these religious traditions. The relative absence of soteriological exclusivism should not, however, be taken to suggest that exclusionary practices are absent from Hindu traditions. Instead of soteriological exclusivism (which is logically difficult, although not impossible, to sustain in a worldview that accepts the idea of reincarnation),[36] one finds forms of exclusivism that are more socio-political in nature. In the modern period, there is Hindutva—literally 'Hindu-ness'—or Hindu nationalism, adherents of which seek to make India into a Hindu nation much as right-wing Christians in the United States seek to make that country into a Christian nation. Hindu exclusivists of this sort do not deny that the religious other might eventually attain salvation. But they do see the religious other, in the here and now, as a second-class citizen of the Indian nation-state. Hindu nationalism, though, is a relatively recent historical phenomenon, rooted in the Indian

---

[35] However, for a counterpoint see Deepak Sarma, *An Introduction to Mādhva Vedānta* (Aldershot: Ashgate, 2003).

[36] This difficulty is of course due to the fact that, in a worldview in which reincarnation occurs, conditions in one's current life that might, in most religions, be seen as precluding one from the possibility of salvation—such as membership in a different religious community, or even in a non-human species—may not obtain in a future lifetime, in which conditions suitable for salvation might obtain. In exceedingly rare cases, such as Dvaita Vedānta, in which members of a particular community are precluded from ever attaining salvation, even in a future lifetime (as Dvaita Vedāntins claim about Advaita Vedāntins), the conditions of the current lifetime that preclude one from attaining salvation now are seen as evidence of a character flaw so deep as to prevent one from ever being reborn in conditions suitable for salvation. Buddhism and Jainism, both of which affirm reincarnation, also affirm that some persons exist who may never reach final liberation from rebirth, though they are not identified with any particular community or specific religious other. Such persons are called, in Buddhism, *icchāntika*, and in Jainism, *abhavya*. In both traditions, this doctrine is a source of discomfort and internal debate, due to a desire to affirm the eventual salvation of all beings. The eventual salvation of all beings (for most, in a future lifetime) is also affirmed in most Hindu traditions.

struggle for political independence and the accompanying discourse of Indian national identity that began in the nineteenth century. As a form of Hindu socio-political exclusivism, the
more ancient analogue of Hindu nationalism takes the shape of forms of social exclusion
rooted in the concept of caste—or more precisely, *jāti* and *varṇa*.

In textual terms, caste-based exclusion is justified by the interpretation of the legal texts of
the Brahmanical sub-tradition of Hinduism: the *Dharma Śāstras*. These texts of the early classical period—from roughly the end of the first millennium BCE and the beginning of the first
millennium CE—define the duties of all members of Hindu society and establish strict internal and external boundaries for Hindu communities based upon a careful delineation of the
persons with whom one may interact without fear of spiritual pollution. Hindu nationalism,
on the other hand, finds its justification in an interpretation of history in which Hindus, who
are portrayed as ever open to and accepting of the beliefs and practices of others, are victim-
ized by the aggressive and proselytizing religious other.

Both forms of socio-political exclusivism—the nationalistic and the caste-based—persist
in contemporary Hinduism, although the same persons do not always practise both types of
exclusion. Indeed, some Hindu nationalists object to caste prejudice on principle, preferring
to view Hindus as one family, in opposition to non-Hindu others. These non-Hindu others
are usually Muslim, Christian, or secular others. Jains, Buddhists, and Sikhs, as persons with
religious traditions native to India, are seen as fellow Hindus in Hindu nationalist ideology,
which typically conflates the terms Hindu and Indian.[37] To be Hindu is to be of Indic origin.
The nationalistic and caste-based practices of Hindu socio-political exclusivism have remarkably little to do with the substantive content of Hindu religious teaching, with which these
practices are, it could be argued, frequently in sharp tension.[38] In more strictly religious, or
theological, terms, Hindu attitudes towards the religious other have more often taken a form
with features of both inclusivism and pluralism.

Sharp distinctions between inclusivism and pluralism are difficult to make with regard to
specific Hindu traditions, or even specific Hindu thinkers. In some places, these traditions or
thinkers sound more inclusivist—emphasizing the superiority of their perspective over the
merely relative truth and efficacy of others—and in some places they sound more pluralistic—
emphasizing the presence of truth and the possibility of spiritual progress in many religions.
If one must generalize, the traditional Hindu attitude towards the religious other can be
described as a radical inclusivism that sees the other as, in some sense, a part of itself. The

---

[37] The observable attitudes of Jains, Buddhists, and Sikhs to being regarded as Hindus range from acceptance to
sharp objections to Hindu 'imperialism'. One sometimes hears the formulation, particularly among Jains, that they
are 'culturally Hindu' while being religiously distinct. The response of specific Buddhists, Jains, and Sikhs seems to
be dependent upon their political relationship to Hinduism as a whole.

[38] An example of Hindu teaching that is in tension with socio-political exclusion would be the often encountered injunctions in Hindu textual sources and in the discourses of living Hindu teachers to see the divine presence
in all beings, *pace* the also often encountered assertion in scholarly writing on Hinduism that defines this religion
as intrinsically rooted in caste prejudice. This essentialist view of Hinduism arises from excessive reliance upon the
Dharma Śāstras as authoritative sources, rather than as reflecting one Hindu ideology among many.

other is part of the definition of self, and vice versa. Hindu inclusivism can take a 'closed' form, as when Hindu authors see other systems of belief and practice as steps on the way to their own. But it can also take a strikingly open form that goes even beyond pluralism in the conventional sense, in which the beliefs and practices of the religious other are not just seen as true, but are freely adopted and assimilated into one's own belief and practice. Interestingly, the inclusivist attitude described here can coexist in the life of the same person with some measure of socio-political exclusivism. It is possible for Hindus to believe, in the abstract, that Christians and Muslims, for example, possess important spiritual truths. The same Hindus may even read Christian and Islamic scriptures appreciatively. But at the same time, they may avoid any significant social interaction with the actual members of these religious communities—with actual Christians and Muslims.

Rather than seeing such 'armchair' acceptance of the religious other as contradictory to socio-political exclusivism, it can be argued that it follows from the logic of caste: one's religion, like one's social status, is a matter of birth that cannot be changed in this life.[39] One can see all religions, like all occupations, as good and necessary, but have no desire to go out and do the work of the other. The traditional Hindu disinclination towards proselytizing can be seen in this light: as a mark of respect for the validity of the religion of the other *for the other*. Mohandas K. Gandhi and Swami Vivekananda, both of whom are frequently cited for their attitudes of inclusivist acceptance towards the religious other, express views on religious conversion that are consistent with this interpretation. Vivekananda, for example, says:

> Do I wish that the Christian would become Hindu? God forbid. Do I wish that the Hindu or Buddhist would become Christian? God forbid. The seed is put in the ground, and earth and air and water are placed around it. Does the seed become the earth, or the air, or the water? No. It becomes a plant, it develops after the law of its own growth; assimilates the air, the earth, and the water, converts them into plant substance, and grows into a plant. Similar is the case with religion. The Christian is not to become a Hindu or a Buddhist, nor a Hindu or a Buddhist to become a Christian. But each must assimilate the spirit of the others and yet preserve his individuality and grow according to his own law of growth.[40]

Gandhi, similarly, says:

> Supposing a Christian came to me and said he was captivated by reading of the *Bhagavat* and so wanted to declare himself a Hindu, I should say to him, 'No. What the *Bhagavat* offers, the Bible also offers. You have not yet made the attempt to find out. Make the attempt and be a good Christian.'[41]

---

[39] See Arvind Sharma, *Hinduism for our Times* (New York: Oxford University Press, 1997).

[40] Swami Vivekananda, *Complete Works*, i (Kolkata: Advaita Ashrama, 1989), 24.

[41] Mohandas K. Gandhi, cited in Robert Ellsberg (ed.), *Gandhi on Christianity* (Maryknoll, NY: Orbis Books, 1997), 14.

Hindus can and do actively seek out cooperation and dialogue with members of other faith communities, and explicitly cite their inclusivist Hindu commitments as their justification for doing so. Vivekananda and Gandhi were famous for their activities in this regard, travelling widely and speaking extensively with persons of other communities. One can find varied approaches in practice, from xenophobic avoidance to enthusiastically active cooperation and dialogue. But both approaches can be seen to have a common basis in the idea that the other is to be affirmed in her otherness, either by letting the other be, or by engaging with the other without seeking to convert the other to what one is oneself. The idea that there will always be religious others—even if self and other are parts of one larger reality—is a distinctive Hindu affirmation, in contrast with theological models that seek to *replace* the other with the self.[42]

The authoritative warrant in Hindu traditions for the inclusivist attitudes exhibited by many Hindus comes in the form of numerous Hindu scriptural pronouncements regarding the multiplicity of paths to the divine: many names for one ultimate truth, many rivers flowing to the one ocean, many paths going up to one mountaintop. An oft-cited verse from the *Ṛg Veda* states that, 'Truth is one, although the wise speak of it in various ways.'[43] There is also the statement of Sri Kṛṣṇa in the *Bhagavad Gītā* that, 'In whatever way people approach me, thus do I receive them. All paths lead to me.'[44] Elsewhere in the epic *Mahābhārata*, of which the *Bhagavad Gītā* forms a portion, one finds the statement that, 'Just as the rain falls from the sky and flows to the ocean, thus do our prayers to all deities reach the one God.'[45] Contemporary Hindu thinkers have picked up these verses and defined Hinduism in a way that makes the acceptance of the religious other that they express a central feature of the Hindu tradition. 'One of the Hindu religion's greatest gifts to mankind is the attitude of religious tolerance and universal harmony,' writes Bansi Pandit, a popular Hindu author.[46] Two of the seven points in the Indian Supreme Court's definition of Hinduism are 'A spirit of tolerance, and willingness to understand and appreciate others' points of view, recognizing that truth has many sides' and the 'Recognition that paths to truth and salvation are many.'[47] A contemporary Hindu catechism states as a central Hindu tenet, 'I believe that no particular religion teaches the only way to salvation above all others, but that all genuine religious paths are facets of God's Pure Love and Light, deserving tolerance and understanding.'[48]

In contemporary Hindu discourse, as these quotations illustrate, an inclusivist Hindu approach to the religious other is sometimes conflated with the secular concept of tolerance. Andrew Nicholson argues, correctly, that this is a distortion of Hinduism, pointing out that:

---

[42] See Paul F. Knitter, *Theologies of Religions* (Maryknoll, NY: Orbis Books, 2010), 19–60.

[43] *Ṛg Veda*, 1: 164: 46c (my tr.).

[44] *Bhagavad Gītā*, 4: 11 (my tr.).

[45] *Mahābhārata*, tr. Chakravarthi V. Narasimhan, 13: 639: 3–4 (New York: Columbia University Press, 1997).

[46] Bansi Pandit, *The Hindu Mind* (Glen Ellyn, Ill.: B. and V. Enterprises, 1998), 353.

[47] Cited in Mary Pat Fisher, *Living Religions*, 4th edn (Upper Saddle River, NJ: Prentice Hall, 2002), 126 and 127.

[48] Satguru Sivaya Subramuniyaswami, *Dancing with Shiva: Hinduism's Contemporary Catechism* (Kauai, Hawaii: Himalayan Academy, 1997), 532.

As presented by European liberal traditions following John Locke, toleration involves the privatization of theological claims. Each sect is treated equally and allowed to thrive or wither on its own without either the support or censure of a laissez-faire state. The citizens of the state are likewise expected to tolerate the private religious convictions of others, with the understanding that these others will also allow them freedom of worship.[49]

The far more radical Hindu approach of inclusivism involves not simply 'tolerating' the fact that others hold different views and engage in different practices from one's own, but actually incorporating the views and practices of others into one's own—albeit on the at least implicit understanding that one's religious perspective forms the broader superstructure or framework in which the views and practices of the religious other are to be assimilated. In the words of Swami Vivekananda, 'We believe not only in universal toleration, but we accept all religions as true.'[50] Elsewhere he refers to tolerance as 'blasphemy'.[51] Gandhi likewise says that, 'We must have the innate respect for other religions as we have for our own. Mind you, not mutual toleration, but equal respect.'[52] Theologically, one may argue that an inclusivist stance is necessary for a religion that affirms its own absolute truth and the essential truth of other traditions without sinking into what Alan Race calls 'debilitating relativism'.[53] In the words of Wilhelm Halbfass, 'Indeed, we may say that any kind of tolerance which is allied with, and committed to, religious absolutism, and which keeps itself free from relativism, skepticism or indifferentism, is by definition inclusivistic.'[54] In classical Indian religious discourse—Hindu, Buddhist, and Jain—inclusivism is expressed in the genre of the doxography—*samuccaya* or *saṃgraha*—in which the views of various traditions are collected and ranked hierarchically as steps to the highest truth.

The highest truth, that is, the *siddhānta*, or 'perfected' view, is that of the tradition of the author of the text in question.[55] But all the other traditions have their places as steps on the way to truth—with materialism typically occupying the starting point—the bottom 'rung' of the 'ladder'—to the highest view. This is clearly different from the purportedly religiously neutral tolerance practised by modern secular governments, or from sceptical indifference to the phenomenon of religious difference. It is a definite religious view. It sees some claims as true and others as false. But it does not therefore reject the view of the other as *wholly* false, for it sees truth as allowing of degrees. From the perspective of the Advaita Vedānta system of Hindu thought, for example, Buddhism is 'more true' than materialism, and Jainism is more true than materialism but less true than Buddhism. It is insufficient to say only that Advaita Vedānta is true and all other views are false, for this would be inadequate to the actual details of what the religious other believes: something to which Indic traditions have been carefully attentive.

---

[49] Nicholson, *Unifying Hinduism*, 185.   [50] Vivekananda, *Complete Works*, i. 3.
[51] Vivekananda, *Complete Works*, ii. 373–4.   [52] Ellsberg, *Gandhi*, 14.
[53] Race, *Christians and Religious Pluralism*, 78, 90.   [54] Halbfass, *India and Europe*, 416.
[55] See Halbfass *India and Europe*, 414, and Deepak Sarma, *Classical Indian Philosophy* (New York: Columbia University Press, 2011).

Probably two of the most renowned Hindu figures of the modern period whose views have shaped popular perceptions among Hindus and non-Hindus regarding how Hindus ought to relate to the religious other are the nineteenth-century Bengali sage, Sri Ramakrishna Paramahamsa (1833–83) and Mohandas K. Gandhi (1869–1948)—the Mahātma or 'Great Soul' who led the non-violent movement for Indian independence from British colonial rule. Ramakrishna is believed to have embodied the principle of Hindu inclusivism through actually practising a range of Hindu and non-Hindu traditions and experiencing the divine in a direct and vivid way by means of each of these practices. His teaching is expressed in the Bengali phrase *yato mat, tato path*, which essentially means that there are as many religions as there are paths to the divine, with each religion corresponding to a different path:

> I have practiced all religions—Hinduism, Islam, Christianity—and I have also followed the paths of the different Hindu sects. I have found that it is the same God toward whom all are directing their steps, though along different paths. He who is called Krishna is also called Shiva, and bears the name of the Primal Energy, Jesus, and Allah as well—the same Rama with a thousand names.[56] God can be realised through all paths. All religions are true. The important thing is to reach the roof. You can reach it by stone stairs or by wooden stairs or by bamboo steps or by a rope. You can also climb up a bamboo pole…Each religion is only a path leading to God, as rivers come from different directions and ultimately become one in the one ocean … All religions and all paths call upon their followers to pray to one and the same God. Therefore one should not show disrespect to any religion or religious opinion.[57]

Gandhi's multi-religious 'experiments with truth' led him to very much the same conclusion, a doctrine to which he referred as *sarva-dharma-sama-bhāva*. He sometimes translates this concept into English as 'the equality of religions', but it may be more fully described as an attitude of equanimity or impartiality towards all religions. In his formulation of this ideal, Gandhi seems to go even beyond inclusivism to embrace an attitude of religious pluralism:

> Religions are different roads converging upon the same point. What does it matter that we take different roads so long as we reach the same goal? In reality there are as many religions as there are individuals. I believe in the fundamental truth of all great religions of the world. I believe that they are all God-given, and I believe that they were necessary for the people to whom these religions were revealed. And I believe that, if only we could all of us read the scriptures of different faiths from the standpoint of the followers of those faiths we should find that they were at bottom all one and were all helpful to one another.[58]

Both Ramakrishna's and Gandhi's approach to the religious other have sometimes led to the popular misunderstanding (and consequent criticism) that Hinduism teaches that there are

---

[56] Swami Nikhilananda, *The Gospel of Sri Ramakrishna* (New York: Ramakrishna-Vivekananda Center, 1942), 60.

[57] Cited in Richards, *Source-Book*, 65.

[58] Richards, *Source-Book*, 156, 157.

no important differences among religious traditions: that the traditional Hindu approach to the religious other is indiscriminate acceptance, rather than an application of the inclusivist principle that another tradition, even if in some ways inadequate from one's own perspective, may contain genuine insight and be beneficial in various ways to its practitioners who should therefore be left to their own devices. As Pravrajika Vrajaprana, a contemporary exponent of the Vedanta tradition of Ramakrishna, explains the teaching of her tradition's founder:

> This is not to say that all religions are 'pretty much the same.' That is an affront to the distinct beauty and individual greatness of each of the world's spiritual traditions. Saying that every religion is equally true and authentic doesn't mean that one can be substituted for the other like generic brands of aspirin.[59]

Using the image of a jigsaw puzzle, in which every piece is different, Vrajaprana explains that the 'harmony of religions' does not involve the negation of religious difference:

> The world's spiritual traditions are like different pieces in a giant jigsaw puzzle: each piece is different and each piece is essential to complete the whole picture. Each piece is to be honored and respected while holding firm to our own particular piece of the puzzle. We can deepen our own spirituality and learn about our own tradition by studying other faiths. Just as importantly, by studying our own tradition well, we are better able to appreciate the truth in other traditions.[60]

CONCLUSION

As mentioned at the outset, Hindu attitudes towards the religious other encompass a spectrum of possibilities. On the one hand, there are certainly some Hindus whose attitudes towards the religious other have been characterized primarily by fear and hatred. Hindu nationalism, being rooted in a historical narrative that emphasizes the victimization of Hindus by religious others characterized primarily by aggression and proselytizing, seeks to exclude non-Hindus from the mainstream of the national life of India, identifying India as a Hindu state where the religious other has only a second-class status. It is primarily a defensive and fear-based mind-set that sometimes manifests in explosions of religious violence, such as those involved in the demolition of a mosque in 1992 believed to be on the site of the birth of Rāma in Ayodhya, or in the brutal slaughter of neighbour by neighbour in the state of Gujarat in 2002.[61]

In contrast, there is the view that Hinduism is the *sanātana dharma*: an eternal and universal religion or way of life that encompasses all forms of religious practice and spiritual aspiration.

---

[59] Pravrajika Vrajaprana, *Vedanta: A Simple Introduction* (Hollywood, Calif.: Vedanta Press, 1999), 56.

[60] Vrajaprana, *Vedanta*, 56–7.

[61] See Martha Nussbaum, *The Clash Within: Democracy, Religious Violence, and India's Future* (Boston: Harvard University Press, 2009).

Hinduism 'is not a religion, but religion itself in its most universal and deepest significance'.[62] Ultimately, from this point of view, there is no religious other. One who holds this view is prompted to say, along with the *paṇḍit* interviewed by Ron Eyre in his television series on the world's religions, *The Long Search*, 'I think at the highest stage there is nobody beyond Hinduism. Everybody is a Hindu.'[63] Hindu inclusivism can be expressed as the view that the other religions of the world are, more or less, forms of Hinduism: that just as the upside-down tree of Hinduism, being made up of branches that have coalesced to form a singular tradition has been able to draw together traditions as diverse as Advaita Vedānta, Pūrva Mīmāṃsā, and devotional movements such as Vaiṣṇavism, Śaivism, and Śāktism, it can similarly assimilate Buddhism, Jainism, Islam, and Christianity, and has indeed done so in various ways that can be traced throughout Hindu history. At the same time, it has also become conventional to think of Hinduism as consisting only of the Brahmanical branches of that tree. But as this chapter has, I hope, shown, the picture is actually more complex than a simplistic equation of *Hindu* with *Brahmanical* is able to capture. Of course, the danger always exists that the inclusivist approach of Hinduism can itself be subverted into a Hindu nationalist argument for Hindu superiority—and such rhetorical moves are, in fact, routinely made.

It is also the case, however, as Hinduism emerges increasingly as a global tradition with an international following—a following, moreover, not confined to expatriate Indians, or the 'Hindu Diaspora' as it is sometimes known, but persons with other ethnic and national origins[64]—that one of the sources of its appeal is its universalism: its inclusivist embrace of the diverse range of human religious behaviour and aspiration in a way that seeks to avoid the kind of sceptical relativism to which more conventional Western notions of tolerance are subject. As with other religious traditions, what remains to be seen in regard to Hinduism is which of its inner trajectories will predominate: that of exclusion and violence, or that of inclusion and harmony.

FURTHER READING

D. N. Jha, *Rethinking Hindu Identity* (London: Equinox, 2009).

Klaus K. Klostermaier, *A Survey of Hinduism*, 3rd edn (Albany, NY: State University of New York Press, 2007).

J. E. Llewellyn (ed.), *Defining Hinduism: A Reader* (New York: Routledge, 2005).

Jeffery D. Long, *A Vision for Hinduism: Beyond Hindu Nationalism* (London: I. B. Tauris, 2007).

---

[62] Sarvepalli Radhakrishnan, *The Hindu View of Life* (London: George Allen & Unwin, 1927), 18.

[63] Ronald Eyre, *The Long Search*, episode 1, 'Hinduism: 330 Million Gods', BBC 1977.

[64] Cf. Philip Goldberg, *American Veda* (Bourbon, Ind.: Harmony, 2010); Lola Williamson, *Transcendent in America* (New York: SUNY, 2010); and F. L. Bakker, *The Struggle of the Hindu Balinese Intellectuals* (Amsterdam: VU University Press, 1993).

Andrew J. Nicholson, *Unifying Hinduism: Philosophy and Identity in Indian Intellectual History* (New York: Columbia University Press, 2010).

Martha Nussbaum, *The Clash Within: Democracy, Religious Violence, and India's Future* (Boston: Harvard University Press, 2009).

Swami Prabhavananda, *The Sermon on the Mount According to Vedanta* (Hollywood, Calif.: Vedanta Press, 1964).

Sarvepalli Radhakrishnan, *The Hindu View of Life* (London: George Allen & Unwin, 1927).

Amartya Sen, *The Argumentative Indian: Writings on Indian History, Culture, and Identity* (New York: Picador, 2006).

Arvind Sharma, *Hinduism as a Missionary Religion* (Albany, NY: State University of New York Press, 2012).

....

CHAPTER 4

Judaism and the Religious Other

ED KESSLER

BIBLICAL JUDAISM

Perhaps the best place to start is with geography.[1] The strip of land along the Mediterranean that became the birthplace of the Hebrew Bible has had various names. But it lies at an extraordinary location, offering the only available land route between Asia and Africa. To the west is the Mediterranean Sea, to the east a mountainous, virtually impassable stony desert. Only two roads, one along the coast, the other along the central mountain chain, allowed a north–south passage. Located between Mesopotamia to the north and Egypt to the south, whoever controlled that strip of land had control of the major land route for trade or military activity between the great empires that rose and fell throughout the period of biblical history. Thus, the geography itself required ongoing relationships with these empires but also determined changing alliances between the Israelites and other neighbouring peoples. Judaism, and the Jewish people, begins with Abraham, initially called Abram, born in Ur, Babylonia, who came to realize that the universe was the work of a single Creator.[2]

The Hebrew Bible recounts how God commanded Abram to leave his home and his family, and how God blessed him and said he would make him a great nation. God established a *berit* (covenant) with Abram and, by extension, with the Jewish people. As we shall see,

---

[1] I am indebted to Jonathan Magonet, formerly principal of Leo Baeck College, who suggested a Jewish study of the Other should begin with the geography of the Bible.

[2] The rabbis tell the following story: 'Abram tried to convince his father, Terach, of the folly of idol worship. One day, when Abram was left alone, he took a hammer and smashed all of the idols in his father's house except the largest one. He placed the hammer in the hand of this idol. When his father returned and asked what happened, Abram said, "The idols began to fight each other, and the biggest smashed all the others." His father said, "Don't be ridiculous. These idols have no life or power. They can't do anything." Abram replied, "Then why do you worship them?" ' Genesis Rabbah, 38. See H. Freedman and M. Simon, *Midrash Rabbah*, Eng. tr. (London: Soncino, 1961).

covenant is a thread that runs through Jewish history, involving rights and duties on both sides: just as Jews have certain obligations to God, so, Jewish theologians suggest, God has certain obligations to the Jewish people.

The Hebrew scriptural texts describe how Abraham migrated to Palestine, but also visited Egypt. His descendants went down to Egypt during a time of famine and settled there, only to be enslaved. Led out by Moses, after forty years' wandering in the desert, they arrived in the land of Canaan about 1200 BCE which they conquered and where they established their own settlement that eventually became a kingdom and, briefly, a small, short-lived empire under King David, around 1000 BCE. This kingdom divided and the Northern Kingdom, Israel, in 722 BCE fell to the Assyrians who removed the population never to return (the so-called 'ten lost tribes'). The same fate of conquest and exile befell the Southern Kingdom, Judah, at the hands of the Babylonians in 586 BCE, leading to the creation of a major Diaspora community. Some seventy years later, under the subsequent Persian Empire, some of the exiles returned, rebuilt the Temple in Jerusalem, and maintained a semi-autonomous existence under Greek and then Roman rule, until its destruction a second time, at the hands of the Romans in 70 CE. While these are the major imperial powers that determined the fate of the Jewish people, throughout this period, different and ever-changing relationships existed with neighbouring peoples, variously identified as near relatives (Moab, Ammon, and Edom), as alien invaders (the Philistines), or as existing neighbours (Syria and Lebanon).

The Hebrew Bible, a library of books from different periods and provenance, edited and re-edited over a period of a thousand years, depicts the Israelites as descendants of Abraham through his son Isaac, grandson Jacob, and Jacob's twelve sons. These represented the twelve tribes who emerged from Egypt to undertake their forty-year journey through the wilderness. Yet the Bible also records that a 'mixed multitude' departed with the Israelites who were also deemed part of the Children of Israel. Around 1000 BCE, when King Solomon built and then dedicated the Temple in Jerusalem, he asked God to answer the prayers of 'foreigners' (*nokhri*) who visited it.[3] These may have included a group of people referred to as *yir'ei adonai*, literally, 'those who fear/are in awe of the Lord', or perhaps they were pilgrims from other nations who came to worship at the Temple in Jerusalem. Following the destruction of the First Temple in 586 BCE and the exile, the prophet Jeremiah sent a letter to the exile community. He had predicted the defeat in his preaching over many decades because of the corruption and rampant injustice he saw around him, and he anticipated exile as punishment for breaking the covenant, though with the possibility of eventual return to the land and restoration. When the destruction actually happened, Jeremiah became the voice of consolation. His letter to the exiles defined the nature of the relationship the exile community should have with its surrounding society, and became the basis for that relationship in all subsequent Diaspora societies until today.

---

[3] 1 Kings 8: 41–3.

Thus says the Lord of hosts, the God of Israel to all the exiles whom I have exiled from Jerusalem to Babylon. Build houses and settle, plant gardens and eat their fruit. Take wives and bear sons and daughters and take wives for your sons and give your daughters to husbands and bear sons and daughters and increase there and do not decrease. And seek the peace of the city to which I have exiled you and pray on its behalf to the Lord, for in their peace will be your peace.[4]

Different biblical witnesses sketch different perceptions of the 'outside' world. At one extreme is the opposite of acceptable behaviour, exemplified by the figure of Amalek,[5] who attacked the Israelites during their wandering in the wilderness. What characterized Amalek as particularly unacceptable was that he attacked the weakest people at the rear and he showed no 'fear of God',[6] a phrase implying no moral values or qualms about murdering helpless people. Haman is another example in his attempts to exterminate the Jewish people in the Book of Esther, only to be prevented at the last minute by Queen Esther. 'Haman' becomes viewed in Jewish history as the archetypal enemy of the Jewish people.

At the other end of the spectrum is the teaching of the prophet Amos that insists that Israel shares much with other peoples, that God has intervened in the history of all nations: 'Are you not like the Cushites to Me, O children of Israel, an oracle of the Lord. Did I not bring up Israel from the land of Egypt, the Philistines from Caphtor (Crete) and the Arameans from Kir?'[7] Yet the same prophet can nevertheless insist on the uniqueness of God's relationship with Israel and hence their greater responsibility: 'Only you have I known from all the families of the earth, therefore I will engage with you for all your wrongdoings!'[8] Another example is found in the books of Isaiah and Micah which speak of a time when all the nations and peoples will flow to Mount Zion in Jerusalem to learn Torah, divine teaching, from God and as a result will cease to wage war.[9] The prophet Isaiah also envisages a time when the two 'superpowers' of the time, Egypt and Assyria, will become a third with Israel as a blessing in the midst of the earth.[10]

If this kind of flexibility is evident at the beginning of Jewish history, a very different strand emerged amongst the leadership returning from the Babylonian exile. Under the Priest Ezra an effort was made to purge the non-Israelite wives married to those Israelites who had remained in the land during the period of exile but had even forgotten how to speak Hebrew. So Nehemiah would comment: 'In those days I saw Jews that had married the wives of Ashdod, Amnon and Moab and their children spoke half in the speech of Ashdod and could not speak the language of the Jews but spoke according to the language of each people.'[11] However, a tough exclusionary approach was not the only line taken. The Book of Ruth is written in direct contradiction to Ezra and Nehemiah's approach. The heroine Ruth is depicted in ideal terms for her sense of loyalty to her Israelite family and she will become the ancestor of King David, the founding figure of the longest lasting biblical monarchy and

---

[4] Jer. 29: 4–7.   [5] Exod. 17: 8–16.   [6] Deut. 25: 17–19.   [7] Amos 9: 7.   [8] Amos 3: 2.
[9] Isa. 2: 1–4 and Micah 4: 1–4.   [10] Isa. 19: 24–5.   [11] Neh. 13: 23–4.

the model for future messianic hopes of restoration. Yet Ruth is a Moabitess, and thus forbidden to enter the Israelite nation as laid down in Deuteronomy.

We need to acknowledge that there is a variety of biblical views of the other. So we simply refer to the Book of Jonah which holds a middle position. Jonah is sent to preach against Nineveh, the capital of Assyria, the empire destined to destroy the Northern Kingdom of Israel, something already an ancient fact at the time of the composition of the book. Jonah's reluctance to go leads him to flee to Tarshish, across the Mediterranean Sea, only to encounter a storm that threatens to destroy the ship in which he is travelling. The sailors pray to their respective gods, but on learning of Jonah's responsibility for the storm, pray to Jonah's God by name and promise to bring sacrifices to God, presumably at the Temple in Jerusalem. When Jonah finally preaches in Nineveh, the citizens and their king repent and 'turn away from their evil ways and the violence that is in their hands'.[12] However, unlike the sailors, the Ninevites never use the divine name for God known to Israel. The implication is that for the author the non-Israelite world contained many peoples who could understand the universal rule of God, like Ruth the Moabitess, but only some of them might make the further step of identifying that God with the God of Israel.

RABBINIC JUDAISM

With the crisis that followed the destruction of the Second Temple in 70 CE by the Romans, the rabbis established schools where they could preserve, apply, and expand their oral tradition. The document that emerged from this activity around 200 CE, the Mishnah, literally 'repetition', became the second founding document of Judaism after the Hebrew Bible. Essentially a codification of the laws that belonged to the oral Torah, it moved far beyond mere legal matters to include also the practices, teachings, and anecdotes of the early rabbis. The Mishnah in turn became the source of study and new layers of commentary crystallized in two vast compilations, each known as Talmud (derived from the verb *lamad* to study); the earlier version, the Palestinian or Jerusalem Talmud, as well as, from out of Judaism of the Diaspora, the Babylonian Talmud. In these new circumstances of exile, the relationship with the dominant power had to be clearly defined. The rabbinic strategy for political survival is summed up in the concept of *dina d'malchuta dina*—'the law of the kingdom is the law'. This submission to the legal system of the dominant power was largely confined to economic matters, however. It left a degree of autonomy in regulating the internal aspects of Jewish society, particularly in areas of religious concern, such as marriage. Effectively it gave Jewish communities a measure of independence for the management of their affairs that was to continue throughout the Middle Ages.[13]

---

[12] Jonah 3: 1.   [13] See J. Magonet, *Talking to the Other* (London: I. B. Tauris, 2003), 29ff.

If this clarified the formal position of the Jewish community, the deeper question of the actual relationship with the non-Jewish world was subject to continuing debate. Certain Jewish ritual requirements, such as the dietary laws, inevitably restricted social interaction with others even before the confinement to ghettos in the medieval period made for almost complete separation. The challenge of defining how one perceived the outside world was expressed in an internal debate between two leading rabbis of the second century CE, Rabbi Akiva and Ben Azzai.

> Rabbi Akiva said: "'You shall love your neighbor as yourself" (Leviticus 19: 18). This is a great principle of the Torah.' Ben Azzai disagreed: 'The verse "This is the book of the descendants of Adam . . . the human whom God made in God's likeness' (Genesis 5: 1) utters a principle even greater'.[14]

When the question was posed, What is the greatest principle of the Torah? Akiva responded with Leviticus 19: 18, 'You shall love your neighbour as yourself'. But in its biblical context the 'neighbour' in question is the fellow Israelite. However, since that verse can be seen as purely internal to the Jewish people, it is countered by the suggestion by Ben Azzai who quotes instead Genesis 5: 1, 'This is the book of the generations of humanity, Adam', which firmly sets the interrelationship of all human beings as the central principle of the Torah. Moreover the continuation of the verse, 'when God created Adam He made him in the image of God', anchors this universal truth in its ultimate source, the element of the divine in every human being. This debate reflects the tension between particularistic and universalistic attitudes we have already seen present in the Hebrew Bible.

How one's duty to one's 'neighbour' is explored is another celebrated principle that is attributed to Hillel, a great teacher of the Pharisees, who lived in the first century BCE. When asked by a proselyte to sum up the whole of Judaism he responded: 'What is hateful to you, do not do to your fellow creature. That is the whole of the Torah. The rest is commentary. Go and learn.'[15] Given the ultimate unity of humanity, the rabbis needed to define the essential obligations towards one another and to God that all human beings and societies should fulfil. Since the rabbis thought in legal categories regarding the demands made on the Jewish people, they applied the same principle regarding the expectations placed upon the rest of humanity. Of particular concern was the worship of false gods and here the rabbis applied the term *avodah zarah* ('foreign worship') to designate idolatry. The minimum requirements for the construction of a civilized society expected of non-Jews became known as the Noachide commandments, which will be discussed below. It is worth emphasizing the rabbinic principle that 'the law of the kingdom is the law' demonstrates that a characteristic feature of rabbinic Judaism is its ability to digest the traditions and customs of surrounding cultures. The

---

[14] *Jerusalem Talmud*, Nedarim 9: 4, 41c.   [15] *Babylonian Talmud*, Shabbat 31a.

fact that rabbinic Judaism survived, despite dispersion, persecution, and its lack of a strong, centralized organization, testifies not only to its resilience but also to an adaptability which included reacting to and to a certain extent being influenced by other religions, notably Christianity and Islam.

MEDIEVAL JUDAISM

In the medieval period there was much discussion among Jews about relations with Islam and Christianity. We will explore this by way of a case study of the significant figure Maimonides (1135–1204 CE), who was a physician, philosopher, and legal authority (Arabic: *Mūsa ibn Maymūn*), and lived his entire life in Muslim countries (Spain, Morocco, Egypt).

Maimonides: A Case Study

Maimonides was a significant influence on later Jewish thinking and no medieval portrait of Judaism would be complete without consideration of him. His magnum opus, *Guide for the Perplexed*, was quickly translated into Latin and used by Christian philosophers including Thomas Aquinas, who refers to 'Rabbi Moses the Egyptian'. Following on from earlier rabbinic discussion, Maimonides and other medieval rabbis reflected on the Noachide Commandments. The book of Genesis portrays Noah as a pious believer who worshipped God through obedience and sacrifice and was given divine commands, including those prohibiting murder and the consumption of blood. He is therefore seen by Judaism (as well as Christianity and Islam) as an archetype of righteousness. Non-Jews were to be defined and treated as monotheists if they adhered to these basic social and religious values. They should establish law-courts; refrain from blasphemy, idolatry, murder, theft, and forbidden sexual relationships such as incest; and not perform vivisection. Maimonides regarded them as 'the pious of the gentile peoples' and worthy of the same eternal bliss guaranteed to Jews who observed the Torah's 613 commands. In the Middle Ages, the concept was widely applied to Muslims and, after some early doubts about the Trinity, was later used in the Jewish theological definition of Christians.

According to Maimonides, both Jesus and Muhammad had a positive effect on the world by propagating monotheism. Indeed, Christianity along with Islam providentially spread knowledge of God and scripture throughout the world, thereby preparing the way for the true Messiah.

> All those words of Jesus of Nazareth and of this Ishmaelite [i.e. Muhammad] who arose after him are to make straight the path for the messianic king and to prepare the whole world to serve the Lord together. As it is said: 'For then I will change the speech of the peoples to a

pure speech so that all of them shall call on the name of the Lord and serve him with one accord' (Zephaniah 3: 9).[16]

One should not conclude that Maimonides was expressing any real tolerance, in the modern sense of the term; the medieval period as a whole was not a period of tolerance. Maimonides insists that Jesus only imagined he was the Messiah. But instead of improving the lot of the Jewish people, Jesus made it incomparably worse. As for Islam, Maimonides was more accepting of its monotheistic character, expressed in a letter in 1165 CE to the inhabitants of Morocco, who had been threatened by the Almohads with conversion, exile, death, or accepting Islam. In the generations that followed, almost all halakhic authorities accepted Maimonides' approach to Islam. One of his best known pieces of advice was to 'listen to the truth from wherever it comes', in which he echoes al-Kindi, one of the first Arab philosophers.[17] Maimonides' statement that 'The pious of the Gentile nations have a share in the world to come' has been frequently cited as evidence of Jewish inclusiveness, although as Marc Saperstein has pointed out, it is unclear whether Maimonides, who excluded idolaters from eligibility, meant to include pious Christians.[18]

THE CHALLENGE OF THE ENLIGHTENMENT AND MODERNITY

The eighteenth-century Age of Enlightenment marked the beginning of modernity. It challenged the intellectual assumptions of the traditional religious and political role of religious authority and witnessed not only the emancipation of Jews in Christian Europe and the granting of equal rights, but also the denigration of Jews and Judaism, rooted in a new form of political and social thinking, called anti-Semitism. Moses Mendelssohn is known as the father of the Jewish Enlightenment (*haskalah*). He argued there was one universal truth, attainable by reason, in which all might share, whether Christian or Jewish or other. In *Jerusalem* (1783) he urged tolerance for other religious groups based upon a common humanity, and regarded the practice of religion as a private affair for the individual. Mendelssohn was an observant Jew who engaged with Christian thinkers, as seen in his open correspondence with the theologian Johann Kaspar Lavater. He argued that rationality was the criterion by which to assess religious claims, and regarded Christianity as deficient in comparison with Judaism.

[16] *Mishneh Torah* (Hilkhot Melakhim 11: 10–12); as cited in J. Rudin, *Christians and Jews Faith to Faith: Tragic History, Promising Present, Fragile Future* (New York: Jewish Lights Publishing, 2010), 128–9.
[17] I am grateful to D. Davies for these remarks on Maimonides. See his *Method and Metaphysics in Maimonides' Guide for the Perplexed* (Oxford: Oxford University Press, 2011).
[18] M. Saperstein, 'Maimonides', in E. Kessler and N. Wenborn (eds), *A Dictionary of Jewish–Christian Relations* (Cambridge: Cambridge University Press, 2005), 283–4.

Politically, the Enlightenment led to Jewish emancipation, that is, to Jews gaining civil rights on a more or less equal footing with other citizens of the countries in which they lived. France in 1791 was the birthplace of Jewish emancipation in Europe and anti-Jewish laws were repealed. The emancipation of Jews was promoted alongside the emancipation of women, slaves, and other religious minorities (Protestant groups in some countries, Catholics in England). Jews gained civil rights on a more or less equal footing with other citizens of the countries in which they lived. Yet, whilst the French Revolution granted Jews citizenship as individuals, it still deprived them of group privileges. In other words, the coming of the modern era resulted in political freedom for individual Jews, but not for the Jewish people *as a community*. So long as Jews identified themselves primarily as individual citizens they were accorded civil rights; but their communal identity was restricted. As Clermont-Tonnerre stated in 1789, 'We must refuse everything to the Jews as a nation and accord everything to Jews as individuals'.[19] Underlying his words is a tension between religious and national identity, a tension existing from the rise of the modern nation-state until today. During the period of the Emancipation, many expected Jews to assimilate or convert to Christianity and significant numbers did indeed convert, amongst them the German-Jewish poet Heinrich Heine who abandoned Judaism only to return to it in later life. His famous remark that his baptismal certificate was an 'admission ticket to European culture' indicated something of the pressure under which Jews remained to conform, at least outwardly, to the dominant faith.

Voltaire exemplified the ambivalence of the Enlightenment. He called for religious tolerance and advocated universal human rights but was not free of the very anti-Jewish prejudices that he ridiculed, discussing Jews in ways that suggested they had innate negative qualities. Voltaire has been seen by some scholars as the father of anti-Semitism, thus associating anti-Semitism and the Holocaust with the emergence of modernity. Wilhelm Marr was the first to use the term 'anti-Semitism' in 1879, but it would be a mistake to differentiate it completely from its much older sister prejudice, anti-Judaism, which has a theological basis. Marr saw Jews as biologically different to model blue-eyed, fair-haired, white Teutons and asserted that Semites, darker skinned than, and inferior to, northern European peoples, could not be assimilated to the majority race and, indeed, were a threat to them. In France, an upsurge of anti-Semitism began in the late nineteenth century, even though the Jewish community there was one of the smallest and most assimilated groups in Europe. The 'Dreyfus Affair' epitomized the disdain held for Jews in French society, particularly among Catholic nationalists. In 1894 Albert Dreyfus, a military man, was arrested and tried for treason. However, it became clear that the evidence was fabricated. Dreyfus was tried again in 1899 and found guilty by a military court, but ten days later he was pardoned by the President of France. The debate about Dreyfus split France. To the French nationalistic and the religious right, Dreyfus the Jew symbolized all the liberal, alien, and de-Christianizing pressures on the traditional

---

[19] Stanislas Marie Adélaïde, *The French Revolution and Human Rights: A Brief Documentary History*, tr. and ed. L. Hunt (Boston: Bedford Books of St Martin's Press, 1996), 88.

Christian order in the country. The Catholic Church through its media gave considerable support to the anti-Dreyfus sentiment sweeping France. The Dreyfus Affair had two major consequences: it motivated Theodor Herzl, a Viennese journalist who covered the trial, to write his book *The Jewish State* in 1896, and it also eventually led to the 1905 law separating church and state in France.

Anti-Jewish attitudes were common also among Protestants, including eminent scholars such as Emil Schurer, who insisted that Judaism was doomed to fail because of its particularism, and Gerhard Kittel, editor of the influential *Theological Dictionary of the New Testament*, who was also a member of the German Nazi party. 'Authentic Judaism', he wrote, 'abides by the symbol of the stranger wandering restless and homeless on the face of the earth'.[20] There were serious outbreaks of anti-Semitism in Russia throughout the nineteenth and early twentieth centuries, when no less than half the world's Jewish population was located within the Russian empire. Pogroms, a Russian word meaning 'devastation' and referring to violent attacks on Jews, regularly took place, the worst being in 1881, 1903, and 1905. While they might be prompted by social and economic factors, they were also coloured by religious ignorance dressed in the garb of zeal. For Adolf Hitler and his Nazi party, race and not religion was the dominant motive for destroying Jews. He espoused a conspiracy view of history: Jews were responsible for Germany's defeat in the Great War of 1914–18. Jews, according to Hitler, were vile, even vermin. Yet if race provided the mythology and motivation for anti-Jewishness, secularized religious language provided the justification. In *Mein Kampf* (1924), Hitler did not hesitate to use overtly Christian language to appeal to a pious audience.

THE SHOAH AND ITS IMPACT

When Poland was occupied in September 1939, Jews were deprived of their belongings and forced into manual labour which Nazis called 'destruction through work'. After Hitler invaded Russia in 1941 Jews there were rounded up, taken to the outskirts of towns, shot, and buried in mass graves. Between October and December 1941, perhaps 300,000 died in this way; and in 1942, a further 900,000. Special troops known as *Einsatzgruppen* were employed for this purpose. From 1941, death by gas was carried out and death camps were built at Chelmno, Auschwitz, Majdanek, Sobibor, Treblinka, and Belzec. After the Wannsee Conference in January 1942, the Nazis began the systematic deportation of Jews from all over Europe to these concentration camps which were designed to carry out genocide. This was the 'Final Solution' policy in action: the extermination of all Jews. At the camps, the ill and the elderly were killed immediately, but the young and fit were put to manual work. At its greatest capacity, the camp at Auschwitz held 140,000. Its five ovens could burn 10,000 a day. Over 1.1 million died at Auschwitz. Thus, when the war ended in 1945 so had ended a whole way of life for

---

[20] Gerhard Kittel, *Die Judenfrage* (Stuttgart: W. Kohlhammer, 1933), 73.

European Jews. Their numbers were decimated—6 million had perished. Of the pre-war Jewish populations of Poland, Latvia, Lithuania, Estonia, Germany, and Austria, less than 10 per cent survived; and less than 30 per cent of Jews in occupied Russia, Ukraine, Belgium, Yugoslavia, Norway, and Romania.

For twenty years after the Holocaust, or *Shoah* (destruction), hardly anything was said or written. It was almost too horrible to mention. Now, there is an enormous literature on the subject. Yet, although the Holocaust is of immense importance, it is misleading if it so dominates the Jewish religious views of the 'other' as to eclipse all other approaches. Jewish responses to the Holocaust tend to fall into two categories. The first, represented by Emil Fackenheim and Elie Wiesel, argues that the Shoah resulted in a rupture in the relationship between Jews and God. The second is to view the events as one would view persecution and oppression during other periods of extreme Jewish suffering. This view is represented by Michael Wyschogrod who states that 'the voices of the prophets speak more loudly than did Hitler'.[21] Fackenheim urged a new commandment, to be added to the 613 biblical commandments, that it was the duty of Jews to survive the trauma of the Shoah and not give Hitler posthumous victory by disappearing.[22] He argued that the Holocaust precipitated an unprecedented need in both Jewish and Christian theology to re-examine the nature of the relationship between man and God. At the heart of his approach is an insistence that a traditional religious response is no longer appropriate in a post-Holocaust world because it fails to provide answers to the unique challenges posed by the Holocaust. For his part, Jonathan Sacks has stated that Christians and Jews 'today meet and talk together because we must; because we have considered the alternative and seen where it ends and we are shocked to the core by what we have seen'.[23] His words echo those of Abraham Joshua Heschel who, in a speech to the Rabbinical Assembly Convention in the United States thirty years earlier, stated that 'Jews and Christians share the perils and fears; we stand on the abyss together'.[24]

In 2000, *Dabru Emet* (Speak truth), a cross-denominational Jewish statement on Christians and Christianity was issued and, commenting on the Holocaust, assessed Christian guilt while separating Christianity from Nazism:

> *Nazism was not a Christian phenomenon.* Without the long history of Christian anti Judaism and Christian violence against Jews, Nazi ideology could not have taken hold nor could it have been carried out . . . But Nazism itself was not an inevitable outcome of Christianity.

---

[21] M. Wyschogrod, 'Faith and the Holocaust', *Judaism*, 20 (1971), 294.

[22] E. Fackenheim, *The Jewish Return into History: Reflections in the Age of Auschwitz and a New Jerusalem* (New York: Schocken Books, 1978), 23–4.

[23] J. Sacks, preface to Helen Fry (ed.), *A Reader of Christian–Jewish Dialogue* (Exeter: Exeter University Press, 1996), p. xi.

[24] H. Kasimow and B. L. Sherwin (eds), *No Religion is an Island: Abraham Joshua Heschel and Interreligious Dialogue* (Eugene, Or.: Wipf & Stock, 1991), 167.

The statement generated much controversy and demonstrated how the Holocaust remains both central to and sensitive in the Jewish–Christian encounter. Some Jews criticized the statement as going too far, remaining convinced that Christians have not forsworn triumphalism; they point to the continuing targeted proselytism of Jews; others express concern that Christians might feel completely exonerated by the Jewish statement. For some Christians, it was troubling to learn that many Jews do view Nazism as the logical outcome of European Christian culture.

In the future, it is possible that Dabru Emet's statement on the Holocaust will mark the end of the first generation of Holocaust theological writings, such as those by Fackenheim. For Christians, a revolutionary shift in the theological understanding of Judaism, and a far more constructive relationship with the Jewish people, has resulted. For Jewish thinkers, such as the author of this chapter, there is a concern that the Holocaust has become the touchstone of Jewish identity and has inculturated Jews to think of themselves as 'victims', and much of the world as 'perpetrators' or 'bystanders'. Jews need to move on to new ways of engaging with the religious 'other'. The risk, otherwise, is that of being not so much grounded in the past as imprisoned by it.

JEWISH VIEWS OF THE OTHER: SOME CONTEMPORARY ISSUES

A number of issues confront Judaism in its relationship to religious others in the contemporary world and which give insight into the wider question of Jewish views of the religious 'other'. Among the more salient there is the challenge of interfaith dialogue, the encounter with Islam, the ongoing situation of the Israeli–Palestinian conflict, the profound matter of memory and identity, and the covenant motif. Some of these have a more ancient resonance; all have contemporary pressing relevance for Jews and Judaism—and for the respective 'others' to which Judaism relates. We shall examine these in turn.

Interfaith Dialogue

The term 'interfaith dialogue' (and the nature of dialogue activity) is often both misconstrued and ill defined. A casual conversation that may add up to no more than a loose restatement of entrenched theological positions is sometimes claimed to be a dialogue. Equally, any communication between persons of two differing religious points of view (e.g. by phone, email or Facebook) may be on occasion described loosely as 'dialogue'. However, dialogue is not synonymous with 'communication'. For dialogue to take place there must be a genuine listening to and hearing of the 'other' who is contributing to the dialogical discourse. For dialogue consists of a direct meeting of two (at least) people and involves a reciprocal exposing of the full religious consciousness of the one with the other. In dialogue each speaks to the other with a full respect of what the other is and has to say. This is never less than personal but it can develop in such a way as to be extended to a group and even to communities. However, it begins with the individual and not with the community.

Such a quest is never easy because it is not merely about the other, nor where the other differs from us. The application of dialogue is perhaps best illustrated in the letters of Jewish philosopher Franz Rosenzweig and Christian theologian Rosenstock-Huessy, which passed between the trenches of the First World War. Rosenzweig's writings emphasize not the subject matter that connects the speaker with the listener but the 'I' confronting the 'Thou'. The word is not only an expression of reality but also a means by which to express it. Speech for Rosenzweig consisted of articulating an awareness and comprehension in living contact with another person, which he called *Sprachdenken*. Thus the use of words in a live encounter was for him more than just talking—something is not only said but something happens. This means that dialogue is dependent upon the presence of another person. It is not difficult to see how Rosenzweig became one of the main sources out of which Martin Buber developed his 'I and Thou' formula. Buber, in his exposition of the I–Thou relationship, maintained that a personal relationship with God is only truly personal when there is not only awe and respect on the human side but when we are not overcome and overwhelmed in our relationship with God. This has implications for Jewish–Christian dialogue—it means that Christians and Jews must meet as two valid centres of interest. Thus, one should approach the other with respect and restraint so that the validity of the other is in no sense belittled. Further, not only is the essential being of the other respected but the world of 'faith' is also treated as valid and genuine; not an 'it' to be carelessly set aside but a distinctive value of belief. An I–Thou relationship is a meeting not of religions but of religious people.

Most recently Emmanuel Levinas, who was greatly influenced by Buber, has argued that the relationship with the 'other' is not an idyllic relationship of communion, or a sympathy through which we put ourselves in the other's place; the other resembles us, but is external to us. For Levinas, the face of the other necessitates an ethical commitment. When people look at each other, they see not only two faces but also the faces of other people, the face of humanity. The relationship becomes less 'I–thou', and more 'we–thou', entailing an ethical commitment to and responsibility for the other person of faith. The responsibility for the other is linked to the human approach to the divine for

> there can be no 'knowledge' of God separated from the relationship with human beings. The Other is the very focus of metaphysical truth and is indispensable for my relation with God. He does not play the role of a mediator. The Other is not the incarnation of God, but precisely by His face, in which he is disincarnated, is the manifestation of the height in which God is revealed.[25]

[25] Emmanuel Levinas, *Totality and Infinity* (Pittsburgh: Duquesne University Press, 1979), 78.

Dialogue, therefore, involves a respect that takes the other as seriously as one would wish to be taken oneself. This is an immensely difficult and costly exercise. We find it all too easy to relate to others in a casual way with a lack of concentration on the reality and good of the other. It is far easier to compare the facts and features of each other's religion than to engage with our dialogue partner on a quest, for example, of the nature and meaning of God's purpose for humanity. In a letter to Rudolph Ehrenberg in 1913 Rosenzweig writes about the saying of Jesus in the Gospel of John (14: 6) that 'No-one can come to the Father except through me'. Rosenzweig does not condemn this saying but asserts that it is true, particularly when one remembers the millions who have been led to God through Jesus Christ.

However, he continues: 'The situation is quite different for one who does not have to reach the Father because he is already with him. Shall I, he asks, become converted, I who have been chosen? Does the alternative of conversion even exist for me?'[26] In these few sentences Rosenzweig introduces us to the crucial question of interfaith dialogue (in this case, Jewish–Christian dialogue)—can Christians view Judaism as a valid religion in its own terms and, of course, vice versa? Directly related to this is the need, from a Christian perspective, for reflection on the survival of the Jewish people, of the vitality of Judaism over 2,000 years and the significance of what Paul called 'the mystery of Israel'.[27] Questions also need to be considered from the Jewish perspective. What was the purpose behind the creation of Christianity? Does the fact that Jesus was a Jew have any implications for Jews?

The Encounter with Islam

In one sense, relations with Islam can be dealt with under the familiar theme of supersessionism, since Muslims traditionally believe that Islam was the final religion revealed by God through the Prophet Muhammad. Islam sees itself as perfecting the two monotheistic religions and the Qur'an calls both Jews and Christians *ahl al-Kitab* (People of the Book).[28] Muhammad's religious practice at first owed much to Arabian Christians and especially Jews: Muslims faced Jerusalem in prayer and fasted during the Day of Atonement.

> Surely those who believe, and those who are Jews, and the Christians, and the Sabians, whoever believes in God and the Last day and does good, they shall have their reward from their Lord, and there is no fear for them, nor shall they grieve.[29]

---

[26] Franz Rosenzweig, *Gesammelte Schriften*, i (The Hague: Martinus Nijhoff, 1913), 132ff.

[27] Before dialogue could begin with Judaism, Christianity shifted from what was, for the most part, an inherent need to condemn Judaism to one of a condemnation of Christian anti-Judaism. This process has not led to a separation from all things Jewish (as proposed by the 2nd-cent. heretic, Marcion, who called for a total separation from the Hebrew Bible and much of the Gospel writings) but, in fact, to a closer relationship with 'the elder brother'.

[28] One consequence of Islamic supersessionism on Jewish–Christian relations is that it provides Christians with an insight into the difficulties raised by traditional Christian supersessionism of Judaism and what is sometimes called replacement theology.

[29] Qur'an 2: 62 (see http://corpus.quran.com).

But after Muhammad failed to gain the support of both other groups, his became a separate religion, claiming to be the fulfilment and reformer of all previous revelations, not just Judaism and Christianity. He expelled two Jewish groups from Medina; finally, a third group was severely treated, the men being killed and women and children sold into slavery. Muhammad showed a similar though less violent ambivalence towards Christians: the Qur'an describes them as 'nearest in love' to the believers,[30] yet condemns their christological and trinitarian beliefs.

Muhammad's ambivalent attitude towards Judaism and Christianity continued into later Muslim history. On the one hand, Jews and Christians were often (not always) well-treated under Muslim rule, regarded (unlike polytheists and atheists) as dhimmis, 'protected people', who were, on payment of a tax, allowed to practise their faith, participate in political and social life, but not seek converts. The dhimmi status and the regulations governing it are traditionally associated with Caliph Umar, as during his caliphate Islam grew rapidly and came to rule over numerous peoples who were not Muslims. For Jews, under Islamic rule life was far easier than for those living under Christian rule.

In their contemporary encounter with Muslims, Jews have much to discuss. Theologically, it is commonly argued that Islam is more similar to Judaism than Christianity since both have problems with Christian trinitarian theology, stress religious law and the centrality of monotheism, and have no priesthood. The 2008 Muslim Letter to the Jewish Community (*Call to Dialogue*), initiated by Muslim scholars at the Centre for the Study of Muslim–Jewish Relations in Cambridge, is an example of a contemporary attempt to demonstrate the commonality between these two faiths.[31] However, the Israeli–Palestinian conflict is a major source of tension between Jews and Muslims, not just in the Middle East but also well beyond.

Judaism, like Islam (and Christianity), has difficulty with its fundamentalists. Jewish fundamentalism generally focuses on issues related to the land and state of Israel and, in recent years, fundamentalists have emerged as a significant political and religious force within Israel as well as in the Diaspora. Some have joined with Christian fundamentalists in calling for the building of a third Temple in Jerusalem. While largely secluded from mainstream society, following a tightly regulated lifestyle, Jewish fundamentalists' beliefs and moral understanding of the world have similarities to those of some radical Christian evangelical communities. Christian allies of Jewish fundamentalists believe the creation of the Jewish state in 1948 and the yet-to-be-built Third Temple are theological prerequisites for the Second Coming of Jesus. However, some of these same fundamentalists also actively seek the conversion of Jews to Christianity.

The Israeli–Palestinian Conflict

Nowhere is the subject of peace and understanding, or perhaps more realistically, violence and misunderstanding, more evident than in the Middle East, and more discussed than in

[30] Qur'an 5: 82.
[31] <http://www.tariqramadan.com/An-Open-Letter-A-Call-to-Peace.1369.html?lang=fr> (accessed May 2012).

the tea rooms and coffee parlours of Jerusalem and Tel Aviv as well as Ramallah and Bethlehem. A story is told about an Israeli and a Palestinian leader meeting with God and asking whether there will ever be peace in the Middle East in their lifetime. 'Of course there will be peace,' God told them. They looked relieved. 'However,' God continued, 'not in my lifetime'. 130 years after the beginning of modern Zionism, a peaceful solution seems some distance away. For most Jews, the centrality of the land of the Hebrew Bible, as well as the survival of over a third of world Jewry, is at stake. The creation of the state of Israel is an ancient promise fulfilled—the ingathering of exiles and the creation of a vibrant nation-state, guaranteeing physical and spiritual security. Christians, for their part, not only disagree as to the place of Israel in Christian theology, but many understandably feel particular concern for Arab Christians who live in Israel and in the future state of Palestine. For many Muslims, the permanent existence of a Jewish state in the Middle East is a religious and political anomaly. It is not an uncommon view that Islamic rule must be returned to the land of Israel. There are, of course, also many Jews, Christians, and Muslims who are deeply concerned about each other, making this a complicated picture to understand. Israel is controversial because it cannot be viewed simply as a geographical and political entity whose emergence is like the establishment of any new state. Political, social, cultural, and religious concerns all affect its place in the Jewish–Christian–Muslim relationship. The encounter between Jews, Christians, and Muslims is sometimes mistakenly transformed into an Israeli–Palestinian or Israeli–Arab conversation, with national identity emphasized far more than religious issues.

For Jews, the will to survive in the Diaspora generated messianic hopes of redemption, which occasionally led to a high level of anticipation and the extraordinary claims of self-appointed messiahs such as Bar Kokhba (d. 135 CE) and Shabbetai Zvi (1626–76 CE). One of the common features of these times of messianic fervour was that the Promised Land became a symbol of redress for all the wrongs which Jews had suffered. Thus, modern Zionism became in part the fusion of messianic fervour and the longing for Zion. Jews took their destiny into their own hands and stopped waiting for a divine solution to their predicament. This was a dramatic break from the Diaspora strategy of survival, which advocated endurance of the status quo as part of the covenant with God. For many Jews, the Jewish state offered the best hope not only for survival in response to the breakdown in Europe in the late nineteenth and early twentieth centuries but also for religious and cultural fulfilment. While Jews may view the creation of the state of Israel as an act of national liberation following nearly 2,000 years of powerlessness and homelessness, many Muslims term the same events 'The Disaster', a time when an Islamic society was uprooted and became a minority in a land that was once *Dar al-Islam*; when over 700,000 Palestinians lost their homes, their land, were displaced, and became (and remain) refugees. Most Jews do not separate Zionism from its deep religious roots within Judaism. However, many Muslims make a distinction between Zionism and Judaism, unwilling to acknowledge that Zionism is an integral component of Judaism and not a 'racist' ideology. Relations between Muslims and Jews are overshadowed by the failure of both communities to address the impact of the

Middle East conflict on our own communities. It is essential to be prepared for conflicting views. An authentic encounter must allow for sharp differences, especially since the modern dialogue is young and vulnerable.

Israel, the only Jewish state in the world, is situated in the heart of the Muslim world and it is essential to foster an environment of friendship so that the peoples of that region—both Israelis and Palestinians—can live as neighbours in the security and peace, as they deserve. Developing good relations is in both their interests, however much their political and religious leaders fail the peoples. Certainly, there is mutual antipathy and prejudice on both sides, thousands of miles away from the military and political conflict, which is given disproportionate attention. Muslim sympathy with the Palestinians is seen by some Jews as threatening to the Jewish community and feeding rising anti-Semitism in the UK and elsewhere in Europe and in many other societies, as well as the Middle East. Likewise, Muslims often see Jews as homogeneous in their support and defence of Israel, unwilling to accept any criticism of the Jewish state. Look in any Jewish or Muslim newspaper and the Israeli–Palestinian conflict will not only receive significant comment (and polemic) but will be reported with ignorant stereotypes which only serve to contribute to the irony that both Muslims and Jews feel vulnerable, misunderstood, and under attack. They share the experience of being minority communities in Europe and the USA, for instance, and have parallel experiences and needs.

Memory and Identity

Unlike national identities, religious identities are sacred to those who hold them and their key events have usually occurred much further in the past than most national events. For example, Jews view the exodus from Egypt as of contemporary significance, as Christians view the death and resurrection of Jesus. How these events are celebrated or commemorated shed light on perceptions of the religious 'other'. Commemorations of past events relate the collective memory of a historical community to an inaugural moment or a founding act. By repetition they help preserve a sense of historical continuity, identity, and even social integration. Collective memory contains a strong conservative force furnishing a community with a sense of historical continuity. By re-enacting these founding moments, the inspiration of the heroic or founding event is preserved and reinforced. However, a preoccupation (some might call obsession) with the past may be harmful. The memory of a founding event that is recollected and re-enacted may become a danger if it results in a negative identity and self-understanding, especially if this becomes the only or primary lens through which reality and the changing world is viewed. For example, the legacy of being a victim has left an enduring mark on the Jewish psyche and impacts on the Jewish encounter with others. A history of being surrounded by oppressive nations has become a feature of Jewish memory and identity, leading to a sense of victimization. Taking to heart the Bible's command to the children of Israel to remember (*zachor*), because 'you were slaves in the land of Egypt', Jews are reminded at Passover, not only to remember that God took them out of the land of Egypt but to remember the suffering of Israel in Egypt;[32] the Torah also reminds them not only to treat the stranger with care but to remember the violence committed against the Israelites by the surrounding nations.

A modern example of a focus upon victimization is the 614th commandment proposed by Emil Fackenheim, as discussed above, in his reflection on the Holocaust. One dangerous consequence of demanding Jewish continuity so as not to give Hitler a posthumous victory is that Jewish identity can easily became Shoah-centred, as can relations between Jews and Christians. The Holocaust reinforced a mentality in the Jewish world that Jews are a small minority and that the Jewish people, even Jews in Israel, are surrounded by hostile non-Jews. Consequently, a Jew will easily construct a negative Jewish identity which, without the positive side of Judaism, will not be of value to be handed down over the generations. A non-Jew will come away with an exclusive picture of the Jew as victim, without an awareness of the positive aspects of Jewish culture. If the Jew disappears from the historical horizons from the death of Jesus in 33 CE and only reappears again when Hitler came to power in 1933, not only will a negative identity be formed but attitudes to the other will also be based on a victim–perpetrator relationship.

One way to disarm an obsession with the past is to adopt a critical approach to it and not become victims of an ideological 'vindication' of the past that is nostalgic, dogmatic, and sometimes irrational. If the past is approached critically, it can reveal new interpretations and understandings of the world that can be liberating and constructive. For example, although reflection on and reaction to the Shoah are essential, positive relations cannot be built solely on responses to anti-Semitism and especially Christian feelings of guilt. Certainly, the past must be remembered and memories have to find a way to be reconciled so that horrors are not forgotten. Otherwise, as George Santayana coined, 'those who cannot remember the past are condemned to repeat it'.[33] However, no healthy and enduring relationship between people is built on guilt. If recent Christian soul-searching in the aftermath of the destruction of European Jewry leads to a new approach and a revision of traditional anti-Jewish teaching, so much the better. However, the future relationship cannot be built on the foundations of guilt. The sense of guilt is transient and does not pass to the next generation; moreover, it is unstable, inherently prone to sudden and drastic reversal. So, it is necessary for Jews and Christians to negotiate a better stance towards a compromised past in order to look forward to a more hopeful future. Indeed, redeeming a compromised past offers grounds for hope in Jewish–Christian relations but also in relations with Muslims and other faith communities.

This might be described as *memoria futuri*,[34] a memory for the future, enabling a more positive memory of the past. For example, Jews could view Diaspora life not primarily in

---

[32]   Deut. 16: 3 refers to unleavened bread as 'the bread of affliction'.

[33]   George Santayana, *The Life of Reason*, i (New York: Charles Scribner's Sons), 284.

[34]   Walter Kasper, President of the Pontifical Commission for Religious Relations with the Jews (2002–10), was the first to promote the concept of *memoria futuri* in a Catholic–Jewish conversation at the Woolf Institute in Cambridge in 2004.

negative terms (as an anti-Jewish environment and exemplifying a continuous history of oppression) but in positive terms (as a fruitful environment facilitating vigorous Jewish existence and dynamic development). Traditionally, Diaspora has been understood as *galut*, 'exile', implying that life outside of Israel is a life *of* exile (an undesirable situation). Indeed, the rabbis understood *galut* as a divine punishment. However, 'diaspora' is a Greek word meaning 'dispersion' (a voluntary situation desirable to the individual), which can be a positive experience for the Jewish people living among the nations of the world, leading to a greater sense of constructive engagement with the 'other'.

Covenant

A covenant (*berit*) is not, as is sometimes mistakenly assumed, a legalistic contract or transaction but is an agreement dependent upon a relationship. Some hold to the view that *berit* is better translated by 'obligation' because it expresses the sovereign power of God, who imposes his will on his people Israel: God promises in a solemn oath to fulfil his word to his people Israel, who are expected to respond by faithfulness and obedience. Jonathan Sacks explained this as follows:

> in a covenant, two or more individuals, each respecting the dignity and integrity of the other, come together in a bond of love and trust, to share their interests, sometimes even to share their lives, by pledging our faithfulness to one another, to do together what neither of us can do alone . . . a contract is about interests but a covenant is about identity. And that is why contracts benefit, but covenants transform.[35]

The language of covenant represents a shift from description to prescription, from what 'is' to what 'ought'; from what human beings *are*, to an ethical statement about what we *may or may not do*.[36] From a Jewish perspective, this is a move from things seen to things heard; from the visual to the practical construction of what might be called today the 'Big Society'. The key metaphors in Judaism are auditory. In the Talmud, phrases referring to knowledge, understanding, or tradition are often variants of the verb *shema*, meaning 'to hear'. The key biblical command is 'Hear, O Israel'.[37] God showed himself to Moses and the Israelites not in the image but in the call. When Elijah perceived God, he heard only a still small voice.[38] In addition, the Bible is not history—what happened sometime else to someone else—but is read in terms of memory, my story, what happened to my ancestors and therefore, insofar as

---

[35] J. Sacks, 'The Relationship between the People and God: An Address to Lambeth Conference' (2008) II. The full text of this address can be found at: <http://www.archbishopofcanterbury.org/articles.php/1063/the-relationship-between-the-people-and-god> (accessed Feb. 2012).

[36] David Hume first articulated this as the 'is–ought problem' in his *A Treatise of Human Nature* (London: John Noon, 1739). Although claims about what ought to be are made on the basis of what is, the logic on which the move from description to prescription is based is uncertain.

[37] Deut. 6: 4.   [38] 1 Kings 19: 11–13.

I carry on their story, to me. The Torah speaks not of moral truths in the abstract but of commands, that is, truths addressed to me, calling for my response. Consequently, much of the Torah is written in the form of narrative, celebrating the concrete, not the abstract; the particular, not the universal.[39]

Narrative truth is not like scientific or logical truth. It does not operate on the either/or of 'true' and 'false'. Narratives contain multiple points of view. For Jews, they are open—essentially, not accidentally—to more than one interpretation, more than one level of interpretation. Nor does the validity of one story exclude another. Stories, including historical narratives, do more than reflect facts about the world. They offer interpretations of the world. They attempt to make sense out of the raw data of events. Narrative constructs and conveys meaning. The rabbinic Bible, the *Mikraot Gedolot*, with its commentaries spanning the centuries ranged around the biblical text, is a starting point. The *Mikraot Gedolot* is rightly regarded as a celebration of the relativity of exegesis and of the enduring, elusive nature of the debate about meaning. The willingness to see a multitude of different possible meanings is in marked contrast to the single 'authentic' meaning, backed by clerical or scholarly authority.[40] Hence the profound difference between thinking, if my faith is true and conflicts with yours, then yours is false. Faith as covenant means, if I and my fellow believers have a relationship with God, that does not entail that you do not. I have my stories, rituals, memories, prayers, celebrations, laws, and customs; you have yours. That is what makes me me, and you you. The truth of one does not entail the falsity of the other. Indeed, the very words 'true' and 'false' seem out of place, as if we were using words from one domain to describe phenomena belonging to another. The idea that truth cannot coexist with falsehood generates narratives of displacement. If I am convinced that I possess the truth while you are sunk in error, I may try to persuade you, but if you refuse to be persuaded, I may conquer or convert you, imposing my view by force in the name of truth. This thinking leads *in extremis* to the dismissive mind-set of, 'I'm right; you're wrong; go to Hell!'

From a Jewish perspective, all relationships between God and humanity are covenantal. None excludes others. God may be with us but also with those who are not like us; with friends but also with strangers. That is why the Torah commands on thirty-six separate occasions to love the stranger. Jewish philosopher, Franz Rosenzweig, argues that both Jews and Christians participate in God's revelation and both are, in different ways, intended by God. Only for God is the truth one; earthly truth remains divided.[41] Contemporary adherents of

---

[39] See E. Wyschogrod, *An Ethics of Remembering: History, Heterology, and the Nameless Others* (Chicago: University of Chicago Press, 1998).

[40] The rabbinic basis for this is found in the following passage: 'In the School of Rabbi Ishmael it is taught: "See, My word is like fire, an oracle of the Eternal, and like a hammer that shatters a rock" (Jeremiah 23: 29). Just as a hammer divides into several sparks so too every scriptural verse yields several meanings' (*Babylonian Talmud*, Sanhedrin 34a).

[41] Rosenzweig was influenced by Jacob Emden who viewed Christianity as a legitimate religion for gentiles. In *Seder Olam Rabbah Vezuta* (1757) Emden wrote positively about Jesus and Paul, utilizing the New Testament in his argument that they had not sought to denigrate Judaism and that their teachings were primarily concerned to communicate the Noachide laws to gentiles.

this position include Israeli scholar David Hartman who argues that a covenant between people and God is predicated on a belief in human dignity. Other religions, especially Christianity and Islam, have their own covenants with God and are called to celebrate their dignity and particularity. This approach may best be called 'Jewish covenantal pluralism'. It begins with the Noachide Commandments,[42] as discussed above, which is an attempt to formulate moral standards for the world without a concomitant demand for conversion to Judaism. As Rabbi Johanan of Tiberias said, 'Whoever denies idolatry is called a Jew'.[43] Therefore, the rejection of idolatry, rather than any doctrinal definition of God, is the key; and these seven commandments provide a theological basis on which to affirm Christianity. A Jewish covenantal pluralist may also turn to the concept of 'Righteous Gentiles', referring to Rabbi Joshua ben Hananya who propounded the view, later generally accepted, that 'the righteous of all nations have a share in the world to come',[44] though they were not converted to Judaism. Judaism does not have an equivalent to *extra ecclesiam non est salus* ('there is no salvation outside the Church'), rather the concept of 'righteous gentiles' provides an opportunity for an affirmation of Christianity. Finally, briefly, one may refer to the principles of *tikkun 'olam* ('establishing the world aright'), *darchei shalom* ('the ways of peace'), and *kiddush Hashem* ('sanctifying God's name', i.e. behaving in such a manner as to bring credit to God), all of which can be brought to govern the Jewish relationship to the religious other.

BACK TO THE BIBLE: A CASE STUDY

Rabbinic interpretations of one key story in the Hebrew Bible, which have clearly been influenced by perceptions of the other—in this case, Christianity—and have implications in general for Jewish perceptions of the religious other, are worth close consideration. The Bible is one key to understanding the relationship between Judaism and Christianity because Jews and Christians shared (and continue to share) a biblically orientated culture. A number of similarities between Jewish and Christian interpretation can be immediately noted, such as an insistence on the harmony of scripture and an emphasis on the sanctity of the text. Consequently, Jewish and Christian interpretations are understandable to many adherents of both religions, noticeably in patristic and rabbinic writings. Both the church fathers and rabbis were close readers of the biblical texts and interested in the detail of scripture. This is illustrated by Origen who commended his Antioch community to 'observe each detail of Scripture, which has been written. For, if one knows how to dig into the depth, he will find a treasure in the details, and perhaps also the precious jewels of the mystery lie hidden where they are not esteemed.'[45] This also aptly describes rabbinic hermeneutics, which seeks to

---

[42] Jacob Neusner *et al.* (eds), *The Tosefta*, Avoda Zara 9.4 (New Haven: Ktav, 1977–86).
[43] *Babylonian Talmud*, Megilla 13a.
[44] Neusner *et al.*, *The Tosefta*, Sanhedrin 13.
[45] *Homilies on Genesis*, 8: 1, L. Doutreleau, *Homélies sur la Genèse: Sources chrétiennes* (Paris: Cerf, 1976).

derive meaning from the detail of scripture. Rabbi Ben Bag Bag, who lived in the first century CE, stated 'turn, turn and turn it again, and you will find something new in it'.[46]

As a piece of writing, Genesis 22—the Sacrifice of Isaac—has everything. It has tension and drama; enough action for a five-act play. Yet it is compressed into eighteen verses. It is packed with energy and dynamism. It is a paradigm of Aristotle's catharsis, arousing both terror and pity. It deals with the biggest themes and touches the deepest emotions. And it seems to have a happy ending. Genesis 22 has been an important story for both Jews and Christians from a very early period. For Jews, from at least as early as the third century CE, the passage has been read on Rosh ha-Shana, the Jewish New Year, and in daily morning prayers. For Christians, from around the same period, the Sacrifice of Isaac was mentioned in the eucharist prayers and the story is read in the period leading up to Easter. A wide variety of themes, central to both Judaism and Christianity, emerge from the commentators' interpretations, including the prediction of Christ's coming, fulfilment of scripture, atonement, and forgiveness. The figure of Isaac is the key, and interpretations reveal an exegetical encounter between Jewish and Christian commentators. In the interpretations of the church fathers, Isaac is portrayed as a youth (unlike some early post-biblical writings such as Josephus and Philo who portray him as an adult). Cyril, for example, describes him as 'small and lying in the breast of his own father'[47] and Eusebius comments that Genesis 22: 13 'did not say, "a lamb", young like Isaac, but "a ram", full-grown, like the Lord'.[48] Other church fathers, such as Chrysostom, portray Isaac as slightly more mature, but who nevertheless retained his youthfulness: 'Isaac had come of age and was in fact in the very bloom of youth'.[49] The rabbinic position was quite different. The rabbis stated that, 'Isaac was 37 years of age when he was offered upon the altar'; another interpretation gave his age as 26 years and a third proposed 36 years.[50] It is significant that, whilst the precise age varied, the rabbis were consistent in their portrayal of Isaac as an adult. None of the rabbinic interpretations, in direct contrast to those of the church fathers, hinted that Isaac might have still been a child. He was a fully developed and mature adult. Both the rabbis and the church fathers also consider in some detail the significance of Isaac carrying the wood:

> *v.6* And Abraham took the wood of the burnt offering, and laid it on Isaac his son; and he took in his hand the fire and the knife. So they went both of them together. *v.7* And Isaac said to his father Abraham, 'My father!' And he said, 'Here I am, my son.' He said, 'Behold, the fire and the wood; but where is the lamb for a burnt offering?' *v.8* Abraham said, 'God will provide himself the lamb for a burnt offering, my son.' So they went both of them together.

---

[46] Pirkei Avot 5: 21, H. Danby, *The Mishnah* (Oxford: Oxford University Press, 1933).

[47] Cyril of Alexandria, *Glaphyra on Genesis*; J. P. Migne, *Glaphyrorum in Genesim* 140–148A (1857–66), 69.

[48] Catena 1277. F. Petit, *La Chaîne sur la Genèse*, Édition Intégrale (Louvain: Peeters, 1995).

[49] R. C. Hill, *Homilies on Genesis* (Washington, DC: Catholic University Press of America, 1986–92).

[50] Genesis Rabbah 55: 4, 56:8; See also *Targum Pseudo Jonathan* in M. Maher (ed.), *The Aramaic Bible. Targum Pseudo Jonathan: Genesis* (Edinburgh: T&T Clark, 1992).

The church fathers viewed it as a model of Jesus carrying the cross. For Melito, Isaac represents Christ and is a model of Christ, who was going to suffer. On the one hand, Isaac paralleled Christ; on the other, he looked forward to Christ.[51] As the Epistle of Barnabas stated, Jesus 'fulfilled the type' that was established in Isaac, pointing forward to the even more amazing deed in the sacrifice of Christ.[52] The rabbis, on the other hand, maintained that Isaac was an adult. His action was not to be interpreted in the light of any later event but had significance in its own right. The rabbis also commented on Isaac carrying the wood and the following passage from Genesis Rabbah 56: 3 does indeed appear to be remarkably similar: ' "And Abraham placed the wood of the burnt-offering on Isaac his son." Like a man who carries his cross (*z'luvo*) on his shoulder.' This interpretation, in one of the oldest and most well-known *midrashim* from fifth-century Palestine, reveals an exegetical encounter. The reference to a cross is an explicit reference to Christianity, which the rabbis have appropriated and dressed in a Jewish garb.

According to the rabbis, Isaac was willing to suffer and give up his life at God's command. The emphasis was not on whether Isaac had actually been sacrificed but on his willingness to be sacrificed, not on martyrdom but on self-offering. Isaac was not forced to offer himself as a sacrifice but willingly gave himself to his father. Isaac's willingness to give up his life represents a rabbinic response to the Christian teaching that Christ was willing to give up his life to His Father. Indeed, so willing was Isaac to give up his life that the rabbis described the Akedah in terms such as 'the blood of the binding of Isaac' or 'the ashes of Isaac'. This is startling because the biblical account explicitly states that the angel stopped Abraham from harming his son and commanded him 'not to do anything' to Isaac. An illustration of this interpretation can be found in the *Mekhilta de Rabbi Ishmael*, Pisha 7 and 11:

> 'And when I see the blood, I will pass over you' (Exodus 13:12 and 25)—I see the blood of the Binding of Isaac. For it is said, 'And Abraham called the name of that place, 'the Lord will see'. Likewise it says in another passage, 'And as He was about to destroy the Lord beheld and repented Him' (I Chronicles 21: 15). What did He behold? He beheld the blood of the Binding of Isaac, as it is said, 'God will for Himself see to the lamb.'

This interpretation clearly suggests that Isaac's blood was shed. Remarkably, the rabbis even suggested that Isaac died and according to the eighth-century CE text, *Pirkei de Rabbi Eliezer* (31), which describes the death of Isaac, and his resurrection, which took place soon after:

> When the sword touched his neck the soul of Isaac took flight and departed but when he heard the voice from between the two cherubim saying, . . . 'do not lay a hand' his soul returned to his body and [Abraham] set him free, and he stood on his feet. And Isaac knew

---

[51] Melito, Fragment 8. S. G. Hall, *Melito of Sardis: On Pascha and Fragments* (Oxford: Clarendon Press, 1979).
[52] *Epistle of Barnabas*, 7.3 in Kirsopp Lake, *Apostolic Fathers* (i), with an Eng. tr. (London: Heinemann, 1912).

the resurrection of the dead as taught by the Torah, that all the dead in the future would be revived. At that moment he opened [his mouth] and said, 'Blessed are You, O Lord, who revives the dead.'

These examples show that rabbinic interpretations of the Binding of Isaac cannot be properly understood without reference to the Christian context. In other words, the rabbis were not only aware of, but were influenced by, Christian exegesis. The large number of shared interpretations, as well as examples of exegetical encounters, indicate the close relationship which existed between Jews and Christians for many hundreds of years, a relationship based on a shared scripture.

CONCLUSION: JEWISH REACQUAINTANCE WITH THE RELIGIOUS 'OTHER'

Although Christian reacquaintance with Judaism has been challenging for Christians—for example, reawakening to Jesus being born, living, and dying a Jew; to reflecting on the fact that the first Christians were Jews and the New Testament is, for the most part, a Jewish work— Jewish reacquaintance with Christianity has also been challenging for Jews. There had been an assumption that Christianity did not influence Judaism and that the influence was one-way, that is, Judaism influenced the development of Christianity. However, as we have seen, the influence has been two-way. Whilst it has been well documented that, after Christianity became the official religion of the Roman Empire, the position of the Jewish communities became more and more precarious, it is not so well known that the rabbis allowed, consciously or not, Christian ideas and interpretations to enter into Jewish thought and life. This happened because dialogue was part of the mainstream of Jewish life. This new reading of the rabbinic writings illustrates not only awareness of Christian teaching but also a willingness to listen, learn, and incorporate those teachings and traditions which were deemed relevant to Jewish life.

When Jews (and Christians) examine post-biblical interpretations they discover a shared emphasis on the importance of certain biblical texts as well as a willingness to be open to, and influenced by, some of each other's teachings. The exegetical encounters which took place so long ago can point the way forward and inspire perceptions of the religious other in the future. This can be likened to an electric cable or plug which has a number of wires, each of them isolated but, together, capable of conducting spiritual and creative energy of great intensity. When the different religious encounters take place a connection is made; when left independent, they remain isolated; combined, they provide light; left alone, their contribution is limited. Witness the following example of a Christian minister who spent a year in Israel:

To be allowed to live and study for a year in Jerusalem has been a formative experience for us all. What we learned that our encounter with Judaism determines our theological thinking still, but also the way in which we read the Hebrew Bible and New Testament. The study of the language, and above all, the discovery of the world of rabbinic interpretations of Scripture in Midrash and Talmud—a world largely unknown to us Christians—has made us understand much anew of what has become alien to us in our own tradition and even forgotten long ago . . . what we have learned here we take with us into our congregations, our schools, our churches. Many of us are engaged today in Jewish–Christian dialogue in a labour of reconciliation, and with other groups whose aim is to secure the traces of history and to offer determined resistance to all new signs of racist thinking.[53]

This view illustrates how a study of Judaism can serve to strengthen Christian faith (and, I would strongly argue, vice versa). The principle should be applied more widely to all faiths. So, in conclusion, I call for the examination of the writings of other faith communities, and for a willingness to examine these writings in a new light. None can escape their obligations in the new framework and this includes an examination of education concerning other faiths. The doors of the seminaries need to be opened to the winds of change. To achieve this, we need scholars to offer a theology of other faiths, and who are willing to put dialogue back into the mainstream.

FURTHER READING

B. and M. Brettler (eds), *The Jewish Study Bible* (Oxford: Oxford University Press, 2004).

M. Brettler and A.-J. Levine (eds), *Jewish Annotated New Testament* (New York: Oxford University Press, 2011).

M. Buber, *I and Thou* (New York: Scribner, 1958).

E. Fackenheim, *To Mend the World: Foundations of Post-Holocaust Thought,* 2nd edn (New York: Schocken, 1981).

A. J. Heschel, *God in Search of Man: A Philosophy of Judaism* (New York: JPS, 1956).

L. Jacobs, *A Jewish Theology* (London: Darton, Longman & Todd, 1973).

E. Kessler, *An Introduction to Jewish–Christian Relations* (Cambridge: Cambridge University Press, 2010).

N. de Lange, *An Introduction to Judaism* (Cambridge: Cambridge University Press, 2000).

J. Magonet, *Talking to the Other: A Jewish Interfaith Dialogue with Christians and Muslims* (London: I. B. Taurus, 2003).

P. Mendes-Flohr and J. Reinharz (eds), *The Jew in the Modern World: A Documentary History* (New York: Oxford University Press, 1995).

J. Sacks, *The Dignity of Difference: How to Avoid the Clash of Civilizations* (London: Continuum, 2003).

---

[53] Pastor Astrid Fiehland, quoted in Fackenheim, *The Jewish Bible After the Holocaust* (Manchester: Manchester University Press, 1988), 104.

CHAPTER 5

Buddhism and the Religious Other

ELIZABETH J. HARRIS

Buddhism emerged from the practice and teachings of Siddhartha Gautama (Pāli: Siddhattha Gotama), the Buddha or awakened one, who, it is now thought, lived in the fifth century BCE, in what is now north-east India.[1] The period was marked by political and socio-economic change, to which the two main strands of religious practice in India, the brahmanical or Vedic, and the *śrāmaṇa* (Sanskrit) or renunciant, responded. The Buddha belonged to the *śrāmaṇa* tradition, which consisted of groups of mendicant spiritual practitioners, usually united around a teacher, and dependent on the patronage of lay people. Conversations, sometimes acrimonious, occurred between different *śrāmaṇa* groups, and between *śrāmaṇa* groups and those within the brahmanical tradition.[2] Buddhism, in effect, consolidated its practices and beliefs in a context of what might now be called interreligious exchange, driven by economic as well as religious conditions.[3] Early Buddhist teaching and the subsequent development of the tradition can be understood accurately only when this context is taken into account.[4]

The *Sutta Piṭaka*: An Authoritative Source on the Religious 'Other'

The historical Buddha's teachings were transmitted orally for several centuries before being written down, to form the *Sutta Piṭaka*, which is the earliest authoritative textual source for

---

[1] Buddhists, however, believe that Siddhartha Gautama was preceded by other Buddhas.
[2] See the *Brahmajāla Sutta* of the *Dīgha Nikāya* (D) within the Pāli texts (D i. 1–46) for a perspective on this diversity. Pāli terms will be used when referring to Pāli texts.
[3] Ellison Banks Findly, *Dāna: Giving and Getting in Pali Buddhism* (Delhi: Motilal Banarsidass, 2003).
[4] Richard F. Gombrich, *How Buddhism Began: The Conditioned Genesis of the Early Teachings* (London and Atlantic Highlands, NJ: Athlone, 1996).

Buddhist attitudes to interreligious exchange.[5] Philologically and doctrinally, it represents a fusion between the actual words of the Buddha, the process of oral transmission, and the concerns of the developing Buddhist community.[6]

Many discourses in the *Sutta Piṭaka* are narratives that show the Buddha conversing with diverse groups and individuals. Invariably, he has the last word about truth. The Pāli texts consistently portray the Buddha as superior to his contemporaries. Nevertheless, a Buddhist response to the religious 'other' with five faces can be identified: adherence to a code of conduct predicated on respectful, non-violent yet rigorous debate; robust teaching of ideas that opposed or challenged those taught by other groups; ridicule of the practices/beliefs of the 'other'; the demotion or subordination of these practices/beliefs; the appropriation and modification of practices/symbols from the religious 'other'.

Respectful Debate

Within Buddhism, clinging to opinions or the view that 'I alone am right' is a hindrance to liberation/enlightenment (*nibbāna*). Liberation can only be attained if such dogmatism is abandoned as 'a seduction of the mind'.[7] Consequently, the Pāli texts encourage respectful but rigorous conversation or debate about truth, within which the judgemental is acceptable.[8] In the *Pāsādika Sutta*, for instance, the Buddha gives this advice to monks who believe that another monk misunderstands the Buddha's teaching:

> If a fellow in the holy life quotes Dhamma in the assembly, and if you think he has either misunderstood the sense or expressed it wrongly, you should neither applaud or reject it, but should say to him: 'Friend, if you mean such-and-such, you should put it either like this or like that: which is the more appropriate?'... If he replies: 'This meaning is better expressed like this than like that', or: 'The sense of this expression is this rather than that', then his words should be neither rejected nor disparaged, but you should explain to him carefully the correct meaning and expression.[9]

Similar advice is given when an offence or dispute comes from outside the Buddhist community:

> Monks, if anyone should speak in disparagement of me, of the Dhamma or of the Sangha, you should not be angry, resentful or upset on that account. If you were to be angry

---

[5] The Pāli texts are called the *Tipiṭaka* (three baskets), because they contain three elements: the discourses (*Sutta Piṭaka*); monastic discipline (*Vinaya*); and the *Abhidhamma*, a scholastic analysis of Buddhist teaching.

[6] Cf. K. R. Norman, *A Philological Approach to Buddhism: the Bukkyō Dendō Kyōkai Lectures 1994* (London: School of Oriental and African Studies, 1997).

[7] Mahinda Palihawadana, 'The Impossibility of Intolerance: A Buddhist Perspective', *Dialogue*, NS 28 (2001), 4.

[8] Elizabeth J. Harris, 'Co-existence, Confrontation and Co-responsibility: Looking at Buddhist Models of Interreligious Relationships', *Swedish Missiological Themes*, 92/3 (2004), 349–69.

[9] D iii. 128, tr. Maurice Walshe, *The Long Discourses of the Buddha* (Boston: Wisdom, 1995), 432; all quotes from the *Dīgha Nikāya* are from this translation.

or displeased at such disparagement, that would only be a hindrance to you. For if others disparage me, the Dhamma or the Sangha, and you are angry or displeased, can you recognise whether what they say is right or not?...If others disparage me, the Dhamma or the Sangha, then you must explain what is incorrect as being incorrect...[10]

A model of reasoned debate is offered, underpinned by the premise that anger is a hindrance for the *nibbāna*-seeker. Its focus, however, is correct understanding of the Buddha's teachings rather than reciprocal interreligious debate.

The *Mahāsīhanāda Sutta* goes further. Kassapa, an ascetic, comes to the Buddha to ask whether the Buddha condemns austerity and self-mortification, whereupon the Buddha raises the deeper question of whether austerities lead to moral progress, continuing:

> Kassapa, there are some ascetics and Brahmins, who are wise, skilled, practised in disputation, splitters of hairs, acute, who walk cleverly along the paths of views. Sometimes their views accord with mine, sometimes they do not. What they sometimes applaud, we sometimes applaud. What they sometimes do not applaud, we sometimes do not applaud; what they sometimes applaud, we sometimes do not applaud, and what they sometimes do not applaud, we sometimes applaud...
>
> On approaching them, I say: 'In these things there is no agreement, let us leave them aside. In these things there is agreement: there let the wise take up, cross-question and criticise these matters with the teachers or with their followers, saying, "Of those things that are unskilful and reckoned as such, censurable to be refrained from, unbefitting a Noble One...who is there who has completely abandoned such things, and is free of them; the ascetic Gotama, or some other venerable teachers?" '[11]

This passage recommends an interreligious ethic that avoids dispute about difference in favour of discussion about what is considered by all to be good. The *Sutta* then shows the Buddha offering himself as the embodiment of that good. The paradigm recommended, rooted in respect, does not, therefore, debar the assertion of the Buddha's superiority.

Teaching Ideas that Opposed Those Taught by Others

Moving to the second response, a focal debate in the Buddha's time concerned the conflict between eternalism (*sassatavāda* or *bhava diṭṭhi*) and annihilationism (*ucchedavāda* or *vibhava-diṭṭhi*). Eternalists, found within the Vedic and the *śrāmaṇa*, were dualists who insisted that the soul and the body were distinct, and that an eternal soul survived death. Annihilationists were materialists; for them, death ended all. The Buddha, in contrast, taught that both positions were traceable to craving, either for eternal existence or a non-accountability that could legitimize sensual indulgence, and taught a 'middle path' between them.

---

[10] D i. 2–3.   [11] D i. 162–3.

All material and non-material elements within a human were impermanent (*anicca*). Dissect one and no unchanging essence or self would be found. Just as the sound of a lute did not lie in any of its component parts, so the identity of a human being did not lie within one element but in the interdependence of five factors (*khandhas*) held together by a process of cause and effect that continued beyond death.[12]

Another contemporary debate related to the efficacy of ritual. Again, the Buddha challenged contemporary practice. In the *Sigālaka Sutta*, the Buddha encounters Sigāla, who, having bathed, is paying ritual homage to the quarters of the earth. When the Buddha asks him the reason for this, Sigāla cites the wishes of his dying father. The Buddha then claims that his actions are wrong and, invited to speak further, explains that true worship lies in avoiding evil deeds and creating wholesome societal relationships.[13] Similarly, in the *Kūṭadanta Sutta*, a Brahmin comes to the Buddha for advice about a sacrifice; in response, the Buddha narrates the story of a ruler who was encouraged to foster economic justice rather than organize a sacrifice.[14]

Ridicule of the 'Other'

The Buddha's challenge to the 'other' occasionally slipped into ridicule, according to the texts. In the *Tevijja Sutta*, two Brahman students disagree on teaching given to them about the path to union with Brahmā and consult the Buddha. The Buddha does not ridicule their aspiration for such union, although it did not feature in his teachings. To this extent, he meets the students where they are. The students' teachers, however, are likened to one who builds a staircase for a palace without knowing the direction of the palace, or someone who seeks for the country's most beautiful girl without being able to describe her. Their fault, the Buddha stresses, is that they do not cultivate Brahmā-like qualities such as loving kindness, compassion, sympathetic joy, and equanimity and therefore cannot know him. The Buddha then presents himself as a fitting guide.[15]

The Subordination of the 'Other'

A form of supercessionism, one aspect of the fourth response identified above, is present in the *Tevijja Sutta*, since the Buddha presents himself as the true Brahman and witnesses the students asking to be lay followers. In the *Kevaddha Sutta*, the subordination of the brahmanical is more graphic. Here, the Buddha narrates to Kevaddha the story of a monk who travels to the realms of the gods with a question about liberation from rebirth. In each realm, the

---

[12] Cf. *Saṃyutta Nikāya* SN iv. 196–7, tr. Bhikkhu Bodhi, *The Connected Discourses of the Buddha* (Somerville, Mass.: Wisdom, 2000), 1253–5.

[13] D iii. 180–93.   [14] D i. 127–49.   [15] D i. 235–51.

gods, unable to answer, send him to a higher one, until he reaches the world of Brahmā. Brahmā, after bluffing about his power, draws Kevaddha aside to admit that only the Buddha knows the answer.[16] In such discourses, early Buddhism reduces the gods of the brahmanical tradition to the level of the mundane, the *laukika*. According to Seyfort Ruegg, the *laukika* becomes what Buddhism shares with other Indian religious groups and the *lokuttara*, the supramundane, becomes what is unique to Buddhism.[17] The former is not stripped of worth. It might lead to a better rebirth. But it could not lead people to ultimate liberation. This distinction became critically important when Buddhism moved from India.

Appropriation of the 'Other'

The appropriation and modification of practices/symbols from the religious 'other' can be illustrated through Gombrich's research into the Buddha's symbolic use of 'fire'.[18] The Pāli texts show the Buddha teaching that the roots of *dukkha* (unsatisfactoriness or suffering) are greed, hatred, and delusion. They fuel craving (*taṇhā*) and are 'fires' to be eradicated. Gombrich argues that this metaphor is an allusion to and appropriation of the three fires that a brahman householder kept alight to symbolize worldly life. Furthermore, he links the Buddha's teaching about the *khandhas* to the same metaphor, through appeal to a text that likens the *khandhas*, when shot through with grasping (*upādāna*), to bundles of fuel (brahman students had to carry bundles of fuel to feed the sacred fires). So, Gombrich argues, the Buddha reinterprets a brahman ritual which, when placed alongside imagery that likens the Buddha to the fire god, Agni, 'looks less like a debate than a takeover bid'.[19]

Exclusivist and Inclusivist Texts

Within these five responses, tension exists between awareness that a Buddhist must transcend clinging to views that would place the 'I' in a position of superiority over the 'other', and the conviction, because of these very teachings, that the wisdom of the Buddha replaces, fulfils, or supersedes other traditions. This tension is also present in the juxtaposition of texts that might now be called exclusivist and inclusivist. At the beginning of a discourse about mindfulness, the *Satipaṭṭāna Sutta*, for instance, the Buddha declares that mindfulness is the one or single (*ekayano*) path for the realization of *nibbāna*.[20] Verse 274 of the *Dhammapada* is similar: 'This is the path—there is no other—for the purification of seeing. Enter upon this one; this

---

[16] D i. 211–23.

[17] David Seyfort Ruegg, *The Symbiosis of Buddhism and Brahmanism/Hinduism in South Asia and of Buddhism with 'Local Cults' in Tibet and the Himalayan Region* (Vienna: Osterreichische Akademie der Wisshenschaften, 2008), 80.

[18] Gombrich, *How Buddhism Began*, 65–72.

[19] Gombrich, *How Buddhism Began*, 72.

[20] But cf. Mahinda Deegalle, 'Soteriological Fundamentalism and Inter religious Dialogue', *Current Dialogue* (June 2001), 9–12, who argues against an exclusivist reading.

is the thwarting of Māra [the personification of evil in Buddhism].'[21] In contrast, some discourses appear inclusivist, although a tendency to take away with one hand what has been given by the other is detectable. In the *Mahāparinibbāna Sutta*, the Buddha declares, inclusively, that true 'ascetics' can be found wherever the Eightfold Path (the Fourth Noble Truth) is present. He adds, however, that other schools are devoid of true ascetics, because they do not contain the Path.[22]

The five responses identified in this section, and tension between the exclusivist and inclusivist, can be seen throughout the history of Buddhism, demonstrating an interplay between texts and practice. Which of them came to the fore in particular contexts, however, and which were supplemented with other responses, was conditioned by socio-economic factors and power relations, as the next section will demonstrate.

BUDDHISM AND OTHER RELIGIONS: A BRIEF HISTORY OF ENCOUNTER

Buddhism and the 'Other' in India

The encounter between Buddhism and the religious 'other' in India after the Buddha's death was dominated by brahmanism, or what may be called emergent Hinduism. Some of Buddhism's differences with brahmanism concerning the self, godhead, caste, epistemology, and ritual have already been illustrated. The extent to which these were underpinned by outright opposition to the brahmanical is contested. Schmidt-Leukel stresses polemic and opposition.[23] Seyfort Ruegg, however, argues for 'a complex historical and religious symbiotic interaction that might, on occasion, also involve critical engagement, struggle ... and anatagonism',[24] in the context of a substratum of symbolism and ideas shared by both. Nevertheless, as Buddhist influence in India grew after the Buddha's death, spreading initially throughout north India, so did Buddhism's critique of and competition with brahmanism.

An attempt to neutralize competition was made by the third-century BCE Mauryan Emperor, Aśoka, who, according to tradition, converted to Buddhism after a blood-filled war. According to his rock and pillar edicts, Aśoka promulgated a pragmatic, ethical Buddhism that stressed respectful, non-manipulative, and tolerant societal relationships. Rock Edict 12 declares:

> Growth in essentials [of all religions] can be done in different ways, but all of them have as their root restraint in speech, that is, not praising one's own religion, or condemning the

---

[21] Valerie J. Roebuck (tr.), *The Dhammapada* (London: Penguin Books, 2010), 54.

[22] D ii. 151. Cf. Kristin Beise Kiblinger. 'Identifying Inclusivism in Buddhist Contexts', *Contemporary Buddhism*, 4/1 (2003), 82–3; *Buddhist Inclusivism: Attitudes Towards Religious Others* (Aldershot: Ashgate, 2005).

[23] Perry Schmidt-Leukel, 'Buddhist–Hindu Relations', in Perry Schmidt-Leukel (ed.), *Buddhist Attitudes to Other Religions* (St Ottilien: EOS, 2008), 143–71.

[24] Seyfort Ruegg, *Symbiosis*, 2.

religion of others without good cause. And if there is cause for criticism, it should be done in a mild way. But it is better to honour other religions for this reason. By so doing, one's own religion benefits, and so do other religions, while doing otherwise harms one's own religion and the religions of others.[25]

This draws on the first response identified in the last section but supplements it with a sixth: peaceful coexistence between religions through mutual respect in the interests of societal harmony. It is a response that reappears in Buddhist history.

When the post-Aśokan Mauryan Empire imploded, the relationship between the brahmanical and the Buddhist became more volatile, yielding an interesting development of the 'subordination' response earlier identified: absorption of practices from the 'other' combined with philosophical subordination or refutation. New forms of Buddhism were emerging by then, eventually to coalesce as the Mahāyāna, the Great Way. Schism, largely driven by dispute over monastic discipline, had previously divided Buddhism.[26] Mahāyāna Buddhism, however, was characterized by another set of factors, including: a philosophical critique directed both at the goal of the *arahant*,[27] which was seen as too individualistic, and at developments within Buddhist scholasticism (*Abhidharma*), the Mahāyāna arguing for the emptiness of all *dharmas* (individual elements that constitute the empirical world); a privileging of the path of the bodhisattva, a Buddha-to-be; a proliferation of Buddhas and bodhisattvas, and devotional practices directed towards them.[28] These were expressed in new *sūtras* attributed to the Buddha. One focus of these *sūtras* was the existing forms of Buddhism, pejoratively called *Śrāvakayāna* (vehicle of the hearers), paralleling attitudes to the non-Buddhist 'other'. The *Saddharmapuṇḍarīka Sūtra* (Lotus Sutra), for instance, represented them polemically as a lesser way, for people of 'small wisdom'.[29] The fragmentary *Bajaur Sūtra*, in contrast, appears to seek continuity between the *Śrāvakayāna* and the new teaching.

Returning to the non-Buddhist 'other', influence from *bhakti* (loving devotion towards deity) within Viṣṇuism and Śaivism (forms of emergent Hinduism) cannot be discounted in the development of Mahāyāna. Its focus, however, was redirected so that buddhas and bodhisattvas became the object of devotion, and a critique was developed. The *Kāraṇḍavyūha Sūtra*, for instance, ranks Hindu deities below the bodhisattvas and declares Śiva to be a potential trickster, who will lead people away from enlightenment, unless he is subordinate to the Buddha.[30] Tantric Buddhism, a form of Mahāyāna Buddhism that was emerging in north-east

---

[25] Rock Edict 12, tr. S. Dhammika, *The Edicts of Asoka: An English Rendering* (Kandy: Buddhist Publication Society, 1993), 14.

[26] About eighteen schools existed by the Common Era. The only ones that survive today trace themselves back to the Theravādins of the first split.

[27] An *arahant* gains enlightenment through the teaching of a Buddha. This remains the goal for Theravāda Buddhists.

[28] See Paul Williams with Anthony Tribe and Alexander Wynne, *Buddhist Thought: A Complete Introduction to the Indian Tradition*, 2nd edn (London and New York: Routledge, 2012), 71–82.

[29] Cf. Burton Watson (tr.), *The Lotus Sutra* (New York: Columbia University Press, 1993), 43.

[30] Schmidt Leukel, 'Buddhist-Hindu Relations', 155–6.

India by the seventh century CE, shows a similar pattern.[31] Buddhist tantra was arguably indebted to Śaivite tantra.[32] A late Buddhist tantric work, the tenth- or eleventh-century *Kālacakra Tantra*, however, refutes all Indian philosophies, including Viṣṇuism, Śaivism, materialism, and Jainism. Only Buddhist Madhyamaka, a non-dualist Mahāyāna philosophy pioneered by Nāgārjuna in the second century BCE, is advocated.[33] Philosophical refutation and subordination, therefore, became the corollary of coexistence with and adaptation of the 'other'.

The Spread of Buddhism outside India

Centrally important in the Buddhist response to the religious systems it encountered when it travelled beyond India was the previously mentioned distinction between the *laukika* and the *lokuttara* (mundane and supramundane). Mundane practices were incorporated into Buddhism through absorption, reformulation, and subordination. Practices that claimed to be supramundane or that held a superior geo-political position evoked a spectrum of responses that included: inculturation; respectful or pragmatic coexistence; assertion of difference; vigorous defensive resistance. Which was chosen was conditioned by power relationships within the local context and, most particularly, the attitudes of the 'other' towards Buddhism.

Sri Lanka

When Buddhism reached Sri Lanka, for instance, in the third century BCE according to tradition, it met a religiosity that recognized good and evil spiritual powers, deities and demons, sorcery and exorcism. Broadly speaking, this was not destroyed but incorporated at the mundane, *laukika*, level. For those who became Buddhist, the Buddhas moved to the top of the cosmic hierarchy with authority over the *lōkōttara*—liberation from rebirth. Deities, spirits, and exorcists remained important but became servants of the Buddha, forming what is now termed 'the little tradition'[34] or 'spirit religion'.[35] Their power persists to the present, renegotiated in contexts of war and economic hardship.[36] Similar patterns can be seen in Cambodia, Myanmar, Laos, and Thailand.[37]

---

[31] Tantric Buddhism offered quick methods to reach enlightenment and techniques to deal with the spirit world through the use of mantras (including *dhāraṇīs*), maṇḍalas, and deity visualization.

[32] Point made by Alexis Sanderson, 'The Influence of Śaivism on Pāla Buddhism', lecture, University of Toronto, 2010.

[33] Vesna A. Wallace, *The Inner Kālacakratantra: A Buddhist Tantric View of the Individual* (New York: Oxford University Press, 2001), 13–17.

[34] See Gananath Obeyesekere, 'The Great Tradition and the Little in the Perspective of Sinhalese Buddhism', *Journal of Asian Studies*, 22 (1963), 139–53.

[35] Cf. Richard Gombrich and Gananath Obeyesekere, *Buddhism Transformed: Religious Change in Sri Lanka* (Princeton: Princeton University Press, 1988).

[36] Cf. Gombrich and Obeyesekere, *Buddhism Transformed*.

[37] See e.g. Donald Lopez, Jr. (ed.), *Buddhism in Practice* (Princeton: Princeton University Press, 1995); John Marston and Elizabeth Guthrie (eds), *History, Buddhism, and New Religious Movements in Cambodia* (Honolulu: University of Hawaii Press, 2004); S. J. Tambiah, *Buddhism and the Spirit Cults of North-East Thailand* (Cambridge: Cambridge University Press, 1975); John Clifford Holt, *Spirits of the Place: Buddhism and Lao Religious Culture* (Honolulu: University of Hawaii Press, 2009).

Ghandhāra

When Buddhism penetrated into the Gandhāran region of north-west India, present-day eastern Afghanistan, and north-western Pakistan, from about the second century BCE, it eventually encountered and appropriated an artistic culture driven by the Graeco-Roman West, through the Kuṣāṇa rulers of the region (first to the third centuries CE). One fruit of this was buddha and bodhisattva images. The earliest images of the historical Buddha arose in two regions, Gandhāra and Mathurā, probably in the late first and early second centuries CE.[38] Significantly, the Gandhāran version was driven by Roman precedents and was probably pioneered by Western sculptors, who draped the Buddha's robes in Roman style and gave him a god-like head. Reliefs modelled on Western precedents depicting the life of the Buddha and *Jātaka* narratives (stories of the Buddha's previous lives) followed.

In addition to such appropriation of the 'other' which served both early Buddhist schools and the Mahāyāna, the *Milindapañha* (The Questions of King Milinda), an influential Buddhist text believed to have been written in the first century CE, points to philosophical engagement with the Graeco-Roman world. It retrospectively represents a conversation about Buddhist philosophy between the Bactrian Greek king, Menander, and a Buddhist sage, Nāgasena.[39] Probably composed, at least in part, by the Sarvāstivāda school of Buddhism, which was strong in Gandhāra and Kashmir, it addresses questions such as the nature of the human person, rebirth, and whether the Buddha was omniscient. In the conversation, Menander's beliefs are unimportant. Following canonical precedent, the conversation is one-way. The Greek poses the questions; Nāgasena responds.

The Encounter with Islam

The rapid movement of Islam from Arabia after Muhammad's death had a considerable impact on Buddhism. Islam moved both west, into North Africa and Spain; and east, into Central Asia (present-day Iran, Uzbekistan, Turkmenistan, and Tajikstan), and north-west India. Buddhists first encountered it in Central Asia in the mid to late seventh century and then in north-west India, first under the Umayyad Caliphate and then under the Abbasids. By this time, according to Elverskog, Buddhists were stronger in the north-east of India than in these areas.[40] Nevertheless, the Chinese pilgrim, Xuanzang, shortly before Islam arrived, calculated that there were 10,000 monks in Bamiyan and 460 monasteries in Sind.[41]

In Islam, Buddhism met a religion that claimed supramundane truth, in a context of imperial dominance, although its veneration of a god and its elevation of heaven might have

---

[38] Benjamin Rowland, 'Gandhara', *Encylopedia of Buddhism*, v (Colombo: Government of Sri Lanka, 1991), 299.

[39] Bactria was a region founded by Alexander the Great, corresponding with much of contemporary Afghanistan. The Bactrian King Demetrius expanded its reach into Gandhāra, the Punjab, and the Indus Valley. This divided with Menander becoming the ruler of the eastern Greek Kingdom (Punjab, Gandhāra, and Kapisa) in the 2nd cent. BCE.

[40] Johan Elverskog, *Buddhism and Islam on the Silk Road* (Philadelphia: University of Pennsylvania Press, 2010), 43–5.

[41] Elverskog, *Buddhism and Islam*, 44.

appeared mundane to Buddhists. That Buddhists chose coexistence, in this context, rather than defensive opposition suggests that Buddhists did not feel threatened by Islam.[42] On the contrary, a common interest in the mercantile brought them together and, as both Berzin and Elverskog demonstrate, Muslim scholars, although they tended to see Buddhism as idolatrous, commented on the tradition and invited Buddhists for doctrinal debates.[43] It is not surprising, therefore, that Buddhism survived in Bamiyan until about the eleventh century. Buddhist scholars were even invited to the House of Knowledge in Baghdad.[44] And Von Hinüber points to the discovery of a Buddhist text translated into Persian by a Muslim as late as the fourteenth century, although, by this time, Buddhism was declining in Central Asia.[45]

The paucity of references to Islam in Buddhist records, however, suggests that the Buddhist choice of coexistence did not imply a reciprocal interest in Islamic doctrine. One exception was the *Kālacakra Tantra* literature, which lists Muslim figures, and refers to Muslim prayer, the halāl method of slaughter, the honour Islam gives to the equality of all people, and the date of the *hijra* (Muhammad's migration from Mecca to Medina).[46] It also contests Muslim belief, for instance, that a birth in heaven could be an ultimate goal.[47] Berzin argues that these references are directed at the late tenth-century eastern Ismāʿīlī Fatimid Muslims, then in control of Multān. He suggests that the barbarians against which Hindus and Buddhists are called to unite in one part of this literature refers to these Shia Muslims, who were threatening the Buddhists and Hindus living in the Sunni Abbasid vassal state in eastern Afghanistan. It could be argued, therefore, that this textual engagement with Islam arose when Buddhists felt threatened. Defensive violence was countenanced in response, although there is no evidence that it was carried out.

Tibet

When Buddhism penetrated the Himalayas into Tibet in two transmissions between the seventh and eleventh centuries CE, it encountered an indigenous tradition within which spirit-mediums helped people cope with an imagined world of local gods, spirits, and deities, malevolent and benevolent. As Samuel argues, Buddhism did not attempt to eradicate belief in this spirit world. Rather, 'Buddhist ritual specialists...became the primary experts in handling' it.[48] Popular narrative, therefore, casts Padmasambhava, one of the first transmitters of Buddhism to Tibet, as a tantric master who could subdue demons, through converting them

---

[42] Elverskog, *Buddhism and Islam*, 48–54.

[43] Cf. Alexander Berzin, 'Buddhist–Muslim Doctrinal Relations: Past, Present and Future', in Schmidt-Leukel, *Buddhist Attitudes to Other Religions*, 212–36; Elverskog. *Buddhism and Islam*, 56–82.

[44] Berzin, 'Buddhist–Muslim Doctrinal Relations', 213.

[45] Oskar von Hinüber, 'Expansion to the North: Afghanistan and Central Asia', in Heinz Bechert and Richard Gombrich (eds), *The World of Buddhism* (London: Thames & Hudson, 1984), 107.

[46] Seyfort Ruegg, *Symbiosis of Buddhism*, 116–17; Berzin, 'Buddhist–Muslim Doctrinal Relations', 214–15. See also J. Newman, 'Islam in the Kālacakra Tantra', *Journal of the International Association of Buddhist Studies*, 21 (1998), 320–3.

[47] Berzin, 'Buddhist–Muslim Doctrinal Relations', 215.

[48] Geoffrey Samuel, *Introducing Tibetan Buddhism* (Abingdon and New York: Routledge, 2012), 13.

to Buddhism. What is now known as the Bön tradition was probably not in existence before Buddhism's coming, but developed after the first transmission, fusing Buddhism with elements from earlier religiosity. Although Buddhist writings about Bön were more negative than accommodating, the two traditions learnt to coexist.[49]

Mongolia

A possible exception to the subordination and absorption of the *laukika* occurred in Mongolia at a later date. According to Wallace, during the 'second conversion' of Mongols to Buddhism towards the end of the sixteenth century, leading lay and monastic Buddhists used violence in 'the forceful replacement of Shamanism (the *laukika*) with Buddhism as the state religion' and 'Buddhist sectarian wars'.[50] Practitioners of shamanism were punished or killed, in a display of exclusivism that was driven as much by political ambition as religious zeal. Walther Heissig, however, presents a less confrontational picture.[51]

China

The transmission of Buddhism to China, and the interreligious dynamic that consequently arose, is complex, historically and geographically. Buddhism probably reached China in the first century BCE through the different routes of the Silk Road, at a time when China's polity was disunited, with Confucianism losing power and Daoism gaining ground.[52] The Buddhism that arrived, however, also lacked unity, since it came from different Buddhist centres, mostly in Central Asia. Gentz stresses the non-elite nature of this early transmission; it was 'an irritating multiplicity of different teachings, traditions, rituals and texts'.[53] Some of these would have appeared similar to Daoist practices, to the extent that the Chinese may not have seen them as foreign.[54] When Buddhist texts were translated into Chinese—Genting suggesting that texts about meditation were first—Daoist and Confucian terminology was used. On the one hand, this changed the meaning of terms such as *dharma*, which became the Dao. On the other, it demonstrated that Buddhism had the capacity to enculturate not only when the existing religiosity could be subordinated but also where the supramundane existed. Nevertheless, the differences between Chinese religion and the Buddhist Indic worldview eventually emerged. Enculturation without recognition of difference became

---

[49] Cf. David Germano and Helmut Eimer, *The Many Canons of Tibetan Buddhism* (Leiden: Brill, 2002); Matthew Kapstein, *The Tibetan Assimilation of Buddhism: Conversion, Contestation and Memory* (Oxford: Oxford University Press, 2000); Geoffrey Samuel, *Tantric Revisionings: New Understandings of Tibetan Buddhism and Indian Religions* (Delhi: Motilal Barnasidass, 2005); Donald Lopez (ed.), *Religions of Tibet in Practice* (Princeton: Princeton University Press, 1997).

[50] Vesna A. Wallace, 'Legalized Violence: Punitive Measures of Buddhist Khans in Mongolia', in Michael K. Jerryson and Mark Juergensmeyer (eds), *Buddhist Warfare* (New York: Oxford University Press, 2010), 91.

[51] Walter Heissig, *The Religions of Mongolia* (Berkeley-Los Angeles: University of California Press, 1992).

[52] Joachin Gentz, 'Buddhism and Chinese Religions', in Schmidt-Leukel, *Buddhist Attitudes to Other Religions*, 174.

[53] Gentz, 'Buddhism and Chinese Religions', 174.

[54] Gentz, 'Buddhism and Chinese Religions', 175.

untenable. Eventually, in the fourth and fifth centuries CE, this led to the emergence of a self-conscious Chinese Buddhism and a new, more oppositional, interreligious dynamic. For instance, 'highly competitive debates'[55] between Daoism and Buddhism occurred, starting in the fifth century, and religious treatises were exchanged.[56] A corollary was that a Chinese Buddhist vocabulary, less dependent on Daoism, developed. In the centuries that followed, however, a harmonious coexistence was reached. In China, therefore, fear of absorption led to an assertion of difference. However, as Gentz stresses, using a study by Gernet, the extent to which differences were stressed was conditioned by local power structures. Where Buddhism was strong, 'conflicts with imperial and other religious institutions' could be risked; where it was weaker, integration and cooperation with other traditions was the pragmatic, safer option.[57]

Encounter with Christianity

Buddhism in China not only had to negotiate a relationship with Daoism and Confucianism but also with Christianity and Islam. Christianity first entered China through members of the Church of the East, probably from Syria, who arrived from the sixth century onwards in the T'ang Dynasty (618–907). Palmer argues controversially, on the evidence of manuscripts found in Dunhuang, narrating the Christian story in Daoist terms, that between the seventh and eleventh centuries a synthesis of Dao, Christ, and Buddha emerged in China as Christians sought to embed Christianity within a Chinese idiom.[58] Lai and von Brück cite facilitating factors such as the presence in both of an ascetic morality and monasticism, a convergence that led the Confucian-dominated Chinese authorities to place Christianity and Buddhism together in state persecutions in the eighth and ninth centuries.[59] This shared victimhood led to the two religions working together on the translation of Christian and Buddhist texts into Chinese.[60] Key to the relationship between the Church of the East and Buddhism, broadly speaking, was that the former showed respect to Buddhism. The Buddhist experience of the Jesuit mission was different. Respect was, therefore, returned. Japanese Buddhists encountered Jesuits before the Chinese, with the arrival of Francis Xavier in 1549. At first, Xavier used Buddhist terminology to communicate Christianity. He changed course when he realized that Christianity was in danger of being seen as another Buddhist denomination.[61] Xavier therefore started to denounce Buddhism, causing Buddhists to respond with 'aggressive

---

[55] Gentz, 'Buddhism and Chinese Religions', 180.

[56] See also Livia Kohn, *Laughing at the Tao: Debates among Buddhists and Taoists in Medieval China* (Princeton: Princeton University Press, 1995).

[57] Gentz, 'Buddhism and Chinese Religions', 185.

[58] Martin Palmer, *The Jesus Sutras: Rediscovering the Lost Religion of Taoist Christianity* (London: Piatkus, 2001).

[59] Whalen Lai and Michael von Brück, *Christianity and Buddhism: A Multi-Cultural History of their Dialogue* (Maryknoll, NY: Orbis Books, 2001), 69.

[60] Lai and von Brück, *Christianity and Buddhism*, 69.

[61] Cf. Urs App, *The Cult of Emptiness: The Western Discovery of Buddhist Thought and the Invention of Oriental Philosophy* (Kyoto: University Media, 2012), 11–17. App argues that Xavier was tricked into presenting an inculturated Christianity by Anjirō, a Japanese convert who later deserted the Jesuits.

propaganda against the foreign intruder'.[62] In other words, when courtesy from the 'other' declined, Buddhists withdrew their courtesy. At the beginning of the seventeenth century, Christianity was proscribed, with Buddhism given responsibility by the state for eliminating it.

China's experience of the Jesuits began in 1582, with the arrival of a group headed by Matteo Ricci (1552–1610). Ricci also privileged enculturation. He wore Chinese dress and sought elite patronage by appealing to the power of Christian ritual and his mastery of 'Learning from Heaven'.[63] He challenged Buddhists to debate and, according to Lai and von Brück, engaged several Buddhist scholars, including Sah-huai Hsüe-Lang, Huang hui, and Chu Hsing.[64] Both elite and rural converts were gained; the latter attracted by their ability to participate in apparently powerful ritual.[65] After his death, the mission continued energetically. The Jesuit mission, however, was eventually opposed by Buddhists and Daoists. Central to this was missionary contempt towards Chinese religiosity, perceived in the insistence that those adopting Christian rites should reject former practices.[66] According to Lai and von Brück, Buddhist leaders also expected respectful and empathetic debate[67] but were disappointed. Some trusted the 'built-in resistance of the Chinese religious landscape',[68] which was generally non-exclusivist, to resist the Jesuits. Others launched a polemical, defensive response, which eventually led to the expulsion of the Jesuits from the province of Fukien.[69]

Tibet also experienced Roman Catholic missionary orders. According to the Dalai Lama, the foundation stone for the first Christian church was laid in 1626, in western Tibet, by missionaries from Goa.[70] Lhasa, however, was only reached in the eighteenth century, by the Capuchins, their first expedition lasting four years (1707–11). More followed, the third arriving in 1716, a year when the Jesuit Ippolito Desideri (1684–1733) also arrived. Desideri mastered Tibetan, studied Buddhist texts under Tibetans, and championed the comparative study of religion, writing extensive 'Notices' on his experiences.[71] Internal evidence within Desideri's writing and Jesuit accounts suggest that Tibetan Buddhists were courteous to him, allowing him to study Buddhism at Shidé Monastery and Sera so that he could better debate with Buddhist lamas. Desideri was apparently allowed to practise Christianity during this

---

[62] Notto R. Thelle, 'Japanese Religions and Christianity', in John Bowden (ed.), *Christianity: The Complete Guide* (London: Continuum, 2005), 652.

[63] Liam Matthew Brockey, *Journey to the East: The Jesuit Mission to China 1578–1724* (Cambridge, Mass.: Harvard, 2007), 57–60.

[64] Lai and von Brück, *Christianity and Buddhism*, 69–70.

[65] Brockey, *Journey to the East*, 95–8.

[66] Brockey, *Journey to the East*, 301, 316, 360.

[67] Lai and von Brück, *Christianity and Buddhism*, 70, suggest that the Buddhist side 'sought to recognise' Christian doctrines in their own scriptures in a pattern that had been used to bring Buddhism, Confucianism, and Taoism into harmony.

[68] Brockey, *Journey to the East*, 299.

[69] Lai and von Brück, *Christianity and Buddhism*, 71–2.

[70] His Holiness the Dalai Lama, *Towards the True Kinship of Faiths: How the World's Religions Can Come Together* (London: Abacus, 2010), 11.

[71] Cf. Leonard Zwilling (ed.), *The Mission to Tibet: The Extraordinary Eighteenth Century Account of Father Ippolito Desideri, s.j.* (Boston: Wisdom Publications, 2010).

time, with some Buddhist monks attending mass. At Sera he debated with Buddhists and began to write treatises that he hoped would prove the superiority of Christianity.[72] Desideri survived political turmoil in Tibet and rivalry with the Capuchins but was eventually forced to leave. According to Zwilling, no Tibetan accounts of the reception of Desideri's treatises exist.[73] It is probable, however, that, because Desideri used Buddhist methods of argument to put forward his own and showed courtesy to Buddhism, courtesy was returned. If the Tibetans had read his *Historical Notices of Tibet*, however, their courtesy might have been stretched, for Desideri, although complimentary about Tibetan culture and character, condemns as the devil's work practices such as the discovery of the reincarnated Grand Lama.[74]

Buddhism and Western Expansionism

The Jesuit mission was one arm of European expansionism. Sri Lanka, Myanmar, and Japan will be used as examples to illustrate further the Buddhist response to the religious 'other', namely Christianity, during the era of Western imperialism.

Sri Lanka

Sri Lanka experienced three European rulers: the Portuguese (1506–1650s); the Dutch (1650s–1790s); the English (1790s–1948). Each evoked different Buddhist responses. The priorities of the Portuguese were at first mercantile, although converts to Roman Catholicism were encouraged through the granting of privileges.[75] Franciscans and then Jesuits arrived from the 1540s and were successful in gaining converts, particularly in the south-west coastal regions. From the 1560s onwards, in the context of the Counter-Reformation, a policy change occurred resulting in the destruction of Buddhist and Hindu places of worship.[76] Under the Dutch, violence stopped but non-Christians suffered legally sanctioned discrimination. The Buddhist response took several forms. The first was violent rebellions from the 1590s; Abeyasinghe cites ten in forty-four years.[77] The second was the development of folk narratives that ridiculed and/or demonized Christianity. These continued into the Dutch period, some presenting Jesus as a 'Carpenter Heretic'.[78] The third was internal revival. Under the

---

[72] Zwilling, *Mission to Tibet*, 43–5.

[73] Zwilling, *Mission to Tibet*, 49.

[74] Zwilling, *Mission to Tibet*, 297–300.

[75] Alan Strathern, *Kingship and Conversion in Sixteenth Century Sri Lanka: Portuguese Imperialism in a Buddhist Land* (Cambridge: Cambridge University Press, 2010), 100.

[76] Strathern, *Kingship and Conversion*, 197.

[77] T. B. H. Abeysinghe, 'Portuguese Rule in Kōṭṭe 1594–1638', in de Silva (ed.), *The History of Sri Lanka*, ii (Delhi: Oxford University Press, 1981), 127–8.

[78] See Elizabeth J. Harris, *Theravāda Buddhism and the British Encounter: Religious, Missionary and Colonial Experience in Nineteenth Century Sri Lanka* (London and New York: Routledge, 2006); see also R. Young and G. S. B. Senanayake, *The Carpenter Heretic: A Collection of Buddhist Stories about Christianity from 18th Century Sri Lanka* (Colombo: Karunaratne & Sons, 1998) consisting of translations of folk narratives that ridicule both Christianity and Saivism; Jesus, for instance, becomes son of Māra, the personification of evil in Theravāda Buddhism.

Dutch, this was centred in the independent Kandyan Kingdom and flowed from there into the Dutch-controlled areas.[79]

Under the British, who conquered the Kandyan Kingdom in 1815, Buddhists encountered Christian missionaries from new, independent, evangelical missionary societies. In 2007, I stated that Buddhists offered five 'faces' to them during the nineteenth century: hospitality and courtesy; a willingness to engage in dialogue about religion and cooperate if mutual benefit was possible; a polite acceptance and tolerance that could mask distrust or even contempt; the wish for reasoned and structured debates to prove the superiority of Buddhism; direct confrontation and opposition. I argued that all five were present throughout the century, but that the first three were dominant when the missionaries first arrived and the last two, at the century's end.[80] In 2012, I added that the kind of 'dialogue' that the monastic Sangha originally sought involved rigorous debate about truth and the contesting of misunderstandings, a form of debate that can be traced back to the Pāli texts. I also added another response: skilled pragmatic decision-making about survival under imperialism.[81]

To expand further, archival material suggests that when the missionaries arrived, from 1805 onwards, the majority of Buddhists, including the monastic Sangha, despite an awareness of folk narratives that subverted Christianity, sought a respectful and pragmatic coexistence with Christianity, with cooperation if mutual interests could be served, a model similar to Buddhism's relationship with Islam in Central Asia. The contempt shown to Buddhism in missionary preaching and writing, however, and the changes in the country's sacred geography due to the increased building of churches and schools, changed this. The missionaries became a threat to the dhamma, demanding defensive action. One early action was to write, on ola leaves, reasoned responses to the Christian critique of Buddhism, which were taken from village to village. When Buddhists gained printing presses, however, in the 1860s, tracts replaced these and, under the leadership of revivalist monks such as Mohoṭṭivattē Guṇānanda, they became more polemical.[82] Buddhist–Christian debates also took place, the last of which, at Pānadurē in 1873, led to the arrival of Western Theosophists to aid Buddhists in their anti-missionary struggle.

In 1888, under Theosophist editorship, an English-language journal, *The Buddhist*, began as a foil to missionary publications. Its first editor, C. W. Leadbeater, for instance, wrote of the religion of the missionaries:

---

[79] See Anne Blackburn, *Buddhist Learning and Textual Practice in Eighteenth-Century Lankan Monastic Culture* (Princeton and Oxford: Princeton University Press, 2001).

[80] Harris, *Theravāda Buddhism*, 191.

[81] Elizabeth J. Harris, 'Memory, Experience and the Clash of Cosmologies: The Encounter between British Protestant Missionaries and Buddhism in Nineteenth Century Sri Lanka', *Social Sciences and Mission*, 25/3 (2012), 265–303.

[82] See Kitsiri Malalgoda, *Buddhism in Sinhalese Society 1750–1800: A Study of Religious Revival and Change* (Los Angeles: University of California Press, 1976); R. F. Young and G. P. V. Somaratne, *Vain Debates: The Buddhist–Christian Controversies in Nineteenth Century Ceylon* (Vienna: Publications of the De Nobili Research Library, 23, 1996); Harris, *Theravāda Buddhism and the British Encounter*.

It cannot live in peace with any other form of faith. It holds that there is but one saviour, but one inspired book, and but one little narrow grass-grown path that leads to heaven. Such a religion is necessarily uncompromising, unreasoning, aggressive and insolent. It has held all other creeds and forms in infinite contempt, divided the world into enemies and friends and amply verified that awful declaration of its founder; 'I came not to send peace on earth but the sword'.[83]

The Sri Lankan revivalist, the Anagarika Dharmapala, took this further. In Sri Lanka, therefore, defence in the face of threat became the dominant response, until the mid twentieth century.

Myanmar

Defensive action also characterized the Buddhist response to Christianity in Myanmar. Britain gained complete control over Myanmar in 1885, although Western missionaries had been active before then, including Roman Catholic orders. American Baptists arrived in 1813 and the Society for the Propagation of the Gospel established a Diocese of Rangoon in 1877.[84] Wesleyan Methodists arrived in Upper Burma in 1887. The first missionary accusation against Burmese Buddhists, as it had been in Sri Lanka, was that they were 'indifferent' or 'lazy'. As Leigh rightly points out, however, ' "Indifference" was the gentlest way in which the Burman could express resistance'.[85] From a Buddhist perspective, 'indifference' was a preferable response to anger. As in Sri Lanka, this changed.

One strategy was to strengthen Buddhists in their own faith through education and religious practice. An affluent lay person, Mrs Hla Oung, founded two Buddhist schools in 1897, one for girls, one for boys. Buddhist monk, Ledi Sayadaw (1846–1923), pioneered an insight meditation (*vipassanā*) revival.[86] Other Buddhist monks—influenced by Sri Lankan revivalism and aided by Western Buddhist monks in Myanmar such as U Dhammaloka (Irish) and Ananda Metteyya (English)—began to pressurize lay Buddhists to resist Christian schools and preaching.[87] Leigh argues that intolerance towards Christianity was evident soon after 1900 and that it increased in the 1920s, led by politicized monks such as U Thawbita and U Tiloka. Missionaries were heckled. Open-air services were disrupted. Christian schooling was boycotted or undermined and Christians were challenged to public debate.[88] Leigh attributes this resistance to nationalism but thereby reduces its religious significance. As in Sri Lanka, missionary contempt for Buddhism was seen as a threat, demanding defence. However, where respect was shown to Buddhism, respect was returned.[89]

---

[83] C. W. Leadbeater, 'Wesak/Wesak Compliments', *The Buddhist*, 1/22 (1889) 173–4.

[84] Michael D. Leigh, *Conflict, Politics and Proselytisation: Methodist Missionaries in Colonial and Postcolonial Upper Burma 1887–1966* (Manchester: Manchester University Press, 2011), 10.

[85] Leigh, *Conflict*, 78.

[86] Patrick Pranke, 'On Saints and Wizards: Ideals of Human Perfection and Power in Contemporary Burmese Buddhism', *Journal of the International Association of Buddhist Studies*, 33/1–2 ([2012] 2011), 461.

[87] Leigh, *Conflict*, 80; cf. Elizabeth J. Harris *Ananda Metteyya: The First British Emissary of Buddhism* (Kandy: Buddhist Publication Society, 1998).

[88] Leigh, *Conflict*, 78–87.

[89] See H. Fielding Hall, *The Soul of a People* (London: Macmillan & Co., 1906).

Japan

Japan was forced to open itself to America in the 1850s. Although Christianity remained pro-scribed until the 1870s, missionaries nevertheless arrived and attempted proselytization in manipulation of the right given to foreigners to practise Christianity, causing an aggressive Buddhist response. Some Buddhists studied Christianity in order to refute it, eventually using Western science for the same end.[90] Even when Japan began to engage positively with the West from the 1870s, tension between Christianity and Buddhism remained. A key figure was Inoue Enryo (1858–1919), who combined Buddhist revivalism with opposition to Christianity.[91]

The Twentieth Century: From Defence to Dialogue

It is impossible to identify within the historical summary above a single Buddhist model for interreligious encounter. Before the twentieth century rigorous debate, reasoned explana-tion, supercessionism, subordination, appropriation, enculturation, coexistence, and defen-sive polemic were all employed, some traceable to the beginnings of Buddhism but each dependent on local conditions. Within all of these except the last, other religious practices could be affirmed as provisional religious paths. In non-polemical contexts, Theravāda Buddhists could accept that the ethics of Christianity or Islam could help humans gain a better rebirth, and Mahāyāa Buddhists, that the long path towards buddhahood, through many lives, need not be walked solely within a Buddhist dispensation. In the twentieth cen-tury, however, with the global growth of interfaith initiatives, and new patterns of religious plurality and religious belonging,[92] some Buddhists found that old strategies were no longer appropriate. Three factors were particularly important: Christian interest in interfaith dia-logue; international and Western interfaith initiatives; Buddhist encounter with the Christian contemplative tradition and Western science.

Christian Interest in Interfaith Dialogue

The 1893 Chicago Parliament of Religions was central to the first of these factors. The courtesy shown to Buddhism by a predominantly Christian organizing team had a profound effect on the Buddhists present. Thelle, for instance, attributes a Buddhist–Christian Conference held in 1896 in Tokyo partly to its influence.[93] Also important, in the context of Japan, was that the courtesy Buddhists met in Chicago was being mirrored in a growing patriotism and appreciation of Japanese traditions among Japanese Christians, making them less of a threat to Buddhists.[94] This trend

---

[90] Notto R. Thelle, *Buddhism and Christianity in Japan: From Conflict to Dialogue 1854–1899* (Honolulu: University of Hawaii Press), 27–33.

[91] Thelle, *Buddhism and Christianity in Japan*, 97.

[92] Cf. Rose Drew, *Buddhist and Christian? An Exploration of Dual Belonging* (London and New York: Routledge, 2011).

[93] Thelle, *Buddhism and Christianity in Japan*, 225–46.

[94] Thelle, *Buddhism and Christianity in Japan*, 163–213.

continued. The National Christian Council Center for the Study of Japanese Religions was founded in 1959, with a journal, *Japanese Religions*, which called Buddhists into dialogue. In 1976, the Nanzan Institute for Religion and Culture at the Roman Catholic Nanzan University was founded, publishing, between 1982 and 2005, the journal, *Inter-Religio*.

In Sri Lanka, Buddhist mistrust of Christianity was lessened through the work of pioneering Christians such as Aloysius Pieris SJ (indologist and liberation theologian), Yohan Devananda (Anglican who pioneered an ashram that sought harmony with Buddhist culture), Tissa Balasuriya OMI, Michael Rodrigo OMI, and Lynn de Silva (Methodist scholar of Pali). In 1974, for instance, the Colombo-based Ecumenical Institute for Study and Dialogue (EISD, formerly the Centre for Religion and Society) pioneered by de Silva and Pieris, began a new series of the journal *Dialogue*, which was to place itself at the cutting edge of Buddhist–Christian exchange, successfully drawing intellectual, English-speaking Buddhists into dialogue.

One theme de Silva asked Buddhists to address was whether non-Buddhists could gain liberation. It drew exclusivist and inclusivist responses. Yatadolawatte Dhammavisuddhi maintained a broadly exclusivist position by pointing to the *Mahāparinibbāna Sutta* passage that states that other religious systems are devoid of the Eightfold Path.[95] He was willing to accept that liberation outside Buddhism was possible but not within these systems, because the teachers within them were not free from the cankers (*āsava*) that prevented liberation. K. N. Jayatilleke, in contrast, inclusively argued that a Buddha was one who 'discovers the truth rather than…has a monopoly of the truth', opening the door for 'others to discover aspects of the truth or even the whole truth for themselves'.[96] He accepted that this could happen within another religious tradition. In both Japan and Sri Lanka, therefore, one trigger for improved Buddhist–Christian relations was a change in the attitude of Christians.

International and Western Interfaith Initiatives

In the context of international interfaith organisations and dialogue, a Japanese lay Buddhist organisation in the Nichiren tradition can be cited: Risshō Kōsei Kai (RKK, Establishment of Righteousness and Friendly Intercourse) founded in 1938. RKK, through its founder, Nikkyo Niwano, was one of the first non-Christian organizations to join, in 1969, the International Association for Religious Freedom.[97] It was also active in the founding of the World Conference on Religion and Peace and the organizing of its first assembly in Kyoto in 1970.[98] Its journal, *Dharma World*, has consistently promoted interfaith understanding, through including articles by internationally recognized non-Buddhist writers.

---

[95] Y. Dhammavisuddhi, 'Does Buddhism Recognize Liberation from Samsara Outside its own Dispensation?', *Dialogue*, NS 13–14 (1986–7), 44.

[96] K. N. Jayatilleke, 'The Buddhist Attitude to Other Religions', *Dialogue*, NS 13–14 (1986–7), 26.

[97] Marcus Braybrooke, *Pilgrimage of Hope: One Hundred Years of Global Interfaith Dialogue* (London: SCM Press, 1992), 52.

[98] Braybrooke, *Pilgrimage of Hope*, 131–41.

An important moment for international engagement between Buddhists and other religions occurred in 1980 when David Chappell (1940–2004), a Christian who later identified as a Buddhist,[99] started the East–West Project from the University of Hawaii to foster academic engagement between Buddhism and Christianity. International conferences were held and a journal, *Buddhist–Christian Studies*, launched. A Japanese chapter of the project began in 1982, becoming the Japan Society for Buddhist–Christian Studies, publishing the *Journal of the Japan Society for Buddhist–Christian Studies*. At the Project's second conference, in 1983, the International Buddhist–Christian Theological Encounter (the Cobb–Abe group), began, led by John Cobb, Christian theologian, and Masao Abe, Zen Buddhist influenced by the Kyōto School.[100] It continued for twenty years. The 1987 conference, drawing 800 people from nineteen countries, gave birth to the Society for Buddhist–Christian Studies (SBCS), which pioneered new forms of structured dialogue, through the journal *Buddhist–Christian Studies* and dedicated publications.[101] In 1997, a parallel organization was founded in Europe, when a group of Christian scholars of Buddhism expanded into the European Network of Buddhist–Christian Studies (ENBCS), which holds a biennial conference, the papers of which are published.[102] Sōka Gakkai (Association for Creating Values), another lay Japanese Buddhist movement, founded in the 1930s, can be cited under this heading. It has more recently become known for the dialogues on global issues between its President, Daisaku Ikeda, and leading global figures from other faiths and ideologies.[103]

Engagement with Christian Mysticism and Western Science

The Kyōto School in Japan illustrates Buddhist engagement with Christian mysticism. Its founder, Nishido Kitarō (1870–1945), looked beyond institutional Christianity to mystics such as Meister Eckhart (*c.*1260–1327) and Western philosophy, and sought to reinterpret Zen in the light of this, particularly the Zen understanding of the non-duality of absolute nothingness (*śūnyatā*). He and his followers then engaged dialogically with the West. Keiji Nishitani (1900–90), for instance, presented a paper in Heidelberg in 1938 on 'Neitzsche and Eckhart',

---

[99] David W. Chappell, 'Religious Identity and Openness in a Pluralistic World', *Buddhist–Christian Studies*, 25 (2005), 9–14.

[100] See Rita M. Gross, 'International Buddhist–Christian Theological Encounter: Twenty Years of Dialogue', *Buddhist–Christian Studies*, 25 (2005), 3–7; Steven Heine (ed.), *Buddhism and Interfaith Dialogue: Masao Abe* (Honolulu: University of Hawaii Press, 1995).

[101] Cf. Rita M. Gross and Terry C. Muck, *Buddhists Talk about Jesus; Christians Talk about the Buddha* (New York and London: Continuum, 2000);—*Christians Talk about Buddhist Meditation: Buddhists Talk about Christian Prayer* (New York and London: Continuum, 2003).

[102] Cf. Perry Schmidt-Leukel, Gerhard Köberlin, and Josef Götz, *Buddhist Perceptions of Jesus* (St Ottilien: EOS, 2001); Perry Schmidt-Leukel (ed.), *Buddhism, Christianity and the Question of Creation: Karmic or Divine* (Aldershot: Ashgate, 2006); John D'Arcy May (ed.), *Converging Ways: Conversion and Belonging in Buddhism and Christianity* (St Ottilien: EOS, 2007); Elizabeth J Harris (ed.), *Hope: A Form of Delusion? Buddhist and Christian Perspectives* (St Ottilien, EOS, 2013).

[103] See Daisaku Ikeda and Majid Tehranian, *Global Civilisation: A Buddhist–Islamic Dialogue* (London and New York: I. B. Tauris, 2003); Ricardo Díez-Hochleitner and Daisaku Ikeda, *A Dialogue between East and West: Looking to a Human Revolution* (London and New York: I. B. Tauris, 2008); Harvey G. Cox and Daisaku Ikeda, *The Persistence of Religion: Comparative Perspectives on Modern Spirituality* (London and New York: I. B. Tauris, 2009).

which drew on Zen to suggest to Christians that the ultimate reality lived out by Jesus was both nothingness and freedom, an 'into-nothingness-and-out-of-nothingness'.[104]

Dialogue beyond Christianity

Buddhist dialogue with Islam in the twentieth century was subordinated to its dialogue with Christianity until the Taliban destroyed the Buddha images at Bamiyan in 2001. Buddhist reactions fell into two categories: vehement denunciation[105] and a call for dialogue so that Muslim misrepresentations of Buddhism could be addressed. One pioneer of the latter was the Taiwanese Dharma Master Hsin Tao, who organized a series of Buddhist–Muslim dialogues. The sixth in the series was held publicly, in 2004, at the Parliament of the World's Religions in Barcelona, on Dharma, Allah, and Governance.[106] Daiseku Ikeda's dialogue with Majid Tehranian also happened at the same time.

A FOCAL DEBATE: THE CONCEPT OF DEITY

The movements outlined above can be further illustrated through Buddhist attitudes to the concept of deity, or God, in other religious systems. The debate can be traced back to the ridiculing of Brahmā's omniscience and the reducing of the gods to the level of the mundane in India. Leaping to the eighteenth century, Desideri, for instance, found that the Tibetans had difficulty with belief in an eternal creator God.[107] We do not know whether this amounted to ridicule. In contexts where the 'other' threatened Buddhism, however, ridicule and even demonization was used. In the polemical atmosphere of seventeenth-century Japan, Suzuki Shōsan's *Ha-Kirishitan* (Refutation of Christianity) judged the Christian God 'a foolscap Buddha'.[108] In the 1873 Pānadurē Debate in Sri Lanka, Mohoṭṭivattē Guṇānanda drew on Western freethinkers such as Bradlaugh and the Sinhala folk imagination to prove that Christians worshipped a demon-like god, a view that, according to Young and Somaratne, 'conformed in the broadest possible manner to that of leading *bhikkhus* [monks] of the era'.[109]

A few decades later, the Sri Lankan Buddhist revivalist, the Anagarika Dharmapala (1864–1933), argued in similar vein. Although he received hospitality from Christians when he travelled to America and even preached in Unitarian Churches, his eventual considered position was that the God of Judaism and Christianity, 'the deity of Horeb',[110] was violent and

---

[104] Shizutero Ueda, 'Jesus in Contemporary Japanese Zen: With Special Regards to Keiji Nishitani', in Schmidt-Leukel *et al.*, *Buddhist Perceptions of Jesus*, 42–58.

[105] See Harris, 'Co-existence, Confrontation and Co-responsibility', 362–5.

[106] Harris, 'Co-existence, Confrontation and Co-responsibility', 365–7.

[107] Zwilling, *Mission to Tibet*, 44.

[108] Thelle, *Buddhism and Christianity in Japan*, 9.

[109] Young and Somaratne, *Vain Debates*, 168.

[110] Anagarika Dharmapala, 'The Repenting God of Horeb', in Ananda Guruge (ed.), *Return to Righteousness: A Collection of Speeches, Essays and Letters of the Anagarika Dharmapala* (Colombo: Ministry of Social Affairs, 1991), 401–25.

capricious. He also condemned the substitutionary, exclusivist theology of the cross beloved of evangelical missionaries as 'monstrously diabolical'.[111] That this theology spoke of an eternal hell for sinners was one reason Dharmapala judged the Christian God negatively. Other Buddhists pointed to the discrepancy between a God of love and the suffering in the world. Ananda Metteyya (Allan Bennett) wrote, possibly autobiographically, of the person who learns that life is *dukkha* (pain-filled):

> If he had faith in God,—in some great Being who had devised the Universe, he can no longer hold it; for any being, now he clearly sees, who could have devised a Universe wherein was all this wanton war, this piteous mass of pain coterminous with life, must have been a Demon, not a God.[112]

The last phrase was repeated to me in 1997 by a Western Buddhist monk who added, 'The weakness of Christianity is its God-belief'. It is blasphemy, he continued, to believe that a God of love could have created such a pain-filled world.[113] In the context of Buddhist modernism,[114] Sri Lankan academic Gunadasa Dharmapala's *A Buddhist Critique of the Christian Concept of God*[115] is also significant in its strident condemnation of the monotheistic concept of God from a Theravāda perspective.

In other contexts, however, less polemical perspectives arose in the twentieth century, as Buddhists were drawn into a dialogue that resulted in some Buddhists drawing parallels between the Christian concept of God and the Buddhist worldview. Bhikkhu Buddhadasa (1906–93), for instance, a Thai scholar monk, moved from suspicion of the religious 'other' to the conviction that religions should cooperate for mutual understanding and to challenge materialism. Controversially, he suggested that the non-personal Dharma of Buddhism was a metaphysical equivalent to the Christian God.:[116]

> No matter what name truth goes by—God, dhamma [Pali; Sanskrit: dharma], Tao, or the laws of nature—it is all one. Its manifestations in different religions may not look the same, but all of them can be seen as various perspectives on the whole. All represent the same truth. In Buddhism the dhamma is the path, the journey, and the realization of the goal of the journey. A similar claim could be made for such terms as *God* and *Tao*.[117]

---

[111]   Guruge, *Return to Righteousness*, 409.

[112]   Ananda Mettteyya, cited in Harris, *Ananda Metteyya*, 25.

[113]   Personal conversation with Ven Sumedha, 1997.

[114]   See David L. McMahon, *The Making of Buddhist Modernism* (Oxford: Oxford University Press, 2008); Harris, *Theravāda Buddhism*.

[115]   Gunadasa Dharmasiri, *A Buddhist Critique of the Christian Concept of God: A Critique of the Concept of God in Contemporary Christian Theology and Philosophy of Religion from the Point of View of Early Buddhism* (Colombo: Lake House, 1974).

[116]   Santikaro Bhikkhu, 'Jesus and Christianity in the Life and Work of Buddhadāsa Bhikkhu', in Schmidt-Leukel et al., *Buddhist Perceptions of Jesus*, 80–103.

[117]   Bhikkhu Buddhadāsa, 'Democratic Socialism', in Donald Swearer (ed.), *Me and Mine: Selected Essays of Bhikkhu Buddhadāsa* (Albany, NY: State University of New York, 1989), 168.

Maurice Walshe, Western convert to Buddhism, appealed to a canonical passage in the *Udāna* (8: 3) to reach a similar position, when invited by de Silva to reflect on Buddhist–Christian relations.[118] He did not deny that the two religions differed, but suggested that the differences could 'to a certain extent be legitimately relativized'. The reality that the *Udāna* speaks of, 'Unborn, Unbecome, Unmade, Uncompounded', namely *nirvāṇa*, argued Walshe, could be seen as an impersonal equivalent to the concept of God. Neither could truly be defined but both could be realized.[119]

Both Buddhadasa and Walshe were criticized. Nyanaponika Mahathera (1901–94), replying directly to Walshe, contested that differences between the two religions could be relativized, declaring that few Christians would be content with 'an impersonal godhead or Ground of Being, and still less with a deified "process of existence"'. He did, however, identify five alternative points of contact, including belief in the 'moral lawfulness' of the universe and the human need for 'liberation/salvation through a spiritual path'.[120] Similarly, Jotiya Dheerasekere, in the same interchange, stated that it would be difficult to find in Buddhism a parallel to 'admission to eternal bliss', implying that the God-centred salvific goal of Christianity bore no resemblance to the goal of Buddhism.[121] Decades later, Paul Williams, when defending his conversion from Buddhism to Christianity against Schmidt-Leukel's claim, on the basis of the *Udāna* passage, that Buddhism and Christianity both speak about the same ultimate reality, declared, 'The Buddhist position is straightforwardly atheist, and Buddhists who are proud of that fact are by no way infected by Orientalism or lacking an understanding of their own religion.'[122]

In Japan, the Kyōto School suggested a different equivalence: between God and *śūnyatā* or emptiness. Masao Abe originally found the Christian concept of God to be unscientific and problematic.[123] Yet, whilst asserting that *śūnyatā* was beyond any concept of one God, he could write:

> [T]he Christian mystics talk about Godhead, 'Gottheit', from which the personal God emerges, and a Christian mystic, Jakob Boehme, spoke about Godhead as 'Das Nichts' ... That

---

[118] 'There is, bhikkhus, a not-born, a not-brought-to-being, a not-made, a not-formed. If, bhikkhus, there were no not-born, not-brought-to-being, not-made, not-formed, no escape would be discerned from what is born, brought to being, made, formed. But since there is a not-born, a not-brought-to-being, a not-made, a not-formed, therefore an escape is discerned from what is born, brought-to-being, made, formed', *The Udāna: Inspired Utterances of the Buddha*, tr. John Ireland (Kandy: Buddhist Publication Society, 1990), 109.

[119] M. O'C. Walshe, 'Buddhism and Christianity: A Positive Approach—With Some Notes on Judaism', *Dialogue*, NS 9/1–3 (1982), 32.

[120] Nyanaponika Mahathera, 'Christianity: Another Positive Approach', *Dialogue*, NS 9/1–3 (1982), 41.

[121] Jotiya Dheerasekere, 'The Individual and Social Dimensions of Salvation in Buddhism', *Dialogue* NS 9/1–3 (1982), 76.

[122] Paul Williams, 'Buddhism, God, Aquinas and Morality: An Only Partially Repentant Reply to Perry Schmidt-Leukel and José Cabezon', in D'Arcy May, *Converging Ways?*, 117–54.

[123] See Masao Abe, 'Kenosis and Emptiness', in Corless and Paul F. Knitter (eds), *Buddhist Emptiness and Christian Trinity* (Mahwah, NJ: Paulist Press, 1990), 5–25; 'Kenotic God and Dynamic Sunyata', in John B. Cobb and C. Ives (eds), *The Emptying God: A Buddhist–Jewish–Christian Conversation* (Maryknoll, NY: Orbis Books, 1990), 3–65.

'Das Nichts' is not nothingness in a negative sense, but rather in a positive sense, because that nothingness or 'Das Nichts' is a source for a personal God. Where Buddhism talks about Emptiness, *Śūnyatā*, roughly speaking it may correspond to the Christian mystic notion of 'Das Nichts' or 'Godhead'.[124]

Ven Ayya Khema (1923–97), German-born convert to Buddhism, towards the end of her life, wrote two books that focused on biblical themes.[125] She also addressed the Eckhart Society, where she found common cause with Abe, the realization of *śūnyatā* being the realization of *nibbāna* within the Kyōto School: 'In the course of talking on the comparison between Christianity and Buddhism and engaging in ecumenical dialogue, I have come to the conclusion that God (or Godhead) and *Nibbāna* are identical—that they cannot be anything else'.[126]

Key to these parallels was the Christian mystical emphasis on self-negating. So, Buddhadasa's presentation on 'No Religion' compared the eradication of the 'I' in the Buddha's teachings with the message in John's Gospel that one must be 'born anew' to gain eternal life.[127] Ayya Khema declared in her Eckhart Society address:

> So those teachers [Buddha and Meister Eckhart] are showing us in undoubtedly unmistakable terms that there is only one thing which is keeping us from total happiness, total peacefulness, and that is 'me'. When 'me' is gone, is gone and then all that remains is the 'All'. And what is that 'All'? God is 'All'.[128]

The last approach I shall mention is that of Rissho Kosei Kai, which speaks of an Eternal Buddha in much the same way as theists might speak about God. Drawing on the *Saddharmapuṇḍarīka Sūtra*, the principal text for Nichiren Buddhists, an inclusivist position embracing theists and non-theists is reached:

> All humans are integrated into one potentiality that all will become Buddhas without exception. This is what 'one Vehicle' (eka-yana) means. Here, we can see universal salvation for all living beings... All teaching taught by the Buddha aim at guiding all people to become Buddhas.[129]

The debate between Buddhism and theism continues and has expanded to embrace the concept of God in Islam.

---

[124] Abe, *Buddhism and Interfaith Dialogue*, 76.

[125] Ayya Khema, *Das Größte ist die Liebe: Die Bergpredigt und das Hohelied der Liebe aus buddhistischer Sicht* (Uttenbuhl: Jhana Verlag, 1999); *Nicht so viel denken, mehr lieben Buddha und Jesus im Dialog* (Uttenbuhl: Jhana Verlag, 2000).

[126] Ayya Khema, 'Mysticism is No Mystery', *Eckhart Review* (Spring 1996), 45.

[127] Swearer, *Me and Mine*, 152–3.

[128] Khema, 'Mysticism is No Mystery', 45.

[129] Michio T. Shinozaki, 'The Thought of the Lotus Sutra as a Philosophy of Integration', *World Faiths Encounter*, 19 (Mar. 1998), 32.

THREE CONTEMPORARY BUDDHIST THINKERS

To illustrate further the breaking down of barriers between Buddhists and other religions, as seen at the end of the last section, three additional thinkers will be examined: the 14th Dalai Lama, Tenzin Gyatso (b. 1935); Thich Nhat Hanh (b. 1926); Rita Gross (b. 1943). All of these extend previously mentioned responses towards a more nuanced inclusivist or pluralist perspective.

The 14th Dalai Lama

The 14th Dalai Lama first encountered other Indic faiths in 1956, when he visited India. The result was that he could no longer 'live in the comfort of an exclusivist standpoint that takes Buddhism to be the only true religion'.[130] After being forced to flee Tibet in 1959, 'the richness and depth of Christianity' was impressed on him when, in 1968, Thomas Merton (1915–68) visited Dharamsala, the location of the Tibetan government in exile.[131] Later, the Dalai Lama was drawn into interfaith events in the West. In 1994, he participated in the annual John Main Seminar, organized by the World Community for Christian Meditation, when, in front of 350 Christians and Buddhists at Middlesex University in England, he responded empathetically to eight passages from the Christian gospels in his first public engagement with Christian texts.[132] He drew parallels between the two religions—tolerance, impartiality, and compassion—whilst not ignoring differences, and, when commenting on Matthew 5: 38–48, stressed, 'According to my own experience, all of the world's major religious traditions provide a common language and message upon which we can build a genuine understanding.'[133] This was followed, in July 1996, by an inter-monastic exchange at Merton's monastery in Kentucky.[134] In 2010, following fourteen more years of interfaith exchange, he was able publicly to declare what he saw as a pluralist standpoint: 'The challenge before religious believers is to genuinely accept the full worth of faith traditions other than their own'.[135] He added, 'The move to a pluralist position of interchange with other religions by no means involves abandoning one's central commitment to one's own faith; it hugely enriches the understanding and practice of one's own religion, as Desideri argued.'[136]

[130] Dalai Lama, *Toward the True Kinship of Faiths*, 6.
[131] Dalai Lama, *Toward the True Kinship of Faiths*, 7–8.
[132] Robert Kiely (ed.), *The Good Heart: His Holiness the Dalai Lama* (London: Rider, 1996), p. ix.
[133] Kiely, *Good Heart*, 45.
[134] See Donald W. Mitchell and James Wiseman OSB (eds), *The Gethsemani Encounter: A Dialogue on the Spiritual Life by Buddhist and Christian Monastics* (New York: Continuum, 1999).
[135] Dalai Lama, *Toward the True Kinship of Faiths*, p. ix.
[136] Dalai Lama, *Toward the True Kinship of Faiths*, 17.

Thich Nhat Hanh

The Vietnamese Thich Nhat Hanh (b. 1926) entered a Zen monastery at 16. Committed to a socially engaged form of Buddhism, he founded Youth for Social Service in 1964 and the Order of Interbeing in 1965. In 1966, he travelled to America 'to help dissolve some of the wrong views' about the Vietnam War[137] and made friends with Christians such as Luther King, Merton, Daniel Berrigan SJ, Hebe Kohlbrugge, and Heinz Kloppenburg. When political realities prevented him from returning, the West became his home. In 1975, conversations between him and Berrigan during the Vietnam War were published, covering topics such as meditation on death, shattering the bridges of the illusion that fuels conflict, exile, self-immolation, building communities of resistance, and Jesus and the Buddha.[138]

Nhat Hanh wrote again of Jesus and the Buddha in two later books.[139] In *Living Buddha Living Christ,* after claiming that his Christian friends had enabled him to see both Jesus and the Buddha as spiritual ancestors,[140] he paralleled the Holy Spirit and mindfulness, because the fruits of love and understanding were the same in each.[141] Living in the presence of God was then equated with the Buddhist idea of 'inter-being' or interconnectedness.[142] Jesus was an enlightened being, an expression of 'the highest spirit of humanity',[143] his hallowed presence and commitment to societal change similar to that of the Buddha. When commenting on the 'I' sayings of John's Gospel such as John 14: 6, he stressed that Jesus was not speaking about an exclusivist theology but a way that all must follow: 'When we understand and practice deeply the life and teachings of Buddha or the life and teachings of Jesus, we penetrate the door and enter the abode of the living Buddha and the living Christ, and life eternal presents itself to us.'[144] The theme of recognizing the living Christ and the living Buddha is expanded in the second book, where, in a teaching context, he declared of the two figures, 'Not only have they met today, but they met yesterday, they met last night, and they will meet tomorrow... There is no conflict at all between the Buddha and the Christ in me.'[145]

Rita Gross

Nhat Hanh's journey into religions other than Buddhism began when he experienced Christians who were non-exclusivist and socially engaged. The Dalai Lama's movement

---

[137] Thich Nhat Hanh, *Living Buddha, Living Christ* (London: Rider, 1996), 4.
[138] Thich Nhat Hanh and Daniel Berrigan, *The Raft is Not the Shore: Conversations toward a Buddhist–Christian Awareness* (Maryknoll, NY: Orbis Books, 1975/2001).
[139] *Living Buddha, Living Christ*; and *Going Home: Jesus and the Buddha as Brothers* (London: Rider, 1999).
[140] Nhat Hanh, *Living Buddha, Living Christ*, 6.
[141] Nhat Hanh, *Living Buddha, Living Christ*, 13–22.
[142] Nhat Hanh, *Living Buddha, Living Christ*, 28–9.
[143] Nhat Hanh, *Living Buddha, Living Christ*, 37.
[144] Nhat Hanh, *Living Buddha, Living Christ*, 55–6.
[145] Nhat Hanh, *Going Home*, 196; cf. Brian J. Pierce OP, *We Walk the Path Together: Learning from Thich Nhat Hanh and Meister Eckhart* (Maryknoll, NY: Orbis Books, 2005).

towards a form of pluralism was conditioned by encounter with Christians in the West. Both, however, tend to cite those parts of Christianity that map most easily onto Buddhism, an inclusivist tendency. Rita Gross, self-confessed pluralist who rejected the Jewish belief of her childhood to become a Western Buddhist feminist scholar and interfaith practitioner, has gone further.[146]

According to Paul Knitter, the following themes have been central to her writings: that truth-claims promoted as final or superior are incompatible with true religious diversity; that monotheistic religions are the biggest sinners in asserting such claims; that religious diversity is a gift and a resource.[147] Religions, Gross has argued, 'are nothing more than highly relative language systems',[148] which, because of their cultural specificity, are incapable of capturing truth completely, although their value can be inestimable to believers. The criterion for judging them, therefore, should be ethical rather than metaphysical, based on whether they help planetary well-being.[149] Religions should also interact for 'mutual transformation'. For example, she has encouraged Buddhists to learn from the 'prophetic inclination' within Judaism and Christianity, suggesting that the absence of a prophetic voice has allowed Buddhists to speak about compassion and yet tolerate 'often extremely repressive social regimes'.[150] Within this call, a robust move away from inclusivism can be detected. The most moving published expression of her interreligious ethic is the record of a conversation she had, in 1999, with Christian feminist theologian, Rosemary Radford Ruether, sister participant in the Cobb–Abe group, in which both participants frankly discuss not only what is liberating in their tradition, but what is problematic.[151]

CASE STUDIES

When taken together, Nhat Hanh, the Dalai Lama, and Rita Gross illustrate key themes in contemporary Buddhist interreligious engagement: inter-monastic dialogue; social engagement; Buddhist women and the 'other'. More can be said about each and also about another key theme: conversion.

---

[146] See: Rita M. Gross and Rosemary Radford Ruether, *Religious Feminism and the Future of the Planet: A Buddhist–Christian Conversation* (London and New York: Continuum, 2001), 25–47.

[147] Paul Knitter, 'Rita Gross: Buddhist–Christian Dialogue about Dialogue', *Buddhist–Christian Studies*, 31 (2011), 79–84.

[148] Rita M. Gross, 'Religious Identity and Openness in a Pluralistic World', *Buddhist–Christian Studies*, 25 (2005), 16.

[149] Gross, 'Religious Identity and Openness', 17.

[150] Rita M. Gross, *Buddhism After Patriarchy: A Feminist History, Analysis, and Reconstruction of Buddhism* (Albany, NY: State University of New York Press, 1993), 134; see also Gross, *Soaring and Settling; Buddhist Perspectives on Contemporary Social and Religious Issues* (New York: Continuum, 1998), 13.

[151] Gross and Ruether, *Religious Feminism*, see also Peggy Morgan, 'Embodiments of Hope in Christianity', in Elizabeth Harris (ed.), *Hope: A Form of Delusion? Buddhist and Christian Perspectives* (St Ottilien: EOS, 2013), 121–41, in which she takes this dialogue as an illustration of 'hope'.

Inter-Monastic Dialogue

Formal inter-monastic dialogue between Buddhism and other religions, particularly Christianity, began in the twentieth century with the work of Merton, although Buddhist–Christian inter-monastic encounter can be traced back at least to the Church of the East in China. Merton tragically died in 1968 at a meeting of L'aide à l'implantation Monastique (AIM—Inter-Monastic Aid) in Bangkok, at which he encouraged his fellow monks 'to devote themselves to serious engagement with the spiritual riches of the East'.[152] In response to this call, AIM in 1973 brought together Christian and non-Christian monks, which resulted in a series of East–West Spiritual Exchanges between Zen and Christian monks. In 1978, two committees/commissions for monastic interfaith dialogue were formed, one based in North America, focusing on the Tibetan tradition, and the other in Belgium and France, focusing on Zen. Further commissions were formed and a newsletter produced for what had by then become Monastic Interreligious Dialogue/Dialogue Interreligieux Monastique (MID/DIM).[153] Today, inter-monastic dialogue is firmly established within Christian monasticism. Buddhists have responded with grace and cooperation and, according to interviews recorded in the MID/DIM journal, have gained much, some recognizing that Christianity had a depth they had not previously seen.[154] One significant project was when four Buddhists, only one a monastic, agreed to comment formally on the Rule of St Benedict, following a Buddhist–Christian encounter at Gethsemani in 1996.[155] It could be argued, however, that this dialogue has been asymmetrical, with Christians gaining more and being more proactive than Buddhists.

Social Engagement

In the twentieth century, some Eastern and Western Buddhists, including Nhat Hanh and Sulak Sivaraksa (lay Siamese Buddhist, b. 1933) coined the term 'Engaged Buddhism', in reaction to forms of Buddhist practice that had seemed to privilege withdrawal, forgetting the centrality of compassionate action in Buddhism.[156] In 1989, the International Network of Engaged Buddhists was founded. Significantly, engaged Buddhists have called people of other religions into collaboration, in a pattern dominated by Buddhist agency in

---

[152] Fabrice Blée, *The Third Desert: The Story of Monastic Interreligious Dialogue* (Collegeville, Mich.: Liturgical Press, 2011), 27.

[153] Accounts of inter-monastic dialogue from a Christian perspective include: Blée, *The Third Desert*; Pierre-Francois de Béthune, *By Faith and Hospitality: The Monastic Tradition as a Model for Interreligious Encounter* (Leominster: Gracewing, 2002); Thomas Josef Götz. 'Catholic Monk, Buddhist Monk: The Monastic Interreligious Dialogue with Japanese Zen', in D'Arcy May, *Converging Ways*, 11–23.

[154] Cf. Karma Pema Tsultrim, 'Comments on the Exchange Program with Tibetans and the American MID', *DIM/MID International Bulletin*, E4 (1997), 14–15.

[155] Cf. Patrick Henry, *Benedict's Dharma: Buddhists Reflect on the Rule of Saint Benedict* (London and New York: Continuum, 2001).

[156] Cf. S. Sivaraksa, *Conflict, Culture, Change: Engaged Buddhism in a Globalizing World* (Boston: Wisdom Publications, 2005).

contrast to inter-monastic dialogue.[157] For instance, Sivaraksa has invited Christian activists to the Spirit in Education (SEM) conferences he has held in Thailand and has been pivotal in the Thai Inter-Religious Commission for Development. Taking another example, Christians have been welcome participants in the Dhammayietras (Walks of Truth) in Cambodia, started by Mahā Ghosānanda in 1992 to encourage non-violence and reconciliation in a context of war.[158] And in Sri Lanka, the Buddhist organization, Sarvodaya, founded by A. T. Ariyaratne to pioneer a Buddhist form of rural development, has developed a more universalist stance that has sought to include people of all religions and none in its vision.[159] Initiatives such as these inspired an SBCS conference in 1996 on 'Socially Engaged Buddhism and Christianity', which included a week-long workshop led by the Dalai Lama, and talks by Ariyaratne and Sivaraksa.

Buddhist Women and the 'Other'

Buddhist women have been involved in inter-monastic dialogue, interreligious social activism, and formal Buddhist–Christian dialogue. For instance, some Western women who have become *bhikkhuṇīs* (Pāli, fully ordained nuns) have found greater understanding from Christian nuns than from Western Buddhists who have rejected the lay/monastic distinction.[160] Ven Dhammananda (Chatsumarn Kabilsingh), pioneer of Buddhist women's ordination in Thailand, has been a member of the Peace Council, an international interreligious group committed to intervention in conflict situations. At the 2004 meeting of the Council in Chiang Mai, she was a key voice in *The Chiang Mai Declaration: Religion and Women: An Agenda for Change.*

Sakyadhita (Daughters of the Buddha), an international Buddhist women's organization, founded in Bodhgaya in 1987, does not focus on interreligious understanding. Education for Buddhist women, ensuring opportunities for higher ordination, creating understanding between different Buddhist schools, and social issues have been more important. However, some members are actively involved in grassroots interfaith work, a fact apparent at the 1998 conference in Cambodia. Trina Nahn-Mijo, for instance, an American Zen practitioner, spoke movingly about her collaboration with a Korean Methodist minister in pressing for the

[157] Cf. Christopher S. Queen and Sallie B. King, *Engaged Buddhism: Buddhist Liberation Movements in Asia* (Albany, NY: State University of New York Press, 1996); Charles S. Prebish and Christopher S. Queen, *Action Dharma: New Studies in Engaged Buddhism* (London and New York: Routledge, 2003); Ken Jones, *The New Social Face of Buddhism: A Call to Action* (Boston: Wisdom Publications, 2003).

[158] Cf. Elizabeth J. Harris, *What Buddhists Believe* (Oxford: Oneworld, 1998), 114–19.

[159] See George D. Bond, *Buddhism at Work: Community Development, Social Empowerment and the Sarvodaya Movement* (Boulder, Colo.: Kumarian Press, 2004); Elizabeth J. Harris, 'The Cost of Peace: Buddhists and Conflict Transformation in Sri Lanka', in Philip Broadhead and Damien Keown (eds), *Can Faiths Make Peace: Holy Wars and the Resolution of Religious Conflicts* (London and New York: I. B. Tauris, 2007), 155.

[160] Karma Lekshe Tsomo, 'Comparing Buddhist and Christian Women's Experiences', in Karma Lekshe Tsomo (ed.), *Buddhist Women across Cultures: Realizations* (Albany, NY: State University of New York Press, 1999), 241–58.

rape of women during war to be seen as an international war crime.[161] And, in a session on 'Dialogues in Religious Diversity', Beth Goldering, a Zen practitioner working interreligiously among the Cambodian poor, stated, 'When I look for spiritual community, I need to find it in a wider context than simply the Buddhist community.'[162]

Conversion as Source of Conflict

The above comment by Goldering and the words of a Catholic participant, Frances Kissling, in the session in Cambodia, however, led one Sri Lankan participant to ask, 'Do we tolerate unethical conversions?' She was referring to the accusation prevalent in Sri Lanka that Christians were using material inducements to convert poverty-stricken Buddhists. Her implication was that Buddhists were too tolerant of this. Fear over Christian proselytization lies in sharp contrast with the interreligious rapprochement present in the other case studies above and demonstrates the persistence of a Buddhist response to the 'other' rooted in defensive action against perceived threat. Continuing to take Sri Lanka as example, by May 2004, mistrust of Christians because of the conversion issue was high enough for a 'Prohibition of Forcible Conversions Bill' to be tabled in Parliament by the Jathika Hela Urumaya (JHU, National Heritage Party). The following month, the Minister of Buddha Sasana within the government presented a similar bill.[163] Neither has yet passed into law but the controversy remains live.[164] The issue gained renewed publicity after the 2004 tsunami. One task of a Commission of Inquiry into unethical conversions appointed by the All Ceylon Buddhist Congress (ACBC) in 2006 was to ascertain whether there was 'evidence to support the view that some relief workers both local and foreign who offered to help out the victims of the December 2004 tsunami disaster made use of that opportunity to convert Buddhists'. The Commission found such evidence and accused 400 NGOs of attempting to convert Buddhists and Hindus.[165] Two months after the report was released in January 2009, a further Commission on Prevention of Unethical Conversions was appointed by the ACBC to receive complaints and initiate legal cases if appropriate. Within the ACBC, Christians remain a force that seeks to destroy the Buddhist identity of the country, necessitating strategies of defence.

---

[161] Trina Nahm-Mijo, 'Engaged Buddhism: "Moving" and Recreating Buddhist Women's Stories', in Karma Lekshe Tsomo (ed.), *Innovative Buddhist Women: Swimming Against the Stream* (Richmond, Surrey: Curzon, 2000), 312–18.

[162] From notes taken by the author at the Cambodia conference.

[163] See e.g. Alexandra Owens, 'Using Legislation to Protect Against Unethical Conversions in Sri Lanka', *Journal of Law and Religion*, 12 (2007), 323–51.

[164] Cf. Elizabeth J. Harris, 'Confrontation over Conversions: A Case Study from Sri Lanka', in D'Arcy May, *Converging Ways*, 37–54.

[165] See Elizabeth J. Harris, 'Buddhism and International Aid: A Case Study from Post-Tsunami Sri Lanka', in Hiroko Kawanami and Geoffrey Samuels (eds), *Buddhism and International Relief Work* (London: Palgrave Macmillan, 2013).

CONCLUSION

This chapter has argued that a fundamental tension lies at the heart of the Buddhist relationship with the religious 'other'. On the one hand, Buddhism teaches that believing only oneself to be right leads away from enlightenment; on the other, there is a conviction that the Buddha's teaching supersedes other systems. This tension has expressed itself variously in history from absorption of the 'other' to supercessionism and polemical defence. Yet, parallel to this, courteous, respectful coexistence and collaboration, in contexts where courtesy has been reciprocated, has flowered, expressing the non-violence and compassion at the heart of Buddhism. Now, in the twenty-first century, global patterns of interreligious encounter and academic study are nurturing greater mutual understanding, convergence, and cooperation between Buddhists and members of other religious traditions.

FURTHER READING

Dalai Lama, His Holiness, *Towards the True Kinship of Faiths: How the World's Religions Can Come Together* (London: Abacus, 2010).

Rita M. Gross and Terry C. Muck (eds), *Buddhists Talk about Jesus: Christians Talk about the Buddha* (New York: Continuum, 2000).

—— and Rosemary Radford Ruether, *Religious Feminism and the Future of the Planet: A Buddhist–Christian Conversation* (London and New York: Continuum, 2001).

Patrick Henry (ed.), *Benedict's Dharma: Buddhists Reflect on the Rule of Saint Benedict* (London and New York: Continuum, 2001).

Robert Kiely (ed.), *The Good Heart: His Holiness the Dalai Lama* (London: Rider, 1996).

Sallie B. King and Paul O. Ingram (eds), *The Sound of Liberating Truth Buddhist–Christian Dialogues in Honor of Frederick J. Streng* (Richmond, Surrey: Curzon, 1999).

Whalen Lai and Michael von Brück, *Christianity and Buddhism: A Multi-Cultural History of their Dialogue* (Maryknoll, NY: Orbis, 2001).

Donald W. Mitchell and James Wiseman OSB (eds), *The Gethsemani Encounter: A Dialogue on the Spiritual Life by Buddhist and Christian Monastics* (New York: Continuum, 1999).

Thich Nhat Hanh, *Living Buddha, Living Christ* (London: Rider, 1996).

Perry Schmidt-Leukel (ed.), *Buddhist Attitudes to Other Religions* (St Ottilien: EOS, 2008).

—— Gerhard Köberlin, and Josef Götz (eds), *Buddhist Perceptions of Jesus* (St Ottilien: EOS, 2001).

J. Abraham Velez de Cea, *The Buddha and Religious Diversity* (London and New York: Routledge, 2013).

CHAPTER 6

Christianity and the
Religious Other

PERRY SCHMIDT-LEUKEL

A range of different factors—such as geographic, ethnic, social, economic, legal, and political, for example—influence and shape interreligious relations. Usually these are so closely intertwined that it is not always easy to unravel which is most responsible for the state of a particular relationship at a given time and place. However, one such factor—or more precisely one subset of factors—has to do with religion itself, namely, for the purpose of this chapter, those elements or factors that are intrinsically connected to the specific beliefs and practices of a religious tradition. Although it is often difficult to isolate religious factors with regard to their degree of impact on a particular interreligious relationship, it is nevertheless possible to look at them in a somewhat isolated way. This may seem artificial, but is nevertheless helpful in order to understand better how the religious aspects operate within this more complex web of factors. At least such an analysis can enable a better grasp of the potential and real force of the religious factors for good or bad and, moreover, understanding what appears as 'good' or 'bad' to whom, and why so. In this sense the present chapter looks at those religious factors that have governed, and still do, Christianity's conception of and relation to its religious others.

In the first section I will attend to the question of how the religious other is constructed in the most authoritative sources of Christianity, the Biblical scriptures, and in some of the main declarations of different Christian churches. Section 2 will present a brief survey of Christianity's relation to various religious others, including other Christians. Finally, section 3 will introduce the main threads of inner Christian positions on how the relationship to religious others should be conceived theologically.[1] As I will try to show, Christian concepts of

[1] I am very grateful to my academic colleagues Reinhard Achenbach, Hermut Löhr, and Jutta Sperber for their valuable suggestions and advice. All errors are, of course, mine.

the religious other were, to a considerable degree, constructed in an a priori manner, that is, as more or less derived from particular forms of Christian (and Jewish) self-understanding. These constructs formed and predetermined Christian encounters with others. Such encounters, however, carry with them the opportunity of becoming more familiar with the other's self-understanding and hence the questioning of any preconceived constructs. As a consequence, the contemporary debates about Christianity's relations to the religious others can be understood as part and process of such questioning.

1. Constructing the Other

Biblical Sources

The Bible, neither the Hebrew Bible, nor the Christian scriptures known as the 'New Testament', does not contain anything like a theology of other religions. As Wesley Ariarajah puts it, 'the Bible is not a book that deals with other faiths or with the question of dialogue with people of other faiths'.[2] In particular the Bible says nothing about the so-called major 'world religions' of Islam (which emerged more than five centuries after the New Testament writings), or Hinduism and Buddhism which were simply unknown to the Biblical authors. Yet the Biblical scriptures—composed over a period of more than six centuries—tell us something about the evolving religions of Judaism and Christianity, not only about their understanding of and interaction with other faiths in their immediate neighbourhood but also about their interaction with each other, including horrific consequences and outcomes.

However, the information that can be obtained from the Biblical scriptures is marked by a pervasive ambiguity: 'The data... are often ambivalent, not to say in apparent contradiction among themselves'.[3] To be sure, the dominant line in both the Hebrew Bible and the New Testament consists of texts and verses that display exclusivist claims in relation to the religious other. These are at times so strong and apodictic that they seem to leave no room for any exception. Yet these are counterbalanced by other texts and verses that not only do present such exceptions but sometimes seem to present them as samples of a universal rule. An understanding of why such contradictory strands exist within the Biblical writings can best be achieved by looking at them from a broadly historical perspective.

Hebrew Bible

Any uncritical reading of the Hebrew Bible is most likely to produce the impression of a stark monotheism along with an uncompromising condemnation of all other gods as man-made idols. Contemporary historical research, however, has produced ample evidence (not only

---

[2] Wesley Ariarajah, *The Bible and People of Other Faiths* (Geneva: World Council of Churches, 1985), p. xii.
[3] See Jacques Dupuis, *Toward a Christian Theology of Religious Pluralism* (Maryknoll, NY: Orbis Books, 1997), 29–30.

based on intra-textual analysis but also on archaeological, in particular iconographic and epigraphic material) that *strictly* monotheistic claims about Israel's god Yahweh were not developed before the time of the Babylonian exile (sixth century BCE) and remained—at least in practice—contested even in the post-exilic period.[4] It appears that originally Yahweh was the tribal deity of the 'Hebrews' or 'Israel' (Exod. 5: 3; Judges 5: 3ff.; Psalm 68: 8) as distinct from the particular deities of other peoples. Their reality was not denied, but they were seen as being less powerful than Yahweh (Exod. 15: 11, Psalm 95: 3). Most importantly, Yahweh was understood as a 'jealous' god (Deut. 5: 9–10) besides whom Israel must not serve any other gods (Exod. 34: 14). Thus the Biblical belief in a singular god began in the mode of henotheism (the preferred one among many) and the sole worship of Yahweh (monolatry) operated as a warranty of Israel's identity and well-being.

This ideally exclusive relationship was marked by the theological concepts of Israel's election by Yahweh and a special covenant between him and his chosen people. In practice, however, exclusive dedication to Yahweh did not mirror Israel's religious reality, which can also be seen from the fact that prophetic figures (Elijah, Hosea, Jeremiah) took a growing polemical stance against the worship of other deities. In parallel to such 'Yahweh alone' movements, the concept or apprehension of Yahweh syncretistically assumed and incorporated features of local Canaanite gods such as El or Baal, or of Jerusalem's sun god and other astral deities. Only when, during and after the Babylonian Exile, polemics against other deities took the radical form of denying their existence, as is particularly evident in the work of Deutero-Isaiah (e.g. Isa. 41: 21–4; 44: 9–20), did the monolatry of henotheism turn into monotheism as such. To the monotheists, Yahweh is the one God 'with no other besides him' (Deut. 4: 35; also 45: 5). By now, worshipping other gods is no longer seen as merely a case of unfaithfulness but as entirely futile because, in fact, there are no other gods. The exclusive loyalty to one particular deity (among others) transmuted into the exclusivist claim of possessing the only true knowledge of God (as the one and only deity *per se*).

Against this background two major motifs of the Hebrew Bible become intelligible: a strong *particularism* according to which Israel alone among the nations knows, and is salvifically related to, the one true God; and an equally strong *universalism* according to which the one true God is the creator of heaven and earth and all its inhabitants.[5] It is between these two motifs that tensions and contradictions arise. In line with the particularist motif the solution of such conflict is eschatological: Israel's role among the nations is understood as being a living testimony to the fact that its own god, Yahweh, is the only God. The nations do not yet know him but, through Israel's testimony, they will come to recognize God truly in the eschatological future (Isa. 45: 14). Even Egypt will then acknowledge Israel's God and be his

---

[4] See e.g. Beate Pongratz-Leisten (ed.), *Reconsidering the Concept of Revolutionary Monotheism* (Winona Lake, Ind.: Eisenbrauns, 2011); Mark S. Smith,—*God in Translation. Deities in Cross-Cultural Discourse in the Biblical World* (Tübingen: J. C. B. Mohr, 2008); Ziony Zevit, *The Religions of Ancient Israel* (London and New York: Continuum, 2003).

[5] Cf. Dupuis, *Toward*, 40; Richard J. Plantinga, 'The Bible and Religious Pluralism', in Richard J. Plantinga (ed.), *Christianity and Plurality: Classic and Contemporary Readings* (Oxford: Blackwell, 1999), 11–25; Veli-Matti Kärkkäinen, *An Introduction to the Theology of Religions* (Downers Grove, Ill.: IVP, 2003), 39–40.

people too (Isa. 19: 19–25). All nations will gather in Zion to praise the true God (Isa. 60: 1–20; 2: 2–5). In line with the universalistic motif we find a more immediate solution: God's care is for all God's creatures in the here and now. There are non-Jewish individuals, like Enoch, Noah, Job, Melchizedek, or Lot, who know and serve the true God. Moreover, God's care is not confined to individuals. As in the Book of Jonah, God worries about the pagan city of Nineveh, sends it a prophet, and delights in its collective repentance (Jonah 3: 10; 4: 9–11). According to Amos (9: 7) God's liberative action is not just for Israel: 'Did I not bring Israel up from the land of Egypt, and the Philistines from Caphtor and the Arameans from Kir?' And according to Malachi (1: 11) God's 'name is great among the nations, and in every place incense is offered to my name'.

Rabbinic Judaism came to combine the eschatological perspective of the particularist motif with some features of the universalistic motif in its teaching of the Noahide laws. Through Noah, God made an everlasting covenant with all people on earth (Gen. 9: 15–17). Whosoever among the gentiles lives by the seven Noahide laws of this covenant—which include abstaining from idolatry—will have a share in the future eschatological salvation.

New Testament

The Hebrew Bible (principally 'Law' and 'Prophets') was the only scripture as such used by Jesus and the early church. Yet to the extent that early Christian groups turned from an inner Jewish sect into a rapidly growing, predominantly non-Jewish ('gentile') movement, whose members did not have to become Jews in order to be Christians, Christianity was soon in need of its own set of canonical writings. All scriptures assembled in the New Testament were composed after Jesus' death within the relatively short period of about 100 years.[6] They do, however, contain a number of sayings which are likely to reflect Jesus' own voice.

In relation to the early development of the Christian faith, one can distinguish three different levels within the New Testament writings: (1) The *faith of Jesus*, expressed in his beliefs about God and his own role; (2) the *faith in Jesus* of his early followers, expressed in beliefs about Jesus; (3) early Christians' *beliefs about believers and non-believers*, that is, about those who share their beliefs in Jesus, those who don't, and those who hold different beliefs. It is not always easy to discriminate clearly between these three levels because at times they are anachronistically conflated into what is presented as Jesus' own teaching. Nevertheless, the distinction is valid in so far as one can determine changes and developments from one level to the next. This is particularly helpful in understanding the construction of the 'religious other'. Tensions between particularism and universalism in the Hebrew Bible remained the matrix underlying Christian developments in this regard.

Academic inquiry into the historical Jesus has seen its own ups and downs. In the first half of the twentieth century the naïve optimism of much of nineteenth-century research gave

---

[6] Assuming the earliest parts (some of Paul's letters) date from the late 40s of the 1st cent. CE and the latest (Jude and 2 Peter) from about 100 years later.

way to a wide-ranging pessimism that one could ever sketch a reliable profile of the historical Jesus. This changed once again with a number of significant studies produced over more recent decades.[7] Historical reconstructions remain cautious, yet something like a consensus on some significant aspects of Jesus' own faith has emerged. First, Jesus did not proclaim *himself* (as the later Gospel of John has it) but God's merciful reign of the coming kingdom of God. Second, Jesus shared the apocalyptic expectations of many of his Jewish contemporaries that the establishment of God's reign on earth is imminent and will be accompanied by transformations of a cosmic dimension. Third, he most likely saw his own role as that of *a* or *the* decisive eschatological prophet,[8] sent to the people of Israel in order to renew it and prepare it for the coming events.

The third point raises the question of how Jesus understood the relationship of Jews and non-Jews to God and God's coming kingdom. Without doubt, Jesus appears to have seen his own mission (and that of his immediate disciples) exclusively to 'the lost sheep of the house of Israel', avoiding the areas of the gentiles and Samaritans (Matt. 10: 5–6; 15: 24). If, however, the manifestation of God's kingdom is confined to the house of Israel, what does that mean for the gentiles? Their exclusion from the salvific acts of God would contradict Jesus' faith in God's boundless mercy and fatherly love, which extends to the whole of his creation (Matt. 6: 25–34), includes friend and foe (Matt. 5: 43–8), and is the central norm of God's rule (Matt. 22: 34–40). According to Sanders, we may therefore assume 'that he expected at least some Gentiles to turn to the God of Israel and to participate in the coming kingdom.'[9] This would place Jesus' own view in line with the expectation of the Hebrew Bible that God will 'redeem his people and constitute a new kingdom, one in which Israel would be secure and peaceful, and one in which Gentiles would serve the God of Israel.'[10]

There are of course not only passages in the Synoptic Gospels where Jesus affirms the existence of a salvific faith among individual gentiles, as in the case of the Syro-Phoenician woman (Mark 7: 24–30; Matt. 15: 21–8), the Roman centurion (Matt. 8: 5–13), the 'Good Samaritan' (Luke 10: 29–37), or the Samaritan leper (Luke 17: 18–19). We also find statements where Jesus commands his followers to preach the Gospel to all nations (Matt. 24: 14; 28: 19; Mark 13: 10; 14: 9; Luke 24: 47) who will join the eschatological feast to the disadvantagement of the Jews (Matt. 8: 11–12). Regarding this 'great commission', it is a common view among Biblical scholars that it does not go back to Jesus himself but rather reflects the later stage of the early church being already actively involved in universal mission. Geza Vermes plausibly argues that

---

[7] e.g.: Geza Vermes, *Jesus the Jew* (London: SCM, 2001); *The Changing Faces of Jesus* (London: Penguin, 2000); Joachim Gnilka, *Jesus von Nazaret: Botschaft und Geschichte* (Freiburg i.Br.: Herder, 1990); H. C. Kee, *What Can We Know about Jesus?* (Cambridge: Cambridge University Press, 1990); E. P. Sanders, *The Historical Figure of Jesus*, London: Penguin, 1993); John P. Meier, *A Marginal Jew: Rethinking the Historical Jesus*, 4 vols. (New York: Anchor Bible, 1991–2009).

[8] See Sanders, *Historical Figure*, 238–9; Vermes, *Changing Faces*, 192–3.

[9] Sanders, *Historical Figure*, 287.   [10] Sanders, *Historical Figure*, 287.

If Jesus had made plain to his apostles that his message was meant for the whole world and not for Jews alone, it would be impossible to explain why according to the Acts of the Apostles the primitive church, and Paul in particular, encountered so much well-nigh insurmountable difficulty apropos the admission of Gentiles into the Christian community.[11]

Gospel records that praise the faith of individual non-Jews may thus either be seen as later constructions in order to create a justification of the mission to the gentiles by grounding it in Jesus' own activity, or as reflecting Jesus' sharing of the universalist motif from the Hebrew Bible that individual gentiles do live in their own proper relationship to the one true God.

The startling shift from Jesus' exclusive mission to Israel to the church's universal mission to the gentiles takes us from Jesus' faith in God to his followers' faith in Jesus. Its principal and central expression was originally the belief in Jesus as the Messiah ('Christ'). While it is far from clear what exactly the concept of 'Messiah' implied, confessing him as the Messiah at least signified that Jesus was seen by his followers as the one crucial messenger sent to, but by and large rejected by, Israel. The fact that in their vast majority Jews did not join the Jesus movement was decisive for the growing conviction that the proclamation of the Gospel should now be to the gentiles (Luke 24: 45ff.; Acts 13: 46) and that the new church made of Jews and gentiles was 'the Israel of God' (Gal. 6: 16), the new people of God (1 Pet. 2: 9–10), heir to the God-given promises (Rom. 8: 17; Gal 3: 29), thereby assuming the paradigmatic role that Israel had had in the Hebrew Biblical tradition.

To the extent that Christian beliefs about Jesus intensified from his confession as the Messiah (Mark 8: 29) to his understanding as the incarnate word (*logos*) of God (John 1: 14, 18), the human image of God (2 Cor. 4: 4; Col. 1: 15) and—in post-New Testament times— to the Son of God in a non-metaphorical,[12] metaphysical sense, finally regarded as the human incarnation of the Second Person of a trinitarian God, the split with Judaism increased. The beginnings of this process are already apparent in the Gospel of John where Jesus appears as the only way to 'the father' (John 14: 6–7) and where 'the Jews', because of their rejection of Jesus, are collectively blamed as those who don't know God (John 7: 28; 15: 21; 16: 3) and are sons of the devil (John 8: 44), or in Matthew where the shift of the mission from the Jews to the gentiles goes along with the collective blaming of the Jewish people for the murder of their Messiah: 'His blood be on us and our children!' (Matt. 27: 25).

Turning to the gentiles implied they were perceived as having the potential to become members of God's new people. This revitalized not only the ancient motif of the eschatological recognition of Israel's God as the one true God. It also implied that God's care for all of his creatures was now seen in terms of God's preparation of the nations for the Gospel—as is particularly evident in the Book of Acts (Acts 10: 34–6; 14: 16–17). This is why Paul, according to Acts (17: 22–31), can even quote from gentile authors (Epimenides, sixth

---

[11] Vermes, *Changing Faces*, 156–7.
[12] Vermes, *Changing Faces*, 183: 'the Jewish attestations of "son of God" are all metaphorical'; similarly Sanders, *Historical Figure*, 243ff.

century BCE) in support of his own message. Nevertheless, Jesus is seen as the only gateway to the participation in God's kingdom and 'there is no other name under heaven given among mortals by which we must be saved' (Acts 4: 12). With the delay of the awaited apocalyptic events, the respective expectations were shifted to the hoped-for 'return' or 'second coming' of Jesus, and finally postponed to an indefinite future. Participation in God's kingdom was thus promised to the believer as happening with the resurrection from the dead at the end of the days.

This leads us to the third level: beliefs about believers and non-believers. Those who share the church's beliefs about Jesus (and thereby, so it is assumed, its faith in Jesus), and mark this by entry into the church through baptism, are saved. Those who don't, are not (as in the late addition to Mark's Gospel—Mark 16: 16). The non-believers were understood as three different groups: (1) Jews who refuse to accept Jesus as their Messiah; (2) gentiles who reject the Gospel and remain faithful to their 'pagan' religions; and (3) 'false believers' who do not share some aspects of the increasingly complex structure of Christian beliefs—in other words, Christians with different theological opinions who, according to the Second Letter of Peter (a late text), are like 'irrational animals... to be caught and killed' (2 Pet. 2: 12). While all of these groups were seen as belonging to the ultimately damned, it was an open question, in this respect, of how to assess those among the gentiles who had never heard the Gospel. Were they in a situation similar to the Jews who lived before Christ? Paul clearly sees them in similar need of the salvation offered in Christ (Rom. 1–3). But he also assumed that at least among Jews salvific faith was possible before Christ, as in the case of his foremost example: Abraham (cf. Rom. 4: 1–12; Gal. 6: 6). Would this possibility also hold for gentiles? Or were they in this respect in a disadvantaged position, as is suggested in Galatians 4: 8–9? The same question can also be raised in relation to the First Letter of John. While it states, unconditionally, that 'everyone who loves is born of God and knows God' because 'God is love' (1 John 4: 7–8), it also holds that 'every spirit that does not confess Jesus is not from God' (1 John 4: 3; see also 5: 12). While the first statement is probably close to Jesus' own faith in God's fatherly love, the second represents the growing exclusivism tying salvation and true knowledge of God to particular forms of Christian orthodoxy. One of the later scriptures of the New Testament keeps affirming that God 'desires everyone to be saved' (1 Tim. 2: 4). Yet this could either be read along the lines of an exclusivist particularism, that is, as a strong incitation to universal mission or, in line with universalism, as an affirmation of God's salvific activity among people of all nations.

Ecclesial Documents

From the Patristic Period to Modern Times

In terms of their reception, two axioms emerging in patristic theology became most influential: first, that seeds of the Divine Logos (*logoi spermatikoi*) can be found throughout the world and second, that there is no salvation outside the church (*extra ecclesiam nulla salus*).[13] These indicate two major divergent theological tendencies: a moderate form of inclusivism, acknowledging the existence of a salvific knowledge of the true God outside explicit Christianity; and a more or less harsh exclusivism confining salvation to those who hold (the 'correct') Christian beliefs. According to Justin Martyr (d. 165) in Jesus Christ the *logos*—the word of God—appeared in its fullness, while fragments or seeds of the *logos* have inspired some people at all times and places to live a god-fearing life. Without bearing this name, these people were 'Christians'. Thus Justin puts patriarchs from the 'Old Testament' (Abraham, Ananiah, Azariah, Mishael, and Elijah, for instance) on the same footing as Greek philosophers such as Heraclitus and Socrates (*1 Apology* 46). This model, versions of which are also found in the writings of Irenaeus (d. *c.*200), Clement of Alexandria (d. before 215), Origin (d. 250), Eusebius (d. 339), Ambrose (d. 397), and Augustine (354–450), involved not only a positive stance on the possible salvation of non-Christians, but enabled the church to draw as much on the Greek philosophical tradition as on the Hebrew Bible in constructing its theology.

The axiom of 'outside the church no salvation' emerged initially from debates among Christians. Having some earlier roots, it appears in its well-known form in the writings of Cyprian (d. 258) who uses it against Christian heretics and schismatics. From the fourth century onwards it is increasingly understood as also referring to those Jews and gentiles who did not become Christians. In the writings of some of the fathers there is, however, an ambiguity about the true borderlines of the church. In line with the theology of the *logoi spermatikoi* some—among them Augustine[14]—held that the church existed from the times of Abel onwards (*ecclesia ab Abel*) and included all Jews and gentiles who had lived in accordance with the *logos*. The true religion was therefore always there and it is only since the coming of Christ that it was identified as the Christian church. Yet when it came to the so-called heretics and schismatics the boundaries of the church were defined along narrow doctrinal lines. In the end, the idea that there is no salvation outside the 'church' in the sense of a particular community defined by its own specific doctrines and institutions predominated. Excluded from salvation were thus (*a*) 'heretics, schismatics' (that is, Christians with other beliefs, held to be false), (*b*) Jews (that is, Jews who had not become Christians), and (*c*) 'pagans' (that is, followers of 'other religions' but not yet perceived in terms of this modern category)—a triad which became standard, as in the following words of Fulgentius of Ruspe (468–533): 'Most firmly hold and by no means doubt, that not only all pagans, but also all Jews, and all heretics and schismatics who die outside the Catholic Church, will go to the eternal fire that was prepared for the devil and his angels.'[15] This view was confirmed by various high-profile

---

[13] See Francis A. Sullivan, *Salvation Outside the Church? Tracing the History of the Catholic Response* (Eugene, Or.: Wipf & Stock, 2002); cf. J. Dupuis, *Toward*, 53–129; Plantinga (ed.), *Christianity and Plurality*.

[14] Augustine, however, also held that there were non-Christians who did not live in accordance with that kind of limited revelation and, moreover, that the seeds of the logos were not given to all. He rejected the idea of a universal salvific will of God in favour of his theory of double predestination. 1 Tim. 2: 4 should thus be read in the sense that no one achieves salvation if God does not wish it. See Sullivan, *Salvation Outside*, 39.

[15] *De fide ad Petrum* 38, 79 (PL 65: 704), cited in Dupuis, *Toward*, 92.

magisterial pronouncements as for example at the Fourth Lateran Council (1215), in the papal bull *Unam Sanctam* (1302), and at the General Council of Florence (1442) which effectively echoes the words of Fulgentius in stating that all who remain outside the Catholic Church, pagans, Jews, heretics, and schismatics, will go to eternal damnation, *even if* they have shed their blood for Christ's name.

The leading figures of the Reformation took the same stance with the only difference being that, to them, the 'heretics and schismatics' were the Catholics. In his *Large Catechism* Luther confirmed that there is neither forgiveness nor holiness outside the Christian church and that '(t)hose who remain outside Christianity, be they heathen, Turks, Jews or false Christians, although they believe in only one true God, yet remain in eternal wrath and perdition.'[16] Any genuine knowledge of God that might exist among non-Christians was seen as insufficient for salvation and as the result of 'natural revelation' (God being recognized through the works of his creation, as in Rom. 1: 18–20). On the basis of the teaching of double-predestination Calvin concluded—like Fulgentius before him[17]—that those who never heard the Gospel do not belong to the divinely elect and are predestined to eternal damnation.[18] Accordingly, the Westminster Confession of 1646 declares that there is no way for the non-Christians to be saved (no. 10.4). Similarly the Anglican Thirty-Nine Articles of Faith reads, in Article 18, that salvation is only in the name of Jesus Christ.

Despite the fact that since the sixth century exclusivism had become Christianity's default position, there have been theological attempts to soften its harsh implication about the eternal damnation of all non-Christians. One such attempt was the view that all who died as unbaptized infants would not go to hell but to the limbo where they would enjoy a kind of natural fulfilment which is less than the supernatural bliss of heaven but certainly much better than hell. To this *limbo puerorum* ('limbo of the children') was added the *limbo patrum* ('limbo of the fathers') as the intermediary place of the Old Testament's patriarchs before their salvation by Christ (in his descent to 'hell'/limbo after the crucifixion) and as the final place for those upright non-Christians who had never heard the Gospel. However, the limbo never became a common view or part of the official teaching of the churches. Another attempt was the idea of the 'baptism by desire', meaning that the serious desire for baptism would count for baptism itself where the person died before the rite was carried out. This idea was sometimes extended to the view that one could impute an unconscious, implicit wish for baptism (*votum implicitum*) in the case of righteous non-Christians who had never heard the Gospel. The Council of Trent affirmed the efficacy of the desire of baptism (DS 1524), but

---

[16] Martin Luther, *Large Catechism*, tr. R. H. Fischer (Philadelphia: Fortress Press, 1959), point 2.3 (see also 2.45; 256).

[17] In line with the teaching of Augustine that God had predestined who would be saved and who would be damned, Fulgentius argued that those Jews and pagans who had never heard the Catholic faith are obviously among the damned. God simply does not want 'that all should be saved and come to the knowledge of the truth…he did not wish to save those to whom he denied the knowledge of the saving mystery'. See Dupuis, *Toward*, 92.

[18] Cf. John Calvin, *Institutes of the Christian Religion* II.6.1; III.21.5–7; III.24.12.

kept quiet on the question of an implicit desire.[19] It was only in 1949 that the magisterium of the Roman Catholic Church officially affirmed, against Leonard Feeney, that 'God also accepts an implicit desire'.[20]

Recent Declarations

After exclusivism having been the dominant Christian position for roughly one and a half millennia, things changed significantly in the twentieth century.[21] The first World Missionary Conference in Edinburgh 1910 was marked by a comparatively sympathetic approach to the non-Christian religions and an appreciation of whatever truth and goodness is found in other faiths as testimony to divine activity in them. The second World Missionary Conference in Jerusalem 1928 was quite specific in acknowledging

> that sense of Majesty of God and the consequent reverence in worship, which are conspicuous in Islam; the deep sympathy for the world's sorrow and unselfish search for the way of escape, which are at the heart of Buddhism; the desire for contact with ultimate reality conceived as spiritual in Hinduism; the belief in a moral order of the universe and consequent insistence on moral conduct which are inculcated by Confucianism.[22]

This anticipates the similarly specific statements in *Nostra Aetate*, the Second Vatican Council's 'Declaration on the Relation of the Church to the Non-Christian Religions' (1965), where the Roman Catholic Church mentions and acknowledges central insights and values in Hinduism, Buddhism, Islam, and Judaism, affirming that

> The Catholic Church rejects nothing that is true and holy in these religions. She regards with sincere reverence those ways of conduct and of life, those precepts and teachings which, though differing in many aspects from the ones she holds and sets forth, nonetheless often reflect a ray of that Truth which enlightens all men.[23]

The declarations of the first two Missionary Councils and of the Second Vatican Council display a return to the inclusivist patristic axiom of the universal presence of the seeds of the *logos* whose unique and full manifestation is found in Jesus Christ. What is strikingly new is the departure from the general designation of non-Christians as 'pagans' to a more differentiated perception of other religious traditions. This is, to a large extent, due to the much better

---

[19] See Sullivan, *Salvation Outside*, 83.

[20] Letter of the Holy Office to Archbishop Cushing (1949), Sullivan, *Salvation Outside*, 137.

[21] For an excellent survey and analysis of discussions within the ecumenical movement see Jan van Lin, *Shaking the Fundamentals. Religious Plurality and the Ecumenical Movement* (Amsterdam and New York: Rodopi, 2002). On the developments with the Roman Catholic Church see Dupuis, *Toward*, 130–79; and Sullivan, *Salvation*, 141–98. On positions of Anglicans, Free Churches, Pentecostal, and Evangelical movements see Kärkkäinen, *Introduction*, 123–50.

[22] From the conference declaration *The Christian Message*, cited in Van Lin, *Shaking*, 94.

[23] *Nostra Aetate* 2. See the official English text at the Vatican's website: <http://www.vatican.va/archive/hist_councils/ii_vatican_council>.

understanding of other faiths that has been gained through improved knowledge of and deepened contacts with them in the course of the later nineteenth and particularly twentieth century. Yet in accordance with the *logos* theology Jesus Christ—and thus Christianity—is understood as the fulfilment of any divinely produced elements in other faiths. This provokes two major questions which came to dominate the debates during the twentieth century. First, is God's activity among people of other faiths to be seen merely as a preparation for the Gospel—or is it in itself of a salvific nature? Second, is it necessary to understand Christianity in any case as the fulfilment of all other religions, or is there room for something like mutual fulfilment, for perceiving the different religions, including Christianity, with their specific strengths and weaknesses, as theologically on a par?

Even after a century of debate the World Council of Churches (WCC) has not come to a conclusive position in relation to the first question, largely due to contrary positions not only between but even more so within their various member churches.[24] The WCC's *Guidelines on Dialogue* (1979) deferred the question, if and how one could speak of God's work among all humankind, to the ongoing theological consideration that should take into account experiences from actual dialogue with non-Christians.[25] Ten years later, in 1989, the World Mission Conference of San Antonio did not come up with an answer but with an affirmation of the WCC's unsolved dilemma: 'We cannot point to any other way of salvation than Jesus Christ; at the same time we cannot set limits to the saving power of God.'[26] Subsequently official declarations tended to avoid the issue, focusing on more practical questions of interfaith dialogue and cooperation.[27]

In contrast, the Roman Catholic Church, since its repudiation of Feeney's views in 1949 and especially since the Second Vatican Council (1962–5), has clearly affirmed the possible salvation of non-Christians. What was, and to some extent still remains, unclear is whether the non-Christian religions themselves, or, more precisely, the 'rays of light' within them, make a positive contribution to this possibility. The 1991 document *Dialogue and Proclamation* declared that

> it will be in the sincere practice of what is good in their own religious traditions and by fol-
> lowing the dictates of their conscience that the members of other religions respond positively

---

[24] See Wesley Ariarajah, 'Power, Politics, and Plurality: The Struggles of the World Council of Churches to Deal with Religious Plurality', in Paul Knitter (ed.), *The Myth of Religious Superiority* (Maryknoll, NY: Orbis Books, 2005), 176–93.

[25] Cf. *Guidelines on Dialogue* (Geneva: WCC 1979), 20–3.

[26] Frederick R. Wilson (ed.), *The San Antonio Report. Your Will Be Done: Mission in Christ's Way* (Geneva: WCC 1990), 32–3.

[27] See e.g. *Ecumenical Considerations for Dialogue and Relations with People of Other Religions* (Geneva: WCC, 2004); Hans Ucko (ed.), *Changing the Present, Dreaming the Future: A Critical Moment in Interreligious Dialogue* (Geneva: WCC, 2006); *Christian Witness in a Multi-Religious World: Recommendations for Conduct* (Geneva: WCC, 2011). See also the Anglican document *Generous Love: The Truth of the Gospel and the Call to Dialogue. An Anglican Theology of Inter Faith Relations* (London: Anglican Consultative Council, 2008) and also *Guidelines for Inter Faith Encounter in the Churches of the Porvoo Communion* (2003), <http://nifcon.anglicancommunion.org/work/guidelines/docs/porvoo.cfm>.

to God's invitation and receive salvation in Jesus Christ, even while they do not recognize or acknowledge him as their savior...[28]

Nine years later, however, the Vatican declaration *Dominus Iesus* (2000) held that genuine 'faith is the acceptance in grace of revealed truth' and must not be identified with 'belief in other religions, which is religious experience still in search of the absolute truth and still lacking assent to God who reveals himself' (no. 7). How much this document reflects divergent and unreconciled tendencies within the Roman Catholic Church is apparent when, in one and the same paragraph (no. 21), it affirms that 'the various religious traditions contain and offer religious elements which come from God' and then continues that '(o)ne cannot attribute to these, however, a divine origin'.[29] Anyway, the main purpose of *Dominus Iesus* is the rejection of a pluralist theology of religions (see section 'Developing Christian Pluralism', p. 143f) which not only abandons exclusivist but also repudiates inclusivist forms of Christian superiority claims.[30]

A Christian pluralist approach to other religions was foreshadowed in 1932 by William E. Hocking's publication of the report *Re-Thinking Missions*. It demanded that the 'relation between religions must take increasingly hereafter the form of a common search for truth'[31] and spoke of 'mission' in the sense of mutual sharing, 'running in both directions, each teaching, each learning, each with the other meeting the unsolved problem of both'.[32] It expressed the bold vision that this process would transform all religions, being no longer divided without losing their distinct identities: 'The names which now separate them lose their divisive meaning; and there need be no loss of the historic thread of devotion which unites each to its own origins and inspirations.'[33] This, according to the report, would foster the coming of God's (universal) kingdom. The report provoked a wave of critical responses from exclusivist minded Christians.[34] Nevertheless, pluralist theologies, with their understanding of interfaith relations in terms of mutual enrichment and mutual fulfilment, returned in more elaborate forms during the last three decades of the twentieth century with the work of Wilfred Cantwell Smith (1916–2000), Raimon Panikkar (1918–2010), John Hick (1922–2012), and others. So far, their views have not entered any official church declarations, although they are constantly present in the debates about an adequate 'theology of religions' and have had a strong impact on many discussions within the World Council of Churches. Some testimony to this is that the statement of the WCC consultation of Baar in 1990 not only affirmed 'the saving presence of God' in other religions but also held that 'the plurality of religious traditions' is 'both the result of the manifold ways in which God has related to peoples and nations

---

[28] *Dialogue and Proclamation*, 29 (Rome: Pontifical Council for Interreligious Dialogue, 1991).

[29] *Dominus Iesus* (Vatican City, 2000).

[30] Cf. Perry Schmidt-Leukel, 'Exclusivism, Inclusivism, Pluralism', in Knitter, *Myth of Religious Superiority*, 28–42.

[31] William E. Hocking (ed.), *Re-thinking Missions: A Laymen's Inquiry After One Hundred Years* (New York and— London: Harper & Brothers, 1932), 47.

[32] Hocking, *Re-thinking Missions*, 46.

[33] Hocking (ed.), *Re-thinking Missions*, 58.   [34] See van Lin, *Shaking*, 134–48.

as well as a manifestation of the richness and diversity of humankind'. Such plurality should therefore not be seen 'as an obstacle to be overcome, but as an opportunity for deepening our encounter with God and with our neighbours'.[35] But, as noted, such statements did not become part of any of the WCC's official declarations.

2. ENCOUNTERING THE OTHER

A comprehensive discussion of Christianity's relation to the 'religious other' ought to include relations to indigenous religions, the Chinese traditions of Daoism and Confucianism,[36] smaller religions like Jainism and Zoroastrianism, newer religions like Sikhism or the Baha'i, and the large variety of new religious movements, and so on.[37] For our present purposes, which is geared to identifying and discussing typical attitudes adopted by Christians towards the religious 'other', the resources used in constructing these attitudes, and significant changes or developments in such attitudes more recently, I shall focus on the so-called 'world religions'. I will also include relations to other Christians for, traditionally, the 'religious other' was not understood by Christianity in terms of 'other religions' (which is a rather modern notion) but, as has been shown, in terms of the triad of 'false Christians, Jews and pagans', which functioned as the underlying paradigm. Islam, for example, was for a long time often perceived as a Christian heresy, not as a form of paganism or 'idolatry'. 'Idolatry' and 'idolaters' were notions applied, during the Middle Ages, to Buddhism and later to Hinduism. Judaism too was not perceived as a different religion either, but as the people of the covenant that had rejected its Messiah. Today the Roman Catholic Church still subsumes its dialogue with Judaism under the rubric of ecumenical, rather than interreligious, relations.[38]

Relations among Christians

The idea that in the beginning there was one genuine, orthodox Christian community from which all others diverged as heretics or schismatics is an ideological *post-facto* reading of the

---

[35] All quotations are from 'Religious Plurality: Theological Perspectives and Affirmations', section II. See *Current Dialogue*, 19 (1991), 47–51.

[36] This is partly covered in J. Gentz and P. Schmidt-Leukel (eds), *Religious Diversity in Chinese Thought* (Basingstoke and New York: Palgrave Macmillan, 2013).

[37] See: Alan Race & Paul Hedges (eds), *Christian Approaches to Other Faiths* (London: SCM, 2008); Charles Wei-hsun Fu and Gerhard E. Spiegler (eds), *Religious Issues and Interreligious Dialogues* (New York: Greenwood Press, 1989).

[38] The Commission of the Holy See for Religious Relations with the Jews works under the aegis of the Pontifical Council for Promoting Christian Unity, not the Pontifical Council for Interreligious Dialogue.

historical reality. The New Testament itself gives evidence that Christianity has been diverse from its inception. There have always been different 'orthodoxies' and different Christians accusing each other as false believers. The formulation of the major creeds was usually accompanied by splits between those who accepted and those who rejected the respective propositions. Smaller 'sectarian' groups often became the victims of brutal persecution by the larger ecclesial institutions, while splits between major groups partly led to long-lasting wars, in particular those following the sixteenth-century Reformation in the West. Such division created an internal 'othering' within the Christian family, so to speak.

Against the long and sanguinary history of intra-Christian conflicts, the rise of the ecumenical movement from early in the twentieth century is comparatively new.[39] The First World Missionary Conference in Edinburgh 1910, where a clear shift in the Christian perception of the religious other became manifest, is usually also identified as the hour of birth of the modern ecumenical movement. It was apparently the same spirit that led Christians to a more sympathetic understanding of each other and of what was now perceived as the 'non-Christian religions'. In the course of the twentieth century the ecumenical movement led to startling developments as, for example, the establishment of the World Council of Churches in 1948 or of many National Christian Councils around the world. A number of churches, particularly among the churches of the Reformation and the Anglican Communion, have entered into full or partial forms of ecclesial communion. With the Second Vatican Council the Roman Catholic Church also committed itself to ecumenism. In 1965 Pope Paul VI and the Ecumenical Patriarch Athenagoras I revoked the mutual anathemas of the great schism of 1054 (without, however, reintroducing full communion). Today, ecumenical dialogues between different Christian denominations are entertained on a regular basis. Some of these dialogues have led to results which would have been unthinkable in preceding centuries as, for example, the *Joint Declaration on the Doctrine of Justification* signed by the Roman Catholic Church and the churches of the Lutheran World Federation in 1999, in which it was agreed that the mutual condemnations of the past do not apply to the self-understanding of the Catholic and Lutheran teachings on justification.

The goal of Christian ecumenism is not just improved relationships, but to visibly express the unity among those who believe in Jesus Christ. Some churches identify the true expression of this unity exclusively with the institutional structures and teachings of their own church. From this perspective the ultimate goal of ecumenism is to unite all under one's own umbrella. Such an inclusivist view acknowledges merely the existence of ecclesial elements or fragments in other Christian denominations. Some other churches, however, have become open to the pluralist idea that the universal church must not be identified with one particular church but exists in a community of churches with legitimate and mutually enriching differences.

---

[39] See Ruth Rouse and Stephen Charles Neill (eds), *A History of the Ecumenical Movement 1517–1948* (Philadelphia: Westminster Press, 1954); Harold E. Fey (ed.), *The Ecumenical Advance: A History of the Ecumenical Movement*, ii. *1948–1968* (London: SPCK, 1970); John Briggs, Mercy Amba Oduyoye, and Georges Tsetsis (eds), *A History of the Ecumenical Movement*, iii. *1968–2000* (Geneva: WCC, 2004).

Christian–Jewish Relations

The rise of Christian anti-Judaism is already evident in parts of the New Testament. As Rosemary Ruether argues, anti-Judaism has been the 'other side' of christology, that is, the Christian confession of Jesus as the 'Christ' ('Messiah') implied and produced the rejection of those Jews who felt unable to agree. This fundamental tension increased considerably with the claim that the messianic promises had found their initial fulfilment in the Christian church.[40] This triggered a number of theological propositions which became standard in the *Adversus Judaeos* ('Against the Jews') literature of the patristic period and determined the Christian attitude to Judaism for more than one and a half millennia:[41] (1) The Jews rejected their Messiah and murdered the Son of God; (2) all suffering of the Jews is therefore a just divine punishment; (3) only the church understands the scriptures of the 'Old Testament' as these point to Jesus; (4) as the 'true Israel' the church replaces Israel; (5) there is no theological value in the continued existence of a Jewish Israel.[42] Anti-Jewish theology turned into anti-Jewish practice[43] when Christianity was privileged under Constantine (272–337) and declared a state cult under Theodosius (347–95). Laws made Jewish life increasingly difficult. From the fifth century on, Jews become frequently the victims of Christian pogroms, forced conversions or expulsion. During the crusades (eleventh–thirteenth centuries), Jewish communities were regularly vandalized by Christian armies. From the twelfth century on, Jews were more and more socially excluded and ghettoized. While their living conditions in Muslim Spain were comparatively much better, this changed dramatically with the *reconquista* and the subsequent introduction of the Spanish inquisition, which was primarily directed against forcefully baptized Jews and Muslims who in secret still observed their old religion. In sixteenth-century Spain, procedures were introduced by which Catholics had to prove their 'purity of the blood' (*limpieza de sangre*), that is, their non-Jewish descent. Christian anti-Judaism thus began to develop into racial anti-Semitism, finally culminating in the atrocities of the Holocaust: 'The racist anti-Semitism which reached its climax of terrorism in the Holocaust would not have been possible without the prehistory of the religious anti-Judaism of the Christian church extending over almost two thousand years.'[44]

Such insights into the connection between Christian anti-Judaism and the Holocaust have contributed decisively to the change in Christian attitudes to Judaism in the years after the Second World War. At the centre of a number of ecclesial documents are unambiguous condemnations of anti-Semitism accompanied by various attempts to overcome the traditional theology of replacement. The latter, however, are not always equally unambiguous. A good example of a remaining tension is the Vatican declaration *Nostra Aetate* which states: 'Although

---

[40] Rosemary Ruether, *Faith and Fratricide: The Theological Roots of Anti-Semitism* (New York: Seabury Press, 1974), esp. 246–51.

[41] Cf. Ruether, *Faith and Fratricide*, 117–82.

[42] According to Augustine, the only reason to let Jews exist is to have them as witnesses to the authenticity of the 'Old Testament'.

[43] See Dan Cohn-Sherbok, *The Crucified Jew: Twenty Centuries of Christian Anti-Semitism* (London: HarperCollins, 1992); Edward H. Flannery, *The Anguish of the Jews. Twenty-Three Centuries of Antisemitism* (New York: Paulist Press, 2004).

[44] Hans Küng, *Judaism* (London: SCM Press, 1992), 236.

the Church is the new people of God, the Jews should not be presented as rejected or accursed by God'.[45] Today, many churches are inclined to admit that God's covenant with Israel has never been revoked, but are less clear when it comes to the question of whether Judaism constitutes an autonomous and equally valid path of salvation. *Nostra Aetate* upholds the church's 'burden...to proclaim the cross of Christ...as the fountain from which every grace flows'. Yet, with *Nostra Aetate* the Roman Catholic Church, like many other churches,[46] committed itself to the goal of 'mutual understanding' and 'fraternal dialogue'. In this respect the declaration functioned as a watershed in Christian–Jewish relations.[47] The Jewish declaration *Dabru Emet*, published on 10 September 2000, acknowledged that '(i)n recent years, there has been a dramatic and unprecedented shift in Jewish and Christian relations'.[48] *Dabru Emet* could even declare that 'Jews and Christians worship the same God'—something that has often been doubted on both sides due to the trinitarian concept of God. Today Christians have begun to take Judaism—not just pre-Christian, but post-Christian, rabbinic Judaism— seriously as a religion in its own right and to strip off traditional prejudices and distortions. However, the crucial question, so clearly raised by Rosemary Ruether four decades ago, of how to confess Jesus as the Christ without any anti-Jewish implications, has not yet found a common Christian answer. For any such answer would imply the admission that a Jewish rejection of this confession may be as justified as its Christian affirmation.[49]

Christian–Muslim Relations

The history of Christian–Muslim encounter is, according to Ludwig Hagemann,

> for the most part a fatal history of polemics and apologetics, of aggression and despair. It had its periods of cultural fertilisation and religious understanding—particularly in some regions of Spain when they were under Muslim rule—but for the most part these are strongly outweighed by competition and confrontation, conquest and reconquest, wars and campaigns, massacres and carnages. Indeed, the history of Christian–Muslim relations is soaked with blood.[50]

Since its inception, Islam spread rapidly in northern, eastern, and western directions and after just one century almost one-third of the Christian world had become part of the Muslim empire. Under Muslim rule, Christians, like Jews, could live as a 'protected community' (*dhimmī*), but were excluded from a number of rights and not permitted to engage in

---

[45] *Nostra Aetate*, clause 4.

[46] Cf. *The Theology of the Churches and the Jewish People: Statements by the World Council of Churches and its Member Churches* (Geneva: WCC, 1988).

[47] Cf. Neville Lamdan and Alberto Melloni (eds), *Nostra Aetate: Origins, Promulgation, Impact on Jewish–Catholic Relations* (Münster & Berlin: LIT Verlag, 2007).

[48] See *Dabru Emet* at <http://www.archden.org/Interreligious/DabruEmet.pdf>.

[49] See E. Kessler, J. T. Pawlikowski, and J. Banki (eds), *Jews and Christians in Conversation* (Cambridge: Orchard Academic, 2002).

[50] Ludwig Hagemann, *Christentum contra Islam: Eine Geschichte gescheiterter Beziehungen* (Darmstadt: Wissenschaftliche Buchgesellschaft, 1999), p. ix (my tr.). See also Hans Küng, *Islam: Past, Present and Future* (Oxford: OneWorld, 2007); J. M. Gaudeul, *Encounters and Clashes: Islam and Christianity in History*, 2 vols. (Rome: Pontificio Istituto di Studi Arabi e d'Islamistica, 2000).

missionary activities. In formerly Christian regions like Armenia, Syria, and Egypt, Christianity gradually shrank to small minorities or disappeared entirely, which was the case in most of North Africa. Since the eleventh century Christian countries succeeded in gradually reconquering Sicily and Spain. The crusaders' armies penetrated into Muslim areas and established for about one hundred years a Christian kingdom in Palestine. From the fourteenth century Islam predominated over Turkey and Greece, as well as the Balkans. In 1453, with the emergence of the Ottoman Empire, Constantinople fell to Muslim rule. In 1529 and again in 1683 Ottoman Muslim troops appeared at the gates of Vienna. In the seventeenth century, after Islam had reached its zenith in territorial expansion, Western Christian nations began to conquer various Islamic countries in the course of their colonial expansion. Just four Muslim nations (Turkey, Iran, Afghanistan, and Saudi Arabia) escaped formal colonization. It is only since the middle of the twentieth century that many Muslim countries have been able to regain their independence. Anti-colonial resentments and the shock of Western colonization still shape much of the current Islamic attitude towards Christianity and the West, while on the Christian side the recovery and resurgence of Islamic nations in post-colonial times have revived deep-seated feelings of a Muslim threat.

The political history of conquest and reconquest mirrors in a sense the theological situation of mutual supersessionism.[51] As much as Christianity sees the divine revelation in Jesus Christ as the climax and fulfilment of God's work in human history, Islam traditionally understands the divine revelation in the Qur'an as surpassing—and in the eyes of many Muslims also replacing—all previous forms of revelation. In Islam Christianity encounters theological claims in relation to itself, which resemble its own traditional claims in relation to Judaism. In the past, theological exchange between Christianity and Islam abounded with harsh polemics and counter-polemics. This has changed to a considerable extent in the second half of the twentieth century. Once more the commitment of the World Council of Churches and of the Roman Catholic Church to interfaith dialogue made a significant contribution to this new climate. The first official dialogue between Christians and Muslims under the auspices of the WCC took place in 1968, followed by numerous dialogical meetings in subsequent years, regularly also involving Roman Catholic participants.[52] The Vatican had set up a commission for Religious Relations with Muslims in 1974 and the Pontifical Council for Interreligious Dialogue started its own official dialogues with Muslims in 1989.[53] Orthodox churches have

---

[51]   See Y. Y. Haddad and W. Z. Haddad (eds), *Christian–Muslim Encounters* (Gainesville, Fla.: University Press of Florida, 1995); Hugh Goddard, *Christians and Muslims: From Double Standards to Mutual Understanding* (Richmond, Surrey: Curzon 1995).

[52]   See Jutta Sperber, *Christians and Muslims: The Dialogue Activities of the World Council of Churches and their Theological Foundation* (Berlin &New York: De Gruyter, 2000); Stuart Brown (ed.), *Meeting in Faith: Twenty Years of Christian–Muslim Conversations Sponsored by the World Council of Churches* (Geneva: WCC, 1989); Douglas Pratt, *The Church and Other Faiths* (Bern: Peter Lang, 2010).

[53]   Cf. Michael Fitzgerald & John Borelli, *Interfaith Dialogue: A Catholic View* (Maryknoll, NY: Orbis Books, 2006), 85–159; Risto Jukko, *Trinity in Unity in Christian–Muslim Relations: The Work of the Pontifical Council for Interreligious Dialogue* (Leiden and Boston: Brill, 2007).

not only been involved in the dialogues of the WCC but also started their own series of dialogues in 1986, particularly under the Ecumenical Patriarchate of Constantinople.[54] Another significant initiative is Building Bridges, a series of annual Christian–Muslim dialogues under the auspices of the Anglican Archbishop of Canterbury, which began in 2002.[55]

Theologically, the key issue is whether Christians and Muslims relate to the same God. While on the Roman Catholic side Pope John Paul II on several occasions answered this in the positive,[56] within the dialogues of the WCC it has never been unambiguously affirmed and at times even been denied by some member churches.[57] That Muslims and Christians have different concepts of God is undisputed and is not the primary reason for Christians' reluctant attitude. Differences about the nature of God (trinitarian or non-trinitarian) and the status of Jesus (divine or not-divine) also apply to Christian and Jewish understandings of God. Nevertheless, Christians find it easier to affirm that Jews and Christians relate to the same God because of the Biblical testimony that the God of Israel is also the God of Jesus. Islam draws on the same tradition, claiming that all three, Jews, Christians, and Muslims, relate to the one God of Abraham. But Islam claims this not on the basis of the Bible but its own scripture, the Qur'an. For Christians to accept the Qur'an as a genuine theological source would implicitly acknowledge the prophetic status of Muhammad, which is inevitable if Christians, in effect, identify the God of Islam with their own God.

Thus there are two mutually closed and opposed hermeneutical circles: if it is the same God, Muhammad had a prophetic role (leading countless people to the true God) and the Qur'an reflects genuine revelation and the Qur'an would thus rightly support the view that the Abrahamic traditions all *relate* to the same God. But, if it is not the same God, Muhammad is a false prophet, and the Qur'an is not a revealed scripture as such and is thus illegitimately sustaining the view that the god of the Qur'an is the same as the God of the Biblical tradition. The position of Christians would become less unambiguous if they admitted a true prophetic function of Muhammad, but in this respect they are—at least on the level of official statements—even more reluctant than in affirming the sameness of God, which inevitably also raises doubts about the seriousness of this latter affirmation. Christian silence about the prophetic status of Muhammad is thus 'to the continuing disappointment...of many Muslims'.[58]

In 2007, 138 Muslim leaders and scholars launched *A Common Word*, an open letter to the leaders of the Christian churches, suggesting that love of God and love of neighbour are central to both communities and form a common basis for peaceful relationships. One background to this initiative is the explicit fear of a Christian–Muslim conflict of an

---

[54] See Andrew Martin Sharp, *Eastern Orthodox Theological and Ecclesiological Thought on Islam and Christian–Muslim Relations in the Contemporary World (1975–2008)* (Leiden: Brill, 2012).

[55] See <http://berkleycenter.georgetown.edu/resources/networks/building_bridges>.

[56] Cf. Jukko, *Trinity in Unity*, 272; Fitzgerald & Borelli, *Interfaith Dialogue*, 119ff.

[57] Sperber, *Christians and Muslims*, 109, 321.

[58] Fitzgerald and Borelli, *Interfaith Dialogue*, 115; see also, from a Muslim perspective, Mahmut Aydin, *Modern Western Christian Theological Understanding of Muslims since the Second Vatican Council* (Washington, DC: Council for Research in Values and Philosophy, 2002), 169ff.

unprecedented, potentially global dimension.[59] Many church leaders and individual Christians replied positively to this extended Muslim hand.[60] Yet whether it will become 'a historic watershed' in the relations between both traditions remains to be seen.[61]

Christian–Hindu Relations

Although Christians have been present in South India since the first half of the first millennium,[62] we do not have much information about Hindu–Christian relations in pre-colonial times. It would appear that early Syrian Christians ('St Thomas Christians') had integrated themselves into the Indian social structure as a kind of caste and coexisted without too much conflict. This changed when the Catholic Portuguese conquered Goa in 1510, by then under Muslim rule. In subsequent decades all mosques and Hindu temples in the region of Goa were destroyed. In 1567 'pagan' and Muslim practices were made illegal. On the suggestion of Francis Xavier the inquisition was introduced in order to identify those who had only nominally converted to Christianity, following the model of the Spanish inquisition. St Thomas Christians now, too, became victims of Roman Catholic repression. From the seventeenth century on, British, Dutch, and French trading companies undertook activities in India, including the establishment of military bases. In the eighteenth century Britain became the dominant power and in 1858 India was formally made part of the British Empire. Under British rule Christian missionary activities grew considerably. Two major approaches in the missionaries' attitude emerged, reflecting the two basic models of the patristic period: an exclusivist one, which considered all Indian forms of religion as idolatrous or even demonic, and an inclusivist approach, which acknowledged certain elements of truth but proclaimed Christ and Christianity as the fulfilment of everything good in the Indian religions. Both approaches nevertheless converge in their ideal and practical goal of ultimately replacing Hinduism with Christianity.[63]

The political dominance and the claimed religious superiority of the West provoked the strong reaction of the so-called Neo-Hindu movement in the nineteenth and early twentieth centuries. It combined the two motives of anti-colonial striving for independence and an anti-missionary striving for a revival and reform of 'Hinduism'. The concept of 'Hinduism' as a religion on its own, encompassing all the various religious traditions and cults that had emerged in India from early Vedic roots, is to a large extent a construct of this movement. Neo-Hinduism

[59] See HRH Prince Ghazi bin Muhammad of Jordan, 'On "A Common Word"', in Ghazi bin Muhammad, M. Volf and M. Yarrington (eds), *A Common Word: Muslims and Christians on Loving God and Neighbor* (Grand Rapids, Mich.: Eerdmans, 2010), 3–17, 7–8.
[60] See <www.acommonword.com>.
[61] Miroslav Volf, 'A Common Word for a Common Future', in Muhammad *et al.*, *A Common Word*, 27.
[62] According to an old legend Christianity was brought to India by the apostle Thomas. Historical evidence for a Christian presence dates from the 6th cent.
[63] Cf. Eric J. Sharpe, *Faith Meets Faith: Some Christian Attitudes to Hinduism in the Nineteenth and Twentieth Centuries* (London: SCM Press, 1977).

replied to the challenge of the Christian mission by its own versions of exclusivism and inclusivism, claiming that Hinduism is rationally and spiritually far more advanced than Christianity. Frequently Neo-Hindu thinkers adopted a rather appreciative attitude to the figure of Jesus[64] but held that Hindu concepts of incarnation (*avatāra*) provide a better framework for understanding his true meaning than the traditional doctrines of Christianity.

In the second half of the twentieth century, after Indian independence, the situation changed in two ways. On the Christian side, a genuine interest in serious dialogue and in spiritual exchange with Hindus became stronger than ever before,[65] while on the Hindu side, in the wake of the nationalist Hindutva movement, anti-Christian resentments are steadily on the rise, suspecting Christian dialogue efforts as just a new missionary strategy.[66] The Christian interest in dialogue with Hinduism emerged from the wish to develop a better inculturated form of Indian Christianity. This, it was understood, cannot be achieved without allowing Christianity to be challenged and eventually transformed by the intellectually powerful theological and philosophical systems of the Hindu tradition and letting Christian spiritual practice be enriched and transformed by Hinduism's large reservoir of contemplative and devotional experience.[67] In addition, many Christians seek to make a contribution to the modernization of the Indian society, particularly in overcoming the inequalities of the caste system. The latter aspect, however, contributes to the difficulties of Hindu–Christian dialogue in so far as this is denounced by Christian critics as a dialogue with the 'oppressors',[68] while members of the Hindutva movement interpret Christian social commitment as an attempt to exploit social issues in order to gain converts.

Christian–Buddhist Relations

The Buddha is first mentioned in Christian writings of Clement of Alexandria (150?–215?) and Jerome (382–420), but we have no evidence that their rather faint awareness of Buddhism was built on any direct contact.[69] Buddhists and Christians probably met first in Central Asia

---

[64] A notable exception to this is Dayananda Saraswaty (1824–83), the founder of the influential *Arya Samaj*.

[65] See Wesley Ariarajah, *Hindus and Christians: A Century of Protestant Ecumenical Thought* (Amsterdam: Rodopi; Grand Rapids, Mich.: Eerdmans, 1991); Jose Kuttianimattathil, *Practice and Theology of Interreligious Dialogue: A Critical Study of the Indian Christian Attempts since Vatican II* (Bangalore: Kristu Jyoti Publication, 1995).

[66] See Sita Ram Goel, *History of Hindu–Christian Encounters AD 304 to 1996* (New Delhi: Voice of India, 1996): 'Hindus are committing a great mistake in regarding the encounter between Hinduism and Christianity as a dialogue between two religions. Christianity has never been a religion; it has always been a predatory imperialism par excellence. The encounter, therefore, should be viewed as a battle between two totally opposed and mutually exclusive ways of thought and behaviour ... as war between the Vedic and the Biblical traditions.' Preface, p. v.

[67] See Harold Coward (ed.), *Hindu–Christian Dialogue: Perspective and Encounters* (Maryknoll, NY: Orbis Books, 1989); Ariasusai Dhavamony, *Hindu–Christian Dialogue: Theological Soundings and Perspectives* (Amsterdam and New York: Rodopi, 2002). See also the *Journal of Hindu-Christian Studies*.

[68] Wesley Ariarajah, *Not without my Neighbour: Issues in Interfaith Relations* (Geneva: WCC, 1999), 79ff.

[69] See David Scott, 'Christian Responses to Buddhism in Pre-Medieval Times', *Numen*, 32/1 (1985), 88–100. See also Wilhelm Halbfass, *India and Europe* (Albany, NY: SUNY, 1988), Paul Ingram, *The Modern Buddhist–Christian*

and China during the seventh and eighth centuries. The Syrian ('Nestorian') Christians presented their Christian beliefs in a way strongly adapted to the conceptuality and spirituality of Buddhism and Daoism and at the same time demonstrated a sometimes startling acknowledgement of God's presence in these faiths.[70] Apart from a few missionaries and adventurers, like William of Rubruck (thirteenth century) or Marco Polo (thirteenth–fourteenth centuries), who found their way to Buddhist countries during the Middle Ages, the next phase of encounter came with Western colonialism, when the Portuguese spread to Sri Lanka, China, and Japan (sixteenth century). The aggressive and highly polemical attitude of Christian missionaries led to serious conflicts in all three areas. In Sri Lanka, a Portuguese colony was established and Buddhists became victims of persecution and expulsion. While in China anti-Christian measures remained comparatively mild, the Japanese rulers of the seventeenth century carried out one of the fiercest persecutions of Christianity ever, leading to the seclusion of the country for more than two hundred years. Yet Japan aside, almost all other Buddhist countries became subject to Western colonization over subsequent centuries. After the Portuguese, the Dutch ruled over parts of Sri Lanka (seventeenth–eighteenth centuries) and were followed in the nineteenth and twentieth centuries by the British, who also conquered Burma and extended their influence over Thailand. France set up its rule over Vietnam, Laos, and Cambodia. China had to endure the presence of British, Portuguese, French, German, and Russian forces. Japan—following the expansionist politics of the West—extended its rule over Korea and parts of China. In the nineteenth century, as a side effect of colonial rule, Buddhist texts became known in the West and attracted converts. Initially Buddhism established itself in Europe without the presence of Asian Buddhists, while in the USA Buddhism was brought by Asian immigrants (often via Hawaii). In Asia, Christianity was often associated with Western imperialism[71] and Buddhism reconstructed as an anti-Christian force serving Asian national interests. In Japan, Christianity met with a renewed open curiosity, but nowhere in Asian Buddhist countries was Christian mission particularly successful, apart from Korea where today the number of Christians comes close to those of the Buddhists. In part, this may be due to the fact that Korea had not suffered domination by a Christian but by a Buddhist colonial power, so that Christians in Korea could present themselves as loyal defenders of Korean self-esteem and independence. In the West, converts usually embraced Buddhism as it was felt to be a more rational and humane non-theistic alternative to Christianity.

Buddhist–Christian dialogue developed primarily after the Second World War. In South-East and South Asian countries, Christians engaged in dialogue because they wanted to

Dialogue: Two Universalistic Religions in Transformation (Lewiston, NY: Edwin Mellen Press, 1988), 2–23; Ninian Smart, *Buddhism and Christianity* (Basingstoke: Macmillan, 1993); Whalen Lai and Michael von Brück, *Christianity and Buddhism* (Maryknoll, NY: Orbis Books, 2001). See also the two international journals dedicated to Buddhist-Christian dialogue: *Buddhist Christian Studies* (University of Hawaii Press) and *Dialogue* (Ecumenical Institute, Colombo).

[70] See Scott, 'Christian Responses'; Martin Palmer, *The Jesus Sutras* (London: Piatkus, 2001).

[71] As the Sri Lankan Buddhist reformist, Anagarika Dharmapala, stated in 1924 (see Ananda Guruge (ed.), *Return to Righteousness*, 439), 'Christianity is a political camouflage. Its three aspects are politics, trade and imperial expansion. Its weapons are the Bible, barrels of whisky and bullets.'

distance themselves from such forms of Christian evangelism as were closely tied to Western colonialism. In Japan, Christian missionaries were interested in adapting to the Japanese culture in order to find better ways of communicating the Gospel. This was also the initial reason why some Christians started to learn Zen meditation. Japanese intellectuals began to study Christianity because they were interested in understanding the connection between the successful technological development of Western countries and its philosophical and religious traditions. In the West, dialogue is often between Christians and Western converts to Buddhism, usually from a kind of comparative perspective in order to arrive at a better understanding of the doctrinal relationship between the two traditions. In China, Buddhist–Christian dialogue is still in its infancy but seems to be developing in the wake of the gradual process of political liberalization.[72] From a theological point of view, one of the key issues in Buddhist–Christian dialogue is still how to interpret Buddhism's non-theistic nature. Is this a form of atheism similar to Western rationalist and materialist atheisms, or is it more an expression of a radically apophatic form of spirituality similar to certain types of Western mysticism? If the former, any commonalities would be reduced to some basic moral values, while the latter allows for the possibility of common roots in the same ultimate reality.

3. Reconstructing Self and Other

Defending Christian Exclusivism

As has been shown, the 'religious other'—those 'outside the church'—was for a long time construed as the triad of 'pagans, Jews and false Christians'. Any theological assessment of them was not that much informed by their specific beliefs and practices but by the fact that they did not share the normative Christian creeds. The otherness of the 'other' was not relevant in terms of the others' own particularity but merely in terms of the general aspect of being different—of simply being 'other'—as such. This a priori perspective has become increasingly challenged through both a better knowledge and understanding of the other and a self-critical reflection on the overall fateful and violent history of Christianity's relation to religious others. Exclusivism, which was Christianity's default position for about one and a half millennia, has thus come under most pressure.

It is undeniable that in the past there was a close connection of acts of intolerant and violent treatment of other Christians and non-Christians with an exclusivist theology that not only denied any positive salvific role to other forms of faith but was also convinced that such forms would lead adherents to eternal damnation. The use of violence appeared to be morally justified, even obligatory, if it served the purpose of protecting one's neighbour from the worst of all evils: hell. Contemporary Christian exclusivists, however, deny any intrinsic

---

[72] This is largely documented in the New Series of *Ching Feng: A Journal on Christianity and Chinese Religion and Culture* publ. by the Christian Study Centre on Chinese Religion and Culture, Hong Kong.

connection between religious intolerance or violence with their exclusivist theology. They insist that the ideal of converting the whole world to Christ can and must be carried out without means of force. That this 'ideal' in itself is perceived by members of other religious traditions as a serious threat is countered by the argument that the right to convert is part of religious freedom.

Looking at the specifics of religious others, exclusivists tend to emphasize the differences from Christianity[73] and downplay any commonalities.[74] Karl Barth, a major exclusivist theologian of the twentieth century, combines both strategies in postulating a radical discontinuity between God's revelation and all forms of religion (including Christianity qua religion) as human phenomena. That is, all commonalities between Christianity and other faiths are relegated to the level of 'religion' while at the same time these commonalities are declared as irrelevant because the only thing to decide the 'truth and falsehood between the religions' ('über Wahrheit und Lüge zwischen den Religionen') is the name Jesus Christ, 'in the entirely formal simplicity of this name' ('in der ganzen formalen Simplizität dieses Namens').[75] A postmodern version of Barth's position can be found in George Lindbeck's exclusivism. For Lindbeck there are no genuine but only apparent commonalities, because religions form autonomous and categorically incommensurable language games. What may appear as the same element in two or more religions is in fact radically different because it operates as part of different 'games'. For example, whatever charitable work a Buddhist does, it is, according to Lindbeck, never the same as Christian *agape* because it is not done in the name of Jesus Christ.[76] Yet how convincing is this construal? In response to Lindbeck one wonders how it could apply to Jesus' parable of the Good Samaritan whom Jesus obviously used as an example of *agape* despite the fact that the Samaritan did not act in the name of Jesus Christ. Lindbeck's neo-Barthian and somewhat Wittgensteinian defence of Christian exclusivism can hardly persuade.

One major problem of exclusivism has always been the question of how it coheres with the faith in a God of boundless love who 'desires everyone to be saved' (1 Tim. 2: 4). The answers of contemporary exclusivists differ. Some exclusivists, like Daniel Strange, deny that a universal salvific will of God really exists.[77] In line with the Augustinian-Calvinist teaching of double predestination such exclusivists hold that only a minority has been elected by God to be saved. This solution does certainly provide exclusivism with coherence, yet at the price of sacrificing faith in a God who equally cares for all his creatures. Other exclusivists find that price too high to be paid. Some of them, like William Lane Craig, speculate that God, even if he wishes so, cannot guarantee the salvation of all, because of human freedom. Nevertheless

---

[73] See e.g. Harold Netland, *Dissonant Voices: Religious Pluralism and the Question of Truth* (Grand Rapids, Mich.: Eerdmans, 1991).

[74] Previously, the standard explanations of parallels between Christianity and other faiths had been demonic imitation (*imitation diabolica*) or, as in case of the Greek religions, borrowing from the Hebrew Bible.

[75] Karl Barth, *Die Kirchliche Dogmatik*, I/2 (Zollikon-Zürich: Evangelischer Verlag, 1960), 376.

[76] See George Lindbeck, *The Nature of Doctrine* (Philadelphia: Westminster Press, 1984), 40, 60–1.

[77] See Daniel Strange, *The Possibility of Salvation Among the Unevangelised* (Carlisle: Paternoster Press, 2002), 284–5, 307–10.

God did create those of whom he knew that they would never freely accept his grace, because their creation served as a means to bring about the greatest number of those who would accept, while at the same time achieving the optimal ratio between those who are and those who are not saved.[78] Even this speculation, however, fails to explain why all non-Christians should belong to those who God cannot save, given that the 'Old Testament' speaks of non-Christians who obviously are believed to be saved.[79] Other exclusivists accept that individual non-Christians might be saved (e.g. by their alleged 'implicit desire'—*votum implicitum*—for baptism, or by some form of post-mortem encounter with Christ), while yet other exclusivists deliberately refrain from answering the question of a possible salvation of non-Christians. So while exclusivists differ on the issue of the salvation of individual non-Christians, all forms of exclusivism have in common that they deny any positive salvific role of the non-Christian religions (or, as with intra-Christian exclusivism, even of other forms of Christianity). This is the main point on which exclusivism differs from inclusivism.

Rediscovering and Adjusting Christian Inclusivism

One of the most influential inclusivist theologies of the twentieth century is Karl Rahner's theory of 'anonymous Christianity', which revitalizes some prominent features of the patristic *logos* theology. According to Rahner, God's universal salvific will encompasses every human being, so that God is in fact gracefully present to all. To the extent that non-Christians respond positively to God's grace by acts of faith, hope, and love they are anonymous Christians. Due to the unique incarnation of God's word in Christ, divine grace has found its clearest expression in the Christian church. Yet the faith of others is not without its own forms of expression of this grace, though less clear (and only implicitly Christian). Other religions entail a 'searching christology', an expectation of an absolute saviour or mediator between God and man, whom only Christians rightly identify as Jesus Christ. Hence Christianity alone is the absolute religion, but non-Christian religions may function as paths of salvation for their adherents as long as these have not yet come to a clear and full recognition of Christ as the absolute saviour.

While exclusivists criticize Rahner as undermining the need for Christian mission, another frequent criticism is that his approach does not do sufficient justice to the differences between Christianity and other faiths. What point is there in labelling as 'anonymous Christians' those who just want to be Jews, Muslims, Hindus, Buddhists, etc.? Against the first objection Rahner emphasizes that the chance of salvation is higher within Christianity (because of its explicit knowledge of Christ as the supreme revelation) so that it still makes sense to bring the Gospel to all. On the second objection Rahner replies that this 'labelling' serves only the intra-Christian purpose of identifying the elements of truth in other religions as related to

---

[78] William Lane Craig, ' "No Other Name": A Middle Knowledge Perspective on the Exclusivity of Salvation through Christ', *Faith and Philosophy*, 6 (1989), 172–88.

[79] See Craig, 'No Other Name', 176, 186.

the divine *logos* which appeared in Christ. In a similar way, according to Rahner, a Roman Catholic who genuinely believes that his church is the one true Church, the Roman Catholic Church will and can appreciate other Christian denominations only by seeing them as 'anonymous Catholics'.[80] This, however, provokes the even stronger objection whether the assumption of such an inner orientation towards Christianity or even Roman Catholicism can do any justice to the particularities of other faiths.

According to Mark Heim, members of other religions who faithfully follow their own traditions cannot be understood, in the sense of Rahner, as being oriented towards a Christian end but pursue their own eschatological goals. Heim therefore proposed the challenging suggestion that several eschatological ends might coexist as real possibilities. Initially he gave this proposal an exclusivist touch, arguing that, for example, God may allow a Buddhist to arrive at *nirvāṇa*, but that *nirvāṇa*, from a Christian perspective, would not be notably different from hell.[81] Later on Heim developed this into the inclusivist[82] suggestion that the eschatological ends of other religions are salvific to the extent that they manifest certain aspects of the Christian end, the beatific vision of God. The Christian end is superior because it involves full knowledge of the trinitarian God whom others only know faintly and incompletely. And the Christian path is superior to all other paths, in that only Christianity prepares its members for this superior end. If members of other religions should also ever arrive at the highest goal, this could only happen if God would lead them there after they have reached their own eschatological end.[83] A similar suggestion has recently been made by Gavin D'Costa according to whom non-Christian religions may lead their adherents to a kind of eschatological limbo where these might have an encounter with Christ enabling them to finally achieve ultimate salvation.[84]

Though inclusivism holds a far more appreciative view of other religions than exclusivism, in the end, it nevertheless implies a negative understanding of religious diversity and so a diminished view of the religious other. In a somewhat simplified way, Christian exclusivism regards other religions as false *because* they differ from Christian faith, while inclusivism sees them as false or deficient *to the extent* they differ. In both cases, however, the reason for a negative assessment is religious difference. As a result, religious diversity can hardly be seen as a value in itself. If Christianity is the only true religion or, as in inclusivism, the uniquely superior religion, then it follows that ideally everyone should belong to Christianity, so implying that in the end all other religions should disappear. Religious diversity can at best be only of a provisional value. It was Jacques Dupuis who realized this problem and tried to amend it by suggesting what he called 'pluralistic inclusivism' or 'inclusive pluralism'.[85]

---

[80]   Karl Rahner, *Schriften zur Theologie*, viii (Einsiedeln-Zürich-Cologne: Benziger Verlag, 1967), 365ff.

[81]   Cf. S. Mark Heim, *Is Christ the Only Way?* (Valley Forge, Pa.: Judson Press, 1985), 146ff.

[82]   See S. Mark Heim, *The Depths of the Riches* (Grand Rapids, Mich.: Eerdmans, 2001), 8.

[83]   See Heim, *The Depths*, 268, 279.

[84]   Gavin D'Costa, *Christianity and World Religions* (Chichester: Wiley-Blackwell, 2009), 159–215.

[85]   See Jacques Dupuis, *Christianity and the Religions* (Maryknoll, NY: Orbis Books, 2002), 95, 255.

According to Dupuis, the plurality of religions needs to be understood as positively willed by God, as rooted in 'the superabundant riches and variety of God's self-manifestation to humankind'.[86] Although Jesus Christ is the centre, climax, and fullness of divine revelation, he is so in a qualitative, not quantitative sense,[87] so that there are elements in other religions which can enrich Christianity. And although Christ is the constitutive cause of salvation for all human beings, this does not mean that all other religions are just provisional. As in the case of Judaism, they can be understood as covenants made by God which have not been 'abolished or revoked'.[88] Dupuis characterizes the relationship between Christianity and other faiths as one of 'mutual asymmetrical complementarity'—mutual and complementary because there is room for mutual learning, asymmetrical because other religions 'can find, and are destined to find, in the Christ event their fullness of meaning', while 'the reverse is not true'.[89] Dupuis's efforts may be seen as squaring the circle. In the end, his attempt to combine the inclusivist claim of Christ's unique superiority with the pluralist understanding of a divinely willed religious diversity leads to a sort of inclusivist double predestination theory: God wants the majority of humankind to be lastingly satisfied with qualitatively lesser forms of revelation. The Roman Catholic Church formally censored and rejected Dupuis's proposal, yet with the argument of leaning too much to genuine forms of religious pluralism.

Developing Christian Pluralism

As is well known, Karl Barth and Karl Rahner developed their exclusivist and inclusivist theologies in an aprioristic way, deriving them not from a consideration of any specific knowledge of other religions but from systematic premises. Despite some claims to the contrary,[90] this is markedly different with religious pluralists.[91] Wilfred Cantwell Smith and John Hick both took off as exclusivists but revised their theologies as a result of a deeper encounter with people of other faiths. Raimon Panikkar began with an inclusivist theology of a broadly Rahnerian type and became a pluralist through his ongoing dialogue with Hinduism. Similar observations apply to a number of other pluralists. In their encounters with the religious other they concluded that Christian superiority claims can no longer be sustained if one looks without bias at the positive and negative aspects of all major religious traditions. They were searching for a theology of religions that is able to understand religious diversity as a diversity of 'equals', neither ignoring nor downplaying the differences, nor abandoning any normative standards by just subscribing to relativism.[92] Whether this has been achieved is still subject to considerable debate, but these motives should not be denied.

---

[86] Dupuis, *Christianity*, 255.   [87] Dupuis, *Toward a Christian Theology*, 249.
[88] Dupuis, *Christianity*, 254.   [89] Dupuis, *Christianity*, 257.
[90] Cf. James Fredericks, *Faith among Faiths* (New York: Paulist Press, 1999), 9–10.
[91] See Perry Schmidt-Leukel, 'Pluralisms' in Race and Hedges (eds), *Christian Approaches*, 85–110; 'Pluralist Theologies', *The Expository Times*, 122/2 (2010), 53–72.
[92] See John Hick and Paul Knitter (eds), *The Myth of Christian Uniqueness* (Maryknoll, NY: Orbis Books, 1987).

It is possible to distinguish between 'monocentric' and 'polycentric' types of pluralism.[93] According to monocentric pluralism, different religions are related in different though equally valid ways to the same Ultimate Reality. This is the view proposed by John Hick, Wilfred Cantwell Smith, Paul Knitter, Alan Race, myself, and many others. The assumption that religions like Judaism, Christianity, Islam, Hinduism, Buddhism, Daoism, etc. are all related to the same Ultimate (known as 'God' in theistic religions), despite their different and even apparently opposed doctrinal statements about this reality, is justifiable if one takes into account the religions' widespread affirmation that the Ultimate, because of its transcendent nature, is necessarily beyond any human words and concepts. Under this premise different concepts cannot be understood as direct descriptions of the Ultimate (which is by definition impossible) but as being related to and expressive of different human experiences with the Ultimate, enshrined in the collective memory of large religious traditions. This implies that, for example, the Ultimate in itself can neither be correctly described as a personal nor as an impersonal reality, but can nevertheless be validly experienced through a range of different personal or impersonal representations. Religious traditions as based on and evolving around such experiences can be assessed as equally 'salvific', if they display the same potential to evoke and sustain a human attitude to the ultimate that is acknowledged as truly salvific on the norms and standards shared by the respective traditions, for example, if they, as Hick suggested, induce a 'transformation from self-centeredness to Reality-centeredness' ('Reality' signifying 'Ultimate Reality' or 'The Real') which is manifested in love and compassion.[94] Influenced by Christian liberation theology, Paul Knitter has expanded this criterion by arguing that the salvific potential must not be taken in a narrow individualistic sense. It rather implies the capacity of the religions to foster human liberation also on a collective, social, and political level so that—from a Christian perspective—it can be seen as their potential to foster the 'Kingdom of God' as itself the, or a, salvific goal.[95]

Polycentric pluralism assumes that different religions are validly related to different 'Ultimates'. This inevitably raises the question of polytheism: can there be different Ultimates without losing their 'ultimate' nature by the sheer fact of not being the sole Ultimate? What would be the relation between such different Ultimates and what would such a view entail regarding the salvific potential of the religions? One notable version of polycentric pluralism has been suggested by process theologians John Cobb and David Griffin.[96] In Alfred North Whitehead's process philosophy the notion of *creatio ex nihilo* (creation out of nothing) is rejected in favour of the idea of a creative divine demiurge. Cobb and Griffin derive from this

---

[93] See Michael Hüttenhoff, *Der religiöse Pluralismus als Orientierungsproblem: Religionstheologische Studien* (Leipzig: Evangelische Verlagsanstalt, 2001), 41–5.

[94] See John Hick, *An Interpretation of Religion,* 2nd edn (Basingstoke and New York: Palgrave Macmillan, 2004), 36–55, 164, 299f.

[95] See Paul Knitter, *One Earth Many Religions* (Maryknoll, NY: Orbis Books, 1995); *Jesus and the Other Names* (Maryknoll, NY: Orbis Books, 1996). This dimension, however, is not absent from Hick. See Hick, *Interpretation,* 303–6.

[96] See John Cobb, *Transforming Christianity and the World* (Maryknoll, NY: Orbis Books, 1999); David Ray Griffin (ed.), *Deep Religious Pluralism* (Louisville, Ky.: Westminster John Knox, 2005).

the existence of three irreducible Ultimates: first, God as a, or the, Supreme Being; second, 'being itself' or pure 'creativity', which is manifested not only in God but also in the cosmos. And since God is eternally creative, there is always some kind of cosmos, which is therefore something like God's body and as such comprises the third Ultimate. These three 'Ultimates' (God, creativity, cosmos) allow for three different religious orientations: 'theistic, acosmic, and cosmic', which exist in a variety of different mixtures and combinations and account for the difference of the religions. But would it not be more appropriate to speak of three different aspects of one complex Ultimate Reality instead of three different Ultimates? Process theologians themselves tend to do so in defence against the accusation of polytheism.[97] This would draw them closer to 'monocentric pluralism.' Yet whether 'polycentric pluralism' is 'pluralist' in the sense of combining the acknowledgement of diversity with *salvific equality* will depend on the question of whether religions with a focus on different aspects of the Ultimate are nevertheless seen as equally salvific.

A similar approach has been developed by Raimon Panikkar for whom the main case for pluralism is the fact that 'reality itself is pluralistic'.[98] He describes this pluralistic nature of reality as a *perichorēsis* or 'circuminsession' of 'World, God and Man' as three different 'dimensions of one and the same reality'.[99] Religions are different ways that induce different experiences of this *cosmotheandric* unity. In Christianity this experience is referred to and induced by the name or symbol of 'Christ',[100] while other religions have their own names, each name functioning as a 'new manifestation and revelation' of this complex unity.[101]

If Jesus Christ is understood as the sole incarnation of the divine word or *logos* and as the unique cause of salvation, Christianity is inevitably superior to all other religions and the pluralist aim of understanding religious diversity as a diversity of equals is unrealizable. In different versions pluralists thus propose an understanding of the presence of the divine in Jesus that no longer implies his exclusive uniqueness or superiority as Saviour and Revealer.[102] At present, this seems to be the main reason why a pluralist theology is still rejected by the Christian churches and the majority of theologians. Yet from a Biblical perspective, informed by a historical understanding, pluralists can rightly claim that *beliefs about Jesus* were formulated in order to share the *faith of Jesus* which was not centred upon him as such, but upon that ultimate divine reality which he called 'Father'. Will it not be possible to share his faith in the boundless goodness of this reality while entertaining different beliefs about Jesus himself?

---

[97] See Griffin, *Deep Religious Pluralism*, 49–50.

[98] Raimon Panikkar, 'The Jordan, the Tiber, and the Ganges', in Hick & Knitter, *The Myth*, 89–116, 109.

[99] Raimon Panikkar, *The Cosmotheandric Experience: Emerging Religious Consciousness* (Maryknoll, NY: Orbis Books, 1993), 72–7.

[100] R. Panikkar, *The Unknown Christ of Hinduism* (Maryknoll, NY: Orbis Books, 1981), 19–20.

[101] Panikkar, *Unknown Christ*, 27–9.

[102] See e.g. Leonard Swidler and Paul Mojzes (eds), *The Uniqueness of Jesus: A Dialogue with Paul F. Knitter* (Maryknoll, NY: Orbis Books, 1997); Roger Haight, *Jesus Symbol of God* (Maryknoll, NY: Orbis Books, 1999); John Hick, *The Metaphor of God Incarnate* (London: SCM Press, 2005).

Outlook

In contemporary Christianity all three positions—exclusivism, inclusivism, and pluralism—have strong defenders. Some theologians suspect that the debate about and between these different approaches has become stuck in an impasse and suggest an alternative—not an alternative position *in*, but an alternative *to* the theology of religions. Instead of disputing whether a salvific knowledge of God is confined to Christianity, or has its superior expression in Christianity, or exists in different yet equally valid forms across several religions, Christian theology should focus on comparisons of specific features, concepts, representatives, and so forth, within other religions and Christianity. If, however, such a 'comparative theology' moves beyond a purely phenomenological comparison, by raising and discussing rather than excluding the question of truth, it will hardly be able to avoid the kind of general questions as discussed in the theology of religions. Instead, it may well be expected that 'comparative theology' will contribute the kind of evidence that would help to strengthen the case of either an exclusivist, inclusivist, or pluralist approach, thereby making an important contribution to the 'theology of religions' debate.[103]

A pluralist theology of religions has been proposed as a model in respect to understanding the 'religious other' from a Christian perspective which would allow for the idea of a mutual fertilization between the religions, in distinction from the exclusivist stance of Christianity over against the religions, or the inclusivist stance of Christianity as the unilateral fulfilment of the religions. A mutual fulfilment or fertilization would have to take the form of a multilateral colloquium that has been variously termed 'universal', 'global', 'world', or more recently 'interfaith' theology. Its vision, as Wilfred Cantwell Smith put it in 1981, is 'a theology that will interpret the history of our race in a way that will give intellectual expression to our faith, the faith of all of us, and to our modern perception of the world'.[104] Within this vision, Christianity's relation to the religious other is no longer understood along the lines of a 'we–they' paradigm but as a relationship within an overarching human community, in which '*some of us* are Christians, *some of us* are Muslims, *some of us* are Hindus, *some of us* are Jews, *some of us* are sceptics',[105] which would indeed constitute a ground-breaking change in understanding Christianity's relation to the religious other.

FURTHER READING

Jacques Dupuis, *Toward a Christian Theology of Religious Pluralism* (Maryknoll, NY: Orbis Books, 1997).

John Hick, *An Interpretation of Religion: Human Responses to the Transcendent* (Basingstoke: Macmillan, 1989).

---

[103] J. Fredericks, *Faith among Faiths* (New York: Paulist Press, 1999); Francis Clooney, *Comparative Theology* (Oxford: Wiley-Blackwell, 2010) and Clooney (ed.), *The New Comparative Theology* (London: T&T Clark, 2010).

[104] Wilfred Cantwell Smith, *Towards a World Theology* (Maryknoll, NY: Orbis Books, 1989), 125

[105] Cantwell Smith, *Towards*, 101 (my emphasis).

Veli-Matti Kärkkäinen, *An Introduction to the Theology of Religions* (Downers Grove, Ill.: InterVarsity Press, 2003).

Jan van Lin, *Shaking the Fundamentals: Religious Plurality and the Ecumenical Movement* (Amsterdam and New York: Rodopi 2002).

Richard J. Plantinga (ed.), *Christianity and Plurality: Classic and Contemporary Readings* (Oxford: Blackwell, 1999).

Alan Race and Paul Hedges (eds), *Christian Approaches to Other Faiths* (London: SCM Press, 2008).

Perry Schmidt-Leukel, *Gott ohne Grenzen: Eine christliche und pluralistische Theologie der Religionen* (Gütersloh: Gütersloher Verlagshaus, 2004).

Perry Schmidt-Leukel, *Transformation by Integration: How Inter-faith Encounter Changes Christianity* (London: SCM Press, 2009).

Wilfred Cantwell Smith, *Towards a World Theology* (Maryknoll, NY: Orbis Books 1989).

Francis A. Sullivan, *Salvation Outside the Church? Tracing the History of the Catholic Response* (Eugene, Or.: Wipf & Stock 2002).

CHAPTER 7

Islam and the Religious Other

DAVID THOMAS

Islam has been involved with other faiths throughouts the entire fourteen hundred years of its history. Its beginnings in seventh-century Arabia were deeply entangled with local forms of polytheism as well as Judaism, Christianity, and other religious traditions of the Middle East, while its later establishment throughout the world brought it into close encounter with the major world religions. Muslims have written at length about the relationship between their own faith and others, though possibilities for acknowledging them have always been limited by the influence of the Qur'ān and the example of Muḥammad. These two primary authorities have exerted unrivalled control over Muslim thinking about other faiths, and they continue to provide the criteria by which the status of other faiths is judged. As long as Muslim approaches to them remain unchanged, it is unlikely that the attitudes that were first formulated in early Islamic times will alter very much or that any innovative suggestions will find widespread acceptance.

Accordingly, the focus of this chapter's discussion of Islam and other faiths will be on the key ideas and motifs that Muslims derive from these sources. The theological flavour this yields is itself significant, for it highlights the very nature of Islam as a religion and so the attitudes and values it presents. This survey will therefore begin with the Qur'ān and the Prophet Muḥammad, for the very foundations of Muslim beliefs and values are found here. From this vantage point Muslim attitudes to other faiths during the period of the early empire can be examined, for it is in this context that Islamic orthodoxy was forged, imparting a legacy that continues to exert an impact on Islamic sensibilities today. The third and final section of this chapter will discuss some key contemporary perspectives on Islam and other religions, noting in particular the work of the Palestinian scholar Ismail Raji al-Faruqi, the Paris-based Mohammed Arkoun, and the US-based Mahmoud Ayoub. Other Muslim authors and approaches could well be included, but space limitations demand careful selection. These three represent both complementary diversity and the theological thrust of much Muslim thinking which is of critical importance when endeavouring to understand the reality of, and possibilities for, Muslim approaches to other faiths in today's world.

THE QUR'ĀN AND THE PROPHET MUḤAMMAD

The Qur'ān and the Prophet lie at the heart of Islamic thought, and they provide not only the main source of attitudes towards other faiths but also the constraint on what is acceptable and what is not. According to orthodox Muslim belief, the Qur'ān was revealed to Muḥammad, a merchant from the Arabian town of Mecca, between 610 and 632 CE. The angel Gabriel confronted him with the first revelation in a cave outside the town and from that point periodically brought him further revelations for the rest of his life. They were communicated as God's final revelation, intended to conclude a succession of revelations stretching back through history. In this is the germ of the traditional Muslim understanding of the relationship between Islam and other religions. To a reader or hearer, the Qur'ān (Arabic 'recitation') as it now appears can seem difficult to access. Close examination often discloses a continuing thread through a *sūra* (chapter), though at first sight it may appear to be a disunited succession of fragments. This means that the Qur'ān's teaching on most topics—and on other faiths in particular—often requires comparison between a number of passages, leading to varying and sometimes conflicting conclusions about the general tenor of what it teaches. Like other scriptures, the Qur'ān contains many shades in its attitudes towards those who are outside or opposed to its immediate circle of recipients, and the task of identifying a prevailing doctrinal view is beset with challenges. Nevertheless, Muslim exegetes discerned at an early stage a dominant line of teachings, and this has more or less remained the norm ever since.

The one prevailing theme in the Qur'ān is the majesty and power of God, who is unique and unlike any other being. It portrays God as the supreme mystery who is nevertheless present to all events, intervening and directing, and cognizant of everything that takes place. This principle, *tawḥīd* (literally, 'the declaration that God is one'), serves as the criterion by which all that is contained in the Qur'ān is expressed. The Qur'ān came into being in an environment that was heavily multi-religious, with Mecca, where Muḥammad lived until his early fifties, a centre of pagan beliefs, while Medina, where he migrated in 622 CE and remained for the rest of his life, the home of tribes of Jews and pagans in addition to those who had accepted Islam. It is entirely likely that in trading centres such as these the Zoroastrian beliefs of the Persian Sassanian Empire and the Christian beliefs of the Byzantine Empire would also be known. In fact, the young Muḥammad is recorded as having a friend (probably Ethiopian) who was a Christian,[1] and Christian teachings would have been circulated through Arabia by missionaries from Nestorian centres in Mesopotamia and from the Christian south. One cannot be certain about Muḥammad's knowledge of the great faiths of the day, though circumstantial evidence suggests that he had more than a mere acquaintance. It is, therefore, not surprising that the Qur'ān refers to these faiths, and to figures familiar from them such as Abraham, Moses, and Jesus, as it comments on the religious complexion of the context into

---

[1] Ibn Isḥāq/Ibn Hishām, *Sīrat rasūl Allāh*, ed. F. Wüstenfeld (Göttingen: J. B. Metzler, 1859–60), i. 115–16; A. Guillaume (tr.), *The Life of Muhammad* (Karachi: Oxford University Press, 1955), 180.

which it first emerged. According to its dominant theme of *tawḥīd*, it is often critical of them. A basic attitude towards the pagans of Mecca to whom Muḥammad first preached his message is given in *Sūra* 109:

> Say: O disbelievers!
> I worship not that which you worship;
> Nor do you worship that which I worship.
> And I shall not worship that which you worship.
> Nor will you worship that which I worship.
> To you your religion, and to me my religion.[2]

Here the Qur'ān makes clear that there cannot be any accommodation between the religion of the Meccans and the teaching of Islam, for the simple reason that the deities of the Meccan cults (if they exist—there is maybe a trace of henotheism in this passage) have no relationship with the God about whom it speaks. This is given a more pungent expression in a slightly later passage, in which the utter difference between the God of Islam and the chief goddesses of Mecca is mockingly set out:

> Have you thought about Al-lāt and al-ʿUzzā
> And Manāt, the third, the other?
> Are yours the males and his the females?
> That indeed would be an unfair division!
> They are but names which you have named, you
> And your fathers for which God has revealed no warrant.   (53: 19–23)

According to the usual interpretation, the Meccans made these three goddesses daughters of the supreme God, but the Qur'ān here retorts that their ascribing daughters to him while priding themselves on having sons points up the ridiculousness of their pagan beliefs. There is literally nothing in them, because they refer to nothing more than names. The pagan Meccans are often referred to as *kāfirūn*, deriving from the verb *kafara*, which in its basic form means 'to conceal' and thence 'to deny' and 'to be indifferent'. The underlying idea would seem to be that the pagans possessed knowledge about the true God, like the rest of humankind, but they turned away from this, concealing it beneath their contrived belief in artificial gods. They are also known as *mushrikūn* ('associators') because they associate other gods with God, and they are rejected in the most uncompromising terms:

> When the sacred months have passed, slay the associators wherever you find them, and take them captive, and besiege them, and prepare for them every ambush.   (9: 5)

² Translations are taken from M. M. Pickthall, *The Meaning of the Glorious Koran* (New York: Dorset Press, 1963), slightly modernized.

There cannot be any kindred feeling between the monotheist Muslims and the polytheist Arabs, so even though agreements may be made for pragmatic reasons, eventually the two groups are heading in such different directions that there must be enmity. While the believers have the potential ability to obey God as he deserves, the polytheists cannot. It is for this reason that God will not pardon them:

> Indeed! God does not forgive a partner being ascribed to him. He forgives everything except that to whom he pleases. Whoever ascribes partners to God, he has indeed invented a tremendous sin.   (4: 48)

It is as though these pagans have not only forgotten about the true God, but in their indifference they have added deities to him from their own invention. As long as they remain in this state, they are beyond retrieval.

The situation is not the same with the followers of the great religious traditions. In places, the Qur'ān speaks about them favourably:

> Indeed! Those who believe, and those who are Jews, and Christians and Sabeans—whoever believes in God and the last day and does right—surely their reward is with their Lord, and there shall no fear come upon them neither shall they grieve.   (2: 62)

Here 'those who believe' are usually identified as the Muslims, and they are ranked on the same level as those from other traditions. This is supported by Q 22: 40, which implies that God protects other places of worship together with the mosques of the Muslims:

> Had it not been for God's repelling some men by means of others, cloisters and churches and oratories and mosques, in which the name of God is often mentioned, would assuredly have been pulled down.

These groups evidently worship God with the same sincerity as the Muslims, and they have the same means of reaching him. This acceptance of Jews, Christians, and Sabeans (a group that is not identified in the Qur'ān, and has been variously explained by exegetes) appears to be linked with the teaching that they resemble Muslims in being sent messengers of their own and having their own scriptures. Thus, for example, Muḥammad is told:

> He has revealed to you the scripture with truth, confirming what was before it, and he revealed the Torah and the Gospel.   (3: 3)

In such verses the Qur'ān and the other two scriptures are linked together as given by God and therefore consistent with one another, at least in essential teachings. Moreover, Muḥammad is typically depicted in the Qur'ān as a prophet like the biblical prophets before him:

> Indeed! We inspire you as we inspired Noah and the prophets after him, and we inspired
> Abraham and Ishmael and Isaac and Jacob and the tribes, and John and Job and Jonah and
> Aaron and Solomon, and we imparted to David the Psalms. (4: 163)

The clear implication of these and similar verses is that God has sent a line of prophetic messengers, among them the great figures familiar from the Bible, and has revealed to each of them a scripture, just as he has revealed the Qur'ān to Muḥammad. This is exemplified in the person of Jesus:

> God will say: Jesus, son of Mary! Remember my favour to you and to your mother, and how
> I strengthened you with the Holy Spirit, so that you spoke to mankind in the cradle as in
> maturity, and how I taught you the Scripture and Wisdom and the Torah and the Gospel.
> (5: 110)[3]

The Qur'ān envisages a repeated cycle of human messengers sent by God to particular communities, each with a message that has been given to him. Since all messages come from God (the Gospel is taught *to* Jesus by God), and all messengers are sent by him, they have the same authority and teach the same things.

This sense of originating equality is important to note, for the Qur'ān appears to enjoin upon Muslims acknowledgement of these earlier messengers and their revelations, and respect for their communities as recipients of a scripture, making them People of the Book. However, in the course of events all has not turned out as it ought to. In principle, the People of the Book should be expected to accept Muḥammad as a divinely guaranteed messenger, and indeed to give him their allegiance. Some appear to do this, but not all (Q 3: 110, 113), and in fact they tend to hold an exclusive attitude that is unwelcoming towards Muslims (Q 3: 25; 57: 29). The Qur'ān does not elaborate on the reasons, though it does go into detail about distortions in the beliefs of the People of the Book:

> The Jews say: Ezra is the son of God, and the Christians say: The Messiah is the son of God.
> That is their saying with their mouths. They imitate the saying of those who disbelieved of
> old. God fights against them. How perverse they are! (9: 30)

Here, these two groups commit the same mistake as the Meccan pagans, associating other, created beings with God and transgressing the cardinal principle of *tawḥīd*. Is this a consequence of their refusal to accept Muḥammad? It appears likely to be at least one reason.

The Qur'ān goes into some detail about Christian doctrinal errors; the Jews tend to be condemned solely on the grounds that they reject the prophetic status of Muḥammad in their exclusiveness, but the Christians are guilty of major misunderstandings. Their primary

---

[3] According to traditional Muslim exegesis, the Holy Spirit is identified here and throughout the Qur'ān as the angel Gabriel, who announced the birth of Jesus to Mary and brought revelation to the prophets.

error is in calling Jesus son of God, but 'the likeness of Jesus with God is as the likeness of Adam. He created him of dust; then he said to him: Be! And he was' (Q 3: 59). Jesus is created just like Adam, and Jesus himself denies anything other than this:

> When God says: Jesus, son of Mary! Did you say to mankind: Take me and my mother for two gods beside God? He will say: Be glorified! It was not mine to utter that to which I had no right. If I used to say it then you know it. You know what is in my mind, and I do not know what is in your mind. Indeed! You, only you are the knower of things hidden. I spoke to them only what you commanded me: Worship God, my Lord and your Lord.   (5: 116–17)

This dialogue between God and Jesus makes it plain that Jesus was no more than a servant of God, subordinate to him and obedient to his will. By definition, he cannot then be divine or equal to God. Thus it follows that any suggestion that God is a tri-unity rather than a singular unity is undeniably wrong:

> Christ Jesus the son of Mary was a messenger of God and his word, which he bestowed on Mary, and a spirit proceeding from him; so believe in God and his messengers. Say not 'Three': desist. It will be better for you, for God is one God: glory be to him: (far exalted is he) above having a son.   (4: 171; see also 5: 73)

The characteristic doctrines of the Christians are erroneous, and distortions of the truth; they have nothing to do with teachings from Jesus himself, and in fact he is on the side of those who condemn them. While it eloquently condemns the Trinity and incarnation, and also the historicity of the crucifixion of Christ (Q 4: 157, 'They [the Jews] did not kill him and did not crucify him') the Qur'ān does not explain how the Christians degenerated from believers in the pure monotheism brought to them by Jesus, just as it does not explain why the Jews refused to acknowledge Muḥammad. It simply intimates that the two religious groups are closed in and exclusive, too haughty and full of themselves to see the truth they have been shown.

One other element in the Qur'ān's condemnation of these groups adds to the picture of what has gone wrong. This is that the People of the Book have somehow tampered with their scripture. What is said about this is cryptic, but it is enough to cast doubt on the ways in which the Jews and Christians have treated their revealed books:

> Do you say that Abraham, Ishmael, Isaac, Jacob and the tribes were Jews or Christians? Say: Do you know better than God? Ah! Who is more unjust than those who conceal the testimony they have from God?   (2: 140)

Here, as well as implying that Judaism and Christianity are recent inventions with no basis in the tradition of belief that stems back to Abraham (who was 'not a Jew, nor yet a Christian, but an upright man who had surrendered (*ḥanīf muslim*)', Q 3: 67), the Qur'ān suggests that they misrepresent the original teachings given to them by hiding part of them. More serious than this,

> Can you entertain the hope that they will believe in you, seeing that a party of them heard the word of God and perverted it knowingly after they understood it?   (Q 2: 75)

The precise meaning of 'perverted it' (*yuḥarrifūnahu*) is not straightforward; it can mean both to alter the meaning of a word and to alter its actual appearance, the latter accusation much the more critical in this context. How or whether this tampering activity on scripture fits in with the distortion of pure monotheism and rejection of Muḥammad as the latest preacher of this doctrine is not explained in the Qur'ān. However, it seems clear that in the environment depicted in these scattered verses the Qur'ān surveys loss of integrity in faith, degeneration in doctrine, and communities that have forgotten or abandoned their original beliefs. The major religious traditions retain possible vestiges in what they read in their texts and proclaim as dogma, but this is overlaid with widespread masses of error. Despite this, it is important to note that the Qur'ān assumes without question that the People of the Book, comprising Jews and Christians, unlike the pagan Arabs, share faith in the one God of Islam. The problem for them is that either they have over-domesticated him as theirs alone or they have admitted accretions that deflect them from pure worship of him. But despite the short-comings in their perceptions, they still retain a connection with him and are therefore not entirely beyond redemption.

This attitude towards the People of the Book is in line with another assumption evident throughout the Qur'ān, that there is only one true God—*tawḥīd* in its pure form—and that therefore everything that takes place is within the compass of his foreknowledge and under his control. This sweeping awareness accounts for some verses that have a dramatically open character when taken alone, and point towards a fundamental acceptance of everything that is done to honour God. A startling example occurs in a passage in which the revelations to Moses, Jesus, and Muḥammad are recalled:

> To you [Muḥammad] we revealed the scripture with the truth, confirming whatever scrip-ture was before it, and a watcher over it. So judge between them by that which God has revealed, and do not follow their desires away from the truth that has come to you. For each we have appointed a divine law and a traced-out way. Had God willed he would have made you one community. But that he may try you by what he has given you. So vie with one another in good works. To God you will all return, and he will then inform you of that in which you differ.   (5: 48)

The thrust of this verse is that, even though Muḥammad's revelation is authentic, it is by God's will that other communities possess their own revelations and follow their own practices. Furthermore, the consequence should not be mutual condemnation but good-natured competi-tion in goodly living which is to be judged by God alone. In the same vein is the following verse:

To each nation have we given sacred rites which they are to perform; so let them not dispute with you [Muḥammad] of the matter, but you summon to your Lord. Indeed! You do follow right guidance.   (22: 67)

The variety of pious rituals (*manāsik*) is condoned by God and actually endowed by him on the different communities. So while Muḥammad's way is authentic, it appears that it is not the only authentic way. Such verses contain considerable potential for continuing Muslim reflection on new ways of understanding and approaching people of other religions.

The inclusive latitude in these and similar verses (e.g. Q 98: 5) typifies an attitude towards faiths other than Islam that recognizes value and truth in them. In the course of history, such verses have usually been interpreted within the broader understanding constructed on the basis of other more negative verses, though their presence in the Qur'ān means that the question of how wrong non-Islamic religions are is kept open. They prevent any simple rejection of everything non-Islamic, and they can even be taken as a prompt to Muslims to investigate these religions, and identify in them what might be right and good, although for all their challenging openness they form only a minor theme in the Qur'ān, and at no time in Islamic history have they been used to challenge the dominant construction that has been placed on its teachings.

This is already apparent in the earliest major biographical account of Muḥammad, written in the mid eighth century by Muḥammad ibn Isḥāq (d. 767), where the story is told of the young Muḥammad, on a trading journey with his uncle, being recognized by the monk Baḥīrā as having the seal of prophethood between his shoulders 'in the very place described in his [the monk's] book'.[4] The implication is that the Christian holy book 'that was in the cell, so they allege, handed on from generation to generation' contained predictions about Muḥammad, as Q 61: 6 and 7: 157 say it does,[5] and also that this monk as a good Christian looks for a prophet who is to come, and acknowledges him readily (understandably, the Christian scholar John of Damascus, writing at about the same time, refers to the monk as an Arian heretic, implying that he was lost in error). Similarly, when a deputation from the south Arabian town of Najrān come to Muḥammad in Medina and enter into a dispute about the nature of their faith, he is able to silence them by reciting verses from the Qur'ān about the true nature of God and Jesus. In response, their leader tells them in private that they know well that Muḥammad is 'a prophet sent by God and he has brought a decisive declaration about the nature of your master'. They return home, taking with them a Muslim who acts as judge between them over financial matters.[6] Again, the clear implication is that there is no resisting the truth in the teachings of the Qur'ān, and that the institution of Islam is so superior to Christianity that Muslims can guide Christians in practical matters.

[4] Ibn Isḥāq, *Sīra* 115–16, ed. Wüstenfeld, 79–80.
[5] Ibn Isḥāq, *Sīra* 115, ed. Wüstenfeld, 79.   [6] Ibn Isḥāq, *Sīra*, 410, ed. Wüstenfeld, 277.

These examples from this early biography of Muḥammad suggest that within a century or so of his death the beginnings of a systematic formulation of the relationship between Islam and Christianity are discernible. In this it is suggested that the earlier faith is a preparation for the later, that its sacred texts predict it, and that it is completed and corrected by it. These are the main lines of the more developed attitude that is spelt out by theological specialists in the early centuries of Islam, and with some variants it remains the same today.

MUSLIM ATTITUDES TOWARDS OTHER FAITHS IN THE PERIOD OF EARLY EMPIRE

Within a few decades of the death of Muḥammad in 632 CE, Arab armies had brought wide areas of the Middle East and North Africa under the rule of Islam, and within a century the empire of the Umayyads stretched from Spain in the west, through the Levant and Fertile Crescent into Iraq and Iran. It was an empire that took in huge numbers of Christians of different kinds, Jews, and Zoroastrians, as well as other faiths. These populations outnumbered the Muslim rulers by a considerable margin, and they often possessed cultural accomplishments and professional expertise that gave them a sense of confidence before their rulers and made those rulers interested to tap their knowledge. The relationship between rulers and ruled was a complicated mixture of respect and deference on both sides before the respective realities of power and learning.

In recognition of the practical needs to govern populations that followed other faiths, and also in fair-minded acknowledgement that their subjects belonged to communities that possessed their own scriptures, as the Qur'ān taught, Muslims identified a legal relationship in which Jews, Christians, and others who were mentioned in their scripture occupied the position of client people, *ahl al-dhimma*, and could be accorded rights in return for accepting responsibilities. It is not clear when this relationship was first codified (it appears to have existed in some form by about 800), though legal experts based it on the authority of the second caliph ʿUmar ibn al-Khaṭṭāb (r. 634–44), and pointed to treaties of surrender that he is supposed to have supervised. These set out the details of the relationship: the client community would enjoy the protection of the Islamic state, and in return they would pay a poll-tax (*jizya*), would not bear arms, and would defer to Muslims by not retaliating if struck and by stepping aside in the road. At some early point they were also required to distinguish themselves in their dress, usually by wearing yellow sashes around their waists, and they were forbidden from building new places of worship or repairing any that fell into ruin.

These were potentially draconian terms, later added to by such stringencies as not teaching the Qur'ān to their children (hence removing a major instrument by which to play a part in society), and not holding public positions that placed them above Muslims. But it is by no means clear that at least in the early centuries they were imposed in any thorough or systematic manner. There are certainly reports that at times of crisis or under rulers who were intent on emphasizing the Islamic character of society they were enforced for a time, but the fact that these reports were actually recorded suggests that at other times the client populations were relatively free to pursue their own lives. It is certainly the case that in early Islamic society before about 900 Christians with expertise in finance, medicine, and translation were prized and respected—a succession of caliphs were treated by a virtual dynasty of medical experts from one family, the Muslim ruler by the Christian professional; a number of Christian translators produced accurate and precise Arabic translations of works from Greek philosophers, mathematicians, physicians, and astronomers for eager Muslim clients.

From the late eighth century onwards, and quite possibly in response to stimuli and challenges from mainly Christian philosophers and theologians, reflection on the nature of faith became an increasingly evident part of the intellectual life of cities such as the capital Baghdad (built by the Abbasid dynasty that had overthrown the Umayyads in 750) and the southern port of Basra. Here, groups of speculative theologians pondered the implications of the Qur'ān and reflected on the nature of transcendent and contingent reality. Most of the leading practitioners belonged to the school of the Mu'tazila ('the withdrawers'), who subscribed to the principles of divine unity and justice. By these they meant that God was both entirely distinct from all other beings and totally undifferentiated in his own being, and was also completely just in his actions, entailing the requirement that humans should have a degree of moral autonomy if they were to be truly worthy of reward or punishment.

While almost everything that was written by these first theological specialists of Islam has been lost, or possibly destroyed by their later detractors, enough is known about the main outlines of their thought to show that they were acutely aware of the claims of other faiths and of the intellectual dimensions of their theologies. Almost every major Mu'tazilī thinker who was active in the ninth- and tenth-century heyday of the school wrote at least one work of refutation against Judaism, Christianity, or the Persian dualist sects, and some challenged individual authors and their ideas. This was almost certainly a part of their endeavour to define the character of distinctive Islamic perceptions of God and his relationship with the world, to be established as much by demonstrating the errors of competing accounts in other religious traditions as by setting out in systematic form the teachings arising from their own scripture.

One of the few thinkers from this period of vigorous theological activity whose works have survived in more than fragmentary form is the singular character of Abū 'Īsā Muḥammad al-Warrāq. He has not been treated well by Muslim historians and the true nature of his thought, as well as details of his biography, are not easy to reconstruct, though he appears to have been active in the mid ninth century and was a follower of the Mu'tazila in his earlier life. But something changed, and in his later years he took a more individual course. Later authors accused him of atheism, Manichaeism, and forms of Zoroastrianism, though there is also a firm tradition that he subscribed to some form of Shī'ism. Whatever his final stance, it would appear that he had more interest in criticizing accepted positions and posing difficult questions about faith than in accepting traditional answers too easily.[7]

Abū ʿĪsā is important because he was keenly interested in the faiths known in his day. He wrote accounts of Judaism, Christianity, and dualist beliefs—the latter being accepted as definitive for centuries by Muslim authors—and his major work, the *Maqālāt al-nās wa-ikhtilāfihim* ('The teachings of people and their differences'), was one of the first examples of the heresiographical tradition in Islam, in which competing teachings from the major faith traditions were described and brought into some form of relationship. Sadly, it was lost in later times and its proper character and full contents can no longer be known.[8] The one work by Abū ʿĪsā that has survived in more or less complete form is his refutation of Christianity, the *Radd ʿalā al-thalāth firaq min al-Naṣārā* ('Refutation of the three Christian sects'), a comprehensive and searching exposé of the deficiencies he saw in the doctrines of the Melkites, Nestorians, and Jacobites (to use the names by which they were known). There is reason to think that this was not untypical of such works from this time, though it was quite probably much fuller than most others, and it sheds significant light on the way in which this other faith was regarded by Muslim thinkers. The *Radd* is divided into three parts. The first is a descriptive account of the main doctrines of the Christian sects, based on what must have been a much fuller account in the *Kitāb al-maqālāt*. It details their teachings about the Trinity, including their differing understandings of what is meant by the term 'Persons', the act through which the divine and human natures united in Christ, including the disagreements between the various sects, and the way in which this unity was affected by the crucifixion. This is one of the most complete accounts of Christian beliefs that have come down from Muslim authors, and it shows the comprehensiveness of Abū ʿĪsā's knowledge, though it also indicates his own preoccupations. For what is striking and instructive from this account is that there is almost nothing in it about the central Christian doctrine of the atonement. Abū ʿĪsā evidently knew about this, because at one point he quotes the Jacobites saying, 'The Divinity was crucified for us', but he makes nothing more of it, except to draw out the implications of the divine nature being affected by death.

The great emphasis upon the interpretations of the Trinity and the act of uniting in this descriptive account points to what must have been Abū ʿĪsā's main aim in the *Radd* as a whole. While it is possible that he was reflecting Christian doctrines as they were presented by ecclesiastical scholars living under Islamic rule, it is more likely that he was reading and implicitly interpreting Christian doctrines according to criteria related to his own concerns. These are nowhere set out in the first part of the *Radd*, but they become clear from the other parts of the work. The second and third parts comprise long and exhaustive arguments against the two main doctrines that Abū ʿĪsā has already described. In the second part he

---

[7] See D. Thomas, *Early Muslim Polemic Against Christianity: Abū ʿĪsā al-Warrāq's 'Against the Incarnation'* (Cambridge: Cambridge University Press, 2002), 21–36.

[8] For an attempted reconstruction, see D. Thomas, 'Abū ʿĪsā al-Warrāq and the History of Religions', *Journal of Semitic Studies*, 41 (1996), 275–90.

demonstrates that according to the account he has given, the Trinity is not logically sustainable, arguing that the relationship between the three Persons and the substance necessarily entails plurality within the Godhead, conflict of activities between them, and internal contradiction within the three Christian sects' depictions of them. And likewise in the third part he demonstrates that the uniting of the divine and human natures entails all manner of irrational consequences in which the divine being ceases to conform to general understandings of what God is like, and again that the christological models put forward by the main sects are logically flawed and lead into multiple contradictions.

The conclusion to which all these arguments point is that Christian doctrines are not logical. Abū ʿĪsā has shown in terms of what may be called straightforward logic and common sense, and on the basis of his own simple summaries of these doctrines, that they fall into contradiction or contravene what is generally held about the being of God. He does not draw the final implication, though his arguments leave little doubt that in his own mind these flawed doctrines and the beliefs they attempt to articulate should be abandoned for a purer form of monotheism. He does not actually say this (at least, not in the surviving parts of his work), but he appears to be suggesting that only Islamic perceptions of God are compatible with reason, and that any right-thinking believer should recognize his error and abandon whatever departs from these.

A further purpose may be discernible behind these implications, which is that forms of belief about the being of God that contradict Islamic beliefs show, by their evident insufficiency, that Islam alone preserves the right way. This can be linked directly with the Qurʾān, which says that it has been revealed to safeguard and preserve previous revelations (Q 3: 3), and asserts that those who diverge from the 'straight way' are in error and are lost. A similar attitude may have been expressed in a work by one of Abū ʿĪsā's earlier contemporaries, the leading scholar of the Basra school of Muʿtazilī thinkers Abū al-Hudhayl al-ʿAllāf (d. between 840 and 850). None of his many works has survived, though later Muslim authors give enough about his thought to show its originality and authoritativeness. He was particularly known for his views about the attributes of God. Other religious thinkers taught that qualities of God, such as his being living, knowing, powerful, and so on derived from attributes of life, knowledge, power, and so on, that had modes of existence within his essence. But Abū al-Hudhayl rejected this, seeing the implicit danger of plurality within God's being as these additional entities could be identified and numbered in addition to his essence itself.

If this inference is not too much of a guess, these two Muslim theologians appear to have held the view that Christianity, and by implication other non-Islamic beliefs, contained grave logical errors and must be abandoned for Islam, the only rationally sound faith. They seem to have thought that something had gone wrong with other faiths, leading to distortions in their beliefs, and that the people who held them must be shown their errors and educated out of them into the truth of Islam. These faiths may contain the odd grain of residual truth, but something serious had happened and they were now no longer any good. Whether any Muslim theologian of the time gave explanations of what exactly had gone wrong cannot be known any longer because so few of their writings survive. However, elements of an explanation do survive, though in disjointed form. The earliest comes from a historian writing at the end of the eighth century who has left an account of the Apostle Paul deliberately giving three of his disciples distorted accounts about the nature of Jesus (evidently to correspond with the christologies of the three main Christian sects in the Islamic world) and sending them out to disseminate them. A fourth disciple, 'the believer', rejected what Paul said, and he and his descendants remained hidden in Arabia, preserving the original teachings about the oneness of God and the humanity of Jesus, until the coming of Islam.[9] In largely similar vein, the Muʿtazilī Abū ʿUthmān al-Jāḥiẓ (d. 869), who was a student of Abū al-Hudhayl, explains that Christians rely on the work of four authors, only two of whom knew Jesus directly, and who may well have colluded together to misrepresent in their four Gospel accounts the original *Injīl* that had been revealed to Jesus.[10] Both these authors detect some form of malevolent intent in the early Christian communities, the result of erroneous teachings being put into circulation, and the implication that the doctrines of their Christian contemporaries are based upon factual distortion in their scripture as well as logical carelessness in their thinking. It is not unlikely that stories of this kind would be known to theologians such as Abū ʿĪsā al-Warrāq and Abū al-Hudhayl al-ʿAllāf and would give them a basis in fact for their demonstrations of the flaws in Christian doctrines. If so, these stories would provide a historical explanation that concurred with their own conclusions, and would confirm them in their attitude that Christianity was in error.

Isolated works such as these, usually in fragmentary form, give only a partial view of what Muslims thought of other faiths in this period. They certainly do not provide any basis for a systematic view that anyone may have held, and in fact they suggest that in this important formative period Muslim theologians were as keen to develop and refine the formulations of their own doctrine of divine unity at the expense of the mistaken alternatives that they refuted as on working out a comprehensive understanding of the status of other faiths. Of course, in the minds of people formed and informed by the Qurʾān there were no other 'faiths' as such, in the sense of traditions of belief and teaching that called for attention alongside Islam. Rather, there were earlier forms of revelation that anticipated Islam as disclosures of the one faith that extended from the beginning of time and were attested to by the prophets and messengers who had come before Muḥammad. These other bodies of doctrine that disagreed with the teachings of Islam were no more than stunted and meaningless human constructions whose pointlessness could easily be exposed by proper scrutiny. In later centuries it is possible to discern forms of considered estimations of non-Islamic faiths and their relationship to Islam itself. One of these is to be found in compendia of theological questions

---

[9] P. van Koningsveld, 'The Islamic Image of Paul and the Origin of the Gospel of Barnabas', *Jerusalem Studies in Arabic and Islam*, 20 (1996), 200–28.

[10] Al-Jāḥiẓ, 'Fī al-radd ʿalā al-Naṣārā', in J. Finkel (ed.), *Thalāth rasāʾil li-Abī ʿUthmān al-Jāḥiẓ* (Cairo: Salafiyya Press, 1926), 24.

that are first known from the beginning of the tenth century and continued to be produced, particularly by members of the Muʿtazilī school, for many hundreds of years.

The innovative thinkers of the ninth century who first developed the outlines of distinctively Muslim theological structures appear to have written works on particular theological issues. It is difficult to be certain about this because in the main only the titles of what they wrote have survived, though if these are reliable guides they indicate separate works on single issues. Then, from about the year 900, large-scale works are recorded in which groups of issues were treated and series of opponents refuted. The best surviving examples date from the mid and late tenth century, and the most elaborate that is known was written by the Muʿtazilī theologian ʿAbd al-Jabbār al-Hamadhānī (d. 1025), one of the most celebrated intellectuals of his day who attracted students and admirers from all levels of society, including senior politicians.

This work, the *Mughnī fī abwāb al-tawḥīd wa-al-ʿadl* ('The summa on topics of divine unity and justice'), which is based on the two main principles of the Muʿtazila, as its title indicates, sets out the whole array of Islamic beliefs and ethical actions. As might be expected, ʿAbd al-Jabbār refers to the views of earlier Muslim thinkers, but more surprisingly he also refers to the teachings of non-Muslim groups that he knows. For example, in book 5 he starts on a long and detailed discussion first of dualist beliefs and secondly of Christianity, with respect to the latter arguing that the doctrines of the Trinity and the uniting of the divine and human natures in Christ are both equally fallacious. Reference back to the preceding books in the *Mughnī* shows why he is doing this: with a view to establishing and defending the Islamic doctrine of *tawḥīd*, the strict and absolute oneness of God, he is turning to these main rival doctrines and exposing their vapidity in order to strengthen his own case. The Trinity presents a model of God that may be regarded as only a relative unity, thus challenging the undifferentiated unity of his own Qurʾān-based conception, while the doctrine of the uniting presents a model in which the Divinity is implicated in the being and experiences of the human Jesus and, more objectionably, is brought into proximity with a contingent essence, in utter conflict with ʿAbd al-Jabbār's own understanding of the way in which the world works. Thus, as he succeeds in demonstrating that these two doctrines have no sense to them and do not withstand rational scrutiny, so he can give support to his own delineation of the being of God. Refutation of rival versions of God proves the truth and effectiveness of his own.

It emerges that ʿAbd al-Jabbār, and probably Abū ʿĪsā al-Warrāq before him, was not interested in Christianity as such (like his predecessor, he knows about the doctrine of the atonement), but only in those aspects which he saw as running most counter to Islam. To restate what has been said with regard to ninth-century Muslim attitudes to other faiths, here a Muslim sees these non-Muslim doctrines not as constituents in whole patterns of belief with integrity of their own—that would be anachronistic—but as aberrances from a tradition of monotheistic faith that has decayed as its bearers have either neglected to safeguard it or have purposely introduced innovations that have resulted in the chaotic disarray that is currently evident in their thought. The same features can be seen in ʿAbd al-Jabbār's rather briefer treatments of Judaism and Hinduism later on in the *Mughnī*. He turns to these at the beginning of his exposition of prophethood, refuting the Hindu denial of prophets in principle and the Jewish denial of prophets after Moses; these are the features that it suits his purpose to attack, because they appear to threaten his Islamic defence of the function of the prophetic messenger.

While these refutations in the *Mughnī* are entirely based on rational argument, they conform in conception to the teaching of the Qur'ān that religion is one, given in a succession of revelations from God through his messengers to their various communities, and that Jews, Christians, Zoroastrians, and others are, or originally were, predecessors of Muslims as holders of essentially identical revealed teachings. Islam is the reaffirmation of this abiding body of truth, and it is the duty of Muslims to defend it. The demonstration that the erroneous teachings that have been insinuated into these earlier forms of the faith are flawed and threadbare is exactly this. It follows that the Muslim attitude towards other religious traditions in the early period of Islam would contain some ambivalence. On the one hand, other traditions should in principle preserve the same elements as Islam, and its predecessors and anticipators should give way to it as the fulfilment of their own beliefs, just as Jesus looked forward to the coming of Muḥammad (Q 61: 6), and during his miraculous Night Journey, when he was taken from Mecca to Jerusalem prior to ascending up to heaven, Muḥammad was accepted as the leader in prayer by all the earlier prophets.[11] On the other hand, however, there may be vestiges of truth in among all the debris of the jumble of beliefs to which these religions cling, and so their followers merit a certain respect as People of the Book. At times, this respect was stronger than others, and with the passing of the centuries it diminished considerably so that *dhimmīs* were treated with increasing harshness by a society in which their continuing existence was sometimes seen as a slur and an anachronistic holdover from a time when they should have recognized the truth, acknowledged their wrong ways, and surrendered to the way of Islam.

It can be seen from these examples, few as they are, that the classical Islamic attitude towards other faiths was reasonably consistent in seeing them as deficient in various ways, either possessing a scripture that had become corrupt and no longer provided the reliable foundation for belief, or relying upon their own traditional and intellectual resources that had led them to similar mistaken results. The norm is Islam and the Qur'ān, and there is no

---

[11] The tendency to portray all faith traditions, not just Christianity and Judaism, as structured like Islam is instanced in the comparison made by the 12th-cent. heresiographer al-Shahrastānī between the Buddha and the mysterious figure of al-Khidr, who is mentioned in the Qur'ān and identified in Islamic tradition as a saintly seeker after spiritual enlightenment (see J. Elverskog, *Buddhism and Islam on the Silk Road* (Philadelphia: University of Pennsylvania Press, 2010), 89), and his portrayal of Hinduism as a form of Sabeanism, a faith mentioned in the Qur'ān, thus making it structurally comparable with the traditions explicitly mentioned in the Qur'ān (see J. Waardenburg, *Muslims and Others: Relations in Context* (Berlin: De Gruyter, 2003), 173–4). It is given practical expression in the recognition among some Muslim law schools of Hindus as *Ahl al-dhimma*, like Jews, Christians, Zoroastrians and Sabeans (Y. Friedmann, 'The Temple of Multān: A Note on Early Muslim Attitudes to Idolatry', *Israel Oriental Studies*, 2 (1972), 176–82), and by the edicts of Mughal rulers of India that for legal purposes Hindus should be treated as *Dhimmīs*.

comparable alternative. Not many centuries after ʿAbd al-Jabbār composed his great theological structure, the Andalusian mystic Ibn ʿArabī wrote the following ecstatic words:

> My heart has become capable of every form:
> It is a pasture for gazelles and a convent for Christian monks,
> And a temple for idols and the pilgrim's kaʿba,
> And the tables of the Torah and the book of the Qurʾān.
> I follow the religion of love: whatever way love's camels take,
>   that is my religion and my faith.[12]

Whereas ʿAbd al-Jabbār articulates a standard Islamic view about other faiths, this effusion has qualities that transcend any single tradition of faith and sets each one against the overarching principle of love. It has the potential to open possibilities of accepting all faiths that were as yet unseen among Muslims at the time of Ibn ʿArabī, although typically of pluralist attitudes it threatens to reduce the delineations of each individual religion to their teachings about a single predetermined principle. Much has been made of this and similar poetic utterances of Ibn ʿArabī and the equally famous mystic Jalāl al-Dīn Rūmī (d. 1273),[13] because it indeed expresses elements in the tradition that are not often witnessed. But it is important to note that it does not in the final analysis strain the tradition by advocating a pluralist acceptance of all faiths, because the criterion of *tawḥīd* is still applied, even though in a refined form stripped from the ritual trappings of Islamic observance. And when it is set against other statements by Ibn ʿArabī, its poetic as opposed to its intellectual character becomes evident. In a letter to the Seljuk Sultan Kaykāʾūs I in about 1213, Ibn ʿArabī advises the ruler to treat his non-Muslim subjects according to Islamic law and to ensure that Islam remains supreme, and he expresses distaste at Christian practices: 'I tell you that among the worst things that can befall Islam and Muslims . . . are the ringing out of church bells, the public display of unbelief and the elevation of words of worship of other than God (*shirk*)'.[14] Here he shows himself more prosaically to be a Muslim of his time, wanting to invoke the regulations contained in the Pact of ʿUmar against offensive elements in church services, and looking on Christians as odious in their misguidedness.

CONTEMPORARY PERSPECTIVES ON ISLAM AND OTHER RELIGIONS

Medieval attitudes towards other religions, fashioned in times when Muslim theological experts were acutely aware of the intellectual stature of the doctrines of others in their

---

[12] *Tarjumān al-ashwāq*, tr. R. Nicholson, *The Mystics of Islam* (London: Routledge, 1963), 105.

[13] See e.g. Reza Shah-Kazemi, *The Other in the Light of the One: The Universality of the Qurʾān and Interfaith Dialogue* (Cambridge: Islamic Texts Society, 2006).

[14] The text is quoted in ʿUthmān Yaḥyā (ed.), Ibn ʿArabī, *Al-futūḥāt al-makkiyya*, 14 vols. (Cairo: al-Hayʾa al-Miṣriyya al-ʿĀmma li-l-Kitāb, 1972–91), iv, 574.

fledgling empire, but also confident of their own political and military superiority as well as their religious correctness, encountered few challenges down to modern times, and in many minds they have continued to provide the framework for thinking about and encountering other believers and their claims. In particular, with regard to Christianity, the portrayal in the Qur'ān of Jesus as a human messenger like other prophets, his denial of divinity, and the errors of Christians in making him Son of God and God a Trinity, all tend to close ears to Christian explanations about the nature of Jesus and of God.

Of course, in recent times Muslims have been confronted with other religions and their claims in new circumstances, with empire a past memory, and political and military ascendancy a thing for now gone. And, like religious scholars in other traditions, Muslim scholars have attempted to emphasize the latitude of the Qur'ān and Islam, and to search out new possibilities for the relationship between their own and other faiths. The Palestinian scholar Ismail Raji al-Faruqi demonstrates how Islam provides the context and the ground rules for what he regards as proper interreligious understanding and exchange. In an essay published in 1980, 'The Role of Islam in Global Inter-Religious Dependence',[15] he claims that Islam 'can supply principles and ideas for the encounter of religions, and forms and structures for their co-existence and cooperation',[16] and goes on to demonstrate how in the case of Judaism and Christianity Islam attests to their truth as revealed religions, and actually identifies with them as confirming their teachings in itself:

> Islam does not see itself as coming to the religious scene *ex nihilo*, but as reaffirmation of the same truth presented by all the preceding prophets of Judaism and Christianity. It regards them as Muslims, and their revelations as one and the same as their own.[17]

In his mind, this supreme agreement between the three scriptural religions transcends lesser differences between them—'Islam treats them as domestic disputes within one and the same religious family'.[18] In the same way, other religions are also from the one divine origin: as the Qur'ān intimates (e.g. Q 35: 24), prophets have been sent to all communities, and since their messages have all been the same, at the core of all beliefs is the one basic element of *tawḥīd*, the oneness of God.[19] In fact, all humans can observe the same principles as those transmitted by the prophets, because all are created with the same intrinsic disposition: 'The true religion is innate, a *religio naturalis*, with which all humans are equipped. Behind the dazzling religious diversity of mankind stands an innate religion inseparable from human nature.'[20]

These are broad claims. They promote Islam as the true religion that is both communicated by prophetic revelation and intuited by natural reason, and they also risk the historical

---

[15] See A. Siddiqui (ed.), *Ismail Raji al-Faruqi, Islam and Other Faiths* (Leicester: Islamic Foundation, 1998). Essays in this collection explore aspects of the relationship between Islam and other faiths.
[16] Siddiqui (ed.), *Ismail Raji al-Faruqi*, 72.   [17] Siddiqui (ed.), *Ismail Raji al-Faruqi*, 75.
[18] Siddiqui (ed.), *Ismail Raji al-Faruqi*, 77.   [19] See Siddiqui (ed.), *Ismail Raji al-Faruqi*, 77–9.
[20] Siddiqui (ed.), *Ismail Raji al-Faruqi*, 84.

characteristics of Islam and other faiths, as well as humanist assessments of the world, by simplifying them into one essential version of belief. But what is the relationship between the Islam that developed through history and this *ideal form of Ur-Religion*[21] that lies behind all manifestations? Faruqi does not inquire into this, accepting, it would seem, that they are identical, and thereby assenting to the claim present in ʿAbd al-Jabbār and others a millennium earlier that this one historical tradition of faith is the full embodiment of truth, and all others succeed or fail in proportion to their agreement with it. The practical outcome of this model, as Faruqi sees it, is that there can be, as there was in the past, a community of faith communities, ʿa universal *Pax Islamica* which recognizes the legitimacy of every religious community, and grants it the right to order its life in accordance with its own religious genius'.[22] This, guaranteed by Islamic law, allows for measures of freedom and equality between religions.

Faruqi's conception here is very much in line with medieval attitudes, and it shares their shortcomings in regarding the historical faiths as all deriving from prophetic articulations of the one divine revelation, and in founding the independence of the religious communities on Islamic precedents and guarantees. It also risks forcing all forms of religion into a small series of preconceived models, relegating their differences to a secondary status where these can supposedly be resolved by reinterpretation and reformulation into the form of true religion that is embodied in Islam. This is a version of inclusivism in all but name. Nevertheless, the conception has distinct virtues, for it allows each faith tradition to preserve its own character and integrity (contrast ʿAbd al-Jabbār's structure, in which no more than selected teachings of the various faiths are employed to adumbrate the truthfulness of their Islamic equivalents by exemplifying the chaotic consequences of teaching the opposite), no matter how precariously. And it sets the conditions for true meeting of faiths on equal terms, as each relies on its own status as a community of believers in its own right. This sense of equality might be intensified if the relationship between Islam in its historical form and the pre-existent communication from God were delineated more fully, and the contingencies and localized expressions of some of its formulations identified and acknowledged.

A scholar whose works begin to do just this in an abstract theoretical model is Mohammed Arkoun. In a brief essay that sums up his earlier thinking, written again in the 1980s,[23] he warns against returning to the kind of debate known from the Middle Ages ʿwhen philosophers and theologians struggled over "truth" by opposing "faith" and "reason"',[24] though he acknowledges the tendency to do so:

---

[21] Siddiqui (ed.), *Ismail Raji al-Faruqi*, 84.   [22] Siddiqui (ed.), *Ismail Raji al-Faruqi*, 91.
[23] M. Arkoun, 'New Perspectives for a Jewish–Christian–Muslim Dialogue', *Journal of Ecumenical Studies*, 26 (1989), 345–52. See also M. Arkoun, *Rethinking Islam: Common Questions, Uncommon Answers*, ed. and tr. R. D. Lee (Boulder, Colo.: Westview Press, 1994), 32–4.
[24] Arkoun, 'New Perspectives', 346.

Members of each community feel obliged to stand up against the others—not to enter into the others' perspectives, but to protect, proclaim and ascertain the specific "values" or unsurpassable "authenticity" of their own religion. Theological references are then used as *cultural systems for mutual exclusion*, never as tools to cross the traditional boundaries and to practice *new* religious thinking.[25]

This is the tendency shown by Faruqi, for all his ecumenical openness. It promotes Islam and the Islamic paradigm, and uses it to interpret other faiths by means of it. Arkoun seeks to find a way of escape from this, and his agenda for doing so ambitiously calls for new ways of teaching religions and history according to comparative methods which are freed from the imperialistic and political tendencies that seek to promote one above the others.

Arkoun's most radical suggestion concerns a new appraisal of revelation, where he also seeks to remove prioritization. He formulates his conception as a description of three hierarchical states. In the first, revelation is the word of God in its transcendent, infinite form, 'unknown to us as a whole, only fragments of it having been revealed through prophets like Jesus'. This is revelation in its eternal, undisclosed state, known only to God. The second state is revelation as it was first transmitted historically, memorized and preserved in oral form in the period before it was written down. And the third stage is when this oral circulation is 'written down and preserved in what I call the *official closed canons*'.[26] He thus envisages a progression from revelation in a state beyond human reach, to its being received in an oral form in which it is still fluid, to its final concretization and preservation in text.

The problem, as he sees it, is that at the present time revelation is no longer accessible except through the concrete text. But, he asks, '[w]ho decided that text A belonged to revelation and text B or C or D did not? Who fixed the number of texts to be included in the canon and then closed the canon?' The various bodies of religious experts were responsible for this, as 'the official "authority" recognised in each "tradition"'. And it has led to the study of revelation possessing an emphatically philological character, as it is the text that becomes the primary object of investigation. But, asks Arkoun, in allusion to developments in linguistics and semiotics, '[w]hat are the roles of the "author" and the "reader", and what is their interacting impact on the text?'[27] And secondly, this kind of linguistic study must be prior to and independent of statements about the theological status of a text.[28] It is this linguistic study that can confirm or challenge theological definitions of revelation, and they remain independent and unchallenged in turn.

Although this is only briefly put, it points to new departures in the comparative study of religion as well as affecting Muslim engagement in interreligious relations. In the first place, it intimates that no religious community can claim to possess direct revelation in its full form, and in fact the historical process by which the revelation was reduced to a text may have

[25] Arkoun, 'New Perspectives', 346.   [26] Arkoun, 'New Perspectives', 349–50.
[27] Arkoun, 'New Perspectives', 350.   [28] Arkoun, 'New Perspectives', 351.

imported presuppositions and relativities into it. In the second place, the text as it is now held is the only means by which the revelation embodied within it can be accessed, and thus it must be studied without preconditions or assumptions, and by employing all the linguistic means available. And in the third place, no religion can claim to have ascendancy, because all have received equally from the one source, and none has the revelation in a fuller or less indirect form than any other. The implication is that, because each historical instance of the revelation is partial, owing to the vicissitudes of its transformation from prophetic utterance to written text, the process of comprehending and interpreting it can fruitfully involve comparisons with the texts of other communities in order to see what elements they contain that can assist fuller understanding. Rivalry between religions thus gives way to cooperation and reciprocal learning.

Arkoun's suggestion is startling in its originality. However, its typically Islamic features are not difficult to identify, for it assumes that revelation takes the form of God's verbal utterance, which has 'been revealed through prophets like Jesus' and is referred to in the Qur'ān 'by such expressions as "the well-preserved table" (*al-lawh al-mahfuz*) or "the archetype of the book" (*umm al-kitab*).'[29] Here revelation is in oral and then written form, as is understood in the Islamic tradition of it being a succession of messages that mediate the divine utterance though a succession of appointed messengers. There is no reference to revelation in a different form from this, for example of the Word of God understood in Johannine terms as God's own selfhood in an individual human life.[30]

A third author who contrasts with Arkoun in showing a detailed and also sensitive knowledge of Christianity is Mahmoud Ayoub. He has written some of the best informed and sympathetic essays on this other faith, though from a clearly Muslim perspective, of any Muslim author past or present. He shows an evident tendency to elide over difficulties and to harmonize similarities at the expense of differences, but he would defend himself by saying that he uses what is available within the range of resources in order to point to ways in which these two faiths can recognize themselves in one another and find the means to respect one another. Typical of Ayoub's approach is the strikingly titled article written in 1993, 'The Miracles of Jesus: Muslim Reflections on the Divine Word'.[31] From a Muslim point of view,

[29] Arkoun, 'New Perspectives', 349.

[30] In a lecture from two years before (*The Concept of Revelation, from People of the Book to Societies of the Book*, Claremont, Calif.: Claremont Graduate School, 11 Mar. 1987), Arkoun acknowledges this crucial difference between the Muslim and Christian perceptions: 'Jesus Christ, as the incarnate Word of God, is homologue to the *Mushaf* [the first written compilation of the Qur'ān] in Muslim representation and to the written Torah in Jewish tradition' (p. 6). But he does not make much of this, and in what he goes on to say he appears to assume the same relationship between the person of Jesus and the written Gospels as between the utterances of Muḥammad and the written text of the Qur'ān: 'Whatever is the original form of the initial revelation, the oral discourse pronounced originally by the mediator between God and mankind has been written down on parchment or paper to become a *book* which I open, read and interpret' (p. 6). This clearly imposes the Muslim model upon early Christian history, and leaves a number of important questions hanging, not least the way in which Christians relate the Gospels to the person of Jesus Christ.

[31] M. Ayoub, 'The Miracle of Jesus: Muslim Reflections on the Divine Word', in A. Siddiqui (ed.), *A Muslim View of Christianity* (Maryknoll, NY: Orbis Books, 2007), 111–16.

this is startling because it seems to promote Jesus to a status above what he is normally given in Islam. Ayoub is aware of this, and says at the beginning that he is motivated not by controversy for its own sake, but by the challenge 'to achieve a consensus of faith and to remind ourselves, our nations, and our societies that our loyalty must be to God alone and not to any human-made institutions' (by which he presumably means the formulations that have been accepted through Islamic history and do not always reflect the Qur'ān faithfully), and by the second challenge to acknowledge and do justice to 'the infinity and openness of God's Word, which transcends human comprehension and yet demands that it be interiorized and understood anew by the people of faith in every age'.[32] He is evidently more interested in exploring the ways in which Muslims and Christians can use the Qur'ān to reach a new understanding of a belief that has provoked contention in the past than to take sides and prove that it is 'right' or 'wrong'.

In the course of the essay Ayoub expounds the teachings of the Qur'ān about Jesus, noting the many mysterious elements about him they reveal. In the final analysis, however, the Qur'ān reminds Christians about the humanity of Jesus, and whatever is said about him must be understood on the basis of this fundamental fact. Hence,

> He is the Word of God and the servant of God and the messenger of God [all titles given to him in the Qur'ān]. He is the Saviour of us all, but what is salvation but healing? A saviour is not simply one who dies for the sins of others but also one who heals the sickness of the human soul; one who infuses life into dead spirits by his own life and spirit. The original meaning of salvation is 'to be healed', 'to be made wholesome', 'to be truly restored to life'. This, according to the Qur'ān, was the mission of Jesus.[33]

Muslims would acknowledge that this estimation is entirely Qur'ānic, while Christians would find little in it to reject although they would wish to go further, and might detect some rhetorical reductionism in the form of words used. It provides possibilities for believers of both traditions to explore further together, because it emanates from both a deep loyalty to the teachings of the one and also an extensive and profoundly sympathetic knowledge of the beliefs of the other. The approach to interreligious attitudes shown in this brief essay strikes a note that is seldom heard. It presupposes extensive knowledge of the other tradition, penetrating beneath its intellectual surface to the spiritual sensitivities that are contained within.

This quality is even more evident in another essay from 1980, with an equally challenging title, 'Towards an Islamic Christology II—the Death of Jesus, Reality or Delusion',[34] that explores the starkest problem that lies between Islam and Christianity, arising from the denial in Q 4:157 that Jesus was killed on the cross. Together with an earlier essay from 1976, it attempts to put forward an Islamic appraisal of Jesus that Ayoub claims amounts to 'a legitimate

---

[32] Ayoub, 'Miracle of Jesus', 111.   [33] Ayoub, 'Miracle of Jesus', 115.
[34] M. Ayoub, 'Towards an Islamic Christology II: The Death of Jesus, Reality or Delusion', in Siddiqui, *Muslim View of Christianity*, 156–83.

Christology',[35] and the 1980 essay itself constitutes an extended analysis of and reflection upon the meaning and ramifications of this and related verses in the light of classical and modern Muslim exegetical works. Some of its concluding observations repay close reading:

> The Qur'an is not speaking here about a man, righteous and wronged though he may be, but about the Word of God who was sent to earth and returned to God. Thus, the denial of the killing of Jesus is the denial of the power of human beings to vanquish and destroy the divine Word, which is forever victorious. Hence the words 'they did not kill him, nor did they crucify him' go far deeper than the events of ephemeral human history; they penetrate the heart and conscience of human beings.[36]

These words address the context of this all-important verse, in which the Jews claimed they killed Jesus, and locate the event of the crucifixion in the relationship between the all-powerful Creator and the all too often recalcitrant creatures. They bring out the point of significance that neither Christian nor Muslim (nor indeed Jew) would deny, that God's will cannot be thwarted. The crucifixion, or non-crucifixion, of Christ is thus a graphic enactment of the rebalancing of this relationship, serving to remind all concerned that although it may be challenged it can never be changed. Ayoub asserts the Islamic teaching of the all-greatness of God (*Allāh akbar*), while at the same time he affords some scope for Christians to see meaning and point in the event. But he does not leave the matter there, for he goes on to suggest that in both traditions' interpretations of the meaning of the event there is a certain partial grasp of a larger truth, but also the potential for a deeper perception of what that truth is:

> The Qur'an insists on 'letting God be God', and this the Muslim community has taken with uncompromising seriousness. The commentators expressed this insistence with eloquence and power, even at the risk of denying man the privilege of being man . . .
> Christianity has insisted, and with equally uncompromising seriousness, on 'letting God be man' in order for 'man to be divine'. The gap between an extreme Islamic and an extreme Christian position on this point is admittedly vast. The difference is, I believe, one of terminology rather than intent. The final purpose of the two communities of faith is one: let God be God, not only in his vast creation but in our little lives as well. Then and only then could man be truly man, and the light of God would shine with perfect splendour in our mouths and hearts.[37]

Setting aside the intractable question of the historicity of the crucifixion, he looks at the underlying tendencies in the two understandings of it. He notes the differences that have maybe been intensified through rivalries, but points to a deeper calling for each to learn from the truth the other holds. While not surrendering its beliefs, Islam can therefore embrace and be enriched by the beliefs of Christianity.

---

[35] Ayoub, 'Towards an Islamic Christology II', 156.   [36] Ayoub, 'Towards an Islamic Christology II', 176.
[37] Ayoub, 'Towards an Islamic Christology II', 177.

Such advocacy would disturb the theologians from the age of Islamic empires for whom the revelation of the Qur'ān was the supreme point of God's communication with his creation, to such an extent that it superseded all others and rendered them superfluous, and particularly so since their recipients had forfeited their claims to conviction by allowing their revelations to become entangled into historical relativism and mistakenness. But it offers a way of cooperation, and of respect and a certain acceptance. Whether it can be multiplied beyond the uniquely difficult relationship between Islam and Christianity, and made into a general principle for working out a theology of the relationship between Islam and other faiths, remains to be seen.

Ayoub's ecumenical openness typifies attempts among a number of Muslim intellectuals to move beyond the restrictions of the past to a more constructive interest in other faiths. Other examples include the Ugandan Badru Kateregga's explorations with the Mennonite Christian David Shenk,[38] the Iranian Majid Tehranian's conversations with the Japanese Buddhist Daisaku Ikeda,[39] and, maybe most important of all, *A Common Word*, an open letter sent by 138 Muslim scholars to Pope Benedict XVI and other Christian leaders.[40] Such gestures give intimations of a recognition that attitudes towards the other that are built on the past are no longer satisfactory, and sometimes even signs of readiness to accord other traditions a status alongside Islam in a pluralistic acknowledgement of their validity. Nevertheless, it is worth noting that, even though *A Common Word* takes the unprecedented step of structuring Muslim dogmatic and ethical teachings according to Jesus Christ's summary of the Jewish Law as given in the Synoptic Gospels, when it is read closely it follows traditional Muslim teachings about the humanity of Jesus by avoiding any verses from the Gospels that suggest he was more than a prophetic teacher.

Conclusion

Ayoub's appreciation of the value that Christianity can yield marks an extreme point in Muslim acknowledgement of other faiths. But it lies well within the Qur'ānic compass, and it does not push some of the possibilities in the scriptural text as far as they might go, for it retains loyalty to the primacy of Islam, while in places the Qur'ān itself, as seen at the beginning of this chapter, includes verses that when taken alone contain a distinct quality of pluralism, recognizing in other traditions qualities that have the potential to lead their followers to the same eternal bliss as it will itself.

[38] B. Kateregga and D. Shenk, *A Muslim and a Christian in Dialogue* (Nairobi: Usima Press, 1980).
[39] Daisaku Ikeda and Majid Tehrenian, *Global Civilization: A Buddhist–Islamic Dialogue* (London and New York: I. B. Tauris, 2003); see also Reza Shah-Kazemi, *Common Ground between Islam and Buddhism* (Louisville, Ky.: Fons Vitae, 2010), and essays in *The Muslim World*, 100/2 and 3 (2010).
[40] <http://www.acommonword.com/the-acw-document>.

The Islamic tradition has rarely gone as far as Ayoub, and it has hardly ever explored the potential in those verses of the Qur'ān that can almost shock with their openness. Rather, there has been a general consensus among Muslims who have thought and written about the faiths (often about Christianity in particular, hence the predominance of the examples concerning this faith in what has been written here) that Islam stands as the supreme embodiment of God's will in its scripture and the intellectual disciplines that have sought to unfold its meaning, and the well-balanced societies that have been constructed on its teachings. It has therefore tended to judge other faiths, or elements within them, on the point of how they conform to the norms of Islam itself.

Above all, it is the criterion of *tawḥīd* that has operated in Muslim attitudes to other faith traditions. Assuming that all religion comes from the one God, as the Qur'ān declares, Muslim authors throughout history have tended to criticize other faith traditions for their lack of scrupulousness in observing belief in the absolute oneness and majesty of God. This remains central in Islam, and will do so as long as the Qur'ān is read. In consequence, Muslims are likely to find they can appreciate or condemn other faiths according to the extent they detect in them the vestiges of this fundamental of their own belief.

FURTHER READING

Z. Karabell, *People of the Book: The Forgotten History of Islam and the West* (London: John Murray, 2010).

I. A. Omar, *A Muslim View of Christianity: Essays on Dialogue by Mahmoud Ayoub* (Maryknoll, NY: Orbis Books, 2007).

L. Ridgeon and P. Schmidt-Leukel (eds), *Islam and Inter-Faith Relations* (London: SCM Press, 2007).

J. Waardenburg, *Muslim Perceptions of Other Religions* (Oxford: Oxford University Press, 1999).

—— *Muslims and Others, Relations in Context* (Berlin: De Gruyter, 2003).

W. M. Watt, *Muslim–Christian Encounters: Perceptions and Misperceptions* (London: Routledge, 1991).

A. Wheatcroft, *Infidels: A History of the Conflict between Christendom and Islam* (London: Penguin, 2004).

PART II

Themes and Issues in Interreligious Relations

CHAPTER 8

Interreligious Conversion

ANDREW WINGATE

I come to this subject from close personal experience of conversion, primarily in South India, and in Britain. In my own doctoral studies, undertaken in India, I came to the realization that conversion movements were not just historical—what had been known as *mass movements*—but also were happening in the contemporary context.[1] These involved three predominant faiths: Hindus, Muslims, and Christians. It was clear that conversion is an immensely complex phenomenon, whether it happened to an individual, a family, a community, or a village, and this was the subject of my research. I studied this subject as a Christian, and it is from that perspective that I write here. But it was a study of both conversion to, and conversion away from, Christianity. On my return to Britain, I continued my interest in conversion issues, especially within these three faiths, but also more broadly. I became conscious that in Europe there were more conversions to Buddhism than any other faith (though Buddhism does not seek conversions as such, only to introduce people to a way of life and meditation). These European conversions are from Christianity, and from those of no religious faith. I became aware too that the phenomenon of 'secret Christians', those who follow Christ but do not take baptism, for fear of the social consequences, or because of wishing to continue on the boundary between two faiths, was a common phenomenon in India, and also to be found in Britain. Interestingly, the television series *Homeland* features a returned American veteran from Iraq who has become a 'secret Muslim'. While still attending church, he prays *salat* secretly in his basement, until discovered by his daughter. He is afraid of his family, and the media, if his practice becomes public, especially when standing for political office.

Conversion is often related to marriage, particularly in Britain, arising as a consequence of the difficulty involved in living, for long periods, in a mixed-faith marriage, and bringing up a mixed-faith family. It is easier for one partner to adopt, or convert to, the faith of the other.

---

[1] Andrew Wingate, *The Church and Conversion: A Study of Recent Conversions to and from Christianity in the Tamil Area of South India* (New Delhi: ISPCK, 1997).

I encountered this within my own family, as my sister married a British Muslim of Pakistani background. Eventually I found myself with two Muslim nephews, Daud and Jawed. The multi-religious and multi-ethnic dimensions of contemporary society found in the West means that such families have become more and more common. In the case of Islam, the normal rule is that a man may marry a woman of 'the book', whether Jew or Christian, and not require her to convert. But, the other way round, a man who marries a Muslim woman is expected to convert. In both cases, the children should be brought up as Muslims, so being given the right and opportunity to choose Islam as adults. I will bring into this chapter a range of contextual examples, mainly from my own experience in South India and in the UK in Birmingham and Leicester. Incidentally, Leicester is the most multi-religious city in Europe.[2] Theory and practice inevitably interact, and theology of conversion comes out both from scripture and tradition, and from direct experience of interaction with converts and their often complex stories. In this chapter, I will attempt to reflect from both ends.

A CRITICAL DISTINCTION: TWO FORMS OF 'CONVERSION'

It is necessary to differentiate between two forms of conversion. On the one hand there is 'conversion' within a faith, and, on the other conversion from one faith to another. This chapter will primarily be concerned with the second, but we should first acknowledge the importance of the first. Within most faiths, there is a concept of lifelong journey, both spiritually and theologically (or ideologically, as in an intellectual development). I think of the prayer of Sam Amirtham, the charismatic founding Principal of the Tamil Nadu Theological Seminary, Madurai. His prayer for his students was, 'Lord, we are not what we ought to be, we are not what we could be, but thank you Lord, we are not what we were.' In Christianity, especially within the evangelical movement, conversion has been seen as an instantaneous phenomenon—a moment when a Christian becomes 'twice born', that is, born again in the Spirit. Such a person is Christian before and after, but is a transformed person in respect of the contours of religious identity in consequence of this second 'birth'. For example, the Methodist Church requires a public testimony to be given by an ordinand bearing witness about how God has moved in their lives and brought them to the point of ordination. This used to require a dateable experience, like that of John Wesley, the founder of Methodism, whose heart was 'strangely warmed' when he was at Aldersgate, at 8.45 p.m. on 24 May, 1738, and heard Luther's interpretation of a passage from the Epistle to the Romans being read. In that moment he understood anew that, indeed, he was saved 'through faith alone'. Other examples of such conversion 'moments' are the obvious ones of Saul becoming Paul, as

---

[2] The census of 2011 shows Leicester has a population 340,000 with Muslims at 61,000, Hindus, 50,000, Sikhs 14,000, and Christians 106,000.

recorded in the New Testament; the conversion of Augustine in the act of taking up an open Bible and reading the presenting passage; and the conversion of Luther himself. Through such narrative accounts, there is recognition of how God moves in mysterious ways in someone's life. In the Catholic tradition, conversion is seen more as a lifelong development—a process of 'sanctification', of being made holy through participation in the sacraments of the church: 'a growing into the measure of the fullness of the stature of Christ'. In the Orthodox churches it will be related to devotion to icons and journeying nearer to heaven in the liturgy. But, in general, throughout the Christian tradition conversion is a recognized description of the faith journey and will often have a moral dimension, as we are called to grow in love of God and of neighbour day by day.

Other faiths, too, have such a concept of daily conversion. In Buddhism, it is a question of learning more of the way of meditation, and of the Buddhist way of life. In Islam, it is found in observance of the five pillars, and, for example, in the pilgrimage journey to Mecca, the haj, which is often seen as a journey of personal conversion, that is, of deepening and discovering anew the already-held faith. Ramadan is an annual period when, apart from the discipline of fasting, time is given consciously to reading the Qur'an, listening to talks, and undertaking extra prayers. Hinduism has a range of disciplines, depending on the type of Hindu group involved. It may be progress through popular devotion (*bhakti marga*) or through the path of knowledge and meditation (*yoga marga*), or through the doing of good works without desiring the fruits of those good works (*nishkama marga*). Sikhism has a measurable stage reached when someone decides to be baptized, when they feel able to fulfil the full demands of the Sikh life. There may also be interdenominational conversion, for example within Christianity, such as from Anglicanism to Catholicism; or within Islam, in taking the spiritual path of Sufism; or within Judaism, from Orthodoxy to Liberalism; within Hinduism, to become a devotee of Krishna, or a follower of a particular guru. Intra-religious conversion is a widely found phenomenon. But it is interreligious conversion which is our focus of attention.

Interreligious Conversion

The key focus of this chapter, conversion from one religion to another, is where a Muslim becomes a Christian, or a Christian becomes a Hare Krishna devotee, or a Christian becomes a Jew, and so on. There are some key challenges we will consider in turn, beginning with the obvious question: just what do we mean by 'conversion'?

What is Conversion?

There is a range of possible definitions which may be considered. The first comes from Mahatma Gandhi: conversion as essentially a matter of 'self-purification and self-realization'. This definition, recognizable to a Buddhist, is very individualistic, and explains other remarks of Gandhi: 'I am convinced, I know, that God will ask and asks us now, not what we label ourselves, but what we are—i.e., what we do. With Him deed is everything, belief without doing is not believing.'[3] And he said to Christian missionaries: 'What do you want to convert Hindus for? If your contact with them enables them, makes them forget untruth, all evil, and brings them a ray of light, is that not enough? Is that not its own reward? Or must you have a mechanical confession from him that he is a Christian?'[4] The deep suspicion of conversion found amongst Hindus can be seen reflected in this comment, in the context of the complex history in recent years of the Hindu–Christian Forum UK, made by the Hindu joint chair: 'In particular for the Hindu members, the topic of conversion seemed to lurk in the background as the "ultimate Christian agenda" and at other times openly being discussed as a barrier to all Hindu Christian relations.'[5]

A second definition of conversion comes from William James: 'The self, hitherto divided and consciously wrong, inferior or unhappy, becomes unified and consciously right, superior and happy in consequence of its firmer hold upon religious realities.'[6] This definition comes from a psychological perspective, based on a consideration of religious experience. Does the conversion make the person feel more integrated and happy in themselves? A third definition is suggested by Albert Gordon who writes of 'ecclesiastical conversion' as a matter of a full and formal shift of allegiance from one to another, different, faith; or, if within one faith-tradition (such as Christianity) from one denomination or church (ecclesia) to another.[7] The strength of this definition lies in the comprehensiveness of what is involved; it is life trans-forming, and so the life of the individual is transformed, at all levels. Other definitions may be gleaned from the likes of Karl Rahner: 'A fundamental decision not wholly accessible to analytical reflection',[8] which warns us against trying to pin down what is essentially a move-ment of the spirit; or from A. D. Nock: 'The reorientation of the soul of an individual... a turning away from a sense of present wrongness at least as much as a turning towards a posi-tive ideal';[9] or R. E. Frykenburg: 'A change (either an event or a process) from one view of life to another, from one set of beliefs or opinions to another, from one party, religion or spiritual state to another.'[10] K. F. Morrison provides two definitions: 'A person embraced a creed, sub-mitted to an institution that taught the creed, and passed through thick and thin, living out the consequences of acceptance and submission', on the one hand, and on the other, more theologically: 'A process of redemption that was initiated, sustained or completed, if at all, by God's action. This involves empathy and identification with all fellow believers.'[11] Another

---

[3] *Young India* (4 Sept. 1924).

[4] These and the following definitions are found in Wingate *The Church and Conversion*, Chapter 10.

[5] Quote from an e mail sent by Ramesh Pattni, 5.8.2012.

[6] W. James, *The Varieties of Religious Experience*, (London and Bombay: Longmans, Green and Co., 1902), 188.

[7] See Albert Gordon, *The Nature of Conversion* (Boston, Beacon Press, 1967).

[8] See article on conversion in Karl Rahner (ed.), *Encyclopedia of Theology* (London: Burns & Oates, 1975), 291–5.

[9] A. D. Nock, *Conversion* (Oxford: OUP, 1933), 7.

[10] R. E. Frykenburg, 'On the Study of Conversion Movements: A Review Article', *Indian Economic and Social History Review*, 17 (1981), 121–38.

[11] K. F. Morrison, *Understanding Conversion* (Charlottesville, Va.: University Press of Virginia, 1992), 89.

scholar simply asserts: 'Conversion is what a group says it is... Genuine conversion is formulated according to the theological convictions of a particular tradition.'[12]

My own definition, based on very wide case-study work in India is as follows: 'Conversion is a process, including a personal decision, taken alone or as part of a group, to centre one's own religious life on a new focus, which one believes is more liberating, in every aspect of that word, and closer to truth. This involves a change of identification within oneself, and normally leads to a change of outward affiliation to a new community, which will affect one's life at various levels, body, heart, mind, and soul; and to tangible changes of behaviour and practice'. This definition aims to bring out the radicalness of the step, one in many ways more upturning than other great decisions in life like choosing a marriage partner, or a career to follow.

Is Conversion an Event or a Process?

Is conversion to be understood as a momentary event, or as a process with some sense of development involved? To explore this, we can look at the so-called 'conversion' of Paul as given in the New Testament.[13] From what we know of Paul's life and background there were years of complex religious, spiritual, and psychological development lying behind, and so leading up to, this event. And there were decades of development after the Damascus Road experience. Moreover, his conversion was not to God as such; there was continuity inasmuch as he remained a Jew of Jews. Rather, within his already-held belief in God he experienced a conversion to Christ and with that a new calling—to become the apostle to the Gentiles.

Most conversions, if not caused by an external event such as falling in love with someone from another faith, take place over a period, and multiple factors are at play. For example, we may consider the case of a British Hindu Punjabi woman in her twenties, and from a large family. As a younger daughter, she found little affirmation, and used to long to go out, which she was allowed to do only to work. She was depressed and identified only loosely with her religion. But each day she passed the cathedral church. One day she went in and sat, and looked at the beautiful stained-glass windows, which told the story of Jesus. Another day she went further and went to sit in a lunchtime service called the 'Holy Eucharist'. Afterwards a woman priest explained the service to her. They became friends, and gradually she learnt of the Christian religion. She read the Bible secretly, and eventually, after some months, decided of her own free will to become a Christian. She felt a deep peace and a sense of being fully loved by God. Sometime after, she took courage into her hands and told her parents. They were predictably negative, reflecting on what they had done wrong that this terrible thing should come upon them. She, however, remained firm in her new-found faith identity. Psychological pressure applied by her parents failed to make her turn back on her decision.

[12] L. Rambo, *Understanding Religious Conversion* (New Haven and London: Yale, 1993), 7.
[13] Acts 9: 1–31; 22: 1–16; 26: 9–18.

As I talked with her, I often felt a sense of 'awe' at the journey she had taken, and the way she could articulate it. Her knowledge of scripture was quite considerable. She quoted, for example, Psalm 27: 13, 'Though my father and my mother forsake me, the Lord will take me up.' Her struggles continued before and after baptism, but I have no doubt that the words conversion and freedom go together in her story. Her determination won her much more freedom of movement, as well as the freedom of her inner spirit. For her, baptism became important, and this she took in an Asian Fellowship. The bishop wanted to baptize her in his cathedral at Easter, as happened with early Christians. But this was too much for her, and would put great pressure on her family. By waiting, and enabling it to happen in a local context, although she did not win over her parents fully, they nevertheless allowed her sister to be present at the baptism on their behalf. Her getting married became an issue too, and though she knew that she could marry anyone of whatever background, she tried to comply with her parents' wishes, and so sought a Punjabi Christian of her own caste background. As can be seen in this story, some ongoing pastoral and theoretical issues are highlighted. What of the attitude of the wider family who do not convert? Can culture be continuous, when joining a new religious community? Let's look at another example.

Ibrahim had been granted political asylum in Leicester. He felt a strong sense of liberation from the oppression he had felt in the Middle Eastern country that he still loved deeply. He left because he had attended some Christian meetings, been reported to the police, tortured, and forced to give up his professional training. His father had been very angry, and his mother had provided the money—he comes from a wealthy family—to travel concealed on a lorry to Europe. The journey of eight days was a nightmare. He had no idea where he was or where he was going until he arrived in Dover. No sooner had he got over this journey than he was 'dispersed' two hundred miles away to Leicester. Here his safe haven was a large 'hotel' where up to four hundred single persons were housed at a time, often two to three to a room. It was not a prison, but sometimes seemed like one, because of its rules and the heavy feel of institutionalization. He was there for more than a year, until his appeal was finally upheld, with a little help from those who could speak for him and be his advocates. Ibrahim came to Leicester as a searcher. He had endured all this suffering because he was not happy with the version of Islam that he had experienced. He was willing to undergo all this privation because of his longing for a new start. In Leicester he attended a Baptist church from the first Sunday after he arrived. Struggling with rudimentary English, which improved week by week, he found out more of the Christian faith. Eventually he decided to seek baptism. Long preparation followed, and this only happened after he had been given asylum. At a moving service of baptism by immersion, before a large congregation, he gave a testimony where somehow he was able to transcend his linguistic difficulties. The key concept in the witness he made was that he felt 'free', 'liberated'; he had found 'life'. Important, too, had been the tangible sense of 'fellowship' he had received within the congregation. He had given up family, country, flat, car, and good prospects all for deprivation, humiliation, and an unknown future where his practical problems were only just beginning. But yet what he was experiencing was 'freedom'; also, for Ibrahim 'freedom' and 'conversion' were inextricably linked.

Yet another example is that of Sajda, a young Muslim woman from a doctor's family. Her mother was an Asian Christian, but the father brought the children up very strictly as Muslims, which is so often the way in mixed marriages. She was given a bicycle for memorizing the whole of the Qur'an. He forbade the mother to take them to church, but this she did when he was away. The atmosphere in the home became very tense, and for Sajda this became linked with a real fear of Islam, with her father's insistent demand for obedience in the name of Allah. She moved towards Christianity, and eventually told her father who said she was no longer his daughter, and that she would go to hell. He even used occult practices against her. Inevitably a divorce followed for her mother. But at last she felt free to be open in her faith. She was now able to attend church as she willed, and she found it to be a place of warmth and community in her troubled life. She felt that the Holy Spirit had been working in her life, and she had experienced this as the Spirit of liberation. She became a social worker, and married another convert, from Hinduism, who also suffered for his faith journey.

A difficult challenge is raised here. If Christians hold an inclusive understanding of God, meaning that God has not left Himself without a witness in any community or culture, and that the Spirit of God can be active outside the church, how do we interpret and understand the dynamics of a story like this? The church, at its best, reveals a God of love, righteousness, liberation, freedom, acceptance, and salvation. That is why above all, I argue, groups and individuals convert to membership. They experience and respond to what Christians refer to as 'God's Grace'. But if such converts then do not experience such realities within the church to which they have joined, and the gap between the gospel—the 'good news' of the grace of God—that is heard, and the church life and culture that is encountered, is too great, could it be that the God in Christ to whom they converted might be better experienced elsewhere? This might be within other forms of Christian fellowship, other than mainline churches. But might God, on occasion, even lead them beyond the Christian fold, to another religion, such as Islam, or Buddhism, or some forms of Hinduism? Perhaps it is that God in Christ meets them there on the way, at least for a time, as they experience something more liberating?

This challenge has been raised for me by individuals in Britain. Take, for instance, the case of an intelligent Scottish woman who converted to Islam, wears full Islamic dress, and plays a full part in her new faith. The stereotype I hear so often is that Islam is a mechanistic religion and that women are oppressed within it. But this woman is a living witness against such thinking. She is articulate and clear about why she is glad to be a Muslim. There is no sense of oppression. Above all she talks of how she has left no God behind for the God found in the Church of Scotland and the Allah of Islam is one and the same. But she now feels liberated because she no longer has to suffer the hierarchy of the church. She also has a personal relationship with God which makes her free. This may not be easy for Christians to hear, but this is her testimony. Another woman Muslim convert speaks of how, through Islam, she now has a direct relationship with God. She feels free because she no longer has to go through a mediator. In these cases the 'conversion' to Islam has opened the way for a more direct and personal faith-relationship with God than previously experienced within the orbit of Christianity.

A similar challenge has been raised by certain conversions to Buddhism. There are now quite a large number of converts of European origin in Britain. Some have found themselves liberated from depression, disillusion, drugs, or alcohol. Buddhism has been a route to personal liberation and new-found identity. But a very different case concerns a Buddhist friend who had been brought up in a strong Roman Catholic family. Conversion came, as so often, in her student years, and again, as so often, by way of a series of seemingly random incidents. She already felt pushed away from her family's faith which she experienced as restricting. Buddhism happened to come to her notice. She has a philosophical mind and was led into the depths of its philosophy. She became a Tibetan Buddhist, and began to share her new faith with Western groups. She became deeply involved in the interfaith movement, and taught Buddhist–Christian dialogue with me. In the more than twenty years I have known her, I have seen her both deepening her conversion to Buddhism, and at the same time relating more affectionately and positively to the Christianity in which she had been brought up, meeting it again as though it were a new thing. Through the openness of her Buddhism she has become free to relate anew to her past.

Is Conversion Individual or Corporate, or Both?

Most converts in South Asia and Africa have converted in families, villages, or in other groups. This is usually for a combination of reasons, but in the Indian context, liberation from oppression, usually caste oppression, is often a central factor.[14] Two recent examples, covering conversion both to and from Christianity, allow us to address the issue of corporate versus individual conversion. It should be noted that it is not the case that village or group conversion necessarily includes all in a village, or all in an extended family. There is still the question of whether an individual opts in or not to a movement taking place. Often conversion takes place in stages, first with pioneers, and then some followers, and only over a long time covering the whole village. These later adherents watch what is happening, and make a decision, depending on the experience of the pioneers. Such conversion movements are more likely to happen in societies where decisions are generally taken corporately. This may apply to study subjects, employment, marriage, and which religion to follow—in the West, the emphasis is on individual decision-making, at every level of life, and is a prime aim of education, to give youth the capacity to take such decisions on their own, with advice, but of their own choosing and on their own responsibility.

[14] A key historical text is J. Pickett, *Christian Mass Movements in India* (New York: Abingdon Press, 1933).

The village of Veerambal is in one of the poorest areas of Tamilnadu. Its Dalit[15] community were living in bonded labour to higher caste landlords who owned all the land. They were treated as slaves, and their women often used as such sexually. In the 1950s they heard the gospel. They heard of a Jesus Christ who loves untouchables and sets them free, and that in the church which he inspired 'there is to be no Jew, nor Greek; no male nor female; no slave nor free'. For them this meant 'no high caste or low caste or Dalit'. They took baptism together, and built a church. The landlords did not like this, and even less so when the converts demanded time off on a Sunday morning to worship. Sunday became a symbol for their true liberation, very much on the lines of one of the Old Testament understandings of Sabbath. In Deuteronomy, Moses prefaces the reading of the ten commandments with 'I am the Lord your God who brought you out of Egypt, out of the land where you lived as slaves'.[16] To observe Sunday and come out of bonded labour to offer their services for a free wage, was an essential corollary to their religious conversion. A battle ensued and three members of the new Christian community were killed. Their descendants will show the visitor today bullet holes in the church walls, a memorial to what they see as their 'exodus' struggle. Eventually, with the assistance of their bishop, Lesslie Newbigin, they won their freedom. They have had many struggles since, and in the new India it is in their interests to revert to Hinduism, since only as Hindus will they get the full help available to Hindu Dalits. But they are quite clear that they have made their choice for freedom. Along with this has gone a sense of dignity, self-respect, and educational attainment as they have taken advantage of Christian schools. For them conversion has meant liberation and freedom as a group.

For others it has not been such a happy story. I researched two villages which had converted to Christianity in earlier days, for reasons similar to Veerambal. But their experience in the church is that, though they gained education, they did not gain acceptance. They remained on the outside. Sometimes this was literally the case: a higher caste Christian said that she was happy to visit them to pray, and mix with them in church. But she must not have them enter her house. Nor may she eat with them, let alone may her children marry any one of them. She agreed that these attitudes were not as Jesus in the gospels would approve—but he had no weddings to arrange! It is not surprising that when an Islamic mission visited the village it had considerable success, not just with Hindus, but also with Christians. The message was clear: in Islam there is equality and liberation from untouchability. There was also a freedom from complicated doctrines such as the Trinity. This they demonstrated in an admission ceremony which I witnessed. Old Muslims embraced new Muslims as part of the event. Food was shared from a common pot, and each person eating had to take a handful of rice from their own plate and place it on the plate of their neighbour. This was a very powerful

---

[15] The term 'Dalit' is the self-designation of those from the so-called outcaste communities, named by Gandhi as Harijans, and designated as 'scheduled castes' in modern India. These are the former so-called 'untouchables', and there are at least 180 million.

[16] Deut. 6: 10–12.

demonstration of how untouchability was being removed at a stroke. Conversion was experienced as social liberation.

An Analysis of Conversion

The kind of human experience found in conversion can be considered from at least four perspectives. The literature on conversion usually focuses on one or other of these. I also think that a 'push–pull' dynamic provides a helpful analysis for understanding the conversion process. It seeks to discern what is 'pushing' a person out of their traditional faith, and what is 'pulling' them towards a new faith. The push factor is not enough on its own. Applied to conversion, this analysis is like understanding immigration—the push factor may be violence in a particular country, or the experience of famine, or lack of educational possibility; the pull factor is the hope and opportunity for a better life of personal freedoms and advancement. We can see the 'push–pull' dynamic played out in the four chief perspectives about conversion.

Religious/Theological

Clearly conversion can be considered from a religious perspective. This can be subdivided into seeing it primarily from the aspect of spirituality and worship—or from theology. What is the journey being taken spiritually or theologically? We take as our example Hindu conversion to Christianity, one of the most common journeys in India or Britain. A push factor here may be lack of peace found in temples, disillusionment with idol worship, or a sense that Hindu beliefs do not satisfy the life questions being asked. Also its very open-endedness may seem unsatisfactory. The religious and spiritual pull factor may be the person of Jesus, as perfect man, or as God; or the centrality of love and Christian ethics. People may be attracted by Christian worship, its togetherness, and sense of fellowship. They may value the idea of a God of justice, siding with the poor, and the ethical and teaching side of the Bible. There may be factors such as a healing experience, or a dream. These pull factors may not be sufficient. The church may be both a 'pull' and a 'push', depending on the character of the local congregation encountered. Hindus may well be pulled, but not when they find they have to give up their symbols, and appear to being tugged in an exclusive direction.

Cultural/Social

Converts very often wish to escape the caste system, particularly, but not exclusively, if they are Dalits or low caste in the Indian context. Even some Brahmins can feel the injustice of a system that puts them on the top for no merit of their own. Independent-minded individuals may wish to revolt against the power of the extended family. A pull factor towards Christianity (and indeed towards Islam) is their egalitarian ideology. In both cases the corporate nature of worship and the apparent cohesiveness of a congregation may attract. On the other hand, the lack of festivals and excitement in the yearly calendar may detract. In practice, communities may not be as they appear, and certainly in India there are caste divisions in the churches. But this may not be known to the potential convert, and anyway is normally less than experienced in wider Hindu society. A block on conversion may be also social and cultural—the diet that involves eating meat; alcohol consumption; so-called Western ways; and the 'low religion' image Christianity often has within Indian society. Such cultural strictures will apply less in the West, where to become a Christian can mean joining the establishment, gaining a step up on the social ladder. But not always.

Personal/Psychological

By far the majority of conversions of individuals are those aged below 30, and especially in student years. A push factor here is the freedom of choice that comes from being away from home. A person is suddenly free. He/she may look for liberation, and a new start. They may feel guilt for what they have done wrong in the practice of this freedom, and search for a new ethic to live by. It is attractive to be 'born again', and is much easier away from home—be it in Chennai, or Mumbai, or London. If someone is in an Indian village, they may long for a better future, if not for themselves, then for their children. The idea of a personal search—the stage of life seen in Hinduism as that of *Brahmacharya*—may result in choices that take a person into a new religion. A psychological element that is a pull factor is the influence of a charismatic individual, whether pastor or layperson. Such persons become *guru* figures, and can provide a model of saintliness or authority. It may be just that they provide friendship at a difficult time. They may offer the assurance of forgiveness. The congregation they lead may provide a place of warmth and welcome, a place where they are known by name. Of course not all congregations are like this. A Muslim convert to Christianity told me that he went to six churches before anyone spoke to him. He was about to give up, when a layperson, much older than him, talked to him, and invited him home for tea. It was there that he was then baptized. Offputting, too, can be the length of training for baptism normally required. Joining Islam is a much simpler process.

Political/Economic/Institutional

This more obviously applies in the Indian context. Village groups may wish to leave behind their bonded labour status economically or their social 'untouchability'. They may become Christians, Muslims, Sikhs, Buddhists; but they see no future in Hinduism as they have experienced it. They have fears in taking a new step, and look for protection, as they face pressures to conform, or lose their meagre labouring work. But there are many church institutions—schools, colleges, hospitals, and other organizations—to which they will have privileged access, or at least they think so. They expect the protection of seemingly powerful clergy if they convert, and emergency aid when things get tough. They appear to have easier access to the West for their children. But these are mostly perceptions rather than reality, although they are powerful nevertheless. A block to conversion here is often the 'colonial' feel of the churches—to join the church may be regarded as betraying the nation. Few of these aspects apply to individual conversion in the West.

These respective tools of analysis can be applied to any journey of conversion, individual or corporate. They can apply, for example, to conversion to Islam, and here the testimonies of Western converts, often women, are very interesting. They value the clear position of women, and liberation from being seen as sexual objects only. Converts to Islam tend to value the apparent simplicity of Islamic theology, and the listed requirements of Islam, the five pillars. The solidarity of worship, shoulder to shoulder, is also recorded as an attraction. These tools can be used between any two faiths, and provide a touchstone of analysis. But there are yet other analytical issues to consider.

Change of Behaviour and Practice

If there is no tangible and observable change, it can be questioned what is the essential validity of the conversion. It may consist of simple but major changes—the holy day changing from Sunday to Friday or vice versa; the celebration of Christmas rather than Eid, or vice versa. There may be considerable changes in the area of segregation of sexes, particularly on public occasions, or at least in how people meet across sexes. It may be in terms of clothing, such as the putting on, or removal of, hijab. It may be in terms of diet. For a man, the question of circumcision may come in, is it expected or not? Reading the Qur'an or the Bible on a regular basis is a big change, and how each is read. It may be about the nature of prayer, and the kind of prayer undertaken. And so we can go on. In India in particular, conversion of a person from a high caste to either Islam or Christianity produces major challenges in terms of behaviour: what kind of food can be eaten, or who can cook it, for example.

How is the Success of Conversion Measured?

What is the measurability of conversion? How do we decide this? At one level, this is simple: does it last? Rates of reversion can be very high. For example, in the 1990s a study was done by Pradip Sudra, of Asian converts to Christianity in Britain. Three-quarters had reverted within two years.[17] This may not have been in terms of belief, which usually remains fixed on

---

[17] See *The Way of Renewal*, Report of the Board of Mission of the Synod of the Church of England (London: Church House Publishing, 1998), 125. This led to the formation of the Alliance of Asian Christians.

Christ—but in terms of outward affiliation, they revert to Hinduism, so powerful is this culturally. In Indian village conversion, reversion also can be found, usually because of pastoral neglect, where Hindu practices re-envelop the convert families, unless there is effective teaching and rooting in the new faith. Maybe the conversion was related to a particular period in life, the revolt of youth, and when that period is over there is a reversion to the normal pattern of life. Maybe the charismatic individual who has been the agent of conversion moves on and there is no group around the convert to nurture them on after this trauma. Even where there is no actual reversion, can we call conversion a 'success' if the person ends in a lonely state, isolated, and sometimes psychologically disturbed? This is unlikely to happen immediately, because the convert has a certain status, and may be valued for the testimony they are asked to give. But what happens when that period inevitably comes to an end? What of the question of a search for truth? Perhaps the new truth no longer satisfies, and guilt can come in at abandoning the old truth. Has conversion led to profound liberation, or the opposite?

Perhaps surprisingly, people often do stick to their new faith through thick and thin, even when the dice are loaded against them. A Methodist minister was a convert to Christianity from Sikhism. He continued to wear one of the five Ks of his Sikh heritage, the silver bangle. This represented the religion of his mother that taught him of God. He faced much wounding opposition to this practice, particularly when he rose to prominence. Yet there was no question of him reverting. Many high-caste converts to Christianity face extreme hostility. But a favourite text for them is often, 'how can I put my hand to the plough, and then look back'.[18]

How do Religion and Culture Relate in these Conversion Stories?

All the above shows how central this question is. It is a highly contextual question: it depends where you are. Where the change of faith is also a change of culture, what faith is, and what culture is, often cannot be unravelled. There is no such thing as pure Buddhism, Islam, Hinduism, or Christianity. Is a convert joining Tibetan, Japanese Zen, Sri Lankan, Thai, or Western Buddhism, for example? Becoming a Muslim in some contexts may be bound up with the Pakistani, Indian, or Arab cultural veneer of the community involved. At the Islamic Foundation in Markfield, outside Leicester, there is an organization specifically established for the support of new Muslims. So also South Asia Concern, a group whose aim is to help Asian converts to Christianity. The Hare Krishna movement is more sensitive to Western Christian converts and their needs than if someone tries to be Hindu within the normal temple culture. Often those in a faith are not able to distinguish between what is faith and what is culture. What is given over as 'of the faith' is actually culture. Children, who attend the madrassas in Leicester every evening, dress in Arab clothing as though that is of the essence of Islam, and are taught that this is how it is. A Brahmin Tamil convert to Christianity told me

---

[18] Luke 9: 62.

that to be accepted in his all-white congregation, where he became a senior official, he had to become a coconut: dark on the outside, and white on the inside.

Some Key Pastoral Considerations

Since conversion can be such a major and often traumatic step, pastoral care of the convert is vital. This applies in whatever pattern the conversion happens, whether individual, family, or group, and from whatever faith to whatever faith. As usual, the context will indicate what is appropriate. The care will need to be both for those who convert, and for the family from which the convert has moved. Such a family may have considerable guilt and reflect on where they went wrong. They need support to talk things through. Two examples of such need for care illustrate the complexity of what is involved. Parents from the Caribbean, living in Birmingham, found that their son had become a Muslim. They felt deeply sad, and also wondered where on earth they had gone wrong. They had failed in their fundamental duty of handing on their Christian faith to their son. Much sensitive counselling was needed for them to accept the new reality, and above all not to take it on themselves. They also needed help to see how they should keep the door open, in the hope that he might return to the fold at some point. At the same time, they could be glad that he had become a pious member of his new faith; he was no extremist, and he had not joined a gang in revolt against society.

The second example is one I was involved in personally. A long-standing Muslim dialogue partner, whom I saw often with his family, telephoned me one day asking me to come over, as he had something to tell me that he could only tell me in person. I arrived, and he poured out his anguish. His daughter had run away with someone she worked with, a Hindu Brahmin. I pointed out she was of age, but he said that, if this came out, there could be trouble between Muslim and Hindu communities in the area. We called the community relations officer within the police, and he undertook to search for the whereabouts of the couple, but pointed out clearly that they had done nothing illegal. They were traced to a Salvation Army Hostel in Scotland, and he undertook to convey any letters. The elder brother wrote a potentially disastrous letter, in effect throwing the woman out of the family if she did not return immediately on her own. Her paramour had betrayed not just her family, but her faith. The father wrote a good letter, assuring her of the continuing love of both her parents, and welcoming the couple back under certain conditions. By now, we knew she was pregnant. The conditions included, predictably, that the Hindu father-to-be should become a Muslim. I advised that only the father's letter should be sent, and wrote my own letter of support. The result was that they returned, married, and he embraced Islam. As time went by, he became the most devout Muslim in the whole family! We can multiply such examples, both from India and from Britain, and it is clear that this theme is a major one. It involves considering the attitude of the whole congregation, and the degree of acceptance and willingness to listen, as well as teach, needed to nurture a convert over a long period. Where marriage is concerned, this is even more crucial—how is a convert to find a suitable partner? This must be a consideration.

Also, if, say, the convert comes out of Hinduism to Christianity, how can an eldest son perform the funeral rites for the father? Here wisdom and pragmatism are needed, rather than rigid rules.

Conversion as Partial Assimilation or 'Belonging'

Can someone remain within one faith community, but be converted to a key element within another? Clearly the answer is yes, since there are many examples of this.[19] There are Buddhist-Christians, or Christian-Buddhists, more usually the former. They remain Christian and often quite involved but, at the same time, they follow Buddhist meditation practices, learn from the teaching of the Buddha as well as from Christ, and may go on Buddhist retreats. Buddhism gives space for this, and I know a Buddhist monk, who always gives space for Christians, if present, to meditate on Christ, using, for example, the loving kindness meditation while the Buddhists meditate on the *Dharma*, or teachings of the Buddha. There are many examples of Hindu Christians. Some are Asian Christians who do not wish to sacrifice their Indianness, and some of the Hindu culture they were brought up to, though they will reject idol 'worship' and the like. One convert calls himself a 'Jesu Bhakter'. He is devoted as ever to Jesus, but using the vocabulary of the Bhakti tradition which he knew as a Tamil Hindu. He wishes to affirm the religious practices of his devout parents, and reject the ultra-Westernization found in the British church of which he is a part. Such boundaries are much less easy to transcend in the case of Islam. It is not conceivable to continue to worship Jesus and be a Muslim (though honouring Jesus as a prophet is part of being a Muslim). As a Muslim, culturally, one can also be a secret Christian—but that is hard to sustain without adherence to a community of Christians. Some Christians follow Sufi practices, particularly in the USA, and love the teachings of Sufi poets such as Rumi. But they remain Christian in their primary religious identity. Some Pakistani Christians, converts from Islam, did for a period hold prayer meetings where they prayed in the physical way of *salat.* Present tensions make that very difficult to even conceive of doing. Jewish-Christians are a significant group— 'Jews for Jesus', for example, believe in Jesus as the Messiah and follow Jewish cultural practices. A good example is found in the writings of Michelle Guinness, who married a Christian priest, and was determined to enable her children to know the Jewish way of life.[20]

Proselytizing: Cross-Faith Conversion-Seeking

Should conversions be sought from people of other major world faiths? This fundamental question raises the issue of our theology, or 'ideology' of religions, and of deepest questions of truth and salvation and, for Christians, the place of mission and evangelism. All religions,

[19] See also Ch. 15.
[20] Michelle Guinness, *Child of the Covenant* (London: Hodder & Stoughton, 1994).

I suggest, have a theology (or ideology) of other faiths, and there are divisions about this within the faiths. Hindus, it is said, are not missionary minded, and we can see that reflected in Gandhi's definition of conversion. But certain Hindu groups are clearly missionary, seeking converts who can follow their way. They seek followers because they believe their way of life and philosophy offers something distinctive to all. They may not condemn others to darkness for not following, but they consider their way is a better way to spiritual fulfilment. At another level, there are repeated attempts, sometimes successful, to reconvert Indian Christians of Dalit background. To be true Indians, they should be Hindu. This Hindutva-style philosophy accompanies the practice of *suddhi*, an ash ceremony conducted in certain *mutts* (monasteries). Muslims and Christians both seek conversions, because they believe that their way, whether of the Qur'an, or of Jesus, is *the* Way, the Truth, and the Life. Evangelism is the natural outworking of this; it is why church and mosque are found throughout the world. The belief that in Islam or in Christianity there is found full salvation and truth has often justified inappropriate means of conversion. But these religions also have an inclusivist strand—any who practise sincerely their own faith, in terms of ethical and spiritual discipline, can be saved through the mercy of God, without converting as such. Another alternative theology has developed in recent times within Christianity, that of pluralism, and there is little impulse here for seeking conversions. None of us have all the truth or a monopoly of salvation, which is relative to the faith practice.

Recent Contributions to the Issue of Conversion

Three recent important documents illustrate the contemporary importance of the topic of conversion within an interreligious context. First, a document titled *Christian Witness in a Multi-Religious World* issued in June 2011 arose out of a series of consultations under the auspices of the World Council of Churches, the Pontifical Council for Interreligious Dialogue, and the World Evangelical Alliance.[21] This significant Christian document was the result of three consultative meetings, the first of which, held in 2006, included representatives of different religions. This meeting affirmed that

> while everyone has the right to invite others to an understanding of their faith, it should not be exercised by violating others' rights and religious sensibilities. Freedom of religion enjoins upon all of us the equally non-negotiable responsibility to respect faiths other than our own, and never to denigrate, vilify or misrepresent them for the purpose of affirming the superiority of our faith.[22]

---

[21] *Christian Witness in a Multi-Religious World: Recommendations for Conduct* (Geneva: WCC, 2011).

[22] 'Assessing the Reality', Lorano, Italy, May 2006; the full text of report is in *International Review of Mission*, 96 (July–Oct.), 2007.

This tone was carried through to the final statement on mission where it was affirmed that 'Religious freedom including the right to publicly profess, practice, propagate and change one's religion flows from the very dignity of the human person which is grounded in the creation of all human beings in the image and likeness of God (Genesis 1.26).'[23] Another principle of the total of twelve agreed to concerns ensuring personal discernment, that is, that 'Christians acknowledge that changing one's religion is a decisive step that must be accompanied by sufficient time for adequate reflection and preparation, through a process ensuring full personal freedom.'[24]

Secondly, there have been a number of joint Muslim–Christian statements about conversion, such as those from Norway, England, and the European Churches. A lead in this was the Church and the Islamic Council of Norway. In 2007, they produced a joint statement as a contribution 'to the on-going international process on the issue of religious freedom and the right to convert.'[25] In this, the universal right to convert was clearly affirmed. The European Churches statement (CEC and CCEE) jointly with Muslim representatives, after a conference in Belgium in 2008 on the theme of being both a European citizen and a person of faith, affirms the right of conversion, including the right, significantly, to leave a religious faith, and to convert to a secular stance of no-faith. It stated:

> As Christians and Muslims we acknowledge the right of freedom of conscience, of changing one's religion, or deciding to live without a religion, the right to demonstrate publicly, and to voice one's religious convictions without being ridiculed or intimidated into silence by prejudice or stereotyping intentionally or through lack of knowledge.[26]

It was much harder for the Muslim delegates, comprising half of the forty-six who participated, to agree to the clause about leaving faith behind, than to change faiths.

Finally I draw attention to the *Goodwill Agreement* between Hindus and Christians on the Hindu–Christian Forum UK, made in 2004. This was a powerful affirmation of the right to convert which was certainly difficult for Hindus to agree to. They also made clear that this was an affirmation for the UK only (and not for India, where anti-conversion laws are increasingly prevalent[27]). Nevertheless, it was a considerable achievement, between a missionary religion, and one that is not normally missionary.[28]

---

[23] Recommendation 7.   [24] Recommendation 11.
[25] <www.kirken.no/english/news.cfm?artid-> (22 Aug. 2007).   [26] Paragraph 9 of final report.
[27] Such laws and regulations were first passed in Arunachal Pradesh in 1978. Legislation of various kinds have been passed in Gujarat (2003), Madhya Pradesh (2006), Chhattisgarh (2006), then Himalchal Pradesh, and on and off in Tamilnadu (2005–8). They are usually called 'Freedom of Religion Bills', and are aimed at protecting Dalits and Tribals from what are seen as pressures to convert. A similar bill has been proposed in Sri Lanka. All such bills unite the churches, as nothing else, in their opposition. Of course, such legislation is part of the reality in many Muslim countries, including the more open Malaysia, where conversion is not allowed for the indigenous Malays, only for Chinese and Indians. This has been so for nearly 200 years, under the Treaty of Malacca, whereby the British got access to Malaya for trade purposes.
[28] See booklet *Bridges and Barriers to Hindu–Christian Relations* (Oxford: Oxford Centre for Hindu Studies, 2011).

CONCLUSION

At the centre of journeys of conversion, from a Christian perspective, is the Spirit 'which blows where it wills'. It is a mystery we are part of, for it is God who converts, not human strategy. J. V. Taylor puts it rather well:

> The most characteristic forms of the action of the Spirit as Creator Redeemer are a constant pressure towards greater personhood, the creation of new occasions for choice, and the principle of self-surrender in responsibility for others. These must be the marks of any evangelism which is truly Christ's evangelism. It must be deeply personal rather than propositional....the truth which converts is the truth *of* Jesus, not the truth *about* Jesus. How strange it is that people who have met the Truth should imagine that they are called to propound truths! How unlike Jesus himself, who would never violate the freedom or responsibility even of his enemies, are those who would win the world with a loud-hailer in one hand and a book of church statistics in the other.[29]

FURTHER READING

Robert Hefner, *Conversion to Christianity: Historical and Anthropological Perspectives on a Great Transformation* (Los Angeles: University of California Press, 1993).

Sebastian Kim, *In Search of Identity: Debates on Religious Conversion in India* (New Delhi: Oxford University Press, 2003).

A. Krailsheimer, *Conversion* (London: SCM Press, 1980).

C. Lamb and M. Darrol Bryant (eds), *Religious Conversion: Contemporary Practices and Controversies* (London and New York: Cassell, 1999).

L. Rambo, *Understanding Religious Conversion* (New Haven and London: Yale University Press, 1993).

R. Robinson and S. Clarke, *Religious Conversion in India* (New Delhi: Oxford University Press, 2003).

J. Seunarine, *Reconversion to Hinduism* (Madras: CLS, 1977).

Gorman Ulf, *Towards a New Understanding of Conversion* (Lund: Teologiska Institutionen i Lund, 1999).

A. Wingate, *The Church and Conversion: A Study of Recent Conversions to and from Christianity in the Tamil Area of South India* (New Delhi: ISPCK, 1997).

---

[29] J. V. Taylor, *The Go-Between God* (London: SCM Press, 1972), 136–7.

CHAPTER 9

Interreligious Dialogue

MARIANNE MOYAERT

However familiar we may be with interreligious dialogue, it remains, certainly in light of history, a remarkable phenomenon. For centuries, adherents of different traditions ignored one another at best—and have fought one another at worst. Although there were interreligious encounters in the past, as a general phenomenon the dialogical 'turn' is new. It is no exaggeration to say that belief in the importance and necessity of dialogue entails a break with the predominantly monological era. Although violent interreligious conflicts continue to ravage the world, there is a growing sentiment that benevolent and respectful contacts between the different religions and their adherents are also possible. The flipside of this growing interest, even popularity, of interreligious dialogue is a certain blurring of the meaning of the term. That is why it is necessary to clarify what precisely is meant by it. In this chapter I want to cast some light on the special dynamics of the dialogue between the religions. Given that interreligious dialogue is a very complex phenomenon, I will explore it from various perspectives: historical, descriptive, etymological, and also philosophical. I will conclude with the crucial questions: What is at stake in interreligious dialogue and how is the tension in the dialogical relationship between identity and openness dealt with? What are the conditions for interreligious dialogue and what fields of tension characterize the dialogue between the religions?

THE EMERGENCE OF INTERRELIGIOUS DIALOGUE

Interreligious dialogue is a relatively recent phenomenon which is usually identified as starting in 1893. In that year, Chicago celebrated the 400th anniversary of Columbus's discovery of America by organizing a World Fair which covered diverse domains such as science, literature, art, and education. The whole event exuded the spirit of the modern ideal of progress. Within the organizing committee it was asked if religion should not also be a part of this festive happening in the form of a 'World's Parliament of Religions'. Not everybody was equally enthusiastic about this proposal: 'Many felt that religion was an element of perpetual discord, which should not be trusted amid the magnificent harmonies of a fraternal assembly of the nations.'[1] However, the conviction that the modern penchant for unity could also be realized in the religious domain was stronger than the opinions expressing distrust. It was this belief in unity that made this great interreligious gathering possible.

In June 1891, the organizing committee sent a letter to the religious leaders of the world, expressing the desire and hope for cooperation between the different religious communities. The World's Parliament of Religions, it was emphasized, was not intended to induce an atmosphere of indifference but, instead, an amiable encounter between people with strong convictions in the hope that they would come closer to the one truth. According to John Henry Barrows, one of the initiators of the event, the reactions were chiefly positive, although there were, as was to be expected, also some negative notes expressed.[2] Among others, the Moderator of the Presbyterian Church to which Barrows belonged rejected the whole initiative. He explained his position as follows: 'The difficulties which I feel rest on the fact that the Christian religion is the one religion. I do not understand how that religion can be regarded as a member of a Parliament of Religions without assuming the equality of the other intended members and the parity of their positions and claims.'[3] The Vatican, too, sounded its disapproval, though the real censure followed only after the parliamentary event: 'In 1895, in a letter to Archbishop Francis Satolli, the Apostolic delegate to the US, Pope Leo XIII officially censured Catholic participation in any "future promiscuous conventions".'[4]

These rejections, however, put us on the trail of what is still the central challenge of interreligious dialogue, namely the tension between identity and otherness. The main question is still that of how one can find a balance between one's own faith commitment and openness to the otherness of the other. A course is constantly being sought between the two extremes of relativism, on the one hand that which ends in indifference and absolutism; on the other, that which ultimately excludes every form of dialogue. Although in a way the challenge is still the same, the general mood has changed quite a bit since then. That is already apparent, for example, from the mere fact that the Vatican, which had such grave objections in 1893, is today one of the great proponents of dialogue between the religions.

Despite this and other negative reactions, the World's Parliament of Religions opened on 11 September 1893. The Liberty Bell of the Columbian Exposition was rung ten times at the beginning of the first meeting, in honour of the ten great religions of the world: Hinduism, Buddhism, Jainism, Zoroastrianism, Taoism, Confucianism, Shintoism, Judaism, Christianity, and Islam. In total, 400 representatives of these different religions were present, of which 150 took the floor during the week of the Parliament to give as thorough a description as possible of their respective

---

[1] J. H. Barrows (ed.), *The World's Parliament of Religions*, i (London: Review of Reviews, 1893), 5.
[2] For the reactions to the letter from the central committee, see Barrows, *World's Parliament of Religions*, 18–61.
[3] Barrows, *World's Parliament of Religions*, 22; other negative reactions came from, among others, the Sultan of Turkey.
[4] M. Braybrooke, *Pilgrimage of Hope: One Hundred Years of Global Interfaith Dialogue* (London: SCM Press, 1992), 29.

traditions.[5] There were, in addition, more than 4,000 people present at the opening session, and that number was doubled on the closing day. One could argue that this first World's Parliament of Religions was more of a Christian forum to which non-Christians were also invited than a true interreligious assembly. That this criticism is not unfounded is obvious if we look at the members of the organizing committee, which consisted of fourteen of Chicago's well-known Protestant Christian leaders, one Jewish rabbi, and a Roman Catholic bishop. Most participants were also Christian, primarily of the liberal Protestant persuasion. Various lectures moreover displayed a strong Christian missionizing tendency and sometimes even an outspoken polemical attitude towards the other religions. The World's Parliament was seen by some Christian participants as the perfect opportunity to proclaim the 'exclusive truth' of Christianity.

Although these facts induce a certain 'relativization' of the whole event, the World's Parliament of Religions was, nonetheless, a milestone. With its intention of advancing a feeling of brotherhood among the various religions, the organizing committee wanted to break with the past in which dealing with the religious other was primarily polemical in character. The World's Parliament offered adherents the opportunity to present their faith or a related theme themselves. As a result, they were not only the topic of study or the object of mission work but also a subject in the encounter. Perhaps the importance of the Parliament was best grasped in the editorial that appeared in the *Chicago Tribune* when the Parliament ended. According to this, Christianity learned from the Parliament that there were no longer godless and heathen people, but Buddhists, Confucians, Hindus, and others: 'Under some of the religions lies the clear idea of divinity, under all lies the clear idea of morality.'[6]

From the Age of Monologue to the Age of Dialogue

The 1893 World's Parliament of Religions has become the symbolic beginning of the interfaith movement that wants to promote positive and constructive relations between the adherents of various religious traditions and considers the ideals of brotherhood, harmony, respect, and openness to be of paramount importance. As the actual catalyst of interreligious dialogue, this largely inflated parliamentary-type event was less important, however. The belief in the importance of interreligious dialogue is more the result of a very long process of a change in mentality in which primarily other factors played a role. This is a process that began centuries ago and is still continuing.

The idea that dialogue is to be preferred above polemics is rooted in the modern ideals of equality, freedom of religion, respect for otherness, and tolerance. The first trigger for this

---

[5] J. M. Kitagawa, 'The History of Religions in America', in J. M. Kitagawa (ed.), *The History of Religions* (Chicago: University of Chicago Press, 1987), 5.

[6] Editorial, *Chicago Tribune*, 24 Sept. 1893.

altered attitude to religious plurality was the painful and dramatic history of the religious wars that ravaged Europe in the sixteenth and seventeenth centuries, which showed how destructive interreligious disagreements could be.[7] These wars have been called 'hermeneutical civil wars' because 'the exegesis of Scripture and the divine commandments led to a hopeless struggle and the cruellest acts'.[8] Only when the insight had grown that discrimination, persecution, and the killing of others in God's name were impermissible could a context arise in which people felt safe enough to discuss one another's beliefs. Tolerance is thus the critical ethical lower limit for interreligious dialogue. To that extent, interreligious dialogue is a child of the modern age and its political choice to bring about the separation of 'church' and 'state', together with the enlightened ideals of democratic pluralism and the recognition of fundamental human rights.[9]

Second, the rise of the interreligious movement occurred in the wake of ecumenical dialogue. Originating in the nineteenth century, ecumenical dialogue wants to break through the divisions that arose in history between Christian denominations by making the unity of Christians visible. Ecumenical dialogue showed that it is possible to maintain positive and constructive relations with people who think and believe differently. The belief gradually grew that something similar should be possible between the different religions. There is an alternative to apologetics and polemics.[10] In that sense, we can also understand why interreligious dialogue is sometimes called the wider ecumenism: one that reaches beyond the community of Christian churches to include the world's great religions.[11]

A third important factor that should be mentioned here is the history of colonization, followed by decolonization after the Second World War.[12] European colonialism was fed ideologically by Western imperialism and a Christian claim to superiority, which resulted in sometimes aggressive missionary activities. Local traditions were portrayed as inferior. They

---

[7]   One of the best known is the Thirty Years' War (1618–48), which was ended by the Peace of Westphalia.

[8]   T. W. A. de Wit, 'De trivialisering van de tolerantie', in M. ten Hooven, *De lege Tolerantie: Over vrijheid en vrijblijvendheid in Nederland* (Amsterdam: Boom, 2001), 88.

[9]   The relationship between religion and modernity (secularization) is not obvious, and can also be thematized in interreligious encounters. Stanley Samartha notes that 'People who are dissatisfied with the consequence of secularism and alarmed by the influence of technology on human life, seem to be looking for signs of the sacred that are deep and mysterious, authentic, significant and persistent which can give direction to and shape the quality of human life. In this context therefore interreligious dialogues are of particular importance.' S. J. Samartha, 'The Progress and Promise of Inter-Religious Dialogues', *Journal of Ecumenical Studies*, 9 (1972), 470.

[10]   The purpose of *apologetic dialogue* is to defend the truth of a particular belief. *Polemical dialogue* goes further than apologetics and maligns the other party in the debate and/or uses insulting language. Arguing by gagging the other is more of an anti-dialogue.

[11]   M. M. Thomas, *Towards a Wider Ecumenism* (Bangalore: Asian Trading Company, 1993); cf. S. M. Heim, *Grounds for Understanding: Ecumenical Resources for Responses to Religious Pluralism* (Cambridge, Mass.: Eerdmans, 1998). Enthusiasm within the ecumenical movement for interreligious dialogue is not shared by all. E.g. George Lindbeck accepts interreligious dialogue is the order of the day, but laments the fact that wider ecumenism is being promoted at the cost of inter-Christian ecumenism. He points out that the intention of interreligious dialogue and of ecumenism are very different: 'The first is a matter of learning how to communicate with strangers and the second, of overcoming estrangement within the family', G. Lindbeck, 'The Unity we Seek: Setting the Agenda for Ecumenism', *Christian Century*, 121 (2005), 29.

[12]   J. B. Cobb, Jr., *Transforming Christianity and the World: Beyond Absolutism and Relativism* (Maryknoll, NY: Orbis Books, 1999), 31.

had nothing whatsoever to contribute to the formation of Western civilizations, not to mention Christianity, and were seen primarily as 'targets for outreach and conversion'.[13] After the Second World War came an end to the so-called colonial era and thus also to the rule of Christianity.[14] Christianity changed from being a privileged partner of those in power into a minority presence with a bad reputation.[15] The unhealthy connection between Christianity and colonial oppression was painfully clear and gave rise to a number of questions. In this context, Samuel Rayan, an Indian Jesuit theologian, posed the following pointed question:

> Imperialist missions have projected Christ as a new, religious Julius Cesar, out to conquer.... We [persons of colonized countries] ask about the subterranean connection between the Western conception of Christ's uniqueness and authority on the one hand and the Western project of world domination on the other.[16]

The belief in the necessity of interreligious dialogue is at least partly inspired by the desire to put the earlier dominant and privileged position of Western Christianity to rights. Gradually, the understanding grew that a non-imperialistic attitude to the world was needed. This understanding is one of the factors that led to the change 'from the age of monologue to the age of dialogue'.[17]

A fourth factor is, without doubt, the Shoah (Holocaust) which cost the lives of 6 million Jews, including 1.5 million Jewish children. Although Nazi anti-Semitism should not be equated with Christian anti-Judaism, the Christian involvement in this catastrophe is undeniable. The Holocaust scholar John Roth states as follows: 'Christianity was not a sufficient condition for the Holocaust, nevertheless it was a necessary condition' for it.[18] It was in Christian soil that Nazism took root. The awareness that the centuries-old Christian 'teaching of contempt'[19] also contributed to this tragedy led to a deep process of reflection in both Roman Catholic and Protestant circles that is still going on today. It is certainly no exaggeration to state that the Shoah is one of the most important factors leading to revolutionary change in the church's attitude *vis-à-vis* Judaism.[20] In that sense, interreligious dialogue is also a post-Holocaust development.[21]

---

[13] J. Hill Fletcher, 'Religious Pluralism in an Era of Globalization: The Making of Modern Religious Identity', *Theological Studies*, 69 (2008), 395.

[14] S. J. Samartha, *One Christ, Many Religions* (Maryknoll, NY: Orbis Books, 1991), 86.

[15] S. B. King, 'Interreligious Dialogue', in C. Meister (ed.), *The Oxford Handbook for Religious Diversity* (Oxford: Oxford University Press, 2010), 103.

[16] S. Rayan, 'Religions, Salvation, Mission', in P. Mozjes and L. Swidler (eds), *Christian Mission and Interreligious Dialogue* (Lewiston, NY: Edwin Mellen Press, 1990), 134.

[17] L. Swidler, J. Cobb, P. Knitter, and M. K. Hellwig (eds), *Death or Dialogue: From the Age of Monologue to the Age of Dialogue* (Philadelphia: Trinity Press International, 1990).

[18] Cited in J. B. Cobb and Ward McAfee (eds), *The Dialogue Comes of Age* (Minneapolis: Fortress Press, 2010), 66.

[19] J. Isaac, *The Teaching of Contempt: Christian Roots of Anti-Semitism* (New York: Holt, 1964).

[20] See M. Guiliani, 'The Shoah as a Shadow upon and a Stimulus to Jewish–Christian Dialogue', in P. A. Cunningham, N. J. Hoffmann, and J. Sievers (eds), *The Catholic Church and the Jewish People: Recent Reflections from Rome* (New York: Fordham University Press, 2007), 54–72.

[21] M. Moyaert and D. Pollefeyt, *Never Revoked: Nostra Aetate as Ongoing Challenge for Jewish–Christian Dialogue*, Louvain Theological and Pastoral Monographs, 40 (Louvain: Peeters, 2010).

Nevertheless, the rise of interreligious dialogue does not have to do only with Christianity's disreputable past. The most important factor by far is the sociological phenomenon of globalization. Migration streams, increased mobility, and changing means of communication have made the world smaller, as it were. At the beginning of the previous century, coming into contact with strange cultures, peoples, and religions remained a remote dream for most people. Today we are confronted willy-nilly with otherness. Cultural and religious diversity are an integral part of our life-world. The religious other is no longer an *abstract figure* but is seen in all her *concreteness* as neighbour, colleague, friend, spouse, etc. 'More and more Christians, along with peoples of other faiths and ideologies, are experiencing *religious pluralism* in a new way—that is they are feeling not only the *reality* of so many other religious paths, but also their vitality, their influence in our modern world, their depths, beauty and attractiveness.'[22] The emphasis is laid on the experience of religious vitality as a (possible) source of spirituality and morality for other religions. Even those who reject the other religions do acknowledge that they are struck by the vitality of the other religions.[23] This positive experience of religious diversity is one of the arguments why 'openness' to the religious other is understood to be a 'virtue'.[24]

Moreover, because of globalization, the awareness of a shared responsibility for this world and the people who live in it has also grown. Globalization causes global problems that can be charted and solved only through global responsibility in a constructive way. People are increasingly coming to the awareness that they have to learn to work together across the boundaries of their religions. According to some, it is even of vital importance to formulate a global ethic on which all the major streams of human culture concur.[25] Our globally interdependent world, so they argue, stands in need of an ethical perspective that transcends cultural and religious differences and 'respects the conditions under which all people in the global community can live in dignity and freedom, without destroying each other's chances of livelihood, culture, society and environment'.[26] Such a shared moral consensus, so the argument goes, can result only from a worldwide dialogue among the religions and ideologies of the world.[27] Especially in the last three decades of the past century several interreligious and intercultural organizations started to make serious efforts at promoting such a dialogue. An important sign of the hope regarding the contribution religions can make here was the ambitious and large-scale interreligious encounter, organized in 1993, in the light of the hundredth

---

[22] John Hick and Paul F. Knitter (eds), *The Myth of Christian Uniqueness*, 2nd edn (Maryknoll, NY: Orbis Books, 1988), pp. vii–xii.

[23] J. G. Stackhouse (ed.), *No Other Gods Before Me? Evangelicals and the Challenge of World Religions* (Grand Rapids, Mich.: Baker Academic, 2001), 11–13.

[24] See H. Küng, 'Dialogability and Steadfastness: On Two Complementary Virtues', in W. G. Jeanrond and J. L. Rike (eds.), *Radical Pluralism and Truth: David Tracy and the Hermeneutics of Religion* (New York: Crossroad, 1991), 237–49.

[25] Cf. Ronald Commers, Wim Vandekerckhove, and An Verlinden (eds), *Ethics in an Era of Globalization* (Aldershot: Ashgate, 2008).

[26] E. Laszlo, *Macroshift: Navigating the Transformation to a Sustainable World* (London: Gaia Books, 2001), 78.

[27] Cf. An Verlinden, 'Global Ethics as Dialogism', in Commers *et al.*, *Ethics*, 187–216.

anniversary of the first World's Parliament of Religions. 'On 4 September 1993 this Parliament passed a "Declaration toward a Global Ethic", in which people of very different religious backgrounds for the first time agreed on a minimum of irrevocable directives which they were already affirming in their own traditions.'[28] The Swiss Roman Catholic theologian, Hans Küng, was the driving force behind this project.[29]

Finally, we see how the necessity of interreligious dialogue can also be argued as an answer to the popular discourse of the clash of civilizations.[30] Those who are engaged in interreligious dialogue hold that now, more than ever before, an alternative to polemics is needed. They promote a case for dialogue and encounter, hoping to stop the spiralling effect of misunderstandings, misapprehensions, annoyances, and violence. Douglas Pratt formulates this challenge as follows: 'Today people of different religions, in pursuit of dialogical relationship with one another, have the possibility of transcending histories of combative clash in favour of a future marked increasingly by cooperative engagement. Religion, in this case, can make things better. At least that is the hope, even if the reality of everyday existence is yet to match.'[31]

The Role of the Vatican and the World Council of Churches

There has been growing interest in interreligious dialogue especially since the end of the 1960s and the beginning of the 1970s. This can be seen in the increase of the number of interreligious encounters, the foundation of a number of interreligious organizations, and the many prominent publications and even journals dedicated specifically to interreligious dialogue. The moment of the true breakthrough of interreligious dialogue happens to coincide, more or less, with the period in which the Vatican on the one hand and the World Council of Churches on the other set to work seriously on interreligious dialogue.[32] Since that time, interreligious dialogue has become 'a permanent and formally endorsed ecclesial activity'.[33] The Second Vatican Council (1962–5) signified a turning point in the relationship between the Roman Catholic Church and 'non-Christian religions'.[34] The council was dominated by an atmosphere of trust, renewal, and openness. Theologically, it was a time of listening to the 'seeds of the Word' in the world, a time of dialogue with the world. Viewed from the

---

[28] H. Küng, *Yes to a Global Ethic* (London: SCM Press, 1996), 2.

[29] M. Moyaert, 'Ricoeur on the (Im-)possibility of a Global Ethics: Towards an Ethics of Fragile Interreligious Compromises', *Neue Zeitschrift für systematische Theologie*, 52 (2010), 440–61.

[30] S. Huntington, *The Clash of Civilizations and the Remaking of World Order* (New York: Free Press, 2002).

[31] D. Pratt, *The Church and Other Faiths: The World Council of Churches, the Vatican, and Interreligious Dialogue* (Bern: Peter Lang, 2010), 18.

[32] 'In a real sense the global face of the Christian Church in the contemporary world is reflected in and through these two institutional structures. The Rome-based Vatican is the locus of authority for the Roman Catholic Church; the Geneva-based WCC is the organisational focus of the ecumenical movement which encompasses the widest spectrum of Christian denominations in its membership.' Pratt, *The Church and Other Faiths*, 21.

[33] Pratt, *The Church and Other Faiths*, 17.

[34] For an extensive study of the relationship between the Roman Catholic Church and non-Christian religions see K. J. Becker and I. Morali (eds), *A Catholic Engagement with World Religions: A Comprehensive Study* (Maryknoll, NY: Orbis Books, 2010).

perspective of the history of theology, this Council was the first in the history of the church to give a positive view of non-Christian religions. The declaration *Nostra Aetate*, on 'the relationship of the Church to non-Christian religions', issued by the Council on 28 October 1965, in particular marks a revolutionary milestone in the history of interreligious relations.

> The Catholic Church rejects nothing that is true and holy in these religions. She regards with sincere reverence those ways of conduct and of life, those precepts and teachings which, though differing in many aspects from the ones she holds and sets forth, nonetheless often reflect a ray of that Truth which enlightens all men.[35]

With this document the Catholic Church sought to establish a new climate in which encounter and dialogue were understood as part of the church's role in the world. As such, *Nostra Aetate* expresses the dialogical spirit of the Second Vatican Council, whose 'intention it was to rally the highest possible majority on the council floor in favor of a change of attitude of Christians and the Church toward the members of other religions'.[36] Although Vatican II did not develop clear theological positions on other religions, it did, by opening up the issue in the direction of interfaith dialogue, mark a new phase in the relationships of the Roman Catholic Church, in all parts of the world, with people of other faiths. As Basset notes, the Vatican's approval and promotion of interfaith engagement implies that the more than 600 million Catholics around the globe are directly invited by the highest authority in their church to so engage.[37] After the Second Vatican Council the importance of interreligious dialogue was confirmed by various initiatives, such as ecclesiastical documents, bilateral encounters, the setting up of various institutions devoted to dialogue,[38] and the days of prayer that were organized several times in Assisi.[39]

Since the 1970s, the World Council of Churches also played an active role in promoting interreligious dialogue. I will mention in particular the interreligious meeting of Ajaltoun in Lebanon (16–25 March 1970), where Christians of various denominations, Buddhists, Hindus, and Muslims (there were no Jews) met together. The purpose was 'to reflect about recent experiences and future possibilities of interreligious dialogue in different contexts, and to draw out lessons for future relations between people of living faiths'.[40] It was a thoroughly international meeting, with participants from seventeen different countries. The *Ajaltoun Memorandum* reads:

---

[35] *Nostra Aetate*, the 'Declaration on the Relation of the Church to Non-Christian Religions', proclaimed by his Holiness Pope Paul VI, on 28 Oct. 1965.

[36] J. Dupuis, *Christianity and the Religions: From Confrontation to Dialogue* (London: Darton, Longman & Todd, 2002), 59.

[37] J. C. Basset, *Le Dialogue interreligieux: Chance ou déchéance de la foi*, Cogitatio fidei, 197 (Paris: Cerf, 1996), 99.

[38] In 1964 Pope Paul VI established the 'Secretariat for Non-Christians' (SNC). It was renamed the Pontifical Council for Interreligious Dialogue (PCID) in 1989 by John Paul II.

[39] Cf. G. Riedl, *Modell Assisi: Christliches Gebet und interreligiöser Dialog in heilsgeschichtlichem Kontext* (Berlin: De Gruyter, 1998).

[40] Samartha, 'Progress and Promise', 467.

The particular object of the Consultation was to gather the experiences of bilateral conversations between Christians and men of the major faiths of Asia with the full participation of members of these faiths, to experiment with a multilateral meeting and to see what could be learned for future relations between people of living faiths....It was the experience of the Consultation that something very new had been embarked upon. It was noted that this was the first time that men of these four faiths had been brought together under the auspices of the World Council of Churches...what was experienced together was felt to be very positive, a matter of general thinking and something to be carried forward urgently.[41]

The great proponent for this meeting, Stanley Samartha, considered interreligious dialogue to be a meeting of commitments: 'The keynote of the consultation was the understanding that a full and loyal commitment to one's own faith did not stand in the way of dialogue.' Faith, according to Samartha, is the 'driving force to and intensification of dialogue'.[42] Following the lead of this conference, the World Council of Churches organized a sub-unit for interreligious dialogue called 'Dialogue between People of Living Faiths and Ideologies', with Samartha as its director.[43] The establishment of this sub-unit marked the recognition of the specificity and importance of interreligious dialogue. The first initiatives to engage those of other religions in dialogue followed quickly. It should be clear that the setting up of the Vatican's Secretariat for Non-Christians and the WCC Sub-unit on Dialogue reinforced the visibility of interreligious dialogue and also underscored its importance. Both religious institutions were very important initiators of interreligious dialogue and have played an important role in dialogue between the religions up until the present.

THE TYPOLOGY OF INTERRELIGIOUS DIALOGUE

Since the 1970s, interreligious dialogue has made unprecedented advances. In this relatively short period, a number of initiatives have emerged, including dialogue groups, encounter centres, interreligious organizations, academic and popular journals, and academic programmes, where the possibilities of interreligious dialogue are studied. Depending on the participants (laypeople, religious leaders, theologians, and monks), the structure (local/international, small/large-scale, bilateral/multilateral), and the themes to be discussed (everyday concerns, ethical challenges, spiritual experiences, doctrinal issues, etc.), interreligious dialogue can take different forms. These can range from encounters between academics in which the exchange of religious ideas is central to those between grassroots groups that are engaged in joint emancipation projects and dialogue, from diplomatic consultations between religious

---

[41] *Study Encounter*, 6/2 (1970), 97–106, cited in S. Samartha, 'Dialogue as a Continuing Christian Concern', *Ecumenical Review*, 23 (1971), 129–42.

[42] *Dialogue between Men of Living Faiths: The Ajaltoun Memorandum* (Geneva: World Council of Churches Publications, 1970), 16.

[43] This later became the Office on Interreligious Religions (OIRR). The name was later changed to 'The Office for', then more recently to 'The Team for', Interreligious Relations and Dialogue (IRRD).

leaders to interreligious prayer meetings in which Buddhist and Christian monks share experiences and insights on meditation practices. They can span the spectrum from encounters focused on action regarding concrete local, national, or ethical challenges (cf. global warming, human rights, etc.) to Scriptural Reasoning groups in which Jews, Christians, and Muslims read one another's scriptures, from personal conversations to international conferences with hundreds of participants, from spontaneous encounters between people who live in the same neighbourhood to colloquia of specialists planned a long time in advance. These different forms of dialogue, each in their own way, promote positive and constructive relations with individuals and communities of other faiths that are directed at mutual understanding and enrichment.

Thomas Michel is right when he says that '[n]arrowing the concept of interfaith dialogue to one type of encounter or identifying it with only one of its forms can limit the richness of what can be hoped for and actually achieved in such encounters'.[44] Nevertheless, it can also be worth our while to mention a number of types, precisely to show something of the diversity of encounters. I will discuss (1) the dialogue of life, (2) the practical dialogue of action, (3) theological dialogue, (4) spiritual dialogue, and (5) diplomatic dialogue.[45] What this typology shows is that there are different forms of dialogue, many reasons to engage in interreligious encounters, a variety of concerns to be addressed, and many themes to be discussed. The *dialogue of life* concerns, in the first place, adherents of a religious tradition who do not have to have official status within their religion, but who simply interact with one another in the context of their daily life. Their coexistence functions as the meeting point for this dialogue, which can take the form of an informal encounter between neighbours around a cup of tea, between parents outside the school, between co-workers in the workplace. In such encounters adherents consciously or unconsciously bear witness to human and religious values that permeate their way of life. People can enrich one another through their daily coexistence and living according to the values that their religious traditions defend. This form of dialogue involves no deliberate or intentional addressing of the difficult theological questions and the complexity of the religious traditions.

Adherents of different religions can also collaborate with others in development, emancipation, and liberation of all of humankind. This practical *dialogue of action* takes shape in the context of collaboration in humanitarian, social, economic, or political fields. The common ground for such dialogue is constituted by the external challenges with which all people are confronted, regardless of their religious traditions. Issues such as migration and asylum, ecological crises, (anti)religious violence, human suffering, economic crises, injustice, and so on, spring to mind in this regard. Via this practical dialogue people learn what drives and

---

[44] T. Michel, 'A Variety of Approaches to Interfaith Dialogue', *Pro Dialogo*, 108 (2001), 342.

[45] For other typologies see e.g. D. L. Eck, 'What do we Mean by "Dialogue"?', *Current Dialogue*, 11 (1986), 5–15; A. Sharma, 'The Meaning and Goals of Interreligious Dialogue', *Journal of Dharma*, 8 (1983), 225–47; E. Sharpe, 'The Goals of Interreligious Dialogue', in John Hick (ed.), *Truth and Dialogue in World Religion: Conflicting Truth-Claims* (Philadelphia: Westminster Press, 1970), 77–95; L. Swidler, *After the Absolute: The Dialogical Future of Religious Reflection* (Minneapolis: Fortress, 1990).

motivates adherents of other religions, what inspires them and gives them strength, and where they draw hope from when a situation seems otherwise to be hopeless. This dialogue nourishes an interreligious solidarity in the awareness of a shared responsibility: where people suffer, injustice happens, or nature is harmed, religions must take action. According to Paul Knitter, '[t]he sharing or converging of different faith perspectives will not only bring about deeper religious cordiality, but it will also call the participants to continue the struggle with greater resolve and bondedness'.[46]

Interreligious *theological dialogue*, sometimes referred to also as the *dialogue of discourse*, is discursive and treats a specific theological topic, such as monotheism and the Trinity, incarnation and avatars, the messiah-ship of Jesus, the role of holy scripture, the problem of salvation, and so forth. The emphasis is on the formulation of *what* is believed and on doctrinal issues. The primary purpose is to come to a reciprocal understanding, perhaps with the hope of resolving prejudicial misunderstanding and so false judgements about each other. In the search for similarities and differences, an attempt is made to penetrate to the precise meaning of certain concepts and ideas. But this form of dialogue is more than a hermeneutical undertaking directed at understanding the other. The question of truth itself is at stake as well; in that sense theological interreligious dialogue is also truly a matter of *truth seeking dialogue*; 'meaning that each participant is willing to seek the truth wherever it may be found, whether inside or outside of the tradition with which he or she identifies'.[47]

Spiritual dialogue, also referred to as the *dialogue of experience*, enables adherents of various religious traditions to learn from one another through prayer and meditation, and is often seen as a greater symbol for interreligious friendship. The starting point here is interiority, that is, spiritual experience, which is the ultimate end of a deep religious quest. It is a matter not so much of insight and understanding on the discursive level as one of contemplation that occurs within the framework of an existential quest for truth. Some people experience a deeper unity with the ultimate dimension of life in spiritual dialogue—an experience that places the belief system of rites and doctrines in an entirely new perspective. Inter-monastic dialogue is well known in this context: 'In all great religious traditions there are individuals and communities that attempt to experience the ideal of the religious life to its fullest and [attempt] to explore the possibilities of their own traditions'.[48] But spiritual dialogue is not reserved only for monks from different traditions. Ordinary believers also ask to celebrate and pray with believers belonging to other religious traditions.

Finally, there is the category of *diplomatic interreligious dialogue*, which has a completely different starting point. It is not so much contemporary society and its common ethical issues but the religious communities themselves that form the horizon against which this dialogue form

---

[46] Paul F. Knitter, *One Earth Many Religions: Multifaith Dialogue and Global Responsibility* (Maryknoll, NY: Orbis Books, 1995), 144.

[47] C. Gillis, *Pluralism: A New Paradigm for Theology* (Louvain: Peeters, 1993), 43.

[48] Basset, *Le Dialogue interreligieux*, 337. Important figures in this regard are Thomas Merton, Bede Griffiths, and Henry le Saux.

takes place. Religious leaders are the central figures here: 'the Hindu brahman, the Buddhist monk, the Jewish rabbi, the Christian pastor, minister or pope, to the extent that they are the heads of religious communities'.[49] The importance of this form of dialogue has been questioned frequently. Doubt is raised about its authenticity: can one speak here really about encounter as such? And the question of tradition and the boundaries of orthodoxy limiting too much the room for 'play' of the dialogue partners is also posed. One speaks, in the end, as a representative of one's tradition. It is true that major doctrinal changes should not be expected from this type of interreligious dialogue. These encounters are too formal in nature for that. But the symbolic importance of this form of dialogue should not be underestimated: diplomatic dialogue implies the willingness of religious leaders and their institutions to leave centuries-old hostility behind them. Religious leaders, who meet one another, shake hands, receive one another hospitably, and sometimes even pray together give a powerful signal to their respective adherents: strong faith convictions should not lead to interreligious animosity.

THE ESSENCE OF DIALOGUE: AN ETYMOLOGICAL PERSPECTIVE

Inspired and enthusiastic arguments for interreligious dialogue are readily forthcoming, but what is frequently missing is actually asking what, specifically, characterizes interreligious dialogue. Very often there is a certain blurring of the understanding of dialogue, thus: 'Dialogue is bandied about with little concern for its meaning, its permissible metaphorical extensions, its dynamics, its ideology'.[50] This has to do, on the one hand, with the practical and applied nature of interreligious dialogue itself. We are at the level of practice, of encounter and action, and not at the level of theory. The vast majority of texts that have been published have been written for a 'lay interfaith audience' without much of a scholarly tone or approach. On the other hand, it is the case that much reflection on the possibilities and difficulties of interreligious dialogue happens in the so-called theology of religions.[51] The question that seems to be primarily important is how Christianity is related to the other religions. Although this question for Christians is inseparable from how they understand interreligious dialogue, reflection on the dynamics of interreligious dialogue is nevertheless of a different order than theological reflection on the relations between the religions. A start at penetrating

---

[49] I am indebted to J. Basset, *Le Dialogue interreligieux*, 329, for these distinctions.

[50] W. Crapanzano, 'On Dialogue', in T. Maranhao (ed.), *The Interpretation of Dialogue* (Chicago: University of Chicago Press, 1990), 269.

[51] Theology, understood as *fides quaerens intellectum*, is concerned specifically with the following two questions: (1) how the challenge of religious diversity can be understood in light of the Christian tradition, and (2) how the Christian tradition can be recontextualized in light of the experiences of believers in the context of religious plurality. The question of how the Christian tradition is related to this context of religious plurality is the main theme of the theology of religions, a discipline that arose in systematic theology during the period around the Second Vatican Council (1962–5).

the very unique nature of interreligious dialogue is an etymological analysis of the word *dia-logos*. That makes it possible to list a few essential characteristics of dialogue. The prefix *dia* puts us on the trail of the ethical dimension of dialogue and the *logos* points to the centrality of the truth question in each dialogue.

Dia and the Ethical Dimension of Dialogue

Dialogue comes from the Greek *dia-logos*, and not from the non-existent *di-logos*, which would mean a duologue. 'Dia' is a prefix that means 'through, between, across, throughout'. The prefix indicates a path, a route. It is thus the direction and not the number of dialogue partners that is, etymologically speaking, determinative for the definition of dialogue—although it is of course the case that there must be at least two people, so that there can be a reciprocal movement. Regardless of the number of participants, the structure of the dialogue is binary and the dialogue partners relate to one another in an 'I–Thou' relationship. This binary structure is dynamic: it concerns a 'true back-and-forth, in which no one is primary or secondary in a definitive way'.[52] The semantic relationship between an 'I' and a 'Thou' can also be denoted as a relationship between a 'self' and an 'other' that stand over against each other. Here we can see the ethical dimension that constitutes the heart of the dialogical encounter. Ethically speaking, dialogical reciprocity points to openness for difference and otherness. There is an ethical prohibition against reducing the other to the known and the familiar.[53] Every dialogue is an encounter with difference and alterity and requires one to be open to and receptive for the other. The religious other is recalcitrant: she does not affirm what is familiar and questions the obviousness of our own familiar frameworks.[54] She makes an appeal, asking to be recognized in her otherness, not to be reduced to what we already know. One can, however, always ignore this appeal coming from the other and reduce her to sameness; and the fact that this is possible at all points to the vulnerability of the other, and hence to the ethical dimension of dialogue.

Logos and Truth-Seeking Dialogue

Logos comes from *legein*, which means 'to speak'. But the former can also mean 'thought'.[55] 'Viewed structurally, it is the reciprocity that characterizes the genre, which also

---

[52] S. Guellouz, *Le Dialogue* (Paris: PUF, 1992), 80.

[53] This making the ethical import of dialogue central can be found very much in so-called dialogical philosophy. This philosophical school of thought caught on after the catastrophe of the First World War with the work of, among others, Ebner, F. Rosenzweig, and M. Buber. But it would not really break through until after the Second World War. Unique to the philosophers who belong to this school is a rethinking of the relation to the other, and not purely as a specific theme within philosophy but as an actual existential dimension. Thus dialogue belongs to the existential structures of being human.

[54] A. Schütz, 'Der Fremde: Ein sozialpsychologischer Versuch', in A. Schütz (ed.), *Nijh* (The Hague: Nijhof, 1972), 59.

[55] Whenever we think of dialogue today, we think first of a personal encounter between two or more people. Here a shift has occurred in the understanding of dialogue, which was originally a literary genre. Literary dialogue had its high point during the Renaissance.

immediately implies that, within a dialogue, only the word that is received by a *"you"* gives life to an *"I"*. But it is no less necessary to remember that only ideas can constitute the content of a dialogue.'[56] What is more, the search for truth belongs to the essence of authentic dialogue. Dialogue is inseparably bound up with a search for truth. That also obtains for interreligious dialogue. As Catherine Cornille correctly remarks, 'Dialogue without concern with the question of truth seems barren, if not inauthentic. It is precisely the thirst for truth which represents the motivation for dialogue, and which distinguishes dialogue from a mere exchange of information about one's respective traditions.'[57] In that sense, dialogue is irreconcilable with both absolutism and relativism: 'Unabridged absolutism makes all dialogue impossible by equating ultimate truth with its expressions. By removing the question of truth, pure relativism removes the existential entry point of dialogue.'[58] In trying to find a balance between relativism and absolutism, we should perhaps view truth as a *regulative idea*, i.e. truth as an ultimate project or goal that orients and directs our search for truth in this age in the knowledge that one will never reach nor possess it. This is truth as a limit idea. The French philosopher, Paul Ricoeur, would argue in this regard for eschatological universalism: 'The unity of truth is "a timeless task only because it is at first an eschatological hope".'[59]

Philosophy and Dialogue

Dialogue is connected deep down with the search for truth and a striving for wisdom. It excludes fanaticism. A fanatic is a person who, convinced that he is absolutely right, locks himself up in his own position and refuses any critical testing or challenge. Dialogue presupposes precisely the engagement of people with critical minds, who question the obvious and also allow others to challenge them. 'What all dialogues have in common is that they always concern a history of a *homo loquens,* who is driven by reason, seeks wisdom.'[60] In that sense, it is not surprising that the existence of dialogue and philosophy have been connected right from the very start. Although the adventure of dialogue begins in Greece with Plato, the philosophical hermeneutics of Hans-Georg Gadamer especially can help us gain a better understanding of what is at stake in the dialogue between the religions. Although he did not engage philosophical hermeneutics with a view to interreligious dialogue, reflection on interreligious dialogue is greatly indebted to Gadamer. His hermeneutical model of conversation often resounds in reflections on interreligious dialogue. As Sallie B. King correctly remarks:

---

[56] Guellouz, *Le Dialogue*, 81.

[57] C. Cornille, 'Meaning and Truth in Dialogue', in F. Depoortere and M. Lambkin (eds), *The Question of Theological Truth: Philosophical and Interreligious Perspectives* (Amsterdam: Rodopi, 2012), 137–55.

[58] Basset, *Le Dialogue interreligieux*, 269.

[59] M. Moyaert, 'Lindbeck and Ricoeur on Meaning, Truth and Translation of Religions', in Depoortere and Lambkin, *Question*, 157–80.

[60] Guellouz, *Le Dialogue* (1992), 257.

'Dialogue and hermeneutics are at base about a very mysterious thing: the process of coming to understand the other'.[61]

Characteristic of Gadamer's thinking is the way in which he defends 'prejudice' which points to the idea that we already carry around with us an understanding because of the religious and cultural tradition to which we belong. It puts us on the trail of the finite and historical being of humankind. 'If we want to do justice to man's finite, historical mode of being, it is necessary to fundamentally rehabilitate the concept of prejudice and to acknowledge the fact that there are legitimate prejudices'.[62] This understanding does not emerge from the emancipation and distancing from one's tradition. We are essentially bound to tradition and to views that have been passed on—without this connection understanding would not be possible. Gadamer points in this perspective to the hermeneutical circle in which understanding occurs. This circle points to the perpetual 'back-and-forth' movement between prior expectations and the strange, a process that is characterized by change, refinement, and correction of those expectations. Understanding always begins with expectations that are replaced by more appropriate insights. But if all understanding already takes place in a pre-structured horizon, how can we ever understand otherness? How can we ever arrive at true openness? Here Gadamer points for the time being to the importance of a hermeneutically trained awareness—the sense that we are historically situated. To be able to become receptive for what does not meet our expectations (anticipations), we must remain aware of the prejudices that cohere with the standards of the traditions in which we ourselves stand. The prejudices we are unaware of will control us and lead us to become fixed in a certain line of thinking. It is prejudices on which we have not reflected that make us deaf to otherness.

The most important condition, however, is that we are addressed by something, that we are moved by something that we are not familiar with, that does not meet our expectations. We become aware of a prejudice only when it is challenged. Understanding begins when we are addressed and challenged by something that interrupts and suspends our own prejudices. 'We now know what this requires, namely the fundamental suspension of our own prejudices. But all suspension of prejudices has the logical structure of a *question*'.[63] Thus, we can be addressed only if we are ready to suspend our own prejudices and to take the other seriously in his appeal for legitimacy. Gadamer proceeds on the basis of the priority of the question and the acknowledgement that one does not know, in the sense of Socrates' *docta ignorantia*. Only those who are aware of their own ignorance and yearn for insight can ask real questions. Gadamer's insights are important for the dialogue between the religions as a practice aimed at doing *justice* to all traditions involved. In the interreligious encounter, all adherents of religions also pledge to do justice to the traditions of the other. Doing justice to the otherness of the other and thus understanding what he stands for is one of the basic principles of each

---

[61] S. B. King, 'Interreligious Dialogue', in C. Meister, *Oxford Handbook*, 107.
[62] H. G. Gadamer, *Truth and Method* (London: Sheed & Ward, 1975), 277.
[63] Gadamer, *Truth and Method*, 299.

encounter. Dialogue can be dialogue only if the focus is on the otherness, when the other can also truly be other, when the strange is not colonized. In interreligious dialogue as well, openness cannot mean that the other is completely understood as such. The understanding of the other does not happen in a neutral space; our own prejudices, commitments, and convictions help to determine how we approach the other and his tradition. Human beings are situated and embodied beings, and we can never fully transcend our historical and cultural context. 'We never see from a God's-Eye point of view, we never think from a neutral place or tabula rasa, but always from a particular point of view rooted in our culture, our language, our worldview, and our own individual life experiences. There is no escaping being rooted in the particular in this way.'[64]

People engaging in dialogue do so by entering the hermeneutical circle, for, either consciously or unconsciously, they bring to their work a specific pre-understanding, a prior set of postulates drawn by their own faith and from their tradition and its theologies.[65] Their attitude is one of humbleness, admitting that 'unavoidably one's own tradition will shape at least the initial horizon for understanding the other tradition'.[66] That is why they do well to be aware of this and to make explicit, as much as possible, their own religious presuppositions when entering the dialogue process. As David Tracy states:

> The dialogue works as a dialogue (and not an exercise in self-aggrandizement) only if the other is allowed—through the dynamic of the to-and-fro movement of questioning—to become in the dialogue itself a genuine other, not a projected other... This movement also implies that one enters a dialogue with one's critical consciousness vigilant and with a knowledge and respect for one's own traditions.[67]

The Dynamics of Interreligious Dialogue: Between Openness and Identity

In interreligious dialogue adherents from various traditions must balance a number of apparently incompatible commitments and conflicting loyalties. Central here is the tension between openness and identity. How can one do justice to difference and otherness without losing one's own identity? How can one hold on to one's own identity without falling into closedness? How can one balance the dimension of testimony in dialogue, which always contains a truth-claim, and at the same time be receptive for the truth in which others are believed to be involved? In the final part of this chapter I will discuss a number of these fields

---

[64] King, 'Interreligious Dialogue', 107.

[65] Stephen Duffy, 'A Theology of the Religions and/or a Comparative Theology?', *Horizons*, 26 (1999), 112.

[66] Werner Jeanrond, 'Toward a Hermeneutics of Love', in Conway and Cornille, *Interreligious Hermeneutics* (Eugene, Or.: Wipf & Stock, 2010), 49.

[67] D. Tracy, 'Western Hermeneutics and Interreligious Dialogue', in Conway and Cornille, *Interreligious Hermeneutics*, 3–4.

which are determinative for interreligious dialogue and point out the tensions that exist between them. It will be immediately clear that interreligious dialogue is marked by a complex interplay of religious commitments and loyalties.

Tradition and Interreligious Dialogue

Interreligious dialogue stands or falls with people who are rooted in a religious tradition that is experienced within a specific faith community.[68] Strongly anchored in their own religion, it is expected by both their faith community and those of other religions that they 'represent' their tradition. People become involved in dialogue not on their own behalf but as representatives of their own tradition. Although this requirement seems self-evident perhaps, an entire field of tension can be found behind this 'demand' that is seldom mentioned. After all, the seemingly *natural claim*—that those who participate must be recognized as representatives by their respective traditions—can function as an exclusionary mechanism. The question of who determines who will be a good and acceptable representative should be asked. One's faith community functions first of all as a point of departure for interreligious dialogue. It forms the 'base camp' from which believers are ready to move out with their tradition and faith convictions. Although tradition can sometimes carry a lot of weight and can sometimes be experienced as 'an undue limitation of religious options',[69] it is precisely this traditional embeddedness that can make dialogue fascinating. Tradition is not just the point of departure; it is also the 'home' to which believers return to catch their breath after these inspiring, challenging, and perhaps also confusing wanderings. Believers will tell their travel stories to this community, hoping not only that those who stayed 'home' will feel addressed by what they have learnt but also that those who stayed 'home' can help them better understand the meaning of these new insights. They must link up constantly with their own faith community. That is why, in addition to interreligious dialogue, an *intra-religious* dialogue must also be undertaken on the question of the meaning of interreligious dialogue, so that a kind of interchange occurs.

From the perspective of the ordinary life of faith, interreligious dialogue is not an obvious choice. Dialogical openness to the religious other and his tradition is not a natural inclination

---

[68] In her approach to interreligious dialogue Helene Egnell remarks that we should not overlook the issue of power in this regard. She asks 'who has the power over discourse, who sets the agenda, who decides what parts of scripture are relevant to the problem or topic under discussion?' See H. Egnell, 'Scriptural Reasoning: A Feminist Response', in D. Cheetham *et al.* (eds), *Interreligious Hermeneutics in Pluralistic Europe* (Amsterdam, Rodopi, 2011), 80. The problem of power and how it impacts on who is invited and who is excluded does not receive a great deal of attention in reflection on interreligious dialogue. For, as is well known, the official, visible representatives or 'spokesmen' of dialogue are nearly always men. From this perspective, it is no wonder that women are underrepresented in Scriptural Reasoning. However, whenever too much emphasis is laid on representation, the critical power of interreligious dialogue can become limited, for one should ask if there is still room from the perspective of representativeness for the dissonant voices, those who are also part of religious communities and play an important role in them.

[69] C. Cornille, *The Im-possibility of Interreligious Dialogue* (New York: Crossroad, 2008), 61.

for most traditions. 'Most religions tend to self-sufficiency rather than to mutual dependency and to something approaching inner complacency rather than to active interest in the other.'[70] From the perspective of history, as we saw, it is primarily non-religious factors that explain the rise of interreligious dialogue. But if the project of interreligious dialogue is to succeed, then it will have to be supported by the religions themselves. In other words, it is necessary to find intrinsic reasons for dialogue, beyond the external ones. That is why traditions themselves must start a process of reflection (and that has started already in many traditions) on the religious meaning of interreligious dialogue. Hence there must always be an intra-religious dialogue on the question of the religious legitimacy of interreligious dialogue.[71]

But there is more at stake than only the question of the religious legitimacy of interreligious dialogue. 'There is', according to David Ford who is himself a Christian theologian involved in the dialogue between Jews, Christians, and Muslims, 'also a case to be made for the positive enhancement of each house'.[72] Interreligious dialogue is not without consequence: consciously or not, people glean certain insights from other traditions. They learn to read their own tradition through the eyes of the other. Shifts in meaning, new interpretations, unexpected insights flow out of this practice. What was strange becomes familiar and what was familiar becomes strange. It is important that believers do not keep these new insights 'for themselves' but take them with them to their particular faith community and share them with their fellow believers. The fruits of the interreligious encounter must also be reflected upon in an intra-religious way. As Cornille puts it:

> Return to the tradition represents an act not only of intellectual and spiritual humility, but also of solidarity with the tradition as a whole, and with individuals who might otherwise never be able to taste the fruits of dialogue. It cannot be denied that interreligious dialogue places high demands on those directly engaged in it, requiring not only solid theological grounding within one's own tradition, but also personal openness, linguistic expertise, and a great deal of religious and spiritual imagination. If, however, dialogue really offers the promise of religious development and spiritual growth, then those who have both the capacity and the opportunity to engage in it also have the responsibility to dedicate their results to the benefits of others and of the tradition as a whole.[73]

Adherents of a religion who participate in interreligious dialogue are struck by what they learn in interreligious dialogue and become convinced of the importance and necessity of doctrinal changes. But it is an entirely different matter to convince the religious 'rank and file' of this. Those who are involved in interreligious dialogue are merely valuable discussion

---

[70] Cornille, *Im-possibility*, 2.

[71] For Christianity, this process of reflection occurs in the so-called theology of religions and the typology of exclusivism, inclusivism, pluralism, and particularism. See M. Moyaert, *Fragile Identities: Towards a Theology of Interreligious Hospitality* (New York: Rodopi, 2011).

[72] D. Ford, *Christian Wisdom: Desiring God and Learning in Love* (Cambridge: Cambridge University Press, 2007), 287.

[73] Cornille, *Im-possibility*, 210.

partners to the extent that they are also at least connected to a specific religious tradition and the community in which the tradition is experienced. Those who give up this connection lose a great deal of their credibility as a discussion partner. Here the importance of intra-religious dialogue comes into view once again. But it is a fact that the dialectic between tradition and dialogue is not obvious. As is often the case,[74] those engaged in dialogue do not find it easy to give feedback to their faith community on the insights they acquire during their encounters.

Commitment as Component of Identity

Religious commitment is analogous to speaking a specific language or belonging to a particular culture or form of life.[75] Adherence to a religion is the result of a long process of socialization and interiorization in which a person learns to speak a particular religious language and learns to perform the rituals, practices, and customs in an appropriate way and to do so in an always changing context. Believers learn to pray and sing, celebrate, and ask forgiveness. By placing their own lives in the larger whole of the tradition to which they adhere, believers learn how to deal with the limits of existence, with conflicts and their own finitude. Rituals, symbols, and narratives structure and order the world and make it possible for human beings to find meaning. Of course each believer has her own religious autobiography, but religious adherence always implies that one's religious character is formed by a preceding tradition.

Religious belonging, however, is much more than speaking a religious language or belonging to a particular tradition. There is also always a commitment to what is ultimately important and hence transcends one's self-interest. Religions introduce something that surpasses human beings. People can only speak about this transcendence because their 'speech' is 'preceded' by tradition. Nevertheless, whoever reduces religion to its preservation without any commitment to transcendence removes its beating heart. Being religious presupposes the acknowledgement of being part of a larger whole and the promotion of a transformation from ego-centeredness to an orientation on what is ultimately important.[76] Because of this commitment, the religious life cannot be reduced to *convention*. Religious commitment also implies *conviction*. Believers, engaging in interreligious dialogue, are somehow compelled by the conviction that the truth they embrace (or does it embrace them?) makes a claim that transcends the boundaries of their own religious community. Believers who take their religious commitment seriously may want to explain their faith conviction and argue with those who think and believe otherwise.

---

[74] For this problem see also Cornille, *Im-possibility*, 78–82.

[75] G. Lindbeck, *The Nature of Doctrine: Religion and Theology in a Postliberal Age* (Philadelphia: Westminster Press, 1984), 33.

[76] John Hick, *An Interpretation of Religion: Human Responses to the Transcendent* (Basingstoke: Macmillan, 1989), 36.

It is, however, clear that faith does not allow itself to be proven; the truth that believers are concerned with does not allow itself to be grasped. Religious truth is never a possession. Any claim to truth will always be a wager. Consequently, religious truth-claims always take the form of a fragile certainty: they can only be attested to in religious testimonies. Thus, inter-religious dialogue takes on the form of *testimony* or *witness* dialogue, which revolves in part around the crucial notion of testimony or witness:

> Dialogue is the space for authentic testimony—on both sides. Interreligious dialogue is not a coming together of scholars in religious studies who compare religions in a neutral and 'objective' way with one another. Every true dialogue is in some deep sense 'religious,' i.e. everyone may, indeed should, bring his faith commitment from the start to every dialogue encounter…He must introduce himself by that which he is and what he believes.[77]

Humility as Criterion for Openness

Giving testimony or bearing witness to one's own faith commitment is an integral part of inter-religious dialogue but does not exhaust the meaning of encounter in any way. Those who engage in interreligious dialogue are not driven exclusively by the desire to bear witness to the truth-claims of their own tradition. Authentic dialogue also presupposes openness to learning from others, the willingness to be interrupted, enriched, changed, and to grow. This presupposes at least that people are open to the possibility that truth can also be found in other traditions and, *mutatis mutandis*, that truth is not exhausted by their own tradition. Unlike the absolutism that claims to 'possess' the truth and the relativism that succumbs to scepticism, we can consider the truth to be a goal that adherents of different religious traditions strive for in the knowledge that they will never arrive at it. A certain awareness of one's own limitations, a certain humility is, from this perspective, an important requirement for the success of inter-religious dialogue that also entails the possibility of growth in faith. Catherine Cornille especially points to the importance of the virtue of humility. Dialogue, she states,

> presupposes humble awareness of the limitation of one's own understanding and experience another possibility of change and growth…Humility…may be understood…to denote a genuine acknowledgment of the limitation and imperfection of one's insights and accomplishments, as indeed of all human realization and self-expression. In dialogue, it is such a humble awareness of the finite and partial nature of one's own understanding that drives one form the same to the other, from complacency to an active search for growth in the truth.[78]

The humility to which Cornille alludes presupposes at least that one renounces 'the possession of truth' and that one expresses instead the wish to be part of the truth—in this

---

[77] T. Sundermeier, 'Grundlagen und Voraussetzungen für das interreligöse Gespräch', *Ökumenische Rundschau*, 49 (2000), 328.
[78] Cornille, *Im-Possibility*, 9.

way also recognizing that other parts of the truth exist outside of one's own religious tradition. No religion can make a valid claim to possess the Truth. It is thus a sign of great religious modesty to understand that one's own access to religion, fundamental though it may be, is a partial access. Others have access to different parts of the Truth. An authentic religious attitude recognizes that truth exists outside of one's own tradition. In other words, interreligious dialogue relies on people who are capable of moving between traditions and who are prepared to welcome religious strangers; people who see themselves as sojourners in search of truth rather than as possessors of the one truth. Only this attitude of humility enables receptivity and openness towards the religious other and the truth to which she is committed.

But the question of what is true, valuable, and worthy of pursuit or praiseworthy in other traditions should be always preceded by *hermeneutical openness*. To judge before gaining a deep understanding would amount to a form of close-mindedness. In this sense, the first requirement of interreligious dialogue is the willingness to *understand* the other in his or her otherness and to avoid reading one's own presuppositions into the religious world of the other. The hermeneutical question if and to what extent one can understand the otherness of the religious other has priority over the *truth* question concerning the *value* of other religions. In other words, *hermeneutical openness* should precede *judgement*. Before judging, before assessing, before appreciating—either positively or negatively—the religious other deserves to be heard and understood.[79] The willingness to understand the other in her otherness precedes the question of the truth of what has been discovered in the other tradition. In this sense, hermeneutical openness *precedes* discernment and judgement.

Hermeneutical Openness

The dialogue between religions presents primarily a hermeneutical challenge. It involves the question of mutual understanding or the degree to which individuals belonging to one religion can grasp the meaning of symbols, teachings, and practices of another. The religious other is the strange other, that is, the other who does not think like me, who eludes me, and whom I do not understand. Interreligious dialogue rests on the confidence of the dialogue partners in the possibility of converting this situation of not understanding into one of understanding. From this perspective, the first form of openness entails the willingness to *understand* the other in his or her otherness and to avoid forms of *Hineininterpretierung* (reading into). The self-understanding or self-interpretation of the religious other is the norm. I call this form of openness *hermeneutical openness*. In interreligious dialogue the religious other asks to be understood in his or her otherness, and hermeneutical openness meets this request precisely: the willingness to be addressed and interrupted by 'an unfamiliarity

---

[79] On the criteria of judgement in interreligious dialogue see Catherine Cornille (ed.), *Criteria of Discernment in Interreligious Dialogue* (Eugene, Or.: Wipf & Stock, 2009).

that does not meet patterns of expectation.'[80] The religious other does not fit completely and without remainder into our preconceptions, as she challenges us to leave the realm of the known. Hermeneutical openness is committed to doing *justice* to her; it is intended to understand other religions in as fair-minded way as possible. Ideally, interreligious dialogue gives way to a viable understanding of the 'other' in which the encountered 'other' is not manufactured to one's own prejudices and expectations. This hermeneutical commitment implies a detailed consideration of religious traditions that are other than one's own.

Not meeting this request for hermeneutical openness is an expression of not taking otherness seriously, which actually amounts to a form of *closedness*. Thus, hermeneutical openness means that the dialogue partners interrupt their own structure of prejudices. It is especially important that the hermeneutical openness is directed at the truly other and not at the image that is formed of the other in one's own tradition.[81] 'We have to learn and, perhaps, be regularly reminded that our most taken for granted beliefs about human failing and flourishing will not necessarily be found in the traditions and texts of other religions.'[82] The sensitivity for otherness must be cultivated. Openness for the other seems, in this perspective, to be the question of the *'listening access to a (strange) culture'*.[83] Dialogue presupposes the obligation of *'listening to a culture'* and *'the heart that listens'*.[84] Openness means being willing to be affected by the insights, questions, desires, and possibly even the experiences of the religious other. This requires a long and patient engagement with the religious tradition of the other. True hermeneutical openness is very demanding, for it presupposes the willingness to truly enter into the 'world' of the religious other.[85]

Enrichment (as Dialogical Reward)

Not infrequently it is said by participants in interreligious dialogue that they have grown through the encounter with the religious other: not only do they understand the particularity of their own faith commitment better, but they also have the idea that they are more strongly anchored or rooted in their own religion without this entailing the end of their dialogical openness. Jews become better Jews; Christians better Christians; Muslims better Muslims. Enrichment can also mean that people look at their own tradition differently. Sometimes *outsiders* are needed for one to see how rich a certain belief or religious text is. But involvement with others can also lead people to develop new sensitivities that were perhaps

[80] B. van Leeuwen, *Erkenning, identiteit en verschil:Multiculturalisme en leven met culturele diversiteit* (Leuven: Acco, 2003), 64.

[81] J. L. Fredericks, 'A Universal Religious Experience? Comparative Theology as an Alternative to a Theology of Religions', *Horizons*, 22 (1995), 86.

[82] W. T. Dickens, 'Interreligious Dialogue: Encountering an Other or Ourselves', *Theology Today*, 63 (2006), 208.

[83] N. Hintersteiner, *Traditionen überschreiten: Angloamerikanische Beiträge zur interkulturellen Hermeneutik* (Vienna: WUV-Universitätsverlag, 2001), 272–3.

[84] R. Facelina, 'Une théologie en situation', *Revue des Sciences Religieuses*, 48 (1974), 320.

[85] See also M. Moyaert, 'From Soteriological Openness to Hermeneutical Openness: Recent Developments in the *Theology of Religions*', *Modern Theology*, 28 (2012), 35–52.

insufficiently or not even present at all in their own tradition. Blind spots or certain exclusionary mechanisms are detected that are difficult to reconcile with the beliefs of one's tradition. Of course, criticism can arise internally, but the external perspective of someone from another religion can also be a catalyst for critiquing a tradition. People also come to value the moral and spiritual values of other traditions more through their actual contact with people from those traditions. One can be impressed by certain ethical guidelines that also usually show a specific view of the world. Another form of enrichment that one can think of is the adoption of certain rituals, symbols, even prayers from different traditions. Adherents of religions can become convinced that a thorough rethinking of certain truth-claims (revelation, salvation, for example) is necessary in light of the insights and experiences that people gain in dialogue. Nevertheless, it can be said that major doctrinal shifts in religious traditions seldom occur.

Discernment in Dialogue

The question of the enriching aspect of interreligious dialogue actually has to do with the question of the *discernment of truth* and the question of criteria for arriving at a well-considered assessment. Whoever says that interreligious dialogue can be enriching recognizes the possibility that truth can be found in another tradition. But on what basis is something determined to be true or not true? This is an especially sensitive point in dialogue, a point where the tension between openness and identity becomes visible again. According to some, it is not appropriate to make judgements about those of other religions and their tradition on the basis of norms and criteria that they do not acknowledge. When other religions are understood and evaluated on the basis of tradition-specific criteria, one is actually making one's own confessional perspective normative, even superior to all other religious perspectives. This does not square with the dialogical attitude of humility as sketched above, and that is why generic criteria must be sought that can be recognized by all religious criteria, *regardless* of their particularity. The pragmatic criterion for truth proposed by the British philosopher of religion, John Hick, is well known. Religions should, according to Hick, be judged on the basis of the degree to which they make the 'transformation from ego-centeredness to Reality-centeredness' possible. This salvific transformation can be perceived best in the moral fruits of the traditions. Religious truth is thus assessed in terms of an ethical principle.[86]

Others dispute that there should be something like universally valid norms that can be recognized within all religious traditions. And even if they do exist, they would never be able to do justice to the particularity of the different traditions. It would be better to recognize that truth is determined intra-textually and that religions employ tradition-specific criteria of truth. Some go even further and claim that tradition-specific criteria are incommensurable and thus question both the possibility and meaningfulness of truth-seeking dialogue. The

---

[86] Hick, *An Interpretation of Religion*, 14.

theologian George Lindbeck is famous for his position in this discussion. He considers it very possible that

> [the different religions] have incommensurable notions of truth, of experience, and of categoreal adequacy, and therefore what it would mean for something to be the most important (i.e., 'God')... Thus when affirmations or ideas from categoreally different religious or philosophical frameworks are introduced into a given religious outlook, these are either simply babbling or else, like mathematical formulas employed in a poetic text, they have vastly different functions and meanings than they had in their original settings.[87]

As always, things are much more complex than presented here, and the discussion does not concern generic criteria or tradition-specific criteria. In reality, it seems that religious adherents make use of both criteria in the context of interreligious dialogue. Clearly, every religion inevitably judges the other according to its own particular criteria. That is in line with what philosophical hermeneutics teaches: there is no helicopter perspective from which the different religions can be surveyed. But 'the content and interpretation of those criteria is by no means fixed and unchanging. On the contrary, not only may different believers and different schools identify different sets of essential criteria within a particular religion, but the understanding of these criteria may also change, at times as a result of the dialogue itself.'[88] It could very well happen that 'the dialogue may also shed new light on the meaning of these very criteria as the internal perspective becomes enriched through engagement with external perspectives.'[89] Just as religions may change through time by coming into contact with other religions and cultural contexts, so will the criteria of discernment develop. This raises doubts about the idea that pure confessional criteria should be operative when judging truth in question. As a matter of fact, religious people also refer to both more generic criteria and to criteria that emerge from dialogue practice itself.[90] It is not a situation of either–or: the reality is much more complex and testifies to a jumble of criteria—both tradition-specific and generic.

CONCLUSION

It is no longer possible to imagine contemporary life without interreligious encounters. People participate in interreligious dialogue for various reasons: out of curiosity, to seek understanding, to collaborate with those of other faiths, out of a desire for a deeper spiritual experience, etc. Interreligious dialogue does not exist in the singular but only in the plural, as

---

[87] Lindbeck, *The Nature of Doctrine*, 49.
[88] Cornille, *Criteria of Discernment*, p. xi.
[89] Cornille, *Criteria of Discernment*, p. xi.
[90] H. Vroom, *Religions and the Truth: Philosophical Reflections and Perspectives* (Grand Rapids, Mich., and Amsterdam: Eerdmans/Rodopi, 1989), 359–75.

a reflection of the variety of people who participate in it: lay people who encounter one another around the cares of everyday life, religious 'activists' who believe in the importance of collaboration in shared challenges, monks in search of spiritual depth, theologians inspired to search for deeper insights, religious leaders who want to show their faith communities that encounter takes precedence over rivalry. But dialogue always presupposes mutual respect, the willingness to listen to the other with a certain attention, the hermeneutical openness to understanding the other, the hope of arriving at deeper insight. In the background, one can always detect the notion that the dialogical turn is a turning point in the history of interreligious relations. People who devote themselves to interreligious dialogue want to show that it can also be different, and that intolerance, conflict, and violence cannot be allowed to have the last word. They want to break with the monological attitude that approaches those of other religions in a, primarily, negative way. In that sense, interreligious dialogue concerns all the positive and constructive interactions between adherents of different religions, who want to encounter one another in a peaceful manner; who want to exchange ideas with one another, and who want to learn from one another's faith.

FURTHER READING

John Cobb and Ward McAfee (eds), *The Dialogue Comes of Age* (Minneapolis: Fortress Press, 2010).

Catherine Cornille (ed.), *Criteria of Discernment in Interreligious Dialogue* (Eugene, Or.: Wipf & Stock, 2009).

—— (ed.), *Interreligious Hermeneutics*, Interreligious Dialogue Series, 2 (Eugene, Or.: Wipf & Stock, 2010).

—— *The Im-Possibility of Interreligious Dialogue* (New York: Crossroad, 2008).

Paul Hedges, *Controversies in Interreligious Dialogue and the Theology of Religions* (London: SCM Press, 2010).

James Heft, *Catholicism and Interreligious Dialogue* (New York: Oxford University Press, 2012).

M. Moyaert, *Fragile Identities: Towards a Theology of Interreligious Hospitality* (New York: Rodopi, 2011).

Douglas Pratt, *The Church and Other Faiths: The World Council of Churches, the Vatican, and Interreligious Dialogue* (Bern: Peter Lang, 2010).

William Skudlarek, *The Attentive Voice: Reflections on the Meaning and Practice of Interreligious Dialogue* (New York: Lantern Press, 2011).

....

CHAPTER 10

Interreligious Majority–Minority Dynamics

PETER C. PHAN AND JONATHAN Y. TAN

Before the Second Gulf War a conversational, if not actually dialogical, encounter between a white American Southern Baptist from Texas and a Muslim from Iraq would have been quite unlikely, even unimaginable. Today, thanks to globalization and migration, it is a routine occurrence in the USA, as well as elsewhere. Despite its frequency, however, such encounter between Christians and Muslims is fraught with tensions and illustrates well the complex and highly charged dynamics of relations between members of a racial, political, cultural, and religious majority and those of the minority. To understand the multifaceted challenges, there is perhaps no more productive site than the meeting of white American conservative Christians and Middle Eastern Muslims. The attitude of these two groups towards each other is generally marked by suspicion and intolerance, and their political outlook vastly complicates their religious relations. American Southern Baptists by and large are opposed to inter-religious dialogue and tend to condemn Islam as a violent religion and the Prophet Muhammad as a purveyor of false doctrines and immorality. The Revd Franklin Graham, son of the famed evangelist Billy Graham and president of the Billy Graham Evangelistic Association, has called Islam 'a very evil and wicked religion'. The Revd Jerry Vines, former president of the Southern Baptist Convention, once referred to Muhammad as a 'demon-possessed paedophile'. On the other hand, Middle Eastern Muslims tend to accuse America of being rabidly pro-Israel and of leading a crusade against Islam. Some groups of them are engaged in mass violence against Americans, whom they regard as 'infidels'.[1]

This chapter will begin with a global snapshot of the current situation of religious diversity and the complexity of majority–minority interreligious encounters across the world

---

[1] See Thomas S. Kidd, *American Christians and Islam: Evangelical Culture and Muslims from the Colonial Period to the Age of Terrorism* (Princeton: Princeton University Press, 2008).

generally, and in Pakistan, India, Sri Lanka, and Malaysia in particular. It will then engage in an in-depth discussion of Muslim–Christian relations in the United States as a paradigmatic case to explore the dynamics of an interreligious dialogue between the religion of the majority and that of a minority. What these countries have in common is the fact that they are multicultural, multi-ethnic, and religiously diverse societies with significant minority religious communities in the midst of a dominant religious majority, for instance Islam in Pakistan and Malaysia, Hinduism in India, Buddhism in Sri Lanka, and Christianity in the United States. We proceed on the basis that a persuasive case can be made that, in the current religious climate, relations between Christianity and Islam are the most strained and bear the most grievous conse-quences, not just in the United States, but also around the world. Indeed, Islam has been on the upsurge, especially in Asia and Africa, making it one of the fastest growing religions in the world. Unfortunately, this has often resulted in growing antagonism and hardening of attitudes towards Christian minorities living in the midst of Muslim majorities in many parts of Asia and Africa, especially in the post-September-11 world. Northern Nigeria has witnessed sectar-ian violence between the Muslim majority and Christian minority populations, resulting in the loss of lives and property destruction.[2] In Lebanon, relations between the dominant Shia majority and the Maronite Catholic minority remain fraught with tension.[3]

The term 'minority' is controversial for its possible pejorative connotations. It is popularly used in the demographic sense to refer to groups of persons of small size in comparison with the total population in terms of, for instance, race, ethnicity, gender, sexual orientation, age, physical abilities, economics, culture, religion, etc. However, it almost always connotes power relations between the minority groups and the majority/dominant group, with the latter, which at times may be numerically small, controlling and occupying positions of power and consequently able to establish economic, political, and legal structures of discrimination against minority groups. Syria is a recent case in point. It comes as no surprise therefore that the discourse on minority groups is inseparably linked with that of rights and policies ensur-ing these rights, such as affirmative action. Hence, instead of the term 'minority', which may have a pejorative connotation, especially when used by the dominant group, the expression 'historically excluded groups' is at times preferred.

We will also examine, from the Roman Catholic perspective, how interreligious dialogue between the dominant and minority religious groups, and among the religious minority groups themselves, can profitably be done. Compared with ecumenical dialogue, interreli-gious or interfaith dialogue engaged in by Christians is of more recent origin. In the Roman Catholic Church such dialogue, which requires a respectful and positive attitude towards

---

[2] See Toyin Falola, *Violence in Nigeria: The Crisis of Religious Politics and Secular Ideologies* (Rochester, NY: University of Rochester Press, 1998) and Rosalind I. J. Hackett, 'Nigeria's Religious Leaders in an Age of Radicalism and Neoliberalism', in Timothy D. Sisk (ed.), *Between Terror and Tolerance: Religious Leaders, Conflict, and Peacemaking* (Washington, DC: Georgetown University Press, 2011), 123–44.

[3] George Emile Irani, 'Between Intolerance and Coexistence: The Vatican, Maronites and the War in Lebanon', in Sisk, *Between Terror and Tolerance*, 49–68.

other religions, was given an official stamp of approval by the Second Vatican Council (1962–5), and in the last fifty years significant efforts have been made at the institutional and grassroots levels to promote religious harmony. However, the problems, theological as well as practical, that are raised by interreligious dialogue, are many and difficult, especially in light of current political and military conflicts.[4]

A GLOBAL SNAPSHOT OF MAJORITY–MINORITY INTERRELIGIOUS RELATIONS

Though our focus is on Muslim–Christian relations within the broader discussion of majority–minority religious encounters, it is highly likely that very similar dynamics are operative in majority–minority encounters involving other religions throughout the world. Indeed, no religion has been innocent of hatred and war, both within itself and against other religious communities, including Judaism, Christianity, Islam, and even religions that uphold non-violence as moral ideals, such as Hinduism and Buddhism, especially when these two are the religions of ethnic majorities embroiled in sectarian conflicts with ethnic minorities, as is the case in India and Sri Lanka.

Sectarian violence against religious minority groups has hit the headlines in the past three decades in many parts of the world—Muslims against Ahmadiyya and Christians in Pakistan, Hindus against Muslims and Christians in India, and Buddhists against Hindus in Sri Lanka. Interreligious conflicts are often linked inextricably to broader socio-economic and political issues. On the one hand, at the grassroots level one often finds harmonious interreligious relations as majority and minority religious groups get along in daily living without any prob-lems: Hindus and Christians making pilgrimages to each other's religious shrines and partici-pating in local communal festivals across religious boundaries, for example.[5] On the other hand, since the 1970s there has been a rise in inter-communal tensions and violence as reli-gion becomes politicized in response to broader economic problems and its consequential political crises and social dislocations.

To worsen matters, in many parts of the world the popular association of Christianity with colonial imperialism often taints interreligious encounters. For many Asian and African nations that have gained independence from their colonial masters since the mid twentieth century, independence and postcolonial consciousness have led to a recovery of national pride and, with it, a massive revival of traditional religions. And Islam, Hinduism, and Buddhism are now not only asserting themselves on the national and international stage, in

---

[4] Cf. Paul Hedges, *Controversies in Interreligious Dialogue* (London: SCM Press, 2010) and Peter C. Phan, *Being Religious Interreligiously: Asian Perspectives on Interfaith Dialogue* (Maryknoll, NY: Orbis Books, 2004).

[5] See Karen Pechilis and Selva J. Raj (eds), *South Asian Religions: Tradition and Today* (New York: Routledge, 2013) and Selva J. Raj and Corinne G. Dempsey (eds), *Popular Christianity in India: Riting Between the Lines* (Albany, NY: SUNY, 2002).

some quarters they are also putting pressure on religious minorities within their midst to abandon Christianity as a colonial relic and foreign import in favour of the local religion of the majority.[6] In addition, increased mobility in today's world has generated large-scale movement of peoples, increasing diversity and plurality, and intensifying tensions between the dominant community in the host countries and newcomer minorities. More problematic is the use of terror and violence by a dominant majority community against a vulnerable minority community to conform to the majority's definition of identity and social belonging. The World Council of Churches was very direct in its 2004 assertion:

> In some parts of the world, religion is increasingly identified with ethnicity, giving religious overtones to ethnic conflict. In other situations, religious identity becomes so closely related to power that the communities without power, or who are discriminated against, look to their religion as the force of mobilization of their dissent and protest. These conflicts tend to appear as, or are represented to be, conflict between religious communities, polarizing them along communal lines. Religious communities often inherit deep divisions, hatreds and enmities that are, in most cases, passed down through generations of conflict. When communities identify themselves or are identified exclusively by their religion, the situation becomes explosive, even able to tear apart communities that have lived in peace for centuries. It is the task of interreligious relations and dialogue to help prevent religion from becoming the fault line between communities.[7]

With the blurring of boundaries between the majority's legitimate quest for a distinctive socio-cultural and religious identity construction and its hostility towards minorities for being different, the unfortunate result is often communal tensions and religious strife, as can be seen in Pakistan, India, Sri Lanka, and elsewhere. Moreover, too often religious identities become intertwined in ethnic conflicts, thereby giving religious overtones to ethnic conflicts, as is the case in Sri Lanka.

Pakistan

From the time of the military dictatorship of the late General Zia Ul Haq to the present day, Pakistan has witnessed an increase in attacks against the Christian minority as alien outsiders, especially through the misuse of controversial blasphemy laws to intimidate and harass Christians.[8] It was against this backdrop that the Roman Catholic Bishop of Faisalabad, John Joseph, shot himself in the head on 6 May 1998 in protest against the execution of a Christian on spurious blasphemy charges.[9] But Bishop Joseph's death

---

[6] Cf. Jonathan Y. Tan, 'Rethinking the Relationship between Christianity and World Religions, and Exploring its Implications for Doing Christian Mission in Asia', *Missiology*, 39/4 (2011), 498–508.

[7] *Ecumenical Considerations for Dialogue and Relations with People of Other Religions* (Geneva: WCC, 2004).

[8] Cf. Owen Bennett Jones, *Pakistan: Eye of the Storm*, 3rd edn (New Haven: Yale University Press, 2009).

[9] Linda Walbridge, *Christians of Pakistan: The Passion of Bishop John Joseph* (New York: Routledge, 2002).

brought no relief to the beleaguered and vulnerable Pakistani Christian minority. The ongoing harassment of Pakistani Christians culminated in the killings of six Christians in Gojra on 1 August 2009 for allegedly desecrating the Qur'an. Christian activists have continued to press for the repeal of blasphemy laws that make it very easy for anyone to single out Christians for harassment.

India

India is an example of a country where religion is caught up in a treacherous mix of caste, race, ethnicity, politics, class, and economics. Since the 1980s, India has witnessed the rise of the militant Hindutva religious movement and its political wing, the Bharatiya Janata Party (BJP), which reject the constitutionally mandated tolerance of Indian Muslims and Indian Christians, on the grounds that these minority religious traditions are foreign and alien to the majority Hindu culture of India.[10] Much of the sectarian interreligious violence by the Hindu majority against the Muslim and Christian minorities has been fomented by Hindu radical groups such as the Vishwa Hindu Parishad (VHP), Rashtriya Swayamsevak Sangh (RSS), Sang Parivar, and Bajrang Dal, which have been accused of coercing Indian Christians and Indian Muslims to abandon their faith and embrace Hinduism, or be killed.[11] Interreligious relations between Hindus and Muslims plunged to their lowest point with the destruction of the Babri Mosque in Ayodhya by Hindutva fundamentalists on 6 December 1992. The ensuing violent clashes between Muslims and Hindus in major Indian cities resulted in more than 2,000 dead and many thousands more injured.[12] Hindu–Christian relations are especially tense and confrontational. The observations of the Indian theologian T. K. John in 1987 are prescient and still hold true in contemporary India:

> [Hindu] critics see Christianity as an alien and complex power structure that threatens to eventually undermine India's culture, national integrity and its religions. They feel that a religion that is disappearing from its former stronghold is being dumped, like so many unwanted drugs, on the Third World where it has to be nourished, supported and propagated by foreign money, control and power, instead of drawing its strength from the soil. They conclude that even current efforts at inculturation (which meet with so much inside opposition) are subterfuge measures to win over hesitant or unwilling recruits to the Christian fold. They accuse the Christian missionaries of taking undue advantage of the poverty, the illiteracy and ignorance of the vast majority of the people, and for the proof of this they point to

---

[10]   See Rowena Robinson, *Christians of India* (Thousand Oaks, Calif.: Sage, 2003) and Robert Eric Frykenberg, *Christianity in India: From Beginnings to the Present* (New York: Oxford University Press, 2008). See also Susan Bayley, *Saints, Goddesses and Kings: Muslims and Christians in South Indian Society, 1700–1900* (Cambridge: Cambridge University Press, 1989).

[11]   Ram Puniyani (ed.), *Religion, Power and Violence: Expression of Politics in Contemporary Times* (Thousand Oaks, Calif.: Sage, 2005).

[12]   Sarvepalli Gopal, *Anatomy of a Confrontation: The Rise of Communal Politics in India* (London: Zed Books, 1993); Arvind Sharma (ed.), *Hinduism and Secularism: After Ayodhya* (New York: Palgrave, 2001).

the fact that they have altogether withdrawn their 'forces' from the more difficult areas like the caste Hindus, the educated and the economically well-off.[13]

Since the 1990s, many Hindutva nationalists have increasingly taken issue with Christian missionary outreach among the Dalits, especially in Gujarat and Orissa, beginning with the cold-blooded murder of the Australian Evangelical missionary Graham Staines and his two young sons Philip and Timothy in 1999 and culminating in the violence and mayhem against Dalit Christians in Orissa by Hindutva agitators in the aftermath of the assassination of the Hindu fundamentalist Swami Laxmanananda Saraswati by Maoist insurgents on 24 August 2008. In the face of vitriol, hate, and exclusivism promoted by right-wing Hindutva militant groups, we may ask whether the quest for interreligious relations between majority and minority groups in this case rather smacks of naivety.

The Statement of the Executive Body of the Catholic Bishops' Conference of India (CBCI) in response to the Orissa violence against Indian Christians is unequivocal in asserting that tit-for-tat responses will only worsen things. One cannot fight religious exclusivism with more religious exclusivism. Rather, one disarms religious exclusivism with an inclusive Christian love. As the Indian bishops explained, 'no matter how great the threat that may confront us, we cannot renounce the heritage of love and justice that Jesus left us' because 'when Jesus went about healing the sick, associating with outcasts and assisting the poor, those works were not allurements but the concrete realization of God's plan for humankind: to build a society founded on love, justice and social harmony'.[14]

In a similar vein, the Catholic Archbishop of Delhi, Vincent Concessao points out that inflammatory missionary tracts which disparage and denigrate Hinduism are counter-productive because 'they give fanatics a battering ram to crush Indian Christianity at large'.[15] Commenting on the increasing tension between Hindus and Christians, the Indian theologian Sebastian Madathummuriyil puts forward the case for the Indian Catholic Church to 're-examine the Church's imperialistic objectives of mission that reflect exclusivist and totalitarian tendencies', as well as to rediscover its identity, 'paying heed to the challenges posed by religious, cultural, ideological, and linguistic pluralism'.[16] In particular, Madathummuriyil thinks that, as a minority community in India, the Indian Catholic Church is well positioned to be a prophetic voice for peace and harmony among Hindus, Muslims, and Christians in India against the backdrop of the Hindutva ideology of homogeneity of religion, culture, and language:

[13] T. K. John, 'The Pope's "Pastoral Visit" to India: A Further Reflection', *Vidyajyoti Journal of Theological Reflection*, 51 (1987), 59.

[14] Catholic Bishops' Conference of India, 'Violence Against Christians: Statement of the Executive Body of the Catholic Bishops' Conference of India', *Vidyajyoti Journal of Theological Reflection*, 72 (2008), 816.

[15] Cited in Francis Gonsalves, 'Carrying in Our Bodies the Marks of His Passion', *Vidyajyoti Journal of Theological Reflection*, 72 (2008), 806.

[16] Cited in Gerald M. Boodoo, 'Catholicity and Mission', *Proceedings of the Catholic Theological Society of America*, 65 (2010), 118.

To be a prophetic Church in the Indian context, then, would imply, on the one hand, forfeiting traditional strategies of mission and, on the other hand, enhancing measures for regaining trust and confidence of both Hindus and Muslims through dialogue in an age of widespread anti-Christian sentiments.[17]

Sri Lanka

Sri Lanka continues to be a nation that is splintered along racial-ethnic and religious fault lines: Sinhalese vs Tamil; Buddhist vs Hindu; and Buddhist vs Christian. The horrors of the long-running internecine strife between the majority Sinhalese and minority Tamil communities have resulted in extremely poisoned relations between these two ethnic communities. It does not help that most Sinhalese are Buddhists while the Tamils are mainly Hindus or Christians, and Sinhalese nationalists have often wrapped their inflammatory political rhetoric in the garments of Buddhist religious pride.[18] Outright civil war between the Tamils and Sinhalese erupted over 'Black July' with anti-Tamil ethnic cleansing riots by the Sinhalese majority that began on 23 July 1983. From 1983 until the military defeat of the Liberation Tigers of Tamil Eelam (LTTE) in 2009, hundreds of thousands died and many more Tamils fled Sri Lanka as refugees. Moreover, the use of Buddhist religious rhetoric to legitimize the civil war against the Tamil minority in Sri Lanka by nationalist political parties such as the Jathika Hela Urumaya (National Sinhala Heritage) Party has poisoned peaceful interreligious relations between the Sinhalese and the Tamils.[19] Significantly, the Jathika Hela Urumaya was led by Sinhalese Buddhist monks who entered politics in 2004 on a Sinhalese Buddhist nationalist platform promoting violence and war to drive the Tamil minority out of Sri Lanka.[20]

On the one hand, there have been attempts by the Sinhalese Buddhist majority to initiate interreligious engagements to bring about peace, reconciliation, and healing across racial-ethnic and religious boundaries. For example, the Sinhalese Buddhist activist, A. T. Ariyaratne, who founded the Sarvodaya Shramadana Movement, a social movement with a successful village-renewal programme that seeks to improve the lives of villagers amidst poverty and civil war, has responded to the sectarian tensions in Sri Lanka by sponsoring peace walks and peace conferences that have promoted reconciliation between the Sinhalese majority and Tamil minority on the basis of shared values that are common to Buddhism, Hinduism,

---

[17] Boodoo, 'Catholicity and Mission', 118.

[18] See Darini Rajasingham Senanayake, *Buddhism and the Legitimation of Power: Democracy, Public Religion and Minorities in Sri Lanka* (Singapore: National University of Singapore Institute of South Asian Studies, 2009), Mahinda Deegalle (ed.), *Buddhism, Conflict and Violence in Modern Sri Lanka* (New York: Routledge, 2006), and Patrick Grant, *Buddhism and Ethnic Conflict in Sri Lanka* (Albany, NY: SUNY, 2009).

[19] See Stanley J. Tambiah, *Buddhism Betrayed? Religion, Politics and Violence in Sri Lanka* (Chicago: University of Chicago Press, 1992); Susan Hayward, 'The Spoiler and the Reconciler: Buddhism and the Peace Process in Sri Lanka', in Sisk, *Between Terror and Tolerance*, 183–200.

[20] Tessa J. Bartholomeusz, *In Defense of Dharma: Just-War Ideology in Buddhist Sri Lanka* (London: Routledge Curzon, 2002).

and Christianity.[21] On the other hand, similar initiatives by the Christian minority have been viewed as 'a sinister plan for pan-Christian domination'.[22]

Malaysia

Contemporary Malaysia is a multi-ethnic, multilingual, multi-religious, and multi cultural society comprising Malays (50.4 per cent), Chinese (23.7 per cent), aboriginals/indigenous (11 per cent), and Indian (7.1 per cent). About 60 per cent of the population of Malaysia is Muslim. Christians are exclusively non-Malays and comprise around 9.0 per cent of the population, followed by Hindus (c.6.5 per cent), and followers of Chinese religions (c.2.5 per cent). At the same time, Malaysia is also a socially and politically volatile society divided by an explosive mix of ethnicity and religion. Although Islam is the official religion of Malaysia and the majority of Malaysians are Muslims, freedom of religion in Malaysia is guaranteed under article 11(1) of the Malaysian Federal Constitution.[23] However, the Malaysian Federal Constitution also empowers the federal and state governments to pass laws against the propagation of non-Muslim religions among the Muslims.[24] The simmering discontent between Malays and Chinese, the two dominant ethnic groups in Malaysia, came to an explosive clash in the series of violent racial riots, stoked by extremist Malay nationalists against the Chinese community, beginning on 13 May 1969.

In the aftermath of these riots, the Malaysian government embarked on a policy of national reconciliation to rebuild a shattered society. In an ironic twist, the cornerstone of the Malaysian government's policy of national reconciliation is the New Economic Policy (NEP) which institutionalized communalism, Malay dominance in nation-building, and Malay sovereignty over the other minority communities in all matters—political, social, and economic. In reality, the NEP resulted in widespread economic inefficiency, corruption scandals, cronyism, and nepotism as a small Malay elite controlled the political and economic levers of powers to the exclusion of ordinary Malays and other races. As the tangible economic benefits of the NEP failed to trickle down to the ordinary Malays in rural communities, the Islamic Parti Islam Se-Malaysia (PAS) emerged to champion Islamization as the alternative to the cronyism and corruption of the NEP. In response to the popularity of PAS's Islamization platform, the ruling political elite adopted a similar policy of Islamization to blunt PAS's tactics.

---

[21] See A. T. Ariyaratne, 'Sarvodaya Shramadana's Approach to Peacebuilding', in David W. Chappell (ed.), *Buddhist Peacework: Creating Cultures of Peace* (Somerville, Mass.: Wisdom Publications, 1999), 69–80.

[22] Jeyaraj Rasiah, 'Sri Lanka', in Peter C. Phan (ed.), *Christianities in Asia* (New York: Wiley-Blackwell, 2011), 57.

[23] Article 11(1) of the Malaysian Federal Constitution states, 'Every person has the right to profess and practise his religion and, subject to Clause (4), to propagate it'.

[24] Article 11(4) of the Malaysian Federal Constitution legalizes all federal and state legislation prohibiting the propagation of non-Muslim religions among Muslims in Malaysia: 'State law and in respect of the Federal Territories of Kuala Lumpur and Labuan, federal law may control or restrict the propagation of any religious doctrine or belief among persons professing the religion of Islam.'

To say that the Malaysian government's heavy-handed programme of Islamization has resulted in increased religious tensions between the majority Muslim and other religious minority communities in Malaysia is an understatement. As a religious minority, Malaysian Christians have found themselves in the direct firing line of legislation and programmes aimed at giving Islam a privileged position over the other religious faiths in Malaysia. For example, federal legislation was passed in 1981 to ban possession of Indonesian translations of the Bible. In response to vociferous protests by Malaysian Christians, a concession was made in 1982 to allow them to use the Indonesian translation for personal devotion and public worship. However, current law prohibits the dissemination and circulation of any Indonesian or Malay translation of the Bible among Muslims in Malaysia. In 1991, legislation was passed by the Malaysian Parliament to prohibit the use in non-Islamic literature of, among other things, the term 'Allah' for God. Malaysian Christians objected to this prohibition of the use of 'Allah' for God, because it impinged on their rights to use these terms in Malay-language translations of the Bible as well as in liturgies and prayer meetings.[25]

Non-Muslims in Malaysia are also rankled by legislation that criminalizes apostasy (*takfir*) by Muslims, as well as the actions of non-Muslims who proselytize their faith to Muslims. These laws against apostasy drew international headlines and condemnation in the case of Lina Joy, who brought a suit before the Malaysian Federal Court to compel the Malaysian National Registration Department to record her change of religion from Islam to Christianity on her identity card after her baptism as a Roman Catholic.[26] On 30 May 2007, her appeal was dismissed by a 2-1 majority, and she and her Christian fiancé were forced to leave Malaysia under threats of violence from Malaysian Muslim activists. More importantly, the Malaysian Federal Court ruling further inflamed interreligious tensions, as non-Muslim minorities perceive this to be yet another nail in the coffin of religious freedom in Malaysia.[27]

In response to pressure from the Malay Muslim majority, the Christian Federation of Malaysia (CFM) was established in 1986 as an umbrella organization for Malaysian Christians that includes the Council of Churches of Malaysia (CCM) representing the mainline Protestant Churches, the National Evangelical Christian Fellowship (NECF) representing the Evangelical, Brethren, and Pentecostal churches, as well as the Malaysian Catholic Church as equal partners. The CFM comprises about 5,000 member churches and encompasses around 90 per cent of the total Christian population of Malaysia. The CFM is also an active member of the Malaysian Consultative Council of Buddhism, Christianity, Hinduism, and Sikhism (MCCBCHS), which was formed in 1983 with the following objectives: (1) to promote understanding, mutual respect, and cooperation among the different religions in Malaysia; (2) to study and resolve problems affecting all interreligious relationships; and (3) to make

---

[25] See Albert Sundararaj Walters, *We Believe in One God? Reflections on the Trinity in the Malaysian Context* (Delhi: ISPCK, 2002).

[26] Jane Perlez, 'Once Muslim, Now Christian and Caught in the Courts', *New York Times*, 24 Aug. 2006: <http://www.nytimes.com/2006/08/24/world/asia/24malaysia.html> (accessed Aug. 2012).

[27] See Albert Walters, 'Issues in Christian–Muslim Relations: A Malaysian Christian Perspective', *Islam and Christian–Muslim Relations*, 18/1 (2007), 67–83.

representations regarding religious matters when necessary.[28] The MCCBCHS has become an organized channel for dialogue between the non-Muslims and the Malaysian government on issues of religious freedom and the impact of encroaching Islamization on the rights of the non-Muslim religious minorities to practise their faith without interference or fear.

AMERICA: 'THE WORLD'S MOST RELIGIOUSLY DIVERSE NATION'?

Whereas there is little contention as to what the United States is geographically, there is a lively debate about the current religious situation of this country, what constitutes a minority,[29] and what interreligious dialogue is and how it should be carried out, especially between religious majority and minority groups, and among the religious minority groups themselves. The United States is irretrievably religiously plural, as hinted at in a recent book by Diana Eck.[30] Its basic thesis is nicely captured on its front cover by an unfurled American flag, with the fifty stars in the upper left-hand corner replaced by the symbols of various religions. Eck's volume, which came out of the Pluralism Project at Harvard University, introduces readers to a 'New America', characterized by not only religious diversity (a sociological datum) but also religious pluralism (a religious and theological challenge to the claim of uniqueness, superiority, and universal necessity for a particular religion). The New America is not only 'Protestant, Catholic, Jew', to invoke another landmark book, published in 1955, by the sociologist Will Herberg,[31] but also Hindu, Buddhist, Muslim, and a lot of other, no less important, religious traditions, such as Jain, Sikh, Baha'i, Zoroastrian, Confucian, Daoist, Native American, Mormon, Seventh-Day Adventist; and the list would be quite lengthy if new religious movements such as New Age and Wiccan are added. The issue then is not *whether* the American religious situation is diverse and pluralistic—it incontrovertibly is—but rather *how* America is to deal with this new phenomenon in all sectors of life, especially religion. It is here that fierce controversies, particularly theological, are raging.

Religious Diversity and Pluralism

Eck is deeply aware that not only are these religions transformed in and by America but also the face of the New America is shaped by this new religious diversity. As she tersely puts it:

---

[28] Paul Tan Chee Ing and Teresa Ee, *Contemporary Issues on Malaysian Religions* (Petaling Jaya: Pelanduk Publications, 1984), 13.

[29] Cf. Michael Mazur, *The Americanization of Religious Minorities: Confronting the Constitutional Order* (Baltimore, Md.: Johns Hopkins University Press, 2004).

[30] Diana Eck, *A New Religious America: How a 'Christian Country' has become the World's Most Religiously Diverse Nation* (San Francisco: HarperSanFrancisco, 2002).

[31] Will Herberg, *Protestant–Catholic–Jew: An Essay in American Religious Sociology* (Chicago: University of Chicago Press, 1955).

'Not only is America changing these religions, but these religions are also changing America'.[32] Eck's sociological and theological accounts of America's religious diversity do not of course go unchallenged, especially by the more conservative Christians who steadfastly hold that America has been and will remain a Christian nation. But that religious diversity has been growing exponentially in America, and steadily since 1965, seems beyond doubt. Recently, the Princeton University sociologist Robert Wuthnow confirmed this new religious phenomenon.[33] New immigrants to the United States include large numbers of Muslims, Hindus, Buddhists, and followers of other religions, and they do not for the most part live in religiously homogeneous enclaves of their own, separated from the rest of the American population, but in the same neighbourhoods as other Americans. Thus, believers of different faiths regularly rub shoulders with one another in daily life.

In her 2006 Presidential Address to the American Academy of Religion, Eck explored the impact of religious pluralism on the academy, civic life, and theology.[34] Wuthnow takes Eck's threefold concern further and asks whether Americans are taking advantage of the opportunities that diversity provides and moving towards a more mature pluralism than they have experienced in the past. Both Eck and Wuthnow rightly point out that with the twin constitutional principles of non-establishment and religious freedom, America possesses a solid legal foundation for religious diversity. But whether Americans privilege *pluribus* over *unum* in their national motto *ex pluribus unum*, and how they understand national unity implied by *unum*, are moot points. However these debates are solved, it is clear that, as Wuthnow has shrewdly noted, 'in our public discourse about religion we [Americans] seem to be a society of schizophrenics'.[35] On the one hand, a large majority of Americans believe that America is a special nation with a divine destiny, a shining city on the hill, a beacon for the world. Furthermore, a large majority of American Christians are convinced that Christianity is the only true, or at least unique, religion; and that America is a nation built on Christian principles. The President is expected to conclude every national address with the phrase 'God bless America'—and 'God' is implicitly taken to refer to the Christian God—otherwise he would be suspected of being a non-Christian at heart (maybe a Muslim or a Mormon)! On the other hand, a majority of American Christians are also convinced that tolerance is a civic and religious virtue conducive to democracy and harmonious living and that religious diversity is to be respected if not promoted. Nevertheless, when American Christians occupy the dominant position and enjoy the controlling power, especially in politics and economics, that they currently do, this religious tolerance remains merely what it is, namely tolerance, and the line between it and intolerance is dangerously thin. Let the others be 'other', the dominant

---

[32] Eck, *New Religious America*, 25.

[33] Robert Wuthnow, *America and the Challenges of Religious Diversity* (Princeton: Princeton University Press, 2005).

[34] Diana Eck, 'Prospects for Pluralism: Voice and Vision in the Study of Religion', *Journal of the American Academy of Religion*, 75/4 (2007), 743–76.

[35] Wuthnow, *America*, 6.

religious group might say, as long as they don't bother us, and above all, do not harm our interests.

Religious Diversity and Power Relations

To the extent that American Christians claim and in fact do exercise dominance in the various arenas of national life, especially religious, this dominance has not gone uncontested and resisted by different non-Christian groups and even by Christians themselves. At the very least, white Americans are now being challenged by the ever-growing presence of non-European immigrants, both documented and non-documented, particularly Hispanic, to imagine an America in which in the near future the so-called ethnic minorities will become the demographic majority.[36] In addition, American Christians are challenged by the non-Christian believers in their midst to rethink their belief in the superiority and universal necessity of Christianity, to reconfigure their modes of interacting with non-Christian believers on the level of both individual and community, to negotiate religiously mixed marriages, and to seek forms of collaboration for the social, political, and religious common good. Clearly, the very identity and the future of both America and American Christianity are at stake, and the way forward to a 'New America' seems to be much more than tolerance and coexistence. In short, nothing less than interreligious dialogue is required.

New Religious Minorities: Challenges and Opportunities

To assure the success of interreligious dialogue in the USA, it is necessary to acknowledge the fact that, in spite of the widespread talk about religious diversity in America, the nation is predominantly Christian and will remain so for the foreseeable future. According to the 2008 US Religious Landscape Survey of the Pew Forum on Religion and Public Life, 76 per cent of the American adult population self-identifies as Christian, whereas the total of non-Christians makes up 4.9 per cent (Jews 1.7 per cent, Muslims 0.6 per cent, Buddhists 0.7 per cent, Hindus 0.4 per cent, other world religions 0.3 per cent, and other native faiths 1.2 per cent).[37] Clearly, non-Christians in America represent a demographic and religious minority. In terms of economic and political power, though there are anecdotal reports of notable successes, especially among Asians, non-Christians remain an insignificant minority. Even so, non-Christian minority groups, as mentioned above, present enormous challenges to America and American Christianity.

The emergence of religious diversity in the USA may be attributed almost exclusively to post-1965 immigration. There is little doubt that globally, migration, either forced or

[36] It was reported by the *Washington Post*, 17 May 2012, that for the first time in history, most of the babies in the USA are members of the minority groups, signalling the dawn of an era in which whites no longer will be in the majority.

[37] See Pew Forum on Religion and Public Life at <http://religions.pewforum.org>.

voluntary, of non-Christians to predominantly Christian countries, has increased exponentially since the Second World War, due often to new instances of violence and war; poverty and natural disasters; political and religious persecution; and globalization. In the USA, the emergence of religious minorities, except Judaism, is the unintended effect of the changes in immigration laws in the 1960s. The Immigration and Nationality Act of 1965, also known as the Hart-Cellar Act, abolishes the system of national-origin quotas and has dramatically increased the number of non-European immigrants, especially from South America, Asia, and Africa. Whereas immigrants from Latin America are predominantly Christian, those from Asia, the Middle East, and Africa bring with them their non-Christian religions, especially Islam, Buddhism, and Hinduism. Migrants, especially transnational immigrants and refugees, by necessity live in a strange land, forced to adjust to unfamiliar and often oppressive circumstances amidst painful experiences of displacement and disorientation. While a great deal of scholarly attention has been given to linguistic, economic, social, political, and cultural challenges facing migrants, relatively little study has been made of their religious situation, especially in the case of non-Christian migrants living in traditionally Christian countries.[38]

The Religious Predicament of Non-Christian Migrants

To facilitate a fruitful dialogue between non-Christian minorities with the Christian majority in the USA and among these religious minorities themselves, it is of utmost importance to recall the special condition of these non-Christians, most of whom are migrants, others American-born but disenfranchised, especially with regard to religion.[39] This religious condition of immigrants may be described as precarious, marginalized, threatened, and endangered. First of all, the religious faith of non-Christian migrants, especially those facing economic poverty, ethnic and racial discrimination, social isolation, and political oppression, is constantly under severe pressure. For their faith to be sustained and developed, worship houses (synagogue, mosque, temple, pagoda, gurdawara, etc.), community fellowship, and, where appropriate, clerical leadership and institutional structures are all absolutely necessary. But unfortunately, whether because of limited financial means or isolation from a supportive close-knit community, these things may not be available to non-Christian migrants. Their faith will remain important, but its practice and expression may well be imperilled for want of necessary support structures.

---

[38] The situation of Christian migrants living—mostly as a tiny minority—in non-Christian countries is often far more difficult than that of non-Christian migrants living in predominantly Christian countries. This 'non-symmetry' deserves careful and greater attention than hitherto accorded.

[39] See Graziano Battistella (ed.), *Migrazioni: Dizionario Socio-Pastorale* (Milan: Edizioni San Paolo, 2010). See also Daniel G. Groody and Gioacchino Campese (eds), *A Promised Land, a Perilous Journey: Theological Perspectives on Migration* (Notre Dame, Ind.: University of Notre Dame Press, 2008); Eleazar S. Fernandez and Fernando S. Segovia (eds), *A Dream Unfinished: Theological Reflections on America from the Margins* (Maryknoll, NY: Orbis Books, 2001).

Secondly, though non-Christian migrants can be economically and educationally success-ful, the number of those who are is very small. As minority religious groups, they are socially marginalized and even politically suspect, especially Muslims in the wake of the 11 September 2001 attacks. There is a temptation for these migrants to abandon their faith and religious practices in order to avoid discrimination and hatred and to move into the social and religious mainstream. Thirdly, the faith of non-Christian migrants is seriously threatened by modern rationality, materialism, and consumerism whose combined onslaught is a most serious men-ace to the faith of the migrants' children. To these, often educated in secular institutions and trained in technical professions, their parents' faith appears quaint, backward, and even superstitious. Christianity, by comparison, is associated with scientific rationality, technologi-cal superiority, and material prosperity, and thus offers a powerfully attractive alternative to their homeland religions.

Lastly, and this is an extremely delicate point but must frankly be acknowledged, the reli-gious adherence of non-Christian migrants in the West is arguably endangered by the ever-present attempt—overt and subtle—of evangelization and even proselytism by Christians. Rare is the case where non-Christians are not pressured—albeit gently—to reject their faith and convert to Christianity, especially if they marry a Christian, attend a Christian school, work in a Christian environment, especially in a country where the celebration of Christian feasts (e.g. Christmas, Easter) are national holidays, and whose way of life is pervaded by Christian symbols, beliefs, and rituals.

These four characteristics of the non-Christian migrants' religious situation—precarious, marginalized, threatened, and endangered—make them extremely vulnerable to the loss of their faith and religious identity. Understandably, they are suspicious of any attempt at inter-religious dialogue, especially by those who hold the reins of power in almost all aspects of life. Interreligious dialogue often appears to them as proselytism through the back door. This fear is of course not unknown to Christians living as a disadvantaged minority in non-Chris-tian lands.

Opportunities for a New Religious Identity

This characterization of the condition of non-Christian migrants in the USA should not however be taken to imply that they are mere powerless victims or passive citizens. On the contrary, recent studies of immigrants in the USA (as well as in Europe) in different disci-plines including anthropology, psychology, economics, politics, and religious studies again and again show how immigrants of all faiths are constantly and actively reshaping their reli-gious identities in response to external and internal pressure.[40] Contrary to the secularization

[40] Cf. Yvonne Y. Haddad, Jane L. Smith, and John L. Esposito (eds), *Religion and Immigration: Christian, Jewish, and Muslim Experiences in the United States* (New York: Altamira Press, 2003); Karen J. Leonard, Alex Stepick, Manuel A. Vasquez, and Jennifer Holdaway (eds), *Immigrants' Faiths: The Transforming Religious Life in America* (New York: Altamira Press, 2006).

thesis, which predicts the death of God in modernity, religion has been a powerful and irreplaceable force shaping and changing the immigrants' constructions of personal and community identity in economic, social, political, and cultural spheres.

In an informative overview of immigration and religion in the USA, the sociologist Alex Stepick argues that there are three obvious and well-established facts about immigrants and religion. First, religion is vitally important in the lives of the majority of immigrants in the USA; for them, God is very much alive. Secondly, immigrant religions are diversifying the American religious landscape, hitherto largely Protestant, Catholic, and Jewish. Thirdly, immigrants practise their religion transnationally, crossing national, cultural, and religious borders, maintaining continuous links with their homeland religions.[41] Stepick also points out that there are several emergent, not yet fully understood phenomena in the religious life of immigrants. All of these have to do with the formation of the immigrants' new religious identity in their adopted country. Uppermost in their minds is the question of which old elements must be preserved and which new elements may and should be adopted to constitute their religious identity. The choice is stark: the homeland religion vs American Christianity; cultural preservation vs assimilation into the American mainstream; native tongue vs English; promotion of cultural and national heritage vs cultivation of religious faith; ethnic particularity or pan-ethnic association; patriarchy vs gender equality; first-generation immigrant vs second-generation youth; individual piety vs structural organization; social networking vs church relationships; spiritual activities vs civic engagement; restriction to the USA vs transnational and transcultural bridge-building.[42] All these tensions not only produce profound anxiety and deep conflict in the immigrants' everyday life but also afford them endless opportunities to create an alternative religious way of life different from both American Christianity and homeland religion that is open, fluid, hybrid, and ever-evolving.

Needless to say, each minority religion in the USA resolves these tensions differently, even within the same religious tradition, depending largely on its location, time, ability for adaptation and change, and theological stance towards modern culture, and more specifically, towards America. In general, the immigrant's religious attitude towards the new culture is either full embrace or total rejection, or most often, a variegated mixture of both. These three approaches, with their myriad varieties and degrees, often produce divisions and subdivisions within each religious tradition (e.g. Orthodox, Conservative, and Reform Judaism; and Shia, Sunni, and Sufi Islam) among immigrant believers and native converts (Middle Eastern, South Asian, and African-American Muslims), or along ethnic, class, national, and regional origins (for instance within Hinduism and Buddhism). Notwithstanding these internal divisions and rivalries, there is no doubt that minority religions in America are alive and well. Many of them, if not all, have built houses of worship, schools and universities, hospitals and

---

[41] Alex Stepick, 'God is Apparently Not Dead: The Obvious, the Emergent, and the Still Unknown in Immigration and Religion', in Leonard *et al.*, *Immigrants' Faiths*, 13–14.

[42] Stepick, 'God is Apparently Not Dead', 14–26.

social services institutions, cultural and recreation centres, and have founded ideologically divergent associations and societies for social and political activism. The question is whether the vitality of these minorities and that of American Christianity will be enhanced by a dialogue among themselves.

INTERRELIGIOUS DIALOGUE WITH NON-CHRISTIAN MIGRANTS: A CATHOLIC EXPERIMENT

As mentioned above, interreligious dialogue was officially approved and encouraged by Vatican II, especially in its Declaration on the Relation of the Church to Non-Christian Religions (*Nostra Aetate*). In the last fifty years, dialogue between the Catholic Church and other religions, in particular Judaism and Islam, has made significant progress, especially under the pontificate of John Paul II.[43] Unfortunately, alongside considerable accomplishments, there have also been events and official statements that seem to hamper interreligious dialogue. In theology, there has been no significant progress towards a more adequate understanding of the salvific role of non-Christian religions beyond the oft-repeated thesis that they contain 'seeds of the Word' and constitute 'a preparation for the Gospel'. Again, perhaps unintentionally, the Vatican rather cast a chill on interfaith dialogue with the condemnation of the (rather moderate) writings on interreligious dialogue of theologians such as Jacques Dupuis. More recently, Pope Benedict XVI created a storm of protest with his 2006 Regensburg address 'Faith, Reason and the University', with his quotation of an offensive remark by the Byzantine emperor Manuel II Palaiologos about the Prophet Muhammad. Fortunately, this mishap led directly to the response of an open letter signed by 138 Muslim leaders, *A Common Word Between Us and You*, initiating a serious dialogue between Christianity and Islam. On balance, Vatican II and its aftermath can be said to have created a highly favourable environment for interfaith dialogue. In the USA, the dialogue between the Catholic Church and Jews, for historical and theological reasons, has obtained pride of place and has achieved momentous results.[44] Dialogue with Muslims, certainly actively pursued since Vatican II, has gained renewed impetus with *A Common Word*. Dialogue with Asian religions is less extensive, although dialogue with Buddhism has been notable, especially in the monastic context.

---

[43] See Francesco Gioia (ed.), *Interreligious Dialogue: The Official Teaching of the Catholic Church from the Second Vatican Council to 2005* (Boston: Pauline Books and Media, 2006).

[44] See Cunningham *et al.* (eds), *The Catholic Church and the Jewish People* (New York: Fordham University Press, 2007) and Philip A. Cunningham *et al.* (eds), *Christ Jesus and the Jewish People Today: New Explorations of Theological Interrelationships* (Grand Rapids, Mich.: Eerdmans, 2011).

A Pastoral Initiative: Catholic Policies for Interreligious Dialogue

The dialogue between Christianity and minority religions of migrants has been advanced by a little-known 2004 document ('Instruction') issued by the Pontifical Council for the Pastoral Care of Migrants and Itinerant People titled *Erga migrantes caritas Christi*. It is the first document of the Roman magisterium to take into account the special religious situation of non-Christian migrants living in traditionally Christian countries, especially Muslims, and to present an extensive treatment of interreligious dialogue with these migrants.[45] In part II ('Migrants and the Pastoral Care of Welcome'), the Instruction speaks of cultural and religious pluralism and the need for inculturation of Christianity (34–6). It insists on the duty of all the local churches to extend to all migrants, irrespective of their religions, assistance, true welcome, and integration (42). It then proceeds to expound the church's pastoral care of Catholic migrants, Eastern Rite Catholic migrants, and migrants of other churches and ecclesial communities (49–58). Lastly, it discusses the church's 'pastoral care' for migrants of other religions in general and for Muslim migrants in particular. This is of immediate interest to us; it is helpful to highlight here the main points of the Instruction's description of the church's mission to non-Christian migrants. The church's mission is said to be first of all 'the witness of Christian charity, which itself has an evangelizing value that may open hearts for the explicit proclamation of the gospel when this is done with due Christian prudence and full respect for the freedom of the other' (59). In addition to acts of charity, the church is called to 'dialogue with these immigrants', albeit that such dialogue must be 'conducted and implemented in the conviction that the Church is the ordinary means of salvation and that she alone possesses the fullness of the means of salvation' (59).

With regard to practical policies, the Instruction calls attention to four matters. First, it does not consider it 'opportune for Christian churches, chapels, places of worship and other places reserved for evangelization and pastoral work to be made available for members of non-Christian religions. Still less should they be used to obtain recognition of demands made on the public authorities' (61). Secondly, while Catholic schools should be open to non-Christian migrants and the latter must not be forced to participate in Catholic worship, the schools' 'own characteristics and Christian-oriented educational programmes' must not be jeopardized. Furthermore, Christian religious instruction, while not to be made compulsory for non-Christian students, 'may be useful to help pupils learn about a faith different from their own' (62). Thirdly, marriage between Catholics and non-Christian migrants 'should be discouraged' (63). Fourthly, the 'principle of reciprocity' should be promoted between Christians and non-Christians in the sense that the 'relationship based on mutual respect and on justice in juridical and religious matters' must be practised not only on the part of

---

[45] See Pontifical Council for the Pastoral Care of Migrants and Itinerant People website: (http://www.vatican. va/roman_curia/pontifical_councils/migrants/doc). References are to paragraph numbers.

Christians' treatment of non-Christian migrants in traditionally Christian countries but also on the part of non-Christians' treatment of Christians in countries where the latter are a minority, especially in matters of religious freedom (64).

With regard to Muslim migrants, the Instruction acknowledges that 'today, especially in certain countries, there is a high or growing percentage'. Given that past relations between Christians and Muslims have been marred by violence and war, the Instruction urges a 'purification of memory regarding past understanding'. However, it reminds Catholics to 'practise discernment' and to distinguish between 'what can and cannot be shared in the religious doctrines and practices and in the moral laws of Islam' (65). Though the Instruction recognizes that there are important similarities between Christians and Muslims, such as 'belief in God the Creator and the Merciful, daily prayer, fasting, alms-giving, pilgrimage, asceticism to dominate the passions, and the fight against injustice and oppression', it expresses the hope that

> there will be, on the part of our Muslim brothers and sisters, a growing awareness that fundamental liberties, the inviolable rights of the person, the equal dignity of man and woman, the democratic principle of government and the healthy lay character of the State are principles that cannot be surrendered.   (66)

With regard to marriage between a Catholic woman and a Muslim man, the need for 'a particularly careful and in-depth preparation' is stressed, and both parties are to be aware of 'the profound cultural and religious differences they will have to face, both between themselves and in relation to their respective families and the Muslim's original environment, to which they may possibly return after a period spent abroad' (67). Furthermore, the Instruction warns the Catholic party that if the marriage is registered with a consulate of the Islamic country of origin, he or she may have to recite or sign documents containing the *shahada*, a practice that it implicitly disapproves as it can imply conversion to Islam. Finally, concerning the baptism of the children, the Instruction urges that the stark differences between the rules of Islam and Catholicism in this matter be made 'with absolute clarity' during the preparation of marriage and that 'the Catholic party must take a firm stand on what the Church requires' (68).

Concerning interreligious dialogue more generally, the Instruction urges Catholics to cultivate 'a convinced willingness' since contemporary societies are becoming increasingly multi-religious. To this end,

> the ordinary Catholic faithful and pastoral workers in local Churches should receive solid formation and information on other religions so as to overcome prejudices, prevail over religious relativism and avoid unjustified suspicions and fears that hamper dialogue and erect barriers, even provoking violence or misunderstanding.   (69)

This dialogue aims at not only finding common points between Christianity and other religions so as to build peace together but also at rediscovering 'convictions shared in each community' (69). Catholics

must never renounce the proclamation—either explicit or implicit, according to circumstances—
of salvation in Christ, the only Mediator between God and man. The whole work of the Church
moves in this direction in such a way that neither fraternal dialogue nor the exchange and sharing
of 'human' values can diminish the Church's commitment to evangelization.   (69)

There is no doubt that *Erga migrantes caritas Christi* marks a significant and much-needed
advance in outlining a detailed policy of the Catholic Church's pastoral care for non-
Christian migrants. On the other hand, for various reasons one may take exception to
several of its practical policies and recommendations. Though the Instruction does
strongly urge all local Catholic churches to extend assistance and welcome to migrants of
all faiths, especially those living in the West, and to help them integrate into their new
environments, its overall tone is indisputably defensive and evangelistic rather than dialogical. In matters regarding the exclusion of non-Christian migrants from using Catholic
places of worship, the preservation of the Christian character of Catholic schools and
educational programmes, the discouragement of marriages between Catholics (especially
women) and non-Christian migrants (especially Muslims), and the application of the
principle of reciprocity, the Instruction's policies are designed to protect the Catholic
Church's interests rather than to promote a genuine interreligious dialogue between
Catholics and non-Christian migrants.

Furthermore, the Instruction at times blurs the line between acts of charity with evangelization, regarding the former simply as a means or a strategy for conversion. While it recommends 'due Christian prudence and full respect for the freedom of the other', the Instruction
sees 'the witness of Christian charity' as 'an evangelizing value that may open hearts for the
explicit proclamation of the Gospel' (59). In light of this statement, non-Christian migrants
can hardly be blamed for accusing Western Catholics of exploiting their economic deprivation for religious gains. Similarly, the Instruction's suggestion that Christian instruction,
while not to be imposed on non-Christian children attending Catholic schools, 'may be useful to help pupils learn about a faith different from their own' (62) will easily be seen by
non-Christian parents as a subtle form of proselytism.

As a whole, *Erga migrantes caritas Christi* does not seem to be sufficiently sensitive to the
peculiarly vulnerable religious plight of non-Christian migrants living in traditionally
Christian countries as described above. The Instruction does not appear to be aware that
Christians and non-Christian migrants living in the West stand in an asymmetrical power
relation. To put matters starkly, Christians are seen as 'givers' and non-Christian migrants are
'receivers'; the former are opulent hosts, the latter often-unwanted guests; the former
endowed with powerful religious structures, the latter with destroyed religious communities.
To non-Christian migrants whose faith is precarious, marginalized, threatened, and endangered, and who depend almost totally on the Christians' charity and welcome for physical
and psychological survival, the church's proclamation that 'the Church is the ordinary means
of salvation and that she alone possesses the fullness of the means of salvation' (59) and that

Christ is 'the only Mediator between God and man' (69) will most probably sound not as a humble confession of the church's faith and a rejection of 'relativism' (62) but as a not-so-subtle 'invitation' to them to abandon their religions and join the church if they want to prosper in their new countries.

In this respect, it is well to remember that, while the Catholic Church itself may not be engaged in crass proselytism, there are other Christian churches that are actively and massively engaged in this practice, especially those advocating the 'prosperity gospel' and those who are adamant that unless one is a Christian one cannot be saved.[46]

Clearly, interreligious dialogue between Catholics and non-Christian migrants, if it is to achieve its true nature and purpose, must be thought anew. First of all, Catholics taking part in interreligious dialogue should be deeply aware of their own vastly superior position of power and the religious vulnerabilities of non-Christian migrants and must never exploit either of them for religious gain. Secondly, they must state, unequivocally and forthrightly, at the outset of the dialogue that they have no intention whatsoever to 'convert' them to Christianity. Indeed, they will be slow in accepting conversions except when they are ascertained to be motivated by purely religious convictions. Thirdly, while steps will be taken to ensure that no human and religious rights of Catholics are violated, their observance should not constitute the *sine qua non* for entering into interreligious dialogue. Indeed, interreligious dialogue may foster such observance without demanding a strict application of the principle of reciprocity. Fourth, interreligious dialogue will always take the fourfold form of common life, common action, theological exchange, and shared religious experience, with the extent and priority of each depending on particular situations and circumstances.[47] This fourfold dialogue might at times make the common use of Christian places of worship not only appropriate but also powerfully effective (as witnessed at a common worship of Christians, Jews, and Muslims—and even non-believers— for healing and forgiveness shortly after 11 September 2001 in a Christian church).

Interreligious dialogue between Christians and non-Christian migrants living in traditionally Christian countries takes on a special urgency since the number of the latter is increasing rapidly. It can be especially difficult because of the extremely vulnerable religious condition of the non-Christian migrants, but this should not discourage interreligious dialogue.

CONCLUSION: MAJORITY–MINORITY DYNAMICS AND INTERFAITH DIALOGUE

Our discussion of interfaith dialogue between religious majority and minority groups shows up a number of pertinent dynamics. Arguably migration is one of the most informative venues

---

[46] Interestingly, according to the 2008 US Religious Landscape Survey of the Pew Forum on Religion and Public Life, seven in ten Americans agree that 'many religions—not just their own—can lead to eternal life'.

[47] See Phan, *Being Religious Interreligiously*.

for the study of interfaith dialogue. The movement of peoples brings about the movement of religions, whether it be Hindu Tamils brought in by the British to work in tea plantations in Ceylon (Sri Lanka), Chinese migrants seeking a better life in colonial Malaya, or Muslims fleeing turmoil in their homelands for a better life in the United States. As people move, whether voluntarily or involuntarily, they bring with them their cultures, religions, and ways of life. And alongside the context of migration, which can often result in a situation where the religious majority is constituted by the native population, for instance the majority German Christians with the minority immigrant Turkish Muslims in Germany, there are many instances where the majority/minority divide falls within the native population—such as Armenian Christians in Iran, Shia Muslims in Iraq, and so on. And it is not always the case that the majority group holds the power, as the situation of Syria has recently highlighted. Nevertheless, as people move from one place to another the challenges of migration—whether voluntary or involuntary—for interfaith relations between the majority community and the minority communities cannot be ignored. And as migration leads to increasing cultural diversity and religious pluralism across the world, some interesting observations can be made. The American sociologist Peggy Levitt, in noticing the close identification between faith, ethnicity, and culture in the identity constructions of Latino and Irish immigrants in the United States, shows how religion plays an important role for migrants. One could say that the overlap between faith, ethnicity, and culture among migrants is so deeply entrenched that they are often hard-pressed to distinguish what is 'national' or 'ethnic' about themselves and what is 'religious', and therefore, when they 'act out these identities, either privately and informally or collectively and institutionally, they express important parts of who they are and pass on these formulations to their children'.[48]

Further, interfaith dialogue engaging majority and minority groups is not restricted to religious matters, but is implicated in all areas of life. In the Asian context, for instance, this issues in a threefold dialogue with Asian cultures, religions, and the poor.[49] Further, all migration, whether voluntary or involuntary, is more than transnational or global population mobility *simpliciter*. It too often results in the commodification and exploitation, leading to the abuse and dehumanizing of the human person. It is often the case that migration 'reveals the vulnerability of people's lives, their insecurity, exploitation, joblessness, uprootedness, political uncertainty and humiliating treatment as outsiders or foreigners'.[50] The 'existential condition of a transnational immigrant and refugee' can include 'violent uprootedness, economic poverty, anxiety about the future, and the loss of national identity, political freedom, and personal dignity'.[51] And in many countries, religious minorities can face the added

---

[48] Peggy Levitt, 'Immigration', in Helen Rose Ebaugh (ed.), *Handbook of Religious and Social Institutions* (New York: Springer, 2005), 397.

[49] See Peter C. Phan, *In our own Tongues: Perspectives from Asia on Mission and Inculturation* (Maryknoll, NY: Orbis Books, 2003), 13–31.

[50] S. Arokiasamy, *Asia: The Struggle for Life in the Midst of Death and Destruction*, FABC Papers, 70 (Hong Kong: FABC, 1995), 9.

[51] Peter C. Phan, *Christianity with an Asian Face: Asian American Theology in the Making* (Maryknoll, NY: Orbis Books, 2003), 8.

pressure of proselytism. In such conditions interfaith dialogue is deeply affected; the pursuit of interreligious relations is an acute challenge.

The power relations that obtain between majority and minority groups is clearly also a hugely influential factor. At times, minority communities experience fear, insecurity, vulnerability, and backlash from the majority community just for being different. The situation of the Roma in Europe is a case in point. Minorities complain about the majority scapegoating them for social ills and pressurizing them to lose their distinctive racial-ethnic or religious features and become fully assimilated in the mainstream of society. It is also the case that, for a migrant population, religious differences and divisions already existing among them in the home country are almost always continued in the host country, and these vastly complicate the dialogue between the majority and minority religions. And in pluralist societies, religious leaders are often challenged to be the source of reconciliation, healing, and peace between their own communities and other communities within their societies; overcoming intolerance and extremism with acceptance and solidarity. However, interfaith dialogue is often carried out not at the official but at the grassroots level, through sharing of daily life, collaboration for the common good, intellectual exchange, and mutual participation in religious activities.

The World Council of Churches' 1979 *Guidelines on Dialogue* hit the mark when it stated that 'dialogue is most vital when its participants actually share their lives together', and went on to explain that where 'people of different faiths and ideologies share common activities, intellectual interests, and spiritual quest, dialogue can be related to the whole of life and can become a style of living-in-relationship' (part III, guideline 6). Authentic dialogue can only arise from genuine relations of mutuality and solidarity between majority and minority communities at the grassroots level. The common good is promoted at all levels when barriers are broken down, bridges are built between majority and minority communities, and goodwill is promoted at grassroots levels to foster reconciliation and harmony and to break the cycle of hate, fear, mistrust, and violence.

FURTHER READING

Tessa J. Bartholomeusz and Chandra Richard De Silva (eds), *Buddhist Fundamentalism and Minority Identities in Sri Lanka* (Albany, NY: SUNY, 1998).

Francesco Gioia (ed.), *Interreligious Dialogue: The Official Teaching of the Catholic Church from the Second Vatican Council to 2005* (Boston: Pauline Books and Media, 2006).

Paul Hedges, *Controversies in Interreligious Dialogue* (London: SCM Press, 2010).

Michael Mazur, *The Americanization of Religious Minorities: Confronting the Constitutional Order* (Baltimore, Md.: Johns Hopkins University Press, 2004).

Peter C. Phan, *Being Religious Interreligiously: Asian Perspectives on Interreligious Dialogue* (Maryknoll, NY: Orbis Books, 2004).

Douglas Pratt, *The Challenge of Islam: Encounters in Interfaith Dialogue* (Aldershot: Ashgate, 2005).

D. R. Senanayake, *Buddhism and the Legitimation of Power: Democracy, Public Religion and Minorities in Sri Lanka* (Singapore: National University of Singapore Institute of South Asian Studies, 2009).

Timothy D. Sisk (ed.), *Between Terror and Tolerance: Religious Leaders, Conflict, and Peacemaking* (Washington, DC: Georgetown University Press, 2011).

....

CHAPTER 11

Fundamentalism, Exclusivism, and Religious Extremism

DOUGLAS PRATT

In this chapter we address the phenomena and interconnectedness of religious fundamentalism, exclusivism, and extremism, for they impact both directly and indirectly upon interreligious engagement. If dialogue and the quest for social harmony and mutual respectful understanding are positive drivers of interreligious relations, then 'fundamentalism' may be identified as the spoilsport, with extremism and exclusivism conspiring against any form of religious détente by opposing, or at the very least undermining, the idea of and opportunities for interreligious engagement. We begin with a discussion of 'fundamentalism' which, despite problems of suitability and applicability, is a term generally used to name a broad religio-political perspective found in most, if not all, major religions. Although many scholars would prefer to excise the word from discourse on religion, and for good reason, it continues nevertheless to enjoy wide coinage. Like it or not, it is part of current vocabulary. So for our purposes we need to critically examine its meaning and gain a more nuanced appreciation for what the term properly refers to. Furthermore, the question can be rightly asked: how may the negative and deleterious dimension of fundamentalism be ameliorated? In order to respond to such a question, we need to begin with understanding. This means we need to identify where the term 'fundamentalism' comes from and what it means.

Following that, we will examine another phenomenon that is often, but not always, related to fundamentalism, namely exclusivism. Here we will both explore its problematic dimensions and pose a radical possibility of habilitating the term so that the root idea of something 'exclusive' can be seen to refer to something needful and positive for interreligious relations. Furthermore, fundamentalism not only connects with the phenomenon of exclusivism; at times it is clearly associated with variant forms of extremism and religiously motivated acts of violence, including terrorism.[1] So we need to discuss the vexed problem of religious

---

[1] See Gabriel A. Almond, R. Scott Appleby, and Emmanuel Sivan, *Strong Religion: The Rise of Fundamentalisms around the World* (Chicago and London: University of Chicago Press, 2003).

extremism and the phenomenon of religiously motivated terrorism. Engaging the question of fundamentalism and attempting a close analysis of it as an ideological trajectory will assist in understanding the link between religion and extremism. I will therefore outline a paradigm of 'fundamentalism' showing how it may be understood as naming an ideological development that begins with the relative harmlessness of an idiosyncratic and dogmatic belief system. It may, in some cases, effectively remain there; there is a sense in which everyone 'knows' what religious fundamentalism refers to. But a particular, generally conservative, narrow, and unyielding belief system, whilst forming the bedrock of what we mean by fundamentalism, is not necessarily all there is to it. For in other cases fundamentalism moves into, or manifests as, an exclusivist withdrawal and oppositional positioning; and in certain circumstances can even go beyond that to the harmful reality of religiously driven and fanatically followed pathways of extremism and allied terrorist activity.

Often, there is a temptation to view such extremism as really beyond religion, largely on account of other social, political, and economic factors, among others, that may have played a part in fomenting any given situation that gives rise to religious extremism. But are such contexts and allied actions so extreme that they are really removed from the religious orbit? Or are they to be understood, also and sometimes especially, from within the frame of religion? If so, might this allow for strategies for their amelioration to be devised by regarding the religious dimension as much a part of a potential solution as it is a part of the underlying problem? These are challenging issues and they raise difficult questions. But interreligious understanding needs to deal with the dark side of religion and so too the negative dimensions of interreligious engagement otherwise, as history has shown all too often, goodwill born of the desire for tolerant and peaceful coexistence can rather quickly evaporate in the heat of intense and combative socio-political changes.

RELIGIOUS FUNDAMENTALISM: ORIGIN AND PROVINCE

The history and meaning of religious fundamentalism is complex. In our day fundamentalism is associated with variant forms of religious extremism and thus religiously oriented terrorism often emanating from, or taking place dramatically within, the Muslim world. In this regard there have been many studies undertaken on so-called Islamic fundamentalism.[2] Rightly or wrongly, it is Islamic extremism and related terrorist activities which are often

---

[2] See Lawrence Davidson, *Islamic Fundamentalism: An Introduction* (Westport, Conn.: Greenwood Press, 2003); Johannes J. G. Jansen, *The Dual Nature of Islamic Fundamentalism* (London: Hurst & Co., 1997); Beverley Milton-Edwards, *Islamic Fundamentalism since 1945* (New York: Routledge, 2005); Bassam Tibi, *The Challenge of Fundamentalism: Political Islam and the New World Disorder* (Berkeley, Calif.: University of California Press, 2002); Peter Antes, 'New Approaches to the Study of the New Fundamentalisms', in Peter Antes, Armin W. Geertz, and Randi R. Warne (eds), *New Approaches to the Study of Religion*, i. *Regional, Critical and Historical Approaches* (Berlin and New York: Walter de Gruyter, 2004), 437–49.

linked to the very idea of fundamentalism.[3] Certainly, movements of a 'fundamentalist' or otherwise extremist type are evident in Islam, but they may be found also in Christianity, in Hinduism, in Judaism, and in other religious communities.[4] A widespread phenomenon and feature of religion *per se*, fundamentalism is not the sole province of any one religion. And the upsurge in the totalizing claims of fundamentalist ideologues, of whatever religion, together with the utilization of globalized communication, transportation, and related modern technologies, means that the issue of religious fundamentalism requires fresh and careful attention. Fundamentalism is much misunderstood; yet it is clear the term tends to evoke a negative reaction of some sort: we none of us regard it with indifference. But what are we to make of it?

The term 'fundamentalism' arose in a uniquely Christian context. For nearly a century it referred to a set of specific Christian beliefs and an allied ultra-conservative attitude. However, usage has since broadened and it has migrated into other, non-religious, arenas of discourse. But it arose, initially, from a series of booklets titled simply *The Fundamentals,* published in America early in the twentieth century and distributed worldwide in order to promote the view that there is a fundamental defining and non-negotiable set of traditional Christian doctrines.[5] These beliefs were promoted as the *sine qua non* for authentic Christianity. True Christianity rests solely on this set of exclusive fundamental doctrines and so, as a distinctive term, 'fundamentalism' arose to refer to this generic idea proposed by the booklets. In an age where theological liberalism had been in the ascendancy, 'fundamentalism' enabled a new countering viewpoint to be identified and promoted.[6] There was abroad the sense of needing to do battle royal for the integrity of the Christian faith, and in this context the badge of fundamentalism was proudly worn. However, subsequent and wider application of the term has not been without problems and difficulties. It does not transfer well into religious contexts other than Christianity, and it is imprecise enough even within the Christian camp. Nevertheless, it is widely used and has attracted considerable scholarly interest.[7]

In some respects fundamentalism may be understood in terms of whatever it is against; it has an oppositional element inherent. Thus the word is often used as 'a pejorative description for anyone who is regarded as having a closed mind with regard to a particular issue.'[8] Peter Lineham, for example, observes that fundamentalism, as a Christian phenomenon, is by no

---

[3] Cf. John L. Esposito, *Unholy War: Terror in the Name of Islam* (New York: Oxford University Press, 2002).

[4] See Mark Juergensmeyer, *Terror in the Mind of God: The Global Rise of Religious Violence* (Berkeley, Calif.: University of California Press, 2000).

[5] James Barr, *Fundamentalism* (London: SCM Press, 1977); George M. Marsden, *Understanding Fundamentalism and Evangelicalism* (Grand Rapids, Mich.: W. B. Eerdmans, 1991).

[6] Martin E. Marty, *Fundamentalisms Compared: The Charles Strong Memorial Lecture 1989* (Underdale, South Australia: Australian Association for the Study of Religions, 1989).

[7] Cf. Lionel Caplan, *Studies in Religious Fundamentalism* (Basingstoke: Macmillan, 1987); Santosh C. Saha (ed.), *Religious Fundamentalism in the Contemporary World: Critical Social and Political Issues* (Lanham, Md.: Lexington Books, 2004).

[8] Bryan Gilling, *'Be Ye Separate': Fundamentalism and the New Zealand Experience* (Red Beach: Colcom Press, 1992), p. xi.

means a simple matter. The root appeal of fundamentalism is often correlated with a sense of moral panic: 'issues which stimulate political action involve a crisis mood that Christian civilisation is at risk. Fundamentalism is after all a popular movement which flourishes by interpreting current issues in simplified and distorted ways.'[9] Much the same sort of reaction, and so association, can be discerned across the Islamic world, as well as elsewhere in the twenty-first century. Given its widening province, fundamentalism has been the focus of a series of notable studies which include both religious and political variants.

One very significant exercise in this regard was the five-year 'Fundamentalism Project' which led to the publication of several substantial volumes.[10] These showed that religious fundamentalism can imply a narrow, strict, and limited metaphysics and set of doctrines, which to a greater or lesser degree hardly impinge on the wider life of a society; or it can mean a worldview perspective that engenders, if not demands, the advocacy of a socio-political ordering and action to achieve an intended outcome. Indeed, 'fundamentalisms look backward and set out to "freeze" some moment, some event, some text or texts from the past as the perfect place in time or space from which to measure' life in the present.[11] An imagined golden age, believed to have pertained at the religion's foundation, is held up as the model and reference point for contemporary reality. In response to the critique that religion—and in particular fundamentalist religion—is but an epiphenomenon riding on what are really political ideas and actions, or that fundamentalism is just a passing fad, such studies have only served to highlight what subsequent history and recent events underscore: religious fundamentalism is a deeply rooted phenomenon that can, and does, give rise to political acts. And a key difference between religiously driven political actions today, in contrast with any previous point in history, is the pervasive context of globalization. Instead of localized, even regional, levels of action, the technology and mentality of a globalized world now allow for a degree of internationalization of the ideologies and activities of so-called fundamentalist movements as never before. If recent events tell us anything, it is that religion, especially in its fundamentalist forms, must not be taken lightly or dismissively ignored.

RELIGIOUS EXCLUSIVISM: REJECTING PLURALITY VS AFFIRMING IDENTITY

Fundamentalism does not exist in a vacuum; it marks out a distinctive response and position, as we shall see more clearly below. As a phenomenon it is often associated with an exclusivist

---

[9]   Peter Lineham, 'The Fundamentalist Agenda and its Chances', *Stimulus*, 14/3 (2006), 8.

[10]   Martin E. Marty and R. Scott Appleby (eds), *The Fundamentalism Project* (1991); *Fundamentalisms Observed* (1991); *Fundamentalisms and the State: Remaking Politics, Economies, and Militance* (1993); *Accounting for Fundamentalisms: The Dynamic Character of Movements* (1994); *Fundamentalisms Comprehended* (1995). All published by the University of Chicago Press, Chicago.

[11]   Marty, *Fundamentalisms Compared*, 1.

stance that reflects a negative response to religious diversity or plurality. Plurality names much of the context of contemporary life; it denotes the present situation of religion in society. Religious plurality is a fact of our time in a way that, arguably, is qualitatively different to almost anything hitherto. Indeed, an affirmation of plurality is a hallmark of so-called postmodernity. As the Australian sociologist Gary Bouma remarks, 'Being consciously multifaith is part of being a postmodern society'.[12] Individual freedoms today juxtapose with accommodating the presence of otherness: that which was formerly 'other' in the sense of being not-present, of being 'over-there', is now on our doorstep and down our street. Today, in just about all quarters of the globe, the religious dimension of any given community is pluriform. And this raises many issues, not the least of which is the manner of relating across religious identities. People of different religious allegiances are neighbours who talk with each other, live together in our various communities, and together address concerns held in common. And such plurality is not only *between* religions; it is also something found *within* religions.

Interreligious engagement and dialogue occur in a context of religious plurality. In a mono-religious context, interreligious relations and engagement is not an issue. Matters of interreligious understanding do not arise. It is the fact of religious diversity, the plurality of religions rubbing shoulders and seeking a mode of peaceful coexistence, which sets the scene. This is what provides the context for interfaith relations and interreligious understanding. And, most importantly, how this diversity is itself perceived, understood, and so responded to, is critical for the nature, style, and eventual success—or otherwise—of interreligious engagement. Thus paradigms of perspective and interpretation in respect to religious diversity govern the nature and extent of this engagement as a lived reality. Broadly speaking, these are the paradigms of exclusivism, inclusivism, and pluralism. They may be regarded as providing options for contending with religious plurality, so setting the scene for interfaith relations and allied dialogical engagements.[13] They denote various means of responding, both cognitively and behaviourally, to religious diversity.

In the context of discourse on interreligious dialogue, exclusivism has been posited as the position inimical to dialogue and against which, through the application of either inclusivism or pluralism, positions of openness to dialogical engagement have been contrasted and advocated.[14] A close analysis shows, however, that exclusivism, inclusivism, and pluralism do not denote three discrete paradigms but that each refers to a range of sub-paradigms that may be better thought of as expressing relative positions upon a continuum.[15] Furthermore, it can be argued that, in the end, the pluralist must necessarily be an exclusivist of some sort such that the paradigm of inclusivism, when pressed, also tends to collapse into some form of

---

[12] Gary D. Bouma, *Australian Soul: Religion and Spirituality in the Twenty-First Century* (Melbourne: Cambridge University Press, 2006), 5.

[13] Cf. Douglas Pratt, 'Contextual Paradigms for Interfaith Relations', *Current Dialogue*, 42 (2003), 3–9.

[14] See e.g. Alan Race, *Christians and Religious Pluralism*, 2nd edn (London: SCM Press, 1993).

[15] Douglas Pratt, 'Religious Plurality, Referential Realism and Paradigms of Pluralism', in Avery Plaw (ed.), *Frontiers of Diversity: Explorations in Contemporary Pluralism* (Amsterdam and New York: Rodopi, 2005), 191–209.

exclusivism.[16] Nevertheless, the critical issue is not so much the oft-criticized paradigm of pluralism, nor even problems raised by inclusivism, but questions posed by the persistence—even growth—of religious exclusivism.

The paradigm of religious exclusivism may be formally defined as *the material identity of particular and universal*. That is to say, religious exclusivism involves the assertion of a particular religion (or form of that religion) as being, in fact, the essence and substance of true universal religion as such, *thereby excluding* all other possibilities. From this viewpoint the exclusivist's religion is the 'Only One Right One' because there can be only one that is right or true. Given the assertion that, from a religious viewpoint, truth and salvation, for example, are universal values, the exclusivist position holds that this universality is materially identified with but one religion, namely that of the exclusivist. Mutually tolerant coexistence of religions is simply not possible. Religions may be spoken of in terms of providing a 'way of life' and a 'path of salvation' in respect of which the position of Christian exclusivism regards all but its own way and path as invalid or void. From the Catholic dogma of *extra ecclesiam nulla salus*, to various conservative Protestant declarations of condemnation of any but their own viewpoint, the 'controlling assumption is that outside the church, or outside Christianity, there is no salvation.'[17] Exclusivism remains a problematic impinging on practical and pastoral dimensions of interreligious relations. Arguably, however, the paradigm of exclusivism comes in at least three variants: open, closed, and extreme/rejectionist. By its very nature exclusivism *per se* is normally hostile to interreligious dialogue or rapport. It impinges on interfaith engagement, most often contributing to outright resistance, or at least the undermining of efforts to engage in it, albeit varyingly so. And this is where nuanced variations of the exclusivist paradigm may be more clearly identified.

An *open exclusivism*, while maintaining cognitive and salvific superiority, for instance, may at least be amenably disposed towards a religious 'other', if only to allow for—even encourage—the capitulation (by way of conversion, for example) of the other. One early twentieth-century 'open' exclusivist, a Christian ecumenical leader who nevertheless affirmed the value of cultural plurality, argued against what he viewed as 'incipient pluralism', namely where syncretism and the notion of a single world-faith are viewed as inexorable outcomes of taking a non-exclusivist line.[18] Similarly, another who for many years was a Christian missionary in Indonesia, popularized and promoted the view that, at the level of human institution, Christianity was no different to other religions in being yet another religion.[19] On this view, Christianity is essentially *other-than* the religions. 'Religion' names the process of human seeking for the divine; Christianity, by contrast, is the sole authentic arena of the divine

---

[16] See e.g. the work of Gavin D'Costa, esp. 'The Impossibility of a Pluralist View of Religions', *Religious Studies*, 32 (1996), 223–32.

[17] John Hick, *God and the Universe of Faiths* (London: Collins, 1977), 121.

[18] W. A. Visser t'Hooft, *No Other Name: The Choice between Syncretism and Christian Universalism* (London: SCM Press, 1963), 88.

[19] See H. Kraemer, *The Christian Message in a Non-Christian World* (London: Edinburgh House Press, 1938).

encountering the human. Christianity stands apart, holding a position of exclusive privilege: 'Christianity understands itself not as one of several religions, but as the adequate and defini-tive revelation of God in history'.[20] Whilst upholding the validity of cultural plurality, the open exclusivism espoused by such ecumenical Christian leaders of the twentieth century at the same time asserted a triumphant Christocentric salvific proclamation and an essentialist, even quasi-fundamentalist, Christian identity. Similarly, other religions may also be regarded by their adherents as the 'natural' religion of human being against which any other may be regarded as deviant or a lesser form. This attitude occurs with some Muslims, for example, on the basis that other forms of religion, such as Judaism and Christianity, had been corrupted over time. Only Islam remains the true faith. Open exclusivism implies openness to some form of relationship with another without expectation of, or openness to, consequential or reciprocal change of self-identity with respect to that relationship. The 'other' is acknowl-edged, but only as an 'antithetical' other whose presence calls forth either or both of patron-izing and polemical engagement.

In contrast to open exclusivism, *closed exclusivism* simply dismisses the 'other' out of hand. Relationship to the 'other', especially the religious other, is effectively ruled out. The 'other' may be acknowledged as having a rightful place, but that place is inherently inferior to that of the closed exclusivist who, *inter alia*, prefers to remain wholly apart from the other. On the one hand, an 'open' exclusivism may yet entertain a 'dialogue' of sorts—perhaps a conversa-tional interaction—if only with a view to understanding the perspective of the other in order, then, better to refute it, or convert its adherents. On the other hand, a 'closed' exclusivism will spurn interaction with another religious viewpoint altogether: imperialist assertion is the only mode of communication admissible.

The third variant is that of *extreme* or *rejectionist exclusivism* which marks a shift from the closed form as such which can be understood simply as the exercise of a right to withdraw into itself. For this third form gives expression to hard-line rejectionist exclusion: the view-point that asserts an exclusive identity to the extent that the fact and presence of an 'other' is actively resisted—even to the point of taking steps to eliminate the other. Examples of such extreme forms of exclusivism can be adduced from within the history of Christianity, as indeed from most religions. Today the more obvious examples are to be found with respect to Islam. Here we see various expressions of Islam claiming to be the only true form of this religion and, in consequence, rejecting—excluding—all other Muslim persua-sions. At the extreme end of this phenomenon the exclusivity entails elimination, as the seemingly never-ending trajectory of mosque bombings and assassinations in some parts of the Muslim world actively testify.[21] The key distinguishing feature denoting extreme/rejectionist exclusivism is the negative valorizing of the 'other'—howsoever defined—with concomitant harsh sanctions and limitations imposed. It is this level of exclusive religion

---

[20] Kraemer, *Christian Message*, 95.
[21] See Mona Siddiqui (ed.), *The Routledge Reader in Christian–Muslim Relations* (Abingdon: Routledge, 2013).

which, in its hostility to variety or 'otherness' (alterity), however that may be identified, inherently invalidates alterity *per se*. It is this level of religious exclusivism which lies at the heart of so much religious strife, not to mention terrorism and insurgency, and thus poses an acute challenge to those who would advocate religious freedoms, toleration, and peaceful coexistence. It is this exclusivism that inheres in the extreme expressions of religious fundamentalism.

A rather sharp question can now be posed. Is there a proper way of speaking of exclusive religion, or of religion in terms of exclusive identity, without necessarily falling into the pit of exclusivist extremism? For it seems that, especially in the context of interreligious engagement and dialogue, if religious identity is not to succumb to syncretistic blurring or relativist reduction, then some measure of exclusivity must necessarily apply. Religious identity, in being discrete, must—as with any discrete identity—incorporate a measure of the 'exclusive' if only as a marker of, or a synonym for, being 'unique'. Uniqueness is a necessary element of identity *per se*. In which case the paradigm of exclusivism, for some time now automatically eschewed by all except, supposedly, fundamentalists, needs to be reconsidered. It needs to be given more nuanced attention so as to allow for a distinction between the stance of exclusion (as in excluding or exclusionary attitudes behaviours) and holding an exclusive identity (as in manifesting distinctiveness and uniqueness). What is of particular interest is the fact that, on the one hand, a measure of exclusivity is logically required for clarity of identity, and that clarity of identity is a necessary prerequisite for dialogical and other engagement; yet, on the other, when taken to an extreme, exclusivity of identity militates against any sort of dialogical rapport by becoming exclusionary; that is, by denying and excluding 'otherness'—and this is a hallmark of extreme religious fundamentalism.

The critical contrast is that, on the one hand, exclusive—or *exclusivity of*—religion is a matter of identity articulation while, on the other, religious *exclusivism* as such is a governing ideological motif. Exclusivity of identity is a requirement for interreligious relational engagement: interlocutors need to know who they are and that their respective identities are mutually exclusive, otherwise dialogue would effectively collapse. Exclusive religion is not a cipher for religious exclusivism. One implicitly validates the variety of religious otherness by way of mutual recognition of and respect for unique religious identity. The other is intent on invalidating such otherness and plurality. Religious exclusivism plays into the hand of ideological extremism; exclusive religious identity allows for the integrity of difference and otherness and thereby the possibility of interfaith relations. The affirmation of a particular, unique, and so exclusive religious identity does not necessarily entail, nor require, a rejection of any 'otherness' or diversity. Religious exclusivity is not the same as religious exclusivism: the one refers to identity uniqueness; the other to an excluding attitude and ideology. The former can be positively, or at least neutrally, disposed towards the fact of religious diversity and plurality, and indeed to engagement with the 'other'; the latter quite clearly is not and instead leans towards extremism.

RELIGIOUS EXTREMISM: RELIGION AND TERRORISM

The ordinarily religious person does not engage in violence as a matter of course. Religions typically espouse values of peace and harmony, even in contexts of challenge and contestation. So the first step in considering religious extremism is to ask an obvious question: what is the meaning of 'extremism'? Mindful of the specific problem of exclusivism, we turn our attention now to an examination of religious extremism as a distinct phenomenon, beginning with a review of the relation of religion and terrorism. Terrorism has many root causes as well as differing frameworks of self-understanding.[22] Religion and terrorism can constitute a powerful mix. Whenever 'religion empowers political terrorism then the terrorism apparently has no limits and acknowledges no boundaries.'[23] Religion is increasingly in the frame as a critical component of contemporary terrorism and political violence.[24] Terrorism expert Alex Schmid has helpfully explored the definition and context of terrorism in terms of 'five conceptual lenses' that provide a multi-perspectival framework comprising crime, politics, warfare, communication, and religious fundamentalism.[25] Terrorism is a multifaceted phenomenon and for Schmid religion provides only a partial perspective on the nature of terrorism. Nevertheless, religion is not to be discounted and may even emerge as the lead factor—especially where there are obvious links between the terrorism and a religion.[26] However, it is not religion *per se* that is the issue to be addressed, rather it is the phenomenon of religious extremism. So what is this extremism?

The term itself evokes a sense of being at the margins, of existing on the boundaries or of functioning at the edges; in other words, extremism suggests—naturally enough—'extremities'. Any organization or group that is in this sense extreme will tend to manifest a tenuous link to whatever is the appropriate 'centre', or else give evidence of a loose connection to the relevant normative tradition. Here, extremism expresses heterodoxy against orthodoxy. But extremism can refer to something else altogether; even, indeed, the opposite of being 'at the margins', and that is: being at—or claiming to be—the centre. In this case the term connotes degrees of intensity or sharpness of focus: extremism suggests fanaticism. In other words, an extremist ideology or group will claim the relevant central position exclusively and, in so doing, will proclaim its normative tradition intensely. Extremism here takes its own wider group identity—its religion or specific religious tradition—to an extreme; not

---

[22] Cf. Walter Reich (ed.), *Origins of Terrorism: Psychologies, Ideologies, Theologies, States of Mind* (Washington, DC: Woodrow Wilson Centre Press 1998).

[23] James Veitch, 'Terrorism and Religion', *Stimulus*, 10/1 (2002), 30.

[24] Cf. Tanja Ellingsen, 'Toward a Revival of Religion and Religious Clashes?', *Terrorism and Political Violence*, 14/37 (2005), 305–32; Susanna Pearce, 'Religious Rage: A Quantitative Analysis of the Intensity of Religious Conflicts', *Terrorism and Political Violence*, 14/37 (2005), 333–52.

[25] Alex Schmid, 'Frameworks for Conceptualizing Terrorism', *Terrorism and Political Violence*, 16/2 (2004), 197–221.

[26] Cf. Juergensmeyer, *Terror in the Mind of God*.

by a move away from the centre, but rather by intensifying its self-understanding and self-proclamation as representing, or being, the centre. Thus, in this mode, extremism expresses an ultra-orthodox outlook in contrast to the relevant orthodoxy. It is important to note, I suggest, that either way religious extremism belongs to a 'tradition'. Such extremism, by definition, has to do with either the extremity or the centring of an existing tradition or religion with which the extremist is concerned: the religious extremist thus requires specific religious identity as the primary reference for self-legitimization.

By contrast, religious cults and other radical alternatives do not belong to a tradition—rather, by definition, they are 'other-than' any normative tradition or religion.[27] That is to say, cults and most other new religious movements (NRMs) are to be distinguished from the religious extremism which I am here addressing. Cult extremists are not to be equated with religious extremists in the strict sense in which I wish to use the term. For *religious* extremists are the extremists *of a religion*; they ought not to be construed as representing a cult, sect, or other form of NRM with the effect, thereby, of being regarded as 'not belonging', and so no longer the putative responsibility (whether in terms of formation or countering) of the religious community whom they claim to represent or with which they are allied. This has been a particular problem in regard to a widespread disavowal from within some Muslim communities that 'Islamic terrorists' are not genuinely Muslim; therefore their espoused Islamism is not to be addressed as it lies outside the purview of the normative tradition. It represents something that is quite beyond the pale so far as the wider community is concerned. This is a position of naïve rejection that construes the extremist as not part of the tradition, and so not representing it. A similar issue has arisen with respect to the Norwegian extremist, Anders Breivik, who clearly manifests some aspects of Christian extremism and sees himself as representing that religion, or at least representing Western European Christian culture, *vis-à-vis* its supposed antipathy to Islam. But it is not easy for a secularized Western Christian culture to recognize him as, indeed, a Christian religious extremist, even when bearing in mind Schmid's caution that terrorism *per se* has no single or simple cause, but with religion being one genuine element nonetheless. So religion cannot be factored out; it clearly played a part in Breivik's extreme ideology that in turn led to his terrorist actions.

As noted, terrorism, as a descriptor for extreme and violent behaviours, is not solely the province of religious fundamentalism. But it can be—and sometimes is—the end-result of a fundamentalist ideological trajectory. This is the issue that faces us today, in both localized and globalized manifestations. It militates against interreligious and inter-communal relations; neighbours who previously coexisted in relative harmony and mutual recognition become implacable foes. Communal relativities give way to absolute hostilities. But an absolutist perspective—arguably at the base of every religion, and certainly the heart of any fundamentalist expression of religion—does not necessarily result in terrorist behaviour. Not all

---

[27] See David Bromley and J. Gordon Melton (eds), *Cults, Religion and Violence* (Cambridge: Cambridge University Press, 2002).

fundamentalists are terrorists. There are many religious fundamentalists who are pacifist in outlook and demeanour. Nevertheless, fundamentalism may lead to terrorism, and in some cases it does. Writing from within an American context, Eugene Gallagher is clear that religious sensibilities lie at the core of many radical right-wing ideologies; in effect, they represent forms of religious—including Christian—extremism. He has noted that any extremist group which 'defines its mission as "religious" is claiming a very powerful form of legitimacy', and its behavioural outworking 'can become particularly problematic and threatening to the social order when a group also espouses a strongly anti-government ideology', for example.[28] Thus, if 'such a group acts or threatens to act on its principles, the need to evaluate its claims to religious legitimacy becomes urgent'.[29] The religious dimension can ill afford to be ignored. Our concern is with religion when it provides primary sanction for an extreme, even violent, line of action. Religious fundamentalism can issue in multifarious forms of extremism.[30] Islamic extremists may have caught attention and headlines; extremism within or arising from other religions, including Christianity, has somewhat less so. But extremism, as with fundamentalism, can be found within the context of virtually all religions, including even Buddhism which is often touted as the exemplar, *par excellence*, of pacifist religion.[31]

A FUNDAMENTALIST PARADIGM: FROM RELIGION TO EXTREMISM

It was in 2005, following the London bombings, that a report of the Home Office of the British government suggested a link between religious fundamentalism and terrorism. This suggestion intrigued me as it was crude and false in leading to the notion, sadly embraced by many, that simply identified religious fundamentalism *per se* with extremism and terrorism. Not all religious fundamentalists are extremists, or at least not in the sense of being violent terrorists. Yet there seems to be a link; but what is it, exactly, and how might it be described and understood? This led me into research that resulted in a concept of fundamentalism as an ideological development that begins with the relative harmlessness of an idiosyncratic and dogmatic belief system; that may move through exclusivist withdrawal and oppositional positioning; and that *sometimes* arrives at the harmful reality of extremism and allied terrorist activity—that is, religiously driven, fanatically followed, pathways of violence.[32]

---

[28] Eugene Gallagher, 'God and Country: Revolution as a Religious Imperative on the Radical Right', *Terrorism and Political Violence*, 9/3 (1997), 63.

[29] Gallagher, 'God and Country', 63.

[30] Cf. Leonard Weinberg and Ami Pedahzur (eds), *Religious Fundamentalism and Political Extremism* (Portland, Or.: Frank Cass, 2004).

[31] Cf. Brian Victoria, *Zen at War*, 2nd edn (Lanham, Md.: Rowman & Littlefield, 2006); Michael K. Jerryson, *Buddhist Fury: Religion and Violence in Southern Thailand* (New York: Oxford University Press, 2011).

[32] See Douglas Pratt, 'Religion and Terrorism: Christian Fundamentalism and Extremism', *Terrorism and Political Violence*, 22/3 (June 2010), 438–56.

As itself a complex phenomenon, religious fundamentalism, I suggest, comprises an inter-connected sequence of factors which collectively and cumulatively describe the development of an ideology and its accompanying mind-set that can lead to certain negative behaviours. I have analysed some twenty factors into a progression of ten sets—or 'features'—of linked pairings of these factors. These are further sub-grouped into three 'phases' so as to yield a paradigm typology involving a sequence of Passive (or 'normative'), Assertive (or 'hard-line), and then Impositional (or 'extremist') forms of fundamentalism.[33] In particular, it is the sequential combination of these features and factors which is important, for it is this inter-connectivity which makes of a typological description a putative paradigm. There are other scholars who have likewise attempted a deeper understanding of fundamentalism by endeav-ouring to identify distinguishing defining features.[34] By contrast, I suggest a more nuanced understanding by way of exploring the dynamics of the sequential development that is argu-ably inherent to the phenomenon and thus exposes the ideological structure of fundamental-ism more precisely.

Passive Fundamentalism

Passive, or normative, fundamentalism comprises six basic defining factors grouped in paired sets in respect to three features—*principal presuppositions, authority derivation,* and *implicit verification.* These describe the heart of religious fundamentalism *per se.* Hence they describe fundamentalism in its 'normative' or 'passive' modality—what, in other words, fundamental-ism is most normally thought to be. It is from this starting point that the ideology of funda-mentalism can be seen to evolve through a hard-line assertive modality and into an impositional extremist modality—thus setting the scene for the execution of violent or ter-rorist acts.

Principal presuppositions

This first feature includes two factors, *perspectival absolutism* and *immediate inerrancy,* which simply note the absoluteness of fundamentalism that rules out the possibility of admitting other perspectives or ideas as to the truth of the matter, and further that the applicable authoritative text or scripture can be read as providing immediate and inerrant knowledge. Fundamentalism, as a mind-set, expresses the modernist project writ large: only one truth, one authority, one authentic narrative that accounts for all, one right way to be. And, of course, declares the fundamentalist, that way is my way.

Further, fundamentalism deems itself privileged in respect to its absolutism, for it implies superiority of knowledge and truth. There is no intermediary or mediating lens through

---

[33] Cf. Douglas Pratt, 'Religious Fundamentalism: A Paradigm for Terrorism?', *Australian Religion Studies Review,* 20/2 (2007), 195–215.

[34] e.g. works cited above by Marsden, Barr, Caplan, and Saha; see also Malise Ruthven, *Fundamentalism: The Search for Meaning* (Oxford: Oxford University Press, 2004).

which variant interpretations may result; what is presented in terms of the absolute text is without error. Knowledge based thereon is sure. However, the assertion of the immediate inerrancy of the text—that is, reading the text as being immediately applicable and providing a non-mediated access to ultimate or divine truth—in fact involves an implicit assertion that there is only one normative interpretive reading allowable, namely that which is undertaken through the fundamentalist's lens. A fundamentalist's presumption of textual immediacy and inerrancy is, of course, but one interpretive option. Nevertheless, from the fundamentalist perspective, alternative and variant interpretations are deemed inherently false or heretical, and so are rejected.

Authority derivation

The second feature extends the presuppositions by way of an *assumption of apodicity* (clarity, non-ambiguity) together with what I call *narrow narrative indwelling*. The former simply holds the authoritative text is unambiguous with respect to meaning. Such texts are not necessarily, or only, scriptural: there are many other possibilities of textual sources upon which a fundamentalist might rely, sometimes even a sense of a secondary scripture that sits alongside the primary scripture. For example it is not only the Qur'an that provides warrant for Islamic extremism but also selected references from texts of *Hadith*, which are often ranked as scriptural, albeit not quite at the same level as the Qur'an. Likewise there are extra-canonical sources, such as creeds and other confessional statements, which can take this role for Christianity. This textual focus is sometimes understood in terms of 'literalism'. But for a fundamentalist the key issue is that the textual authority is such that the text itself provides pellucid expression of truth, whether in terms of an abstract universal, or in respect to a pragmatic or programmatic articulation of the values and views espoused by the fundamentalist *as* the truth. Paradoxically, of course, any so-called 'literalist' reading is itself an act of interpretation.

It is often assumed, falsely, from a fundamentalist perspective that a 'direct' reading of the text can be made so as to avoid the murky waters of interpretation; that is, there is no need to apply any sort of intellectual critique or scrutiny of the text: meaning can be immediately understood; the text at hand is clear in its composition. More particularly, the modern fundamentalist approach most often takes an approach of factual correspondence: that which is true is a statement of fact—the truth of any matter is in the correspondence between claim and fact. Hence the message conveyed by the text is regarded as apodictic; for the religious fundamentalist the scripture is read as a compendium of more or less clear fact.

Allied to the assumption of apodicity is the factor of narrow narrative indwelling. Arguably, all religious people 'indwell', to a greater or lesser degree, their respective religious narrative. That is to say, the paradigms, models, values, and so on which are given within the religious narrative—the scriptural record as well as ancillary histories/stories and so forth—provide the life references, points of meaning, and frameworks of understanding that inform a religious individual's existence and identity. Where the narrative base is broad, the religious life that indwells therein likewise reflects breadth. But where the base is narrow, the resultant religious life is correspondingly confined. It is a mark of the indwelling of a fundamentalist that the narrative base is distinctly narrow; indeed, this very narrowness often marks a fundamentalist out from the wider religious tradition and community which, by contrast, will have a tendency to admit a wider reading of its narrative and so a capacity to indwell it with a greater measure of interpretive flexibility.

Implicit verification

The third feature of passive fundamentalism combines the factors of *narrative correlation* and *rhetorical corroboration*. Principal presuppositions granted, and the derivation of authority established, the evolving fundamentalist perspective begins now to move from a variant conservative expression of a religious worldview to a more intentional advocacy of religious viewpoint as being, *par excellence*, the expression of authenticity and truth applicable for, or to, all. The fundamentalist's verification of their position marks the closure of the passive phase. A deepening of the correlation between the religious narrative espoused, and the reality, or *Sitz-im-Leben*, of the religious community concerned, is the first of the pair of factors involved. Of course, some such measure of narrative correlation is a quite normal feature of religion. Any religion will normally proffer some degree of correlation between its narrative and the 'real world' in which the followers of the religion live—otherwise religion would reduce to a simple and obvious fairy-tale. However, a distinction can be made between the broader traditions of a religion whose narrative correlation will be relatively loose, flexible, or at least provisional, and the fundamentalist whose degree of correlation will be that much tighter, intense, and so inflexible. For a fundamentalist the correlation will be such as to yield an unambiguous outcome.

Allied to narrative correlation is the factor of rhetorical corroboration. Here the discourse of fundamentalism can be more readily tested, perhaps. For in the articulation of narrative correlation there is likely to be found a corresponding intensification of a corroborating rhetoric that situates, endorses, and justifies the fundamentalist perspective *vis-à-vis* the judgements and assessments made about the external world in terms of narrative correlation. Rhetoric will be sharp and self-affirming; judgements will be clear and reflective of both the correlation factor and also as the corroboration factor. Thus the perspective of the fundamentalist derives implicit verification and the scene is set for the next phase.

Assertive Fundamentalism

The second phase reveals a deepening and strengthening of the ideology of fundamentalism, and its application both real (in terms of fundamentalist groups) and potential (in respect to the wider society in which the fundamentalism concerned is situated). It involves four features, each again comprising a pair of linked factors, namely *epistemological construction, identity structure, contextual scope,* and *condemnatory stance*. Together these reveal how, as an ideological trajectory, what we refer to as 'fundamentalism' is in reality a complex phenomenon and cannot be regarded as applying uniformly in all cases. This very complexity highlights the need for both nuanced understanding and cautiously critical appreciation, especially given that where interreligious relations and understanding may be said to be desperately needed it is often in contexts where religious sensibilities and identities are deeply held and valued to the point of being superficially identified as representing a 'one-size-fits-all' fundamentalism.

Epistemological construction

This first feature of an assertive fundamentalism involves the interplay of *hard factualism* and *applied necessity*. That is to say, fundamentalism hardens, and becomes more self-assertive, as it tightens its grip on what is understood to be knowable, and how what is knowable is known. The range of what is admitted as genuine knowledge is truncated: 'real' knowledge is reduced to facts that are held to be true—all else belongs to the realm of falsehood. Some hard-line fundamentalists reject scientific hypotheses and theories which, in their view, challenge or deny the 'facts' as they believe them to be. This focus on facts—and so the reading of scripture as a compendium of God-given 'facts' to be relied upon implicitly—brings with it a dimension of necessariness to the fundamentalist's construction of knowledge. In effect, the fundamentalist's scripture is regarded as 'The Book of Facts'. Thus the fundamentalist perspective on knowledge is regarded, by the fundamentalist, as necessarily true. Alternative approaches to knowledge, to ascertaining truth and falsity, as well as meaning and value, are necessarily ruled out. Hence an applied necessity of perspective obtains in respect to the focus on God-given 'facts' as the essential content of knowledge.

Identity structure

The emergence of a distinct structure of identity is the second feature of the assertive phase of fundamentalism. It involves the juxtaposition of what might be called *communitarian intent* with *individual constraint*. Individual fundamentalist identity necessarily reflects the identity of the fundamentalist community: the stronger, more hard-line or assertive the fundamentalism, the tighter this relation. Communitarian intent denotes the way in which a fundamentalist group places value, to a greater or lesser degree, upon membership of the specific fundamentalist community, and upholding its values and norms as essential such that the identity of individuals within the community is proscribed. Thus the factor of individual constraint is the necessary corollary, and the two factors go together to form the structure of fundamentalist identity. These factors apply very obviously to sectarian groups of one sort or another, but they can also apply more widely within a religion, thus giving the appearance of the religion *per se* as inherently 'fundamentalist'. In the case of Islam, for example, the communitarian ideal of the *Umma* can mean that withdrawal from the community on account of a change in individual religious identity is viewed as apostasy: effectively a treasonable offence attracting severe sanction in some quarters. Thus Islam can present as a fundamentalist religion *per se*—at least in terms of the passive category; and seemingly often with a hard-line edge. But that does not mean Islam, as a religion, is *necessarily* inherently violent. Nevertheless, this fourth set of factors contributes to a predisposition and justification of violent behaviour. Evidence for this can be adduced from within the history of Christianity, for instance. And today there are Christian churches, denominations, and sects for whom the essential dynamic of a fundamentalist identity structure would certainly apply.

Contextual scope

The next feature has to do with an ideological hardening by way of holding together an *ideological exclusivism* with an *inclusivist polity*, thus forming the contextual scope of fundamentalism. On the one hand, religious fundamentalism excludes, virtually automatically, anything that relative to it appears 'liberal'; that admits of, for example, any limitation, provisionality, otherness, openness, or change. It excludes religious liberalism of any ilk. Similarly, variant secular fundamentalisms often attempt to exclude religion *per se*, on much the same sorts of grounds. Ideological exclusivism works in multiple directions. On the other hand, religious fundamentalism displays a propensity to include, in respect to considerations of the policies and praxis of social organization, all others that fall within its frame of reference or worldview understanding. Thus, paradoxically, the excluding of all other ideological variants and perspectives necessarily implies the wholesale inclusion of a society in terms of the outworking of polity considerations.

Here, fundamentalist ideology does not see itself as one among many, or even a dominant-yet-still-one among many. Rather it sees itself as the one to which the many are subsumed and so gathered into the fold, as it were, such that there is no room for alterity of any sort. This may still appear innocuous, especially if the fundamentalists concerned are a minor or marginalised group in terms of the wider society in which they exist, or where such an inclusivist stance finds a more benign setting within a normative or orthodox religious tradition. Nevertheless, at this juncture the fundamentalist, for whom polity inclusiveness is a primary element, is now poised to become impositional—to act on this inclusivism in terms of an explicit polity, whether covertly (as in the religion known as the Church of Jesus Christ of Latter Day Saints vicariously baptizing the dead) or overtly (as in the Taliban's insistence that everyone in Afghanistan live according to their application of Islam). The apparent paradox of fundamentalism evincing both exclusivism and inclusivism as two of its core features is resolved. And so, for example, the fundamentalism of a resurgent Islamist perspective naturally insists not just that all Muslims should live according to Islamic law, but that all members of the society in question, irrespective of religion, should likewise submit to this law code—understood, of course, to transcend human values and codes by virtue of being 'God's law'—or be made so to do.

Condemnatory stance

The fourth feature of assertive hard-line fundamentalism denotes a move into negative values. The motif of condemnation is manifest in the holding and articulating of *negative judgemental values* and the exercise of what may be called a *pietistic tyranny*. Assertive fundamentalism is distinguished by strident assertions of a condemnatory or judgemental sort; it is in the expression of judgemental values that such hard-line fundamentalism displays its real stance towards any who would dissent from within, or oppose from without. Inherent in this is often a deprecating attitude towards others, whether in regard to virtually any other (the world at large), or focused on specific others (particular groups of categories of people such as Jews, Blacks, or gays). Such judgementalism can be found, for example, in the generalized sense of dismissal of all outside the fundamentalist fold, or as in the sweeping condemnation of (Western) society found within some expressions of contemporary Islamic rhetoric. It can also be found in a more targeted sense, as in variant forms of both political and religious fundamentalism that dehumanize opponents, or as in contemporary instances of Islamic anti-Semitic rhetoric and the decrying of Israel.

More particularly, it is in the inward application of judgemental values—that is, applying such values for the purpose of control and censure within the fundamentalist's own community—that the factor of pietistic tyranny may be discerned. This is where assertive fundamentalism shows itself to be truly hard-line. The faith values it espouses—its 'piety'—becomes, in effect, a tool of tyranny: newlywon converts must cut themselves off from their family of origin (as with the Moonies, for example); or members of the community must have no social intercourse with anyone who is not in fellowship with them (as with the Exclusive Brethren, for instance). The advocacy by one religious community that its members should have no truck with those of any other, or a different, community may be evidence of pietistic tyranny in action. As constituted by these two factors—judgemental values and pietistic tyranny—the feature of condemnatory stance sets the seal on the assertive phase and sets the scene for the next phase, that of impositional fundamentalism.

Impositional Fundamentalism

What began as 'merely' or 'benignly' passive fundamentalist ideology, by the time it reaches this last stage, transforms or evolves into something of a distinctly radicalized and/or impositional nature such that extreme actions, including violent behaviours and even terrorism, may be contemplated, advocated, and engaged. We observe here an ideological development not only under way but reaching its zenith. It is this final, impositional, phase which, necessarily including and building upon the second two features of the preceding assertive phase (*contextual scope* and *condemnatory stance*), denotes the terminal trajectory of an ideological development that began with passive fundamentalism. For, it is out of this last phase, and as its logical *terminus*, that religiously motivated terrorism springs. The three features of this phase are identified as *value application*, *explicit justification*, and *enacted extremism*.

Value application

The first, the application of discriminatory values, occurs where alterity, or 'otherness' (however defined and applied), is negated and, as a necessary corollary, the superiority of the self is asserted. Thus *alterity negation* and *self-superiority assertion* are the two factors comprising this particular feature of value application. The discriminatory negation of otherness is per-haps critical at this juncture, for the scene set by the preceding features of contextual scope and condemnatory stance now emerges into a devaluing and dismissal of a multiplicity of forms of 'otherness'. Often, such alterities may be demonized. A religious 'other' may be cast as 'satanic', or at least seriously and significantly labelled as a hostile opponent, and so hos-tilely regarded. One way or another the fundamentalist is here applying negative valuation to 'otherness' as such, with a corresponding assertion of self-superiority *vis-à-vis* such 'other'. Thus, for example, my God is greater than your god. My truth reigns over your ignorance. The authenticity of my faith contrasts with the feeble delusion you entertain. My laws express the divine reality directly which is infinitely superior to the laws which derive merely from human ideas. And so we might go on. The scene is now well set for the next feature—the rendering of an explicit justification not just for a viewpoint but also for actions premised on that viewpoint. For the second feature comprises a justifying process for both the ideology espoused and any actions it implies.

Explicit justification

Once all the preceding features are in place, it is but a short step to the penultimate pair of factors that signals the expression of fundamentalist extremism in some form of direct politi-cal action: *sanctioned imposition* and *legitimated violence*. The former sees the very imposition of the fundamentalist's views and polity as, in fact, sanctioned by a higher or greater author-ity, however that is conceived. This point of reference transcends the local, particular, ordi-nary taken-for-granted freedoms of everyday life; it embraces and promotes the requirement to be, live, and do in accord with the fundamentalist's ideological dictates. The sanctioning of a programme of imposition leads naturally to the next factor. Here, extremist violence is legitimated and a platform of justification is established, at least in the mind of the imposi-tional fundamentalist. In other words, once there is in place a sense of transcendent sanction for any set of particular programmatic actions, the way to the legitimizing of violent behav-iours to achieve the outcomes driving the programme is eased. Muslim, as well as other sui-cide bombers provide an example of the outworking of the sequential progression of the features of fundamentalism that culminate in extreme actions. Sanctioned imposition and legitimated violence are the two sides of the chief coin of justification in the currency of extremism.

So we are brought to the final feature of the sequential paradigm of fundamentalism as it connects to extremism, namely 'enacted violent extremism' with the penultimate factor of *manifest contempt* and the end-result factor: the religiously motivated *terrorist act*. On the one hand, manifestations of contempt, as an expression of negative judgements and the negation of the 'other', are often instantiated in various contemptible behaviours—intimidation, coer-cion, violent and destructive actions directed at non-human symbolic targets (works of art, places of worship), and so on. Such behaviours may be *ad hoc*, simply manifesting an under-lying contempt in a comparatively spontaneous fashion. If an aim as such could be adduced, it would be to assert superiority, impose an ideology, or enforce subjugating submission; but not necessarily inculcate terror *per se*, even if the behaviours are in themselves terrorizing.

On the other hand, there is certainly the phenomenon of intentionally organized terrorism, where extremism knows no bounds: the terrorizing of a targeted populace that is itself both means and end. It is only thus that the extremist ensures that a duly sanctioned imposition can be brought about as, for example, in Afghanistan in recent years. Not only was it the case of advocating that all Muslims ought to submit naturally to the Sharia but, according to the fundamentalist ideals of the Taliban, all of society should be made to submit, like it or not; for enforced submission is an inherent element of its extreme application of an otherwise comparatively passive Islamic ideal (peaceful submission to God by way of living according to divine law or Sharia). Submission to the dictates of the fundamentalist is at this juncture a matter of necessary imposition, as Afghani women found to their cost. And the alternative to even an involuntary submission is outright destruction: hence, from the Taliban's extremist perspective, even the Buddha 'idols' had to be destroyed. How else does the extremist ensure that the imposition that has been sanctioned can actually be effected? Otherness—alterity—has to be eliminated if it cannot be made to submit, for submission is the necessary corollary of an ideology of imposition. And history provides plenty of examples of that.

CONCLUSION

I have endeavoured to describe a typological paradigm structure that demonstrates a sequential and cumulative ideological development which highlights the nature of the link between religious fundamentalism and extremism. Of course, the two are not necessarily related. But they can be; and in certain cases they are. The trick is to discern the difference: where is fundamentalism likely to result in extremism, even terrorism? To the extent that we can sensibly use the term we can say that not all fundamentalists, of whatever religion, are terrorists. It is fundamentalist religion of a more 'extreme' type that reveals a propensity for violent behaviour and terrorist modalities. My hypothesis is that all forms and expressions of religious fundamentalism begin with, or at least include, the three features which denote the passive phase. Much conservative religiosity would identify with this phase and would not be overly troubled by that. Indeed, variant forms of reactionary conservatism across both Christianity and Islam, as well as other religions, would easily classify as expressive of passive fundamentalism. A passive fundamentalist group to all intents and purposes 'minds its own business' so far as the rest of society is concerned; an assertive group perhaps somewhat less so, but an impositional group does not.

Some religious groups or movements clearly go beyond the passive phase such that we may identify them as belonging to the second, hard-line assertive, phase. Most typically sectarian movements, for example Jehovah's Witnesses, the Unification Church, the Exclusive

Brethren[35] tend to fit within the more overt 'assertive' phase. But arguably there are some which, having incorporated all the marks of a hard-line assertive fundamentalism, then go further to manifest what, perhaps, can be best described as variant forms of an 'impositional' fundamentalism; for example, in the United States, the 'World Church of the Creator'.[36] An impositional fundamentalism wants to see things change to fit its view of how things should be, and will take steps to make its views known and, if need be, act imposingly to bring about change—by covert or overt interventions. It is here that we discover the propensity for fundamentalism to yield to terrorism. This may be seen also in the example of the so-called Phineas Priesthood.

The name comes from an account in the Hebrew Bible—the Christian 'Old Testament'— where it is recorded (Numbers 25) that Phineas, an Israelite priest, killed an Israelite man and a Midianite woman by running them through with a spear while they were engaging in a sexual act within the precincts of the Tabernacle. In the Bible, Phineas is commended for having prevented Israel's fall to idolatrous practices brought in by Midianite women, as well as putting a halt to the desecration of God's sanctuary. For some this provides justification for 'doing God's Will' by using violent means. In the USA such individuals have been identified as terrorists for, among other things, the planning and/or execution of the bombing of FBI buildings, abortion clinic bombings, and the like. Such individuals acting either alone or in the context of a loose-knit right-wing extremist movement are sometimes denoted as 'lone wolf' operatives. But the essential ideology and extreme dynamics are much the same, as was borne out by the 2011 case of the Christian-oriented right-wing extremist Anders Breivik, noted above.

It is the underlying dynamic of an ideological development which the paradigm outlined above attempts to map. To be sure, there are examples of non-religious movements of protest, such as anti-vivisectionists or environmental activists, who will give evidence of all three phases—albeit in some modified form—of the fundamentalist paradigm. There will certainly be expressions of a relatively passive or normative sort (for example, people who hold sympathetic views and provide passive financial support); dimensions of a hard-line assertive approach (people who publicly advocate the movement's views and policies); and from time to time instances of a clear impositional polity at work wherein disruptive, even violent, actions will take place (by people who are the 'extremists' of the movement). But the key difference between such secular groups oriented to a cause, and contemporary forms of religious fundamentalism that are inclined to an impositional activism and so extremism, is that the former are highly specialized and focused—it is relatively clear as to who are the protagonists, who the target—and the latter rather more wide-ranging in terms of scope and likely arena of application.

---

[35] This offshoot of the English Plymouth Brethren is active in Australia and New Zealand, as well as elsewhere. It is a highly sectarian and fiercely exclusive group that exercises tight control over its members; cf. David Barrett, *The New Believers: Sects, 'Cults' and Alternative Religions* (London: Cassell, 2001).

[36] George Michael, 'RAHOWA! A History of the World Church of the Creator', *Terrorism and Political Violence*, 18/4 (2006), 561–83.

FURTHER READING

Mia Bloom, *Dying to Kill: The Allure of Suicide Terror* (New York: Columbia University Press, 2005).

John L. Esposito, *Unholy War: Terror in the Name of Islam* (New York: Oxford University Press, 2002).

Michael K. Jerryson, *Buddhist Fury: Religion and Violence in Southern Thailand* (New York: Oxford University Press, 2011).

Mark Juergensmeyer, *Terror in the Mind of God: The Global Rise of Religious Violence* (Berkeley, Calif.: University of California Press, 2000).

Joseph E. B. Lumbard (ed.), *Islam, Fundamentalism, and the Betrayal of Tradition* (Bloomington, Ind.: World Wisdom, 2004).

George M. Marsden, *Understanding Fundamentalism and Evangelicalism* (Grand Rapids, Mich.: W. B. Eerdmans, 1991).

Martin E. Marty and R. Scott Appleby (eds), *Fundamentalisms Comprehended* (Chicago: University of Chicago Press, 1995).

Malise Ruthven, *Fundamentalism: The Search for Meaning* (Oxford: Oxford University Press, 2004).

Brian Victoria, *Zen at War*, 2nd edn (Lanham, Md.: Rowman & Littlefield, 2006).

Leonard Weinberg and Ami Pedahzur (eds), *Religious Fundamentalism and Political Extremism* (Portland, Or.: Frank Cass, 2004).

CHAPTER 12

Encounter as Conflict: Interfaith Peace-Building

ANNA HALAFOFF

Our so-called postmodern, even 'ultramodern',[1] world is characterized by increased human interaction, both real and virtual, enabling previously unimaginable encounters between diverse individuals and groups. These encounters have produced both conflict and peace-building opportunities among people of different cultures, religions, and political orientations. This chapter focuses particularly on encounters between religious persons and groups as they confront common social and environmental issues. While scholars largely ignored the role of religion in contributing to and ameliorating social problems in the twentieth century,[2] religion has come to occupy a prominent place in the public sphere at the turn of the twenty-first century, largely due to its association with violent extremism. Although there is no doubt that religion continues to play a role in cultures of violence, both direct and structural, the peace-building capacity of religion is often overlooked within academic discourses. This chapter therefore examines the interfaith movements' commitment to peace-building activities in order to illustrate that religions have long played, and continue to play, a role in conflict transformation. It draws from work undertaken as part of the Netpeace study, conducted from 2006 to 2009, which examined the interfaith movement's response to global risks—such as terrorism and climate change—in Australia, the United Kingdom, and the United States of America.[3] A total of fifty-four semi-structured in-depth interviews were conducted throughout 2007–8 with leading interfaith practitioners in all three countries.

---

[1] See Jean-Paul Willaime, 'Religion in Ultramodernity', in James A. Beckford and John Wallis (eds), *Theorising Religion: Classical and Contemporary Debates* (Aldershot: Ashgate, 2006), 77–89.

[2] Cf. James A. Beckford, 'The Sociology of Religion and Social Problems', *Sociological Analysis*, 51/1 (1990), 1–14.

[3] This chapter draws on the author's Ph.D. thesis published as *The Multifaith Movement: Global Risks and Cosmopolitan Solutions* (Dordrecht: Springer, 2013). A complete list of participants in the Netpeace study is listed in the book.

Respondents' remarks are tagged including the participant's surname, the year of the interview, and the country in which they reside, for example, [Patel 2007, USA]. The findings of this study show that interfaith and multi-actor peace-building networks, including religious and non-religious actors, can transform conflicts into peace-building opportunities.

Religion, Peace, and Conflict

The first Parliament of the World's Religions (PWR),[4] held in Chicago in 1893, is commonly described as the beginning of the interfaith movement, and the second PWR,[5] held in Chicago 100 years later, as signifying the movement's 'coming of age'.[6] Global interfaith engagement expanded significantly in the 1990s, as evidenced by the 1993 PWR and the formation of a number of major interfaith organizations with headquarters in the USA.[7] Following the 11 September 2001 terrorist attacks and the 2005 London bombings, a dramatic rise in interfaith engagement occurred, particularly in Western societies, as interfaith initiatives were implemented as peace-building strategies in the wake of these tragedies.[8] Conflict, whether at the personal or societal level, often acts as a trigger for deeper awareness and understanding to develop between parties whose differences previously seemed irreconcilable. It follows that tensions between religious persons and groups can best be addressed, and the foundations for peaceful religiously diverse societies can be established, through embodied interfaith encounters.

Religion and Social Problems

Enlightenment thinkers held the assumption that religion would eventually decline and cease to be a public force and that whatever religions were to remain in modern times would be reasonable and tolerant. These views led to the development of theories of secularization among sociologists of religion, such as Max Weber, Emile Durkheim, Thomas Luckmann,

---

[4] The 1893 Parliament of the World's Religions (PWR) was originally titled the World's Parliament of Religions (WPR). The Council for the Parliament of the World's Religions (CPWR) was established to coordinate the 1993 PWR and future PWRs. CPWR is now simply called the Parliament of the World's Religions (PWR). I have used Parliament of the World's Religions (PWR) throughout the text to describe all WPR, CPWR, and PWR events in order to avoid confusion.

[5] The 1993 PWR, commonly described as the second PWR, was actually the third. The second, much smaller PWR was held in Chicago in 1933, convened by the World Fellowship of Faiths (WFF); see Marcus Braybrooke, *Pilgrimage of Hope* (London: SCM Press, 1992), 39.

[6] Braybrooke, *Pilgrimage of Hope*, 7–8.

[7] See Eck, *A New Religious America*; Peter Kirkwood, *The Quiet Revolution: The Emergence of Interfaith Consciousness* (Sydney: ABC Books, 2007).

[8] See Eck, *A New Religious America*, pp. xiii–xix; Gary D. Bouma, Sharon Pickering, Anna Halafoff, and Hass Dellal, *Managing the Impact of Global Crisis Events on Community Relations in Multicultural Australia* (Brisbane: Multicultural Affairs Queensland, 2007), 61–6, 106; Kirkwood, *Quiet Revolution*, pp. v–vi; Gustav Niebuhr, *Beyond Tolerance: Searching for Interfaith Understanding in America* (New York: Viking, 2008), 5–7, 10–11.

and Niklas Luhmann, who assigned an increasingly privatized and thereby marginalized role to religion in modernity.[9] As a result, the vast majority of sociologists of religion showed relatively little interest in religious responses to the emerging problems posed by industrialization and capitalism for much of the twentieth century. However, religions, far from disappearing from public life, have increased their influence in the public sphere throughout the world in the latter half of the twentieth century.

Following the end of the Second World War and the collapse of the Japanese and British Empires, the steady process of decolonization, coupled with the 'human rights revolution' centred on a commitment to equality of all peoples, led to rising demands for justice, autonomy, equitable participation, and self-organization among indigenous, cultural, and religious groups.[10] This period also led to a rise in immigration from previous colonies to Western countries and consequently to the creation of increasingly multicultural and interfaith societies, particularly in parts of Europe, the UK, the USA, Canada, Australia, and New Zealand. As Gary Bouma states, 'the fact and experience of diversity preceded the institutionalisation of diversity', and as a result societies were forced to choose between repressive or tolerant policies.[11] This eventually led to the legitimation of a pluralist worldview in Western societies, evident in policies of multiculturalism, as diverse cultural and religious groups acted within the democratic system to introduce rights for previously excluded minorities.

During the 1970s and 1980s, as a result of policies of multiculturalism, immigrants were encouraged to maintain some of their cultural practices and identities and political institutions were reformed to accommodate them. As a result of these developments the interfaith movement expanded in Western societies as diverse cultural and religious groups strengthened their participation in the ultramodern public sphere during this period.[12] However, while a growing respect for cultural pluralism characterized Western societies in the 1970s and 1980s, undercurrents of cultural and religious exclusivity remained, evident in majority cultures' frequently hostile attitudes to indigenous and immigrant communities acquiring rights and autonomy.[13]

Processes of decolonization and globalization led not only to an increase in rights accorded to immigrant and indigenous communities, but also to a global rise of critiques of Western

---

[9] See José Casanova, *Public Religions in the Modern World* (Chicago: University of Chicago Press, 1994), 5–6, 17–19, 35.

[10] Jürgen Habermas, 'Learning by Disaster? A Diagnostic Look Back on the Short Twentieth Century', *Constellations*, 5/3 (1998), 313; cf. Will Kymlicka and Christine Straehle, 'Cosmopolitanism, Nation-States, and Minority Nationalism: A Critical Review of Recent Literature', *European Journal of Philosophy*, 7/1 (1999), 74–5; Mary Kaldor, *Global Civil Society: An Answer to War* (Cambridge: Polity 2003), 144–5.

[11] Gary Bouma, 'From Hegemony to Pluralism: Managing Religious Diversity in Modernity and Post-Modernity', in Gary D. Bouma (ed.), *Managing Religious Diversity: From Threat to Promise* (Melbourne: Australian Association for the Study of Religions, 1999), 14.

[12] Cf. Eck, *A New Religious America*; Paul Weller, *Religious Diversity in the UK: Contours and Issues* (London: Continuum, 2008), 179–80.

[13] Will Kymlicka, 'Do We Need a Liberal Theory of Minority Rights? Reply to Carens, Young, Parekh and Forst', *Constellations*, 4/1 (1997), 76.

capitalism. While capitalist modernity promised to deliver economic benefits and equal rights for all, by the mid to late twentieth century it was becoming increasingly clear, especially with the spread of global communication systems, that capitalism had fallen well short of providing these benefits except to a very small proportion of the world's population, largely at the expense of the life-world and the majority of its citizens.[14] According to Jean-Paul Willaime, the term 'ultramodernity', which he coined in 1998, best describes our current era as '(a) we have not left modernity behind and (b) we are actually in a stage of radicalisation of modernity'.[15] Willaime aligns his term ultramodernity with Marcel Gauchet's observation that we live in a time of 'major discontinuity which is compatible with an underlying continuity'.[16] The major discontinuity lies in a shift 'from a logic of certainty to uncertainty' wherein the modernist belief in progress has become subject to considerable doubt and where 'nothing escapes close critical examination'.[17] According to Willaime, in ultramodernity the so-called secular ideals of modernity that marginalized and criticized religion and 'set themselves up as new certainties' are being de-absolutized, resulting in 'the disenchantment of the disenchanters'.[18] A period of *radical reflexivity* thereby categorizes the ultramodern era in which social movements and diverse cultural and religious groups have played an increasingly critical role in the public sphere.

Globalization became increasingly viewed as a process of global 'marketization and Americanization' that threatened to destroy the environment, cultural and religious identities, values, and livelihoods.[19] Pressing concerns about the survival of humanity meshed well with religious discourses of end times and religious responses to social problems elicited radical narratives of overturning existing orders and re-establishing new orders in their place. As a result of these transformations religions came to play a central mobilizing role among social movements of people questing for self-determination, political participation, and equitable and sustainable development, seeking to defend the life-world against state and market penetration.[20] These religious movements, violent and non-violent, frequently evoked theological rhetoric of justice to question the legitimacy of state and market forces. Islamic movements spoke of empowering the 'disinherited', liberation theology of liberating the 'poor', and the 'velvet' revolution of 'the power of the powerless'.[21] The Satyagraha movement in India, the Civil Rights Movement in the USA, the Iranian and Nicaraguan revolutions of 1979, the Solidarity Movement in Poland, the spread of liberation theology through Latin America, Asia, and Africa, conflicts in Northern Ireland and former

---

[14] See Habermas, 'New Social Movements', 35; – 'Learning by Disaster?', 314–15.

[15] Willaime, 'Religion in Ultramodernity', 78.

[16] Marcel Gauchet, *La Démocratie Contre Elle-Même* (Paris: Gallimard, 2002), p. xv.

[17] Willaime, 'Religion in Ultramodernity', 78–9.

[18] Willaime, 'Religion in Ultramodernity', 79.

[19] James A. Beckford, *Social Theory and Religion* (Cambridge: Cambridge University Press, 2003), 11.

[20] Cf. Casanova, *Public Religions*, 4–5, 228; Habermas, 'New Social Movements', 35;—*The Theory of Communicative Action*, ii. *Lifeworld and System: A Critique of Functionalist Reason* (Cambridge: Polity Press, 1987), 396; Beckford, 'The Sociology of Religion and Social Problems', *Sociological Analysis*, 51/1 (1990), 6–8, 11.

[21] Casanova, *Public Religions*, 4–5.

Yugoslavia, the Salman Rushdie affair in the UK, and the rise of the Christian right's influence on American politics provide further evidence of this phenomenon.[22]

Dramatic advances in information and communications technologies in the 1980s led to a dawning 'global circumstance'[23] and the realization of the interconnectedness of global problems and their solutions. According to Habermas, the process of globalization 'sharpens our awareness of the growing interdependence of our social arenas, of shared risks, and the joint networks of collective fates'.[24] However, while an increased awareness of interconnectedness created a perception of 'oneness' among an emerging global citizenry, it also heightened differences, thereby threatening ontological security.[25] On the one hand, this led to a rise of social movements and international non-governmental organizations (NGOs) and UN agencies—the so-called 'tamed' social movements and networks—which embodied 'a growing global consciousness' and 'sense of a common humanity', and on the other, a rise of 'new wars' and fundamentalist movements.[26] In addition, the more liberal, 'reasonable and tolerant' forms of religion, such as the interfaith movement, while undoubtedly increasing their presence in the ultramodern public sphere, have been challenged by a simultaneous rise in exclusive and conservative forms of religion and identity politics.[27] Therefore, by the end of the twentieth century religions could be described as not only playing a more public role but also an increasingly ambivalent one by promoting both cultures of violence and cultures of peace in ultramodern societies.[28]

Will Kymlicka and Keith Banting note how attitudes towards immigrants have swung between periods of openness and periods of 'backlash and retrenchment' in response to local and international events and concerns.[29] During the 1970s and 1980s policies of multiculturalism and pluralism received broad community support. However, by the 1990s, processes of globalization and the demise of the welfare state had already begun to exacerbate existing prejudices against immigrant communities. Fears abounded that an influx of immigrants would undermine solidarity, and thereby pose a threat to social cohesion and economic security, as immigrants would either take jobs away from locals or become a welfare burden on the state. Despite the fact that ultramodern global labour markets depend on immigrants,

[22] Casanova, *Public Religions*, 3; cf. William Sims Bainbridge, *The Sociology of Religious Movements* (New York: Routledge, 1997), 331–9.

[23] Roland Robertson, 'The Sacred and the World System', in Phillip E. Hammond (ed.), *The Sacred in a Secular Age: Toward Revision in the Scientific Study of Religion* (Berkeley, Calif.: University of California Press, 1985), 347–58.

[24] Habermas, 'Learning by Disaster?', 318.

[25] Mary Kaldor, *New and Old Wars: Organized Violence in a Global Era* (Cambridge: Polity, 1999), 2–4, 6; cf. Beckford, *Social Theory and Religion*, 109.

[26] Kaldor, *Global Civil Society*, 144–5.

[27] Martin E. Marty and R. Scott Appleby, *The Glory and the Power: The Fundamentalist Challenge to the Modern World* (Boston: Beacon Press, 1992), 11–13; Kaldor, *New and Old Wars*, 6.

[28] R. Scott Appleby, *The Ambivalence of the Sacred: Religion, Violence, and Reconciliation* (Lanham, Md.: Rowman & Littlefield, 2003).

[29] Will Kymlicka and Keith Banting, 'Immigration, Multiculturalism, and the Welfare State', *Ethics and International Affairs*, 20/3 (2006), 281.

following 11 September 2001 and the London bombings of 2005, Western governments hardened their immigration policies and multiculturalism was widely criticized, particularly within the UK and the EU, for contributing to ghettoization and cultural relativism, thus hindering processes of integration and threatening the stability of ultramodern societies.[30] The events of 11 September 2001 and subsequent terrorist attacks on 12 October 2002 in Bali, and on 7 and 21 July 2005 in London, had the deleterious effect of creating a wave of Islamophobia and 'migrantophobia' throughout Western societies.[31]

In addition, the global war on terror waged by the USA and its allies 'squeeze[d] the space for global civil society'.[32] The anti-globalization movement postponed or cancelled protests and women's and environmental initiatives ceased to receive public funding. However, the global peace movement expanded its circle to include more religious communities, especially Islamic groups, and mass demonstrations in opposition to the war in Iraq were held throughout the world. The interfaith movement also increased dramatically in size and number during this period, and actually enjoyed growing state support, particularly in the UK and Australia, as interfaith initiatives began to be included in peace-building strategies to counter extremism and advance social cohesion.

Religious and Interreligious Peace-Building

Religious peace-builders Douglas Johnston and Cynthia Sampson have argued that, due to the growing public role of religions during the 1990s, state actors could no longer afford to ignore religious dimensions in a world in which religion played an increasingly prominent role in both perpetuating *and* ameliorating conflict. Following the end of the cold war, conflicts arose derived largely from clashes of cultural and/or religious communal identity. Rivalry between nationalities or religions was exacerbated by economic competition and rising expectations regarding quality of life fuelled by the processes of globalization.[33] Conventional diplomacy, geared as it was towards resolving conflicts between nation-states, was unprepared to deal with these new conflicts, which centred on principles of self-determination, freedom, and justice. In addition, as existing international law discouraged outside nations and international organizations from becoming involved in conflicts within nation-states, they were ill prepared to deal

---

[30] Kymlicka and Banting, 'Immigration, Multiculturalism', 300; Brian S. Turner, *Religious Diversity and Civil Society: A Comparative Analysis* (Oxford: Bardwell Press, 2008), 1–2; Charles Taylor, 'Foreword: What is Secularism?', in Geoffrey Brahm Levey and Tariq Modood (eds), *Secularism, Religion and Multicultural Citizenship* (Cambridge: Cambridge University Press, 2009), pp. xiii–xiv; Geoffrey B. Levey, 'Secularism and Religion in a Multicultural Age', in Levey and Modood, *Secularism, Religion and Multicultural Citizenship*, 3.

[31] Eck, *A New Religious America*, pp. xiii–xix; Bouma *et al.*, *Managing the Impact of Global Crisis Events*, 5–6, 48–53, 65–8; Niebuhr, *Beyond Tolerance*, 5–7, 10–11.

[32] Kaldor, *Global Civil Society*, 148.

[33] Douglas Johnston, 'Introduction: Beyond Power Politics', in Douglas Johnston and Cynthia Sampson (eds), *Religion, the Missing Dimension of Statecraft* (Oxford: Oxford University Press 1994), 3; Cynthia Sampson, 'Religion and Peacebuilding', in I. William Zartman and J. Lewis Rasmussen (eds), *Peacemaking in International Conflict: Methods and Techniques* (Washington, DC: United States Institute of Peace Press, 1997), 274.

with these 'new wars'. This created a vacuum in which religious organizations, among other civil society actors, became involved in conflict resolution, mediation, and 'track II (nonofficial) diplomacy', effecting non-violent social change 'from the middle'.[34]

According to religious peace-building theory, there are several factors that predispose religions and religious leaders to peace-building and conflict prevention, amelioration, and resolution: religious communities have extensive networks for communication and action; injustice can give rise to conflicts and religions provide mandates for non-violent resistance to injustice; in situations where there is state corruption or collapse, religious institutions and leaders provide moral authority and have the trust and respect of the people; processes of reconciliation are often informed by religious concepts; and religious actors are engaged with communities at the grassroots level.[35] Faith-based peace-making draws on religious texts and narratives of peace, justice, repentance, and forgiveness to aid the peace-building process. Faith-based peace-building can be undertaken within single faith communities as well as between faith communities.[36] Religious peace-building has also been described as including education, conflict resolution, and reconciliation, and socio-political change through non-violent means.[37] Religious peace-builders, who use these methods advocating non-violence and pluralism, are present within all major religious traditions.

The interfaith movement has focused on peace-building since its inception at the turn of the twentieth century. Interreligious peace-builders have long sought to transform exclusive attitudes into more pluralist perspectives and to provide detailed methodologies for the peaceful resolution of conflict influenced by theological and philosophical principles derived from their faith traditions.[38] Religious traditions provide detailed methodologies for personal and collective peace realization insofar as most religions advocate the importance of virtues and ethics and of cultivating one's good qualities. Many religions also advocate the need for transforming a self-centred, adversarial individualism or group dynamics into cooperative, compassionate mutuality and global responsibility. It is this reflexive nature of religion, particularly its emphasis on taking personal responsibility, which lies at the foundation of religious peace-building and conflict transformation.[39] It is also an undervalued aspect of religions. Reflexivity, applied to self and society, is not solely a product of modernity; rather, it is a quality inherent to many religious and spiritual traditions that well predate modern and ultramodern eras.

While all of the major religions proclaim peace as a worthy pursuit and ultimate goal at both the individual and collective social level, there are many conflicting theories of how this

---

[34] Johnston, 'Introduction: Beyond Power Politics', 3–4.

[35] Sampson, 'Religion and Peacebuilding', 275; David Little and Scott Appleby, 'A Moment of Opportunity? The Promise of Religious Peacebuilding in an Era of Religious and Ethnic Conflict', in Harold Coward and Gordon S. Smith (eds), *Religion and Peacebuilding* (Albany, NY: State University of New York Press, 2004), 3.

[36] David R. Smock, *Religious Contributions to Peacemaking: When Religion Brings Peace, Not War* (Washington, DC: United States Institute of Peace, 2006), 37–8.

[37] Sampson, 'Religion and Peacebuilding', 274.

[38] Mohammad Abu-Nimer, 'Conflict Resolution, Culture, and Religion: Toward a Training Model of Interreligious Peacebuilding', *Journal of Peace Research,* 38/6 (2001), 686, 701.

[39] Sampson, 'Religion and Peacebuilding', 276.

common goal can best be achieved. There is a prevalent view, frequently expressed at inter-faith events, that religions in their pure forms advocate only peace and that they have been misused for political ends. However, Perry Schmidt-Leukel argues that there must be religious predispositions towards conflict, or it would not be possible to exploit religions for political purposes. The claim of superiority inherent in all major religions and therefore the existence of 'mutual superiority claims' render 'mutual supersession' and therefore predisposition to conflict inevitable.[40] In addition, most religions also justify the use of violence and war in order to protect or defend one's religion and religious values from external threats. This conviction of undertaking a holy duty and its corresponding absence of guilt or moral dilemma is what makes religious violence especially dangerous and problematic. Mark Juergensmeyer warns that simplifying religious violence as purely a political strategy negates this symbolic aspect of religious violence and in particular its long association with what he describes as 'Cosmic War'. Thus, when 'life struggles' are merged with cosmic struggles and a cause has been sacralized, violence becomes legitimized.[41] It follows that enemies are demonized and therefore dehumanized. Multiple theologies not only lay the ground for Cosmic War, but they also proclaim that its proponents will ultimately be victorious and rewarded. Martyrdom offers hope, and it restores pride to the suffering and the oppressed by exalting and ennobling the defiant. Consequently, the triumph sought by Cosmic War over the forces of evil is one that is not easily abandoned. Juergensmeyer argues that what makes religious violence particularly savage and relentless is that its perpetrators have placed religious images of divine struggle and Cosmic War at the service of worldly political battles. For this reason, acts of religious terrorism serve not only as tactics in a political strategy but also as evocations of a much larger spiritual confrontation.

In addition to legitimizing direct violence, whether in the form of war or terrorism, religious traditions are often hierarchical, patriarchal, didactic, and discriminatory, thereby legitimizing cultures of structural violence directed against indigenous people, women, homosexual people, children, 'other' religious and cultural groups, and all forms of non-human life.[42] Scholars who highlight the ambivalent nature of religion, rather than positing religion as either entirely problematic or peaceful, argue that it is precisely religions' role in promoting these cultures of violence, be they direct or structural, that predisposes religious actors to advance cultures of peace in their stead.[43] By understanding how religion legitimates violence, rather than denying that it does, religious peace-builders are well equipped to address the root causes of social problems. These religious peace-builders not only have the potential to transform their own faith traditions, but they can also be valuable allies for state actors in

---

[40] Perry Schmidt-Leukel (ed.), *War and Peace in World Religions* (London: SCM Press, 2004), 3–7.

[41] See Mark Juergensmeyer, *Terror in the Mind of God: The Global Rise of Religious Violence* 3rd edn (Berkeley, Calif.: University of California Press, 2003), 158–83.

[42] Appleby, *Ambivalence of the Sacred*, 237.

[43] Johnston, 'Looking Ahead: Toward a New Paradigm', in Johnston and Sampson (eds), *Religion, the Missing Dimension of Statecraft*, 332; Appleby, *Ambivalence of the Sacred*, 240.

collaboratively addressing issues of common security. By challenging the aspects of religion that promote cultures of violence, interfaith peace-builders occupy an ideal position to offer an alternative role for religion, one that valorizes religious diversity, and affirms a commitment to non-violent methods of conflict transformation and the highest peace-building principles of their traditions.

Ultramodern Interfaith Encounters

The findings of the Netpeace study explain how the interfaith movement has responded to crisis events and how interfaith encounters continue to be implemented as effective peace-building strategies to counter risks in contemporary societies. Several participants in the study recounted how interfaith organizations were formed during the 1960s and 1970s, alongside other social movements, to combat global inequities and to campaign for human rights. The World Conference of Religions for Peace, with its focus on nuclear disarmament, global warming, and economic and social justice, was described as a pioneer in the field of interfaith peace-building particularly in the 1970s and 1980s. Participants also described how a significant shift occurred within interfaith engagement from dialogue to common action during this period and how a new concern with addressing economic inequities emerged within the interfaith movement during the 1980s. Maurice Glasman, Director of the Faith and Citizenship Programme at London Metropolitan University, recalled how religious communities in the UK became increasingly concerned about the economic pressures affecting families and young people. At the end of the twentieth century, as states became weaker and markets became stronger, religious organizations played an increasingly critical role in the public sphere by responding to local and global problems of growing inequality, commodification, and atomization produced by market forces.

Netpeace study participants also stated that environmental issues became a key focus for interfaith organisations in the early 1990s, primarily in the USA, as illustrated by the comments of Fletcher Harper, Executive Director of GreenFaith:

> during the 1990s... there has been a growing awareness of serious challenges to human well-being and ecological wellbeing due to human activity... increasing numbers of religious leaders are aware of this and see this as something that they are morally called to respond to.
>
> [Harper 2008, USA]

In addition, Eboo Patel, Executive Director of the Interfaith Youth Core, explained how, during the early 1990s, an international awareness of global issues led to a rise of social movements and a plethora of international conferences focused on areas of common concern, including environmental, women's, and human rights issues. According to Patel, these initiatives formed 'the beginning of an architecture for global living' [Patel 2007, USA]. According to Paul Knitter, Paul Tillich Professor of Theology at Union Theological

Seminary, the interfaith movement responded accordingly, cementing its focus on more practical issues of ethics, human rights and environmental sustainability [Knitter 2007, USA].

Many participants also affirmed that the dramatic rise in immigration to Western societies during the 1960s and 1970s produced a corresponding increase in interfaith engagement and consequently a growing respect for religious diversity. Dirk Ficca, Executive Director of the Council for a Parliament of the World's Religions, and Shaykh Ibrahim Mogra, Chair of the Interfaith Relations Committee of the Muslim Council of Britain, described how living in increasingly diverse societies created the impetus for interfaith initiatives in the latter half of the twentieth century:

> [F]or the first time in history, since the 60s, large, diverse, ethnic, cultural and religious communities are living next door to each other in metropolitan areas in ways that have never happened before...In your school, at the supermarket, in every aspect of most major cities' cultural life, people of different traditions are bumping into each other, so there's a need to find a way to live together. [Ficca 2007, USA]

And Mogra opined:

> I think there has been on-going migration of non-Christian religious communities into what we call the West, and clearly when such communities move into any part of the UK...they become visible, they make friendships, they go to work or take their children to school...so that initial interaction...feeds the need for people to want to get to know each other in a better way. [Mogra 2007, UK]

Netpeace participants explained how increased mobility coupled with growing global communication systems also contributed to the rise of interfaith engagement in ultramodernity. According to Patel, not only was the 'interactional' nature of ultramodernity enabled by the increased movement of people, but it was also aided by the growth of global communication systems. And Ficca described this process as leading to a 'more deep weaving of our systems' and a heightened sense of interconnectivity. Many participants stated that this unprecedented access to information increased contact between people and facilitated understanding of increasingly diverse local communities. As Stephen Shashoua, Director of the Three Faiths Forum in Britain, illustrates here, it also awakened a sense of global empathy and a corresponding need to know one's new neighbours:

> viewing the global neighbourhood through the new technologies we were feeling that the world was much closer, realising the neighbours...from across the world were actually, they were right next to us...poverty around the world, [was] always very high on the list but now a more direct relationship with those specific countries, and also with that global understanding of other [contexts], led to...an increased curiosity of knowing the neighbour that lived within your locality, so I think the global led to the local in that way.
>
> [Shashoua 2008, UK]

Many participants also affirmed that the end of the cold war stimulated a new interest in religions' role in conflict and peace-building, and thus in interfaith engagement. William F. Vendley, Secretary General of Religions for Peace, claimed that the end of the cold war had an even greater impact than September 11 on the process of 'religion re-emerging in the domain of political science, in the domain of statecraft', because during the cold war period religion was 'largely submerged' and consequently had no place in government departments, think-tanks, or in political science [Vendley 2007, USA]. According to him, it was the USSR's demise that 'brought not simply ethnicity, but religion, which is just about 2 cm below the soil of even the most secular nationalism…to the fore'. Joseph Camilleri, Director of the Centre for Dialogue at La Trobe University, agreed that, with the collapse of Communism, 'the lid was taken off [religion] but in the taking off of the lid that also brought a number of simmering or latent conflicts to the surface' [Camilleri 2008, AUS]. Mohammed Abu-Nimer, Director of the Peace-building and Development Institute at American University, Washington, DC, also stated that the end of the Cold War increased the visibility of religious and ethnic identities, previously subsumed under Soviet rule, and that as religion was increasingly perceived as 'a provocateur of conflict' its role in conflict resolution and peace-building became increasingly prominent [Abu-Nimer 2008, USA]. And Harper explained how this led religious actors to challenge prevalent discourses in which religion was largely associated with conflict and fundamentalism, which in turn led to a rise in interfaith engagement at the turn of the twenty-first century:

> over the previous 30 years and certainly the previous 20 to 25 years…many ascendant religious groups, often but not always religiously conservative, had contributed toward sectarian strife and…the polarising of relationships between people, and…there are a large majority of people of faith who want their religious tradition and their community to play a positive role in both mediating and lessening conflict…so…some of the increase of activity is related to the stepping forward of many people of goodwill from a range of religious traditions who want to see their religion play a constructive role rather than one that might tend to increase tension.   [Harper 2008, USA]

As David R. Smock, Vice-President of the Centre for Mediation and Conflict Resolution at the United States Institute of Peace stated, 'in places where religion is one of the sources of conflict…it's particularly incumbent upon religious actors to be peacemakers' [Smock 2007, USA]. Abu-Nimer also recalled how a new emphasis on second-track diplomacy and the power of religious actors to influence the dynamic of conflict began to emerge in the 1990s, evident in the research undertaken by Douglas Johnston, which was frequently mentioned by participants as a highly significant and undervalued body of work.[44]

A rise of multi-actor peace-building networks, including religious actors, also occurred in the 1990s in response to pressing social and environmental issues alongside the increase of

---

[44] Johnston and Sampson, (eds), *Religion, the Missing Dimension of Statecraft.*

interfaith networks.[45] A ground-breaking initiative of this period was the World Faiths Development Dialogue (WFDD), established in 1998 by James Wolfensohn, the then President of the World Bank, and the then Archbishop of Canterbury, George Carey, to create partnerships between faith and development actors to address the problems of poverty. The 1999 PWR in Cape Town, attended by over 7,000 people, also released *A Call to the Guiding Institutions* such as the UN and global IGOs to play a role in building peaceful, just, and sustainable societies.[46] The Millennium World Peace Summit of Religious and Spiritual Leaders was also convened, on 27 August 2000, at the United Nations in New York.

Despite long-held suspicions and resistance, Netpeace participants described how these developments reflected a growing recognition among state actors, IGOs, and NGOs of the need to partner with religious communities, at both the local and the global level in response to common crises. For example, Chris Seiple, President of the Institute for Global Engagement, recounted that due to religions' ambivalent role in both perpetuating and ameliorating ultra-modern risks at the turn of the twenty-first century, it became critical for state actors and global institutions to form partnerships with religious actors and to develop greater understanding of religion at this time:

> All these issues we face here are global and they have two characteristics. One is [that] no single entity can solve them in and of themselves, state or non-state. The second is it's not a question of if, but when you partner. Here are all the players, NGOs are the new player on the stage since the 90s and... religions are the new player that nobody knows how to talk to, they have always been there, but these guys, government, military, UN have been uncomfortable dealing with them... [but] you gotta (sic) understand religion...
>
> [Seiple 2007, US]

Indeed, R. Scott Appleby described the emergence of a new 'secular–religious' model of diplomacy as a promising recent development, and has attributed 'the building of strong secular and religious networks and coalitions' as the key to its success, as such collaborations can draw upon expertise and resources from diverse sectors.[47] James A. Beckford similarly asserted the importance of cooperative responses to social problems through 'networks, campaigns, and movements', which challenge distinctions between public and private religion and the spheres of religion and politics.[48]

The need for multi-actor peace-building networks, including religious actors, intensified following the events of September 11. As briefly described above, there was a dramatic increase in interfaith engagement in the USA, the UK, and Australia in response to the events of September 11 as interfaith initiatives were implemented as peace-building and

---

[45] Sandy Bharat and Jael Bharat, *A Global Guide to Interfaith: Reflections from around the World* (Winchester: O Books, 2007), 243.

[46] See Marcus Braybrooke, *Interfaith Witness in a Changing World: The World Congress of Faiths, 1996–2006*; available online at <www.religion-online.org>.

[47] Appleby, *Ambivalence of the Sacred*, 255.

[48] Beckford, 'Sociology of Religion and Social Problems', 9, 11.

counter-terrorism strategies in response to this crisis event.[49] The interfaith movement has been described as a 'quiet revolution' of 'mostly unrecognised efforts' by diverse religious communities to create a more peaceful world.[50] However, as Chloe Breyer, Executive Director, of the Interfaith Centre of New York, noted, the events of September 11 put the interfaith movement 'on a map in a mainstream way that it hadn't been before' [Breyer 2007, USA] as public displays of solidarity among faith leaders condemning violence increased the visibility of the movement. Netpeace participants described how the events of September 11 also lent more urgency to interfaith engagement and intensified the need for understanding among diverse communities. Consequently, the interfaith movement gathered strength and a greater awareness of the importance of cooperation and understanding across faith communities emerged at both the local and global level. In addition, subsequent to September 11, interfaith engagement was identified as a potential solution to counter religious extremism, which suddenly propelled it to centre of world attention. Indeed, Sr. Joan Kirby, the Temple of Understanding's United Nations representative, exclaimed how after September 11, 'it's as if the wave is cresting. There's such enormous interest in interfaith dialogue and cooperation, from the grassroots all the way to the United Nations!' [Kirby 2007, USA]. Although September 11 and the need to counter religiously motivated terrorism created 'a new sense of urgency' for interfaith initiatives, it is critical to recognize that this momentum was building in the interfaith movement well before 2001, and particularly during the 1990s, as described above.

The 2002 Bali bombings and the 2005 London bombings also led to an increase of interfaith encounters in the UK and Australia. Netpeace participants stated that the 'home-grown' nature of the terrorists involved in the London bombings at once increased fears and prejudices and also provided greater impetus for interfaith engagement in both the UK and Australia. Participants also stated that interfaith networks that were well established after September 11 enabled quicker and more effective responses to these crisis events. Netpeace participants explained how Muslim communities suddenly became more 'visible' after September 11, due to increased media attention, thereby heightening awareness of Islam and of Muslims in Western societies. Consequently, a new imperative to include Muslim communities in interfaith activities arose within the interfaith movement. Interfaith initiatives provided a platform for Muslim communities to differentiate themselves from terrorists, to dispel negative stereotypes of Muslims, and to affirm their commitment to non-violent principles. September 11 was thereby seen as a notable turning point for Muslim interfaith engagement in that Muslim communities became more proactive in initiating dialogue and educational activities to dispel negative stereotypes and misconceptions perpetuated by the media and in promoting the peace-building aspects of Islam.

---

[49] Cf. Eck, *A New Religious America*, pp. xiii–xix; Bouma *et al.*, *Managing the Impact of Global Crisis Events*, 6, 22–6, 55, 57–60; Kirkwood, *Quiet Revolution*, pp. v–vi; Niebuhr *Beyond Tolerance*, pp. xxii, 5–7, 10–11.

[50] Kate McCarthy, *Interfaith Encounters in America* (Piscataway, NJ: Rutgers University Press, 2007), 2.

Netpeace participants also described the rise of multi-actor peace-building networks after the events of September 11. Notable developments included: the Interreligious and International Peace Council (IIPC), first held in New York in 2003; the Tripartite Forum on Interfaith Cooperation for Peace (Tripartite Forum), which includes UN and NGO faith-based actors; the World Economic Forum's (WEF) Council of 100 Leaders (C-100) founded in 2004; and the meeting of religious leaders that took place in Russia prior to the G8 meeting in 2006/7. Moreover, participants explained that a heightened emphasis on interfaith youth initiatives also emerged in the USA, UK, and Australia, with a focus on countering extremism and home-grown terrorism following September 11 and the London bombings. There was also a significant rise in women's interfaith initiatives as women's interfaith networks were formed in the USA, Australia, and the UK after September 11 and the Bali and London bombings.

Netpeace participants also recounted how, following the release of Al Gore's *An Inconvenient Truth*, the issue of climate change broadened interfaith participation. For example, in Australia major religious and faith organizations joined together in 2006 to make a *Common Belief* statement on climate change. Melanie Landau, a Lecturer in Jewish Studies at Monash University, and Shashoua, explained how growing global environmental concerns have high-lighted the interdependent nature of life and the need for collaborative responses aimed at countering risks:

> [There's] a recognition, even if it's not overt, that we can't do it alone...environmental [risks] for example, there's just this realisation of maybe a common destiny. [Landau 2008, AUS]

> When I was a kid I remember having a conversation with my father, and we had discussed what will bring world peace and he said an external threat, and so a UFO coming down putting us all in harm's way and we have to band together for our survival, now the external threat is now the environment, and so it's an internal threat because it depends on us as well. Is this the only way? [Shashoua 2008, UK]

Embodied Interfaith Encounters and Conflict Transformation

Many Netpeace participants described how these interfaith initiatives act as peace-building strategies by increasing opportunities for contact and communication among people of diverse faiths, thereby contributing to greater levels of understanding across faith communities. Mehmet Ozalp, Chief Executive Officer of Affinity Intercultural Foundation, explained how interfaith engagement enables a more authentic level of awareness to develop between faith traditions as representatives of religious communities share knowledge about themselves and their religions directly:

> [In the past] we tended to explain other's faith[s] from our own frame of reference, this is a big problem...one of the key initiatives that we [now] have is to find out about each other's

faith...from the followers of that faith; how do they understand it...this is a very important aspect of interreligious dialogue, that we should see each other in their own frame of reference, and momentarily even get into that frame of reference in order to understand it, even if we disagree, even if we come out of it, and this is very important, in appreciation of the other.   [Ozalp 2008, AUS]

Ozalp further explained how post-September-11 interfaith engagement provided an opportunity to prevent 'generalisations...for the Western world [that] all Muslims are potential terrorists, [and] in the Muslim world [that] the whole Western world is out to get them...generalisations that really do not serve anything for peace'. As Sherene Hassan, Interfaith Officer at the Islamic Council of Victoria, Australia, stated, 'people only fear the unknown', and interfaith engagement provided an effective strategy for 'normalising Muslims' in the broader community, which had previously had little contact with Muslim communities:

> Most of the people that I'm presenting to have never met a Muslim before, the only Muslims they have met or the only Muslims they are familiar with are those on the television, the most extreme examples. So it's just a matter of normalising Muslims, of people being able to see Muslims in a normal light, that they meet me, I'm a teacher, my husband's a doctor, I talk about just everyday experiences and not just about my religion—I talk about the football team that I barrack for...it's about dispelling misconceptions and myths...[it's] about normalising Muslims.   [Hassan 2008, AUS]

Ficca similarly described how, through increased contact, interfaith engagement provides 'positive experience of difference' and thereby humanizes 'the other'. In this regard, Ozalp stated that 'we tend to dehumanise issues and matters, and...when we meet at interfaith dialogue we realise our humanity above all, so we are all human beings, we are not just this scary monster that is sometimes portrayed'. In addition, Mogra explained how public affirmations of friendship and collaboration between religious communities assist in diminishing negative stereotypes pertaining to religion, instead affirming its peace-building role in the wider community:

> non-religious society always felt that the problems of the world are because these religions can't get along, they don't see eye to eye and they are always fighting and causing these wars. What the religious communities can now demonstrate is, look, we are friends, we can live together, we agree to disagree and we can do things together...so that's another benefit where wider society can begin to regard religion as an asset rather than a liability, where they see the positive contributions of religious communities to society as a whole and I think it will make life for religious people easier and better, because we become part and parcel, an accepted component of society.   [Mogra 2007, UK]

And Rachel Woodlock, a Researcher for the Centre for Islam and the Modern World at Monash University, likewise remarked:

> when you are told that religion is the cause of problems in the world...it gives you a sense of satisfaction that you're doing something different, that this isn't true for you and your

experiences, that your religious practice is not about violence it's about peace-building and about connecting with other human beings.   [Woodlock 2008, AUS]

These actor perspectives reveal that interfaith initiatives can dispel misconceptions and fears, and act as peace-building strategies following crisis events by assisting in normalizing and humanizing the so-called 'other'. In the wake of September 11, as 'othering' shifted to Muslim communities, interfaith initiatives provided opportunities not only to develop a greater understanding of Islam and Muslims but also to show that the majority of Muslims condemned these violent attacks. The interfaith movement demonstrated that different religions were capable of uniting for peace, thereby challenging the prevalent view propagated in the popular media at that time that religions—and Islam in particular—were exclusively sources of violence. Consequently, the interfaith movement enabled a greater understanding of the peace-building potential of religion in the ultramodern public sphere.

Several participants in the Netpeace study also explained that for interfaith engagement to be truly effective at the local and global level it needs to be embodied in role models, in personal stories, and real relationships, as illustrated by Umar Faruq Abd-Allah, Chairman of the Board and Scholar-in-Residence of the Nawawi Foundation:

> I'm a person who, by nature, loves ideas and books and history and all sorts of abstractions…[however] human beings don't understand that well. What they do understand is other human beings and that for ideas to be meaningful, they must have human voices, they must have human faces and the Civil Rights Movement…that becomes meaningful when it's personified by Dr Martin Luther King, with his persona, his voice, his face, his courage, and so that is something that I got from interfaith. I got that from Eboo Patel…   [Abd-Allah 2007, USA]

Similarly, Nurah Amatullah, Executive Director of the Muslim Women's Institute for Research and Development, described how real relationships between individuals from diverse traditions provide the best foundations for interfaith collaboration:

> it is evident in the state of religion and the academy and its relationships with government and other actors [which] has meaning and validity in relationships like ours. So, if not our faiths, our individual faiths, you [Anna Halafoff] being Buddhist, me being Muslim and the teachings of those traditions to respect each other, to hold human life sacred, to be courteous, to be hospitable. If individually we did not hold those values and practise them, and therefore cultivate a relationship in the practice of those teachings, we would not have a relationship, and we have a relationship that I value, so it is in these types of exchanges that the beauty of those things, of those teachings really become manifest and that is what counts. It's not a theological debate about texts…it's how we understand our traditions, how we practise them and how they inform our engagement [with] the other.   [Amatullah 2007, USA]

Knitter, in a similar vein, remarked that

> The best way, maybe the only way, [is] to break down some of our deeply rooted…prejudices…of superiority and exclusivity that we have inherited in our religious

traditions... [and] the best way to start questioning that is through friendships with people from other religions. When a human being enters into a relationship...genuinely caring for another human being, and respecting another human being, and then realising that that other human being follows a totally different religious path; that is one of the most effective ways for self-reflection. And...we see the evils that can come out of religion in terms of violence, but that being the occasion for greater cooperation. [As a result of this] greater cooperation...friendships are developing. And once those friendships come, I think there's ever-greater hope that there can be real openness, genuine, genuine collaboration, genuine respect and affirmation of each other.   [Knitter 2007, USA]

These actor perspectives demonstrate that interfaith engagement is most effective when it is embodied, whether in role models, in personal stories, or in real relationships and friendships. In fact, it is these friendships that hold the interfaith movement together. Many Netpeace participants also described how interfaith initiatives concurrently affirm common values across faith traditions and respect for diversity. They recounted how interfaith initiatives provide opportunities to discover commonalities among diverse faiths, which in turn affirms the highest human qualities and values. According to Ibrahim Abdil-Mu'id Ramey, Director of the Human and Civil Rights Division at the Muslim American Society Freedom Foundation in the USA, religion acts as a 'container of values' as religions provide 'universal understandings' of non-violence, justice, and guidance on how best to conduct human relationships and economic transactions to avoid doing harm to others [Ramey 2007, US]. Amatullah similarly described how religious traditions can affirm the highest of human ideals and also the 'sanctity and sacredness' of all life [Amatullah 2007, US]. And Landau also explained how 'each faith is at its highest when it reticulates back to a sense of shared humanity...and planet' [Landau 2008, AUS]. As Ramey argued, 'the best practices of religions certainly have a role to play in shaping human events and moving human events forward' by affirming common values, in particular respect for all life' [Ramey 2007, US].

Netpeace participants explained how self-reflexive religious processes of striving for personal improvement can lead to the questioning of societal norms, especially materialist values, and thereby provide the impetus to find more equitable and sustainable means of developing personal and collective happiness. They also confirmed the arguments of religious peace-builders that religious actors must question what is wrong with contemporary society, including their own traditions, and seek religious means to remedy these situations. Toh Swee-Hin, Director of the Multi-Faith Centre at Griffith University in Queensland, Australia, described how interfaith engagement, by reflexively challenging cultures of violence, both direct and structural, can enable faith leaders to reform their respective traditions:

The eternal challenge...is that faith communities have to also engage in intra-faith dialogue, so when it comes to human rights...there may be doctrines or institutional practices over centuries that...are clear violations of human rights of particular groups, sectors, women, children, different sexual orientations, and that's a challenge for all faith communities but...we are seeing more openness in faith communities to do it...So interfaith dialogues will hopefully help us raise some of those difficult issues of internal transformation.

[Toh 2008, AUS]

As Charles Gibbs, the Executive Director of the United Religions Initiative, remarked, we are 'seeing a drama for the future of humanity being played out', with the question therefore: will we 'go the way of fear and hatred and division, violence and destruction, or will we find a different way?' [Gibbs 2007, USA]. He also suggested that 'the best of the interfaith movement is shining a light on a different way, a way [in which] we can invest in cultivating the technologies of peace and mutual understanding and respect', drawing on spiritual and religious traditions as resources. Further, he noted that while humanity has expended an enormous amount of effort on perfecting the ability to be violent, we have invested comparatively little in perfecting the ability to be peaceful. Despite the fact that the negative aspects of religion have dominated the media since 11 September 2001, the interfaith movement has continued to grow and to seek collaborative solutions to global crises.

Similarly, Sylvie Shaw, a Lecturer in Religion and Spirituality Studies at the University of Queensland, Australia, compared the steady growth of peace-building movements, including the interfaith movement, to 'an underground river':

When you go to Central Australia, you'll see the white ghost gums, and they're growing, they're quite flourishing, but it's completely dry on the surface. So underneath, the roots are down there, they're tapping into the water that's allowing the growth of the desert to bloom. But occasionally, when it rains, there's an inundation and overflow, and that allows the Berlin Wall to fall down, or Apartheid...or a big demonstration to happen, and then it goes back and continues to bubble on...the underground movement that's there, that bubbles up every now and again in Seattle or Genoa, in multifaith and interfaith. It's not on the surface, but it's such an important development, and there are so many people involved, that it can shift, and so the interfaith can meet with the environment [movement] can meet with the social justice [movement] and we can turn things around.   [Shaw 2007, AUS]

CONCLUSION

This chapter has focused on the interfaith movement's capacity to transform conflicts into peace-building opportunities. While secularization theory predicted the demise of religion, instead religious actors have increasingly played a prominent role in the ultramodern public sphere, most notably as critics of the spread of global capitalism. Processes of capitalist globalization not only threatened traditional ways of life, but also alerted humanity to the interconnectedness of global problems and their solutions. In response to the threats posed by global capitalism, religious movements, including the interfaith movement, arose alongside other peace-building social movements of this period in defence of the life-world and its citizens to advance common human and environmental security.

However, by the mid 1990s, the optimistic moment created by the end of the cold war and the plethora of social movements that sought more inclusive, non-violent, multilateral forms of governance was replaced by a regressive decade characterized by the rise of conservative governments and fundamentalist religious movements that routinely employed direct and structural violence in order to impose their regimes upon citizens. The environmental movement and women's movement were all but silenced during this period. However, the peace movement and the interfaith movement gathered strength and momentum, especially following September 11 and the wars in Afghanistan and Iraq. As religion frequently played a central role in the public sphere in discourse around these conflicts, religious peace-builders united in interfaith activities to develop greater understanding of diverse communities and the underlying causes of these tensions. According to peace-building principles, religious actors from diverse traditions acted as both critics *and* partners of state actors, advising on policies to counter the underlying causes of terrorism and to build more genuinely inclusive and peaceful societies.

It follows that despite, *and also* as a result of, religions' capacity to incite both structural and direct violence, religions have played a peace-building role in ultramodern societies, as evidenced by the increase in interfaith encounters at the turn of the twenty-first century. While the peace-building capacity of religion is often overlooked within academic discourses, the findings of the Netpeace study demonstrate that interfaith initiatives have been implemented to collaboratively counter global risks and advance common security in increasingly religiously diverse societies. Understanding interreligious relations involves an appreciation not only of religion's role in conflict but also its role in conflict transformation.

FURTHER READING

R. Scott Appleby, *The Ambivalence of the Sacred: Religion, Violence, and Reconciliation* (Lanham, Md.: Rowman & Littlefield, 2003).

James A. Beckford, *Social Theory and Religion* (Cambridge: Cambridge University Press, 2003).

——— and John Wallis (eds), *Theorising Religion: Classical and Contemporary Debates* (Aldershot: Ashgate, 2006).

Marcus Braybrooke, *Pilgrimage of Hope: One Hundred Years of Global Interfaith Dialogue* (London: SCM Press, 1992).

José Casanova, *Public Religions in the Modern World* (Chicago: University of Chicago Press, 1994).

Harold Coward and Gordon S. Smith (eds), *Religion and Peacebuilding* (Albany, NY: State University of New York Press, 2004).

Diana Eck, *A New Religious America: How a 'Christian Country' has Become the World's Most Religiously Diverse Nation* (New York: HarperOne, 2001).

Douglas Johnston and Cynthia Sampson (eds), *Religion, the Missing Dimension of Statecraft* (Oxford: Oxford University Press, 1994).

Mark Juergensmeyer, *Terror in the Mind of God: The Global Rise of Religious Violence*, 3rd edn (Berkeley, Calif.: University of California Press, 2003).

Perry Schmidt-Leukel (ed.), *War and Peace in World Religions* (London: SCM Press, 2004).

CHAPTER 13

Interreligious Engagement in the Public Sphere

NICHOLAS ADAMS

This chapter addresses eight challenges that face interreligious engagement in the public sphere. Its aim is to assess a series of contradictions that emerge from the contributions of a range of well-known recent writers on the role of religion in the public sphere, including John Neuhaus, John Rawls, Jürgen Habermas, Robert Audi, Nicholas Wolterstorff, and Diana Eck. These figures have attracted much commentary in recent years. What distinguishes this account is its focus on the implications for interreligious engagement that their thinking raises. My account faces the difficulties and questions posed by considering questions of ethics and politics, and identifies a number of practical tasks that need to be discharged in the academy if these questions are to be pursued fruitfully; it names the challenges of naming and categorization of the themes and issues that might be investigated in relation to the public square; it considers questions of how procedural and substantive issues are to be framed; it considers the relation between learning about religious life and the practical action that is required in the public sphere; it questions the received wisdom that supposes that the goal of public engagement is to maximize agreement between parties; finally it examines the tension between a conception of service by a particular religious tradition to wider society as it stands and a conception of transforming that wider society and conforming it to the vision of a particular religious tradition; the last section returns to the question of local particularities. The overall task of this chapter is to name the obstacles to thinking clearly about this topic, rather than to answer those questions in a premature way.

A TRANS-ATLANTIC DEBATE

The first challenge relates to the extensive and growing bibliography on the role of religious life in the public sphere, or 'public square', and the difference between the European and

American approaches to the subject. As soon as the discussion gets started, we are faced with the two geometrical shapes—spheres and squares. Jürgen Habermas's influential *The Structural Transformation of the Public Sphere* characterized the public sphere as a place of free public enquiry and formation of opinion.[1] His account has two notable features: it is bourgeois; and it is discursive rather than executive. Richard John Neuhaus's influential *The Naked Public Square* characterized the public square as the arena of American democratic debate.[2] Unlike Habermas's account it is not restricted to the bourgeois classes, and it includes both discursive and executive bodies. This preliminary attempt to sort out spheres and squares is not so neat, however. Talk of spheres tends towards a more European context of discussion, whereas talk of squares often identifies an American geographical and political focus. Spheres may sound more informal, non-institutional, and somewhat abstract, where squares may evoke physical civic space and even a certain concrete pageantry and performance, but in practice—in the literature—these terms bleed freely into one another. Habermas's investigations into the public sphere in the late 1950s were motivated by a sense that discursive spaces were under threat in late modernity; his *Habilitationsschrift* was directed quite consciously against Carl Schmitt's mocking of democracy, in the early twentieth century, as 'endless conversation' (itself an image drawn from Friedrich Schlegel in the early nineteenth century). Habermas sought to marry historical inquiry into the forms of bourgeois formation of opinion (especially in coffee houses and through newspapers) with a retrieval of viable models for social and political discussion in a post-war Europe. He desired to retrieve conversation as a core theoretical category, and to place his proposals on a secure historical footing. Religion plays a rather minor role in this narrative.

Neuhaus's considerations of the public square arose under quite different conditions in a different country (the USA) and in a different time (the early 1980s). It was focused on questions of what he called 'religious politics and political religion', and the rise of Jerry Falwell and the increasing influence of the Moral Majority in American public political discourse. His book tried to make sense of the peculiarly American constitutional separation of church and state in a context where traditional Lutheran voices like his own were increasingly squeezed out between an aggressive opposition between secular humanists and militant evangelical Christians. This was a situation further complicated by the fact that the aggression of the secular humanists might have been a rhetorical invention of the Christians: describing the American situation was itself a contested matter, for Neuhaus. The 'naked public square' described, for Neuhaus, a forum of public discussion where religion was forbidden to play a meaningful part. His book argued strongly against such a state of affairs.

We can already see two problems emerging for any informed discussion of interreligious engagement in the public sphere. The first is the difference between the European and

---

[1] Jürgen Habermas, *The Structural Transformation of the Public Sphere: An Inquiry into a Category of Bourgeois Society* (Cambridge, Mass.: MIT, 1989).

[2] Richard John Neuhaus, *The Naked Public Square: Religion and Democracy in America* (Grand Rapids, Mich.: Eerdmans, 1984).

American contexts. The European discussion kick-started by Habermas covers a wide sweep of history extending back to the seventeenth century and tries to make sense of a series of transformations extending into roughly the middle of the twentieth. The American debate joined by Neuhaus invokes the eighteenth-century American Constitution, to be sure, but its primary focus is the corrosive (for Neuhaus) effects of the Moral Majority on religious participation in political life. It is difficult to know how (or if) the European discussion can answer American questions, or how (or if) the American discussion is relevant to European problems. The second problem is the question of religious life itself. For the European context, in Habermas's work, the primary categories are 'the political' and 'the discursive', with a significant emphasis on European history. In the American context, in Neuhaus's account, the primary categories are 'religious politics' and 'political religion', with much less of an emphasis on history *per se*. Thomas Howard's recent *God and the Atlantic* has begun the work of sorting through these complexities, in a sophisticated and persuasive fashion, but this kind of question is often placed to one side in considerations of religious engagement in public life.[3] It must be placed centre-stage at the start.

CATEGORIES OF ENGAGEMENT

A second challenge emerges as one investigates in more detail the questions posed by scholars in the USA as they consider questions of religious engagement in the public square. Such scholarship is in nearly every case motivated by a problem of some kind—a problem in American culture that calls for study, in the first place, and, second, a response in the light of that study. It turns out, however, that there is no single problem addressed in various ways, but various perceived problems which are approached in a strikingly uniform fashion. To display this interesting feature, it is a worthwhile exercise to show how studies of religious engagement in the public sphere frame their material, and how they describe the problems they seek to confront. The categories in use for describing religious engagement in public are locally particular and are not readily applicable to new contexts. It is not obviously possible that more widely applicable categories of analysis can plausibly be generated. The question of interreligious engagement in the public sphere or square has become more urgent since the attacks on the World Trade Center in New York in 2001. The single most significant development since then has been a concern to understand Islam, both in its Middle Eastern context and in its diaspora forms in North America and Europe. A concern with terrorism has led to a distorting dual focus on Arabic-speaking Islam (which is in fact a numeric minority in Islam worldwide) and on English-speaking Islam (which is generally a tiny minority in countries with a Christian majority, despite its prominence in the media). There is much less study of

[3] Thomas Howard, *God and the Atlantic: America, Europe and the Religious Divide* (Oxford: Oxford University Press, 2011).

South Asian Islam (Indonesia, India, Malaysia, Pakistan, Singapore, Bangladesh) or the indigenous Islam that borders on Europe (Morocco, Tunisia, and Turkey). However, interest in religious engagement in the public sphere, and indeed the literature that shapes the scholarly imagination on these questions, predates 2001. We can look briefly at four pre-2001 studies which set the agenda for much of the scholarship which follows, and display the frameworks within which their work is conducted.

Neuhaus's 1984 *The Naked Public Square* identifies the rise of the moral majority, and its domination of religious public discourse, as the most immediate problem. This provoked a strong reaction from both liberal Christians (among whom Neuhaus counts himself) and 'militant secularists'. These two groups now make common cause against the Christian right. Such an unlikely coalition, Neuhaus suggests, is a creation of the moral majority itself: without the strident rhetoric of Jerry Falwell and others, such an alliance between natural opponents would not have come about. Neuhaus poses the issue as one of patriotism and a desire to do justice to the distinctive benefits of American political and religious life: 'The American experiment is today being rudely tried by militants both rude and respectable who are busily creating the enemy they claim to fear'.[4] That enemy is what the militant fundamentalists call 'a conspiracy against religion'. Neuhaus suggests that the coalition between liberal Christians and militant secularists is wrong-headed—disastrously so—in its attempt to create a 'naked public square' in which questions of religion are divorced from (and kept away from) practices of public deliberation. He invokes Martin Luther King Jr. and Jerry Falwell as figures who, alike, rightly (in his view) advocate the close bond between religious belief and public virtue.[5] But he sees a much more dangerous alliance between the militant religious right and the militant secularists: they are both undermining the legitimacy of religious public political identity, and they are being unwittingly aided by liberal Christians. The challenge Neuhaus articulates is for those who form the large majority of Christians in the USA (namely those who are not part of the Protestant mainline, which is a numerical minority, despite its prominence in the media) to promote forms of public virtue that are rooted in religious identity, and to refuse a separation of church and state that threatens such a vision:

> The public square is not a secular and morally sterilized space but a space for conversation, contention, and compromise among moral actors. Compromise is not mere fudging, then. It is not morally compromising. Within a universe compromised by fallen humanity, compromise is an exercise of moral responsibility by persons who accept responsibility for sustaining the exercise that is called democracy.[6]

This rhetoric nicely encapsulates Neuhaus's principal theological and social concerns. The moral majority too closely identifies Christianity, America, and civilization in such a way as to insist that to pursue one simply is to pursue the other two. Neuhaus takes the view

---

[4] Neuhaus, *Naked Public Square*, 188.   [5] Neuhaus, *Naked Public Square*, 78ff.
[6] Neuhaus, *Naked Public Square*, 128.

(drawing on H. Richard Niebuhr) that this is a case of Christ being identified with culture. What is needed, he claims, is a new vision of 'the church militant' in which Christianity is in the service of culture, but through a commitment to Christ's power to transform it, not by accommodating church life to American culture.[7] In summary, Neuhaus sees the problem as a false opposition of church and state. This opposition is consciously promoted by militant secularists. Right relations between church and state are undermined by the actions of this militant religious right. The common good is threatened by the unwitting collusion of liberal Christians, who wrongly see a 'naked public square' as a solution to the problems caused by the religious right. The solution proposed by Neuhaus is a renewed commitment to a religiously informed public virtue.

The European situation in the late 1950s (Habermas) and the American context of the early 1980s (Neuhaus) is not ours in the twenty-first century. Questions of religious life and public debate are moreover not confined to Europe and the USA. Every country in the world faces locally particular questions about the relation of religious life to public debate, and quite different pictures emerge if one travels to China, Egypt, India, Indonesia, Pakistan, Russia, Saint Lucia, Saudi Arabia, Singapore, South Africa, and Sweden (and nearly everywhere else). There is no single history, and thus no single set of philosophical and political categories, that can describe or transform these different contexts of political life. This plurality of local particularities is made ever more complex by continual intellectual exchange between them. It is likely that those debating questions of interreligious engagement in the public sphere in St Petersburg or São Paulo have read Habermas and Neuhaus. Categories travel: those forged in one context are adapted in another, often without much thought about the differences between such contexts. Geographical particularities are of course accompanied by religious particularities. Countries like the USA or Russia, with strong Christian majorities (although with quite distinct kinds of Christianity, with distinct histories) are quite different from countries like Egypt or Iran, which have strong Muslim majorities (with distinct denominations with different histories). It is only through attention to local particularities that terms like 'public sphere', which has a Christian origin, can be made applicable in Muslim-majority countries.[8]

POLITICS AND RELIGIOUS CONVICTION

A third challenge arises when we turn to a series of debates that correlate politics and religious conviction by way of the 'liberal' arguments of Robert Audi, on the one hand, and the

---

[7] Neuhaus, *Naked Public Square*, 225.

[8] See Dale Eickelman and Armando Salvatore, 'The Public Sphere and Muslim Identities', *European Journal of Sociology*, 43/1 (2002), 92–115; Dale Eickelman and Jon Anderson, *New Media in the Muslim World: The Emerging Public Sphere* (Bloomington, Ind.: Indiana University Press, 2003); Armando Salvatore, *The Public Sphere: Liberal Modernity, Catholicism, Islam* (London: Palgrave Macmillan, 2007).

'theologically oriented' arguments of Nicholas Wolterstorff which present challenges to the separation of church and state in the USA, especially as this is displayed in changes in political action and legal judgement, on the other.[9] Audi offers a defence of a certain conception of a 'neutral' state in which religion and politics are kept separate at institutional and individual levels. His arguments are self-consciously rational and appeal to common sense: he limits his arguments to those that in his view any reasonable person would accept. Wolterstorff presents arguments on behalf of an 'impartial' state in which religion and politics are intertwined, but in which the state does not favour any particular religious tradition.[10] Wolterstorff's arguments start with a consideration of history, rather than a statement of rational principles, and he acknowledges a geographical limitation to the discussion: it must focus on the contemporary USA without overgeneralizing this case. He advances arguments that will be persuasive to any person who takes seriously such things as history, geography, and the particularities of education in a particular community.

Audi's arguments are reminiscent of late seventeenth-century philosophical arguments in which it is presupposed that trains of religious reasoning will, if correct, be perfectly harmonious with trains of what Audi calls 'secular' reasoning. In cases where such threads of reasoning contradict each other, the task is to discover which arguments are already largely settled. Where a novel strand of religious reasoning contradicts a well established moral insight, it should be supposed by the religious persons that there is some undiagnosed error in their religious thinking. Conversely, where a novel strand of moral reasoning contradicts a well established religious insight, such as an unambiguous scriptural injunction, that moral reasoning should be investigated for error.[11] In this account there is some vagueness in the relation of 'secular' to 'moral' arguments: they seem at times interchangeable. There is also a pressing need to identify the peculiar characteristics of 'religious' thinking, in order to differentiate it from 'secular' reasoning. Using the word 'religion' is notoriously difficult and some social anthropologists who have done fieldwork in Christian communities have even suggested that one can produce good accounts of Christian communities and their practices without using the word at all.[12] Audi is a philosopher (in the analytical tradition) and instead of fieldwork he proposes a system of classification in which religious traditions display a concern with 'five kinds of evidential grounds' that are not shared by secular traditions. These are scripture, the community's authority, tradition, religious experience, and natural theology.[13]

Audi's philosophical rationalism is displayed in his suggestion that while these five 'sources of religious obligation' are historically interdependent, they are logically independent, in the

---

[9] Robert Audi and Nicholas Wolterstorff, *Religion in the Public Square: The Place of Religious Convictions in Political Debate* (Lanham, Md.: Rowman & Littlefield, 1997).

[10] Audi offers an alternative contrast, namely between being 'neutral *toward* religion' and 'neutral *among* religions'; see Audi and Wolterstorff, *Religion in the Public Square*, 128.

[11] Audi, 'Liberal Democracy and Religion in Politics', in Audi and Wolterstorff, *Religion in the Public Square*, 21.

[12] Timothy Jenkins, *Religion in English Everyday Life: An Ethnographic Approach* (London: Berghahn, 1999).

[13] Audi, 'Liberal Democracy', 10.

sense that support for a particular obligation from one of these five sources does not 'entail' support from any of the other four.[14] This particular argument is important to Audi, because it makes it possible to consider cases where such sources contradict each other (producing relatively weak commitments to a particular obligation) or where a number of them agree with each other (producing relatively strong commitments). Like many such systems of classification, it is not clear what force this taxonomy has, and it is not obvious why it is to be preferred over rival systems of classification. Such a rival system of classification is offered by Neuhaus, for example: the distinctive marks of religious life for Neuhaus are the operation of particular categories such as grace, sin, repentance, idolatry, and so forth. One might say that Audi's identification of epistemological generalities does not sit easily with Neuhaus's identification of 'grammatical' particularities.[15] The acid test of any taxonomy of religious life is that it should be recognizable to religious persons and bear some relation to their native categories. Those who find this line of critique of Audi persuasive should note, however, that grammatical considerations come at a significant cost: it becomes much more difficult to offer generalizations. Audi's use of very general notions such as scripture and tradition offers the possibility of covering a wide range of phenomena. Categories such as grace and sin are obviously particular to a much narrower range of practices. Neuhaus's categories are not so much generally 'religious' as specifically 'Christian'. We will return to the question of generalization later.

Another deep question to pose to Audi concerns what one might call his 'system of reason'. Audi's arguments are driven by certain striking primary categories: these concern motivations, principles, considerations, obligations, judgements, and decisions. He organizes these into a system, with a logical hierarchy, whose purpose is to map and adjudicate the rationality (or lack of it) displayed in particular forms of judgement. Human action is framed by these categories, and then evaluated in a way that identifies more and less rational forms of reasoning. Like many such systems of reason, one does not notice what is missing from it unless one is familiar with rival frameworks, in which such phenomena as habits and passions (to take David Hume's favourite examples) play a central role. Similarly, Audi's locus of reasoning is individual more often than it is institutional; it favours freedom more often than it favours order; it privileges persuasion over coercion; it focuses on native common sense at the expense of acquired education, and so on. The deeper problem, however, is that it treats certain categories as mutually exclusive, and it assumes that this opposition is simply obvious. The most obvious exclusive pairs are religious/secular; religious/political; religious/moral; rationale/motivation; history/principle; and public/private. Were one to experiment with substituting hyphens for slashes, an alternative way of thinking would emerge that would not constitute a counter-argument, but a fundamentally different imagination.

Wolterstorff's arguments are evidence of just such a different imagination. Where Audi's arguments are organized rationally, Wolterstorff investigates histories; where Audi appeals to

---

[14] Audi, 'Liberal Democracy', 12.   [15] Cf. Nicholas Lash, *Easter in Ordinary* (London: SCM Press, 1988).

the necessities of logic, Wolterstorff appeals to the contingencies of education; where Audi sees (and emphasizes) binary oppositions, Wolterstorff sees distinct terms that are in relation to each other: he emphasizes both the distinctness and the relations. This has a profound effect on Wolterstorff's descriptions of such things as institutions, laws, and (most importantly) liberal democracy. For Audi these things are expressions of principles, of obligations, of (in a word) reason. For Wolterstorff, there are certainly such things as principles, obligations, and reasons, but the concrete entities one encounters, and in which one participates, in the world are not expressions in a system of reason, but are historical products that are subject to complex inter-relations of continuity and change. Wolterstorff's argument is rather simple: any history that one cares to rehearse will be overwhelmingly religious at its core, on any familiar meaning of the word 'religious'. Of course, it is commonplace for religious life to be written out of certain kinds of explanation which treat categories such as 'the economic' or 'the political' as if these were quite independent of religious life; but such editing out is manifestly ludicrous, he claims:

> The people in Leipzig assembled in a meeting space that just happened to be a church to listen to inspiring speeches that just happened to resemble sermons; they were led out into the streets to protest marches by leaders who just happened to be pastors. Black people in Capetown were led on protest marches from the black shanty-towns into the center of the city by men named Tutu and Boesak—who just happened to be bishop and pastor, respectively, and who just happened to use religious talk in their fiery speeches.[16]

Wolterstorff rejects any historically oriented account that fails to do justice to the religious dimension of that history. This leads him to investigate the particular historical developments displayed in the works of John Locke, and then the revised form that Locke's 'liberal position' takes in the more recent philosophy of John Rawls. Wolterstorff's repeated critique of the liberal position (which he sharply distinguishes from the ideal of liberal democracy, to which he is committed) is that it is insufficiently attentive to history, and—in its appeal to universal standards of common sense—insufficiently attentive to matters of education. The problem with Rawls, for Wolterstorff, is in part Rawls's tacit assumption (inherited—historically!— from the Enlightenment) that rationality is hard-wired. Against this, Wolterstorff insists that rationality is learned.[17]

It is also striking that where Audi produces a system of classification in which to evaluate the judgements of religious and secular persons, Wolterstorff more often interprets texts, citing a substantial paragraph on which he offers commentary. Taken alongside the observation that where Audi offers a system of reason, Wolterstorff offers a historical narrative, one can see two quite distinct ways of thinking in operation. The reader of this debate is thus in an

---

[16] Wolterstorff, 'The Role of Religion in Political Issues', in Audi and Wolterstorff, *Religion in the Public Square*, 81.

[17] Wolterstorff, 'Role of Religion', 98.

interesting position: it is not only the arguments that invite evaluation and comparison; it is the entire intellectual shape of their forms of thought that needs to be considered. Nowhere is this more evident than in Audi's consideration of how a commitment to freedom of speech plays out when people must decide whether to permit a Nazi group (in Audi's words) to 'present its case'. For Audi this is a question of principle (freedom of speech) and of paranoia (fear of Nazis), and it is for him rationally decidable, so long as all parties agree to be 'rational civilized people'.[18] There is no sense at all that the history of Nazism—a history of which reasoners are part—might play a role in one's judgements. I have drawn particular attention to issues of framing rather than particular arguments for two reasons. First, Audi and Wolterstorff do not show that they have noticed how differently each other thinks. In their essays on each other's initial statements, they engage principally (indeed almost solely) with each other's arguments rather than the shape of each other's intellectual projects. Second, the arguments go nowhere: there are no significant concessions on either side, at the level of argument, but only claim and counter-claim. In their second round of essays they show quite clearly that they understand each other yet remain almost entirely unmoved by each other's arguments on the most important points. This does not appear to be a debate where views are changed.

I suspect that views on these issues are unlikely to be changed so long as such different intellectual frameworks are juxtaposed seemingly without either side noticing. A consideration of Neuhaus's *The Naked Public Square* and the gentlemen's debate in Audi and Wolterstorff's *Religion in the Public Square* reveals a dimension of the literature that needs to be confronted in any attempt to make sense of interreligious engagement in the public sphere: it is often concerned with debates between Christians and secularists, and is driven by the categories that these debates generate.

INTERFAITH ENGAGEMENT

A fourth challenge concerns the lack of fieldwork on interfaith engagement, in a range of countries, which makes generalization difficult. Claims about interfaith engagement are constantly in danger of overgeneralization. Two edited collections of essays, produced almost simultaneously, with almost identical titles taken from a clause in the American Pledge of Allegiance, which is often made each day in America's schools raise significant issues in this regard.[19] The pledge, which reads: 'I pledge allegiance to the flag of the United States of America, and to the republic for which it stands, one nation under God, indivisible, with

---

[18] Audi, 'Wolterstorff on Religion and Politics', in Audi and Wolterstorff, *Religion in the Public Square*, 132–3.
[19] Marjorie Garber and Rebecca Walkowitz (eds), *One Nation Under God? Religion and American Culture* (London: Routledge, 1999); R. Bruce Douglass and Joshua Mitchell (eds), *A Nation Under God? Essays on the Fate of Religion in American Public Life* (Lanham, Md.: Rowman & Littlefield, 2000).

liberty and justice for all', was composed in 1892 and adopted by Congress in 1942 with the phrase 'under God' only officially added when Eisenhower signed it into law in 1954.

Both books place this added phrase in question, in two different attempts to make sense of the relation between religious self-understandings and American identity. Garber and Walkowitz do not offer a strong organizing principle for their volume, but arrange matters in a loose fashion under four subheadings: civility, law, practice, and conversion. The opening essay by Diana Eck concerns itself with the variety of religious life in America, and with two accompanying phenomena, each of which calls for analysis. The first is what Eck calls 'the controversies of the American public square', which in 1999 were apparently only just beginning.[20] The second is the failure by the academy to take religious life sufficiently seriously, and to make proper use of religious categories, in social analysis of American culture. The latter is a common complaint by scholars of religion in nearly every field: in the face of intense and persistent religious everyday life, in every country, it remains the case that attentiveness to that religious life remains a specialized subject, 'religious studies', rather than a dimension that pervades economic, political, sociological, philosophical, and ethical investigation. Eck herself names the problem as a tendency to treat religious life as 'a bounded set of ideas, institutions, and practices'; religious traditions are, she says, 'more like long historical arguments reconfigured around the issues of each generation than like dogmas passed along in a box from one generation to the next'.[21]

Eck, like Wolterstorff, frames her analysis against a backdrop of historical change, rather than fixed analytical categories. She notes that non-Christian religious traditions in the 1970s in America were not visible—especially architecturally—in the same way that Christianity was hewn into the urban landscape in cathedrals and churches. Changes in that urban landscape, with the building of new temples, mosques, and Gurdawara (Eck does not consider the visibility of Judaism in this context—perhaps because it is more focused on the home), are partial triggers for the controversies that attend a renegotiation of the public square and the place of religion within it. Eck notes that there are challenges to researching salient features of American life relating to the changing public square. One of the most striking is the fact that acts of violence (such as the numerous acts of arson against non-Christian religious buildings in the USA) attract press coverage and leave an imprint in local judicial proceedings. Violence is much easier to find (and, over the few years between Eck's essay and this one, especially much easier to find on the internet). By contrast the many stories of accommodation, transformation, understanding, and cooperation remain generally invisible and inaudible, because they leave little or no record. The available evidence (if one means newspaper articles, court cases, warrants for arrest) suggests that the religious public square is awash with violence and little else. The two arguably most memorable public square stories of 2010 in the USA, for example, were the so-called 'Ground Zero Mosque', and the Dove

---

[20] Diana Eck, 'The Multireligious Public Square', in Garber and Walkowitz, *One Nation*, 4.
[21] Eck, 'Multireligious Public Square', 5.

World Qur'an-burning controversy. Stories of peaceful life together do not attract the same attention yet these are, Eck persuasively argues, a much better indicator of what the future holds.[22]

There is also an important distinction to be made between discrete events with a determinate cause, such as an act of violence, a request for planning permission, or a court case involving religious actions in public schools, and events that follow a religious calendar, such as festivals, fasts, and New Year's celebrations. Eck's analysis suggests that calendrical events offer a rich resource for charting transformations of the public square: they take place repeatedly, and one can discern changes between one year and the next, especially in cases where there is a marked rise in visibility, or where a state official from one religious tradition publicly acknowledges a festival from another.[23] It is possible to develop this insight and suggest that a focus on high-profile one-off events may distort one's perception of the state of interreligious encounters in the public sphere, whereas attention to festivals and other events repeated in the yearly cycle may provide a more reliable everyday sense of how things lie. As before, in the case of the comparison of Audi and Neuhaus on the question of how one describes religious traditions, such an approach will not yield widely generalizable results: attentiveness to questions of interreligious engagement in religious festivals will be locally particular, and will not readily yield insight into matters beyond the specific geographical context in view. It would appear that the Pluralism Project directed by Eck, which forms the basis for many of Eck's insights, has been successful precisely because it gathers together locally particular cases, rather than trying to generalize about 'America' or 'religion' too hastily.

The other essays in this collection describe various aspects of American culture in ways that draw attention to its religious and interreligious dimensions: it represents a useful snapshot of the state of affairs before September 2001. There is, for example, an essay on 'Islamic Law and Muslim Women in America' by Azizah al-Hibri, which presents a fascinating account of the public voices of American Muslim women, especially scholars, and the repudiation of Western secular feminism by them that is necessary if their work is to be credible to Muslims outside North America.[24] This essay is also important because it presents an account of Islam, by a Muslim, in a bibliography that at that time was overwhelmingly represented by Catholic, Protestant, and Jewish voices.

This representation can be seen in the other volume with almost the same title, published a year later, edited by R. Bruce Douglass and Joshua Mitchell. Where the Garber and Walkowitz book has an emphasis on minorities, with a special sensitivity towards women's public voices in American religion, Douglass and Mitchell explore more traditional theological and political questions, largely within mainstream Catholic and Protestant perspectives, with two essays (one on covenant, one on Jewish contributions to the public square)

---

[22] Eck, 'Multireligious Public Square', 11. [23] Eck, 'Multireligious Public Square', 15.
[24] Azizah al-Hibri, 'Islamic Law and Muslim Women in America', in Garber and Walkowitz, *One Nation*, 128–43.

by Jewish scholars. The Douglass and Mitchell volume explores classic themes within the frame of the role of religion in American public discourse, such as reason and revelation, the enduring influence of the Enlightenment (and its belief in the waning of religious life), questions of religious meaning as an important qualification (and transformation) of the bare freedom made possible by democracy, the power of the state over marriage, the increasing prominence of Catholic voices in the political sphere, the role of the university in public debate, the tendency of some churches to conform to the world (or at least to 'America'), the challenge of Christian anthropology to liberal conceptions of human beings as 'free standing, self-possessing, self-defining, self-naming creatures',[25] questions of same-sex marriage, and—finally—on the significance of doubt and hesitation for religious persons acting in the public square.

The volume as a whole is a useful compendium of then-current debate within the mainstream churches of America about the relation of doctrine to political speech, and the challenges that face religious and non-religious folk as they try to engage each other in mature political debate. It is especially significant as a public utterance by a group who are arguably increasingly inaudible: those Christians who are the numerical majority, who take the teachings of the long tradition seriously, and whose views are not readily assimilable to strident fundamentalist Biblicism and which are ignored by the 'new atheism' of our own time. The book's principal failure, from the point of view of this chapter, is the reluctance by its contributing authors to consider in any detail the practical question of how Christians (and perhaps Jews) engage with Muslims, Sikhs, Hindus, and others in the public square. The dominant picture is of a struggle between the long Christian tradition and the Enlightenment, marked by a series of attempts to rescue America from its Enlightenment (and thus secularizing) inheritance. This picture is, however, complicated by the inclusion of Jewish voices. Elliott Dorff, in his essay on Jewish voices in the public square, reminds the reader that the late eighteenth century was not a period of catastrophe for Jews, in the way that it is sometimes portrayed by some Christians as disastrous for Christian theology:

> The Enlightenment was a breath of fresh air for Jews. For the first time since the time of the Maccabees, they were to be accepted as full citizens, eligible for voting, university education, government service, residence anywhere in the realm, and equal treatment in the courts. This was, indeed, a new world.[26]

Other Jewish thinkers would doubtless disagree; Dorff himself acknowledges that he grew up in the 1950s and 1960s when Jewish leaders were loudly supportive of a thick wall between church and state.[27] Yet he has also changed his mind, he says, about what the separation of church and state should mean. Dorff suggests there are strong Jewish reasons to resist a naked

---

[25] Jean Bethke Elshtain, 'How Should We Talk?', in Douglass and Mitchell, *Nation Under God?*, 167.
[26] Elliott Dorff, 'The King's Torah', in Douglass and Mitchell, *Nation Under God?*, 204.
[27] Dorff, 'King's Torah', 218.

public square, and to support forms of public debate where religious identity and religious arguments play a full role.

In sum, these four books, published between 1984 and 2000, offer a useful display of the concerns of religious scholars in the academy, as they deliberate about the place of religious voices in the public square in America. It is a varied picture, comprising more conservative voices seeking to make sense of historical developments and the unavoidable changes that accompany them, and more experimental voices seeking to do justice to the multi-religious political and social landscape. It is worth noting in passing that Eck makes the excellent point that 'multi-religious' is a description of how things are, whereas the word 'pluralism' denotes a project. I follow her in this chapter in speaking of 'plural' rather than 'pluralist' societies.

These studies concern the American landscape, and because the American literature has such a strong influence on the shape of discussions about interreligious engagement in the public sphere beyond America's borders it has been worthwhile spending a little time becoming familiar with some of its details, although we have barely scratched the surface. What are often presented as the principal discussions of interreligious engagement in the public sphere are, in fact, locally particular; and concerned almost exclusively with what is actually a tiny minority of the world's population. There are important differences between North America and Europe, and between North and South. No single nexus of debates, no single set of categories, can hope to embrace the local particularities of Los Angeles, Bradford, Dhaka, and Hong Kong. It is true that universities in these four cities resemble each other, and this is because they are in various ways heirs of the new German universities of the early nineteenth century. Debates in universities are likely to bear family resemblances for this reason. But the everyday lives of their inhabitants are not like this, and the political structures within which questions of interreligious engagement in the public sphere are decided are often deeply dissimilar. Once one deals with contexts in which democracy is quite different (or even absent), where corruption is endemic, where power is concentrated in the hands of a few families, where the media are state-controlled, where high-quality education is not publicly provided, where courts are instruments of the ruling parties, and where Christian communities need to be protected by the state from Islamist violence, the nostrums of American debate melt into air.

THE MEANING OF 'RELIGION'

The meaning of 'religion' is vague and porous. This poses our fifth challenge. It is difficult to stabilize the term sufficiently to specify what count, or do not count, as 'religious' concerns. Furthermore, if the public sphere is taken to be the arena in which opinion is formed, and in which debates are held, and if we are concerned with interreligious encounters in that arena, it is worth reflecting on what areas of intellectual life are the focus of such opinion, and which themes are debated. I propose three broad possibilities for grouping such interreligious encounter. The first we might call 'religious' concerns. These include such things as freedom of religion, religious exceptions to general laws, religious accommodations within particular social settlements, and the limits of permissible practice in state-funded schools. The second we might call 'moral' concerns and they include such matters as abortion, medical research, euthanasia, animal rights, environmental ethics, same-sex marriage, and so forth. The third we might name 'comprehensive' concerns. Rather than denoting a particular field of questions that might be supposed to concern 'religious' people, this would insist that all human action, in its entirety, is properly the concern of religious life, and that economic and foreign policy are matters for religious deliberation just as vitally as the school curriculum of religious studies provided for pupils aged 12.

These three broad categories reflect a fairly intuitive division of kinds of issue, at least when considered in the context of legislation. The first is concerned with laws that affect a particular group. Are Muslim taxi-drivers permitted to refuse service to customers carrying alcohol? Are Christians entitled to wear crucifixes at work? Must Jewish abattoirs stun animals prior to slaughter? The second is concerned with laws that affect everyone, where particular traditions may have explicit doctrinal settlements relating to the issues concerned. Is it permissible to undertake stem-cell research? Should voluntary euthanasia be legalized? May same-sex couples be married and enjoy the same privileges as heterosexual married couples? The third is concerned with all laws, regardless of whether religious traditions have explicit doctrinal positions. Should capital gains tax be levied at the same rate as income tax? Should prisoners be entitled to vote? Should national corporations be permitted to export arms to countries with poor human rights records? It becomes obvious, and rather swiftly, that the way one treats issues of these kinds is a reflection on how narrow or broad one's conception of 'religion' is. It is possible to conceive of religious issues being constrained to issues that affect religious communities; or to have a broader conception of religious issues as those in which religious communities have a particular stake; or to have a maximally broad conception of religious issues as embracing any issues whatsoever, given that religion embraces all of life.

This, again, is too neat a classification. The issue of abortion might be considered to come under the second heading of 'moral' concerns, on the grounds that it is an issue that affects everyone, and is an issue on which the Roman Catholic Church, for example, has a particular clear doctrinal position. But it could also come under the first heading of 'religious' concerns, on the grounds that particular pieces of legislation particularly affect, and constrain, Roman Catholic institutions. Similarly, the issue of US foreign policy *vis-à-vis* Israel might come under the heading of 'religious' concerns, on the grounds that it affects Jewish communities in the USA, or it could be what I have called a 'comprehensive' concern, because it is a foreign policy issue that has no explicit religious dimension (at least from the point of view of some of those responsible for formulating such foreign policy). Two further examples might be the 'Make Poverty History' campaign of 2005, in which churches and other religious groups had a highly visible public presence, or—on a smaller scale—the 'Anti-Usury Campaign' in

London in 2009, in which Jewish, Christian, and Muslim community leaders came together to lobby for restrictions on the rate of interest that banks can charge, with a focus on unjust credit-card interest charges.[28] These puzzles—which we might call puzzles of scale—are multiplied when one considers the complex relationship of 'religious' action and the growing phenomenon of community organizing in Britain and the USA. All kinds of alliances are possible within the range of activities that might be counted as community organizing, some of them overtly religious in tone (like the anti-usury campaign in London) and some of them characterized by rhetoric that is much broader (such as community organizing involvement in the living wage campaign). There is a growing literature on community organizing, including critical studies of it, but as yet there is not a substantial body of study of the relation of religious identity and community organizing.[29] A consideration of the topics that might be addressed in a context of interreligious engagement in the public sphere turns out to require a certain unavailable clarity on what is meant by 'religion' in relation to action in the public sphere. It is possible to gain clarity on certain issues, but one must pay a price, such as ignoring highly complex (and under-researched) local phenomena such as community organizing.

PUBLIC SPHERE INTERRELIGIOUS ENGAGEMENT: PHILOSOPHICAL CONSIDERATIONS

Notwithstanding Chapter 17 below, and the recently concluded UK 'Religion and Society' project (2007–12), there is an overall lack of case studies and fieldwork in relation to wider contexts of Western urban religious life. Without them it is difficult to take generalizations about religious life seriously, and dangerous to make proposals for solving its problems. However, in this section we will consider the challenge of certain philosophical questions that relate to understanding interreligious engagement in the public sphere. The two most important figures here are Jürgen Habermas and John Rawls, whom we might characterize as explicitly 'liberal' voices in the public sphere. Although these two figures disagree with each other on a range of issues, they share a commitment to a recognizable style of inquiry which is a particular feature of Anglo-American philosophy: identifying principles which guide human action. This is a form of inquiry that was first practised systematically by Immanuel Kant, in the latter part of the eighteenth century. It rests on three beliefs: human action is guided by principles; these principles can be identified; they can be organized into a system of reason.

---

[28] <http://www.makepovertyhistory.org> and see: <http://www.guardian.co.uk/commentisfree/belief/2009/jul/22/debt-interest-religion-usury>. See also <http://www.citizensuk.org/> and <http://www.10percentisenough.org>.

[29] See e.g. James DeFilippis, Robert Fisher, and Eric Shragge, *Contesting Community: The Limits and Potential of Local Organizing* (Piscataway, NJ: Rutgers University Press, 2010); John Atlas, *Seeds of Change: The Story of ACORN, America's Most Controversial Antipoverty Community Organizing Group* (Nashville, Tenn.: Vanderbilt, 2010).

These are widely held beliefs among certain philosophers, and they are one way of organizing moral inquiry. Its most significant intellectual rival was established by David Hume and J. G. Herder, also in the eighteenth century, and developed significantly by G. W. F. Hegel in the early nineteenth century, who supposed (i) human action is guided by habits; (ii) these habits can be studied; (iii) limited generalizations can be made on the basis of such study. Whether one takes the Kantian route or the Hume/Herder path depends on what kind of philosopher one is, and how much fieldwork one is prepared to do. The Kantian route holds out the promise of a high degree of generalization, and has the disadvantage that its pronouncements may be somewhat imaginary and not borne out by the facts. The Hume/Herder path holds out the promise of amassing a vast number of case studies, and has the disadvantage that its insights cannot easily be generalized.

This way of classifying questions of method is intended to be more practically useful than distinguishing procedural from substantive approaches in ethics, which is the more common way to sort out some of the problems identified here. According to this way of thinking, there are forms of ethical reasoning focused on procedure, largely associated with Kant, and forms of ethical reasoning focused on conceptions of the good life, largely associated with Hegel (and going back to Aristotle's *Nicomachean Ethics*). Procedural approaches are said to focus on 'right' action; substantive approaches, by contrast, focus on 'the good'. Quite apart from the fact that this distinction now seems rather dated, and fails to take account of approaches that are indebted to both Kant and Hegel (rather than choosing between them), it fails to identify the more important difference: between approaches that overgeneralize on the basis of considering ideas, and approaches that generalize in a more limited way on the basis of cases, whether these are historical or fieldwork studies. I propose to distinguish between idealizing approaches, and fieldwork approaches. Rawls and Habermas are highly influential on contemporary thinking about the role of religion in the public sphere. Both are practitioners of idealizing approaches: they do not conduct or take much notice of the relevant historical or fieldwork studies, and they generalize not from sets of cases, but through the practice of considering others' ideas and evaluating their strengths and weaknesses. Rawls is important because he is one of the best-known philosophers to be concerned in a deep way with how social unity can be achieved in situations (like that of the USA) where there is a wide variety of institutional, cultural, and religious diversity. Rawls's most important conceptual bequests are the notions of 'overlapping consensus' and 'comprehensive doctrines'. The two terms are related.

The idea of a 'comprehensive doctrine' is a classic expression of Rawls's belief that human action is guided by principles. Rawls (like Kant) affirms the idea that there are 'reasonable citizens', who are persons who wish to live in a society where there is broad agreement on certain principles, which make common life possible in the face of social diversity. Reasonable citizens are not distinguished by their particular beliefs about what is good or bad, right or wrong, just or unjust, but by the fact that their particular beliefs form a coherent whole which guides their thought and action. This coherent whole is a 'comprehensive doctrine'. The scope of a 'comprehensive doctrine' is rather vague. In some contexts it might mean 'Christianity', in others 'Protestant', in still others 'Free Church of Scotland'. The important feature, in Rawls's account, is not how broad it is, or what it contains: it is the fact that there are different comprehensive doctrines in play. A modern society can be expected to include a variety of comprehensive doctrines, however they are defined, and thus a 'liberal' society cannot be guided by any single comprehensive doctrine. To take comprehensive doctrines seriously is to be concerned with the coexistence of different traditions. Rawls says much more than this, however: he proposes that a 'political' conception should be independent of a 'comprehensive doctrine', for it is what permits reasonable citizens, with different comprehensive doctrines, to agree to live together peaceably.

The idea of an 'overlapping consensus' is a way of addressing one of the most significant problems for approaches to ethics which are approached, as Rawls's is, through a system of ideas. It can be posed as a question: What motivates people to commit themselves to conceptions such as political liberalism, which are products of a system of ideas rather than historically transmitted and embodied? The notion of an overlapping consensus is intended to act as a kind of bridge between comprehensive doctrines and products of the system of reason. Rawls's idea is that there are areas of overlap between different comprehensive doctrines; that such areas of overlap can be identified; and that they can be articulated in such a way as to motivate rational citizens to cooperate. More informally, you and I may disagree on a range of things, and belong to strongly divergent traditions, but on *this* and *this*, our traditions agree; and we can use this as a basis for common liberal commitments. The basic idea is that we can agree on the same thing, but for different reasons. When applied to interreligious engagement in the public sphere, Rawls's ideas provide a framework that comes from none of the comprehensive doctrines represented, to which each tradition might nonetheless be committed, so long as there is sufficient overlapping consensus.

Habermas is important for two reasons. First, he attempts to identify 'universal' features of human reason in the face of divergent traditions; second, he has in recent years placed a concern with religious traditions more centrally in his theoretical work. The most important conception in his earlier work is the 'ideal speech situation'; in his later work it is that there can be 'translation' between the languages of particular traditions and more generally operative public discourse. We can take each of these briefly in turn. The 'ideal speech situation' is part of Habermas's lifelong project to produce a coherent body of philosophical reasoning between Kant and Hegel, by which Habermas means taking seriously Kant's attempts to identify transcendental conditions for cognition, and doing justice to Hegel's insight that all human action is historically specific. Habermas's earlier work is marked by a certain kind of formalism, and repeated attempts at precise definitions of terms. He tried out a number of formulations of the ideal speech situation, in various texts, and in his summary of it some years later he compresses it as follows:

1. Every subject with the competence to speak and act is allowed to take part in a discourse.

2a. Everyone is allowed to question any assertion whatever.

2b. Everyone is allowed to introduce any assertion whatever into the discourse.

2c. Everyone is allowed to express his attitudes, desires and needs.

3. No speaker may be prevented, by internal or external coercion, from exercising his rights as laid down in (1) and (2).[30]

The basic idea is that everyone can participate; everyone can question each other, make cognitive claims, and say how they feel; no one can bring coercion to bear. Habermas often speaks in the same context of the 'unforced force of the better argument'. The purpose of the ideal, in Habermas's work, is to formalize the conditions for dialogue, in a way that articulates a standard by which practice can be judged. Its significance for interfaith engagement is its influence on a range of (mostly Christian) thinkers interested in questions of religious dialogue. The idea of 'translation' between particular traditions and discourse in the public sphere is a much later development in Habermas's work and its significance is contested. The background to this claim is a shift in his work away from a belief that religious forms of thought will gradually be replaced by more rational forms, to a more sympathetic view that religious forms of thought continue to be indispensable to the modern imagination. This has led most commentators on Habermas to reassess his work, and to discern a new direction in which he is no longer a secularist.

Habermas, in his more recent work, holds the following views. Religious traditions are bearers of moral intuitions that would otherwise be absent in a culture. Religious traditions educate their members to be moral persons. They transmit strong motivations towards moral action that would otherwise be absent in a culture. Religious traditions advocate care for the vulnerable in society; they are the bearers of hopes that would otherwise be difficult to sustain. These views are quite close to those of Immanuel Kant's *Religion within the bounds of mere reason*, in that the focus is on the moral dimensions that are transmitted through religious life. Habermas also makes a strong distinction between rational claims and religious claims. A rational claim, for Habermas, is one that is in principle unreservedly open to question. This is an echo of one of the conditions (2a) of the ideal speech situation just cited. A religious claim, by contrast, is one which the religious community may be unwilling to open to question: it is held to be inviolable. This is a key distinction for Habermas, and amounts to an insistence that in rational argument any axiom can be converted into a hypothesis, whereas in religious argument certain axioms are protected.[31] Habermas here echoes views from Kant's *Conflict of the Faculties*, which assigns to theology the task of defending certain claims, and to philosophy the task of questioning them. A picture emerges from this way of viewing religious life. On the one

---

[30] Jürgen Habermas, *Moral Consciousness and Communicative Action* (Cambridge, Mass.: MIT, 1990), 86.
[31] Jürgen Habermas, *Between Naturalism and Religion* (Cambridge: Polity, 2008), 129.

hand, religious traditions carry important moral insights which would otherwise be attenuated; on the other hand, religious traditions block fully rational discussion of such insights: they become (in a striking phrase) 'discursively extraterritorial'.[32]

Against this background, Habermas makes his proposal about how religious claims are to be handled in the public sphere. He encapsulates his contribution as follows:

> Religious traditions have a special power to articulate moral intuitions, especially with regard to vulnerable forms of communal life. In corresponding political debates, this potential makes religious speech into a serious vehicle for possible truth contents, which can then be translated from the vocabulary of a particular religious community into a generally accessible language.[33]

Religious traditions have a language that is saturated with their own history, a language that makes sense for those that speak it. If its truth-claims (and Habermas is most interested in moral claims) are to become publicly available, they must be translated into a language that others can understand. In other words, the moral treasures of religious traditions can only become effective in the public sphere if they are exchanged for hard currency. To stick with the monetary metaphor, they need to be cashed. There are many problems with this view, of which two stand out. The first is that such a way of thinking supposes that religious language is just a shell for the kernel of non-religious truth within. The second is that it makes an artificial and over-emphatic separation between different kinds of language: the contemporary language of the public sphere is in strong historical continuity with the (Christian) religious languages that Habermas thinks need translating. He seems to confuse an insight into the relation between axioms and hypotheses (which is at least defensible) and a view of what languages are (which is much less defensible).

We can now take stock. Rawls's notion of 'comprehensive doctrines' comes quite close to Habermas's notion of 'religious languages' and Rawls's notion of 'overlapping consensus' seems to have something in common with Habermas's notion of 'translation'. They are by no means identical, but the basic thrust is discernible: if different traditions are to participate in the public sphere they need to do something other than just be themselves: they need to affirm the public sphere and be intelligible to each other within it. Rawls and Habermas share an insistence that areas of possible agreement need to be sifted out of those traditions, either as 'overlapping' or as 'translated' bits of tradition. However critical one is of Rawls and Habermas, they have clearly identified a problem, and they offer a solution. The problem is that the language of the public sphere cannot simply be the language of one single tradition. The public sphere comprises a variety of traditions and their languages. There need to be laws binding on all. There need to be political institutions which embrace all. There need to be schools where all can send their children. The solution they offer is that there should be a 'liberal' or 'rational' settlement of some kind. Both figures draw on Enlightenment

---

[32] Habermas, *Between Naturalism*, 129–30.   [33] Habermas, *Between Naturalism*, 131.

philosophy—supremely that of Kant—to frame their imaginations for what such a settlement should look like. Where the critique should fall is a contested matter. It is commonplace in philosophical discussions to find fault with the privileging of procedural over substantive issues. That is, Rawls and Habermas are often criticized for placing too much weight on how participants in discussion arrive at judgements, and too little weight on what those judgements actually are. It is commonplace in theological discussions to object to the privileging of the Enlightenment over the Renaissance or over high medieval intellectual achievements. That is, Rawls and Habermas are too indebted to a tradition which neglects memory, tradition, authority, and, above all, doctrine, in a way that falsely opposes faith and reason. It is less common to suggest that the fault lies in the tendency to overgeneralize and to pay too little attention to fieldwork and case studies. It is less common, because this criticism would apply just as strongly to many critics of Rawls and Habermas. Arguably it is what is needed, however. We need more studies of religious life that are attentive to local particularities, and which are hesitant about generalization.[34]

DIALOGUE AND DISAGREEMENT

The seventh challenge relates to the fact that it is not obvious that liberal models of dialogue provide the necessary framework for containing persistent disagreements. Furthermore, it is difficult to attract more conservative members of religious tradition into interreligious dialogue. Interestingly, one of the lessons of the ecumenical movement within Christianity is that, after half a century or more of intra-faith dialogue, there is almost no prospect of arriving at agreement and unity in the foreseeable future. This is not a lament, pessimistic grumble, or melancholy sigh. It is a simple statement of the facts. Ecumenical initiatives do not produce unity. But they do increase understanding, and in fact enable different denominations to discover from each other where their doctrinal, liturgical, and pastoral distinctivenesses lie. There is even a project, originating in the UK, devoted to exploring the significance of long-term disagreement for future ecumenical action.[35]

The ecumenical reality is a lesson that can fruitfully be appropriated in interfaith engagement in the public sphere. This volume contains a number of essays exploring the possibilities for agreement and consensus in interreligious engagement. These often involve what one might call 'liberal' strategies for mutual accommodation. I mean by this the expression of a desire to discover a common humanity in the midst of religious difference. This idea is expressed in many ways in interfaith encounters: the core idea is that in the midst of our traditions' different doctrinal commitments, or liturgical particularities, or pastoral practices,

---

[34] For two exemplary fieldwork approaches to religious life, see Susan Friend Harding, *The Book of Jerry Falwell: Fundamentalist Language and Politics* (Princeton: Princeton University Press, 2001) and Timothy Jenkins, *Religion in English Everyday Life*.

[35] See the 'receptive ecumenism' section at <www.centreforcatholicstudies.co.uk>.

we are nonetheless, at a fundamental level, all human, and we should seek to foreground our humanity. This is not a matter of discarding differences, or playing down our particularities: it is more a matter of seeing them as embellishments—valued embellishments—of an unadorned common essence. Another familiar variation of this theme, one that is more extreme, is the idea that there is a 'religious essence' to traditions of worship which is shared. This might be a commitment to God's unity (shared by Jews, Christians, and Muslims) or a concern to discern truth in scriptures (even if the particular scriptures are not shared). This rhetoric is a variant of Aristotle's distinction between substances and accidents, in which certain basic features are substantial, and others (such as particular doctrines or practices) are accidental. It also has a family resemblance to Rawls's 'overlapping consensus' and Habermas's notion of 'translation'.

Such liberal strategies work well for interreligious engagement between liberals and it has clear benefits for common action in the public sphere. It is, however, somewhat limited, both intellectually and practically. It is limited intellectually because the narrative of a common humanity is itself historically particular, and has grown up as a particular liberal strategy, with a distinct genealogy, but is transmitted and articulated in ways that conceal that historical particularity. It is advantageous to conceal it, because the narrative of a common humanity is highly portable if it is not tied to a particular (in this case European) philosophical tradition. It is limited practically because the religious folk who most need to engage each other are those who do not believe that there is anything more substantial than doctrinal commitments or practices of worship: their prayers are their identity, not accidental clothing of a naked essence. The challenge is to reach those who are not liberal, which in this case means those who are not concerned to reach agreement. In situations where there is no prospect of such agreement, there is a need for sustaining disagreement in a generous and generative way.

What, then, is the right kind of interreligious engagement in the public sphere for those who do not believe that talk of common humanity should trump doctrinal particularity, and who engage each other in the friendly but firm belief that persistent long-term disagreement is a distinguishing mark of our common endeavours? The answer to this question is deceptively simple: better disagreements. An example can clarify this. One of the most common discussions to unfold when Christians and Muslims who are new to interfaith engagement get to know each other is the difference between Christian views of Jesus and Muslim views of Muhammad. There is a great deal of exploration of the fact that Christians hold Jesus to be divine whereas Muslims hold Muhammad to be human. The first sign that 'better disagreement' is being achieved is when Muslims grasp that Christians hold Jesus to be divine *and human*, and when a discussion of the Chalcedonian formula is brought into play. But as Daniel Madigan has repeatedly argued, a more fruitful dialogue will be held if Muslims and Christians compare not Jesus and Muhammad, but Jesus and the Qur'an.[36] This discussion

---

[36] See Daniel Madigan, 'Mutual Theological Hospitality', in D. Linnan and W. El-Ansary (eds), *Muslim and Christian Understanding: Theory and Application of 'A Common Word'* (London: Palgrave Macmillan, 2010), 57–67.

will start to be about the incarnation of God's word. And a sign that 'better disagreement' is being achieved will be when differences in the conceptions of 'incarnation' and 'word' come to the fore.

This is a compressed account: a complex interplay of doctrinal and worship-oriented mutual discovery is encapsulated in this brief example. The main point is that Muslims and Christians are not going to get very far in this discussion if they are trying to discover their common humanity. The quest for unadorned essence leads away from this kind of doctrinal exploration, not more deeply into it. But if Christians and Muslims wish to improve the quality of their disagreements, because they know these disagreements are persistent and long-term, then such ever-deeper doctrinal investigations are vital. I have heard well-meaning Christians tell their Muslim colleagues that the humanity of Jesus is more important than his divinity, in the hope that this will improve the prospects for fruitful dialogue. The same can be heard in discussions of the oneness and threeness of God in discussions of tri-unity, as if the first line of the Nicene Creed is the essential claim, and everything that follows is mere embellishment. This is the friendly face of doctrinal disaster. What are needed are schools for learning higher quality disagreement. I have found the practice of scriptural reasoning to be exemplary in this regard. It is a well-developed practice where members of different traditions (typically Jews, Christians, and Muslims, although it is not restricted to them) meet together to study each other's scriptures, and to meditate on the generativity of the texts in conversation and in the lives of those who study them at home. Space prevents a proper discussion of this practice here: there is a ready bibliography of essays that describe it.[37] One of the fruits of scriptural reasoning is its production of myriad cases of interreligious engagement from which limited generalizations might be attempted. This is not the same as fieldwork, but it is a step in the right direction for those who identify overgeneralization as one of the main obstacles to making sense of interreligious engagement in the public square. It also provides almost endless cases of persistent disagreement which nonetheless generate understanding and collegiality around the table.

MULTIPLE INTERRELIGIOUS PUBLIC SPHERE ENGAGEMENTS

The final challenge engages an attempt to articulate a desire for interreligious engagement in the public sphere to serve the common good in society and not merely produce more understanding, or the safe handling of long-term disagreements. Any account of the public sphere

---

[37] David Ford, *Christian Wisdom: Desiring God and Learning in Love* (Cambridge: Cambridge University Press, 2007), 273–303; Nicholas Adams, *Habermas and Theology* (Cambridge: Cambridge University Press, 2006), 234ff.; Nicholas Adams, 'Scriptural Reasoning and Interfaith Hermeneutics', in David Cheetham *et al.*, *Interrreligious Hermeneutics in Pluralistic Europe* (Amsterdam: Rodopi, 2011), 59–78.

that rings true to the core identities of religious traditions will be theological. No single account of the public sphere will therefore be satisfactory. There need to be multiple accounts, from multiple traditions, and these will very likely be dissonant. Interreligious engagement has to be more than community anger management. The religious traditions which come together in interreligious engagement in the public sphere do not, by and large, promote a vision in which only the goods of a particular community are valued. My own Christian tradition has at its heart a concern for the whole world, for example, and this concern is mirrored in many other traditions, in a variety of ways.

The public sphere is neither a religious sphere nor a secular sphere. It is religious and secular. Religious life often defines itself in opposition to the secular, and secular life often defines itself in opposition to the religious: in such a public context, there is no prospect of finding a purely religious or purely secular form of life. The crucial question concerns how a religious and secular public sphere, where the religious and the secular often define themselves against each other, can serve the common good, at the same time as pursuing questions of truth. Traditions must surely engage each other from the heart of their identities, their practices, and their beliefs if the common good is to be served. Meetings at the margins, in the safe spaces where nothing is at stake, may produce friendly encounters, but they are unlikely to do any heavy lifting. It is the most authoritative voices in the traditions that need to be brought into conversation, even when they seem to be the ones that provoke the strongest suspicion from members of other religious traditions. Questions of revelation must be part of the conversation, and difficult discussions about law, idolatry, prophethood, and polytheism are unavoidable if our societies' deepest problems, including debt, racism, religious violence, youth unemployment, rising food inequalities, and the increasing scarcity of water, are to be tackled in a practically effective way by members of different religious traditions.

Members of religious traditions need to risk upsetting each other if they are to work together. This displays not a desire to disturb, but a willingness to share what matters most deeply. It might seem irresponsible to advocate a public sphere saturated with contestation at a time when Europe is seeing a resurgence of far-right political parties whose goal is to polarize and to provoke. But the kinds of public sphere where generative conversations unfold will probably be far from television cameras or radio microphones. Today's mass media are not conducive to conversation: their bread and butter is the theatrical false opposition, the ten-minute interview, the fifty-minute report. What are needed are three-hour text-study sessions and three-day working parties, resourced by deliberative scholarship that identifies and works through the more complex problems.

Two religious issues, one deeply challenging, and one more hopeful, will probably remain close to the centre of any pursuit of the common good. The challenging issue is that which goes under the description of conversion, proselytization, or mission. Certain religious traditions, especially Christianity and Islam, aim to attract others to their traditions. It is likely that the young people who have most to offer in service to the common good—those with the most energy and imagination—are also likely on occasion to be those most enthusiastically committed to promoting their traditions to others. The public sphere will not be merely an arena of discussion and compromise: it is also potentially a zone of transformation and conversion. That makes it risky and sometimes dangerous. Unless those who are involved in interreligious engagement in the public sphere are willing openly to address this possibility, and to develop responses to it that are true to the heart of their religious identities, the prospects for the common good seem poor. The more hopeful issue is one that involves thinking in an explicitly theological way: it is the commitment in nearly every religious tradition to transcendence. There is no 'neutral' articulation of transcendence which connects every tradition effortlessly; nor is it desirable to identify any 'essential' transcendence that plays out in different 'accidental' ways in different traditions. But transcendence nonetheless seems to be one of those generative themes that produces close family resemblances between traditions. To phrase it in a recognizably Christian idiom: human action, especially human speech, is not the last word, and can never be the decisive criterion by which divine or human action is to be judged. Humans are not the final authority. Human rationalities, however sophisticated and impressive, cannot trump God's wisdom. We thus should not fear our disagreements, nor be anxious about our rival claims to truth. This is because we do not possess any final truth, and cannot defeat our opponents with absolute certainty. To acknowledge God's transcendence is to know how vulnerable we are to being placed in the wrong, even (and especially) where we are most emphatic about being in the right. This is one of the lessons of the book of Job. This is a recognizably Christian idiom, but it seems that nearly every other religious tradition has resources for articulating insights that bear a strong resemblance to it. It can sound rather preachy in the context of a scholarly investigation into the public sphere, but anything more restrained risks a radical failure to do justice to what lies at the heart of religious identities.

FURTHER READING

Nicholas Adams, *Habermas and Theology* (Cambridge: Cambridge University Press, 2006).

Robert Audi and Nicholas Wolterstorff, *Religion in the Public Square: The Place of Religious Convictions in Political Debate* (Lanham, Md.: Rowman & Littlefield, 1997).

Craig Calhoun, Mark Juergensmeyer, and Jonathan VanAntwerpen, *Rethinking Secularism* (Oxford: Oxford University Press, 2011).

Dale Eickelman and Jon Anderson, *New Media in the Muslim World: The Emerging Public Sphere* (Bloomington, Ind.: Indiana University Press, 2003).

——and Armando Salvatore, 'The Public Sphere and Muslim Identities', *European Journal of Sociology*, 43/1 (2002), 92–115.

David Ford, *Christian Wisdom: Desiring God and Learning in Love* (Cambridge: Cambridge University Press, 2007).

Jürgen Habermas, *Between Naturalism and Religion* (Cambridge: Polity, 2008).

Thomas Howard, *God and the Atlantic: America, Europe and the Religious Divide* (Oxford: Oxford University Press, 2011).

John Rawls, *Political Liberalism* (New York: Columbia, 2005).

Armando Salvatore, *The Public Sphere: Liberal Modernity, Catholicism, Islam* (London: Palgrave Macmillan, 2007).

—— and Dale Eickelman, *Public Islam and the Common Good* (Leiden: Brill, 2006).

CHAPTER 14

Dialogue, Liberation, and Justice

MARIO I. AGUILAR

This chapter outlines some of the challenges arising from the late twentieth century acceptance of world religions as important for people's lives by virtue of the ubiquitous presence of
world religions throughout the world, on the one hand, and as themselves living traditions
involved in human and social dialogue aimed at liberation from oppression and working for
justice in society, on the other. Following from the assumption that religious diversity is not
a problem but a human reality, it suggests that the main areas of dialogue to be explored theoretically and in practice during the twenty-first century are: (1) the strengthening of a central
dialogue of a common humanity, thus including non-theistic traditions such as Buddhism,
humanism, and atheism; (2) the work of world religions for a common liberation of human
beings from any aspects of life that could prevent them from expressing their full personal
and communal dignity; and (3) the promotion of a model of dialogue that publicly proclaims
justice as a central component of all world religions and that connects all religious traditions
with the secular creation of states that foster justice for all their members. It is at this point in
human history that postmodern reflections arising from the end of the Cold War, and the
challenges to sectarian discourses after 9/11 bring together positive and exciting possibilities
for an interreligious dialogue based on universal acceptance of difference.

As Eric Hobsbawm rightly states, 'most history in the past was written for the glorification
of, and perhaps for the practical use of, rulers'.[1] Hierarchies and social differentiation—
including religious—with their attendant inequalities were taken as *de rigueur*. However, during the twentieth century a rediscovering of equality arose through the reconstruction of
multiple histories and, in the process, religious diversity has been reassessed. Indeed, it is in
this wider socio-political context that the contemporary phenomenon of dialogue between

---

[1] Eric Hobsbawm, *On History* (London: Abacus, 1998), 267.

the religions has arisen. For, arguably, interreligious dialogue had to take place within the ending of the colonial period because it was the role of the colonizer that gave centrality to one religious tradition over another. It is this centrality that has been reimagined in the post-coloniality of political and religious elites.[2] Processes of colonial ordering became post-colonial processes of disordering that could be negotiated without the presence of armies or establishment colonial manifestations of an established religion such as imperial Christianity.[3] Thus, by the 1950s reflections and actions related to an interreligious dialogue between the world religions had a considerable shift with, for example, the role of Mahatma Gandhi in fostering the equality of religions and their importance within the foundations of a new post-colonial state.[4] The importance of this post-colonial dialogue was not undermined with Gandhi's assassination; however, in this case, the partition of India with all its atrocities reminded others of the ills provided by political, religious, and social sectarianism in the name of politics—a guilt passed in turn onto religious practitioners.[5] In the European climate at the end of the Second World War many voices suggested that one way of fostering a post-colonial peaceful dialogue towards independence was the unity of a secular and a religious dialogue.[6]

Within such dialogue there was the possibility of the arrival of a system that would bring justice to the independent nations and a clearer freedom of religious practice.[7] The independent movements in Asia spoke of a new utopian and dialogic world, namely that led by the reflections and actions of Mahatma Gandhi who was to become a beacon of religious respect and diversity. Though his dream was shattered immediately by the religious violence that arose all over the Indian subcontinent after independence, and within the history of democratic states in Asia, it made a major impact nevertheless on the religious dialogue that was to follow.[8] For nobody could deny that in Asia there were millions of people who colourfully celebrated their religious convictions in day-to-day life and the new Asian leaders of independent nations, with the exception of China, were supported not just by Western Christianity but by millions of Muslims, Hindus, Sikhs, and Buddhists.[9] However, the equal rights proclaimed by the newly born states did not reach many of the religious divisions, distrusts, and

---

[2] Jost Dülffer and Marc Frey (eds), *Elites and Decolonization in the Twentieth Century* (Basingstoke and New York: Palgrave Macmillan, 2011).

[3] For a socio-historical analysis of ordering-disordering, see V. Y. Mudimbe, *The Invention of Africa: Gnosis, Philosophy and the Order of Knowledge* (Bloomington, Ind., and London: Indiana University Press and James Currey, 1988).

[4] Dennis Dalton, *Mahatma Ghandi: Non-Violent Power in Action* (New York: Columbia University Press, 1993).

[5] D. C. Jha, *Mahatma Ghandi: The Congress and the Partition of India* (London: Sangam, 1995).

[6] See the historical complexity shown by Sucheta Mahajan, *Independence and Partition: The Erosion of Colonial Power in India* (New Delhi and Thousand Oaks, Calif.: Sage Publications, 2000).

[7] Cf. Joan Vincent (ed.), *The Anthropology of Politics: A Reader in Ethnography, Theory and Critique* (Malden, Mass., and Oxford: Blackwell, 2002).

[8] See John C. Hawley (ed.), *Writing the Nation: Self and Country in the Post-Colonial Imagination* (Amsterdam: Rodopi, 1996).

[9] Long before these 20th-century processes the Philippines, the only nation with a majority of citizens who considered themselves Christians (Roman Catholics), had already become independent from the Spanish Empire. See Ninian Smart, *The World's Religions* (Cambridge: Cambridge University Press, 1998), ch. 16: 'South Asia and Reactions to Colonial Intervention'.

animosities that historically had been accumulated within countries ruled by colonial empires in which, for the most part, precedence was given to Christianity. Thus, the change that was to impact issues and practices within an interreligious dialogue came about because of the reflections on faith and practice that were triggered, for the most part, by the changes in lifestyle and diversity in belief and non-belief that took place in Europe, the United States, and the post-colonial independent nations trying to achieve progress through a new economic dependency.

With respect to momentous shifts that occurred within Christianity, as the principle colonial religion *par excellence*, the advent of the Second Vatican Council (1962–5) marked a doctrinal change within the Roman Catholic Church with respect to other faiths. And at around the same time, the World Council of Churches (WCC), formed in 1948, had also begun to rethink the respect and value accorded to other world religious traditions. This was especially so in Asia and Africa in regard to those religious traditions that were very much part of a socio-cultural (re)construction of society and nations then emerging and irrupting within the world. One of the prominent issues within those initial religious dialogues was the possibility that religious traditions had an impact on development, state-building, poverty eradication, and the liberation of peoples from foreign oppression, inequality, and situations of ignorance. Issues of social inequality and injustice were expressed in real terms, for example, in a lack of schooling and openness to a wider world; these spoke of phenomena that religious-sponsored schools, for example, could help to eradicate.[10]

These changes in outlook and ideas did not immediately influence the ongoing social processes of the so-called 'developing nations' but rather created a framework of 'dialogue in equality' that was to become more pronounced within the twenty-first century. Within such dialogues the stress was clearly on the importance of spirituality and the spiritual contribution of world religions to society. Prayer meetings in Assisi by leaders of the main religions of the world (first convened by Pope John Paul II in 1986), and visits by the Pope to synagogues, mosques, and temples, provided a larger world with signs of a will to perceive other religions as positive and an honest attempt at leaving behind centuries of distrust and common attacks on other people's religions. The Anglican Communion played an important role as many of its churches remained located within countries in which Christianity remained a minority religion. Other Christian World Communions, such as the Lutheran and Reformed, also pursued interreligious engagement in concert with the wider ecumenical programme promoted through the World Council of Churches. But of particular note for our purposes, and which will provide the primary focus for this chapter, is the change that was wrought in and through the Roman Catholic Church, the single largest Christian denomination.

---

[10] For a critical discussion on issues of development in a post-colonial setting, see Jeffrey Haynes, *Religion and Development: Conflict or Cooperation?* (Basingstoke and New York: Palgrave Macmillan, 2007).

Interreligious Relations After Vatican II

It was in 1959 that three events took place which triggered a deeper interaction between religious and political projects of liberation and non-theistic traditions. First, in January 1959 the armies of liberation of Fidel Castro attained victory in what it was to be known as the Cuban Revolution. Second, in March 1959 the 14th Dalai Lama left his homeland of Tibet to start a lifelong exile in India. Third, in the same month Pope John XXIII called a council of the bishops of the worldwide Roman Catholic Church, to be known as the Second Vatican Council, to discuss the identity and role of the church in the modern world.

John XXIII clarified that the council should emphasize the positive aspects of the modern world, seeking always the justice of the Kingdom of God and implementing a magisterium that should be pastoral in nature: 'the church should contribute to the unity of humankind and present its teachings in ways understandable to people who live in the modern world'.[11] John XXIII could be deemed a radical initiator of movements for religious dialogue in that he spoke about the church of the poor and his own wish for a church that could be less monarchic and more understood by the contemporary world, especially that of Europe. Years later, it is a fact that new developments on dialogue and a very strong process of secularization in Europe have made some of the fresh and inclusive insights of Vatican II less relevant to most people. Indeed, it is possible to argue that there has been an effort, from some quarters within the hierarchy of the church, to forget or at least diminish the influence of the council during the pontificates of John Paul II and Benedict XVI. The return to more centralized authority reminiscent of the church pre-Vatican II has meant a shift from the model of a servant church advocated at the Council to that of a dogmatic teaching church under Benedict XVI. As a result, there has been less room for collegial cooperation between local churches and less decision-making power assigned to the local Episcopal Conferences.[12]

This model affected modes and ways of fostering dialogue between Christians and those of other faiths as well as to those of no faith. John Paul II and Benedict XVI each became a sign of dialogue by their appearances at world events of interfaith prayer such as the occasions in Assisi, and they visited synagogues and mosques, showing enormous respect for other faiths, particularly those of the Abrahamic traditions, Muslims and Jews.[13] However, their teaching concerning dialogue with other religions reinforced the necessary primacy of the Catholic Church as 'the church of Christ' and, notwithstanding the work of the Pontifical Council for Interreligious Dialogue (PCID) and its predecessor, the Secretariat for Non-Christians (SNC), relatively little encouragement to continue interreligious dialogue was actually given to Christian communities which were already engaged in dialogue on the ground. In many cases, however, local dialogical initiatives and encounters, involving

---

[11] Robert J. Schreiter, 'The Impact of Vatican II', in Gregory Baum (ed.), *The Twentieth Century: A Theological Overview* (Maryknoll, NY: Orbis Books, 1999), 159.

[12] See the role of the bishop in *The Code of Canon Law* (London and Sydney: Collins, 1983), §§ 375–430.

[13] See Peter Hebblethwaite, *Introducing John Paul II: The Populist Pope* (London: Collins, 1982).

Catholics as well as other Christians, continued unabated. In the case of Christian–Buddhist relations there was an increase in the appreciation of Buddhist philosophy and meditation by Christians in many places, and particularly among the youth of Europe. In fact, a number of Christians started asserting a dual belonging to different religious traditions, mostly to Christianity and Buddhism.[14]

As a result of these changes in emphasis of the past thirty years, I would argue it is crucial to re-examine the teachings of Vatican II regarding interfaith dialogue and to revisit the spirit of the council regarding dialogue with other human beings, particularly with those who do not adhere to a belief in a creator God, such as Buddhists, in order to critically discuss inter-religious relations and dialogue in respect to the motifs and concerns of liberation and justice. To maintain appropriate focus we will first address the issues of conscience and human dignity, paying close attention to critical documents and outcomes emanating from Vatican II and the important encyclical of Pope Paul VI, *Ecclesiam Suam*. Attention will then turn to the dialogue for liberation, and the quest for justice through the agency of interreligious relations, through the lens of Christian (Catholic) engagement with Buddhism. We thus come at the more general matter of interreligious dialogue, liberation, and justice through a twofold case study: developments in Catholic Christian thought on the one hand, and Christian–Buddhist dialogical relationships on the other.

THE ISSUES OF CONSCIENCE AND HUMAN DIGNITY

Two issues for discussion became central within Vatican II: conscience and human dignity.[15] Without agreement on the freedom of conscience given by God to all human beings, and therefore the assertion of the dignity of each human being made in the image of God, further discussions on an inclusive church that is also involved in interreligious dialogue would have been extremely difficult.[16] Thus it is difficult to separate the key Vatican II document on other religions, *Nostra Aetate*, from documents such as those on the Constitution of the Church (*Lumen Gentium*), the Pastoral Constitution on the Church in the Modern World (*Gaudium et Spes*), and the Declaration on Religious Liberty (*Dignitatis Humanae*).

Dignitatis Humanae (issued 7 December 1965) significantly made religious freedom of the individual part of official church teaching.[17] This was a complete about-face, given that a previous pope, Pius IX, had included in his *Syllabus of Errors* any works related to religious

---

[14] Rose Drew, *Buddhist and Christian? An Exploration of Dual Belonging* (London: Routledge, 2011) and Paul F. Knitter, *Without Buddha I Could Not Be a Christian* (London: Oneworld, 2009). See also Ch. 15.

[15] See Mario I. Aguilar, *Church, Liberation and World Religions: Towards a Christian–Buddhist Dialogue* (London: T&T Clark, 2012).

[16] See Ann M. Nolan, *A Privileged Moment: Dialogue in the Language of the Second Vatican Council 1962–1965* (Bern: Peter Lang, 2006).

[17] *Dignitatis Humanae*, §§ 1–2; cf. John Paul II, *Essays on Religious Freedom* (Milwaukee: Catholic League on Religious and Civil Rights, 1984).

(and political) pluralism.[18] Indeed, prior to Vatican II, as Pratt notes, the Roman Catholic Church 'had lived wholly within its own worldview framework: resistant to winds of change and slow to adapt; in effect content with the status quo of received tradition' and further that 'any acknowledgement of the "religiously other"…was, at best, rather muted'.[19] *Dignitatis Humanae* was indeed a radical change that was particularly needed by Catholics living in mostly Protestant societies such as the United States. It argued that there is no recognition of a church's authority by a believing state; rather the church's authority adheres to freedom rather than to the establishment.[20] The ground for this change in doctrine, breaking with the tradition stemming from the emperors of Western Christendom, Constantine, Justinian, and Charlemagne, comes from a thorough examination of the dignity of the human individual.[21] This right to individual freedom extends to groups of believers and it includes freedom of enquiry, association, communication, finance, public testimony, worship, and common moral endeavour.[22] *Dignitatis Humanae* puts a newly strong emphasis on individual conscience, stating that 'it is through this conscience that man sees and recognizes the demands of the divine law'.[23]

For a contemporary generation of Catholic Christians that has enjoyed the fruits of Vatican II it is difficult to grasp the enormous and central change that this emphasis on the freedom of the individual meant—to Catholics and non-Catholics alike. It must be remembered that, at the time of the council, Catholics were restricted in their freedom of belief, public testimony, communication, worship, and moral guidance.[24] For example, the publication of the Index of forbidden books meant Catholics were formally banned from reading many works by non-Catholics and, in order to publish anything themselves on issues of religion and morality, they needed an episcopal imprimatur, that is, a permission to publish; while all Catholic clerics needed an imprimatur for absolutely anything they were intending to publish. Control of what was read, and written, was tight. Furthermore, Catholics could not attend other churches' worship; thus they were under the control of a clearly hierarchical system that was accountable to the Holy Office. But, as a result of Vatican II, all this changed: 'the windows of tradition were thrown open to allow a new breeze of thinking to blow through, and a new light of sensitivity to illuminate' this church.[25]

---

[18] See also James Tunstead Burtchaell CSC, 'Religious Freedom (*Dignitatis Humanae*)', in Adrian Hastings (ed.), *Modern Catholicism: Vatican II and After* (London: SPCK; New York: Oxford University Press, 1991), 118–25.

[19] Douglas Pratt, *The Church and Other Faiths: The World Council of Churches, the Vatican, and Interreligious Dialogue* (Bern: Peter Lang, 2010), 169.

[20] *Dignitatis Humanae*, § 6.

[21] Owen Chadwick, *Catholicism and History: The Opening of the Vatican Archives* (Cambridge: Cambridge University Press), 1978.

[22] *Dignitatis Humanae*, §§ 4–7.

[23] *Dignitatis Humanae*, § 3.

[24] Tunstead Burtchaell, 'Religious Freedom (*Dignitatis Humanae*)', 120.

[25] Pratt, *The Church and Other Faiths*, 170.

Nostra Aetate

The Declaration on the Relations of the Church to Non-Christian Religions (*Nostra Aetate*, October 1965) was truly the work of the council because nobody would have predicted beforehand that the fathers of the council would engage with other religions apart from Judaism.[26] It was a process of reflection that was clearly aided by Pope John XXIII and was prepared through the appointment of Cardinal Bea as the president of the Secretariat for Promoting Christian Unity. Bea was also asked to work on a 'schema' on the Jews, a particular preoccupation of the council. In the event this was abandoned because of considerations about ongoing political animosity between Arabs and Jews. This was providential in that the schema was then diversified. A new schema was thus introduced containing three chapters on the Christian churches, one on the Jews, and a fifth dealing with religious freedom. Discussions were influenced heavily by the possibility that words about the Jews could endanger the existence of Christians within Israel and Palestine as well as a fear of a reaction by Muslims if they were to be mentioned within paragraphs on ecumenism, or paired with Jews. Thus, even when there was no clear discussion on religious freedom it was clear that the council document had to evolve to include other religions.

In May 1964 Pope Paul VI, the successor to John XXIII who had died in June 1963, solved the impasse by giving more importance to relations with other religions, expressed through the founding of a special secretariat for the development of relations with other religions (Secretariat for Non-Christians). Three months later Paul VI issued his encyclical *Ecclesiam Suam*, the most comprehensive church document related to the spirituality of dialogue. In September 1964 the text on dialogue presented to the council was broadened as to include mention of Muslims and other religions as well as Jews. As a result of this process of extended preparation, the declaration *Nostra Aetate* was approved at the first vote in November 1964 and finally promulgated on 28 October 1965. Even though this seems a detailed account, in fact it is somewhat a simplified version of the true complexity, but sufficient to show how such a momentous change in the attitude and orientation of the Catholic Church had occurred, and how interrelated issues and developments were then able to flow.

Already at the start of the document the fathers of the council outlined the common human need to ask questions about life and death, judgement, sinfulness, and indeed human life as a whole.[27] Further, *Nostra Aetate* recognized the existence of religions belonging to advanced civilizations that have systematized some of these answers to the questions about life and death.[28] It mentions Hinduism and Buddhism, suggesting that 'Buddhism in its various forms testifies to the essential inadequacy of this changing world. It proposes a way of life by which men [sic] can, with confidence and trust, attain a state of perfect liberation and reach supreme illumination either through their own efforts or by the aid of divine help.'[29]

---

[26] For the history of the document and a critical analysis see Donald Nicholl, 'Other Religions (Nostra Aetate)', in Hastings, *Modern Catholicism*, 126–34.

[27] *Nostra Aetate*, § 1.   [28] *Nostra Aetate*, § 2.   [29] *Nostra Aetate*, § 2.

The sentence that follows was something of a bombshell, outlining a newness of the acceptance of diversity that marked an end to the enmity of many centuries between the Catholic Church and other religions. For the fathers of the council state plainly that:

> The Catholic Church rejects nothing of what is true and holy in these religions. She has a high regard for the manner of life and conduct, the precepts and doctrines which, although differing in many ways from her own teaching, nevertheless often reflect a ray of that truth which enlightens all men [sic].[30]

However, the document also stressed the fact that for Christians the way to 'the fullness' of religious life is found in Christ.[31] Christians are to engage 'with prudence and charity into discussions and collaboration with members of other religions', preserving and encouraging other faiths while bearing witness to their own. And regarding Islam, the document makes a clear connection between the roots of faith in Abraham and the daily life of prayer, almsgiving, and fasting that connects Christians and Muslims.[32] There is a plea to forget a past with 'many quarrels and dissensions' between Christian and Muslims and a fresh call is made to promote 'peace, liberty, social justice and moral values'.[33]

The document, initially concerned with Christian–Jewish relations, certainly stresses the roots of both faiths in Abraham, Moses, and the Prophets, recalling the fact that although the Jews did not recognize Jesus as the Messiah, nevertheless they remain 'very dear to God'.[34] Thus, there is a common spiritual heritage that should be encouraged by biblical and theological studies and through what the council calls 'friendly discussions'.[35] It was at this point that the document dealt with the most difficult historical stumbling block of Christian–Jewish relations: the death of Christ. The passage of John 19: 6 where the Jewish authorities and the people themselves press for the death of Christ was used through the centuries to accuse the Jews of deicide, an account that contributed to anti-Semitism within the Christian community. *Nostra Aetate* was absolutely clear in stating that 'neither all Jews indiscriminately at that time, nor Jews today, can be charged with the crimes committed during his passion'.[36] The terrible charge of killing the Son of God, of deicide, was finally and formally expunged—at least in terms of Catholic teaching. In the *Nostra Aetate* text a warning follows for those who distort the truth of the Gospel, together with an affirmation that the church 'reproves every form of persecution against whomsoever it may be directed'.[37] Finally, the document condemns any discrimination or harassment against people because of race, colour, and condition in life or religion.[38]

On the basis of this seminal document arising from Vatican II that the Catholic Church went a long way to establish a principle of respect and cooperation with other religions which would have been unthinkable at the start of the twentieth century. But this was not the only

---

[30] *Nostra Aetate*, § 2.   [31] *Nostra Aetate*, § 2.   [32] *Nostra Aetate*, § 3.
[33] *Nostra Aetate*, § 3.   [34] *Nostra Aetate*, § 4.   [35] *Nostra Aetate*, § 4.
[36] *Nostra Aetate*, § 4.   [37] *Nostra Aetate*, § 4.   [38] *Nostra Aetate*, § 5.

Vatican II output to signal momentous change in Christian orientation towards people of other faiths.[39]

Ecclesiam Suam

The council established a magisterial principle of inclusion for the world religions that was based not on an exceptional state of affairs but on a return to an inclusivist understanding of church and a refreshed sense of a spirit of dialogue. Both understandings were set up by Paul VI in the encyclical letter 'On the Church' (*Ecclesiam Suam*) promulgated on 6 August 1964. The encyclical manifested an openness that had been denied previously; however, this openness was a significant necessity in order to enhance the work of the church. According to Cardinal F. König, President of the Secretariat for Non-Believers, in an interview given to Vatican Radio, 'the Church was called to dialogue, but only in order to carry out its proper task, namely the saving proclamation of Christ'.[40] The first of Pope Paul VI's encyclicals, *Ecclesiam Suam* is divided into three parts: self-awareness, renewal, and dialogue, and it describes the church as entrusted with one task, 'to serve society'.[41] Within this service the church must reflect 'on its own nature, the better to appreciate the divine plan which it is the Church's task to implement'.[42] For the church, according to Paul VI, belongs to the world 'even though distinguished from it by its own altogether unique characteristics'.[43] Further, 'the Church is deeply rooted in the world'; 'it exists in the world and draws its members from the world'.[44] It is bound to feel the tensions and the pressures of an ever-changing world.[45] Thus, it is necessary, according to Paul VI, to revisit the church's own existence in the scriptures and the apostolic tradition.[46] Again and again he stressed the importance of the conciliar deliberations on the church and laid the foundational principle for a church immersed in the world, defined as 'in the world, but not of it'.[47] He reminded readers of John XXIII's word for the council, 'aggiornamento', and his own adherence to it as a significant marker of the need for the church to be immersed in the contemporary world and to look for the 'signs of the time'.[48]

One of the important points for the renewal of the church in general and the renewal of ecclesiastical life in particular mentioned by Paul VI was 'the spirit of poverty, or rather, the zeal for preserving this spirit'.[49] Such is the centrality that Paul VI gives to the spirit of poverty that he asserts: 'it is a fundamental element of that divine plan by which we are destined to win the Kingdom of God, and yet it is greatly jeopardized by the modern trend to set so

---

[39] Cf. Pratt, *The Church and Other Faiths*.
[40] Ricardo Burigana and Giovanni Turbanti, 'The Intersession: Preparing the Conclusion of the Council', in Giuseppe Alberigo (ed.), *History of Vatican II*, iv. *Church as Communion: Third Period and Intercession September 1964–September 1965* (Maryknoll, NY: Orbis; Leuven: Peeters, 2003), 610.
[41] *Ecclesiam Suam*, § 5.   [42] *Ecclesiam Suam*, § 18.   [43] *Ecclesiam Suam*, § 18.
[44] *Ecclesiam Suam*, § 26.   [45] *Ecclesiam Suam*, § 26.   [46] *Ecclesiam Suam*, § 26.
[47] *Ecclesiam Suam*, § 49.   [48] *Ecclesiam Suam*, § 50.   [49] *Ecclesiam Suam*, § 54.

much store by wealth'.[50] The Pope recognizes the difficulties that everyone has on keeping a spirit of poverty and announces particular canonical regulations and directives regarding poverty so as to highlight clearly that 'spiritual goods far outweigh economic goods, the possession and use of which should be regulated and subordinated to the conduct and advantage of our apostolic mission'.[51] Regarding wealth, the Pope encourages the understanding of economics and the actual use of wealth not as a source of tension but to help those who are in need; thus wealth should be used 'justly and equitable for the good of all' and ultimately redistributed.[52] Together with the spirit of poverty, charity emerges as 'the very heart and centre of the plan of God's providence'.[53] Paul VI uses the word 'charity' instead of 'love' and argues strongly following the hymn of love (1 Corinthians 13) that 'charity is the key to everything. It sets all to rights. There is nothing which charity cannot achieve and renew'.[54]

The third part of *Ecclesiam Suam* deals with the issue of dialogue and particularly with dialogue with the world, which is inclusive of

> those human beings who are opposed to the light of faith and the gift of grace, those whose naive optimism betrays them into thinking that their own energies suffice to win them complete, lasting, and gainful prosperity, or, finally, those who take refuge in an aggressively pessimistic outlook on life and maintain that their vices, weaknesses and moral ailments are inevitable, incurable, or perhaps even desirable as sure manifestations of personal freedom and sincerity.[55]

Christians differentiate themselves from the world without indifference to, fear of, or contempt for, the world; on the contrary the church is distinguished from humanity in order to become closer to humanity by showing more concern and more love for all.[56] Thus, the church must enter into dialogue with the world because it has something to say; a message to give and a communication to make.[57]

A significant theological motif threading through the encyclical, and later resonating in other documents pertaining to dialogue, is the history of recognition that the church must engage in dialogue, in a conversation, with the world[58] and that, furthermore, such dialogue arises out of the experience of God in prayer; indeed, God Himself is 'the noble origin of this dialogue'.[59] Dialogue happens between the church and the world, and between the church and other faiths because of the undergirding dialogue of God with creation and, in fact, the very salvific and providential process whereby the dialogue established by the Father who sent his Son, and who is in dialogue with us through the church, provides a paradigm of dialogue that should be established with the whole of humanity.[60] In his reflection, Paul VI stressed the fact that God initiated this dialogue first in love and this is an important characteristic of the church's dialogue with others: it should be initiated by the church without

---

[50] *Ecclesiam Suam*, § 54.
[51] *Ecclesiam Suam*, § 54.
[52] *Ecclesiam Suam*, § 55.
[53] *Ecclesiam Suam*, § 56.
[54] *Ecclesiam Suam*, § 56.
[55] *Ecclesiam Suam*, § 59.
[56] *Ecclesiam Suam*, § 63.
[57] *Ecclesiam Suam*, § 65.
[58] *Ecclesiam Suam*, § 69.
[59] *Ecclesiam Suam*, § 70.
[60] *Ecclesiam Suam*, § 71.

waiting for others and in the spirit of love.[61] In fact, as God's dialogue was not initiated on merit or with particular objectives, but entered freely, without coercion, in a spirit of conversational openness, so the same process of dialogue with others in 'human friendliness, interior persuasion, and ordinary conversation' is expected of the church.[62]

Within Paul VI's teachings dialogue is catholic (universal), perseverant with the church taking the initiative; thus, dialogue becomes the method for relational engagement between the church and the world.[63] In order to respect a human being's freedom and dignity Paul VI suggests that dialogue has the following characteristics: (i) it should be intelligible, (ii) it should be humble, truthful, and peaceful, (iii) it should carry confidence in the power of words as well as in the goodwill of the other party, and (iv) it should be conducted with the prudence of a teacher.[64]

In the final part of *Ecclesiam Suam* Paul VI provided a positive view of developments and changes in the world, stating that:

> All things human are our concern. We share with the whole of the human race a common nature, a common life, with all its gifts and all its problems. We are ready to play our part in this primary, universal society, to acknowledge the insistent demands of its fundamental needs, and to applaud the new and often sublime expressions of its genius.[65]

Among the most difficult sectors of society with whom the church could dialogue Paul VI mentioned those who followed atheism and communism.[66] Among the very positive partners in dialogue Paul VI mentioned those who seek and work for peace, those who share a faith in One God (Jewish and Muslim) and those who follow Afro-Asiatic religions.[67] Thus, regarding those who follow non-Christian religions Paul VI asserted:

> We desire to join with them in promoting and defending common ideals in the spheres of religious liberty, human brotherhood, education, culture, social welfare, and civic order. Dialogue is possible in all these great projects, which are our concern as much as theirs, and we will not fail to offer opportunities for discussion in the event of such an offer being favourably received in genuine, mutual respect.[68]

Finally, Paul VI referred to those who share a belief in Christ, stressing the commonalities between the Christian churches rather than the differences.[69] The fact that representatives of all the Christian churches were present at the Second Vatican Council was already a sign of the things to come. As a result of all those reflections, dialogue emerged as central to the life of the church. Among the many foci for dialogue, the motifs of justice and liberation have long rung out; and among the many contexts and partners to dialogue, engagement between Christians and Buddhism provides us with a distinctive field of study and illumination.

---

[61] *Ecclesiam Suam*, §§ 72–3.   [62] *Ecclesiam Suam*, §§ 74–5.   [63] *Ecclesiam Suam*, §§ 76–8.
[64] *Ecclesiam Suam*, § 81, cf. § 79.   [65] *Ecclesiam Suam*, § 97.   [66] *Ecclesiam Suam*, §§ 99–104.
[67] *Ecclesiam Suam*, §§ 106–7.   [68] *Ecclesiam Suam*, § 108.   [69] *Ecclesiam Suam*, § 109.

DIALOGUE FOR LIBERATION

The inclusion of Buddhism within any interreligious dialogue suggests that a shift from a dialogue centred solely on religious traditions that uphold the existence of a God has taken place. For it must always be remembered that Buddhism is a non-theistic tradition. As such it neither upholds a belief in a Creator God or a creation out of a divine existence and will; nor, as normative Catholic teaching would assert, belief in an end of biological life associated with a judgement by a divine being leading to an eternal existence of the soul either close to God (Heaven) or far away from God (Hell). Instead, Buddhists uphold a belief in a continual reincarnation depending on good deeds and, for some, a final exiting of this cycle of life and rebirth. The main prize that could be attained by a Buddhist is the cessation of personal suffering, a daily reality for all sentient beings.

What can unite theistic and non-theistic religions is the self-affirmation that these two ways of explaining the physical and metaphysical worlds will not be able to reconcile their explanations. Instead, these two kinds of semantic and interpretative traditions can come together if they locate human beings and creation—that is, all sentient beings in the Buddhist sense—at the centre of a daily understanding and a common action. There is no doubt that the word 'liberation' as a trope has been used to describe positive processes in which human beings, and indeed the whole of creation, have managed to come out of situations—both material and spiritual—that have oppressed them and made them suffer. There are enormous possibilities within an interreligious dialogue between Christianity and Buddhism because of the dialogue that can arise out of the common use of the trope 'liberation' as well as because a search for liberation creates, as a result, justice for those who finally are assumed as free, as equal, as dependent, and as interconnected sentient beings.

If Buddhism has historically considered a final enlightened moment and the liberation from the senses as central to a Buddhist path to Enlightenment, Christianity has been less confident in such processes of liberation. Further, as a majority religion in the Western hemisphere, Christianity has not managed to assert its central role within a just society and at its best it has lived through golden periods of ethical practice in which it has tried to ameliorate the power of institutional structures in order to promote the effectiveness of the Christian message within society. However, as a result, forms of Christianity that challenged the dichotomy between body and soul, or between religious ascetic practices and an incarnational theology within a body of politics, also became suspect yet necessary in the latter part of the twentieth century.

The fact that liberation from suffering, expressed in both personal sin and structural sin, became central to certain forms of Christian thinking such as liberation theology in Latin America was a result of the discussions of Vatican II, but it was also disliked by others. For the advent of Vatican II not only opened theoretical new thinking on interreligious relations, but also required new thinking and new ways of dialogue by the episcopal conferences of the Catholic Church. Through the reflections of the Latin American bishops in Medellin (1968) and Puebla (1979) the centrality of those who suffer ('the poor') and those who are treated unjustly ('the marginalized') acquired a central place in theological reflections of liberation from sin, oppression, and poverty. Thus, the 'theology of liberation' outlined by the Peruvian theologian Gustavo Gutiérrez provided the term 'liberation' as a metaphor and trope related to prayer and work that could enable the reflection on suffering by human beings and their own determination to leave those cycles of poverty and oppression and to attain liberation.

The term 'liberation' associated with Buddhism has expressed clearly the possibility that, after recognizing suffering as a fact, the Buddhist is able to achieve liberation by detachment from material things and by the acquiring of unity with a common humanity. This is a process that requires a spiritual revolution and self-awareness, on the one hand, and a material change of life preferences and actions, on the other. The difference expected in a Buddhist from all other realms of understanding is the realization that all human beings have the same desires and senses, and that all human beings have the capabilities of accepting their suffering condition and making their actions not only beneficial to their own liberation but also to others. For the right action towards others and to a sentient world not only brings liberation to them, but also to all sentient beings around them. Thus, a process of Buddhist liberation that seems an individual and selfish path becomes a communal path whereby the one achieving liberation would not exit the cycle of life (*samsara*) until all others have done so.

The case of the Tibetan Dalai Lamas is striking because, already considered an image and manifestation of the Lord Buddha having achieved liberation, they 'come back' to accompany, teach, lead, and comfort Tibetans in their path.[70] Thus they become Bodhisattva, beings that, despite the fact that they want, and have the capacity, to leave the cycle of life (*samsara*), they return to this cycle, renounce the peace of an individual salvation, work to deliver all beings from suffering, and so become 'Buddhas for the sake of others'. Thus, we read in the Bodhicharyāvatāra:

> And now as long as space endures,
> As long as there are beings to be found,
> May I continue likewise to remain
> To drive away the sorrows of the world.
>
> (10.55)
>
> The pains and sorrows of all wandering beings—
> May they ripen wholly on myself.
> And may the virtuous company of Bodhisattvas
> Always bring about the happiness of beings.
>
> (10.56)[71]

---

[70] Mario I. Aguilar, *The Rising of the Dalai Lamas in Tibet: From the First to the Fourth 1391–1617* (Santiago: Fundación Literaria Civilización, 2011).

[71] Shāntideva, *The Way of the Bodhisattva*, 2nd rev. edn (Boston: Shambhala Publications, 2011), 10.55–6.

Liberation, understood in the Bodhicharyāvatāra, becomes an interreligious trope because it allows the dialogue with other traditions, such as Christianity or Islam, to be engaged through the trope of an action for others as well as by and for an individual. Within Christianity liberation from poverty and suffering becomes part of the life and work of the saints and those involved in saving others while following a path of individual piety and devotion. The giving of 'alms' as a pillar of Islam, and as a necessity for a Christian who is to attain eternal life, requires the giving of the self as well as a change in a lifestyle for the sake of the liberation that is to come.

Within Christianity the term 'liberation' became widely used after Vatican II when the values of a Christian Gospel that empowered followers who looked after the sick, the poor, the lonely, the prisoners, and the marginalized of society were also understood as a challenge to an unjust society that did not allow for the dignity of human beings, created by God, to be realized within the modern state. The Buddhist perspective of helping the alleviation of suffering and the care for all sentient beings brings them in one purpose together with the actions of Christianity where love of God and neighbour come together as a cause and effect of liberation from sin. Grace as the absence from sin in Christianity relates closely to compassion as the absence of attachment and selfishness in Buddhism. Further, compassion for all sentient beings either through the example of the Good Samaritan in the Gospel or the respect and care for all sentient beings in the teachings of the Buddha, creates a relational axiomatically connected notion not in ideals or theologies but in practice.

INTERRELIGIOUS RELATIONS THROUGH JUSTICE

It is the application of interreligious dialogue that has been lacking because another truism, not readily accepted by all, is that human beings practise different religions and belong in their own way to the tradition that is more familiar to them. Reflections on religious diversity have exhausted the way forward simply because, in the words of Rita Gross, 'religious diversity is normal'.[72] She has expressed further the positive connotation of this fact of life, commenting that 'I have been deeply aware of the normality and joy of religious diversity for so long now that it is almost impossible for me to imagine the feelings of someone troubled by religious diversity'.[73] The relations between two or more religious traditions centre upon the metaphysical realities of a spiritual world, understood as cause and effect of personal deeds, consequences arising out of one's ethical behaviour, respect, and cooperation with others, finally understood as different from each other. These characteristics locate cooperation outside the self-centred realms of the religious self—pointing to a landscape of interreligious relations that operates within society, within the world, and within the present and future of

---

[72] Rita M. Gross, 'Excuse Me, But What's the Question? Isn't Religious Diversity Normal?', in Paul F. Knitter (ed.), *The Myth of Religious Superiority: A Multifaith Exploration* (Maryknoll, NY: Orbis Books, 2005), 76.

[73] Gross, 'Excuse Me', 76.

a world in which religious practitioners meet and interact. The relations *ad intra* that created the invention of difference and strife have been superseded by the secularized world. Thus, religious traditions have cooperated in interfaith councils, groups, and commonly organized public events in order to make the point about the importance of metaphysics within an ever-growing globalized and materialistic world. This state of affairs has not pushed the different religious traditions to utilize their place in the world but it has made them recognize their similarities, common hopes, and common values.

I suggest that there is a place and location within a reflection on interreligious dialogue that dwells on the respect of difference. Difference understood not as an opposition of 'truths' but difference as a variety of ritual practices and adherence to beliefs with a complementarity of a common path of life. For religion, as a practice of an order and as an explanation, is only a means to an end and not an end in itself.[74] Thus, the start of any dialogue requires the acceptance of different doctrinal understandings as exemplary bases for causation in dialogue. It is in difference that the centrality of the Christ or of a Creator God is put aside in order to dialogue about the centrality of human beings and all sentient beings within the history and future of justice, injustice, suffering, and liberation as divine justice. Thus, dialogue brings the acceptance of difference and the common understanding of suffering as poverty, injustice, and ignorance. The difficulties of any dialogue arise from assertions of centrality, superiority, and absoluteness where dialogue then is only a polite way of discussing what is already known. However, from a Christian perspective, I would argue the acceptance of difference suggests a human diversity that speaks of the beauty and complexity of God's creation rather than a negation of God's possibilities within God's plans and actions for this world in which all religious traditions interact.

It is necessary at this stage of a discourse on interreligious relations based on difference to remember the interpretations provided by two central interpreters of the hermeneutics of suffering within Christianity and Buddhism: Rje Tsong Khapa, founder of the Gelugpa, the religious monastic order of the Dalai Lama; and Gustavo Gutiérrez, pastoral and intellectual founder of a theological movement for liberation within Christian theology. Tsong Khapa writes:

> Resoluteness regarding insight into the characteristics of suffering phenomena is the path of confrontation which is the antidote to the ten afflictions pertaining to the suffering of the desire realm to be abandoned by means of the path of seeing: the view of the transitory aggregates, the extreme views, the false views, arrogance with regard to one's own view, arrogance regarding one's own propriety and conduct, doubt, desire, anger, pride, and ignorance.[75]

---

[74] This is clearly expressed within Buddhism whereby the practice of ritual actions and meditation is only a vehicle towards enlightenment. Buddhism is a good vehicle but it is not the only one and certainly within the common journey Christians have used more than one 'vehicle', see Sallie King, 'A Pluralistic View of Religious Pluralism', in Knitter, *Myth of Religious Superiority*, 88–101.

[75] Rje Tsong Khapa, *Ocean of Reasoning: A Great Commentary on Nāgārjuna's Mūlamadhyamakakārikā* (New York: Oxford University Press, 2006), 473.

The centrality of Tsong Khapa's emphasis on the attitudes and attachments of human beings resonates within the challenges and theological adherences shown by Gustavo Gutiérrez. For example, Gutiérrez, assuming the historical plight of the poor and the marginalized, suggests that poverty constitutes suffering and oppression. He argues that 'poverty and its causes are opposed to the will to life and fellowship with God that are inscribed in God's creation' and further, 'poverty is an evil'.[76] Instead, a life of poverty and detachment that is personally and voluntarily adhered to leads to an agency of freedom and the practice of a religion that can be understood and shared by others in different traditions. Thus, we are free to love others and we recognize that we also share some responsibility for the existence of unjust 'social mechanisms'.[77]

In one of his theological assessments of the poor and marginalized within society and the Christian commitment to them Gutiérrez writes: 'To be a disciple of Jesus is to make his messianic practice our own. Our discipleship is our appropriation of his message of life, his love for the poor, his denunciation of injustice, his sharing of bread, his hope for resurrection.'[78] Suffering and the life of the poor suggests an injustice within the world, the existence of societies in which not everything is well, societies in which the poor do not have a voice and where some enrich themselves at the expense of those who suffer. If Buddhists recognize suffering and its causes as a needed realization in order to seek an exit from a world of suffering, Christianity has looked at a Kingdom of God that is 'here and now' but 'not yet', a realization that brings the desire to arrive at the eternal Kingdom but 'not yet' because of God's care for human beings here and now.[79] In the words of Leonardo Boff, 'the acta and facta of Jesus (his praxis) are to be seen as historifications of what the kingdom of God signifies concretely, i.e., a liberative change in the existing situation'.[80]

CONCLUSION

It is clear that the creation of just or unjust structures within society can be the responsibility of many religious traditions and of the non-theistic traditions as well. The search for justice proclaimed in Christianity arising out of the ministry of Jesus (for example, Luke 4) is complemented by the Buddhist's care for all sentient beings that are part not only of a human

[76] Gustavo Gutiérrez, 'Friends of God, Friends of the Poor', in his *The Density of the Present: Selected Writings* (Maryknoll, NY: Orbis Books, 1999), 154–5.

[77] Gustavo Gutiérrez, *We Drink from our own Wells: The Spiritual Journey of a People* (London: SCM Press, 1983), 99.

[78] Gustavo Gutiérrez, 'The Historical Power of the Poor', in his *The Power of the Poor in History: Selected Writings* (London: SCM Press, 1983), 96.

[79] See also Jon Sobrino SJ, 'Central Position of the Reign of God in Liberation Theology', in Ignacio Ellacuría SJ and Jon Sobrino SJ (eds), *Mysterium Liberationis: Fundamental Concepts of Liberation Theology* (Maryknoll, NY: Orbis; Blackburn, Victoria, Australia: CollinsDove, 1993), 350–88.

[80] Boff further suggests that 'In that sense Jesus moves towards the project of those who are oppressed'; see Leonardo Boff, *Jesus Christ Liberator: A Critical Christology of our Time* (London: SPCK, 1980), 282–3.

society but locate themselves within an interconnected ecological system of wider planetary implications. Thus, the call of Jesus of Nazareth to bring Good News to the poor is complemented by the call of the Dalai Lama as the manifestation of the Lord Buddha to heal all sentient beings through compassion. Within a framework of liberation and justice any interreligious relations foster and help to develop an attitude of openness to the liberation of all sentient beings that live and interact within nations and states. Thus, the influence of interreligious relations and their cooperation challenge the suffering that could arise out of injustice within society and the history of human beings. In this context both Christianity and Buddhism suggest that good deeds towards other human beings, and towards creation, are signs of goodness—with the possibility of an eternal reward for Christians and the accumulation of *karma* in order to exit the cycle of life and suffering for Buddhists. Any dialogue, religious, non-religious, or interreligious, between the religions of the book (Christianity, Judaism, and Islam) and the religions of reincarnation, *samsara*, and liberation (Buddhism and Hinduism) starts with these assertions of difference and diversity and ends with reaffirmations of commonality and openness.

Arguably, in the end what makes this cooperation for justice and the dialogue that arises out of such cooperation possible is the acceptance that one tradition (Christianity) believes in a Creator as a Supreme Being and the other (Buddhism) believes in creation and the cycle of life informed by energy and matter. However, both have humans and animals at the centre of creation and share an ethical attitude of respect towards sentient beings. They share a common human journey and the central belief that justice would bring peace to a world explained in a different manner. The 'presence of Spirit' ultimately suggests in the words of Sallie King that 'with the acceptance of one's own no-ultimacy comes the humility to accept that other religions can manifest Truth, too'.[81]

FURTHER READING

Ricardo Burigana and Giovanni Turbanti, 'The Intersession: Preparing the Conclusion of the Council', in Giuseppe Alberigo (ed.), *History of Vatican II*, iv. *Church as Communion: Third Period and Intercession September 1964–September 1965* (Maryknoll, NY: Orbis; Leuven: Peeters, 2003), 453–615.

Rita M. Gross, 'Excuse Me, But What's the Question? Isn't Religious Diversity Normal?', in Paul F. Knitter (ed.), *The Myth of Religious Superiority: A Multifaith Exploration* (Maryknoll, NY: Orbis Books, 2005), 75–87.

Gustavo Gutiérrez, 'Friends of God, Friends of the Poor', in *The Density of the Present: Selected Writings* (Maryknoll, NY: Orbis Books, 1999), 147–56.

—— 'The Historical Power of the Poor', in *The Power of the Poor in History: Selected Writings* (London: SCM Press, 1983), 75–107.

---

[81] Sallie King, 'A Pluralistic View of Religious Pluralism', in Knitter, *Myth of Religious Superiority*, 101.

Eric Hobsbawm, 'On History from Below', in *On History* (London: Abacus, 1998), 266–86.

Donald Nicholl, 'Other Religions (Nostra Aetate)', in Adrian Hastings (ed.), *Modern Catholicism: Vatican II and After* (London: SPCK; New York: Oxford University Press; 1991), 126–34.

Robert J. Schreiter, 'The Impact of Vatican II', in Gregory Baum (ed.), *The Twentieth Century: A Theological Overview* (Maryknoll, NY: Orbis Books; Ottawa, Ontario: Novalis; London: Geoffrey Chapman, 1999), 158–72.

CHAPTER 15

Multiple Religious Belonging

CATHERINE CORNILLE

One of the phenomena spawned by the experience of religious plurality is that of multiple religious belonging, or of hybrid religious identities. This may take various forms, from a free and piecemeal combination of elements from a variety of religious traditions to a more selective appropriation of diverse teachings and practices, guided by a set of normative principles often grounded in one or the other tradition. The relationship between multiple religious belonging and interreligious dialogue is somewhat ambivalent. Profound dialogue with other religious traditions often leads to identification with some of their teachings and/or practices, and thus to some form of multiple belonging on the part of the dialogically engaged individual. And individuals who identify with different religions tend to engage spontaneously in some form of personal and internal dialogue.

Furthermore, multiple belonging has at times been regarded as a virtual condition for interreligious dialogue. Many of the pioneers of interreligious dialogue in the twentieth century have been seen as belonging in various degrees to more than one religion.[1] On the other hand, multiple religious belonging may also become an impediment to serious interreligious dialogue insofar as it tends to move away from commitment or belonging to any particular religious tradition and its engagement in dialogue. In short, the expression 'multiple religious belonging' covers a diversity of kinds and degrees of belonging to more than one religious tradition. In this chapter I will offer a typology of multiple religious belonging in order to then reflect on the relative import of such belonging for interreligious dialogue.

---

[1] One notable example of this is Raimon Panikkar, who famously declared about his journey into other religions that 'I "left" a Christian, "discovered" myself a Hindu, "returned" a Buddhist, all the while remaining a "Christian".' In his *The Intra-Religious Dialogue* (New York: Paulist Press, 1998) he suggests that all understanding of the religious other requires some degree of 'convincement', meaning that 'we cannot understand a person's ultimate convictions unless we somehow share them' (34).

TYPES OF MULTIPLE RELIGIOUS BELONGING

The term 'multiple religious belonging' has come into use in the West since around the turn of the twenty-first century. Two edited volumes which have played an important role in this dissemination of the term are Jacques Scheuer and Denis Gira's *Vivre de plusieurs religions: Promesse ou illusion?*,[2] and my own *Many Mansions: Multiple Religious Belonging and Christian Identity*.[3] Both volumes approach the phenomenon mainly from the perspective of the fascination among Western Christians with various forms of Hindu or Buddhist teachings and practices.[4] The term rapidly came to also refer to Jews who had become profoundly involved in the teachings and practices of Buddhism (Jubus), and then to any form of identification with two or more religious traditions. While a relatively new term and phenomenon in the West, in fact multiple religious belonging has existed for centuries in various parts of the world, and has manifested itself in many different ways. I here distinguish five forms of multiple belonging, based on the contexts in which it is used and the deeper motivations guiding the process of belonging to more than one religion: *cultural belonging, family belonging, occasional belonging, believing without belonging,* and *asymmetrical belonging.* While the first two types of multiple belonging may be regarded as involuntary or based on social and cultural contexts, the latter three types are more deliberate and based on personal need or choice.

Cultural Belonging

One of the most ancient and prevalent forms of multiple belonging is primarily associated with *cultural* identity. Here, one comes to belong to different religions as a result of belonging to a particular culture in which various religions have come to assume particular and complementary roles. For example, prior to the Cultural Revolution, the religious life of most Chinese was shaped by a mixture of Confucian, Taoist, and Buddhist elements, each focusing on particular dimensions of life. And modern Japanese often claim to be Shinto, Buddhist, and Christian, and possibly also members of a new religion, depending on the occasion or the personal and ritual need. The religions are here viewed from a vitalistic perspective serving particular this-worldly needs or offering added aesthetic value to particular ritual moments. But the particular configuration of religious services is here determined by the culture itself, or by the way in which particular religions have adapted to the cultural matrix.

---

[2] Jacques Scheuer and Denis Gira, *Vivre de plusieurs religions: Promesse ou illusion?* (Paris: Les Éditions de l'Atelier, 2000).

[3] Catherine Cornille, *Many Mansions: Multiple Religious Belonging and Christian Identity* (Maryknoll, NY: Orbis Books, 2002).

[4] In 2011, two monographs appeared, approaching the topic again from the Christian perspective: Gideon Goosen, *Hyphenated Christians; Toward a Better Understanding of Dual Religious Belonging* (Berlin: Peter Lang, 2011) and Rose Drew, *Buddhist and Christian?: An Exploration of Dual Belonging* (London and New York: Routledge, 2011).

Family Belonging

A second type of multiple religious belonging is based on *family* identity. As more and more marriages take place between individuals belonging to different religious traditions, the children born from such couples are often raised with some exposure to the religions of both parents. While some families may choose to raise their children predominantly in one or the other tradition, children tend nevertheless to partly identify with the religion of both parents. As in the previous case, this involves an involuntary form of multiple religious belonging. One identifies with more than one religion not by choice, but by virtue of belonging to a particular familial constellation. Unlike the previous instance, however, a synthesis between the different religions is not necessarily given, but must be achieved by the individuals themselves.

Occasional Belonging

In the course of history, multiple religious belonging has often been a matter of *situational identity* as it has taken the form of *occasional and need-based* identification with any number of different religious traditions and practices. This manifests itself in particular in popular forms of religiosity which are based less on questions of logical coherence of the teachings of different religions than on the efficacy of particular religious practices. Nowhere is the reality of multiple religious belonging more evident than at temples, shrines, or religious sites which are believed to possess miraculous powers. Individuals from any and all religious traditions tend to flock to such sites in the hopes of partaking in the healing or other powers believed to be actively present. In India, for example, Christians may visit Hindu miraculous shrines,[5] and Hindus will visit Christian shrines. African Christians, on the other hand, often continue to visit traditional African healers, and many Brazilian Christians admit to also participating in and belonging to the healing religions of Santeria and Candomble. Here, identification with particular traditions or practices usually lasts as long as a particular problem exists, though the effectiveness of any particular practice may lead to more enduring loyalty or identification.[6] While this type of multiple belonging is generally identified with popular religiosity and healing rituals, it may also be seen to include some forms of spiritual seeking which temporarily tap into the resources of a particular religion to fulfil more psychological or spiritual needs.

---

[5] For numerous examples of this, see Selva Raj and Corinne Dempsey, *Popular Christianity in India: Riting Between the Lines* (Albany, NY: SUNY, 2002).

[6] For numerous examples of this type of popular mixing, see Devaka Premawardhana, 'The Unremarkable Hybrid: Aloysius Pieris and the Redundancy of Multiple Religious Belonging', *Journal of Ecumenical Studies*, 46/1 (2011), 76–101.

Believing without Belonging[7]

The fourth instance of multiple religious belonging may be referred to as a matter of *eclectic belonging* as it involves *deliberate and unlimited identification with belief elements from different religious traditions*. Exposure to the reality of religious plurality has led to a tendency to form one's own religious identity by picking and choosing from among the teachings and practices of different religions. The most recent Western expression of this development is often traced back to the Theosophical movement, founded by Helena Blavatsky and Henry Steel Olcott. It is based on a rejection of all religious claims to exclusive and absolute truth and on recognition of all religions as containing elements of truth. Rather than doctrinal claims, it is personal experience and judgement which forms the basis for the validity and truth of particular teachings and practices. Though one may speak here of multiple religious belonging in the broad sense of the term, it might be more aptly designated as 'believing without belonging' or multiple religious non-belonging.

Asymmetrical Belonging

A fifth type of multiple religious belonging is a product of *asymmetrical identity* in that it involves *belonging primarily to one religion while also identifying with another*. This also entails a deliberate or voluntary act on the part of an individual. But unlike in the previous case, it involves primary grounding in a particular religious tradition and acceptance of its criteria of religious identity and belonging. Here, individuals tend to identify predominantly with one tradition which becomes the basis and norm from which one comes to selectively identify with elements from one or more other traditions. Thus, this involves a somewhat unequal sense of belonging to more than one tradition. In some cases, multiple belonging may lead to a shifting of a sense of primary belonging from one religion to another, or to a genuine sense of dividedness between two traditions, one tradition being normative in certain areas of life and the other in other areas. A special case of this may be found in individuals who identify with the symbolic framework and scriptural tradition of one religion and with a hermeneutic or interpretative framework of another. This is the case, for example, with Christian theologians who have come to use the philosophical frameworks of Hinduism or Buddhism to reinterpret Christian faith.[8] The question of whether or not this is a case of multiple belong-

---

[7] This expression was first used by Grace Davie in her book, Religion in Britain since 1945: *Believing without Belonging* (Oxford: Wiley-Blackwell, 1994).

[8] e.g. Christian theologians such as John Keenan and Joseph O'Leary have come to use Buddhist Madhyamika categories to reinterpret Christian faith. See John Keenan, *The Meaning of Christ: A Mahayana Theology* (Maryknoll, NY: Orbis Books, 1989), and his other works including *I am/No Self: A Christian Commentary on the Heart Sutra* (Leuven: Peeters, 2011). For Joseph O'Leary, see his *Religious Pluralism and Christian Truth* (Edinburgh: Edinburgh University Press, 1996), and more recently his 'Skillful Means as a Hermeneutic Concept', in C. Conway and C. Cornille (eds), *Interreligious Hermeneutics* (Eugene, Or.: Wipf & Stock, 2010), 163–83. John Thatamanil, on the other hand, uses categories and views of the Hindu tradition of Advaita Vedanta to reinterpret traditional Christian notions of God, creation, and the human predicament in his *The Immanent Divine* (Minneapolis: Fortress Press, 2006).

ing depends on the possibility of severing a religion from its traditional hermeneutical framework and reinterpreting it from a radically different perspective.

DEGREES OF MULTIPLE RELIGIOUS BELONGING

Though the expression 'multiple religious belonging' has become part of common discourse it may, in fact, be something of a misnomer. The term suggests a measure of equal belonging to two or more religious traditions. However, I would argue that such equal belonging is both theoretically impossible and concretely impracticable, at least when belonging is understood in terms of the self-understanding of particular religions.[9] The literature on multiple religious belonging has come to approach the phenomenon predominantly from the perspective of the subject who claims to belong to a particular religion. However, all forms of religious belonging involve a subjective as well as an objective pole, a confession by an individual as well as recognition of that confession by the tradition itself.[10] I may claim to be a Hindu, but if no Hindu recognizes me as such, that claim remains meaningless. Most religions tend to prefer, if not require, single and undivided commitment and belonging from their members. This may be attributed to religious jealousy or possessiveness. But it may also be seen as part of the logic of religious identity and belonging, justifiable on theological, practical, and spiritual grounds.

On theological grounds, the idea of equal belonging to two or more religions may be regarded as a contradiction in terms. While different religious traditions may have much in common, no two religions are perfectly compatible. Belonging to one always excludes, to some extent, belonging to another. This may be of minimal concern to individuals who practise multiple belonging, oriented as they tend to be towards practical efficacy, rather than logical coherence. However, insofar as religions do include a theoretical or philosophical dimension, multiple belonging can only be practised by effectively ignoring this dimension. Even on a practical level, multiple belonging is difficult to engage, as Paul Griffiths has clearly shown. As he argues, it is 'performatively impossible to belong to both at once—in much the same way that it's performatively impossible to be a sumo wrestler and a balance-beam gymnast'.[11] Certain religious expectations, such as the dedication of all of one's charitable giving or volunteer time to particular religious causes, exclude the possibility of multiple belonging.

---

[9] For a more critical assessment of multiple religious belonging from the perspective of the self-understanding of religions, see my 'Mehrere Meister? Multiple Religionszugehörigkeit in Praxis und Theorie', in Reinhold Bernhardt and Perry Schmidt-Leukel (eds), *Multiple religiöse Identität* (Zurich: Theologischer Verlag Zurich, 2008), 15–35.

[10] As even Panikkar pointed out, religious belonging is a matter not only of the individual but also of the tradition to which he or she claims to belong. With regard to Christian belonging, he proposed that 'the criterion for Christian identity lies ultimately in the sincere confession of a person, validated by a corresponding recognition of a community'. Raimon Panikkar, 'On Christian Identity: Who is a Christian?', in Cornille, *Many Mansions?*, 123.

[11] Paul Griffiths, *The Problem of Religious Diversity* (Oxford: Blackwell, 2001), 13.

On a spiritual level, religions tend to advocate the importance of complete surrender of self as a necessary condition for spiritual growth and for attaining the highest state of spiritual realization. Insofaras such surrender requires commitment to one particular religious path and discipline, multiple religious belonging would in this context probably be regarded as an impediment to spiritual growth.

Since multiple religious belonging is thus arguably undesirable, if not impossible from the point of view of the religions themselves, it involves primarily a subjective experience of identifying with elements from two or more religions. However, in most cases, individuals who claim to belong to multiple religions tend to identify to various degrees with the different religions. One sees that one religion, usually the religion of birth, tends to remain dominant, while elements from other religions which are compatible with the dominant religion are selectively integrated. In some cases, individuals may wittingly or unwittingly come to identify primarily with another religion, while remaining attached to elements of their birth religion. In either case, multiple belonging rarely involves an equal sense of belonging to different religions, or a desire to fulfil all of the requirements for belonging as set out by the tradition itself. As such, the term multiple religious belonging tends to be used in a very broad sense.

MULTIPLE RELIGIOUS BELONGING AND RELIGIOUS PLURALISM

While many individuals who practise multiple religious belonging are less concerned with theoretical theological coherence than with the concrete efficacy of their practices, some do try to develop a broader religious framework in which such practice might make sense. In her book, *Buddhist and Christian?*, Rose Drew collected accounts from several Christian theologians who also identify with Buddhism. Most of these theologians adhere to a form of theological pluralism, which, she states, 'is crucial to full and authentic dual belonging, for if Buddhism is affirmed as superior, it is hard to see how one can claim authentic Christian belonging and, if Christianity is affirmed as superior, it is hard to see how one can claim authentic Buddhist belonging'.[12] In classical pluralist mode, most tend to affirm the unity and unknowability of ultimate reality or what Drew calls 'a monocentric understanding of the ultimate orientations of Buddhism and Christianity'.[13] With regard to many of the mutually exclusive teachings of Buddhism and Christianity (such as the nature of the afterlife and the continuing existence of an individual self), many of those who claim dual belonging seem to adopt an attitude of agnosticism, or treat them as 'bracketed questions'.[14] Emphasis is placed

---

[12] Drew, *Buddhist and Christian?*, 222.   [13] Drew, *Buddhist and Christian?*, 208.
[14] Drew, *Buddhist and Christian?*, 210.

on the distinction between the ultimate truth itself and the religious teachings and practices as means to, but not identical with, that ultimate truth.

Using a classical Buddhist image, which has become popular among pluralists, Paul Knitter refers to religious languages and symbols as 'fingers pointing to the moon'; thereby justifying his own foray into both Buddhism and Christianity.[15] The focus of religious commitment and belonging is thus here defined not so much in terms of established religious identities, but in terms of the ultimate reality which lies beyond religious boundaries. Since this ultimate reality is the origin and goal of all religions, multiple religious belonging is believed to be reconcilable with the self-understanding of all religions.

One of the pioneers of multiple belonging who rejects the pluralist solution is Roger Corless. Having studied and practised Buddhism and Christianity for many years, he came to realize that the two traditions could not be reconciled in terms of their own self-understanding. Instead, he regarded his own engagement with the two traditions as a *tertium quid*, a personal synthesis which could not be claimed to be either fully Christian or fully Buddhist, but which could still function as the basis for dialogue between the two traditions.[16] This unified ultimate reality then becomes the focus of commitment and the grounds for the possibility of commitment to more than one tradition.[17] Corless squarely recognized, however, that this personal synthesis was neither authentically Christian nor Buddhist. 'Unless one's formal Buddhist and Christian practices are clearly distinguishable from each other,' he stated, 'how can one be sure that one is an authentic practitioner of either tradition?' And he believed that, if one is not practising authentically within each tradition, 'one will undermine the dialogue between them'.[18]

While multiple religious belonging in the full sense of the term may require a pluralist view of religious truth, a more qualified understanding of the phenomenon as identifying with elements of another religion may fit with more inclusivist approaches. Gideon Goosen, for example, defines religious hybridity or dual religious belonging as a process which occurs 'when a person has a first major religion and draws on a second to a greater or lesser degree, according to the criteria of doctrine, practices and actions'.[19] Arguing from a Christian perspective, Goosen suggests that one may still recognize Jesus Christ as the 'apex of revelation',[20] while acknowledging elements of truth in other religions. Here, multiple belonging thus involves a primary commitment and belonging to one religion, while belonging only in a very limited and derivative sense to a second tradition.

---

[15] Paul Knitter, *Without Buddha I Could Not Be a Christian* (Oxford: Oneworld, 2009), 59–73.

[16] See *Buddhist and Christian?*, 45–8, 214. Corless referred to this as a 'coinherent superconsciousness' which he later also came to identify with forms of eco-spirituality.

[17] *Buddhist and Christian?*, 207.

[18] Quoted by Rose Drew in *Buddhist and Christian?* 187.

[19] Drew, *Buddhist and Christian?*, 19.

[20] Gideon Goosen, *Hyphenated Christians*, 131.

RELIGIOUS BELONGING AND
INTERRELIGIOUS DIALOGUE

The term 'interreligious dialogue', like 'multiple religious belonging', has been applied to many different types of encounter between members of different religions, from the high level and formal meeting of leaders of different religions to friendly exchanges among different believers; from grassroots collaboration between religions in common social or political projects to the in-depth study of the other religion with an eye on learning from one another and deepening or enriching one's own religious tradition. All of these forms of dialogue presuppose a sense of belonging to one or the other tradition.

Among the conditions for the possibility of interreligious dialogue I laid out in *The Im-Possibility of Interreligious Dialogue*, commitment or belonging to a particular religious tradition constitutes the most obvious, but also the most paradoxical condition.[21] Firm commitment to a particular religion tends to reduce interest in and openness towards other religious traditions. Insofar as each religion claims to offer the fullness of the means of salvation, and insofar as commitment is an all-embracing and lifelong project, believers may feel little inclination to also explore the teachings of other religions. As such, dialogue also requires some degree of doctrinal humility and hospitality or receptivity towards the truth of other religions. However, insofar as those conditions are fulfilled, commitment to a particular tradition and to the project of advancing its truth remains an important requirement for dialogue.

The conception and ritual markers of religious belonging of course differ from one tradition to the next. Whereas some religions require a formal rite of initiation, others are content with a more informal dedication of oneself to particular teachings and practices. And while birth marks the reality of belonging to ethnic religions, other religions tend to require a more voluntary and explicit sign of commitment. Though the boundaries of belonging may at times be somewhat fluid, most religions do have basic requirements to be fulfilled in order to be recognized as a member of the tradition (signing of forms, payment of dues, passage through moments of initiation, and so on). Such belonging to a tradition does not guarantee knowledge about the tradition or a desire to engage in dialogue. But it is the willingness to speak from and for a particular tradition which distinguishes genuine interreligious dialogue from purely personal spiritual seeking.

The importance of religious belonging for interreligious dialogue is thus based on a conception of dialogue as an engagement between two traditions with their histories, worldviews, doctrines, rituals, and schools of thought. While it is true that dialogue occurs between individuals, rather than between traditions, it is the sense of accountability to the other as a representative of a tradition, and to the tradition for what one has learnt from the other that

---

[21] Cornille, *Im-Possibility of Interreligious Dialogue*. The other conditions elaborated in the book are humility, interconnection, empathy, and generosity.

marks the dialogue as genuinely interreligious. With regard to the other, it entails the responsibility to represent not only one's own private opinion, but a long history of reflection and transmission of particular teachings, insights, and experiences. Interreligious dialogue moreover requires a willingness to testify not only to the contents but also to the truth of a particular set of beliefs and practices.[22] Religious belonging lends the authority of tradition to the voices in dialogue. This of course requires a certain basic knowledge of one's own tradition, combined with the humility to admit that one does not know, understand, or agree with particular aspects of the tradition. It also presupposes transparency about one's own situated place as belonging to a particular school, sect, or subtradition within the religion as a whole. Dialogue indeed does not take place between a Christian and a Muslim, but between, for example, a conservative European Roman Catholic and a liberal Shiite Muslim. This transparency about one's religious identity and belonging offers confidence and purpose, as well as subtlety and nuance, to the dialogue.

In addition to providing a solid ground from which to engage in dialogue with the other, the condition of religious belonging also assures the possibility of enrichment through dialogue, not only for the individual involved, but for the whole tradition. Engagement in interreligious dialogue from a sense of commitment and belonging implies a desire to share the fruits of the dialogue with a larger community of believers. Since the practice of interreligious dialogue tends to be the privilege of a limited few who have the interest, the expertise, and the luxury to explore the teachings and practices of other religions, it is only through a willingness to communicate one's insights and experiences with the larger tradition that this tradition may also participate in the process of learning and growth. To be sure, many traditions and believers may not be receptive to the fruits of dialogue, and individuals who have engaged in advanced forms of dialogue are, at times, marginalized if not effectively punished by their respective traditions. But it is only through continued or at times renewed commitment to a particular religion that dialogue may hope to move religions forward.

One of functions of religious commitment in dialogue is that of providing participants with a particular normative framework through which to discern the truth and value of the teachings and practices of the other. This may be regarded by some as a limiting factor in the dialogue in so far as interreligious dialogue is often regarded as a completely open pursuit of truth. From this perspective, the normative conceptions of truth of any particular religion may be seen to represent an impediment to open dialogue. However, when dialogue is viewed as an engagement between religious traditions with their developed traditions and conceptions of truth, such criteria become an essential foundation for constructive dialogue. Rather than one's own taste and judgement, they represent a genuinely religious source and basis for assessing the truth and validity of another religion.

---

[22] For more on this, see my 'The Role of Witness in Interreligious Dialogue', *Concilium* 1 (2011), 61–70.

In the process of dialogue, one religious tradition thus tends to function as a basis for both understanding and judging the other. This normativity functions on both an epistemological level and a level of judgement. In the attempt to grasp the meaning of particular teachings and rituals of the other tradition, believers tend to use their own familiar categories and draw analogies with their own tradition. It is on the basis of similarities and analogies that one then comes to also understand differences and particularities of the respective traditions. The other thus always comes to be understood through the lens of one's own religious tradition. This may be seen to involve some degree of distortion, as one can never fully understand the other from within. But the experiences and insights of the outsider may still prove fruitful and productive, both for the outsider and for the insider. For the outsider, the very attempt at understanding the other from within opens new religious vistas and experiences which may come to enrich one's own tradition. And for the insider, they may come to shed new light on one's own all too familiar teachings and practices.[23] In the process, the other thus functions as a catalyst which sheds new light on traditional teachings and at times offers new ways of interpreting traditional teachings or new ways of attaining particular religious or spiritual states and experiences.

In addition to their epistemological and hermeneutical role, the doctrinal and practical teachings of one's tradition also function as the norm to evaluate the truth and validity of the teachings and practices of the other. This has been a point of contention between pluralist and all other approaches to the religious other. Whereas pluralists regard this religious normativity as a residue of religious imperialism and arrogance, inclusivists regard it as an inevitable component of religious commitment and identity. Insofar as dialogue takes place between representatives of particular religions, the basic worldview and belief system of that tradition will inevitably function as the basis against which the teachings and practices of the other religion are judged. Thus, insofar as all religions judge one another in this fashion, it may actually serve as an expression of equality between participants in dialogue.[24]

While the notion of normativity often evokes a sense of judgement of the other on the basis of fixed principles, there are different ways in which it may operate in the dialogue. Some may use it as a maximal principle of discernment, allowing truth or validity only in those teachings and practices which are the same as one's own. Others may use it as a minimal principle, allowing for the possibility of truth and validity in whatever teachings and practices are not in contradiction with one's own. The latter approach allows for considerable openness to discovering new insights in other religions. In the actual practice of dialogue, the principle of normativity tends to operate spontaneously, rather than reflectively or self-consciously. One tends to be drawn to elements in other religions which complement one's

---

[23] Mikhail Bakhtin refers in this context to the importance of 'exotopy', of the creative understanding which can only come from standing outside the culture (or religion). See Tsvetan Todorov, *Mikhail Bakhtin: The Dialogical Principle* (Minneapolis: University of Minnesota Press, 1984), 109.

[24] For more on religion-specific criteria used in dialogue, see Catherine Cornille (ed.), *Criteria of Discernment in Interreligious Dialogue* (Eugene, Or.: Wipf & Stock, 2009).

own tradition or which fill particular religious or spiritual needs. This generally arises from certain internalized religious attitudes and desires which are shaped within a particular tradition.

In addition to its complexity, the idea of the normativity of a particular religion may also be understood in dynamic terms. Not only is it not always clear what the essential criteria are within a particular religion which may serve as a basis for judging another, but religious norms and criteria may themselves shift and change, at times as a result of the dialogue. Engagement with other religions and hermeneutical frameworks may indeed affect the way in which one comes to understand or interpret certain central teachings of one's own tradition, which in turn will colour one's understanding and judgement of the other. As such, belonging to a tradition and viewing other religions from a particular normative perspective may be understood as a dynamic process which itself may come to shift and change in the process of dialogue.

MULTIPLE RELIGIOUS BELONGING AS AN OBSTACLE FOR INTERRELIGIOUS DIALOGUE

Since the expression 'multiple religious belonging' covers a large spectrum of degrees and kinds of belonging, its relationship to and relevance for interreligious dialogue is equally varied. The most extreme or literal forms of multiple religious belonging present a challenge and even an obstacle for interreligious dialogue. For arguably multiple religious belonging generally represents a retreat from fully belonging to any one particular religion, or an indifference to the specific criteria of belonging to particular religions as such. As pointed out above, most forms of multiple religious belonging focus on the practical or this-worldly efficacy of religions, rather than on their logical or theological truth and coherence. Focused as they are on the immediate well-being of the individual, they tend to ignore the larger questions of what one religion might be able to offer to the other.

The experience of multiple religious belonging also often arises from, or can lead to, a somewhat tentative or lukewarm commitment to any one particular religion. Such multiple belonging may at times involve a painful separation from the religion one is most familiar or comfortable with. For some, multiple belonging indeed does involve a process of identifying with the teachings and practices of another religion, while yet remaining nostalgically attached to one's originating—most often therefore family—tradition. It then takes the form of an oscillation between traditions in which one becomes normative in some religious matters and the other in others. This means that those who experience multiple belonging do not fully embrace either religion on its own terms, but rather choose to live in the tension between irreconcilable or competing worldviews. In relinquishing full commitment or belonging to any one tradition, they thus also abandon the willingness or ability to speak from or for either tradition. This is probably what characterizes the experience of many 'Jubus' (Jewish-Buddhists), who remain ethnically connected to their Jewish roots but have come to identify philosophically and experientially with the Buddhist tradition. It is certainly the case for a good number of Christians (or former Christians) who have developed strong sympathies for particular elements of Buddhist thought and practice, but do not feel inclined to fully convert to Buddhism while neither being able to return to fully embrace their Christian roots.

As mentioned, one way in which the experience of multiple religious belonging comes to be resolved is by recourse to a pluralist view which locates truth in a reality transcending all religious traditions as the ultimate focus of commitment. But the pluralist solution for the possibility of multiple belonging tends to clash with the self-understanding of religions. All the same, the main challenge for interreligious dialogue is its tendency to disregard the particulars of religious teaching and practice, as Mark Heim[25] has so convincingly argued, and thus its disinterest in advancing the truth of particular religions through detailed and constructive dialogue. All the same, these radical or extreme forms of multiple religious belonging may still be instructive for the religions engaged in dialogue. The very inability or unwillingness to fully commit or belong to a particular religion may be an occasion for critical self-examination on the part of the religion. And the appeal of specific teachings and practices in other religions may equally prompt reflection on what may be lacking or in need of further development in one's own religion. Multiple religious belonging tends to arise from a sense of insufficiency or lack in any one particular religion. This may lead to a search for truth in another religion, or it may result from an engagement with other religions which brings home a discrepancy between what one tradition has to offer and one's own religious experience or thirst. The experience of multiple religious belonging thus points to a certain hiatus within a particular tradition or to areas which do not offer satisfactory insight or experience.

The ways in which individuals attempt to reconcile different religious loyalties may also become edifying for the process of dialogue. If we take the recent work of Paul Knitter as an example of multiple religious belonging, as he himself suggests, then the ways in which he draws from Buddhist sources in order to address certain areas which he perceives as lacunae or theological conundrums, may come to inform, both positively and negatively, the way in which Christian (and maybe Buddhist) thinkers deal with the questions raised. Knitter admittedly represents a somewhat ambivalent example of pure multiple belonging, since he himself claims to be still primarily a Christian, writing for Christian readers, but still opening himself to the possibility of being judged unorthodox by fellow Christians.[26] Other attempts to integrate Buddhist and Christian teachings and practices, as in the case of Ruben Habito, Sallie King, or Roger Corless, can equally shed light on the ways in which different religions fulfil various religious desires and needs, and in which they may potentially come to be reconciled.

The inability or unwillingness to choose for one or the other religions, and the desire to persist in the unresolved tension between religious traditions may itself also become edifying

---

[25] S. Mark Heim, *Salvations: Truth and Difference in Religion* (Maryknoll, NY: Orbis Books, 1995).

[26] Knitter, *Without Buddha*, pp. xiii–xiv.

for interreligious dialogue. Not only does it reveal a certain form of courage to depart from the trodden path, it also places into sharp relief the fault-lines, or breaking points, between religions which do not allow for easy or ready harmonization in one direction or the other. In their own varied attempts at integration of certain aspects of different religions, individuals who claim multiple religious belonging offer concrete options or proposals to be considered in the process of interreligious dialogue.

MULTIPLE RELIGIOUS BELONGING AS A MEANS TO DIALOGUE

While multiple religious belonging in the full and oxymoronic sense of the term may represent an impediment for genuine interreligious dialogue, a more qualified understanding of the term as referring to the phenomenon of belonging to one religion, while yet identifying with certain elements of another may in fact be regarded as a condition for a constructive dialogue between religions. Here, interreligious dialogue is understood as a process not merely of friendly exchange of information, but also of mutual learning and argumentation. The desire to learn from another religion always arises from a deep identification with particular teachings and practices, or from multiple religious belonging in the broadest sense of the term. Most of the pioneers of interreligious dialogue were individuals who went far into the study and exploration of other religions, often at first with the intent of rendering Christianity more intelligible to the other. This was the case with a missionary such as Henri Le Saux. In an attempt to understand Hinduism from within, Le Saux became the disciple of several Hindu gurus (including Ramana Maharshi and Gnanananda) and took on the Hindu lifestyle of a wandering ascetic or *sannyasi*. In the process of immersing himself in the contemplative traditions of Hinduism, Le Saux attained very profound and transformative spiritual experiences and insights. As a result, he dedicated the rest of his life to reconciling (often unsuccessfully and with a great deal of torment and frustration) these with his Christian faith.[27] Many of the other pioneers of inculturation and interreligious dialogue, such as Raimon Panikkar, Aloysius Pieris, or Louis Massignon, were individuals who became captured to a greater or lesser degree by elements of truth and value they encountered in other religious traditions. Panikkar later came to speak of the importance of 'convincement' or acceptance of the truth of a particular religious teaching or practice in order to come to a full understanding of it, and to render it meaningful for dialogue.[28] It is, indeed, only insofar as one is moved or inspired by a teaching or practice in another religion that one will seek to incorporate it in one's own religious life and in the life of one's primary religion of belonging.

---

[27] This torment is powerfully expressed in his journal, *La Montee au fond du Cœur: Le Journal intime d'un moine Chrétien-sannyasi Hindou 1948–1973* (Paris: OEIL, 1986).

[28] Panikkar, *Intra-Religious Dialogue*, 34.

While the experience of multiple belonging was often experienced as a shock and a source of some suffering and confusion by the early pioneers of dialogue, it has become considerably less traumatic and disorienting in recent decades, as information about other religions is readily accessible and as religious attitudes towards other religions have become considerably more open and receptive. Comparative theologians not only within Christianity, but also in Buddhism or Judaism, have come to dedicate their career to the study of another religion, somewhat more deliberately identifying with certain teachings and practices, and exploring the possibilities of their appropriation or integration within their own religions. One type of comparative theology or interreligious dialogue which merits attention in the context of multiple religious belonging is that of Christian theologians such as John Keenan, Joseph O'Leary, and John Thatamanil, who have come to use the philosophical framework of other religions, in particular Mahayana Buddhism or Advaita Vedanta, in order to rethink fundamental Christian principles and ideas. This work has opened up revolutionary, innovative, and challenging ways of understanding the fundamentals of Christian faith. The theologians engaged in this exercise view it as a way to overcome the metaphysical challenges of our times. The question of whether or not this represents a form of multiple religious belonging hinges on the possibility of separating the teachings of a religion from the philosophical framework in which it has traditionally been expressed. If that is indeed the case, then the work of these scholars may be regarded as a modern version of Thomas Aquinas's use of Aristotelian concepts to express Christian faith. If, however, religions are essentially tied to the metaphysical framework in which they were originally expressed, then this surely qualifies as a challenging case of multiple religious belonging.

In the context of interreligious dialogue multiple religious belonging often functions as a temporary or transitional state. An individual might come either to deliberately or inadvertently identify with the teachings or practices of another religion and then seek to integrate these within, or at least bring them into dialogue with their own religion. This process of dialogue may involve the rediscovery of elements within one's own tradition which have been forgotten or marginalized. Or it may involve the integration of insights and experiences which are reconcilable with one's religion and which bring new life to the tradition. The question of whether or not multiple belonging remains a more permanent state then depends on whether or not elements from the other religion eventually come to be successfully integrated within one's primary religious tradition.

CONCLUSION

Both 'interreligious dialogue' and 'multiple religious belonging' are notoriously vague and somewhat general terms or categories, covering a variety of types and degrees of engagement with various religious traditions. Interreligious dialogue may refer to the simple encounter of individuals of different traditions all the way to the systematic engagement of scholars of one religion with the teachings and practices of another, as takes place in the discipline of comparative theology. Multiple religious belonging may equally range from a selective identification with certain teachings and practices of another religion all the way to the experience of initiation in various religions and the attempt to live in the tension between two entirely different religious traditions. Taken in the most general sense, all forms of multiple religious belonging involve some degree of inter- or intra-religious dialogue. In the case of multiple religious belonging as cultural identity, the religions coexisting in a particular culture tend to consciously or unconsciously interact with and influence one another. Even though each religion occupies a specific and compartmentalized role in the lives of individuals, one may find various attempts to integrate the different religions or to appropriate elements from one religion into another.[29] Individuals born from parents with different religious identities also often attempt to integrate the different religions into their own life and thus perform some kind of internal dialogue. This type of personal or internal dialogue takes place all the more with individuals who come to integrate elements from different religions into their own personal synthesis.

While using the expressions 'multiple religious belonging' and 'interreligious dialogue' in these broad senses of the terms thus points to various convergences and connections, it may not actually help to come to a clear understanding of each phenomenon in itself and in relation to the other. The term 'interreligious dialogue' refers, strictly speaking, only to those forms of engagement with the religious other which take place within the framework of religious traditions and which are oriented to the enrichment not only of individuals but of the traditions themselves. This understanding of interreligious dialogue presupposes a clear sense of identification with and belonging to a particular religion which remains the normative framework from which one engages the other religion. When interreligious dialogue is understood in this sense, then some types of multiple belonging may have only limited relevance.

One of the characteristics of the experience of multiple religious belonging is its focus on this-worldly efficacy, rather than theological coherence. The truth and efficacy of particular teachings and practices tends to be measured in terms of personal or subjective needs and fulfilment, rather than in terms of their theological or philosophical coherence. And insofar as the experience of multiple religious belonging arises from a certain dissatisfaction with or detachment from particular religions, it will not likely result in a desire to change or enrich those traditions themselves. While, for some, multiple religious belonging may represent a temporary state which is aimed at advancing the dialogue, for others it may in fact become a flight from the difficulties of dialogue. As Roger Corless astutely remarked: 'Unless one's formal Buddhist and Christian practices are clearly distinguishable from each other...how can one be sure that one is an authentic practitioner of either tradition?' and if one is not

---

[29] A famous example of this in China may be found in the Neo-Confucianism of Zhu Xi (1130–1200) which manifests profound influences from both Taoism and Buddhism.

practising authentically within each tradition, he reasoned, 'one will undermine the dialogue between them'.[30]

The expression 'multiple religious belonging' may also benefit from more nuance or precision. It tends to be used to refer to any form or degree of identification with more than one religious tradition, ranging from experiences of being inspired by or attracted to a particular teaching or practice of another religion to a sense of full identification with two (or more) traditions, or a loss of primary identification with either. This raises questions about the appropriateness of using the term 'belonging' in all cases. Such a term would presuppose at least a desire to fully belong to more than one tradition and to live up to its requirements for membership. This—relatively rare—occurrence might be distinguished from multiple religious identification, or hybrid religious identity, which emphasizes the subjective experience of identifying with elements from different religious traditions. Though radical forms of multiple belonging, understood as full identification with two or more traditions, may be a contradiction in terms, the experience of partial identification with elements from different religions is rather common and may be regarded as a condition for advanced and constructive interreligious dialogue. Dialogue presupposes a primary identification with a particular set of religious teachings and practices. But it is also served by an ability to empathize and identify with teachings and practices of another religion, and thus to assess their value and importance for one's own religious tradition. It is indeed the experience of being deeply moved or inspired by the teachings of another religion which leads to the desire to integrate those teachings and experiences within one's own tradition.

One of the critical issues in the relationship between interreligious dialogue and multiple religious belonging concerns the very notion of religious belonging itself. Every tradition has its own particular criteria of belonging, and these criteria may shift and change through time. Some religions have clear lines of authority determining whether or not someone belongs, while others are less discriminating. Some focus the criteria of belonging on questions of orthodoxy, while others focus more on orthopraxis. Interreligious dialogue has been an area in which the boundaries of belonging have at times been challenged and stretched. Insofar as it involves openness to the presence of truth in other religions and the introduction of new ideas, practices, and experiences in one's own, it may be seen to threaten classical notions of religious identity and belonging. As such, individuals who themselves believe they firmly belong to a particular tradition may come to find themselves unwittingly and against their own desire on the margins or outside their own tradition. Dialogue thus raises the question of the extent to which one may identify with elements from another religion and integrate those elements in one's own tradition while still fully belonging to that religion. This question can only be addressed from within the boundaries of particular religions and case by case. But it is one of the most interesting and challenging questions which may have a significant impact on the self-understanding of religions and on the future of interreligious dialogue.

[30]   Quoted by Rose Drew in *Buddhist and Christian?*, 187.

FURTHER READING

John Berthrong, *The Divine Delhi: Religious Identity in the North American Cultural Mosaic* (Maryknoll, NY: Orbis Books, 1999).

Catherine Cornille (ed.), *Many Mansions? Multiple Religious Belonging and Christian Identity* (Maryknoll, NY: Orbis Books, 2002).

John D'Arcy May, *Converging Ways? Conversion and Belonging in Buddhism and Christianity* (Sankt Ottilien: EOS, 2007).

Rose Drew, *Buddhist and Christian? An Exploration of Dual Belonging* (London: Routledge, 2011).

Gideon Goosen, *Hyphenated Christian: Toward a Better Understanding of Dual Religious Belonging* (Oxford: Peter Lang, 2011).

Paul Knitter, *Without the Buddha I Could Not Be a Christian* (Oxford: Oneworld, 2009).

Peter Phan, *Being Religious Interreligiously* (Maryknoll, NY: Orbis Books, 2007).

Jacques Scheuer and Denis Gira, *Vivre de plusieurs religions: Promesse ou illusion?* (Paris: Les Éditions de l'Atelier, 2000).

Perry Schmidt-Leukel and Reinhold Bernhardt (eds), *Multiple religiöse Identität* (Zurich: Theologischer Verlag Zurich, 2008).

CHAPTER 16

Boundaries and Encounters

DAVID R. VISHANOFF

Benedict Anderson famously defined a nation as 'an imagined political community . . . imagined as both inherently limited and sovereign'.[1] A group of people would not constitute a nation if they did not regard themselves as separate and independent from other people. This does not come about necessarily or inevitably, but only because at some point those people choose, consciously or unconsciously, to take their attention off what they have in common with others, and focus instead on one or more differences in ethnicity, language, geography, culture, or religion, which they elevate to the status of national boundary markers in their collective imagination. Are religions likewise imagined rather than natural communities, created and sustained by a group's choice to give themselves a collective identity by treating certain differences as boundaries, while ignoring other differences and overlooking equally real commonalities? If so, what does that mean for interactions that take place across those boundaries? Are they always exercises in self-definition—encounters with imagined 'others' who are nothing but reflections of the boundaries by which each party defines itself? Or can interactions transcend and modify those boundaries, so that each party's conception of the other is transformed by the encounter, and its own identity is modified in the process?

Scholars of religion have not yet agreed on any definition of religious community as clear and eloquent as Anderson's definition of a nation, or any general theory of religious boundaries and interactions; but their studies of specific cases are rich in theoretical insight into the many ways in which religious people construct their identities, maintain their boundaries, and then proceed to cross those boundaries to interact and communicate with others. This chapter draws together several of those insights and case studies into a systematic account of religious boundaries and encounters.[2]

---

[1] Benedict Anderson, *Imagined Communities: Reflections on the Origin and Spread of Nationalism*, rev. edn (London: Verso, 2006), 6.

[2] The research and thinking behind this chapter owe a great debt to the diligent and theoretically insightful assistance of Whitney Patterson, whose work was supported by the Honors Research Assistantship Program of the University of Oklahoma Honors College.

Boundaries

The notion of interreligious encounter presupposes the existence of a boundary across which interaction takes place. Interaction is a broad term, encompassing any form of active relationship between people, whether the action be verbal, symbolic, or concrete, and whether the participants be members of the same or different communities. Let us use the term 'encounter' more narrowly to designate interaction with an 'other', face to face across some kind of dividing line. Why are religions so distinct from each other that interactions between their adherents constitute encounters, with all the sense of strangeness, adventure, and even danger that this word evokes? In other words, why is religion itself divided up into several clearly demarcated religions? The answer lies partly in the peculiar story of how modern Westerners developed their concept of religion.

The religious communities out of which modern Europe grew tended to think of religion as something that they had and that others lacked. Not that medieval European Christians did not recognize the existence of other belief systems; they were certainly aware of Islam, for instance, but they tended to speak of it as a falsification of true religion, or some kind of demonic counter-religion, rather than a complete religion in its own right, parallel to Christianity, giving its own answers to the same set of questions. (Muslims returned the favour, portraying medieval Christianity as a corruption of the true religion of Abraham, Ishmael, Isaac, and Jacob.) In this premodern schema, there was only one religion, and boundaries were drawn between followers of this true religion, heretics who distorted the true religion, and people who were simply irreligious. There were plenty of others, but no genuinely religious others.

The idea that there are in the world many comparable religious systems—that 'you have your religion and I have mine'—rests upon a generic concept of 'religion in general' that came to dominate Western thinking only in the modern period. Colonial ventures gave Europeans an unsettling new awareness of foreign beliefs and practices, which they rendered less threatening by classifying them as more or less developed forms of 'religion'. Some regarded them as precursors to the more sophisticated religion of modern Christianity, while others romanticized them as survivals of a universal human spirituality uncontaminated by the ritual, doctrinal, and institutional complexities that they despised. Both attitudes required identifying some generic phenomenon called religion that each of these foreign systems embodied to some degree. Friedrich Schleiermacher (d. 1834) famously identified the essence of religion as a 'feeling of absolute dependence'. Rudolf Otto (d. 1937) described it as a feeling of 'the numinous', an a priori idea of something holy and wholly other, of which all religious systems are developments and schematizations. Other modern scholars focused not on religious experience but on shared ethical norms such as love for humanity or the golden rule, which they found expressed in all the great religions.

All the so-called great religions were found to have their own core doctrines, scriptures, rituals, founders, and theories of salvation, so that they could stand alongside Christianity as comparable systems in which different sacred things played the same basic roles: *salat* was Muslim prayer, *nirvana* was Buddhist salvation, the Vedas were the Hindu Bible, and so on. This construction of parallel religious systems lumped together diverse people, texts, and practices, while projecting onto all of them various features of Protestant Christianity. In India, for example, numerous non-Muslim religious traditions were conflated by the British colonial administration under the label of Hinduism, even though they worshipped rival deities in different ways and recited different scriptures in different languages. This was justified by British scholars' discovery of the monistic teachings of the Upanishads, which resonated with their own Unitarian convictions, and allowed them to explain all the different deities, texts, and rituals of India as just so many expressions of what they took to be an essential element of Hinduism (and of all genuine religion): worship of the One.

It is easy, in retrospect, to critique this facile construction of separate, parallel, and internally homogeneous religions. More difficult is appreciating why it was so attractive to modern Europeans. Postcolonial theorists have offered one explanation: Europeans wanted other religions as mirrors in which to study, critique, or defend their own. Religions were imagined, often from a great distance, as foils for Europeans' insecurities about Christianity, which was under threat. The Enlightenment critique of tradition as a basis of power and knowledge, the Reformation critique of the Church's institutional authority, and the wars of religion that followed the Reformation had all undermined the idea that Christianity should be the foundation of political power, social order, and knowledge itself. Some Christians, desiring to preserve a legitimate role for Christianity, argued that its authority was never meant to encompass politics, law, or scientific knowledge, but only special kinds of knowledge and certain private dimensions of life. Christianity was thus defended against the charge that it was anti-scientific, irrational, and the cause of bloodshed, by being relegated to the private domains of personal belief, experience, and devotional practice. This move defined a new and separate dimension of life called religion—not a particular religion, but religion in general, which all people could share despite their differences. This was a very useful concept, because it facilitated the study of colonized peoples, and made possible the dream of a religiously pluralistic society in which Protestants, Catholics, and possibly even others could live side by side under a religiously neutral government. This idea of generic religion, manifested in a plurality of religions, was a corollary of secularization, and it remains crucial to the project of secular pluralism.

This means that our habitual way of looking at religions—as discrete, bounded, comparable entities sharing certain universal features—is not natural or neutral; it is an ideological construct. It serves the project of pluralistic secular democracy, and at the same time hinders our understanding of particular human beings who do not share all the essential elements of religion, or who do not stay within the boundaries we draw between religions. Joel Robbins has pointed out this problem among anthropologists, who have been so committed to thinking of religions and cultures as stable entities with clear boundaries that they have been largely unwilling to recognize the possibility of people crossing or straddling those boundaries. When anthropologists talk about conversion, they tend to assume that people never really leave their religion, but only take on certain outward markers of their new religion while remaining essentially a member of their old one, even if they claim to be completely transformed. Similarly, anthropologists tend to understand syncretism as an old religion taking on the veneer of a new religion, not as a real mixture or a creative new religious identity.[3] The discipline of religious studies has now largely rejected such essentialist conceptions of religions, at least in principle, and is therefore able to focus more and more on phenomena that cross or blur religious boundaries. This textbook is an example of that progress, though the very word 'interreligious' in its title shows how much our thinking still depends on the notion that individual religions are separate but parallel instances of 'religion in general'.

The modern concept of religion also shapes our understanding of human interaction. Our decision to study *religious* boundaries and encounters foregrounds certain dimensions of the people we are trying to understand—their personal beliefs, experiences, and devotional practices—while drawing our attention away from racial, gender, economic, linguistic, and other aspects of their identities. This choice can have very concrete consequences. It can change an interaction that might have proceeded on the basis of commonalities into one focused on religious difference. At the end of this chapter we will return to the consequences and moral significance of our scholarly habit of treating religions as distinct instances of a single phenomenon called religion, separated by boundaries that turn interactions into encounters.

Religions and their boundaries, however, are not just the fictitious constructions of academics. Human beings have long occupied themselves with erecting what we call religious boundaries between themselves and others. If the anthropologist Émile Durkheim was even partly right when he said that religion's primary function is to sacralize and thus sustain communities, then every religion must have ways of setting its adherents apart from others. How and where those boundaries are drawn may seem somewhat arbitrary, but it is not inconsequential. Though they are imagined constructs, religious boundaries are quite real in the sense that they have very concrete effects. As Eileen Barker notes, 'In locating religious identities, as with all other aspects of life, we need to draw the line somewhere. But how and where it is drawn can lead to very different consequences and to very different challenges for both "them" and "us".'[4] For example, the category of Hinduism, however artificial it may be, has been used by Indian nationalists to gain political advantage or even to spark riots against Indian Muslims.

Boundaries are real in another sense as well: they are not usually constructed out of thin air, but out of empirically observable differences. Almost any kind of difference can be used

---

[3] Joel Robbins, 'Crypto-Religion and the Study of Cultural Mixtures: Anthropology, Value, and the Nature of Syncretism', *Journal of the American Academy of Religion*, 79 (2011), 408–24.

[4] Eileen Barker, 'We've Got to Draw the Line Somewhere: An Exploration of Boundaries that Define Locations of Religious Identity', *Social Compass*, 53 (2006), 212.

as a boundary: 'religious' differences defined by practices, doctrines, symbols, institutions, sacred texts, or sacred spaces; social differences defined by lineage, race, ethnicity, nationality, language, culture, or geographical location; and even individual differences marked by personal choices, narratives, and self-identifications. As an illustration of the use of practices to construct religious boundaries, consider the widespread practice of eating. What could be more universal, a better expression of human unity and goodwill? Yet few practices are so ritualized and loaded with meaning. One of the most important meanings people assign to their food is who it binds them to, and who it separates them from.

David Freidenreich, in a rich and detailed study of Jewish, Christian, and Islamic food laws, has shown how many different ways there are to construct religious boundaries out of rules for eating.[5] He argues that as long as the ancient Israelites thought of themselves mainly as an ethnic community, their food laws were not intended to divide them from the groups around them. Once they defined themselves as a religious community, however, they began to view the differences between their own food and others' food as communal boundary markers.[6] They did not all agree on just how high a barrier their food laws should be—a wall barring interaction with others, or just a line in the sand identifying who is who. During the second century BCE, certain Jews in Alexandria observed Biblical food laws to identify themselves as Jews, but not to avoid contact with non-Jews; on the contrary, they ate food prepared by gentiles, at the same table as gentiles, as long as the food met Biblical requirements.[7] Hellenistic Jews in Judaea, on the other hand, were more concerned to avoid assimilation into gentile society, and therefore condemned the consumption of gentile food simply because it was prepared by gentiles, even if its ingredients were acceptable.[8] Several centuries later, Judaean sages still upheld those restrictions on food prepared by gentiles, but ceased to regard them as social boundaries: the Mishnah presented them as based not on the identity of the preparers *per se*, but on the prohibited ingredients that might contaminate the food of gentiles even accidentally. The sages of the Mishnah discussed at length how to avoid even the slightest chance of any Jewish wine being used by gentiles for idolatrous libations (which would make the rest of it prohibited), all the while taking for granted that Jews and gentiles were drinking the same wine together at the same table.[9] Another rabbi, however, whose views are preserved in the Palestinian Talmud, objected to such free interaction, and interpreted those same food laws as social boundaries, analogous to the rules prohibiting intermarriage with non-Jews.[10] This social barrier was systematically reinforced in the Babylonian Talmud, which worried aloud that eating or drinking with gentiles might lead to intermarriage.[11]

[5] David M. Freidenreich, *Foreigners and Their Food: Constructing Otherness in Jewish, Christian, and Islamic Law* (Berkeley, Calif.: University of California Press, 2011).

[6] Freidenreich, *Foreigners and Their Food*, 14, 17–26, 31–2.

[7] Freidenreich, *Foreigners and Their Food*, 32–4, 44–6.

[8] Freidenreich, *Foreigners and Their Food*, 35–40, 45–6.

[9] Freidenreich, *Foreigners and Their Food*, 47–8, 52–9.

[10] Freidenreich, *Foreigners and Their Food*, 60–2.   [11] Freidenreich, *Foreigners and Their Food*, 72–6.

Freidenreich's historical analysis demonstrates that differences between the eating practices of two religious communities do not inevitably constitute boundaries: they have to be interpreted as such,[12] and they can be reimagined in various ways from group to group, from place to place, from generation to generation, and even from rabbi to rabbi.[13] The learned Jew Saul of Tarsus demonstrated this yet again when he became Paul the follower of Christ. He did not reject Jewish food laws—he continued to regard them as entirely appropriate for Jewish followers of Christ—but he downplayed their significance in an effort to efface the boundary between Jews and gentiles within the nascent Christian community. He did, however, draw a sharp line between Christians and the pagan society around them by asking all Christians to observe one particular Jewish food law—the prohibition against food offered to idols. He did not want them to stop interacting with their society, so he urged them to go ahead and eat the food sold in the market or served in non-Christian homes without asking whether it had been offered to idols.[14] His rule allowed for interaction, but framed that interaction as an encounter across a clear religious boundary.

Ironically, the very success of Paul's mission to the gentiles eventually undermined his attempts to unite them with Jews and distinguish them from pagans. As sacrificial rituals declined in the Christianized Roman Empire, abstention from meat offered to idols no longer set Christians apart. A new 'other' had to be found, and the now largely gentile Church found that other in the Jews, whose literal understanding of the Law of Moses was a convenient antithesis to Christianity.[15] Even in areas where no Jews lived, Catholic canon lawyers warned sternly against eating their food, or compared Jewish observances to idolatrous sacrifices. Their concern cannot have been actual social interaction with real Jews; they seem to have been imagining quasi-idolatrous, legalistic Jews representing everything that Christians were not. Freidenreich notes that canons forbidding Christians to eat with Jews were promulgated especially by Catholic councils in areas they had recently taken over from Arian Christians, and he suggests that they emphasized those dietary rules so as to appear more Christian than the relatively tolerant Arians they had displaced.[16]

This illustrates a curious feature of religious boundaries: they are often constructed for a group's own internal purposes, with very little concern for, interest in, or knowledge of the other.[17] Jewish sages did the same with gentiles, constructing their otherness 'as a contrasting background against which to define Jewish identity',[18] with precious little attention to how gentiles actually lived or how they understood themselves. In the Talmud 'a non-Jew is, by definition, an idolater, and wine touched by an idolater is, by definition, treated as if it has been offered in libation'—even though the gentiles surrounding the Talmudic sages were,

---

[12] See esp. Freidenreich, *Foreigners and Their Food*, 5.
[13] See esp. Freidenreich, *Foreigners and Their Food*, 8–9, 15–16, 45–6, 52, 60, 63–4, 67, 69, 81, 84, 127.
[14] Freidenreich, *Foreigners and Their Food*, 78, 89–96, 127.
[15] Freidenreich, *Foreigners and Their Food*, 103, 107–12, 116.
[16] Freidenreich, *Foreigners and Their Food*, 113–23, 127.
[17] See esp. Freidenreich, *Foreigners and Their Food*, 10, 59, 70–1, 76, 83, 114, 174–5, 209–12, 223.
[18] Freidenreich, *Foreigners and Their Food*, 66.

increasingly, Christians and Zoroastrians rather than idolaters.[19] Another striking example is certain Muslim scholars' prohibition against eating a duck or goose prepared by a Jewish butcher. The problem was not that the butcher was Jewish; the Qur'an explicitly permits Muslims to eat the food of Jews. Nor was the duck or goose itself the problem; both are perfectly acceptable under both Islamic and Jewish food laws. The problem was that the Qur'an said that Jews were forbidden to eat animals with undivided toes, and Muslim scholars took this to include web-footed birds. They therefore imagined, mistakenly, that ducks and geese did not satisfy Jewish food laws, and therefore were not covered by the Qur'an's permission to eat Jewish food.[20] They managed to construct a boundary out of a difference that did not actually exist.

Freidenreich's rich study provides many more examples of how differences (real or imagined) in rules about eating were used to construct boundaries between Jews, Christians, and Muslims. These boundaries were constructed and understood in different ways by different parties, but all agreed that the boundaries were there. Ironically, food laws could be used to construct such recognizable boundaries only because the groups they divided actually had a great deal in common. Freidenreich's work reveals how similar were the legal questions, the scholastic arguments, the ways of interpreting scripture, the notions of impurity, and the basic dietary and cultural practices by means of which various groups of Jews, Christians, and Muslims defined the different kinds of boundaries that they imagined to exist between them. Each group's boundaries would have been unintelligible to the others, were it not for their shared assumption that preparing food imbues it with the identity of the preparer, that sharing food binds people together, and that avoiding one another's food sets people apart.[21] For a boundary to be visible from both sides there must be some shared symbolic vocabulary that transcends and thus belies the boundary itself.

Other practices besides eating, of course, can serve similar functions: think of clothing, or rituals of worship, initiation, or excommunication. Doctrines can play similar roles: recall how the early Christian church councils sought to draw a fine line around Christianity using the subtlest of theological formulas. The same is true of sacred symbols, texts, institutions, and spaces. For example, the Qur'an symbolically encompassed Jews and Christians within the bounds of the believing community by forcefully affirming their prophets (though it reimagined them in the image of Muhammad) and their scriptures (though it redefined them as divinely authored books of law). At the same time, it declared Jews and Christians to be in fact disbelievers because of doctrines such as the divine sonship of Ezra and Jesus, and because of the institutional authority they accorded to rabbis and priests. Perhaps the most visible and public sign of the growing barrier between Muslims and non-Muslims was a spatial reorientation from praying towards Jerusalem to praying towards Mecca. This bodily marker soon came to stand all by itself for Muslim identity: early theologians referred to the visible Muslim community as *ahl al-qibla,* 'the people of [our] prayer direction'.

---

[19] Freidenreich, *Foreigners and Their Food*, 71.
[20] Freidenreich, *Foreigners and Their Food*, 185–9.
[21] Freidenreich, *Foreigners and Their Food*, 3–4, 7, 173–4, 181, 224.

These doctrinal, symbolic, and practical differences are called 'religious' because they concern aspects of life that fall within our modern concept of religion. We consider doctrine an essential part of religion, and we regard diet as religious when it becomes the subject of sacred law, but we tend to put politics in another category. When religious people construct their own boundaries, however, they do not always make that distinction. They may identify religious boundaries with what we call social divisions—political, ethnic, or cultural differences, whether real or imagined. A political state, for instance, can be linked strongly or weakly to a certain religious identity, or it can be sharply distinguished from it: some Christians in the United States call passionately for the recovery of what they imagine to be a Christian national past that sets their country apart from non-Christian nations, while others insist that the whole point of the American political experiment was to dissociate national from religious identity, so that religious boundaries can criss-cross the nation freely. Another kind of imagined social grouping is ethnicity, whose boundaries are constructed out of real or imagined differences in ancestry or group history. Sometimes ethnic and religious identities are conflated, or serve to reinforce one another, as when immigrant ethnic communities adopt heightened religious observance and symbolism as a way of avoiding assimilation. Alternatively, immigrants may become more open to their host culture by dissociating the religious and ethnic dimensions of their identity. Zoroastrians, for example, traditionally regard themselves as an ethnically bounded religious community, but in the United States intermarriage threatens that identity, and they have faced that threat by redefining themselves as an essentially religious group whose boundaries can expand to include non-Persian spouses as long as they convert to the religion.[22]

Other social characteristics that can be used to define religious boundaries include language, geography, nationality, race, culture, and lineage. Each of these can be reimagined so as to reconstruct the boundaries of a community in new ways. Steven Ramey[23] has studied a striking example of this in Northern India, where Hindus who left Sindh when it became part of Muslim-dominated Pakistan in 1947 have taken their Sindhi identity as a kind of religious identity that defies the conventional boundaries between Hindus, Sikhs, and Muslims. The Sikh tradition had influenced Sindh considerably, and was not always regarded as separate from Hinduism there, so when the Hindu Sindhi immigrants arrived in Lucknow, India, and established their community centre, one Sindhi symbol they enshrined in it was a copy of a scripture conventionally identified as Sikh, the Guru Granth Sahib, which they displayed prominently for veneration. Some of these Sindhi immigrants also participated in Sufi teaching lineages and rituals, without considering themselves Muslims. The government usually categorized them as Hindus, but mainstream Indian Hindus regarded them with some suspicion, so they took concrete symbolic steps to highlight their view that the

---

[22] Fenggang Yang and Helen Rose Ebaugh, 'Transformations in New Immigrant Religions and Their Global Implications', *American Sociological Review*, 66 (2001), 282.

[23] Steven W. Ramey, 'Challenging Definitions: Human Agency, Diverse Religious Practices and the Problems of Boundaries', *Numen*, 54 (2007), 1–27.

Guru Granth Sahib was in fact a Hindu text: they installed *murtis* (sculptures) of various Hindu deities around it, mounted a large Om above it, and placed alongside it a copy of the Bhagavad Gita, in a place of apparently equal honour—though they paid far more attention to the Guru Granth Sahib. They also began to adopt more Indian Hindu wedding and funerary customs. They insisted, however, that their Sindhi mixture of Hindu, Sikh, and even Islamic identities was not a mixture at all, but a perfectly legitimate and distinctly Sindhi form of Hinduism. As they saw it, they were not engaged in syncretism or the blending of religions; it only appeared that way to others who artificially separated what had once belonged together. Nor were they blurring religious boundaries in an attempt to be inclusive; they just thought the government had drawn its religious boundaries in the wrong place. They employed Indian Hindu culture and symbols in an effort to convince others to accept them within the conventional bounds of Hinduism, while insisting that their Sindhi scriptures, teaching lineages, and geographic origins constituted a legitimate religious identity in its own right.

Ramey's illuminating analysis points out one additional level on which religious people draw boundaries. We have discussed both religious symbols and social differences as boundary markers; Ramey adds the personal choices by which individuals define and narrate their own identities and locate themselves within the competing sets of boundaries that society traces around them. One man Ramey interviewed told his story as one of transition from a Sindhi Hindu identity towards a more mainstream Indian Hindu identity, marked by the gradual and deliberate replacement of Sindhi rituals that other Indians regarded as Sikh with rituals they identified as Hindu. Ramey argues that scholars should acknowledge individuals as agents who draw their own versions of boundaries, for their own purposes, by their choice of vocabulary, symbols, and practices, and by the way they tell their own stories.

Another vivid illustration of how individuals redefine themselves in violation of conventional boundaries is Eliza Kent's study[24] of a small, secret, intergenerational network of crypto-Christian women in Sivakasi, India, who, in response to the teaching of Anglican missionaries early in the twentieth century, came to identify themselves privately as Christians. They met in one another's homes for lessons and prayer, and tried to avoid worshipping Hindu deities or eating food offered to them, but they did not openly reject Hinduism. They continued to participate in Hindu rituals their husbands expected of them, including the worship of family deities, though they sometimes employed subterfuges such as marking their faces with powder instead of the sacred ash that they considered to have been offered to idols. In social and ritual terms, they remained Hindus, but their personal narratives set them apart as Christians.

Religious, social, and individual differences only become boundaries when they are actively envisioned as such. Imagined religious boundaries are real in that they have concrete

---

[24] Eliza F. Kent, 'Secret Christians of Sivakasi: Gender, Syncretism, and Crypto-Religion in Early Twentieth-Century South India', *Journal of the American Academy of Religion*, 79 (2011), 676–705.

effects on people's lives, and they are usually grounded in empirically observable differences, but their status as boundaries depends on the human symbolic labour that constructs and maintains them. They do not mark fundamental, natural, or intrinsic divisions; they emerge from religious peoples' conscious or unconscious choice to highlight certain differences while overlooking equally real similarities. Indeed, were it not for those similarities, there would be no need to erect the boundaries, nor would the boundaries be visible to those on both sides if there were no shared concepts, symbols, or discourses out of which to build them. They derive their strength from the very continuities and commonalities that they appear to deny. Although they are the products of contingent choices, boundaries come to be so taken for granted that they appear just as natural, inevitable, and immovable as the hills and streams that divide up the countryside. Yet they can still be contested, negotiated, blurred, or redrawn. We have seen that they are imagined differently, and assigned greater or lesser significance, by different groups and individuals at different times. They sometimes serve to inhibit encounters with the other, but often they are intended only to give a group an identity by contrasting it with others, not to prevent interaction. Boundaries may overlap and intersect. They are permeable: individuals and whole communities can cross them, straddle them, or redraw them altogether. Whenever they are drawn or redrawn, it is always for some purpose, and that purpose usually has much more to do with the self than with the other. Boundaries help a religious community to define its own identity by way of contrast. They therefore tell us a great deal about the group that constructs them, but notoriously little about the other, who is sometimes imagined in an inaccurate or very rudimentary way. Boundaries are more like mirrors than fences.

ENCOUNTERS

Where there are boundaries, interactions become encounters. When people interact across a religious boundary, that boundary is activated: it frames the relationship and shapes each party's perception of the other. The other whom each person encounters is therefore partly an imaginary construct, and a projection of the same drive for self-definition that led to the creation of the boundary in the first place. How does this affect the interaction? Does it reduce the other to an imagined entity, an anti-self, defined entirely by the boundary that the self constructs for its own internal purposes, with little regard for the other's own self-understanding? Is the outcome of an encounter predetermined by the way the other is imagined, with no possibility for new understanding to change the course of the relationship? Or are the boundaries fragile enough, the commonalities that span them deep enough, and the communication that takes place across them genuine enough that each party's understanding of the other changes, and the boundaries are reimagined or even redrawn? If so, encounter will inevitably lead to some alteration in each party's own sense of identity, since the boundaries were part of what defined that identity to begin with.

We will address these questions using several examples of religious encounter, ranging from polemic and conflict to appropriation, assimilation, cross-fertilization, cooperation, and dialogue. Like our examples of boundaries, these interactions take place at several levels: they are engagements with other peoples' practices, doctrines, deities, spaces, texts, institutions, social characteristics, and personal identities. Once again we will begin with religious practices. Unfortunately, David Freidenreich's rich study of the construction of boundaries through food laws cannot tell us exactly how or when laypeople actually crossed those boundaries,[25] but many other encounters involving practices have been well documented.

Michelle Voss Roberts cites the example of lay Christians in India who sometimes adopt elements of Hindu practice such as the observance of caste distinctions, head-shaving rituals, and animal sacrifices at Christian shrines.[26] This interaction—this use of 'someone else's ritual'—constitutes an interreligious encounter because it involves reaching across a conventional religious boundary. That boundary is usually thought of as defined primarily by differences in belief, which scholars and religious elites often treat as the most important component of religious identity. Voss Roberts argues, however, that ritual practice is equally constitutive of religious identity, especially for ordinary laypeople. When these Christians perform 'Hindu' rituals, therefore, those rituals are just as constitutive of their own religious identity as the beliefs that make them Christians. That means they have a second identity defined by a second boundary: they are not just Christians transgressing a doctrinal boundary to engage in the practices of others; they are also members of a ritually defined Indian community engaged in their very own religious practices. That ritually defined community includes both Indian Christians and Hindus, but excludes non-Indian Christians (as well as Indian untouchables). Viewed in this light, what looked like an encounter with the practices of a religious other now looks like participation in the Christians' own community—or, rather, one of their own communities. They have a hybrid identity: they are doctrinally Christian and ritually Indian.[27] Hybrid religious identities are common, and recognizing this can help defuse the rhetoric of religious difference that so often fans conflict in India.

The religious encounter cited by Voss Roberts does not create new boundaries or modify old ones; it simply reveals and highlights an alternative way of drawing boundaries—an alternative choice about which differences and similarities to emphasize—that has been overlooked by observers, and that even the participants themselves may never have articulated explicitly, though they embody it in their actions. Such alternative boundaries blur the borders that we are accustomed to see between religions. Often, however, scholars and religious adherents alike find the conventional boundaries better suited to their purposes, and sometimes they go to great lengths to defend or actively reinforce them, as illustrated by the following case.

---

[25] As noted by Freidenreich, *Foreigners and Their Food*, 9–10.
[26] Michelle Voss Roberts, 'Religious Belonging and the Multiple', *Journal of Feminist Studies in Religion*, 26 (2010), 50.
[27] See Voss Roberts, 'Religious Belonging and the Multiple', esp. 49–52.

In the nineteenth century, when British colonial administrators and Orientalist scholars were still trying to sort the religious chaos of India into clearly demarcated religions, Buddhists and Hindus both venerated an image of the Buddha in a Hindu-controlled temple at Bodhgayā, where the Buddha was said to have achieved enlightenment. Both the Buddhists and the more numerous Hindus performed typically 'Hindu' rituals, adorning the image with paint, clothing, and sandalwood paste. We might conclude that here too, as in the previous example, the conventional boundaries between religions (which Orientalist scholarship did much to reify) did not fit the communities of ritual practice that actually existed in India. The supposed 'encounter' of shared ritual was not encounter at all, but merely interaction among members of a single ritually defined Indian community. Orientalists misperceived this as a transgression of boundaries because their paradigm caused them to ignore what the participants shared.

This misperception, however, was not simply a failure of understanding; it was an active attempt, by Orientalists and by a particular Buddhist leader whom they influenced, to create a more absolute boundary between Hinduism and Buddhism than the worshippers themselves felt was necessary. Anagarika Dharmapala, a Sri Lankan Buddhist educated in Christian schools, was influenced in his early years by the Theosophical movement, which (in very modern fashion) regarded Hindu and Buddhist devotion as expressions of a common religious essence. Eventually, however, Dharmapala adopted the Orientalists' scorn for Hindu 'idolatry' and 'syncretism', as well as their high regard for Buddhism as a rational antithesis to such sensuous superstition. He therefore set out to restore Bodhgayā to Buddhist control, and to what he considered properly Buddhist rituals. He argued that the ritual practices which both Hindus and Buddhists observed at Bodhgayā were strictly Hindu, and therefore constituted a contamination of what he regarded as a strictly Buddhist shrine. The image of the Buddha, he complained, had been turned into an idol of Vishnu. His efforts culminated in a failed attempt to place a new image of the Buddha in the temple and ceremonially install it following Buddhist rituals. This led to an extended court battle, at the end of which control of the site was peacefully handed over to Buddhists; but Hindus continue to visit it today, and continue to perform 'Hindu' rituals there.[28]

Did Dharmapala's agenda for Bodhgayā stem from a refusal to understand the Hindu pilgrims (and even the Buddhist ones) on their own terms? Did his adoption of Orientalist categories blind him to the boundaries and commonalities embodied in the pilgrims' shared practices? Did he refuse to perceive the pilgrims accurately because he needed an idolatrous 'other' with which to contrast his refined conception of Buddhism? The very question should prompt us to reflect on the power of scholarly categories to shape concrete political reality. In this case a court gave the force of law to an Orientalist boundary. That boundary, however, did not result from a simple misunderstanding of the religious communities that existed on the ground; it was a deliberate attempt to construct a new definition of Buddhism and give it

---

[28] Jacob N. Kinnard, 'When Is the Buddha Not the Buddha? The Hindu/Buddhist Battle over Bodhgayā and Its Buddha Image', *Journal of the American Academy of Religion*, 66 (1998), 817–39.

a new position *vis-à-vis* the Hindu community in India. By refusing to imagine religious boundaries as the pilgrims did, and by deliberately promoting a sharper boundary between Hinduism and Buddhism, Dharmapala reframed the interaction taking place in the temple as an encounter that violated the separateness and uniqueness of Buddhism. He reframed Hindus as 'others' whose practices made them idolaters, and he sought to redefine Buddhism as the opposite of idolatry—just as Jews and Christians sought to define themselves as anti-idolaters through their food laws.

In contrast to such active rejection of commonality, we may cite examples of the deliberate appropriation of others' practices. Sociologists Fenggang Yang and Helen Ebaugh[29] studied immigrant religious communities in the United States and observed what we might be tempted to call the pervasive influence of American Protestant Christianity on the worship practices of both Christian and non-Christian immigrants. The Chinese Buddhist Hsi Nan Temple in Houston, for example, adopted practices such as Sunday worship, pews, hymns, expository sermons, congregational responses, and alternating between standing and sitting over the course of a service. It also broadened the range of its activities to include social and cultural functions such as weddings, which were not performed at Buddhist temples in China. Some of these practices were deliberate imitations of Christian ones, initiated after one of the monks visited several churches. Yang and Ebaugh found, however, that many immigrants did not attribute their adoption of Protestant practices to Christian influence or social pressure to assimilate; instead they justified these changes by re-examining the foundations of their own religious traditions, and deciding that some of their former practices were merely cultural rather than essentially Buddhist and could therefore be changed. This enabled them to accommodate the practices of other religions without calling into question the uniqueness or superiority of their own religion, or feeling that they were stepping outside its boundaries. For instance, a monk at Hsi Nan Temple argued that its involvement in social and cultural matters was a recovery of Buddhism's early tradition of social engagement, which was only lost when monks and nuns were forced into seclusion in remote areas under the Ming dynasty. From this monk's perspective, the changes made by the Hsi Nan Temple were not a case of influence or cross-fertilization between Christianity and Buddhism; they were a recovery of the Temple's own religious tradition. The Buddhists of Houston consciously reached across an acknowledged religious boundary and appropriated the practices of others, and thus lessened the barriers between themselves and other Americans; but they did not thereby deny or mitigate that boundary in their own thinking. Rather, they maintained that boundary by reimagining the borrowed practices as rooted in their own religion, and thus in effect denied that their encounter with American Protestantism had really been transformative.

These examples demonstrate that encounters with the practices of others can blur conventional boundaries and reveal alternative ways of drawing boundaries, so that groups that were

---

[29] Yang and Ebaugh, 'Transformations in New Immigrant Religions'.

considered separate can be seen as members of a single ritually defined community. Yet there is a strong urge to reassert conventional boundaries and deny the transformative and unitive effects of ritual encounter. A religious community's desire for a distinct identity of its own often blinds it to the embodied reality of shared practice.

A similar tension can be observed in doctrinal encounters: dialogue and even polemic can result in communities of shared theological discourse, yet both are plagued by the almost inescapable need to imagine others in terms that serve one's own purposes. This is most obvious in doctrinal polemic: the parties often 'talk past one another' because their arguments proceed on the basis of a distorted understanding of the other's doctrine, or of concepts and assumptions that the other does not share. To take but one example of this commonly observed phenomenon, consider Swami Dayananda Saraswati (1824–83), a wandering ascetic who founded the Hindu nationalist Arya Samaj movement. Among his many criticisms of the Bible and the Qur'an was the charge that their concepts of mercy and forgiveness were unjust because they ignored the law of *karma*.[30] Swami Dayananda had engaged Christians in live debate, and he undoubtedly realized that this argument would have no traction with them. His goal was not to persuade Christians or Muslims, but to persuade his fellow Hindus of the value of a strict doctrine of *karma* for refuting foreign religions. Certain Hindu devotional movements, which Dayananda opposed, had questioned the absoluteness of *karma*. By mocking Christians and Muslims for their disregard of *karma*, Dayananda was taking a stab at those Hindu groups as well, and showing that a strong doctrine of *karma* could help Hindus to resist the Christian colonialists. His writing may have had the form of polemic directed at others, but he was not really addressing them; the only community his argument was likely to convince was his own, and the only argument he could really hope to win was one that was taking place among Hindus. His polemic did not really reach across the boundary between Hindus and others; it merely reinforced that boundary, while reaching across an internal boundary to persuade his fellow Hindus.

Theological dialogue differs from polemic in its intent: it generally seeks to overcome religious boundaries rather than reinforce them. Yet it too is subject to the distorting power of imagined boundaries. Dialogue that is too intent on breaking down boundaries and discovering commonalities often leads each party to imagine the other in its own image, and to gloss over troubling differences. In such cases, dialogue produces new imagined boundaries that are just as much projections of the self as the old boundaries were. Dialogue can be transformative, and it is often professed that genuine dialogue requires openness to the possibility of one's own identity being transformed by the encounter. When self-transformation becomes the goal of encounter, however, one must question whether dialogue has led to a transformed understanding of the other, or just a new self-image. The other may still be serving as a mirror for exploration of the self.

---

[30] Swami Dayananda Saraswati, *Light of Truth: Or an English Translation of the Satyarth Prakash*, tr. Chiranjiva Bharadwaja, new edn (New Delhi: Sarvadeshik Arya Pratinidhi Sabha, 1975), 220–1, 622, 652–3.

Despite this pitfall, both dialogue and polemical debate necessarily undermine some aspect of the boundary across which they occur, because both require the development of some kind of shared theological discourse. Even persuasion and evangelism require the development of a vocabulary that transcends that boundary, as pointed out by La Seng Dingrin in his study of Adoniram Judson (1788–1850), an American missionary to Burma. Judson claimed that Christianity had 'no point of contact' with Buddhism, yet he found it necessary to use terms derived from the Pali language of the Buddhist scriptures to convey his Christian message.[31] Such shared vocabulary, engendered by the encounter itself, creates a new community of discourse that crosses theological boundaries. This commonality is easily overlooked, however, because polemic, evangelism, and even dialogue are premised and focused upon the boundary between two religions, and therefore tend to draw attention away from the continuities that make the encounter possible.

Like practices and doctrines, deities themselves can be the focus of religious encounter. Joel Robbins, in his study of the Urapmin of Papua New Guinea, notes that when they converted to a charismatic form of Christianity they retained their belief in nature spirits. Whereas many anthropologists would view this as syncretism, or evidence of the superficial nature of their conversion, Robbins argues that these beings were thoroughly integrated into a Christian view of God: the Urapmin retained in their religious world only those spirits to which they could assign a reduced role, such as causing illness, which they did not wish to attribute to the Christian God, while they abandoned the cult of ancestors because their identity as creators impinged on the role of the Christian God.[32] Eliza Kent, in her study of crypto-Christians in Sivakasi, notes that they continued to believe in Hindu deities, but reclassified them as demons to fit within their Christian framework of belief.[33] The Hindus who venerated the image of the Buddha at Bodhgayā assimilated him into a Hindu framework as the ninth incarnation of Vishnu; Orientalists came to view this as a case of mistaken identity, but from the perspective of the Hindus it was a natural way of accounting theologically for a figure already embraced by their ritual practice.[34] These examples illustrate the permeability of religious boundaries: even deities can be borrowed from others. Yet they also illustrate the seemingly irresistible drive to reframe the religion of others so that it fits within one's own paradigms, rather than seek to comprehend the religion of others as they themselves understand it. Michelle Voss Roberts notes that New Age movements in the United States have been criticized for just such a self-serving reinterpretation of Hindu goddesses such as Kali, who are used to express New Age values with little regard for the meanings assigned to them by Hindus.[35] Even the way one refers to someone else's deity is a matter of

---

[31] La Seng Dingrin, 'Is Buddhism Indispensable in the Cross-Cultural Appropriation of Christianity in Burma?', *Buddhist-Christian Studies*, 29 (2009), 3–22.

[32] Robbins, 'Crypto-Religion and the Study of Cultural Mixtures', 416–19.

[33] Kent, 'Secret Christians of Sivakasi', 681, 687.

[34] Kinnard, 'When Is the Buddha Not the Buddha?' 828–34.

[35] Voss Roberts, 'Religious Belonging and the Multiple', 45.

self-interest: English-speaking Christians who want to encourage a negative and oppositional view of Islam typically insist on calling the God of Muslims Allah, while more affirming Christians, as well as Muslims wishing to be affirmed in Western societies, insist on translating Allah as God.

Sacred spaces are a particularly conflict-prone aspect of religion, because their uniqueness and concreteness make them difficult to share and easy to fight over. Nevertheless, sacred spaces are sometimes shared for long periods, as we saw concerning Bodhgayā, even if the groups sharing them give them very different interpretations. And sometimes groups competing for the same space actually share very similar interpretations of it. Jerusalem has long been regarded as a site of great apocalyptic significance by both Christians and Muslims, who share very similar views about its connection to Jesus and his expected return. Although the memory of the Crusades makes Jerusalem a symbol of opposition between Christians and Muslims, their shared interpretations of the city illustrate how much the two communities owe to a common Near Eastern apocalyptic tradition.

Encounters centred on sacred texts tend to be less violent than encounters at sacred spaces, perhaps because texts are easier to share and harder to monopolize in an age of popular literacy and mass communication. Nevertheless, because they have come to be regarded as symbols of their respective religious communities, violence directed at scriptures can still inflame conflict, as when the Christian pastor Terry Jones sparked rioting in Afghanistan by publically burning a copy of the Qur'an at his church in Gainesville, Florida, in 2011. Protestant values have led many modern students of religion to regard scriptures as the sources or defining components of religious traditions, and it is often thought that 'going to the source' of another religion will ensure a genuine understanding of the other. It turns out, however, that others' scriptures are remarkably easy to reframe, reinterpret, or even modify to serve one's own purposes. Muslim polemicists, for example, have a long tradition of quoting the Bible to refute the divinity of Jesus, but to do this they often select texts that present Jesus as human, and interpret these literally, while arguing that texts that appear to support the divinity of Jesus should be read metaphorically. This ignores the way most Christians have historically understood these texts, and thus renders the polemic an assault against a straw man—an exercise in self-reassurance rather than interreligious engagement.

Some religious people have embraced the scriptures of others, but even this apparently radical effacement of boundaries often turns out to be an exercise in self-affirmation. The Hindu reformer Rammohun Roy (1772–1833), for instance, translated and published extracts from the Gospels in order that his fellow Hindus might take the words of Jesus to heart;[36] yet an examination of his excerpts quickly reveals that he included only those high-minded ethical teachings that he sought to promote in his own reforms of Hinduism, while excluding

---

[36] Rammohun Roy, *The Precepts of Jesus, the Guide to Peace and Happiness, Extracted from the Books of the New Testament Ascribed to the Four Evangelists: To Which Are Added, the First and Second Appeal to the Christian Public, in Reply to the Observations of Dr Marshman, of Serampore, from the London Edition* (New York: B. Bates, 1825).

stories of miracles and other such superstitions, the like of which he wanted to eradicate from Hinduism. He was especially fond of the harsh words Jesus spoke against the ritualism of the Pharisees, because they supported the criticism that Roy himself was making against the traditional Brahmin priestly establishment. To affirm such a selective portrait of the other is merely to paint a portrait of oneself.

Another nineteenth-century Indian who affirmed the Bible, the Muslim modernist Sayyid Ahmad Khan (1817–98), went so far as to publish his own extensive commentary on the first eleven chapters of Genesis and the first five chapters of Matthew; yet he too read the Bible through his own lens and for his own purposes, recognizing as divine revelation only those portions that satisfied the Islamic criterion that scripture must stem directly from a prophet such as Moses or Jesus, not from the prophet's followers.[37] His commentary was a symbolic gesture of goodwill towards the British, but the scripture he encountered was hardly the same one that his Christian interlocutors saw in the pages of the Bible.

The Qur'an itself embraced the Bible in the sense that it retold many of its stories, and affirmed the revealed status of the Torah of Moses, the Psalms of David, and the Gospel of Jesus. This was a deliberate attempt to draw a religious boundary that included Jews and Christians, but the people it included, like the books it affirmed, were imagined constructs. The Christians whom the Qur'an affirmed were essentially Muslims, though there is considerable debate today about exactly how Muslim the Qur'an required Christians to be. The Gospel was represented as a book of law spoken by God to Jesus, quite unlike the third-person narratives about Jesus that Christians regarded as canonical. The Biblical book of Psalms was quoted briefly in the Qur'an,[38] and medieval Muslim authors actually produced a complete Islamic version of 'the Psalms of David'. This Islamic book of Psalms was a rewriting of the Biblical Psalms in a Qur'anic idiom, presented as divine address to the prophet David rather than as human prayers to God. Its contents were drawn almost entirely from Islamic sources rather than the Bible. Consequently, modern scholars have treated these Islamic Psalms as a mere forgery, almost completely devoid of any real engagement with the Bible. Nevertheless, like the Qur'an's own construction of an imagined Bible, this rewriting of the Psalms betrays and indeed highlights an underlying continuity in the literary and symbolic world inhabited by Jews, Christians, and Muslims.[39]

In modern times scriptures have become an especially intriguing locus of religious encounter because they have come to function as symbols representing entire religious communities, they are readily accessible to outsiders, and they are open to multiple interpretations. For these very reasons, encounters involving scriptures are subject to the same tendency

---

[37] Syud Ahmud, *The Mohomedan Commentary on the Holy Bible*, part I (Ghazipur: by the author, 1862), 20–2, 31, 39.

[38] Q 21: 105 quotes Ps. 37: 29.

[39] David R. Vishanoff, 'An Imagined Book Gets a New Text: Psalms of the Muslim David', *Islam and Christian–Muslim Relations*, 22 (2011), 85–99; 'Why Do the Nations Rage? Boundaries of Canon and Community in a Muslim's Rewriting of Psalm 2', *Comparative Islamic Studies*, 6 (2010), 151–79.

towards distorted perception of the other that we have noted in encounters focused on practices, doctrines, and deities. Imagining the other in such a way as to reflect one's own assumptions and concerns appears to be a common feature of all types of religious interaction, perhaps because the boundaries across which encounters take place are constructed precisely for the purpose of defining and understanding the self.

Other loci of religious encounter could be enumerated and illustrated. Religious institutions play an important role in both marking and crossing boundaries. Denominational organizations formalize many of the theological, ritual, and cultural divisions in American Protestantism, and other institutions are then formed to overcome those divisions. Interdenominational mission agencies, social service organizations, and ecumenical councils, some stretching across not only denominational but also religious lines, provide opportunities for encounter and cooperation. Ecumenical groups are inherently fragile, because they undermine the role of boundaries in constructing group identities; yet they also reflect and reinforce new kinds of boundaries that are vying to replace traditional ones. The modern concept of a plurality of parallel religions that all embody a common essence called 'religion' has led to more and more religious people wishing to identify themselves not as belonging to a single religion, but as members of a larger, more diffuse community of believing or spiritual human beings. This new identity is articulated by means of new boundaries that divide pluralists from exclusivists, or modernists from fundamentalists, while cutting across conventional religious boundaries. These new identities and boundaries are concretized by interdenominational and interreligious cooperation at the institutional level.

Even as religious institutions unite their members, they necessarily create new divisions and new others. Yet the very process by which such institutions are formed within modern political and legal structures gives them an uncanny similarity to one another. As Yang and Ebaugh observe, American immigrant institutions such as the Hsi Nan Temple in Houston soon become incorporated as non-profit organizations with bylaws, boards of lay trustees, and formal but voluntary memberships wielding some degree of congregational authority. They do so, in spite of their long traditions of hierarchically governed institutions, because this is what the legal structures of modern states demand, and because religious participation in modern democracies has become so much a matter of voluntary association that institutions must become more responsive to their members in order to survive. As Yang and Ebaugh point out, this shift towards congregational institutions does not just result from the 'Americanization' of immigrants; increasingly it characterizes religious institutions around the globe.[40] The concepts and mechanisms by which modern religious institutions operate give them a unity of form that belies the very boundaries that they were created to reinforce or overcome.

Religious encounter can also be about social characteristics such as lineage, race, ethnicity, nationality, language, culture, and geographic location. Early twenty-first-century conflicts

---

[40]   Yang and Ebaugh, 'Transformations in New Immigrant Religions', 273–5, 283–4.

between Christians and Muslims in Nigeria are a case in point: the strife is framed in explicitly religious terms, as though the enforcement of Sharia law were the main point of dispute, but the divisions and tensions between the two communities are just as much ethnic, political, economic, and geographic as they are religious. The choice to focus on a religious difference gives the conflict a transcendent quality, and paints the other as someone whose presence cannot be tolerated, rather than someone with whom economic or political differences can be negotiated.

Religious encounter also occurs at the level of individual self-definition. Our modern concept of religion makes it more a matter of individual than social identity. We consider people's religion to be determined primarily by how they tell their own stories, and how they choose to locate themselves within the various sets of boundaries that society has drawn. Individuals cross those boundaries in various ways, including conversion, crypto-religion, and multiple religious belonging.

Conversion involves moving one's whole self, or at least the core of one's identity, across a religious boundary. As Joel Robbins has pointed out, many anthropologists have been so committed to the idea that culture and religion are deeply embedded and enduring webs of meaning and practice, from which individuals have little power to extract themselves, that they have been reluctant to countenance the possibility of fundamental religious transformation, and have been prone to dismiss claims of conversion as only skin-deep: missionaries may have managed to impose on their victims a veneer of Western religious and cultural forms, but the converts' fundamental ways of thinking and engaging the world necessarily remain unchanged. If these anthropologists are right, then even in conversion the other with whom one becomes identified is not genuinely understood, but remains a construct imagined and embraced for one's own purposes and in one's own interests. Robbins objects, however, that, while it may not be possible to simply discard one's cultural or religious system, it is possible to rearrange it so that lingering elements of one's old framework are made secondary to the controlling ideas and narratives of the new religion, as in the case of the Urapmin, who retained their beliefs in various spirits only insofar as they could integrate them into their new Christian framework.[41] If Robbins is right, then crossing a religious boundary by individual conversion is a form of religious encounter that allows a genuine understanding and sharing of at least the central features of another religion.

In crypto-religion a person deliberately retains the outward forms of a dominant religious tradition while secretly identifying with another religion. One example, already mentioned, is the crypto-Christian women of Sivakasi: socially they remained entirely within the ritually demarcated boundaries of Hinduism, but at the level of their personal narratives and beliefs they were Christians. Multiple religious belonging, which is addressed by Catherine Cornille's Chapter 15, is identification with aspects of two or more religious traditions; for example, drawing rituals from Buddhism while reciting Christian creeds. Like crypto-religion, multiple religious belonging may be particularly appealing, or even necessary, for those on the margins of conventionally

---

[41] Robbins, 'Crypto-Religion and the Study of Cultural Mixtures'.

defined religions, for whom conventional boundaries are not adequate to describe their experience, and who do not have the power to redefine the publically recognized religious boundaries within which they must locate themselves.[42] Increasingly, however, religious elites are also choosing to identify themselves as Buddhist Christians or Christian Muslims. Such identification, often publically proclaimed, is not just an effort to negotiate existing boundaries; it contributes to the redrawing of religious boundaries along new lines to create an interreligious community of human beings who are religious in a more modern, generic sense.

We may question to what extent such multiple religious belonging reflects genuine engagement with another religion as its adherents understand it, and to what extent it involves recasting the other religion in terms of one's own categories and aspirations. The modern concept of generic religion expressed in multiple traditions suggests that it is quite possible for an individual to combine religious expressions from two religions without violating their fundamentals, but might not most adherents of those religions—especially those who view their religion as uniquely true—object that what has been adopted is not their religion at all, and that their religion can only be understood and adopted in its entirety? This is an important question, both for scholars and for those who would belong to multiple traditions; but if we adopt the modern premise that individuals are free to choose and define their own religion, and if we do not wish to exclude marginalized groups from participating in the definition of their own religion, then we must count converts, crypto-religious people, and people who claim multiple religious traditions as real members of those traditions. That means counting their understanding of those traditions as genuine understanding, even if it differs from how most adherents understand the religion. They may have distorted the other in self-serving ways, but once they choose to identify themselves as part of that other religion, their understanding of it becomes partly constitutive of it. Crossing religious boundaries by individual conversion, crypto-religion, or multiple religious belonging thus leads, by definition, to genuine understanding—not because the distorting power of imagined boundaries has been overcome, but because understanding the other now means understanding oneself. Joining the other can be the ultimate means of reshaping the other in one's own image.

These examples of religious encounter at various levels illustrate several features of religious encounter that follow naturally from the observations we made about religious boundaries. We saw how various religious, social, and individual characteristics can serve as symbols for entire communities, so that differences in those areas are elevated to the status of boundaries; we have now seen that those same kinds of characteristics can be shared or engaged across boundaries: interactions can involve religious practices, doctrines, deities, spaces, texts, and institutions; they can be driven by social identities or characteristics; and they can take place at the level of personal narratives, whether those be publically declared, private, or even secret. We noted that these characteristics only become boundary markers if someone chooses to regard them as such; we now see that rituals like clothing an image can just as well

---

[42] See Voss Roberts, 'Religious Belonging and the Multiple', 44, 57–62.

be shared as disputed, and in that case the interaction hardly constitutes an encounter at all, since encounter occurs only when it is thought of as taking place across a boundary. Just as boundaries can be imagined in different ways and even in different places by different groups and individuals, so an interaction can be viewed by one person (Anagarika Dharmapala, for example) as a dangerous encounter or influence, while another person (a pilgrim at Bodhgayā) does not focus on the same boundary and therefore views the interaction as an innocuous rubbing of shoulders in a shared ritual. What appears to one person as an immovable social barrier that prohibits interaction may be to someone else a purely conceptual boundary that can be crossed at will in daily life. Sometimes an encounter reinforces the boundary across which it takes place, but sometimes it reveals that there is as much continuity as difference, or that other boundaries are more important. We noted that boundaries often intersect or overlap, and interaction can shift the focus from one boundary to another, or even draw a new boundary in a new place, as happens when individuals or institutions attempt to straddle conventional religious groups. These dynamics of boundary crossing can occur in all manner of encounters: conflict, polemic, appropriation, assimilation, cross-fertilization, cooperation, dialogue, or the sharing of practices, texts, and even deities.

When a boundary is activated in the imagination so that an interaction comes to be viewed as an encounter, does the imagined boundary so dominate each party's conception of the other that there is no genuine interaction or communication, but only an imagined encounter with an imagined anti-self that serves each party's own internal agenda of self-definition? We have seen that polemic is often directed at doctrinal straw men, others' deities are often reimagined even as they are adopted, and others' texts are quoted selectively or even rewritten for one's own purposes. Every boundary has a purpose, and in every encounter the boundary across which it takes place is activated and made to frame the interaction for some specific purpose, which usually has more to do with the goals of the person who initiates the encounter than with those on the other side. We have seen people such as Dayananda Saraswati and Rammohun Roy critiquing or embracing elements of another religion for the purpose of intramural argument with their fellow Hindus. It appears that frequently religious encounter does indeed take place with an imagined and even a quite distorted other. This should not be surprising. Interactions may be real and concrete relationships between real people, but insofar as they are encounters with religious others across boundaries that are imagined as mirrors for one's own identity, they are also encounters with oneself. This appears to be true to some extent even when an individual adopts the other religion, as in conversion or multiple religious belonging.

Religious encounter, therefore, can readily become an attempt to use the other for one's own ends. The most visible and effective boundaries are typically defined by those with the most power, and encounters across them often serve the purposes of the powerful, as when Anagarika Dharmapala employed the Orientalists' boundaries to gain control of Bodhgayā for Buddhists. Yet we have also seen that even the powerless are able to reconstruct their own boundaries, and create new communities of shared discourse or practice, precisely by reaching across conventional boundaries and affirming commonalities that those boundaries had pushed into the background. Just as we said that the construction of a recognized boundary requires some common symbolic vocabulary that is shared across and thus belies the boundary, so we have seen that encounters require some kind of shared focal point such as a shared ritual practice, a way of translating theological terms, or a common legal structure for institutional organization. The encounter itself, therefore, qualifies the absoluteness of the boundary, and highlights an alternative boundary that joins the two parties in a single community of some kind.

Since communal boundaries are a key ingredient of group identity, the modification of boundaries that can result from encounter modifies or at least reframes the identities of the participants in some way, and makes them less absolutely other. The very act of interacting around a particular thing requires the establishment of some common discourse about it, which in turn has the potential to change the way each party views its relationship to the other, and thus how it views itself. When this happens, the encounter is no longer purely encounter, but partly interaction with someone who shares some aspect of one's own identity. This has the potential to make interaction genuinely about the other person, precisely because he or she is no longer imagined strictly as an anti-self. When people think of themselves as engaged in a religious encounter, they tend to interact with their own construct of the other as a mirror or foil for their own identity; but when they think of themselves as in an interaction with someone who falls on their own side of at least some boundaries, there is a greater opportunity for them to hear and understand the other without the distorting lens of an imagined boundary. An encounter may be well-intentioned and affirming, or it may be adversarial, but as long as the encounter itself forces a modification or qualification of the boundary, so that some commonality with the other is acknowledged, then it is possible for the other to be perceived anew, and the self's identity to be reframed in a slightly new way. This redrawing of boundaries does not guarantee that understanding has been improved: one may reimagine the other—and oneself—in new but still very distorted ways. Nevertheless, our examples show that, despite the distorting power of imagined boundaries, interreligious encounter is not necessarily just an illusion.

CHALLENGES

In asking how boundaries are constructed in the imagination, and how they affect the interactions that take place in light of those boundaries, I have emphasized a strong tendency for boundaries to be imagined for the sake of defining one's own identity, and, consequently, for encounters to consist of interactions with an imagined anti-self rather than with real human beings understood in their own terms. I have not claimed that this is always or inevitably true, only that it poses an ever-present analytical and moral challenge, both for religious studies scholars and for religious people attempting to engage members of other traditions.

For scholars of religion, this chapter highlights the pitfall of assuming that there are natural, intrinsic boundaries between religious groups. Boundaries are not simply fictions—we have seen that they are quite real in the sense that they are often constructed out of real differences, they are experienced by religious communities as real, and they can have concrete effects on people's lives. Boundaries are also very useful analytical tools: thinking requires sorting, classifying, and drawing boundaries, and as long as we remain open to reimagining them in new ways, boundaries can help to generate new insights into people and their religions. Nevertheless, scholarly categories and boundaries are epistemologically and morally ambivalent. They may obscure as much as they reveal. Orientalists were unable to see Hindus and Buddhists as members of a community of shared Indian ritual practice, and anthropologists, according to Joel Robbins, have been reluctant to take conversion seriously because they have tended to regard cultural and religious boundaries as impermeable.

Scholars' categories are also sometimes adopted by the very people the scholars study, and this can have concrete effects on those people's lives, as when the stark boundary that Orientalists drew between Hinduism and Buddhism contributed almost directly to the transfer of power at Bodhgayā. Scholars, therefore, have a moral obligation to consider how the boundaries they assume or create compare with the boundaries imagined by the people they study, and how their scholarly categories may affect the ways in which those people interact—pushing Indian pilgrims, for example, to regard themselves as members of rival groups rather than participants in a common ritual tradition, and thus potentially contributing to the kind of interreligious conflict over sacred spaces that has plagued modern India. It is morally incumbent upon scholars to look for inadequacies in their categories and imagined boundaries, and to keep trying out new boundaries in their attempts to understand religious people. If they do not, they may end up compartmentalizing people for their own scholarly purposes, or dismissing them as marginal cases if they do not fit their categories, rather than treating them as religious agents in their own right who contribute just as much as scholars to the definition of religious boundaries and communities.

Being aware of the ideological origins of their own concept of religion, scholars also have a moral responsibility to be honest about the goals for which they employ it. If they embrace wholeheartedly the secular democratic vision of religious pluralism that the concept of generic religion was designed to support, it behoves them to at least acknowledge how the people they are categorizing may wish to resist that project by drawing their own boundaries. Those who adopt a more postmodern critical stance have a responsibility not only to critique scholarly categories and boundaries, but also to reconstruct them along new lines that promote the interests of the marginalized, or that at least acknowledge their ways of imagining their own religious identities. All modern scholars of religion share a special duty not to let their tendency to isolate religion from other dimensions of human life lead them to neglect the non-religious commonalities that unite people across religious lines, lest their own scholarship, by highlighting religious divisions, contribute to conflict and even violence.

Some scholars, of course, are also religious people, and many of them pursue forms of interreligious encounter or dialogue on their own account. I hope that these scholars find in this chapter an even stiffer challenge: a moral imperative to be continually suspicious of their own efforts at encounter with religious others. Merely to frame an interaction with another human being as an instance of interreligious encounter is to highlight a certain boundary across which the interaction takes place, and thus to push into the background the numerous commonalities that exist across that boundary, and without which neither the boundary nor the encounter would even be possible. Framing an interaction that way makes one's interlocutor an imagined other, and one must always suspect, therefore, that it makes one's encounter with that person an exercise in constructing one's own identity, rather than an act of attentive listening and coming to understand a fellow human being on his or her own terms. The resulting distortion in one's conception of the other is not neutral; it can have concrete consequences as important as the difference between peace and conflict. Even if one's image of the other is deliberately constructed with the intent of encouraging harmony and tolerance, it may still represent a violation of the other's identity and self-understanding, and this, I suggest, is an even more fundamental moral harm than physical conflict.

FURTHER READING

Benedict Anderson, *Imagined Communities: Reflections on the Origin and Spread of Nationalism*, rev. edn (London: Verso, 2006).

Eileen Barker, 'We've Got to Draw the Line Somewhere: An Exploration of Boundaries that Define Locations of Religious Identity', *Social Compass*, 53 (2006), 201–13.

David M. Freidenreich, *Foreigners and Their Food: Constructing Otherness in Jewish, Christian, and Islamic Law* (Berkeley, Calif.: University of California Press, 2011).

Eliza F. Kent, 'Secret Christians of Sivakasi: Gender, Syncretism, and Crypto-Religion in Early Twentieth-Century South India', *Journal of the American Academy of Religion*, 79 (2011), 676–705.

Jacob N. Kinnard, 'When Is the Buddha Not the Buddha? The Hindu/Buddhist Battle over Bodhgayā and Its Buddha Image', *Journal of the American Academy of Religion*, 66 (1998), 817–39.

Steven W. Ramey, 'Challenging Definitions: Human Agency, Diverse Religious Practices and the Problems of Boundaries', *Numen*, 54 (2007), 1–27.

Joel Robbins, 'Crypto-Religion and the Study of Cultural Mixtures: Anthropology, Value, and the Nature of Syncretism', *Journal of the American Academy of Religion*, 79 (2011), 408–24.

Michelle Voss Roberts, 'Religious Belonging and the Multiple', *Journal of Feminist Studies in Religion*, 26 (2010), 43–62.

CHAPTER 17

Interreligious Cooperation

PAUL WELLER

'Interreligious cooperation' is a form of interreligious relating and at times dialogue that implies a specific and distinctive set of characteristics and intentions. In particular, it is often focused either on the possibilities presented by action that can be undertaken together by people of various religions, and/or by shared consultation around policies or programmes. The goals may be varied. Interreligious dialogue may be required in order to clarify the basis for action, or an action may lead into interreligious dialogue as an expression of it. 'Interreligious cooperation' may also be part of, or directed to the improvement of interreligious relations. But equally it may not be focused so much, or at all, on relations between religious groups, but rather on what people from various religions cooperating together might contribute to the wider society in which they live—for example, in the relief of suffering, the upholding of human rights, or as a challenge to economic and/or political injustice. This chapter will explore a range of questions and issues in relation to concrete examples of interreligious cooperation, including: the role and place of confidence-building; the question of who will cooperate with whom and on what basis (who's in and who's out and why); the possibilities and limitations connected with different organizational and structural forms for cooperation (for example, through a formalized, and aspiring to be representative, council or in a more loosely structured Network).

There is also the question of who initiates such interreligious cooperation (from within, across or beyond particular religions); the range of aims and goals in interreligious cooperation; the advantages and disadvantages of 'narrow front' cooperation (for example, in work in a specific field, such as the promotion of peace) in comparison with 'broad front' forms of cooperation (such as in general councils of religions); the differences between interreligious cooperation organizations (established for long-term existence) and initiatives set up for particular temporary purposes. And in exploring these questions and issues it is important to contextualize the examples discussed in terms of their specific historical and social location.

THE CHANGED CONTEXT FOR INTERRELIGIOUS COOPERATION

The end of the nineteenth century and beginning of the twentieth saw the emergence of a relatively new phenomenon in the history of religions. Historically speaking there have been many examples of interreligious controversy and conflict, as well as of interreligious dialogue. Instances of interreligious cooperation between individuals and, sometimes, between groups, can also be found. Within religiously diverse neighbourhoods, families composed of people of different religions have cooperated together over many generations in relation to the basic needs of human life, while in places of work, individuals and groups of different religions have cooperated together in various ways, at various levels, and for various purposes. In particular, trade and commerce have often formed an at least minimal shared material ground for exchange and cooperation between groups of varied kinds, including different cultural and religious groups. Indeed, David Hart goes so far as to propose trade as an illuminating model for understanding and developing a broader interreligious engagement: 'religious conversation is part of the give and take of human exchange. It is neither more nor less than that, and takes place within the many different types of trading activities we engage in.'[1] However, what is new in the period known as 'modernity' has been the emergence of more *organized* and *specific* forms for interreligious cooperation. In this regard, the more recent historical and contemporary developments in interreligious cooperation both reflect and partake in the wider societal changes that characterize modernity as set out by Max Weber in his analysis of the emergence of *Gesellschaften* (societies) out of *Gemeinshaften* (communities), and the associated development of organizational rather than more organic forms of relating and cooperating. Thus the focus of this chapter is on particular *organizations* engaged in interreligious cooperation. And whilst the examples are drawn from the UK experience, the lessons suggested have wider applicability.

Explicitly understood, interreligious cooperation in modern organizational forms goes back only just over a century. Marcus Braybrooke[2] traces the aetiology of these quintessentially modern forms of interreligious cooperation back to the World's Congress of Religions[3] that was convened in Chicago in 1893. That was followed in 1933 by the First International Assembly of the World Fellowship of Faiths,[4] held also in Chicago during its

---

[1] D. Hart, *Trading Faith: Global Religions in an Age of Rapid Change* (Ropley: O Books, 2006), 94.

[2] M. Braybrooke, *Inter-Faith Organisations, 1893–1979: An Historical Directory* (Lampeter: Edwin Mellen Press, 1980); and *Pilgrimage of Hope: One Hundred Years of Global Interfaith Dialogue* (London: SCM Press, 1992).

[3] J. Barrows (ed.), *The World's Parliament of Religions* (Chicago: The Parliament Publishing Co., 1893); and R. M. Seager, *The World's Parliament of Religions: The East–West Encounter, Chicago, 1893*, (Indianapolis: Indiana University Press, 1995).

[4] C. Weller (ed.), *World Fellowship: Addresses and Message by Leading Spokesmen of all Faiths, Races and Countries* (New York: Liversight Publishing Corporation, 1936).

second World's Fair. In more recent times the project of the Chicago Congress has been 'commemorated' and its project revived by a Council for the Parliament of the World Religions[5] which has organized successor events in Chicago (1993), Cape Town (1999), Barcelona (2004), Melbourne (2009), and with another planned to take place in Brussels in 2014. Another early initiative, but which took place in Europe rather than the USA, was the Religions of the Empire Conference[6] organized in 1924 in London by Sir Denison Ross and which was held in conjunction with the British Empire Exhibition. One of those who took a prominent part in that conference—the explorer and mystic Sir Francis Younghusband—went on to convene the World Congress of Faiths in 1936[7] which subsequently established itself as an interreligious organization that has continued its work down to the present day.

In the case of the USA-based events, the religious freedom and diversity of the New World played a significant role in their genesis. In the case of the UK-based ones, it was the colonial and imperial projects of nineteenth- and early twentieth-century Europe that turned out, in many ways, to provide a significant catalyst for a growth in consciousness about religious diversity and plurality. This came about through the engagement in colonial contexts of a significant number of administrators, members of the armed forces, and Christian missionaries who had already been exposed to the texts, ideas, and beliefs of a variety of religions. Many became involved in early interreligious initiatives when back in the metropolis. However, although these were pioneering and important developments relative to the perspectives and positions of the majority of the world religious traditions at the time, these international events and their associated organizations were often seen as being in a religiously peripheral position. As such, they were thought to exist primarily for individual interfaith enthusiasts from within the world religious traditions, or else as events and organizations within which people from more socially and religiously marginalized religious traditions could find both a measure of acceptance by people of other religions as well as a public platform. Thus these earliest initiatives tended to be more *international* in form than national or local; and they also tended to be *multilateral* rather than focusing on relationships between two or three particular religions. But it was with the development of more national forms of interreligious cooperation—initially emerging out of international initiatives—that a greater engagement began to be secured from the organized religious 'mainstreams'. We shall touch on two.

---

[5] See J. Beverluis (ed.), *A Sourcebook for the Community of Religions: The Council for a Parliament of the World's Religions* (Chicago: The Council for a Parliament of the World's Religions, 1993); and H. Küng and K-J. Kuschel (eds), *A Global Ethic: The Declaration of the Parliament of the World's Religions* (London: SCM Press, 1993).

[6] W. Hare (ed.), *Religions of the Empire: A Conference of Some Living Religions within the Empire* (London: Duckworth, 1925).

[7] A. Millard (ed.), *Faiths and Fellowship: The Proceedings of the World Congress of Faiths, held in London, July 3rd–17th, 1936* (London: J. M. Watkins, 1937); M. Braybrooke, *A Wider Vision: A History of the World Congress of Faiths* (Oxford: One World, 1996).

The Council of Christians and Jews

In 1942, partly as a response to the situation of Jews in Nazi Europe, a Council of Christians and Jews (CCJ) was formed and, following the ending of the Second World War, in 1946 an international conference of Christians and Jews was held in Oxford. At that conference it was decided to plan for an International Council of Christians and Jews (ICCJ).[8] Its tasks became all the more urgent as the full truth emerged concerning the Holocaust of European Jewry. For various reasons the ICCJ did not formally meet until 1975 in Hamburg, Germany, although an International Consultative Committee of organizations concerned with Christian–Jewish cooperation was in existence from 1962 onwards. In 2012 thirty-eight national Councils of Christians and Jews were linked with the ICCJ, including the CCJ in the UK. However, prior to this body, the London Society for Christians and Jews had existed as an initiative of the Liberal Jewish movement.[9]

With the emergence of the CCJ there came a structure that was both more national and also more inclusive of the diversities and official representative bodies of both Jews and Christians in the UK. Linked with this national organization today there are also thirty-five local CCJ branches. The CCJ sets out its founding and continuing aims as being to '(1) promote religious and cultural understanding between Christians and Jews, (2) work for the elimination of religious and racial prejudice, hatred and discrimination, particularly antisemitism, and (3) promote religious and racial harmony on the basis of ethical and social teachings common to Christianity and Judaism'.[10]

Religions for Peace

Also developed at an international level is the organization now called Religions for Peace, but originally known as the World Conference of Religions for Peace (WCRP).[11] In its conception, composition, and activity this has been an explicitly inter- and multi-religious organisation. As its name already makes clear, it is focused on the contribution that religions may be able to make to the preservation, establishment, and development of peace in the world. Its work also involves bringing about interreligious dialogue, albeit specifically focused on overcoming conflict rooted in religious differences. It holds an international assembly every five years and its international body has consultative status in the United Nations Economic and Social Council (ECOSOC), as well as with UNESCO and UNICEF. Following a long history of attempts to convene a global interreligious

---

[8] B. Simpson and R. Weyl, *The International Council of Christians and Jews* (Heppenheim: ICCJ 1988); and M. Braybrooke, *Children of One God: A History of the Council of Christians and Jews* (London: Valentine Mitchell, 1991).

[9] G. Yates (ed.), *In Spirit and in Truth: Aspects of Judaism and Christianity: A Symposium* (London: Hodder & Stoughton, 1934).

[10] <http://www.ccj.org.uk/Groups/172746/Council_of_Christians/About/ Position_Statements.aspx>.

[11] See J. H. Taylor and G. Gebhardt (eds), *Religions for Human Dignity* (Geneva: World Conference on Religion and Peace, 1986); and H. A. Jack, *A History of the World Conference on Religion and Peace* (New York: World Conference on Religion and Peace, 1993).

conference focused on issues related to peace, the WCRP met in Kyoto in 1970. At that event it was agreed to form an organization which would take forward the impetus from the conference through at least four programmes. These were designed to initiate interreligious seminars and conferences at all levels in order to create a climate for the peaceful resolution of disputes among and within nations without violence; encourage the establishment of national and regional committees for peace; develop an interreligious presence at the United Nations and other international conferences, through which the influence of religion could be directly exerted to resolve conflicts; and encourage the further development of the science of interreligious dialogue for peace. The organization, Religions for Peace, has seventy-five national affiliates and a number of regional bodies. A European Committee of the WCRP was formed in 1975 and a UK and Ireland Chapter (later separating out into a distinct UK Chapter and an Irish Chapter) was also formed at that time, which today is called Religions for Peace (UK). At the European level, and linked with Religions for Peace internationally, there is a Religions for Peace Europe, and a European Council of Religious Leaders.

THE INTER FAITH NETWORK FOR THE UK: A CASE STUDY

Most of the multi-religious (as distinct from bilateral or multilateral) organizations developed at an international rather than national or regional level. At the same time, the articulation between international and national levels—as, for example, in Europe, historically, through the Religions for Peace organization—underlines the importance of identifying and learning lessons from national-level examples of cooperation. The significance of this interplay is likely to grow as, in broader economic and political terms, regional and continental forms of organization become ever more important and lead to the emergence of new initiatives for interreligious cooperation. In Europe, this includes the emergence of the European Network on Religion and Belief (ENORB)[12] to which this chapter will, in its concluding section, return after an analysis of the context, history, and development of the Inter Faith Network for the UK. Although the Network[13] belongs to a specific national context, analysis of a national organization in which learning to cooperate and being willing to do so have been at its heart for over a quarter of a century will bring into a focus a range of wider key

---

[12] <http://www.enorb.eu>.
[13] See P. Weller, '"Inheritors Together": The Interfaith Network for the United Kingdom', *Discernment: A Christian Journal of Inter-Religious Encounter*, 3/2 (1988), 30–4; 'Das "Inter Faith Network for the UK": Eine neue Initiative in den interreligiösen Beziehungen', in J. Lähnemann (ed.), *Das Wiederwachen der Religionen als pädagogische Herausforderung: Interreligiöse Erziehung im Spannungsfeld von Fundamentalismus und Säkularismus* (Hamburg: E. B.-Verlag Rissen, 1993); 'The Inter Faith Network for the United Kingdom', *Anglo-Indian Historical Review: A Journal of History*, 20/1 (1994), 20–6.

issues, opportunities, challenges, strengths, and limitations from which it might be possible to glean lessons of relevance applicable to various wider contexts and settings.

While the UK saw many important pioneering initiatives in interreligious cooperation, generally speaking these remained somewhat peripheral and tangential to the focus, concerns, and organizational priorities of the majority religious groups, communities, and organizations. From within the religious 'mainstreams' they were often perceived—and sometimes were— places within which 'enthusiasts' (for inter-religious goodwill), 'refugees' (from specific religious communities), and 'seekers' (after spirituality) focused their energies.[14] This was partly inevitable because, despite the very broad cultural and religious diversity of its imperial and colonial extensions, until the last quarter of the twentieth century what might be called the 'religious landscape'[15] of the UK was itself not very religiously plural. However, from the post-Second World War period onwards—and accelerating particularly via the New Commonwealth immigration of the mid-to-late 1950s and the 1960s—the 'Empire came home'. As part of this, it also gradually became clear that the UK was becoming 'home' to an increasing range of different religious groups, making it perhaps the country with the broadest range of religious diversity in Europe in terms of substantial communities of Muslims, Hindus, and Sikhs, as well as other religious groups, all joining Christians and the already established Jewish presence.[16]

Between the period of the initial immigration and the outbreak in 1988–89 of the decade-long *Satanic Verses* controversy[17] that clearly signalled the 'return' of religion in relation to identity and politics, the groundwork was laid for the foundation, in 1987, of the Inter Faith Network for the UK. Significantly, the emergence of the Network as a national-level organization only took place after the prior development at the local level, from the early 1960s onwards, of a number of pioneer initiatives for interreligious cooperation—such as the Wolverhampton Inter Faith Group, founded in 1974. The emergence of such local initiatives occurred because it was in particular localities that the composition of the population had changed most substantially, and the new challenges and opportunities of living together in an increasingly religiously plural society became most sharply delineated and impossible to avoid. National-level consciousness of these issues, and the development of new initiatives to engage with them, only followed when sufficiently widespread local change meant they could no longer be seen as important only for particular localities and not for the country as a whole.

In July 2012 the Network celebrated its silver jubilee. Its formal establishment had followed two years of extensive preparatory consultation by its founding director (from 1987 to 2007), who, in September 1984, had taken leave of absence from his employment in the civil service in order to map the emerging interreligious architecture of the UK and to see how greater linkages might be forged across already existing initiatives. The outcome of a consultative

---

[14] P. Weller, 'Inter-Faith Roots and Shoots: An Outlook for the 1990s', *World Faiths Encounter*, 1 (1992), 48–57.

[15] P. Weller, *Religious Diversity in the UK: Contours and Issues* (London: Continuum, 2008), 8–58.

[16] P. Weller (ed.), *Religions in the UK: Directory, 2007–10* (Derby: Multi-Faith Centre at the University of Derby, in association with the University of Derby, 2007).

[17] P. Weller, *A Mirror for our Times: 'The Rushdie Affair' and the Future of Multiculturalism* (London: Continuum, 2009).

process during 1986 and 1987 signalled sufficient mutual trust among the Network's founding affiliates to affirm the degree of understanding, recognition, and commitment recorded in the founding resolution. At the inaugural June 1987 meeting the organizations initially constituting the Network stated that:

> We meet today as children of many traditions, inheritors of shared wisdom and of tragic misunderstandings. We recognise our shared humanity and we respect each other's integrity in our differences. With the agreed purpose and hope of promoting greater understanding between the members of the different faith communities to which we belong and of encouraging the growth of relationships of respect and trust and mutual enrichment in our life together, we hereby jointly resolve: that the Inter Faith Network for the United Kingdom now be established.[18]

Network of Networks

The Network's founding aims were to 'advance public knowledge and mutual understanding of the teachings, traditions and practices of the different faith communities in Britain, including an awareness both of their distinctive features and of their common ground and to promote good relations between persons of different religious faiths'. The nature and structure of the Network is one that necessitates interreligious cooperation[19] of a quite complex and multilayered kind. First, the Network is neither an individual membership organization, nor—in an important sense—does it have an existence of its own apart from the existence of its affiliated organizations and groups. Because of this, the Network itself is perhaps most aptly described as a 'network of networks' or an 'organization of organizations'. And in many ways it is this which is characteristic both of its strength as well as of its limitations. The Network was explicitly *not* set up as a Council of Faiths for the UK. The creation of such a body was advocated by some on the basis it 'would simply be to give institutional form to a process which has been gathering force over the years'.[20] But the majority of those who were involved

---

[18] Quoted in Inter Faith Network for the UK, *20 Years: Milestones on the Journey Together towards Greater Inter Faith Understanding and Cooperation* (London: Inter Faith Network for the UK, 2007), 12.

[19] It should be noted that the Inter Faith Network itself has (with the exception of its *Statement on Inter-Religious Relations*—see further, below) tended to use the terminology of 'faith communities' and 'inter-faith relations' and their variants more than that of 'religions' and 'interreligious relations' and their variants. Partly as a consequence of this, and the Network's growing national profile over the years, when UK government and other public bodies began to engage more with issues of religion and public life, they more often than not also adopted that terminology, rather than the terminology more generally used in this chapter. Interestingly, when Sir Francis Younghusband founded the World Congress of Faiths he also deliberately chose the terminology of 'faiths', but with a different purpose. In his case, it was in order to be able to include within the WCF both humanists and followers of what today are known as 'New Religious Movements', rather than restricting membership to the generally accepted world religious traditions alone. The Network, by contrast, while using the terminology of 'faiths' has so far understood itself (at least in terms of the range of its national affiliated bodies—see further below) as engaging primarily with the generally accepted 'world religious traditions' with significant communities in the UK.

[20] S. Lamont, *Church and State: Uneasy Alliances* (London: Bodley Head, 1989), 204.

felt that a project to create a Council of Faiths would be an attempt at forced growth in a context within which a more modest and realistic enterprise was needed rather than the construction of a grand design which, when tested by the realities of interreligious relations, might prove to be only a chimera of wishful thinking. Therefore, the 'looser' and more inclusive structure of the Network was what emerged. In this the Network did not seek to supplant existing international, national or local interreligious initiatives. Rather, it sought to 'link' them in order to encourage the wider sharing of the experience and expertise already held within these organizations, so that their wealth of human and material resources might be better known and more fully accessible, both to all the Network's categories of affiliated organizations and for the benefit of the wider society.

The word 'link' is, in fact, one that is found very frequently in the Network's articulation of itself and its work. And in connection with this the Network originally used the looser word 'affiliation' rather than the perhaps harder edged word 'membership', although the latter has come to be used more in recent years. At the time of its foundation, the Network linked sixty organizations in four categories of affiliation; twenty-five years on it linked 200 organizations. In its Annual Report for 2010–11,[21] the Network states that it 'works with its member bodies and other agencies to help make the UK a place marked by mutual understanding and respect between people of different religions where all can practise their faith with integrity' and that its 'way of working is firmly based on the principle that dialogue and cooperation on social action can only prosper if they are rooted in respectful relationships which do not blur or undermine the distinctiveness of different religious traditions'.

As a result of its fourfold structure of affiliation, the Network includes the diverse perspectives of interreligious enthusiasm, academic study, and community representation in a framework which embraces both the local and national dimensions of interreligious activity in the plural society of the UK. The strength of this is that these diverse standpoints and perspectives can come into interaction with each other. At the same time, it is inevitable that the diverse interests represented by the four categories of affiliated bodies, when combined with the varieties of religious tradition, can give rise to a wide spectrum of expectations and therefore a degree of tension which it has sometimes been difficult for the Network to hold together in balance. At the same time, tension is a feature of an organization that is alive rather than one that is moribund. And the tensions which are inherent in the structure of the Network have, on the whole, so far proved to be creative and mutually stimulating.

One of these tensions is that between the representative bodies of the various religions and organizations in the other categories of affiliation. Although the Network has never aspired to be a Council of Faiths, from the beginning one of the things that distinguished it from other interreligious initiatives operating at a national level in the UK was that it was judged important that representative bodies from the various religious communities should

---

[21] Inter Faith Network for the UK, *Promoting Mutual Respect and Understanding: Annual Report, 2010/11* (London: Inter Faith Network for the UK, 2011), inside cover.

be at its heart. In this way it was planned that it should not become a kind of club for like-minded interfaith enthusiasts, but rather would have the possibility of engaging with the broad streams of the religious communities and traditions of the UK and their representative and consultative structures and processes. The Network also links national organizations and UK branches of international organizations that are specifically dedicated to aspects of inter-religious relating (some of which are focused on the contribution of religions to peace, others on dialogue between religious traditions more for its 'own sake') and various religions (some of which are bilateral, others trilateral, and others multilateral in their focus) including, for example, the Council of Christians and Jews and Religions for Peace (UK). From 2001 onwards, the Network had also convened these bodies together in what had been the first regular meeting for a specific category of Network affiliates, prior to the development of the Faith Communities Forum. Eventually included within this category of membership has been the linking of the Inter Faith Council for Wales/Cyngor Rhyng-greyfyddol Cymru (founded in 2004); the Northern Ireland Inter Faith Forum (founded in 1993); and the Scottish Inter Faith Council (founded in 1999).[22] From 2005 onwards the linking bodies within the four nations of the UK (England, Wales, Northern Ireland, and Scotland) have met together regularly with each other and with the Network.

With the growth, during the period of the New Labour governments, of the role in England of the then Regional Development Agencies and Regional Assemblies, a pattern of regional-level interreligious initiatives also developed such as the Northwest Forum of Faiths and 'faithsnetsouthwest'. From 2006 onwards, jointly with the Faith Based Regeneration Network, the Inter Faith Network facilitated meetings of these forums in an informal link initiated by the 'English Regional Faith Forums Network'. In a number of cases, these regional develop-ments were perhaps less 'bottom up' in their emergence than many local interreligious initia-tives, in so far as many of the religions involved have not had such extensive regional-level infrastructures in comparison with their local or national organizational presence. Therefore, following the formation of the Conservative-Liberal Coalition government and the with-drawal of the public funding that had been a central part of the budgets of many of these regional bodies, a number have struggled and others (such as the Faiths Forum for the East Midlands) have been dissolved. As noted above, the Network also links local interreligious groups of various kinds, such as the Leicester Council of Faiths, the Cambridge Inter-Faith Group, the Coventry Multi-Faith Forum, and so on. Some, but not all, are members of the Inter Faith Network. Those which are members of the Network are not branches of the Network, but independent entities in their own right and in some cases were in existence before the Network was established. They are very diverse in terms of local contexts, histo-ries, constitutions, compositions, aims, and methods of working. The majority are in locali-ties characterized by a high degree of ethnic diversity and visible religious plurality, but there are also groups formed to promote greater understanding of religious diversity in

---

[22] P. Weller, *Time for a Change: Reconfiguring Religion, State and Society* (London: T&T Clark, 1995), 73.

geographical areas that are less visibly diverse. Some include people from a wide variety of different religions while others, reflecting their local demography, are mostly composed of people of two or three religious traditions; some are very informal groupings of individuals, while some are formally representative bodies in consultative relationships with their local public authorities.

The Network also links educational and academic bodies specializing in interreligious relations, such as the Religious Education Council for England and Wales; the Shap Working Party on World Religions in Education; and the Centre for Christianity and Interreligious Dialogue at Heythrop College, University of London. This category of affiliation is not intended for any academic or educational organization engaged in the study of religion and religions. Rather, it is for those which are specifically concerned with, and contributing from an academic perspective to, the relational dimensions of religions, particularly with reference to the UK context. In many ways during the history of the Network this has been the least central and most difficult to incorporate into its life. But it has also been an important part of the Network's overall balance. The Network's affiliation structure means that, although there are sometimes those both within and beyond it who want the Network to assume a number of roles or tasks which might increase its visibility, it often holds back from doing so because it sees some of these roles or tasks as more properly belonging to one of its affiliated bodies. And because of the Network's overall approach, one of its central functions is as a means of communication between its affiliated bodies and their diverse interests, resources, and contributions to one another, to government, to public bodies, and to the wider society.

A Means of Communication

As one means of bringing its overall constituency together for communication, the running of its affairs, and to address major issues of contemporary common concern, the Network organizes annual national meetings at which all its affiliated organizations have representation and at the end of which are its annual general meetings. But although this public coming together of the Network is an important expression of a mutual commitment and growing community, the Network is not primarily about the public visibility of such meetings, or about the making of public statements on particular issues or topics. It is rather more about the difficult and often almost invisible, but nevertheless critical, tasks of cementing relationships, building trust, and extending communication. From the beginning, one of the things that the Network facilitated was an exchange between the richly diverse, but sometimes struggling, local initiatives. As the Network says of itself, it 'links, shares good practice between, and supports with advice and information the growing pattern of inter faith initiatives in the UK at national, regional and local levels'.[23] Thus, over the years, the Network has sponsored and serviced

---

[23] Inter Faith Network for the UK, *Promoting Mutual Respect* (2011) inside cover.

regular regional consultations or 'link meetings' between local interreligious initiatives in the various regions of England, and also in Scotland, Wales, and Northern Ireland. Meetings of this kind have not only benefited local groups, but they have also been a means by which the Network's national staff could keep in touch with the day-to-day concerns of grassroots interreligious work. In this way, as well as in others, such local groups have been able to contribute to the formation of the Network's agenda at a national level. Furthermore, these link meetings have also always been open to all local interreligious initiatives whether affiliated to the Inter Faith Network or not. In this way a certain dynamic of relationship has been maintained so that Network affiliation does not convey an exclusivity that might imply that only local interreligious initiatives affiliated to the Network are worthwhile.

One of the features over the twenty-five years of the Network's development has been the very substantial growth in the number of local interreligious initiatives.[24] This took place particularly during the period of the New Labour governments which, through mechanisms such as City Partnerships, encouraged places of worship and local religious organizations, as civil society organizations, to contribute to the generation of 'social capital'.[25] As local government became increasingly active in this area, the Network has articulated part of its role as being, on the one hand, that 'in cooperation with the Scottish, Welsh and Northern Irish national inter faith linking bodies and Regional Faith Forums in England, [it] fosters local inter faith cooperation and offers advice on patterns of local inter faith initiatives suitable to a particular local area as well as helpful contacts',[26] while, on the other, it 'assists member organisations and other agencies, such as local authorities and other public bodies, to help strengthen their inter faith programmes and good practice'.[27] An early example of this was that, following extensive consultation over drafts of the document, in 1999 the Inter Faith Network published the first edition of *The Local Inter Faith Guide*.[28] This provided advice on the setting up and running of local interreligious initiatives and was followed up by, in 2002, *Faith and Community*.[29] In 2003, in partnership also with a range of relevant bodies, the Network published *Partnership for the Common Good*,[30] while in 2005 a second edition of *The Local Inter Faith Guide* was published.[31] Externally, the Network also played a role in

[24] Inter Faith Network for the United Kingdom, *Local Inter Faith Activity in the UK: A Survey* (London: Inter Faith Network for the UK, 2003).

[25] R. Furbey et al., *Faith as Social Capital: Connecting or Dividing?* (Bristol: Policy Press, 2006).

[26] Inter Faith Network for the UK, *Promoting Mutual Respect* (2011), inside cover.

[27] Inter Faith Network for the UK, *Promoting Mutual Respect*.

[28] Inter Faith Network for the UK, *The Local Inter Faith Guide: Faith Community Cooperation in Action* (London: Inter Faith Network for the UK in association with the Inner Cities Religious Council of the Department for the Environment, Transport and the Regions, 1999).

[29] Local Government Association, *Faith and Community: A Good Practice Guide for Local Authorities,* 1st edn (London: Local Government Association Publications, 2002).

[30] Inter Faith Network for the UK, *Partnership for the Common Good: Inter Faith Structures and Local Government* (London: Inter Faith Network for the UK in association with the Local Government Association, the Home Office, and the Inner Cities Religious Council of the Office of the Deputy Prime Minister, 2003).

[31] Inter Faith Network for the UK, *The Local Inter Faith Guide: Faith Community Co-operation in Action,* 2nd edn (London: Inter Faith Network for the UK in association with Inner Cities Religious Council and the Office of the Deputy Prime Minister, 2005).

facilitating some of the consultation with religious groups by the UK Government Home Office that led to the 2004 *Working Together* document.[32] This included a number of recommendations intended to help government departments 'improve their engagement with citizens from the faith communities in matters of national policy'[33] and suggested 'various approaches which the faith communities themselves can adopt to get the most out of their dealings with Government'.[34]

The follow-through of the *Working Together* report led to the 2006 foundation of the Faith Communities Consultative Council in order to act as a focus for communication between government and civil servants on the one hand, and religious communities and interreligious bodies on the other. In due course, responsibility for convening this was moved to the Department for Communities and Local Government where, in 2009, the perspectives and contributions of the Faith Communities Consultative Council were complemented by appointment of an Expert Panel on Faith advising the Secretary of State for Communities, other Ministers, and Civil Servants in the Department for Communities and Local Government. This panel was composed of a group of academics and community actors with substantial knowledge of the religious traditions and communities in the UK, but not acting as formal representatives of any of them. However both bodies were abolished in the summer of 2010 following the formation of the Conservative-Liberal Coalition government, in the light of different approaches that the newly elected government wished to take to the engagement of religious communities and groups in working towards its vision of a 'Big Society'.

Developing Shared Approaches

Over the years the Network has engaged with its affiliated organizations in a variety of consultative exercises. As its annual report for 2010–11 puts it, the Network 'proceeds by consensus wherever possible and not making statements on behalf of member bodies except after full consultation'.[35] As early as 1990, the Network had launched a 'Values in a Multi-Faith Society Project' and in 1991, a 'Faith in Public Life Programme', both of which have continued to provide a broad framework for the ongoing agendas and specific initiatives undertaken by the Network. One of these specific initiatives was a process that, as early as 1991, resulted in the Network's *Statement on Inter Religious Relations*, which represented the first multilaterally developed and agreed statement of its kind in the UK. By their endorsement of it, the Network's affiliated organizations at that time took a new step forward in interreligious cooperation and laid a solid foundation for the building of increased communication, consultation, and trust among the religious communities of the UK.

[32] *Working Together: Co-operation between Government and Faith Communities: Recommendations of the Steering Group Reviewing Patterns of Engagement between Government and Faith Communities in England* (London: Home Office Faith Communities Unit, 2004).

[33] *Working Together*, 1.

[34] *Working Together*, 2.

[35] Inter Faith Network for the UK, *Promoting Mutual Respect* (2011), inside cover.

This document included a series of headline statements along with a more extended commentary. Together with publication and sale of the whole document, the highlighted summaries were separately and freely distributed and, over the years, have frequently been used in various forums as a focus for discussion and debate on issues in interreligious relations, being reissued and reprinted by the Network in 2006. It refers to recognition of the

> need to respect the integrity of each other's inherited and chosen religious identities, beliefs and practices. To be able to live by our traditions, share our convictions, and act according to our consciences are freedoms which we all affirm and which we wish the framework of society to uphold. But these freedoms must never be used in order to pressurise others into changing their religious identities, beliefs or practices.[36]

This paragraph, together with its more developed commentary, had been one of the most difficult to frame and agree during the preceding consultation process, touching, as it does, upon some of the most sensitive historical and contemporary issues in the relationships between people of different religions. The outcome reflected a measure of the cooperative spirit, but the sensitivity of these issues was soon further underlined by the announcement by the Christian Churches of Britain and Ireland of the 1990s as being a Decade of Evangelism, as well as the responses to this of other religions in the UK. The inception of this decade led to the Network undertaking further 'confidence-building' work which issued in the publication of a booklet on *Mission, Dialogue and Inter Religious Encounter*.[37] This included a briefer *Code of Practice on Building Good Relations with People of Different Faiths* that was even more widely circulated and used than the earlier *Statement on Inter Religious Relations*, and was translated into a variety of community languages precisely in order to encourage its wider dissemination and use. Essentially, the Code embodies what it describes as a 'shared ethic of inter religious encounter',[38] on the basis that 'if there is to be a sound basis for trust between us, we need to treat each other in all our dealings in a consistently principled way'.

A Source of Reliable Information

Since 1998 the Network has maintained an office in central London which has supported another aspect of its work, namely, that it 'runs a helpline and publishes resources to help people working to promote good inter faith relations'.[39] Religious traditions and communities, and especially minority ones, often feel that they suffer from ignorance among the general population as well as misinformation and distortion in their depiction by the

---

[36] Inter Faith Network for the UK, *Statement on Inter Religious Relations* (London: Inter Faith Network for the UK, 1991), paragraph 11.

[37] Inter Faith Network for the UK, *Mission, Dialogue and Inter Religious Encounter* (London: Inter Faith Network for the UK, 1993).

[38] Inter Faith Network for the UK, *Mission, Dialogue and Inter Religious Encounter*, 11.

[39] Inter Faith Network for the UK, *Promoting Mutual Respect* (2011), inside cover.

public media. In the light of this, one of the important roles played by the Network office and its staff has been the provision of a central point of reference for enquiries from member organizations, other religious organizations, government departments, the media, and the general public. In addition, the Network has also undertaken planned and proactive work to provide information about the religions of the UK and the relationships between them. Initially, in 1988, the Network produced a *Handbook of Affiliated Organisations*[40] which included contact details and summary information on the organizations affiliated to it. Growing out of that, and extending beyond it, between 1991 and 2003, the Network collaborated (initially) with one of its affiliated organizations, the University of Derby's Religious Resource and Research Centre, and (then) with the Multi-Faith Centre at the University of Derby, in developing and taking forward the Multi-Faith Directory Research Project.

When the directory project began, while some religions in the UK had their own published directories (for example, Jews and Christians), others (such as Hindus and, at the time, Muslims) had no comprehensive published directory and no multi-religious reference work existed. Therefore, the project aimed to fill a lacuna in providing an overview work of reference for a general professional readership that included collated contact details for local places of worship, religious organizations, and interreligious initiatives throughout the country. It combined this with introductory descriptions about the religions and their organizations in the UK in ways that sought to reflect their own self-understanding and to be academically defensible. The first edition of the directory was published in 1993.[41] It was followed by revised, updated, and expanded editions in 1997[42] and 2001.[43] By the time of the 2007 edition,[44] the directory had become a self-standing project and publication, the Network having withdrawn from continuing direct involvement as it had fulfilled its original aim of meeting a need. But arising from an agreement with the broader directory project, in 2004 the Network produced the first edition of its publication, *Inter Faith Organisations in the UK: A Directory*,[45] which provided contact and other summary information on interfaith organizations operating at all levels of the UK, from national, through regional, to local. This has been followed by further editions, the most recent of which was published in 2009 and includes details on around 260 organizations working at UK, national, regional, and local levels to promote good interfaith relations.[46]

---

[40] Inter Faith Network for the UK, *Handbook of Affiliated Organisations* (London: Inter Faith Network for the UK, 1988).

[41] P. Weller (ed.), *Religions in the UK: A Multi-Faith Directory* (Derby: University of Derby in association with the Inter Faith Network for the UK, 1993).

[42] P. Weller (ed.), *Religions in the UK: A Multi-Faith Directory* (1997 edn).

[43] P. Weller (ed.), *Religions in the UK: Directory, 2001–03* (Derby: Multi-Faith Centre at the University of Derby in association with the Inter Faith Network for the UK, 2001).

[44] Weller (ed.), *Religions in the UK* (2007).

[45] Inter Faith Network for the UK, *Inter Faith Organisations in the UK: A Directory* (London: Inter Faith Network for the UK, 2004).

[46] Inter Faith Network for the UK, *Inter Faith Organisations in the UK* (2009 edn).

In addition to such works of reference, the Network has also produced for its member organizations a series of regular circulars covering both the business of the Network itself and also the key issues with which it has been concerned. In addition, it has also produced wider briefing notes. From 1996 to 2008, a regular newsletter called *Inter Faith Update* was produced in order to highlight and disseminate information on the Network's activities and other inter-religious initiatives. Since 2009 the Network has circulated an e-bulletin which also gives details of developments on public policy issues of particular interest and concern to faith communities. From 1999 onwards, the Network has also maintained a website that gives information on its activities, provides web links to its affiliated organizations' own websites, and from which many of the Network's publications and reports can be downloaded in PDF format.

A Channel for Shared Representations

Although the Network is not a Council of Faiths it says of itself that it 'fosters joint working by the faith communities on social issues'.[47] On occasion, the Network has been able to give some general expression to the common concerns of its affiliated bodies, such as, in its earliest years, during the discussions which led up to the passing into law of the 1988 Education Reform Act (which, amongst other major changes, brought in new legislation to strengthen emphasis on Christianity with regard to the content of collective worship and religious education in publicly funded schools). Although the Network did not seek to make representations on specific draft clauses of the proposed legislation, it was nonetheless active in expressing the broad concerns of its affiliated organizations during the discussions on, and amendments to, the Bill as it went through Parliament. In addition, briefing papers were issued to the Network's affiliated organizations to assist them in their own activity and representations on this matter. The wider question of how the Network should relate to matters of social and political concern has not been an easy one to resolve. Although it was clear that an interreligious organization could not ignore the political dimensions of life, it was also clear that on many issues there is, not surprisingly, no unanimity of position and perspective among the affiliated organizations. Indeed, on such matters, the internal diversity of religious and interreligious organizations is often as great as the diversity that exists between them. The Network has therefore sought carefully to delineate the ways in which either it or its officers act publicly and collectively by developing an explicit *Policy on the Making of Network Statements*. At the same time, the Network has been proactively engaged in seeking ways to ensure that all of its affiliated organizations are adequately consulted on matters of concern to them so that they can fully participate in social and political debate such as when, for example, consultations took place on changes to the law governing charitable organizations.

---

[47] Inter Faith Network for the UK, *Promoting Mutual Respect* (2011), inside cover.

Inclusive Engagement with Public Bodies

One of the aims of the Network includes reference to 'the common ground' between the religions. The Network says of itself that it 'provides a trusted neutral, non-denominational framework for people of different faiths to discuss issues of shared concern, reflecting on both the distinctive aspects and the common ground of their individual traditions' and that it 'arranges seminars and conferences and carries out research to pursue particular issues in greater depth, such as building good relations on campus, and developing bilateral dialogues'.[48] The *Statement on Inter Religious Relations*[49] had claimed that

> We hold in common ideals of compassion, service, justice, peace, and concern for the environment. We also believe that popularity, money and power should never be accepted as the sole determining factors in individual or social life. We also acknowledge that many of those who are without a religious commitment also uphold these ideals.

However, also recognizing the problems involved in making broad claims to shared values the statement had also acknowledged that 'both within and between our communities there are significant differences in the ways in which we translate these values and ideals into ethical judgements concerning specific personal and social issues', while also holding that 'a recognition of the extent to which we share a range of common values and ideals can contribute to a wider sense of community in our society'.

Resulting in the publication of a report,[50] starting in 1996 the Network facilitated a process around these issues by bringing together a range of the key individuals and organizations involved in values debates to explore the possibilities and problematics of this agenda, including representatives of the Values Education Council, the School Curriculum and Assessment Authority, and a range of representatives from various religious traditions. Over the years the Network has also been active in trying to facilitate the participation and inclusion of the UK's diverse religious communities. For example, the Network worked closely with the Inner Cities Religious Council, which had been founded in 1992 as a national government-established forum for advice to government from religious community representatives on a range of inner-city regeneration and policy issues.[51] Both the Inter Faith Network and the Inner Cities Religious Council worked together with the Commission for Racial Equality in exploring the case for new legislation to respond to religious, as distinct from racial and ethnic discrimination. The Network also helped to facilitate consultation undertaken by the Office for National Statistics that eventually led to the inclusion of questions on religious identity in the 2001 decennial Census for England and Wales, and for Scotland.

---

[48] Inter Faith Network for the UK, *Promoting Mutual Respect*.

[49] Inter Faith Network for the UK, *Statement* (1991), paragraph 4.

[50] Inter Faith Network for the United Kingdom, *The Quest for Common Values: Report of a Seminar Organised by the Inter Faith Network for the UK, 10th December, 1996* (London: Inter Faith Network for the UK, 1997).

[51] C. Beales, 'Partnerships for a Change: The Inner Cities Religious Council', *World Faiths Encounter*, 8 (1994), 41–6.

The Network contributed to a religiously inclusive consideration and planning of events intended to mark the millennium year 2000, including the development of a set of practical guidelines.[52] Of particular significance, it worked with the religious communities, and with the assistance of government, to create the Act of Commitment by the Faith Communities of the United Kingdom[53] which took place in the Royal Gallery of the House of Lords as part of the official millennium celebrations. This theme was echoed almost a decade later when the Network was involved in work with the religious communities and Lambeth Palace in the development of a statement to mark the first Inter Faith Week in England, and which had a particular focus on cooperation for the common good. Since its inception in 2009, the Inter Faith Week has become a major programme of the Inter Faith Network.[54] It took as its model the long-standing Scottish Inter Faith Week. It is designed to increase the involvement of people across England, Wales, and now also Northern Ireland in dialogue and cooperation, both of which form an explicitly identified part of the week, as is also that of dialogue between those of religious and non-religious beliefs.

A Mediator in Controversy

If the Network cannot avoid matters of social and political concern, then its credibility would certainly be called into question if it did not try to engage with issues of interreligious conflict, controversy, and relations, the tackling of which lie at the heart of its own rationale. However, this is far from simple. And where religious conflicts overlap with wider social and political issues it is even more challenging for the Network. The controversy[55] that in late 1988 and early 1989 broke around Salman Rushdie's novel, *The Satanic Verses*,[56] and which continued for a decade to arouse passions and debates, posed a severe test to the stability and robustness of the Network. Early in the autumn of 1988, a number of Muslim individuals and organizations inquired of the staff about the Network's stance on the issues raised. While many individuals and organizations within the Network sympathized with the hurt of the Muslim community and felt that freedom of expression should not be allowed to jeopardize good community relations, the problem which such situations posed to the Network soon became apparent in internal discussions on the issue. Alongside those of a variety of religious traditions who, on the basis of liberal social, political, and religious ideas, defended Rushdie's freedom to publish such a book, there were also Network-affiliated organizations (such as

---

[52] *Marking the Millennium in a Multi-Faith Context: Guidelines for Events Organisers* (London: Churches and Other Faiths sub-group of the Millennium Co-ordinating Group, 1998).

[53] <http://www.interfaith.org.uk/rcommit.htm>.

[54] For an evaluation of Inter Faith Week and a range of examples of the kind of activities undertaken within its framework and the complexities of interreligious cooperation involved, see Inter Faith Network for the UK, *Inter Faith Week 2009: A Report and Evaluation* (London: Inter Faith Network for the UK, 2009).

[55] Weller, *Mirror for our Times.*

[56] Salman Rushdie, *The Satanic Verses* (London: Viking Penguin, 1988).

the Friends of the Western Buddhist Order—FWBO)[57] which opposed the invocation of any law of blasphemy on specifically religious grounds, arguing that any such laws represented a danger to religious freedom.

By the time that Ayatollah Khomeini's *fatwa* was issued and Salman Rushdie went into hiding, the pressure for the Network to publicly do or say something was intense and eventually its officers felt that it was their responsibility to issue a statement. This was done with some hesitation, since at that point the Network had no agreed procedure for issuing public statements and there was concern about how the affiliated organizations might react if the officers were perceived to be saying things on their behalf with which they might not agree. The statement[58] that was eventually issued inevitably walked a tightrope between not being able to take up a clearly unified position in relation some of the substantive issues of the debate, whilst attempting to be specific enough to be of some value. As it transpired, despite the media's clamour for comment, the Network's statement was hardly reported, perhaps because it did not claim to offer clear-cut solutions but stated, rather, that 'there are difficult and divisive issues here which require more considered public debate in a calmer atmosphere as we develop the appropriate social framework for our life together in a multi-faith society. This will take patience, tolerance and commitment as we forge a shared vision of such a society.' However, many of the local inter religious initiatives affiliated to the Network found the officers' statement helpful in formulating their own local responses to the crisis that had developed around the controversy.

The Network's overall response to the Rushdie affair demonstrated its growing maturity as a framework for interreligious communication and cooperation and led to a wider recognition of the Network's potential role in such matters by significant public bodies such as the government-appointed and funded Commission for Racial Equality (CRE). The then Commission for Racial Equality (now superseded by the Equality and Human Rights Commission) was set up by the Race Relations Act of 1976 with the duties, among others, of working towards the elimination of discrimination, promoting equality of opportunity and good relations between persons of different racial groups, and, when required by the Secretary of State or when it otherwise thought necessary, drawing up and submitting to the Secretary of State proposals for amending it. In 1989 the Network and the CRE entered into a partnership to sponsor a joint seminar, which drew together people from various religions, the media, and the law, to discuss legal provisions for curbing blasphemy.[59] The consensus of this seminar was that the then current blasphemy law did not provide a helpful or hopeful way forward. In a second joint seminar, held in October of 1990, the participants moved on to debate the alternatives of abolition without replacement or the introduction of new legislation

---

[57] See FWBO, *Statement* (Norwich: Office of the Western Buddhist Order, 1990).

[58] See 'The Rushdie Affair—A Documentation', *Centre for the Study of Islam and Christian–Muslim Relations*, 42 (1989), 18–19.

[59] Inter Faith Network for the UK, *Law, Blasphemy and the Multi-Faith Society* (London: Inter Commission for Racial Equality, 1990).

focused on the protection of believers rather than of beliefs, and to explore the possible role of self-regulatory codes of conduct in the media and publishing world.[60]

A Bridge between the National and International

Where religious and political issues are primarily located overseas, the Network has found itself in an even more difficult position than in relation to that posed by the *Satanic Verses* affair which, although it had international ramifications, was a controversy that was focused, in the first instance, in the UK itself. For example, if the Network were directly to have tried to address the religious dimensions of all the conflicts in the Middle East, Sri Lanka, Fiji, and other locations that could be seen to have interreligious dimensions, then it might easily have put into jeopardy other things that it might have been possible for it to achieve in the UK. Because of this it was agreed that the Network should only engage with issues and its officers only issue statements on matters that have a direct bearing upon interreligious relations in the UK. However, of course, even such a 'limitation' in focus as this has not always been so clear-cut, because religions in the UK are also connected with wider global religious families and so what happens in other parts of the world has an impact upon the state of interreligious relations in the UK.

The complex and sensitive relationship between the international and the national, the need for the Network to make some response, and the potential value of such response to those trying also to engage with such issues in a responsible way at local levels has been repeated in a number of such occasions including, for example, in 1992, when the Babri Mosque in Ayodhya, India, was demolished and in the wake of which a number of Hindu places of worship in the UK (including in the author's home city of Derby) were attacked, and then following the 9/11 (2001) Al-Qaeda attacks on the World Trade Center and the Pentagon in the USA. In connection with this, the Network's Executive Committee issued a document which sought to bring a measured assessment to bear at a time of great emotional tension that had, in some instances, resulted in hostility being experienced and attacks being made on Muslim individuals and property, as well as people thought to be Muslims.[61]

However, despite their importance at such times, public statements have not seemed to offer the best way forward for the Network's activities. Rather, it has best been able to act as a low-key facilitator of informal conversations, personal contacts, and confidence-building measures, with the intention that even where conflict and controversy exist they should not result in a loss of communication, and also in order to promote a sense of shared responsibility for each other's welfare across the religions. It was therefore this kind of approach that followed the UK's own experience of a mass terror attack on London Transport on 7 July

---

[60] Inter Faith Network for the UK, *Law, Respect for Religious Identity and the Multi-Faith Society* (London: Commission for Racial Equality, 1991).

[61] Executive Committee, Inter Faith Network for the UK, *Reflections on Recent Events* (London: Inter Faith Network for the UK, 2001).

2005, in response to which the Network brought forward the publication of guidance that it had already been engaged in preparing with its member bodies.[62]

Lessons for Interreligious Cooperation

National Initiatives: Lessons from the Inter Faith Network

One of the distinctive features of the development of the Network is that its emergence clearly had a 'bottom up' quality that differentiates it from superficially similar initiatives in a number of other European countries where more 'statist' or 'corporatist' models of relating to religious groups have led to some national governments themselves trying to convene various bodies for interreligious cooperation.[63] The groundwork for the Network's development as national-level organization for interreligious cooperation both was, and arguably could only be, laid after the development of local-level initiatives generated sufficient 'critical mass' of attention and concern and when 'mainstream' national communities and their associated organizations also started to develop a 'felt need' for mechanisms to facilitate mutual interaction and cooperation. It is significant that this took place both prior to, and independently of, any substantial UK government engagement in issues of interreligious cooperation, which involvement really only began with the 1992 foundation of the Inner Cities Religious Council. It then developed further in the early years of the first (1997–2001) New Labour government's 'communitarian' political project, in which religious groups were seen as civil society partners having something important to contribute in the development of what the American social theorist Robert Putnam[64] called 'social capital'. It grew further following the 2001 disturbances in the former northern mill towns and the global repercussions of the 9/11 attacks on the USA and the UK Government's subsequent emphasis on 'social cohesion', reaching a peak following the impact of the 'social policy shock'[65] delivered as a consequence of the 7/7 (2005) London Transport bombings, following which the government tried even more overtly and directly to become a co-actor in the development of initiatives for interreligious cooperation.

While, increasingly, the Network has engaged in partnership working with both government and other public bodies, and its budget also incorporates a proportion of public funding, its relationship with government has been an independent one which has allowed it to maintain a critical distance, while it has sought to ensure its work is not completely dependent on

---

[62] Inter Faith Network for the UK, *Looking After One Another: The Safety and Security of our Faith Communities* (London: Inter Faith Network for the UK, 2005).

[63] M. Braybrooke, 'Interfaith in Europe', in S. Gill, G. D'Costa, and U. King (eds), *Religion in Europe: Contemporary Perspectives* (Kampen: Kok Pharos, 1994), 201–13.

[64] R. Putnam, 'Bowling Alone: America's Declining Social Capital', *Journal of Democracy*, 2 (1995), 65–78; and *Bowling Alone: The Collapse and Revival of American Community* (New York: Simon & Schuster, 2000).

[65] Weller, *Religious Diversity in the UK*.

public funding, but is also financed by charitable trusts and by faith community sources as well as directly from its affiliated organizations. To this extent, the Network could be seen as one of the 'parallel worked alternatives' that are important to develop as potential exemplars for the shape of an emergent new 'socio-religious contract' in which a more inclusive approach to the relationships between religion(s), state, and society could be embodied, that would not presuppose the social or legal dominance of one religious tradition relative to others, and that also would not entail the incorporation of organized religion(s) into government(s) nor their complete detachment from it.[66] Indeed, a 'combination of such initiatives legitimated by the state and public bodies alongside the continued development of local inter-faith councils and inter-faith initiatives emerging from within a vigorous wider voluntary sector, offers the most constructive way forward'.[67]

Issues for, and Evaluation of, the Inter Faith Network

One of the challenges for interfaith cooperation is that, because of the structure of many (though not all) religious communities and groups, women have not always been able to play as full and as public a role in some interreligious leaderships as do many men. Given the general age profile of religious leaderships, this can also apply to young people. Historically women have, in fact, often played a significant and leading role, especially in the development of local interreligious initiatives in the UK. But the Network has also sought, from its earliest days, to address women's participation and contribution. The Network has also tried to address the participation of young people through a number of avenues.[68] The task of trying to ensure as inclusive as possible an engagement for women and young people of various religions in opportunities and issues for interreligious cooperation among themselves, and also in terms of their wider contributions across the religions and to the wider society, is likely to continue to remain challenging both for the Network and for the religious communities themselves and their representative organizations.

Engagement with other diversities that the Network has perhaps not yet even begun to contemplate (such as with people of different sexual orientation within and across religions) may in future years emerge and prove yet more challenging. In recent years, however, there have already been two other sets of issues which the Network has not found it easy to deal with or fully to resolve. The first has been that of enquiries about affiliation to the Network's category of national representative religious bodies, received from organizations that can often be seen by many as being outside of the religious 'mainstream'. Most recently and particularly, this has seen the question of Pagan membership raised regularly at network Annual General Meetings, culminating at the Network's silver jubilee AGM in

---

[66] Weller, *Time for a Change*, 214–15.
[67] Weller, *Time for a Change*, 214.
[68] Cf. Inter Faith Network for the UK, *Connect: Different Faiths Shared Values* (London: Inter Faith Network for the UK in association with TimeBank and the National Youth Agency, 2004).

a formal application for such membership from the Druid Network. There are already Pagan individuals active within the Network—for example, as members of some national and local interreligious initiatives, a number of which provide for Pagan affiliation, while others do not. But the question has been focused on the legitimacy or otherwise of applications from Pagan national religious organizations to affiliate to the Network as national representative bodies. On one side of this debate are arguments made on a pragmatic stance that, since some 'mainstream' religious groups that might find such affiliation problematic, and/or there is a perception that Pagan affiliation in this category may also affect the standing of the Network with government and other public bodies, the time is not ripe to welcome such affiliation. On the other side of the debate are those who point out that, on numerical grounds, the national Census shows there are more Pagans in the UK than there are people of some other religious traditions (for example, Jains and Zoroastrians) which have national representative organizations affiliated to the Network and that Pagan traditions can have a claim—albeit in more modern forms—to have some continuity with the original religious traditions of these islands.

Others have pressed the point that, since the Network is in receipt of public funds, they feel it to be discriminatory and contrary to at least the spirit of equality and human rights law and policies in relation to the protected characteristics of 'religion or belief' that Pagans should be excluded from this category of affiliation. At the same time it remains the case that, under the Equality Act 2012, religious organizations can provide a rationale for certain carefully defined exemptions (which include some limited exemptions bearing upon their self-definition of patterns of membership). The arguments relating to public funding and equality and diversity law and policy have also been used relative to the possibility of Humanist organization affiliation to the Network. As with Pagans, it is also the case there are numbers of Humanists involved in the Network through other organizational categories of affiliation—for example, in local and national interreligious initiatives, and through the academic and educational bodies affiliated to it. At the same time, while Pagans clearly come within the category of 'religions' and thus the Network's focus specifically on inter-*religious* dialogue, relations, and cooperation, most Humanists do not see themselves as 'religious', and most religious people would share that view. So, while to some extent the arguments around Pagan and Humanist affiliation have some similarities, the issues are also to another extent, distinct. Nevertheless, in 2004 the Network was involved in helping to establish a national Religion and Belief Consultative Group that was brought into existence in parallel with the development of the Equality and Human Rights Commission and its remit to work across all the equalities 'strands' and 'protected characteristics' under equalities and human rights law, including that of 'religion or belief' itself, which is intended to cover both religious believers, and also the non-religious. This Group involved the British Humanist Association and the National Secular Society, as well as representative bodies from across a range of religious communities in the UK. However, once the emphasis of the group started to move into the direction of perhaps becoming a formal advisory body on 'religion or belief' for the Equality and Human Rights Commission, the Group splintered and came to an end with the with-drawal from it of major Christian representative bodies, thus underlining the challenges of attempting this kind of collaborative work.

The issues that have emerged for the Network around the various possible forms of Pagan, Humanist, and other involvement in its life and work are not likely to go away, and will remain difficult ones for the Network to chart a way through. But whatever the outcome of contin-ued debate around questions of affiliation, it has proved possible—for example in relation to Humanists—for the Network to undertake some collaborative initiatives across these divides. It remains to be seen whether there might be scope for the Network to engage with Pagans in a similar way to an initiative of that kind undertaken with Humanists. And, of course, debates around these matters have been ongoing at the level of local interreligious organizations, with different positions being taken up by different groups.[69] The diversity of approach itself means that the Network as a whole does not have a common mind on these matters and, although some of the strongest reservations come from some of the national representative bodies in a number of religions, even among and across all of these there is not unanimity of viewpoint on all matters. Cooperation must be constantly negotiated. However, although challenges remain, at the level of a national initiative the Inter Faith Network for the UK represents a model that now has a quarter of a century of accumulated experience in the specific religious, social, and political context, aspects of which may be transferable to other national contexts, and other aspects of which may not.

Whatever may be the Network's strengths and limitations, and whatever the future holds, in its first twenty-five years the Network has, overall, made a worthwhile and enduring con-tribution to the evolution of the UK as a multi-religious society and to a positive engagement with the implications of that on the part of religious groups themselves, the state, and other public bodies in the wider society. At the time of the Network's tenth anniversary celebra-tions, a former Archbishop of Canterbury, George Carey, stated: 'There is no other organisa-tion which provides such a trusted forum between all the main faith communities in the United Kingdom. We must do all we can to ensure its future, since the task of building bridges of understanding between these faith communities can only become increasingly important.' Arguably this evaluation proved to be correct, holds good for today, and it is likely to do so for at least the immediately foreseeable future. At the same time, the experience gathered in the course of the Network's development and operation is likely, in the future, to need com-plementing. For example, whatever the current challenges and crises being faced by the European Union (and especially in the Eurozone), across the world regional and continental forms of economic, political, and social organization are growing in importance and this seems to be a trajectory of regionalization that is only likely to increase, even if its current organizational forms face upheavals and changes as part of their development.

---

[69] R. Herne, 'The Challenge of Paganism within Inter Faith Work', *World Faiths Encounter*, 23 (1999), 32–7.

EMERGENT EUROPEAN POSSIBILITIES FOR INTERRELIGIOUS COOPERATION

In this context, concluding this chapter with a return to the more international level of consideration at which it began, both the potential need for more regional and continental levels of interreligious cooperation, and the relationship between these and national initiatives, are likely to grow in significance. Thus Article 17 of the Treaty of Lisbon states, with regard to religion and belief, that the European Union

> Respects and does not prejudice the status under national law of churches and religious associations or communities in the Member States.
>
> Equally respects the status under national law of philosophical and non-confessional organisations.
>
> Recognising their identity and their specific contribution, the Union shall maintain an open, transparent and regular dialogue with these churches and organisations.

Interreligious cooperation is an imperative for the religious communities of Europe and the societies and states of which they are a part, both because of the need to deal creatively with Europe's own religious diversity, but also because of a need to understand, and relate to, the diversity of the wider world within which Europe is set. As part of an attempt to engage with this orientation from the European Union (EU), including the EU's Lisbon Treaty commitment to holding an 'open, transparent and regular dialogue' with 'churches' and with 'philosophical and non-confessional organisations', a fragile new initiative, the European Network on Religion and Belief (ENORB), has recently begun to be developed. It is part of ENORB's aims to try, at a European level, to link existing national-level interreligious frameworks and to stimulate their development where they do not currently exist. A statement on ENORB's website (September 2012) explains that an Exploratory Group is currently working with the following aims:

> To bring religious and non-religious groups together to work in partnership and in dialogue with the European Union, on EU policy priorities, with particular reference to the 'economic, social and territorial cohesion' of Europe.
>
> To build a common European Platform to combat discrimination and prejudice, and promote harmony and shared values between different religious and non-religious traditions, through joint activities including dialogue, exchanges and social actions for the common good.
>
> To develop a shared language between religions, philosophical organisations, and politicians on key issues and policies for the future of Europe.[70]

The approach of ENORB contrasts with that of the Inter Faith Network by its explicit aim to engage with not only religious organizations, but also those of with a non-religious

---

[70] <http://www.enorb.eu>.

philosophical and ethical orientation. In many ways this takes account of the strong tradition of *laïcité* in France and reflects the historical patterns that developed in a number of member states of the EU, such as the Netherlands and Belgium, where consultation from public bodies has for many years been extended on a more equal basis to both religious and non-religious philosophical-ethical groups.

At the same time, given the challenges that can already be involved in interreligious working alone, ENORB's vision is a bold and ambitious and it may or may not prove able to carry through the scope of this extended vision, either with regard to breadth of religious and non-religious participation or depth of connection with individual countries. ENORB is, as yet, a fragile initiative with a potentially large gap between vision and reality. And yet twenty-five years ago, that was also the case with the consultations that eventually led to the formation of the Inter Faith Network for the UK. In pursuing an initiative such as ENORB—as well as in other initiatives for interreligious and/or religion and belief cooperation in various national and regional/continental contexts, it is likely that the experience of the Inter Faith Network for the UK will remain one that it will be helpful for others to reflect on when charting new ways forward in our religiously pluralizing and globalizing world.

FURTHER READING

J. Beverluis (ed.), *A Sourcebook for the Community of Religions: The Council for a Parliament of the World's Religions* (Chicago: The Council for a Parliament of the World's Religions, 1993).

Marcus Braybrooke, *A Wider Vision: A History of the World Congress of Faiths* (Oxford: One World, 1996).

——*Children of One God: A History of the Council of Christians and Jews* (London: Valentine Mitchell, 1991).

——*Pilgrimage of Hope: One Hundred Years of Global Interfaith Dialogue* (London: SCM Press, 1992).

Inter Faith Network for the UK, *20 Years: Milestones on the Journey Together towards Greater Inter Faith Understanding and Cooperation* (London: The Inter Faith Network for the UK, 2007).

H. A. Jack, *A History of the World Conference on Religion and Peace* (New York: World Conference on Religion and Peace, 1993).

Free downloads of relevant documents available as follows:

Inter Faith Network for the UK, *The Local Inter Faith Guide:* <http://www.interfaith.org.uk/publications/lifg2005.pdf>.

——*Local Inter Faith Activity in the UK:* <http://www.interfaith.org.uk/publications/lifsr-web.pdf>.

UK Government, *Working Together: Co-Operation Between Government and Faith Communities:* <http://webarchive.nationalarchives.gov.uk/20120919132719/www.communities.gov.uk/documents/communities/pdf/151393.pdf>.

....

CHAPTER 18

The Future of Engagement: Emerging Contexts and Trends

DAVID CHEETHAM, DOUGLAS PRATT,
AND DAVID THOMAS

It goes without saying that the world today is a vastly different place to what it was one hundred years ago. At the dawn of the twentieth century the globe could be relatively neatly mapped and colour-coded in terms of nationhood and religion. Christian lands; Muslim lands; Confucian lands of China; Buddhist and Hindu lands, and the great swathe of undifferentiated pagans, heathens, and 'others': for the most part the 'religious other' was literally 'elsewhere'. And although the reality for many had been centuries of relative religious plurality—Hindus, Buddhists, Muslims, Sikhs, and Jains mutually coexisting in South Asia, for example—by contrast the religious diversity with which Christians in the West had to deal on a daily basis was wholly internal: Catholic vs Protestant; dissenter, freethinker, and a smattering of secular agnostics all vying for legitimacy in the face of *de facto*, if not *de jure*, identification of state and religion—in the form, usually, of a specific Christian church. It was Christian overseas missionary workers, whether in evangelical outreach or humanitarian succour mode, who related to the really religious 'others'. On the home front the diversity of Christian denominations for the most part maintained their barricades of true faith over against each other. Notwithstanding the religious diversity that has in fact accompanied all great religious traditions, at the outset of the twentieth century many societies, and certainly Western ones, were arguably more or less religiously homogeneous, or at least were dominated by one major religion; but not any more. In the intervening century everything has changed. As a result, interreligious relations have moved from the exotic to the everyday; the religious 'other' of days past is the religious neighbour of today.

Early in the twentieth century a 'Christian' nation—such as Australia or a New Zealand—would return a census figure showing some 95 per cent or more of the population identifying as Christian. Europe and North America would have been much the same. By the end of the first decade of the twenty-first century that proportion had dropped to around 50 per cent. In the UK, the proportion of the population identifying as Christian in 2001 was 72 per cent, by 2011 that had dropped to 59 per cent. Christianity will soon be a minority religion in many heretofore Christian lands. And this demographic shift is not just a matter of the loss of religion *per se* coupled with a concomitant rise in secular identities; it also reflects shifting demographics of the religious 'other'. For, since the middle of the twentieth century, in the aftermath of the Second World War, the globe has experienced huge immigration—and refugee—flows as never before. The formerly distant, 'elsewhere' other has become the neighbour, the co-worker, the 'other-next-door'; the rich diversity of religious otherness is unavoidably and ubiquitously present. The context of interreligious relating is now, for many, a matter of daily intercourse and regular social engagement. And whereas around the middle of the twentieth century Christian churches in many Western societies, imbued with the spirit of ecumenical détente, formed cooperative councils at local, regional, and national levels, nowadays one is more likely to find multi- or interfaith councils in their stead. Patterns of interreligious relating have irrevocably changed. As we might imagine, it is not all roses and plain sailing. Attitudes and perceptions of the religious 'other', deeply forged in terms of interreligious histories, can often predominate and so skew prospects for contemporary interfaith engagement.

So it was to the question of the religious 'other' that we turned in Part I of our book. How religions and their communities have conceived, regarded, and so related to—or not—the religious other with which they have had contact has impacted and very often defined the parameters of relationship. We explored various understandings of the religious 'other' from the perspective of major influential world religions. There is no single viewpoint. Negative conceptions of the other have their counterpoint in varyingly positive apprehensions of otherness. But the key lesson for the future is that the historically negative need not be finally determinative. From within each religion there can be a legitimate positive, appreciative, and embracing regard for the 'other'. At the very least the sheer presence of that which is other invites the response of curiosity and inquiry: who is this other? Who is my religious neighbour? Mutual education and the happily human propensity to give and receive hospitality, to forge solid cooperative communal relations and social harmony if only for the sake of enlightened self-interest—we prosper better and do well in a context of harmony rather than in a climate of hostility—would seem the obvious and sensible response to the lived reality of social and religious diversity. But all too often this is not the case; or if it is, it must be worked at in the face of apathy, ignorance, and even outright antipathy. One of the pressing challenges that can be seen in many contexts, it would seem, is that of actively recognizing, accepting, and so engaging with the religious other that is present in the local environment. And this highlights a pressing trend: the pervasive undermining effect of ignorance. Indeed, it is the combating of ignorance—whether innocent, blind, or culpable—that is a continuing task facing all those who see the need for promoting interreligious relations as a key element of contemporary social reality.

Overcoming the resistance of ignorance is no easy task. On the one hand there is *innocent* ignorance, or ignorance *simpliciter*; namely the situation of a naïve 'not-knowing' which yields the direct and unequivocal 'don't know' response when a question of knowledge or perception of a religious 'other' is posed. However, this allows opportunity for correction through the provision of information and the processes of education, for such ignorance implies no intentional prejudice on the part of the one who is innocently ignorant. Such a person is open to knowledge; the cognitive deficit is acknowledged and corrected. On the other hand, *blind* ignorance is something else again. It is ignorance born of an intellectual stubbornness, or a cognitive barrier that effectively prevents any 'seeing' or 'knowing', except that which has been dictated by the already-held worldview perspectives. Blind ignorance implies some measure of shutting out the prospect of change through new knowledge. There is nothing necessarily malicious about this; rather it reflects the widespread phenomenon of closed-minded conservatisms. In this case knowledge of the other is so utterly prescribed by the worldview of the knower that no alternative perspective or image is admissible. Here the notion of applying a corrective simply through provision of information is inadequate. Any educational process, if attempted, will require sustained and careful execution to effect any real change. For even if change is unwelcome or resisted, the premise of this mode of ignorance is basically that of cognitive inertia which, in principle, can be overcome, albeit often at great cost. Indeed it is this type of ignorance that yields to the great changes in social ordering and cultural life as happened, for instance, in the momentous changes brought about in the USA by the civil rights movement in the twentieth century. With sustained great effort the deleterious effects of blind ignorance can be reversed.

However, there is yet a third kind of ignorance that goes beyond even that occasioned by the blinding effect of a limited perspective and an intransigently closed mind. This third kind is *culpable* ignorance, that is, an active ignoring: the deliberate refusal to know; the avoidance of the challenge of cognitive change; the reinforcement of a prejudicial perspective by deliberately shunning any evidence, argument, or perspective to the contrary. This is a level of ideologically driven ignorance born of an active dismissal of alternative possibilities; the out-of-hand rejection of options presented for alternate ways of thinking, understanding, and interpreting. It prefers the already-held fixed position as a final word on a matter, irrespective. This goes hand-in-glove with the attitude and mind-set that harbours most forms of fundamentalism or extremism. It produces an intentional 'won't know' or 'not wanting to know' response. It is resistant to any information contrary to its own; it is inimical to the educational process; it treats cognitive change as effectively, if not actually, treasonable. This form of ignoring the reality of the religious and cultural other can apply to either or both of a host community and an immigrant or otherwise 'new' religious or cultural subset within a society. It becomes the seed-bed of social disruption and the retreat into mutually exclusionary religious identities. This presents those promoting interreligious engagement with perhaps the greatest challenge, for it signals an a priori deep resistance to any form of positive interreligious relations.

In order properly to relate to any other, it is necessary to both acknowledge the existence of the other and take the first step of mutual introduction: to establish a basis for mutual relational engagement. It is the engagement of people with one another across religious boundaries and identities that lies at the heart of interreligious relations. If we had to sum up what it is all about, perhaps we might say something like: interreligious relations have to do with how well religious people are able to accommodate people of other religions. Of course, where a religious identity is inherently exclusive with, as a corollary, otherness tightly and negatively defined, then clearly the likelihood of any cross-religious engagement, whether in terms of a mode of dialogue or an act of practical cooperation, is very low indeed. Alternatively, where a religious identity is not threatened by the presence of an 'other', perhaps even actively seeks to relate to a religious other, some form of interreligious engagement is much more likely to occur. But, as with any relationship, it requires the parties to it to equally engage, more or less, and so participate. And therein is the rub: to what extent will religious individuals and communities co-equally engage in interreligious relations in the future? The settings for engagement are many and various. Interreligious relations are often the product of a tension between contexts of dissonance, where some historical or current underlying tension exists; and the quest for consonance, where differences are ameliorated by virtue of a climate of peaceful coexistence and harmoniously respectful interpersonal relationships.

Each religious identity is unique and is to be understood and respected on its own terms. To that extent religions are legitimately 'exclusive' in that each religion is uniquely what it is. There is no suggestion that the exclusive uniqueness whereby religions are undeniably different one from the other is to be abrogated by virtue of promoting some kind of syncretistic synthesis. Otherness remains important; relationships can only occur between two or more 'others' who bring to that relationship their uniqueness and exclusive identities. But that exclusiveness is not the same as the exclusionary attitudes which are inimical to the religious other; here religious exclusivism denotes the rejection of otherness. Openness to, and relationship with, a religious other requires a sense of being grounded in a unique—exclusive—identity on the one hand, and an abjuring of an attitude and a priori position of exclusion *of* the other—exclusivism—on the other. How religious communities live and perceive themselves within a multi-religious context, which is the case globally and more and more so locally, will be the litmus test for the future of interreligious engagement. Self-understanding and responding to religious plurality are current concerns that lead the way into twenty-first-century interfaith relations. Indeed:

> one of the critical issues of our time is discovering what it means to be both true to our own faith and authentically open to relationship with a person of another faith—to know and hold the truths that comprise the substantial beliefs of our religion, yet recognize, and where appropriate acknowledge and respect, the beliefs and perspectives that comprise the truth proclaimed by another religion.[1]

---

[1] Douglas Pratt, *Being Open, Being Faithful: The Journey of Interreligious Dialogue* (Geneva: WCC, forthcoming), 149.

Importantly, the faith-identity to which an individual may wish to be true is not necessarily a matter of identifying with one discrete religion as such. As has been noted in many quarters, religious-identity boundaries are today much more porous and fluid than in times past. This is very much the case with the new context in which religious encounter and engagement takes place, at least in the West. In Western secular societies in particular it is not uncommon for people to self-identify as in some way 'spiritual' but disavow allegiance to any one specific religious institution. For many, religion is only one way of construing wider human experience and both the loyalty to a specific religious tradition and the engagement between traditions are pursuits of the few and the elite. Furthermore, it can be argued that in this context religious self-definition is no longer by simple labels such as Roman Catholic or Anglican, nor even Christian or Hindu. The model of an individual being secure in their loyalty to one faith tradition no longer holds as strongly as it used to. Of course, the new fundamentalisms are to a large extent reactions to this religious individualism. Yet the phenomenon of fluid religious identity and so belonging is gaining ground. What of interreligious relations in such a context? They may become chaotically democratic, or they may cease to be meaningful. While it is difficult to predict what may eventuate, this trend must at least be acknowledged, for patterns of religious allegiance and interaction that have predominated over the last century may not be useful much longer. And so we move quite naturally from reflecting on religious identity and otherness to the matter of issues pertinent to interreligious relations as covered in Part II.

The issue of cross-religious conversion, that is, of seeking to persuade individuals to change their religious identity and belonging in favour of another continues to be a vexed issue for interfaith relations in many contexts. For some religions, notably Christianity and Islam, the notion of having a message to proclaim and a mission to offer this message, and actively seek the response of acceptance of the message and its implications for identity and belonging, is a deeply embedded component. Too often, perhaps, colonial Christian imperialism in the early modern era functioned to obliterate the 'other' by virtue of conversion (both to the Christian religion and to a Western lifestyle, set of values, and so forth), and so thereby enabling the reception of the 'lost' other into 'saved' and even 'authentic' humanity. The disjunction of unsaved/saved, or lost/authentic, was often expressed in terms of a purity/impurity binary: lost humanity required a special cleansing in order to be purified and made authentic. The secular equivalent of this process amounted simply to cultural assimilation—the suppression of the language and customs of the other; enticed or enforced processes of removal from the sphere of 'otherness' to the realm of cultural acceptability. These two trajectories— religious and secular—at times colluded as, for example, in Australia's history of dealing with its Aboriginal population. Today the critical question to ask is: can religions equally manifest and present their identity and self-understanding to a wider public (what some might refer to as bearing witness or 'proclamation'), yet resile from the action of proselytization? Can such religions see themselves as simply part of a market-place of possibility? Can each religion uphold the validity of the religion of the other *for the other*? Can a value be accorded to not attempting to convert the other from a sense that each religion is right and proper for a given person or group in accordance with particular circumstances, location, and era? Or is it the case that deeply held convictions as to the nature of reality necessarily impel religions to postures of overriding superiority? The tension between these polar positions will continue to play its part in the unfolding of interreligious relations.

Without doubt there has been an upsurge of interest in interreligious dialogue since the middle of the twentieth century and, rather ironically, in the twenty-first century this interest and engagement has been spurred on by the tragic events of 9/11 and their aftermath. Whilst dialogue and interfaith engagement involving Islam and Muslims have since tended to predominate, in fact there are many multifaith and bilateral dialogical engagements taking place. Interreligious dialogue has had a chequered history, but a steadily expanding one nevertheless. Dialogue occurs in different modalities and with varying levels of engagement. A mixture of high-level and sharply focused intellectual dialogues is actively pursued in many quarters; equally the phenomenon of broad-based interfaith dialogical activities that embrace many religions, and which have a more general community enrichment and social engagement focus, are occurring around the globe. A plethora of interfaith councils, committees, organizations, and occasional forums bear testimony to the lively future for dialogical engagement. The cross-religious quest for peace is perhaps one of the more notable and long-standing examples of interfaith cooperation of the past century or so. It is a never-ending quest and challenge. And where there are differentials such as those encapsulated by a majority–minority relational context, then there is also scope for considerable development and challenge to take place. Religion is often a key factor that has been formally and often intentionally overlooked, despite all evidence of its pervasive influence and impact. Indeed, noting four momentous events since the late twentieth century—the Islamic revolution in Iran, the collapse of Communism, the attacks of 9/11, and the recent Arab Spring—Linda Woodhead comments that each 'had to do with religion as well as politics' and yet they 'took us by surprise—academics and politicians alike. Had we not airbrushed religion out of our world view, might we not have been able to anticipate and understand a little better?'[2]

In some situations religion is the predominant actor in the political space of the public sphere. In many others, especially secular Western societies, religions and their spokespeople must struggle to find a platform and to have their voice heard. Many issues swirl around the broader arena of cross-religious engagements within the public domain. Fundamentalism and extremism are not just issues internal to religion; they manifest within, and at times significantly impinge upon, societies and public life. So, too, matters of countering conflict with peace-building, and the seeking of justice and the pursuit of liberation of one sort or another. Engagement in interreligious relations has a broad purview. And one arena where this can be seen is education. For example, a major book series, 'Religious Diversity and Education in Europe', committed to investigation and reflection on the changing role of religion and

---

[2] Linda Woodhead, 'Restoring Religion to the Public Square', *The Tablet*, 28 Jan. 2012, 7.

education, gives voice to this important dimension of religious engagement in the public domain. The series is premised on the fact that globalization and plurality are influencing all areas of education, including religious education. The inter-cultural and multi-religious situation in Europe demands a re-evaluation of the existing educational systems in particular countries as well as new thinking more broadly.[3] And there has been a very significant scholarly uptake in this field of research and reflection.[4] A solid argument for a positive correlation between religious education and democratic conduct has been put forward by one political scientist supported with empirical evidence from a study by the European Monitoring Centre on Racism and Xenophobia.[5] Such studies highlight a pressing need to map out education strategies that will give recognition to religious diversity rather than perpetuate divisions. It is argued, for example, that religious education 'complements civic education…Religious education in the form of interreligious education has shown to be able to contribute to inter-cultural understanding, tolerance and harmony'.[6] Jean-Paul Willaime,[7] in addressing the French secular context, states

> *laïcite* no longer functions as an alternative system to religion, but rather as a regulating principle for the pluralism of both the religious and the non-religious convictions existing in civil society…In France as elsewhere, ultra-modernity inquires about the place and role of religious faith.[8]

Historically, secular authorities 'have…been suspicious of religion, which has been relegated to the private sphere'.[9] And the traditional distrust of religion continues and is seen in more militant forms of *laïcite*, 'reactivated by three things—concerns about cults and the practices of new religious movements, the head-scarf affair in schools, and growing evidence of religious extremism in world events'.[10] But none of this prevents teaching about religions; it rather suggests a greater need to do so. Indeed, there is an urgency that has been recognized by the Debray report at the highest levels of French education. It noted and promoted the need to move 'from a laïcite of ignorance (in which religion does not concern us) towards a laïcite of understanding (where understanding becomes our duty)'.[11]

---

[3] Cf. Robert Jackson, Siebren Miedema, Wolfram Weisse, and Jean-Paul Willaime (eds), *Religion and Education in Europe: Developments, Contexts and Debates* (Münster: Waxmann, 2007), esp. vol. iii.

[4] Wolfram Weisse, 'Introduction', in Jackson *et al.*, *Religion and Education in Europe*, 9.

[5] A. Hasenclever, 'Geteilte Werte—Gemeneinsamer Frieden? Überlegungen zu zivilisierenden Kraft von Religionen und Glaubensgemeinschaften', in H. Küng and D. Senghaas (eds), *Friedenspolitik: Ethische Grundlagen internationaler Beziehungen* (Munich: Piper, 2003), 288–318.

[6] Jackson *et al.*, *Religion and Education in Europe*, 17.

[7] Jean-Paul Willaime, 'Teaching Religious Issues in French Public Schools: From Abstentionist Laïcite to a Return of Religion to Public Education', in Jackson *et al.*, *Religion and Education in Europe*, 87–101.

[8] Willaime, 'Teaching Religious Issues', 89.

[9] Willaime, 'Teaching Religious Issues', 89.

[10] Willaime, 'Teaching Religious Issues', 90.

[11] R. Debray, *L'Enseignement du fait religieux dans l'école laïque: Rapport au ministre de l'Education Nationale* (Paris: Odile Jacob, 2002), cited in Jackson *et al.*, *Religion and Education in Europe*, 93.

However, the utopian vision of a secular society positively predisposed to religious diversity is under threat from both religious extremism and reactionary forces that may be either religious or non-religious. The point is made by philosopher Martha Nussbaum.[12] With reference to the contemporary upsurge of reactionary intolerance, she observes: 'Our situation calls urgently for searching critical self-examination, as we try to uncover the roots of ugly fears and suspicions that currently disfigure all Western societies.'[13] A right metaphysics is required to address the difficulties now attendant upon religious narrative and its pragmatic expressions. Such examination, according to Nussbaum, should focus on three key ingredient principles: equal respect for all citizens and transcending religious differentiation; rigorous critique of inconsistencies and exceptions; and the cultivation of an imaginative capacity or the exercise of a sympathetic imagination and critical empathy. Nussbaum notes of the *burqa* and *niqab* bans implemented in France, Belgium, and Italy that the numbers of actual wearers involved is a relatively tiny minority. Ultra-modern pluralist societies are heterogeneous; yet pressures to assert homogeneity (as in dress-code limitations) are on the rise. Nussbaum points out that fear, as a narcissictic emotion requisite for self-preservation, is at the same time destructive of heterogeneity and the acceptance of ultra-alterity—especially when based on falsehood and enflamed by propaganda and prejudice or ideologies, whether religious or otherwise, such as anti-Semitism, for example. 'First, fear typically starts from some real problem... Second, fear is easily displaced onto something that may have little to do with the underlying problem but serves as a handy surrogate for it... Third, fear is nourished by the idea of the disguised enemy.'[14] She concludes:

> Our current climate of fear shows that people are all too easily turned away from good values and laws, in a time of genuine insecurity and threat. Our time is genuinely dangerous... many fears are rational, and appeals to fear have a role to play in a society that takes human life seriously. Still, at this point, the balance has all too often shifted in the other direction, as irresponsibly manufactured fears threaten principles we should cling to and be proud of.[15]

If there is one single issue around which the future of interreligious relations is likely to swing, it has to be that of contending with religious diversity, which is the contemporary critical problematic of religion *par excellence*. It has global sweep and relevance.[16] The term 'diversity' simply names the state of affairs that reflects a plurality of items within a field of otherwise sameness. Instead of one ruling power we have, in many modern societies, a diversity of political parties vying to take their place in the ruling chamber, thus reflecting, and contributing to, the modern social diversity that makes for democracy. Instead of all

---

[12] Martha C. Nussbaum, *The New Religious Intolerance: Overcoming the Politics of Fear in an Anxious Age* (Cambridge, Mass.: Belknap Press, 2012).

[13] Nussbaum, *New Religious Intolerance*, 2.

[14] Nussbaum, *New Religious Intolerance*, 23.

[15] Nussbaum, *New Religious Intolerance*, 244.

[16] Cf. J. Gentz and P. Schmidt-Leukel (eds), *Religious Diversity in Chinese Thought* (Basingstoke and New York: Palgrave Macmillan, 2013).

members of a nation or state belonging to one religion, or owning even the same allegiance and identity within one overarching religious tradition, there has ever been a measure of diversity of religious identity now exacerbated by the globalized mixture that sees all religions effectively everywhere, or near enough to something like that. Thus, contending with religious diversity, as the value-neutral fact or state of affairs, is the underlying issue to the problem of exclusivist extremism, which in turn expresses a value-laden ideological position that is taken in response to the fact of plurality. This fact has been responded to ideologically in terms of the paradigms of rejection (or 'exclusivism'), incorporation (or 'inclusivism'), and affirmation (or 'pluralism').[17] Of these, exclusivism, which relates also to fundamentalism and is varyingly linked to extremism and terrorism, constitutes the critical problematic wherein contending with diversity yields a reactionary and nugatory response: plurality, or diversity, is rejected. This is made manifest in varying expressions of intolerance—the denial of diversity and the rejection of alterity.[18] We see this expressed in many contemporary situations within society—with respect to gender identities, racial, or ethnic groupings, as well as with religious allegiance and identity. In general terms such rejection is a matter of attempting to maintain a state of uniformity and a defence of 'tradition'.

At the same time, religion often yields to a 'fixation with the fixed', to that which offers seductive intimations of immutability. In a threatening context of change and challenge, recourse to the unchangeable and the security of what is presumed to be a received tradition of unyielding sameness; or alternatively the attempt to return a society to such a state once thought to exist in some pure form, now lost or besmirched and so requiring extraordinary effort to recover, lies at the heart of religious reaction that attempts to reinforce a closed identity structure, and is inclined to take extreme action against those perceived to threaten it by violating its norms. We see this demonstrated most vividly in the actions of the Taliban in Afghanistan who will eliminate all alterity that threatens their narrative, their ethics and experience, and their metaphysics—whether girls seeking an education, young people enjoying their time of youth, fellow Muslims who follow a more mystical and peaceful way, or indeed anyone and anything perceived to embody a threatening 'otherness'. These are not the only examples; they are among the more recently obvious and dramatic. So, too, the frenzy whipped up across the Muslim world in the wake of the video *The Innocence of Muslims*, posted on YouTube. This anti-Islamic video was initially written and produced in California in 2011. After it was uploaded onto the internet in 2012 it gained widespread notoriety and was widely condemned as propaganda, and it provoked a hostile reaction from many parts of the Muslim world. In effect it promoted a form of culpable ignorance: Islam and its Prophet

---

[17] Cf. Paul Hedges, *Controversies in Interreligious Dialogue and the Theology of Religions* (London: SCM Press, 2010); Alan Race and Paul M. Hedges, *Christian Approaches to Other Faiths* (London: SCM Press, 2008); Douglas Pratt, 'Pluralism, Postmodernism and Interreligious Dialogue', *Sophia*, 46/3 (Dec. 2007), 243–59.

[18] Douglas Pratt, 'Religious Identity and the Denial of Alterity: Plurality and the Problem of Exclusivism', in Paolo Diego Bubbio and Philip Andrew Quadrio (eds), *The Relation of Philosophy to Religion Today* (Newcastle-upon-Tyne: Cambridge Scholars Publishing, 2011), 201–15.

were portrayed in highly demeaning ways, and this was advocated as the truth of the matter. In such cases, the perception of a religious other as manifesting a threat to boundary and identity yields a paradoxical extreme action that, in turn, transgresses otherwise acceptable norms of behaviour, value, and narrative. The Norwegian extremist Andres Breivik killed fellow citizens in a 2011 rampage as a way of expressing rejection of Islam as a cultural and religious threat to European identity. In 2009 the Swiss took fright at four minarets in their country and resolved that no more should appear, and in so doing transgressed their own constitution and European conventions. Muslims, incensed by depictions of the Prophet and his followers as violent and criminal, react by fomenting violence and crime. What is it that links all these differing expressions of extremism which have religion somewhere in the frame? They are varyingly representative of the response of a harsh exclusivism to the fact and manifestation of diversity; a denial of diversity/otherness in favour of uniformity and 'tradition' and the corresponding tendency to take extreme actions.

Contending with religious diversity, and so contending with the presence of religious 'others' are two sides of the interreligious coin. And in the process of relating to another, a self is defined.[19] The very act of mutual self-introduction that commences any form of two-way relationship provokes a moment of self-reflection: each must be prepared to respond to the question: who are you? One recent trend to emerge from out of the arena of interreligious engagement is the self-reflective task of asking what relating to a religious other means for the sense of religious 'self'. So, for example, in recent years the Interreligious Dialogue and Cooperation team of the World Council of Churches has embarked on a study process under the generic title of 'Christian self-understanding in a religiously plural world'. This is very much a twenty-first-century development born of the experience of interreligious relations during the second half of the twentieth century. A series of bilateral studies have been pursued,[20] and a major statement on the subject is due to be considered by the General Assembly of the WCC in November 2013. Although the need to reflect on what interreligious engagement means for the self-understanding of the parties so engaged may be a major concern in some Christian quarters, it is, in principle, something needful for all religions in today's multi-religious world.

Furthermore, contending with and relating to a religious other implies having a view, a concept, of the other and what such relating means. This, indeed, is what undergirds our volume of reflections and discussions. And it points to a major developing trend that is presently referred to as interreligious theology. But can there be 'interreligious theology' as such? Or is it more a case of confessional theology undertaken in an interreligious perspective? Or both? Of course, the use of the term 'theology' might be viewed as problematic—it suggests a theistic religion engaged in self-understanding. However, if we grant that 'theology' names

---

[19] Cf. Paul Heck, *Common Ground: Islam, Christianity, and Religious Pluralism* (Washington, DC: Georgetown University Press, 2009).

[20] See recent edns of *Current Dialogue*.

the intellectual reflection upon matters of ultimate religious concern irrespective of the nature, or not, of any theistic perspective, then the term may legitimately refer to the intellectual quest implied by any self-reflective religious ratiocination. It is arguably not quite the same as the phrase 'religious ideology' which could be regarded as naming the broad arena of religious self-reflection of which 'theology' might be regarded as a subset. However, for our purposes, 'theology' can be taken to name the intellectual self-reflection and articulation of religion as such. The phrase 'religious ideology' rather suggests a wider set of principles, worldview presuppositions, and the like that empowers religious engagement within the wider world, for example. Thus we might say that an interreligious theology is a trans-confessional quest, the attempt at a new way of confessional self-understanding in a multi-religious context. It may well be the product of various bilateral dialogues, something that has been referred to as 'theology after dialogue'.[21]

In the context of developing an interreligious theology a critical question that is raised has to do with the legitimacy of using the scriptural resource of another religion. On the one hand this can be decried as a matter of 'raiding' or 'inappropriate use' of the scriptural sources of another tradition; on the other this can be countered by stressing the genuine motivation of enriching one's own tradition by way of deeply engaging with another. This has been the intent and experience of the process of Scriptural Reasoning. In his chapter on Judaism, Ed Kessler draws attention to the relativity of exegesis and 'the enduring, elusive nature of the debate about meaning'. Recently, this midrashic style of hermeneutics has been a deep inspiration for the Scriptural Reasoning movement, with its emphasis on the improvised hermeneutics possible when members of Abrahamic traditions meet to 'reason' around their sacred texts. However, although it is clearly a creative and flexible method of engagement, it is not clear that it is a style that recommends itself equally to all traditions. After all, it is possible that a hermeneutical openness and spiritual *reverie* in one tradition looks undisciplined to another. Illustrating precisely this issue, the Islamic scholar Tim Winter claims that Scriptural Reasoning is 'not method, but rather a promiscuous openness to methods of a kind unfamiliar to Islamic conventions of reading'.[22] Of course, in an attempt to understand and interpret texts from other traditions an 'outsider' may legitimately comment by way of utilizing linguistic and historical tools in humble acknowledgement of the contributive value of the text of the other to the sense of the outsider's religious self.

Such constructive theology can only take place within the context of, and for, a particular faith community. No single theology can embrace the diversity of all faiths, despite some grandiose attempts at doing something like that. A confessional theology of religions may offer a perspective on religious others consonant with the principles and perspectives of the confession concerned, even challenging and extending it. But there is no possibility of an

---

[21] See Douglas Pratt, *The Church and Other Faiths: The World Council of Churches, the Vatican, and Interreligious Dialogue* (Bern: Peter Lang, 2010).

[22] Tim Winter, 'Qur'anic Reasoning as an Academic Practice', in David Ford and C. C. Pecknold (eds), *The Promise of Scriptural Reasoning* (Oxford: Blackwell, 2006), 109.

external vantage point from which to offer a confessional-inclusive, trans-confessional 'theology' of religion *per se*. It may be possible to offer a confessional-neutral theory or philosophy of religion, but all too often such attempts tend to fall short. In an interreligious context there is a necessary dimension of 'give-and-take'. A two-way engagement of learning and gaining occurs. But a confessional theology of religion cannot presume to 'give', it can only take. Nevertheless, a new paradigm, of offer and reception—as in the newly emerging perspective of 'receptive ecumenism'[23] within the Christian orbit—might offer a way forward. The point is to acknowledge the prospect of a subtle, yet significant, change in the interreligious dialogical dynamic. Rather than each religion attempting to quarry from another, with perhaps the prospect of conjoining that with wholly internal perspectives in an attempt to 'give' back to the other a resolution that is still predominantly one's own and not the other's, the shift occurs in starting not from what one regards as worthwhile and so 'takes', to humbly awaiting what is offered by the other and from the other's perspective. It becomes a matter of receiving this for reflection and consideration, then in the context of that dynamic mutually applying and jointly engaging in a process of shared reflection on response, reaction, and potential meaning, without in the first instance attempting to 'resolve' anything, but rather seeking, and being open to, genuinely novel insight, interpretation, and so new construction of idea and conception. It was the scholar of religion Wilfred Cantwell Smith who expressed the view that the point of interreligious engagement was to arrive at a place where, instead of a process of a religious 'us' talking about a religious 'them' and maybe reflecting upon what the 'them' means for 'us', it is the 'we' of religions engaged in talking and reflecting together about the religious 'us'. The future of religion lies in dedicated interreligious engagement; religions ignore each other at their ultimate peril; understanding the future of religion amounts to understanding the present reality, and the immediate prospects, of interreligious relations.

---

[23]   Cf. Paul D. Murray (ed.), *Receptive Ecumenism and the Call to Catholic Learning: Exploring a Way for Contemporary Ecumenism* (Oxford: Oxford University Press, 2008).

BIBLIOGRAPHY

Abe, Masao, *Buddhism and Interfaith Dialogue* (Honolulu: University of Hawaii Press, 1995).

Abu-Nimer, Mohammed, 'Conflict Resolution, Culture, and Religion: Toward a Training Model of Interreligious Peacebuilding', *Journal of Peace Research*, 38/6 (2001), 685–703.

Abhedananda, Swami, *Christ the Yogi* (Whitefish, Mont.: Kessinger Publishing, 2005).

Adams, Nicholas, *Habermas and Theology* (Cambridge: Cambridge University Press, 2006).

Adélaïde, Stanislas Marie, *The French Revolution and Human Rights: A Brief Documentary History*, tr. and ed. L. Hunt (Boston Mass.: Bedford Books of St Martin's Press, 1996).

Aguilar, Mario I., *The Rising of the Dalai Lamas in Tibet: From the First to the Fourth 1391–1617* (Santiago: Fundación Literaria Civilización, 2011).

—— *Church, Liberation and World Religions: Towards a Christian–Buddhist Dialogue* (London: T&T Clark, 2012).

Ahmud, Syud, *The Mohomedan Commentary on the Holy Bible* (part I, Ghazipur: by the author, 1862; part II, Aligarh: by the author, 1865).

Alberigo, Giuseppe (ed.), *History of Vatican II*, iv. *Church as Communion: Third Period and Intercession September 1964–September 1965* (Maryknoll, NY: Orbis; Leuven: Peeters, 2003).

Almond, Gabriel A., R. Scott Appleby, and Emmanuel Sivan, *Strong Religion: The Rise of Fundamentalisms around the World* (Chicago and London: University of Chicago Press, 2003).

Anglican Consultative Council, *Generous Love: The Truth of the Gospel and the Call to Dialogue: An Anglican Theology of Inter Faith Relations* (London: Anglican Consultative Council, 2008).

Antes, Peter, Armin W. Geertz, and Randi R. Warne (eds), *New Approaches to the Study of Religion*, i. *Regional, Critical and Historical Approaches* (Berlin and New York: Walter de Gruyter, 2004).

App, Urs, *The Cult of Emptiness: The Western Discovery of Buddhist Thought and the Invention of Oriental Philosophy* (Kyoto: University Media, 2012).

Appleby, R. Scott, *The Ambivalence of the Sacred: Religion, Violence, and Reconciliation* (Lanham, Md.: Rowman & Littlefield, 2000).

Ariarajah, Wesley, *The Bible and People of Other Faiths* (Geneva: World Council of Churches, 1985).

—— *Hindus and Christians: A Century of Protestant Ecumenical Thought* (Amsterdam: Rodopi; Grand Rapids, Mich.: Eerdmans, 1991).

—— *Not without my Neighbour: Issues in Interfaith Relations* (Geneva: WCC, 1999).

Arkoun, M., *The Concept of Revelation, from People of the Book to Societies of the Book* (Claremont, Calif.: Claremont Graduate School, 1987).

—— 'New Perspectives for a Jewish–Christian–Muslim Dialogue', *Journal of Ecumenical Studies*, 26 (1989), 345–52.

—— *Rethinking Islam, Common Questions, Uncommon Answers*, ed. and tr. R. D. Lee (Boulder, Colo.: Westview Press, 1994).

Armour, Ellen, 'Theology in Modernity's Wake', *Journal of the American Academy of Religion*, 74/1 (2006), 7–15.

Arokiasamy, S., *Asia: The Struggle for Life in the Midst of Death and Destruction*, FABC Papers, 70 (Hong Kong: FABC, 1995).

Audi, Robert, and Nicholas Wolterstorff, *Religion in the Public Square: The Place of Religious Convictions in Political Debate* (Lanham, Md.: Rowman & Littlefield, 1997).

Avari, Burjor, *India: The Ancient Past* (New York: Routledge, 2007).

Aydin, Mahmut, *Modern Western Christian Theological Understanding of Muslims since the Second Vatican Council* (Washington, DC: Council for Research in Values and Philosophy, 2002).

Babylonian Talmud, ed. I. Epstein (London: Soncino, 1935–82).

Bainbridge, William Sims, *The Sociology of Religious Movements* (New York: Routledge, 1997).

Bakker, F. L., *The Struggle of the Hindu Balinese Intellectuals* (Amsterdam: VU University Press, 1993).

Barker, Eileen, 'We've Got to Draw the Line Somewhere: An Exploration of Boundaries that Define Locations of Religious Identity', *Social Compass*, 53 (2006), 201–13.

Barnes, Michael, *Theology and the Dialogue of Religions* (Cambridge: Cambridge University Press, 2002).

Barr, James, *Fundamentalism* (London: SCM Press, 1977).

Barrett, David, *The New Believers: Sects, 'Cults' and Alternative Religions* (London: Cassell, 2001).

Barrows, J. H. (ed.), *The World's Parliament of Religions* (Chicago: Parliament Publishing Co.; London: Review of Reviews, 1893).

Barth, Karl, *Die Kirchliche Dogmatik*, I/2 (Zollikon-Zürich: Evangelischer Verlag, 1960).

Bartholomeusz, Tessa J., *In Defense of Dharma: Just-War Ideology in Buddhist Sri Lanka* (London: Routledge Curzon, 2002).

Basset, J. C., *Le Dialogue interreligieux: Chance ou déchéance de la foi*, Cogitatio fidei, 197 (Paris: Cerf, 1996).

Battistella, Graziano (ed.), *Migrazioni: Dizionario Socio-Pastorale* (Milan: Edizioni San Paolo, 2010).

Baum, Gregory (ed.), *The Twentieth Century: A Theological Overview* (Maryknoll, NY: Orbis Books, 1999).

Bauman, Zygmunt, *Life in Fragments* (Oxford: Blackwell, 1995).

Bayley, Susan, *Saints, Goddesses and Kings: Muslims and Christians in South Indian Society, 1700–1900* (Cambridge: Cambridge University Press, 1989).

Beales, C., 'Partnerships for a Change: The Inner Cities Religious Council', *World Faiths Encounter*, 8 (1994), 41–6.

Bechert, Heinz, and Richard Gombrich (eds), *The World of Buddhism* (London: Thames & Hudson, 1984).

Becker, K. J., and I. Morali (eds), *A Catholic Engagement with World Religions: A Comprehensive Study* (Maryknoll, NY: Orbis Books, 2010).

Beckford, James A., 'The Sociology of Religion and Social Problems', *Sociological Analysis*, 51/1 (1990), 1–14.

—— *Social Theory and Religion* (Cambridge: Cambridge University Press, 2003).

—— and John Wallis (eds), *Theorising Religion: Classical and Contemporary Debates* (Aldershot: Ashgate, 2006).

Bellah, Robert, *Beyond Belief: Essays on Religion in a Post-Traditional World* (London and New York: Harper & Row, 1970).

Bernhardt, Reinhold, and Perry Schmidt-Leukel (eds), *Multiple religiöse Identität* (Zurich: Theologischer Verlag Zurich, 2008).

Béthune, Pierre-Francois de, *By Faith and Hospitality: The Monastic Tradition as a Model for Interreligious Encounter* (Herefordshire: Gracewing, 2002).

Beverluis, J. (ed.), *A Sourcebook for the Community of Religions: The Council for a Parliament of the World's Religions* (Chicago: Council for a Parliament of the World's Religions, 1993).

Bhagavad Gītā, tr. George Thompson (New York: North Point Press, 2008).

Bharat, Sandy, and Jael Bharat, *A Global Guide to Interfaith: Reflections from around the World* (Winchester: O Books, 2007).

Blackburn, Anne, *Buddhist Learning and Textual Practice in Eighteenth-Century Lankan Monastic Culture* (Princeton and Oxford: Princeton University Press, 2001).

Blée, Fabrice, *The Third Desert: The Story of Monastic Interreligious Dialogue* (Collegeville, Mich.: Liturgical Press, 2011).

Bodhi, Bhikkhu (tr.), *The Connected Discourses of the Buddha* (Somerville, Mass.: Wisdom, 2000).

Boff, Leonardo, *Jesus Christ Liberator: A Critical Christology of our Time* (London: SPCK, 1980).

Bond, George D., *Buddhism at Work: Community Development, Social Empowerment and the Sarvodaya Movement* (Bloomfield: Kumarian Press, 2004).

Boodoo, Gerald M., 'Catholicity and Mission', *Proceedings of the Catholic Theological Society of America*, 65 (2010), 117–18.

Bouma, Gary D. (ed.), *Managing Religious Diversity: From Threat to Promise* (Melbourne: Australian Association for the Study of Religions, 1999).

—— *Australian Soul: Religion and Spirituality in the Twenty-First Century* (Melbourne: Cambridge University Press, 2006).

—— Sharon Pickering, Anna Halafoff, and Hass Dellal, *Managing the Impact of Global Crisis Events on Community Relations in Multicultural Australia* (Brisbane: Multicultural Affairs Queensland, 2007).

Bowden, John (ed.), *Christianity: The Complete Guide* (London: Continuum, 2005).

Braybrooke, M., *Inter-Faith Organisations, 1893–1979: An Historical Directory* (Lampeter: Edwin Mellen Press, 1980).

—— *Children of One God: A History of the Council of Christians and Jews* (London: Valentine Mitchell, 1991).

—— *Pilgrimage of Hope: One Hundred Years of Global Interfaith Dialogue* (London: SCM Press, 1992).

—— *A Wider Vision: A History of the World Congress of Faiths* (Oxford: One World, 1996).

Briggs, John, Mercy Amba Oduyoye, and Georges Tsetsis (eds), *A History of the Ecumenical Movement*, iii. *1968–2000* (Geneva: WCC, 2004).

Broadhead, Philip, and Damien Keown (eds), *Can Faiths Make Peace: Holy Wars and the Resolution of Religious Conflicts* (London and New York: I. B. Tauris, 2007).

Brockey, Liam Matthew, *Journey to the East: The Jesuit Mission to China 1578–1724* (Cambridge, Mass.: Harvard, 2007).

Brodeur, Patrice, 'From the Margins to the Centers of Power: The Increasing Relevance of the Global Interfaith Movement', *Cross Currents*, 55/1 (2005), 42–53.

Bromley, David, and J. Gordon Melton (eds), *Cults, Religion and Violence* (Cambridge: Cambridge University Press, 2002).

Bronkhorst, Johannes, *Greater Magadha: Studies in the Culture of Early India* (Leiden and Boston: Brill, 2007).

Brown, Stuart (ed.), *Meeting in Faith: Twenty Years of Christian–Muslim Conversations Sponsored by the World Council of Churches* (Geneva: WCC 1989).

Bubbio, Paolo Diego, and Philip Andrew Quadrio (eds), *The Relation of Philosophy to Religion Today* (Newcastle-upon-Tyne: Cambridge Scholars Publishing, 2011).

Byrne, Peter, *Prolegomena to Religious Pluralism: Reference and Realism in Religion,* (London: Macmillan, 1995).

Caplan, Lionel, *Studies in Religious Fundamentalism* (Basingstoke: Macmillan, 1987).

Casanova, José, *Public Religions in the Modern World* (Chicago: University of Chicago Press, 1994).

Catholic Bishops' Conference of India, 'Violence Against Christians: Statement of the Executive Body of the Catholic Bishops' Conference of India', *Vidyajyoti Journal of Theological Reflection,* 72 (2008), 814–17.

Chadwick, Owen, *Catholicism and History: The Opening of the Vatican Archives* (Cambridge: Cambridge University Press, 1978).

Chappell, David W. (ed.), *Buddhist Peacework: Creating Cultures of Peace* (Somerville, Mass.: Wisdom Publications, 1999).

—— 'Religious Identity and Openness in a Pluralistic World', *Buddhist–Christian Studies,* 25 (2005), 9–14.

Chattopadhyaya, Debiprasad, *Lokāyata: A Study in Ancient Indian Materialism* (New Delhi: People's Publishing House, 1959).

Cheetham, David, *Ways of Meeting and the Theology of Religions* (Aldershot: Ashgate, 2013).

—— et al. (eds), *Interreligious Hermeneutics in Pluralistic Europe* (Amsterdam: Rodopi, 2011).

Chia, Edmund, *Thirty Years of FABC: History, Foundation, Context and Theology,* FABC Papers, 106 (Hong Kong: FABC, 2003).

Christian Witness in a Multi-Religious World: Recommendations for Conduct (Geneva: WCC, 2011).

Church of England, *The Way of Renewal,* Report of the Board of Mission of the Synod of the Church of England (London: Church House Publishing, 1998).

Clooney, Francis, *Comparative Theology: Deep Learning across Religious Borders* (Oxford: Wiley-Blackwell, 2010).

—— (ed.), *The New Comparative Theology: Thinking Interreligiously in the 21st Century* (London: T&T Clark, 2010).

Cobb, John B., *Transforming Christianity and the World: Beyond Absolutism and Relativism* (Maryknoll, NY: Orbis Books, 1999).

—— and Christopher Ives (eds), *The Emptying God: A Buddhist-Jewish-Christian Conversation* (Maryknoll, NY: Orbis Books, 1990).

—— and Ward McAfee (eds), *The Dialogue Comes of Age* (Minneapolis: Fortress Press, 2010).

Code of Canon Law, The (London and Sydney: Collins, 1983).

Cohn-Sherbok, Dan, *The Crucified Jew: Twenty Centuries of Christian Anti-Semitism* (London: HarperCollins, 1992).

Commers, Ronald, Wim Vandekerckhove, and An Verlinden (eds), *Ethics in an Era of Globalization* (Aldershot: Ashgate, 2008).

Conway, C., and Catherine Cornille (eds), *Interreligious Hermeneutics* (Eugene Or.: Wipf & Stock, 2010).

Corless, Roger, and Paul F. Knitter (eds), *Buddhist Emptiness and Christian Trinity: Essays and Explorations* (Mahwah, NJ: Paulist Press, 1990).

Cornille, Catherine, *Many Mansions: Multiple Religious Belonging and Christian Identity* (Maryknoll, NY: Orbis Books, 2002).

—— *The Im-Possibility of Interreligious Dialogue* (New York: Crossroad, 2008).

—— (ed.), *Criteria of Discernment in Interreligious Dialogue* (Eugene, Or.: Wipf & Stock, 2009).

Cornille, Catherine, 'The Role of Witness in Interreligious Dialogue', *Concilium*, 1 (2011), 61–70.

Coward, Harold (ed.), *Hindu–Christian Dialogue: Perspective and Encounters* (Maryknoll, NY: Orbis Books, 1989).

——and Gordon S. Smith (eds), *Religion and Peacebuilding* (Albany, NY: State University of New York Press, 2004).

Cox, Harvey G., and Daisaku Ikeda, *The Persistence of Religion: Comparative Perspectives on Modern Spirituality* (London and New York: I. B. Tauris, 2009).

Craig, William Lane, ' "No Other Name": A Middle Knowledge Perspective on the Exclusivity of Salvation through Christ', *Faith and Philosophy*, 6 (1989), 172–88.

Cunningham, Philip A., N. J. Hoffmann, and J. Sievers (eds), *The Catholic Church and the Jewish People: Recent Reflections from Rome* (New York: Fordham University Press, 2007).

——*et al.* (eds), *Christ Jesus and the Jewish People Today: New Explorations of Theological Interrelationships* (Grand Rapids, Mich.: Eerdmans, 2011).

Dalai Lama, His Holiness, *Towards the True Kinship of Faiths: How the World's Religions Can Come Together* (London: Abacus, 2010).

Dalton, Dennis, *Mahatma Ghandi: Non-Violent Power in Action* (New York: Columbia University Press, 1993).

Danby, H., *The Mishnah* (Oxford: Oxford University Press, 1933).

D'Arcy May, John (ed.), *Converging Ways: Conversion and Belonging in Buddhism and Christianity* (St Ottilien: EOS, 2007).

Davidson, Donald, 'On the Very Idea of a Conceptual Scheme', *Proceedings and Addresses of the American Philosophical Association*, 47 (1973–4), 5–20.

Davidson, Lawrence, *Islamic Fundamentalism: An Introduction* (Westport, Conn.: Greenwood Press, 2003).

Davie, Grace, *Religion in Britain since 1945: Believing Without Belonging* (Oxford: Wiley-Blackwell, 1994).

Davies, D., *Method and Metaphysics in Maimonides' Guide for the Perplexed* (Oxford: Oxford University Press, 2011).

D'Costa, Gavin (ed.), *Christian Uniqueness Reconsidered: The Myth of a Pluralistic Theology of Religions* (Maryknoll, NY: Orbis Books, 1990).

——'The Impossibility of a Pluralist View of Religions', *Religious Studies*, 32 (1996), 223–32.

——*The Meeting of Religions and the Trinity* (Edinburgh: T&T Clark, 2000).

——*Christianity and World Religions: Disputed Questions in the Theology of Religions: An Introduction to the Theology of Religions* (Oxford: Wiley Blackwell, 2009).

Deegalle, Mahinda (ed.), 'Soteriological Fundamentalism and Inter-Religious Dialogue', *Current Dialogue* (June 2001), 9–12.

——*Buddhism, Conflict and Violence in Modern Sri Lanka* (New York: Routledge, 2006).

DeFilippis, James, Robert Fisher, and Eric Shragge, *Contesting Community: The Limits and Potential of Local Organizing* (Piscataway, NJ: Rutgers University Press, 2010).

Depoortere, F., and M. Lambkin (eds), *The Question of Theological Truth: Philosophical and Interreligious Perspectives* (Amsterdam: Rodopi, 2012).

Dhammavisuddhi, Y., 'Does Buddhism Recognize Liberation from Samsara Outside its own Dispensation?', *Dialogue*, NS 13–14 (1986–7), 40–51.

Dhammika, S. (tr.), *The Edicts of Asoka: An English Rendering* (Kandy: Buddhist Publication Society, 1993).

Dharmasiri, Gunadasa, *A Buddhist Critique of the Christian Concept of God: A Critique of the Concept of God in Contemporary Christian Theology and Philosophy of Religion from the Point of View of Early Buddhism* (Colombo: Lake House, 1974).

Dhavamony, Ariasusai, *Hindu–Christian Dialogue: Theological Soundings and Perpectives* (Amsterdam and New York: Rodopi, 2002).

Dheerasekere, Jotiya, 'The Individual and Social Dimensions of Salvation in Buddhism', *Dialogue*, NS 9/1–3 (1982), 73–82.

Dialogue and Proclamation: Reflections and Orientations on Interreligious Dialogue and the Proclamation of the Gospel of Jesus Christ (Rome: Pontifical Council for Interreligious Dialogue, 1991).

Dickens, W. T., 'Interreligious Dialogue: Encountering an Other or Ourselves', *Theology Today*, 63 (2006), 203–14.

Díez-Hochleitner, Ricardo, and Daisaku Ikeda, *A Dialogue between East and West: Looking to a Human Revolution* (London and New York: I. B. Tauris, 2008).

Dignitatis Humanae, Declaration on Religious Liberty, Vatican II (Vatican City, 1965).

Dingrin, La Seng, 'Is Buddhism Indispensable in the Cross-Cultural Appropriation of Christianity in Burma?', *Buddhist–Christian Studies*, 29 (2009), 3–22.

Dominus Iesus (Vatican City, 2000).

Doniger, Wendy, *The Hindus: An Alternative History* (New York: Penguin, 2009).

Douglass, R. Bruce, and Joshua Mitchell (eds), *A Nation Under God? Essays on the Fate of Religion in American Public Life* (Lanham, Md.: Rowman & Littlefield, 2000).

Doutreleau, L, *Homélies sur la Genèse: Sources chrétiennes* (Paris: Cerf, 1976).

Drew, Rose, *Buddhist and Christian? An Exploration of Dual Belonging* (London and New York: Routledge, 2011).

Duffy, Stephen, 'A Theology of the Religions and/or a Comparative Theology?', *Horizons*, 26 (1999), 105–15.

Dülffer, Jost, and Marc Frey (eds), *Elites and Decolonization in the Twentieth Century* (Bsaingstoke and New York: Palgrave Macmillan, 2011).

Dumoulin, Heinrich, *Christianity Meets Buddhism* (LaSalle, Ill.: Open Court, 1974).

Dupuis, Jacques, *Toward a Christian Theology of Religious Pluralism* (Maryknoll, NY: Orbis Books, 1997).

—— *Christianity and the Religions: From Confrontation to Dialogue* (Maryknoll, NY: Orbis Books; London: Darton, Longman & Todd, 2002).

Ebaugh, Helen Rose (ed.), *Handbook of Religious and Social Institutions* (New York: Springer, 2005).

Ecclesiam Suam, Paul VI, Encyclical 'On the Church' (Vatican City: 1964).

Eck, Diana L., 'What do we Mean by "Dialogue"?' *Current Dialogue*, 11 (1986), 5–15.

—— *A New Religious America: How a 'Christian Country' has Become the World's Most Religiously Diverse Nation* (San Francisco: HarperSanFrancisco, 2002).

—— 'Prospects for Pluralism: Voice and Vision in the Study of Religion', *Journal of the American Academy of Religion*, 75/4 (2007), 743–76.

Eickelman, Dale, and Jon Anderson, *New Media in the Muslim World: The Emerging Public Sphere* (Bloomington, Ind.: Indiana University Press, 2003).

—— and Armando Salvatore, 'The Public Sphere and Muslim Identities', *European Journal of Sociology*, 43/1 (2002), 92–115.

Ellacuría, Ignacio, SJ, and Jon Sobrino SJ (eds), *Mysterium Liberationis: Fundamental Concepts of Liberation Theology* (Maryknoll, NY: Orbis; Blackburn, Victoria: CollinsDove, 1993).

Ellingsen, Tanja, 'Toward a Revival of Religion and Religious Clashes?', *Terrorism and Political Violence*, 14/3 (2005), 305–32.

Ellsberg, Robert (ed.), *Gandhi on Christianity* (Maryknoll, NY: Orbis Books, 1997).

Elverskog, Johan, *Buddhism and Islam on the Silk Road* (Philadelphia: University of Pennsylvania Press, 2010).

Encylopedia of Buddhism (Colombo: Government of Sri Lanka, 1991).

Esposito, John L., *Unholy War: Terror in the Name of Islam* (New York: Oxford University Press, 2002).

Eyre, Ronald, *The Long Search*, episode 1, 'Hinduism: 330 Million Gods' (London: BBC, 1977).

Facelina, R., 'Une théologie en situation', *Revue des Sciences Religieuses*, 48 (1974), 311–21.

Fackenheim, Emil, *The Jewish Return into History: Reflections in the Age of Auschwitz and a New Jerusalem* (New York: Schocken Books, 1978).

—— *The Jewish Bible After the Holocaust* (Manchester: Manchester University Press, 1988).

Falola, Toyin, *Violence in Nigeria: The Crisis of Religious Politics and Secular Ideologies* (Rochester, NY: University of Rochester Press, 1998).

Fernandez, Eleazar S., and Fernando S. Segovia (eds), *A Dream Unfinished: Theological Reflections on America from the Margins* (Maryknoll, NY: Orbis Books, 2001).

Fey, Harold E. (ed.), *The Ecumenical Advance: A History of the Ecumenical Movement*, ii. *1948–1968* (London: SPCK, 1970).

Findly, Ellison Banks, *Dāna: Giving and Getting in Pali Buddhism* (Delhi: Motilal Banarsidass, 2003).

Finkel, J. (ed.), *Thalāth rasā'il li-Abī 'Uthmān al-Jāḥiẓ* (Cairo: Salafiyya Press, 1926).

Fisher, Mary Pat, *Living Religions*, 4th edn (Upper Saddle River, NJ: Prentice Hall, 2002).

Fitzgerald, Michael, and John Borelli, *Interfaith Dialogue: A Catholic View* (Maryknoll, NY: Orbis Books, 2006).

Flannery, Edward H., *The Anguish of the Jews: Twenty-Three Centuries of Antisemitism*, rev. edn (New York: Paulist Press, 2004).

Fletcher, J. Hill, 'Religious Pluralism in an Era of Globalization: The Making of Modern Religious Identity', *Theological Studies*, 69 (2008), 394–411.

Ford, David, *Christian Wisdom: Desiring God and Learning in Love* (Cambridge: Cambridge University Press, 2007).

—— and C. C. Pecknold (eds), *The Promise of Scriptural Reasoning* (Oxford: Blackwell, 2006).

—— Ben Quash, and Janet Martin Soskice (eds), *Fields of Faith: Theology and Religious Studies for the Twenty-first Century* (Cambridge: Cambridge University Press, 2012).

Fredericks, James, *Faith among Faiths* (New York: Paulist Press, 1999).

Fredericks, J. L., 'A Universal Religious Experience? Comparative Theology as an Alternative to a Theology of Religions', *Horizons*, 22 (1995), 67–81.

Freedman, H., and M. Simon, *Midrash Rabbah*, Eng. tr. (London: Soncino, 1961).

Freidenreich, David M., *Foreigners and their Food: Constructing Otherness in Jewish, Christian, and Islamic Law* (Berkeley, Calif.: University of California Press, 2011).

Friedmann, Y., 'The Temple of Multān: A Note on Early Muslim Attitudes to Idolatry', *Israel Oriental Studies*, 2 (1972), 176–82.

Fry, Helen (ed.), *A Reader of Christian–Jewish Dialogue* (Exeter: Exeter University Press, 1996).

Frykenberg, Robert Eric, *Christianity in India: From Beginnings to the Present* (New York: Oxford University Press, 2008).

—— 'On the Study of Conversion Movements: A Review Article', *Indian Economic and Social History Review*, 17 (1981), 121–38.

Furbey, R., et al., *Faith as Social Capital: Connecting or Dividing?* (Bristol: Policy Press, 2006).

Gadamer, H. G., *Truth and Method* (London: Sheed & Ward, 1975).

Gallagher, Eugene V., 'God and Country: Revolution as a Religious Imperative on the Radical Right', *Terrorism and Political Violence*, 9/3 (1997), 63–79.

Garber, Marjorie, and Rebecca Walkowitz (eds), *One Nation Under God? Religion and American Culture* (London: Routledge, 1999).

Gauchet, Marcel, *La Démocratie Contre Elle-Même* (Paris: Gallimard, 2002).

Gaudeul, J. M., *Encounters and Clashes. Islam and Christianity in History*, 2 vols. (Rome: Pontificio Istituto di Studi Arabi e d'Islamistica, 2000).

Gentz, J., and P. Schmidt-Leukel (eds), *Religious Diversity in Chinese Thought* (Basingstoke and New York: Palgrave Macmillan, 2013).

Germano, David, and Helmut Eimer, *The Many Canons of Tibetan Buddhism*, tr. Geoffrey Samuel (Leiden: Brill, 2002).

Gill, S., G. D'Costa, and U. King (eds), *Religion in Europe: Contemporary Perspectives* (Kampen: Kok Pharos, 1994).

Gilling, Bryan (ed.), *'Be Ye Separate': Fundamentalism and the New Zealand Experience* (Red Beach: Colcom Press, 1992).

Gillis, C., *Pluralism: A New Paradigm for Theology* (Louvain: Peeters, 1993).

Gioia, Francesco (ed.), *Interreligious Dialogue: The Official Teaching of the Catholic Church from the Second Vatican Council to 2005* (Boston: Pauline Books and Media, 2006).

Gnilka, Joachim, *Jesus von Nazaret: Botschaft und Geschichte* (Freiburg i.Br.: Herder, 1990).

Goddard, Hugh, *Christians and Muslims: From Double Standards to Mutual Understanding* (Richmond: Curzon, 1995).

Goel, Sita Ram, *History of Hindu–Christian Encounters AD 304 to 1996* (New Delhi: Voice of India, 1996).

Goldberg, Philip, *American Veda* (Bourbon, Ind.: Harmony, 2010).

Gombrich, Richard F., and Gananath Obeyesekere, *Buddhism Transformed: Religious Change in Sri Lanka* (Princeton: Princeton University Press, 1988).

—— *How Buddhism Began: The Conditioned Genesis of the Early Teachings* (London and Atlantic Highlands, NJ: Athlone, 1996).

Gonsalves, Francis, 'Carrying in our Bodies the Marks of His Passion', *Vidyajyoti Journal of Theological Reflection*, 72 (2008), 801–7.

Goosen, Gideon, *Hyphenated Christians: Toward a Better Understanding of Dual Religious Belonging* (Berlin: Peter Lang, 2011).

Gopal, Sarvepalli, *Anatomy of a Confrontation: The Rise of Communal Politics in India* (London: Zed Books, 1993).

Gordon, Albert, *The Nature of Conversion* (Boston: Beacon Press, 1967).

Gottschalk, Peter, *Beyond Hindu and Muslim* (New York: Oxford University Press, 2005).

Grant, Patrick, *Buddhism and Ethnic Conflict in Sri Lanka* (Albany, NY: SUNY, 2009).

Griffin, David Ray (ed.), *Deep Religious Pluralism* (Louisville, Ky.: Westminster John Knox, 2005).

Griffiths, Paul, *The Problem of Religious Diversity* (Oxford: Blackwell, 2001).

Groody, Daniel G., and Gioacchino Campese (eds), *A Promised Land, a Perilous Journey: Theological Perspectives on Migration* (Notre Dame, Ind.: University of Notre Dame Press, 2008).

Gross, Rita M., *Soaring and Settling; Buddhist Perspectives on Contemporary Social and Religious Issues* (New York: Continuum, 1998).

Gross, Rita M., and Terry C. Muck (eds), *Christians Talk about Buddhist Meditation: Buddhists Talk about Christian Prayer* (New York: Continuum, 2003).

—— and Rosemary Radford Ruether, *Religious Feminism and the Future of the Planet: A Buddhist–Christian Conversation* (London and New York: Continuum, 2001).

—— and Terry C. Muck (eds), *Buddhists Talk about Jesus: Christians Talk about the Buddha* (New York: Continuum, 2000).

—— 'Religious Identity and Openness in a Pluralistic World', *Buddhist–Christian Studies*, 25 (2005), 15–27.

—— 'International Buddhist-Christian Theological Encounter: Twenty Years of Dialogue', *Buddhist–Christian Studies*, 25 (2005), 3–7.

Guellouz, S., *Le Dialogue* (Paris: PUF, 1992).

Guillaume A. (tr.), *The life of Muhammad* (Karachi: Oxford University Press, 1955).

Guinness, Michelle, *Child of the Covenant* (London: Hodder & Stoughton, 1994).

Guruge, Ananda (ed.), *Return to Righteousness: A Collection of Speeches, Essays and Letters of the Anagarika Dharmapala* (Colombo: Ministry of Social Affairs, 1991).

Gutiérrez, Gustavo, *The Power of the Poor in History: Selected Writings* (London: SCM Press, 1983).

—— *We Drink from Our Own Wells: The Spiritual Journey of a People* (London: SCM Press, 1983).

—— *The Density of the Present: Selected Writings* (Maryknoll, NY: Orbis Books, 1999).

Habermas, Jürgen, 'New Social Movements', *Telos*, 49 (1981), 33–7.

—— *The Theory of Communicative Action*, ii. *Lifeworld and System: A Critique of Functionalist Reason* (Cambridge: Polity Press, 1987).

—— *The Structural Transformation of the Public Sphere: An Inquiry into a Category of Bourgeois Society* (Cambridge, Mass.: MIT, 1989).

—— *Moral Consciousness and Communicative Action* (Cambridge, Mass.: MIT, 1990).

—— 'Learning by Disaster? A Diagnostic Look Back on the Short 20th Century', *Constellations*, 5/3 (1998), 307–20.

Haddad, Yvonne Y., and W. Z. Haddad (eds), *Christian–Muslim Encounters* (Gainesville, Fla.: University Press of Florida, 1995).

—— Jane L. Smith, and John L. Esposito (eds), *Religion and Immigration: Christian, Jewish, and Muslim Experiences in the United States* (New York: Altamira Press, 2003).

Hagemann, Ludwig, *Christentum contra Islam: Eine Geschichte gescheiterter Beziehungen* (Darmstadt: Wissenschaftliche Buchgesellschaft, 1999).

Haight, Roger, *Jesus Symbol of God* (Maryknoll, NY: Orbis Books, 1999).

Halafoff, Anna, *The Multifaith Movement: Global Risks and Cosmopolitan Solutions* (Dordrecht: Springer, 2013).

—— and David Wright-Neville, 'A Missing Peace? The Role of Religious Actors in Countering Terrorism', *Studies of Conflict and Terrorism*, 32/11 (2009), 921–32.

Halbfass, Wilhelm, *India and Europe: An Essay in Understanding* (Albany, NY: SUNY, 1988).

—— *Philology and Confrontation: Paul Hacker on Traditional and Modern Vedanta* (Albany, NY: SUNY, 1995).

Hall, H. Fielding, *The Soul of a People* (London: Macmillan, 1906).

Hall, S. G., *Melito of Sardis: On Pascha and Fragments* (Oxford: Clarendon Press, 1979).

Hammond, Phillip E. (ed.), *The Sacred in a Secular Age: Toward Revision in the Scientific Study of Religion* (Berkeley, Calif.: University of California Press, 1985).

Harding, Susan Friend, *The Book of Jerry Falwell: Fundamentalist Language and Politics* (Princeton: Princeton University Press, 2001).

Hare, W. (ed.), *Religions of the Empire: A Conference of Some Living Religions within the Empire* (London: Duckworth, 1925).

Harris, Elizabeth J., *Ananda Metteyya: The First British Emissary of Buddhism* (Kandy: Buddhist Publication Society, 1998).

—— *What Buddhists Believe* (Oxford: Oneworld, 1998).

—— 'Co-existence, Confrontation and Co-responsibility: Looking at Buddhist Models of Inter-Religious Relationships', *Swedish Missiological Themes*, 92/3 (2004), 349–69.

—— *Theravāda Buddhism and the British Encounter: Religious, Missionary and Colonial Experience in Nineteenth Century Sri Lanka* (London and New York: Routledge, 2006).

—— 'Memory, Experience and the Clash of Cosmologies: The Encounter between British Protestant Missionaries and Buddhism in Nineteenth Century Sri Lanka', *Social Sciences and Mission*, 25/3 (2012), 265–303.

—— *Hope: A Form of Delusion? Buddhist and Christian Perspectives* (St Ottilien, EOS, 2013).

Hart, D., *Trading Faith: Global Religions in an Age of Rapid Change* (Ropley: O Books, 2006).

Hart, David Bentley, *The Beauty of the Infinite: The Aesthetics of Christian Truth*, (Grand Rapids, Mich.: Eerdmans, 2003).

Hastings, Adrian (ed.), *Modern Catholicism: Vatican II and After* (London: SPCK; New York: Oxford University Press, 1991).

Hawley, John C. (ed.), *Writing the Nation: Self and Country in the Post-Colonial Imagination* (Amsterdam: Rodopi, 1996).

Haynes, Jeffrey, *Religion and Development: Conflict or Cooperation?* (Basingstoke and New York: Palgrave Macmillan, 2007).

Hebblethwaite, Peter, *Introducing John Paul II: The Populist Pope* (London: Collins, 1982).

Heck, Paul, *Common Ground: Islam, Christianity, and Religious Pluralism* (Washington, DC: Georgetown University Press, 2009).

Hedges, Paul, *Controversies in Interreligious Dialogue and the Theology of Religions* (London: SCM Press, 2010).

Heim, S. Mark, *Is Christ the Only Way?* (Valley Forge, Pa.: Judson Press, 1985).

—— *Salvations: Truth and Difference in Religion*, (Maryknoll, NY: Orbis Books, 1995).

—— *The Depths of the Riches* (Grand Rapids, Mich.: Eerdmans, 2001).

—— *Grounds for Understanding: Ecumenical Resources for Responses to Religious Pluralism* (Cambridge, Mass.: Eerdmans, 1998).

Heine, Steven (ed.), *Buddhism and Interfaith Dialogue: Masao Abe* (Honolulu: University of Hawaii Press, 1995).

Heissig, Walter (tr. Geoffrey Samuel), *The Religions of Mongolia* (Berkeley, Calif.: University of California Press, 1992).

Henry, Patrick (ed.), *Benedict's Dharma: Buddhists Reflect on the Rule of Saint Benedict* (London and New York: Continuum, 2001).

Herberg, Will, *Protestant-Catholic-Jew: An Essay in American Religious Sociology* (Chicago: University of Chicago Press, 1955).

Herne, R., 'The Challenge of Paganism within Inter Faith Work', *World Faiths Encounter*, 23 (1999), 32–7.

Hewitt, Harold (ed.), *Problems in the Philosophy of Religion: Critical Studies of the Work of John Hick* (London: Macmillan, 1991).

Hick, John (ed.), *Truth and Dialogue in World Religion: Conflicting Truth-Claims* (Philadelphia: Westminster Press, 1970).

—— *God and the Universe of Faiths* (London: Collins, 1977).

—— *Problems of Religious Pluralism* (London: Macmillan, 1985).

—— *An Interpretation of Religion: Human Responses to the Transcendent* (Basingstoke: Macmillan, 1989; 2nd edn, Basingstoke and New York: Palgrave Macmillan, 2004).

—— *The Metaphor of God Incarnate*, 2nd, rev. edn (London: SCM Press, 2005).

—— and Paul F. Knitter (eds), *The Myth of Christian Uniqueness* (Maryknoll, NY: Orbis Books, 1987).

Hintersteiner, N., *Traditionen überschreiten: Angloamerikanische Beiträge zur interkulturellen Hermeneutik* (Vienna: WUV-Universitätsverlag, 2001).

Hobsbawm, Eric, *On History* (London: Abacus, 1998).

Hocking, William E. (ed.), *Re-thinking Missions: a Laymen's Inquiry after One Hundred Years* (New York and London: Harper & Brothers, 1932).

Holt, John Clifford, *Spirits of the Place: Buddhism and Lao Religious Culture* (Honolulu: University of Hawaii Press, 2009).

Home Office, *Working Together: Co-operation between Government and Faith Communities: Recommendations of the Steering Group Reviewing Patterns of Engagement between Government and Faith Communities in England* (London: Home Office Faith Communities Unit, 2004).

ten Hooven, M., *De lege Tolerantie: Over vrijheid en vrijblijvendheid in Nederland* (Amsterdam: Boom, 2001).

Howard, Thomas, *God and the Atlantic: America, Europe and the Religious Divide* (Oxford: Oxford University Press, 2011).

Hume, David, *A Treatise of Human Nature* (London: John Noon, 1739).

Huntington, S., *The Clash of Civilizations and the Remaking of World Order* (New York: Free Press, 2002).

Hüttenhoff, Michael, *Der religiöse Pluralismus als Orientierungsproblem: Religionstheologische Studien* (Leipzig: Evangelische Verlagsanstalt, 2001).

Ikeda, Daisaku, and Majid Tehranian, *Global Civilisation: A Buddhist–Islamic Dialogue* (London and New York: I. B. Tauris, 2003).

Ing, Paul Tan Chee, and Teresa Ee, *Contemporary Issues on Malaysian Religions* (Petaling Jaya: Pelanduk Publications, 1984).

Ingram, Paul, *The Modern Buddhist-Christian Dialogue: Two Universalistic Religions in Transformation* (Lewiston, NY: Edwin Mellen Press, 1988).

Insole, Christopher, *The Politics of Human Frailty: A Theological Defence of Political Liberalism* (Notre Dame, Ind.: University of Notre Dame Press, 2004).

—— and Harriet Harris (eds), *Faith and Philosophical Analysis* (Aldershot: Ashgate 2005).

Inter Faith Network for the UK, *Handbook of Affiliated Organisations* (London: Inter Faith Network for the UK, 1988).

—— *Law, Blasphemy and the Multi-Faith Society* (London: Commission for Racial Equality, 1990).

—— *Law, Respect for Religious Identity and the Multi-Faith Society* (London: Commission for Racial Equality, 1991).

—— *Statement on Inter Religious Relations* (London: Inter Faith Network for the UK, 1991).

—— *Mission, Dialogue and Inter Religious Encounter* (London: Inter Faith Network for the UK, 1993).

—— *The Quest for Common Values: Report of a Seminar Organised by the Inter Faith Network for the UK, 10th December, 1996* (London: Inter Faith Network for the UK, 1997).

—— *The Local Inter Faith Guide: Faith Community Cooperation in Action* (London: Inter Faith Network for the UK in association with the Inner Cities Religious Council of the Department for the Environment, Transport and the Regions, 1999).

—— *Local Inter Faith Activity in the UK: A Survey* (London: Inter Faith Network for the UK, 2003).

—— *Partnership for the Common Good: Inter Faith Structures and Local Government* (London: Inter Faith Network for the UK in association with the Local Government Association, the Home Office, and the Inner Cities Religious Council of the Office of the Deputy Prime Minister, 2003).

—— *Connect: Different Faiths Shared Values* (London: Inter Faith Network for the UK in association with TimeBank and the National Youth Agency, 2004).

—— *Inter Faith Organisations in the UK: A Directory* (London: Inter Faith Network for the UK, 2004, 2009).

—— *Looking After One Another: The Safety and Security of our Faith Communities* (London: Inter Faith Network for the UK, 2005).

—— *The Local Inter Faith Guide: Faith Community Co-operation in Action,* 2nd edn (London: Inter Faith Network for the UK in association with Inner Cities Religious Council and the Office of the Deputy Prime Minister, 2005).

—— *20 Years: Milestones on the Journey Together Towards Greater Inter Faith Understanding and Cooperation* (London: Inter Faith Network for the UK, 2007).

—— *Inter Faith Week 2009: A Report and Evaluation* (London: Inter Faith Network for the UK, 2009).

—— *Promoting Mutual Respect and Understanding: Annual Report, 2010/11* (London: Inter Faith Network for the UK, 2011).

Ireland, John (tr.), *The Udāna: Inspired Utterances of the Buddha* (Kandy: Buddhist Publication Society, 1990).

Isaac, J., *The Teaching of Contempt: Christian Roots of Anti-Semitism* (New York: Holt, 1964).

Jack, H. A., *A History of the World Conference on Religion and Peace* (New York: World Conference on Religion and Peace, 1993).

Jackson, Robert, Siebren Miedema, Wolfram Weisse, and Jean-Paul Willaime (eds), *Religion and Education in Europe: Developments, Contexts and Debates* (Münster: Waxmann, 2007).

James, William, *The Varieties of Religious Experience* (London and Bombay: Longmans, Green & Co., 1902).

Jansen, Johannes J. G., *The Dual Nature of Islamic Fundamentalism* (London: Hurst & Co., 1997).

Jaspers, Karl, *The Origin and Goal of History,* tr. Michael Bullock (New Haven: Yale University Press, 1953).

Jayatilleke, K. N., 'The Buddhist Attitude to Other Religions', *Dialogue,* NS 13–14 (1986–7), 11–39.

Jeanrond, W. G., and J. L. Rike (eds), *Radical Pluralism and Truth: David Tracy and the Hermeneutics of Religion* (New York: Crossroad, 1991).

Jenkins, Timothy, *Religion in English Everyday Life: An Ethnographic Approach* (London: Berghahn, 1999).

Jerryson, Michael K., *Buddhist Fury: Religion and Violence in Southern Thailand* (New York: Oxford University Press, 2011).

Jerryson, Michael K., and Mark Juergensmeyer (eds), *Buddhist Warfare* (New York: Oxford University Press, 2010).

Jerusalem Talmud, see B. Benrend (ed.), *Talmud Yerusahalmi: Kemo she-nidpas be venetsi'ah bi-shenat,* Krotoschin, 5282 (1866).

Jha, D. C., *Mahatma Gandhi: The Congress and the Partition of India* (London: Sangam, 1995).

Jha, D. N., *Rethinking Hindu Identity* (London: Equinox, 2009).

John, T. K., 'The Pope's "Pastoral Visit" to India: A Further Reflection', *Vidyajyoti Journal of Theological Reflection,* 51 (1987), 58–66.

John Paul II, *Essays on Religious Freedom* (Milwaukee: Catholic League on Religious and Civil Rights, 1984).

Johnston, Douglas, and Cynthia Sampson (eds), *Religion, the Missing Dimension of Statecraft* (Oxford: Oxford University Press, 1994).

Jones, Ken, *The New Social Face of Buddhism: A Call to Action* (Boston: Wisdom Publications, 2003).

Jones, Owen Bennett, *Pakistan: Eye of the Storm,* 3rd edn (New Haven: Yale University Press, 2009).

Juergensmeyer, Mark, *Terror in the Mind of God: The Global Rise of Religious Violence* (Berkeley, Calif.: University of California Press, 2000; 3rd edn, 2003).

Jukko, Risto, *Trinity in Unity in Christian–Muslim Relations: The Work of the Pontifical Council for Interreligious Dialogue* (Leiden and Boston: Brill, 2007).

Kaldor, Mary, *New and Old Wars: Organized Violence in a Global Era* (Cambridge: Polity, 1999).

—— *Global Civil Society: An Answer to War* (Cambridge: Polity, 2003).

Kapstein, Matthew, *The Tibetan Assimilation of Buddhism: Conversion, Contestation and Memory* (Oxford: Oxford University Press, 2000).

Kärkkäinen, Veli-Matti, *An Introduction to the Theology of Religions* (Downers Grove, Ill.: InterVarsity Press, 2003).

Kasimow, H., and B. L. Sherwin (eds), *No Religion is an Island: Abraham Joshua Heschel and Interreligious Dialogue* (Eugene, Or.: Wipf & Stock, 1991).

Kateregga, B., and D. Shenk, *A Muslim and a Christian in Dialogue* (Nairobi: Usima Press, 1980).

Kawanami, Hiroko, and Geoffrey Samuels (eds), *Buddhism and International Relief Work* (London: Palgrave Macmillan, 2013).

Kee, H. C., *What can we Know about Jesus?* (Cambridge: Cambridge University Press, 1990).

Keenan, John, *The Meaning of Christ: A Mahayana Theology* (Maryknoll, NY: Orbis Books, 1989).

—— *I am/No Self: A Christian Commentary on the Heart Sutra* (Leuven: Peeters, 2011).

Kellenberger, James (ed.), *Inter-Religious Models and Criteria* (London: Macmillan, 1993).

Kent, Eliza F., 'Secret Christians of Sivakasi: Gender, Syncretism, and Crypto-Religion in Early Twentieth-Century South India', *Journal of the American Academy of Religion,* 79 (2011), 676–705.

Kessler, E., and N. Wenborn (eds), *A Dictionary of Jewish–Christian Relations* (Cambridge: Cambridge University Press, 2005).

—— J. T. Pawlikowski, and J. Banki (eds), *Jews and Christians in Conversation* (Cambridge: Orchard Academic, 2002).

Khapa, Rje Tsong, *Ocean of Reasoning: A Great Commentary on Nāgārjuna's Mūlamadhyamakakārikā* (New York: Oxford University Press, 2006).

Khema, Ayya, 'Mysticism is No Mystery', *Eckhart Review* (Spring 1996), 44–57.

Kiblinger, Kristin, 'Identifying Inclusivism in Buddhist Contexts', *Contemporary Buddhism*, 4/1 (2003) 79–97.

—— *Buddhist Inclusivism: Attitudes towards Religious Others* (Aldershot: Ashgate, 2005).

Kidd, Thomas S., *American Christians and Islam: Evangelical Culture and Muslims from the Colonial Period to the Age of Terrorism* (Princeton: Princeton University Press, 2008).

Kiely, Robert (ed.), *The Good Heart: His Holiness the Dalai Lama* (London: Rider, 1996).

King, Rolfe, and David Cheetham (eds), *Contemporary Practice and Method in the Philosophy of Religion* (London: Continuum, 2008).

Kinnard, Jacob N., 'When Is the Buddha Not the Buddha? The Hindu/Buddhist Battle over Bodhgayā and Its Buddha Image', *Journal of the American Academy of Religion*, 66 (1998), 817–39.

Kirkwood, Peter, *The Quiet Revolution: The Emergence of Interfaith Consciousness* (Sydney: ABC Books, 2007).

Kitagawa, J. M. (ed.), *The History of Religions* (Chicago: University of Chicago Press, 1987).

Kittel, Gerhard, *Die Judenfrage* (Stuttgart: W. Kohlhammer, 1933).

Klostermaier, Klaus K., *A Survey of Hinduism*, 3rd edn (Albany, NY: SUNY, 2007).

Knitter, Paul F., *One Earth Many Religions: Multifaith Dialogue and Global Responsibility* (Maryknoll, NY: Orbis Books, 1995).

—— *Jesus and the Other Names* (Maryknoll, NY: Orbis Books, 1996).

—— (ed.), *The Myth of Religious Superiority: A Multi-faith Exploration* (Maryknoll, NY: Orbis Books, 2005).

—— *Without Buddha I Could Not Be a Christian* (Oxford: Oneworld, 2009).

—— *Theologies of Religions* (Maryknoll, NY: Orbis Books, 2010).

—— 'Rita Gross: Buddhist-Christian Dialogue about Dialogue', *Buddhist-Christian Studies* 31 (2011), 79–84.

Kohn, Livia, *Laughing at the Tao: Debates among Buddhists and Taoists in Medieval China* (Princeton: Princeton University Press, 1995).

Koningsveld, P. van, 'The Islamic Image of Paul and the Origin of the Gospel of Barnabas', *Jerusalem Studies in Arabic and Islam*, 20 (1996), 200–28.

Kraemer, H., *The Christian Message in a Non-Christian World* (London: Edinburgh House Press, 1938).

Kulke, Hermann, and Gunther-Dietz Sontheime (eds), *Hinduism Reconsidered* (New Delhi: Manohar, 2001).

Küng, Hans, *Judaism* (London: SCM Press, 1992).

—— and K.-J. Kuschel (eds), *A Global Ethic: The Declaration of the Parliament of the World's Religions* (London: SCM Press, 1993).

—— *Yes to a Global Ethic* (London: SCM Press, 1996).

—— and D. Senghaas (eds) *Friedenspolitik: Ethische Grundlagen internationaler Beziehungen* (München: Piper, 2003).

—— *Islam: Past, Present and Future* (Oxford: OneWorld, 2007).

Kuttianimattathil, Jose, *Practice and Theology of Interreligious Dialogue: A Critical Study of the Indian Christian Attempts since Vatican II* (Bangalore: Kristu Jyoti Publication, 1995).

Kymlicka, Will, 'Do we Need a Liberal Theory of Minority Rights? Reply to Carens, Young, Parekh and Forst', *Constellations*, 4/1 (1997), 72–87.

—— and Keith Banting, 'Immigration, Multiculturalism, and the Welfare State', *Ethics and International Affairs*, 20/3 (2006), 281–304.

Kymlicka, Will, and Christine Straehle, 'Cosmopolitanism, Nation-States, and Minority Nationalism: A Critical Review of Recent Literature', *European Journal of Philosophy*, 7/1 (1999), 65–88.

Lähnemann, J. (ed.), *Das Wiederwachen der Religionen als pädagogische Herausforderung: Interreligiöse Erziehung im Spannungsfeld von Fundamentalismus und Säkularismus* (Hamburg: E. B. Verlag Rissen, 1993).

Lai, Whalen, and Michael von Brück, *Christianity and Buddhism: A Multi-Cultural History of their Dialogue* (Maryknoll, NY: Orbis Books, 2001).

Lake, Kirsopp, *Apostolic Fathers* (I), with Eng. tr. (London: Heinemann, 1912).

Lamdan, Neville, and Alberto Melloni (eds), *Nostra Aetate: Origins, Promulgation, Impact on Jewish–Catholic Relations* (Münster and Berlin: LIT Verlag, 2007).

Lamont, S., *Church and State: Uneasy Alliances* (London: Bodley Head, 1989).

Lash, Nicholas, *Easter in Ordinary* (London: SCM Press, 1988).

Laszlo, E., *Macroshift: Navigating the Transformation to a Sustainable World* (London: Gaia Books, 2001).

Leadbeater, C. W., 'Wesak/Wesak Compliments', *The Buddhist*, 1/22 (1889), 172–4.

van Leeuwen, B., *Erkenning, identiteit en verschil: Multiculturalisme en leven met culturele diversiteit* (Leuven: Acco, 2003).

Leigh, Michael D., *Conflict, Politics and Proselytisation: Methodist Missionaries in Colonial and Postcolonial Upper Burma 1887–1966* (Manchester: Manchester University Press, 2011).

Lekshe Tsomo, Karma (ed.), *Buddhist Women across Cultures: Realizations* (New York: SUNY, 1999).

—— (ed.), *Innovative Buddhist Women: Swimming Against the Stream* (Richmond: Curzon, 2000).

Leonard, Karen J., Alex Stepick, Manuel A. Vasquez, and Jennifer Holdaway (eds), *Immigrants' Faiths: The Transforming Religious Life in America* (New York: Altamira Press, 2006).

Le Saux, Henri, *La Montee au fond du Cœur: Le Journal intime d'un moine Chrétien-sannyasi Hindou 1948–1973* (Paris: OEIL, 1986).

Levinas, Emmanuel, *Totality and Infinity* (The Hague: M. Nijhoff; Pittsburgh: Duquesne University Press, 1979).

—— *Otherwise than Being, or, Beyond Essence* (The Hague: M. Nijhoff, 1981).

—— *Difficult Freedom: Essays on Judaism* (London: Athlone Press, 1990).

Levey, Geoffrey Brahm, and Tariq Modood (eds), *Secularism, Religion and Multicultural Citizenship* (Cambridge: Cambridge University Press, 2009).

van Lin, Jan, *Shaking the Fundamentals: Religious Plurality and the Ecumenical Movement* (Amsterdam and New York: Rodopi, 2002).

Lindbeck, G., *The Nature of Doctrine: Religion and Theology in a Postliberal Age*, (Philadelphia: Westminster Press, 1984).

—— 'The Unity we Seek: Setting the Agenda for Ecumenism', *Christian Century*, 121 (2005), 28–31.

Lineham, Peter, 'The Fundamentalist Agenda and its Chances', *Stimulus*, 14/3 (Aug. 2006), 2–14.

Linnan, D., and W. El-Ansary (eds), *Muslim and Christian Understanding: Theory and Application of 'A Common Word'* (London: Palgrave Macmillan, 2010).

Llewellyn, J. E. (ed.), *Defining Hinduism: A Reader* (New York: Routledge, 2005).

Local Government Association, *Faith and Community: A Good Practice Guide for Local Authorities*, 1st edn (London: Local Government Association Publications, 2002).

Long, Jeffery D., *A Vision for Hinduism: Beyond Hindu Nationalism* (London: I. B. Tauris, 2007).

—— *Jainism: An Introduction* (London: I. B. Tauris, 2009).

Lopez, Donald (ed.), *Buddhism in Practice* (Princeton: Princeton University Press, 1995).

—— *Religions of Tibet in Practice* (Princeton: Princeton University Press, 1997).

Luther, Martin, *Large Catechism,* tr. R. H. Fischer (Philadelphia: Fortress Press, 1959).

McCarthy, Kate, *Interfaith Encounters in America* (Piscataway, NJ: Rutgers University Press, 2007).

McIntosh, Jane, *A Peaceful Realm: The Rise and Fall of the Indus Civilization* (Boulder, Colo.: Westview Press, 2002).

MacIntyre, Alasdair, *Whose Justice? Which Rationality?* (London: Duckworth, 1996).

—— *After Virtue: A Study in Moral Theory,* 3rd edn (Notre Dame, Ind.: University of Notre Dame Press, 2007).

McMahon, David L., *The Making of Buddhist Modernism* (Oxford: Oxford University Press, 2008).

Magonet, J., *Talking to the Other* (London: I. B. Tauris, 2003).

Mahābhārata, tr. Chakravarthi V. Narasimhan (New York: Columbia University Press, 1997).

Mahajan, Sucheta, *Independence and Partition: The Erosion of Colonial Power in India* (New Delhi and Thousand Oaks, Calif.: Sage Publications, 2000).

Maher, M. (ed.), *The Aramaic Bible: Targum Pseudo Jonathan: Genesis* (Edinburgh: T&T Clark, 1992)

Malalgoda, Kitsiri, *Buddhism in Sinhalese Society 1750–1800: A Study of Religious Revival and Change* (Los Angeles, Calif.: University of California Press, 1976).

Maranhao, T., (ed.), *The Interpretation of Dialogue* (Chicago: University of Chicago Press, 1990).

Marsden, George M., *Understanding Fundamentalism and Evangelicalism* (Grand Rapids, Mich.: W. B. Eerdmans, 1991).

Marston, John, and Elizabeth Guthrie (eds), *History, Buddhism, and New Religious Movements in Cambodia* (Honolulu: University of Hawaii Press, 2004).

Marty, Martin E., and R Scott Appleby (eds), *Fundamentalisms Compared: The Charles Strong Memorial Lecture 1989* (Underdale, South Australia: Australian Association for the Study of Religions, 1989).

—— *The Fundamentalism Project* (Chicago: University of Chicago Press, 1991).

—— (eds), *Fundamentalisms Observed* (Chicago: University of Chicago Press, 1991).

—— *The Glory and the Power: The Fundamentalist Challenge to the Modern World* (Boston: Beacon Press, 1992).

—— (eds), *Fundamentalisms and the State: Remaking Politics, Economies, and Militance* (Chicago: University of Chicago Press, 1993).

—— (eds), *Accounting for Fundamentalisms: The Dynamic Character of Movements* (Chicago: University of Chicago Press, 1994).

—— (eds), *Fundamentalisms Comprehended* (Chicago: University of Chicago Press, 1995).

Mazur, Michael, *The Americanization of Religious Minorities: Confronting the Constitutional Order* (Baltimore, Md.: Johns Hopkins University Press, 2004).

Meier, John P., *A Marginal Jew: Rethinking the Historical Jesus,* 4 vols. (New York: Anchor Bible, 1991–2009).

Meister, C. (ed.), *The Oxford Handbook for Religious Diversity* (Oxford: Oxford University Press, 2010).

Merleau-Ponty, Maurice, *The Prose of the World,* tr. John O-Neill (London: Heinemann, 1984).

Michael, George, 'RAHOWA! A History of the World Church of the Creator', *Terrorism and Political Violence*, 18/4 (2006), 561–83.

Michel, T., 'A Variety of Approaches to Interfaith Dialogue', *Pro Dialogo*, 108 (2001), 342–51.

Migne, J. P., *Glaphyrorum in Genesim* (1857–66).

Milbank, John, *Theology and Social Theory: Beyond Secular Reason*, 2nd edn (Oxford: Blackwell, 2005).

Millard, A. (ed.), *Faiths and Fellowship: The Proceedings of the World Congress of Faiths, held in London, July 3rd–17th, 1936* (London: J. M. Watkins, 1937).

Milton-Edwards, Beverley, *Islamic Fundamentalism since 1945* (New York: Routledge, 2005).

Mitchell, Donald W., and James Wiseman OSB (eds), *The Gethsemani Encounter: A Dialogue on the Spiritual Life by Buddhist and Christian Monastics* (New York: Continuum, 1999).

Morrison, K. F., *Understanding Conversion* (Charlottesville, Va.: University Press of Virginia, 1992).

Moyaert, M., *Fragile Identities: Towards a Theology of Interreligious Hospitality* (New York: Rodopi, 2011).

—— 'From Soteriological Openness to Hermeneutical Openness: Recent Developments in the Theology of Religions', *Modern Theology*, 28 (2012), 35–52.

—— 'Ricoeur on the (Im-)possibility of a Global Ethics towards an Ethics of Fragile Interreligious Compromises', *Neue Zeitschrift für systematische Theologie*, 52 (2010), 440–61.

—— and D. Pollefeyt, *Never Revoked: Nostra Aetate as Ongoing Challenge for Jewish–Christian Dialogue*, Louvain Theological and Pastoral Monographs, 40 (Louvain: Peeters, 2010).

Mozjes, P., and L. Swidler (eds), *Christian Mission and Interreligious Dialogue* (Lewiston, NY: Edwin Mellen Press, 1990).

Mudimbe, V. Y., *The Invention of Africa: Gnosis, Philosophy and the Order of Knowledge* (Bloomington, Ind., and London: Indiana University Press and James Currey, 1988).

Muhammad, Ghazi bin, M. Volf, and M. Yarrington (eds), *A Common Word: Muslims and Christians on Loving God and Neighbor* (Grand Rapids, Mich.: Eerdmans, 2010).

Murray, Paul D. (ed.), *Receptive Ecumenism and the Call to Catholic Learning: Exploring a Way for Contemporary Ecumenism* (Oxford: Oxford University Press, 2008).

Netland, Harold, *Dissonant Voices: Religious Pluralism and the Question of Truth* (Grand Rapids, Mich.: Eerdmans, 1991).

Neuhaus, Richard John, *The Naked Public Square: Religion and Democracy in America* (Grand Rapids, Mich.: Eerdmans, 1984).

Neusner, Jacob, *et al.* (eds), *The Tosefta* (New Haven: Ktav, 1977–86).

Newman, J., 'Islam in the Kālacakra Tantra', *Journal of the International Association of Buddhist Studies*, 21 (1998), 320–3.

Nhat Hanh, Thich, *Living Buddha, Living Christ* (London: Rider, 1996).

—— *Going Home: Jesus and the Buddha as Brothers* (London: Rider, 1999).

—— and Daniel Berrigan, *The Raft is Not the Shore: Conversations toward a Buddhist–Christian Awareness* (Maryknoll, NY: Orbis Books, 1975 and 2001).

Nicholson, Andrew J., *Unifying Hinduism: Philosophy and Identity in Indian Intellectual History* (New York: Columbia University Press, 2010).

Nicholson, R., *The Mystics of Islam* (London: Routledge, 1963).

Niebuhr, Gustav, *Beyond Tolerance: Searching for Interfaith Understanding in America* (New York: Viking, 2008).

Nikhilananda, Swami, *The Gospel of Sri Ramakrishna* (New York: Ramakrishna-Vivekananda Center, 1942).

Nock, A. D., *Conversion* (Oxford: Oxford University Press, 1933).

Nolan, Ann M., *A Privileged Moment: Dialogue in the Language of the Second Vatican Council 1962–1965* (Bern: Peter Lang, 2006).

Norman, K. R., *A Philological Approach to Buddhism: The Bukkyō Dendō Kyōkai Lectures 1994* (London: School of Oriental and African Studies, 1997).

*Nostra Aetate, Declaration on the Relation of the Church to Non-Christian Religions, Vatican II (Vatican City, 1965).

Nussbaum, Martha, *The Clash Within: Democracy, Religious Violence, and India's Future* (Boston: Harvard University Press, 2009).

—— *The New Religious Intolerance: Overcoming the Politics of Fear in an Anxious Age* (Cambridge, Mass.: Belknap Press, 2012).

Obeyesekere, Gananath, 'The Great Tradition and the Little in the Perspective of Sinhalese Buddhism', *Journal of Asian Studies*, 22 (1963), 139–53.

Ochs, Peter, 'Comparative Religious Traditions', *Journal of the American Academy of Religion*, 74/1 (2006), 125–8.

O'Leary, Joseph, *Religious Pluralism and Christian Truth* (Edinburgh: Edinburgh University Press, 1996).

Olivelle Patrick (tr.), *Upaniṣads* (New York: Oxford University Press, 1996).

—— *Dharmasūtras* (New York: Oxford University Press, 1999).

Orsi, Robert (ed.), *The Cambridge Companion to Religious Studies* (Cambridge: Cambridge University Press, 2012).

Owens, Alexandra, 'Using Legislation to Protect Against Unethical Conversions in Sri Lanka', *Journal of Law and Religion*, 12 (2007), 323–51.

Oxford Centre for Hindu Studies, *Bridges and Barriers to Hindu–Christian Relations* (Oxford: Oxford Centre for Hindu Studies, 2011).

Palihawadana, Mahinda, 'The Impossibility of Intolerance: A Buddhist Perspective', *Dialogue*, NS 28 (2001), 1–17.

Palmer, Martin, *The Jesus Sutras: Rediscovering the Lost Religion of Taoist Christianity* (London: Piatkus, 2001).

Pandit, Bansi, *The Hindu Mind* (Glen Ellyn, Ill.: B. and V. Enterprises, 1998).

Panikkar, Raimon, *The Unknown Christ of Hinduism* (Maryknoll, NY: Orbis Books, 1981).

—— *The Cosmotheandric Experience: Emerging Religious Consciousness* (Maryknoll, NY: Orbis Books, 1993).

—— *The Intra-Religious Dialogue* (New York: Paulist Press, 1998).

Pattison, George, *A Short Course in Philosophy of Religion* (London: SCM Press, 2001).

Pearce, Susanna, 'Religious Rage: A Quantitative Analysis of the Intensity of Religious Conflicts', *Terrorism and Political Violence*, 14/3 (2005), 333–52.

Pechilis, Karen, and Selva J. Raj (eds), *South Asian Religions: Tradition and Today* (New York: Routledge, 2013).

Pennington, Brian K., *Was Hinduism Invented? Britons, Indians, and the Colonial Construction of Religion* (New York: Oxford University Press, 2005).

Petit, F., *La Chaîne sur la Genèse*, Édition Intégrale (Louvain: Peeters, 1995).

Phan, Peter C., *Christianity with an Asian Face: Asian American Theology in the Making* (Maryknoll, NY: Orbis Books, 2003).

—— *In our own Tongues: Perspectives from Asia on Mission and Inculturation* (Maryknoll, NY: Orbis Books, 2003).

Phan, Peter C., *Being Religious Interreligiously: Asian Perspectives on Interfaith Dialogue* (Maryknoll, NY: Orbis Books, 2004).

—— (ed.), *Christianities in Asia* (New York: Wiley-Blackwell, 2011).

Pickett, J., *Christian Mass Movements in India* (New York: Abingdon Press, 1933).

Pickthall, M. M., *The Meaning of the Glorious Koran* (New York: Dorset Press, 1963).

Pierce, Brian J., OP, *We Walk the Path Together: Learning from Thich Nhat Hanh and Meister Eckhart* (Maryknoll, NY: Orbis Books, 2005).

Plantinga, Richard J. (ed.), *Christianity and Plurality: Classic and Contemporary Readings* (Oxford: Blackwell, 1999).

Plaw, Avery (ed.), *Frontiers of Diversity: Explorations in Contemporary Pluralism* (Amsterdam and New York: Rodopi, 2005).

Pongratz-Leisten, Beate (ed.), *Reconsidering the Concept of Revolutionary Monotheism* (Winona Lake, Ind.: Eisenbrauns, 2011).

Prabhavananda, Swami, *The Sermon on the Mount According to Vedanta* (Hollywood, Calif.: Vedanta Press, 1964).

Pranke, Patrick, 'On Saints and Wizards: Ideals of Human Perfection and Power in Contemporary Burmese Buddhism', *Journal of the International Association of Buddhist Studies,* 33/1–2, 2012 (2011), 453–88.

Pratt, Douglas, 'Contextual Paradigms for Interfaith Relations', *Current Dialogue,* 42 (2003), 3–9.

—— *The Challenge of Islam: Encounters in Interfaith Dialogue* (Aldershot: Ashgate, 2005).

—— 'Pluralism, Postmodernism and Interreligious Dialogue', *Sophia,* 46/3 (Dec. 2007), 243–59.

—— 'Religious Fundamentalism: A Paradigm for Terrorism?', *Australian Religion Studies Review,* 20/2 (2007), 195–215.

—— 'Religion and Terrorism: Christian Fundamentalism and Extremism', *Terrorism and Political Violence,* 22/3 (June 2010), 438–56.

—— *The Church and Other Faiths: The World Council of Churches, the Vatican, and Interreligious Dialogue* (Bern: Peter Lang, 2010).

Prebish, Charles S., and Christopher S. Queen, *Action Dharma: New Studies in Engaged Buddhism* (London and New York: Routledge, 2003).

Premawardhana, Devaka, 'The Unremarkable Hybrid: Aloysius Pieris and the Redundancy of Multiple Religious Belonging', *Journal of Ecumenical Studies,* 46/1 (2011), 76–101.

Puniyani, Ram (ed.), *Religion, Power and Violence: Expression of Politics in Contemporary Times* (Thousand Oaks, Calif.: Sage, 2005).

Purcell, Michael, *Levinas and Theology* (Cambridge: Cambridge University Press, 2006).

Putnam, R., 'Bowling Alone: America's Declining Social Capital', *Journal of Democracy,* 2 (1995), 65–78.

Queen, Christopher S., and Sallie B. King, *Engaged Buddhism: Buddhist Liberation Movements in Asia* (Albany, NY: SUNY, 1996).

Race, Alan, *Christians and Religious Pluralism: Patterns in the Christian Theology of Religions* (Maryknoll, NY: Orbis Books, 1982; 2nd edn, London: SCM Press, 1993).

—— and Paul M. Hedges (eds), *Christian Approaches to Other Faiths* (London: SCM Press, 2008).

Radhakrishnan, Sarvepalli, *The Hindu View of Life* (London: George Allen & Unwin, 1927).

Rahner, Karl, *Schriften zur Theologie,* viii (Einsiedeln-Zürich-Cologne: Benziger Verlag, 1967).

—— (ed.), *Encyclopedia of Theology* (London: Burns & Oates, 1975).

Raj, Selva J., and Corinne G. Dempsey (eds), *Popular Christianity in India: Riting between the Lines* (Albany, NY: SUNY, 2002).

Rambo, L., *Understanding Religious Conversion* (New Haven and London: Yale University Press, 1993).

Ramey, Steven W., 'Challenging Definitions: Human Agency, Diverse Religious Practices and the Problems of Boundaries', *Numen,* 54 (2007), 1–27.

Rawls, John, *The Law of Peoples with 'The Idea of Public Reason Revisited'* (Cambridge, Mass.: Harvard University Press, 1999).

Reich, Walter (ed.), *Origins of Terrorism: Psychologies, Ideologies, Theologies, States of Mind* (Washington, DC: Woodrow Wilson Centre Press, 1998).

Richards, Glyn (ed.), *A Source-Book of Modern Hinduism* (London: Curzon, 1985).

Ricoeur, Paul, *On Translation*, tr. Eileen Brennan (Abingdon and New York: Routledge, 2006).

Riedl, G., *Modell Assisi: Christliches Gebet und interreligiöser Dialog in heilsgeschichtlichem Kontext* (Berlin: De Gruyter, 1998).

Robbins, Joel, 'Crypto-Religion and the Study of Cultural Mixtures: Anthropology, Value, and the Nature of Syncretism', *Journal of the American Academy of Religion,* 79 (2011), 408–24.

Robinson, Rowena, *Christians of India* (Thousand Oaks, Calif.: Sage, 2003).

Roebuck, Valerie J. (tr.), *The Dhammapada* (London: Penguin, 2010).

Rose, Gillian, *Mourning Becomes the Law: Philosophy and Representation* (Cambridge: Cambridge University Press, 1996).

Rosenzweig, Franz, *Gesammelte Schriften*, i (The Hague: Martinus Nijhoff, 1913).

Rouse, Ruth, and Stephen Charles Neill (eds), *A History of the Ecumenical Movement 1517–1948* (Philadelphia: Westminster Press, 1954).

Roy, Rammohun, *The Precepts of Jesus, the Guide to Peace and Happiness, Extracted from the Books of the New Testament Ascribed to the Four Evangelists: To Which Are Added, the First and Second Appeal to the Christian Public, in Reply to the Observations of Dr Marshman, of Serampore, from the London Edition* (New York: B. Bates, 1825).

Rudin, J., *Christians and Jews Faith to Faith: Tragic History, Promising Present, Fragile Future* (New York: Jewish Lights Publishing, 2010).

Ruether, Rosemary, *Faith and Fratricide. The Theological Roots of Anti-Semitism* (New York: Seabury Press, 1974).

Rushdie, Salman, *The Satanic Verses* (London: Viking Penguin, 1988).

Ruthven, Malise, *Fundamentalism: The Search for Meaning* (Oxford: Oxford University Press, 2004).

Saha, Santosh C. (ed.), *Religious Fundamentalism in the Contemporary World: Critical Social and Political Issues* (Lanham, Md.: Lexington Books, 2004).

Salvatore, Armando, *The Public Sphere: Liberal Modernity, Catholicism, Islam* (London: Palgrave Macmillan, 2007).

Samartha, S. J., 'Dialogue as a Continuing Christian Concern', *Ecumenical Review,* 23 (1971), 129–42.

—— 'The Progress and Promise of Inter-Religious Dialogues', *Journal of Ecumenical Studies,* 9 (1972), 463–76.

—— *One Christ, Many Religions* (Maryknoll, NY: Orbis Books, 1991).

Samuel, Geoffrey, *Introducing Tibetan Buddhism* (Abingdon and New York: Routledge, 2012).

—— *Tantric Revisionings: New Understandings of Tibetan Buddhism and Indian Religions* (Delhi: Motilal Barnasidass, 2005).

Sanders, E. P., *The Historical Figure of Jesus* (London: Penguin, 1993).

Saraswati, Swami Dayananda, *Light of Truth: Or an English Translation of the Satyarth Prakash,* tr. Chiranjiva Bharadwaja, new edn (New Delhi: Sarvadeshik Arya Pratinidhi Sabha, 1975).

Sarma, Deepak, *An Introduction to Mādhva Vedānta* (Aldershot: Ashgate, 2003).

—— *Classical Indian Philosophy* (New York: Columbia University Press, 2011).

Savarkar, Vinayak Damodar, *Hindutva* (New Delhi: Hindi Sahitya Sadan, 2003).

Scheuer, Jacques, and Denis Gira, *Vivre de plusieurs religions: Promesse ou illusion?* (Paris: Les Éditions de l'Atelier, 2000).

Schmid, Alex P., 'Frameworks for Conceptualizing Terrorism', *Terrorism and Political Violence,* 16/2 (2004), 197–221.

Schmidt-Leukel, Perry (ed.), *War and Peace in World Religions* (London: SCM Press, 2004).

—— (ed.), *Buddhism, Christianity and the Question of Creation: Karmic or Divine* (Aldershot: Ashgate, 2006).

—— (ed.), *Buddhist Attitudes to Other Religions* (St Ottilien: EOS, 2008).

—— 'Pluralist Theologies', *The Expository Times,* 122/2 (2010), 53–72.

—— *Transformation by Integration. How Inter-faith Encounter Changes Christianity* (London: SCM Press, 2009).

—— Gerhard Köberlin, and Josef Götz (eds), *Buddhist Perceptions of Jesus* (St Ottilien: EOS, 2001).

Schütz, A. (ed.), *Nijh* (The Hague: Nijhof, 1972).

Scott, David, 'Christian Responses to Buddhism in Pre-Medieval Times', *Numen,* 32/1 (1985), 88–100.

Seager, R. M., *The World's Parliament of Religions: The East–West Encounter, Chicago, 1893* (Indianapolis: Indiana University Press, 1995).

Segal, Robert, 'All Generalisations are Bad: Postmodernism on Theories', *Journal of the American Academy of Religion,* 74/1 (2006), 157–71.

Sen, Amartya, *The Argumentative Indian: Writings on Indian History, Culture, and Identity* (New York: Picador, 2006).

Senanayake, Darini Rajasingham, *Buddhism and the Legitimation of Power: Democracy, Public Religion and Minorities in Sri Lanka* (Singapore: National University of Singapore Institute of South Asian Studies, 2009).

Seyfort Ruegg, David, *The Symbiosis of Buddhism and Brahmanism/Hinduism in South Asia and of Buddhism with 'Local Cults' in Tibet and the Himalayan Region* (Vienna: Osterreichische Akademie der Wissenschaften, 2008).

Shah-Kazemi, Reza, *Common Ground between Islam and Buddhism* (Louisville, Ky.: Fons Vitae, 2010).

—— *The Other in the Light of the One: The Universality of the Qur'ān and Interfaith Dialogue* (Cambridge: Islamic Texts Society, 2006).

Shāntideva, *The Way of the Bodhisattva,* 2nd rev. edn (Boston, Mass.: Shambhala Publications, 2011).

Sharma, Arvind, 'The Meaning and Goals of Interreligious Dialogue', *Journal of Dharma,* 8 (1983), 225–47.

—— *Hinduism for our Times* (New York: Oxford University Press, 1997).

—— (ed.), *Hinduism and Secularism: After Ayodhya* (New York: Palgrave, 2001).

Sharp, Andrew Martin, *Eastern Orthodox Theological and Ecclesiological Thought on Islam and Christian–Muslim Relations in the Contemporary World (1975–2008)* (Leiden: Brill, 2012).

Sharpe, Eric, *Faith Meets Faith: Some Christian Attitudes to Hinduism in the Nineteenth and Twentieth Centuries* (London: SCM, 1977).

—— *Comparative Religion: A History,* 2nd edn (London: Duckworth, 1986).

Shinozaki, Michio T., 'The Thought of the Lotus Sutra as a Philosophy of Integration', *World Faiths Encounter,* 19 (Mar. 1998), 26–38.

Siddiqui, A., (ed.), *Ismail Raji al-Faruqi, Islam and Other Faiths* (Leicester: Islamic Foundation, 1998).

—— (ed.), *A Muslim View of Christianity* (Maryknoll, NY: Orbis Books, 2007).

Siddiqui, Mona (ed.), *The Routledge Reader in Christian–Muslim Relations* (Abingdon: Routledge, 2013).

Silva, K. M. de (ed.), *The History of Sri Lanka*, ii (Delhi: Oxford University Press, 1981).

Simpson, B., and R. Weyl, *The International Council of Christians and Jews* (Heppenheim: ICCJ, 1988).

Sisk, Timothy D. (ed.), *Between Terror and Tolerance: Religious Leaders, Conflict, and Peacemaking* (Washington, DC: Georgetown University Press, 2011).

Sivaraksa, S., *Conflict, Culture, Change: Engaged Buddhism in a Globalizing World* (Boston: Wisdom Publications, 2005).

Smart, Ninian, *The World's Religions* (Cambridge: Cambridge University Press, 1998).

—— *Buddhism and Christianity: Rivals and Allies* (Basingstoke: Macmillan, 1993).

Smith, J. Z., *Relating Religion: Essays in the Study of Religion* (Chicago: University of Chicago Press, 2004).

Smith, Mark S., *God in Translation: Deities in Cross-Cultural Discourse in the Biblical World* (Tübingen: J. C. B. Mohr, 2008).

Smith, Wilfred Cantwell, *Towards a World Theology* (Maryknoll, NY: Orbis Books, 1989).

Smock, David R. (ed.), *Religious Contributions to Peacemaking: When Religion Brings Peace, Not War* (Washington, DC: United States Institute of Peace, 2006).

Sperber, Jutta, *Christians and Muslims: The Dialogue Activities of the World Council of Churches and their Theological Foundation* (Berlin and New York: De Gruyter, 2000).

Stackhouse, J. G. (ed.), *No Other Gods Before Me? Evangelicals and the Challenge of World Religions* (Grand Rapids, Mich.: Baker Academic, 2001).

Strange, Daniel, *The Possibility of Salvation among the Unevangelised* (Carlisle: Paternoster Press, 2002).

Strathern, Alan, *Kingship and Conversion in Sixteenth Century Sri Lanka: Portuguese Imperialism in a Buddhist Land* (Cambridge: Cambridge University Press, 2010).

Subramuniyaswami, Satguru Sivaya, *Dancing with Shiva: Hinduism's Contemporary Catechism* (Kauai, Hawaii: Himalayan Academy, 1997).

Sugirtharajah, Sharada, *Imagining Hinduism: A Postcolonial Perspective* (London: Routledge, 2003).

Sullivan, Francis A., *Salvation Outside the Church? Tracing the History of the Catholic Response* (Eugene, Or.: Wipf & Stock, 2002).

Sundermeier, T., 'Grundlagen und Voraussetzungen für das interreligiöse Gespräch', *Ökumenische Rundschau*, 49 (2000), 318–31.

Swearer, Donald (ed.), *Me and Mine: Selected Essays of Bhikkhu Buddhadāsa* (New York: SUNY, 1989).

Swidler, L., *After the Absolute: The Dialogical Future of Religious Reflection* (Minneapolis: Fortress, 1990).

—— and Paul Mojzes (eds), *The Uniqueness of Jesus: A Dialogue with Paul F. Knitter* (Maryknoll, NY: Orbis Books, 1997).

—— J. Cobb, P. Knitter, and M. K. Hellwig (eds), *Death or Dialogue: From the Age of Monologue to the Age of Dialogue* (Philadelphia: Trinity Press International, 1990).

Tambiah, Stanley J., *Buddhism and the Spirit Cults of North-East Thailand* (Cambridge: Cambridge University Press, 1975).

Tambiah, Stanley J., *Buddhism Betrayed? Religion, Politics and Violence in Sri Lanka* (Chicago: University of Chicago Press, 1992).

Taylor, J. H., and G. Gebhardt (eds), *Religions for Human Dignity* (Geneva: World Conference on Religion and Peace, 1986).

Taylor, J. V., *The Go-Between God* (London: SCM Press, 1972).

Thatamanil, John, *The Immanent Divine* (Minneapolis: Fortress Press, 2006).

Thelle, Notto R., *Buddhism and Christianity in Japan: From Conflict to Dialogue 1854–1899* (Honolulu: University of Hawaii Press, 1987).

Theunissen, Michael, *The Other: Studies in the Social Ontology of Husserl, Heidegger, Sartre and Buber* (Cambridge, Mass.: MIT Press, 1984).

Thomas, D., 'Abū 'Īsā al-Warrāq and the History of Religions', *Journal of Semitic Studies*, 41 (1996), 275–90.

——*Early Muslim Polemic against Christianity: Abū 'Īsā al-Warrāq's 'Against the Incarnation'* (Cambridge: Cambridge University Press, 2002).

Thomas, M. M., *Towards a Wider Ecumenism* (Bangalore: Asian Trading Co., 1993).

Thompson, George (tr.), *Bhagavad Gītā* (New York: North Point Press, 2008).

Tibi, Bassam, *The Challenge of Fundamentalism: Political Islam and the New World Disorder* (Berkeley, Calif.: University of California Press, 2002).

Todorov, Tsvetan, *Mikhail Bhaktin: The Dialogical Principle* (Minneapolis: University of Minnesota Press, 1984).

Tsultrim, Karma Pema, 'Comments on the Exchange Program with Tibetans and the American MID', *DIM/MID International Bulletin*, E4 (1997), 14–15.

Turner, Brian S. (ed.) *Religious Diversity and Civil Society: A Comparative Analysis* (Oxford: Bardwell Press, 2008).

Ucko, Hans (ed.), *Changing the Present, Dreaming the Future: A Critical Moment in Interreligious Dialogue* (Geneva: WCC, 2006).

Veitch, James, 'Terrorism and Religion', *Stimulus*, 10/1 (2002), 26–37.

Vermes, Geza, *The Changing Faces of Jesus* (London: Penguin, 2000).

——*Jesus the Jew* (London: Collins, 1973; SCM Press, 2001).

Victoria, Brian, *Zen at War*, 2nd edn (Lanham, Md.: Rowman & Littlefield, 2006).

Vincent, Joan (ed.), *The Anthropology of Politics: A Reader in Ethnography, Theory and Critique* (Malden, Mass., and Oxford: Blackwell, 2002).

Vishanoff, David R., 'Why do the Nations Rage? Boundaries of Canon and Community in a Muslim's Rewriting of Psalm 2', *Comparative Islamic Studies*, 6 (2010), 151–79.

——'An Imagined Book Gets a New Text: Psalms of the Muslim David', *Islam and Christian–Muslim Relations*, 22 (2011), 85–99.

Visser t'Hooft, W. A., *No Other Name: The Choice between Syncretism and Christian Universalism* (London: SCM Press, 1963).

Vivekananda, Swami, *Complete Works* (Kolkata: Advaita Ashrama, 1989).

Voss Roberts, Michelle, 'Religious Belonging and the Multiple', *Journal of Feminist Studies in Religion*, 26 (2010), 43–62.

Vrajaprana, Pravrajika, *Vedanta: A Simple Introduction* (Hollywood, Calif.: Vedanta Press, 1999).

Vroom, H., *Religions and the Truth: Philosophical Reflections and Perspectives* (Grand Rapids, Mich., and Amsterdam: Eerdmans/Rodopi, 1989).

Waardenburg, J., *Muslims and Others: Relations in Context* (Berlin: De Gruyter, 2003).

Walbridge, Linda, *Christians of Pakistan: The Passion of Bishop John Joseph* (New York: Routledge, 2002).

Wallace, Vesna A., *The Inner Kālacakratantra: A Buddhist Tantric View of the Individual* (New York: Oxford University Press, 2001).

Walsh, Maurice (tr.), *The Long Discourses of the Buddha* (Boston: Wisdom, 1995).

Walshe, M. O'C., 'Buddhism and Christianity: A Positive Approach—with Some Notes on Judaism', *Dialogue*, NS 9/1–3 (1982), 3–39.

Walters, Albert, *We Believe in One God? Reflections on the Trinity in the Malaysian Context* (New Delhi: ISPCK, 2002).

—— 'Issues in Christian–Muslim Relations: A Malaysian Christian Perspective', *Islam and Christian–Muslim Relations*, 18/1 (2007), 67–83.

Warrier, Maya, and Simon Oliver (eds), *Theology and Religious Studies: An Exploration of Disciplinary Boundaries* (London: T&T Clark, 2008).

Watson, Burton (tr.), *The Lotus Sutra* (New York: Columbia University Press, 1993).

Wei-hsun Fu, Charles, and Gerhard E. Spiegler (eds), *Religious Issues and Interreligious Dialogues* (New York: Greenwood Press, 1989).

Weinberg, Leonard, and Ami Pedahzur (eds), *Religious Fundamentalism and Political Extremism* (Portland, Or.: Frank Cass, 2004).

Weller, C. (ed.), *World Fellowship: Addresses and Message by Leading Spokesmen of All Faiths, Races and Countries* (New York: Liversight Publishing Corporation, 1936).

Weller, Paul, ' "Inheritors Together": The Interfaith Network for the United Kingdom', *Discernment: A Christian Journal of Inter-Religious Encounter*, 3/2 (1988), 30–4.

—— 'Inter-Faith Roots and Shoots: An Outlook for the 1990s', *World Faiths Encounter*, 1 (1992), 48–57.

—— (ed.), *Religions in the UK: A Multi-Faith Directory* (Derby: University of Derby in association with the Inter Faith Network for the UK, 1993 and 1997).

—— 'The Inter Faith Network for the United Kingdom', *The Anglo-Indian Historical Review: A Journal of History*, 20/1 (1994), 20–6.

—— *Time for a Change: Reconfiguring Religion, State and Society* (London: T&T Clark, 1995).

—— (ed.), *Religions in the UK: Directory, 2001–03* (Derby: Multi-Faith Centre at the University of Derby in association with the Inter Faith Network for the UK, 2001).

—— (ed.), *Religions in the UK: Directory, 2007–10* (Derby: Multi-Faith Centre at the University of Derby, in association with the University of Derby, 2007).

—— *Religious Diversity in the UK: Contours and Issues* (London: Continuum, 2008).

—— *A Mirror for our Times: 'The Rushdie Affair' and the Future of Multiculturalism* (London: Continuum, 2009).

Williams, Paul, with Anthony Tribe and Alexander Wynne, *Buddhist Thought: A Complete Introduction to the Indian Tradition*, 2nd edn (London and New York: Routledge, 2012).

Williamson, Lola, *Transcendent in America* (New York: New York University Press, 2010).

Wilson, Frederick R. (ed.), *The San Antonio Report: Your Will Be Done. Mission in Christ's Way* (Geneva: WCC, 1990).

Wingate, Andrew, *The Church and Conversion: A Study of Recent Conversions to and from Christianity in the Tamil Area of South India* (New Delhi: ISPCK, 1997).

World Council of Churches, *Dialogue between Men of Living Faiths: The Ajaltoun Memorandum* (Geneva: World Council of Churches Publications, 1970).

World Council of Churches, *Guidelines on Dialogue with People of Living Faiths and Ideologies* (Geneva: World Council of Churches Publications, 1979).

—— *Ecumenical Considerations for Dialogue and Relations with People of Other Religions* (Geneva: WCC, 2004).

Wüstenfeld, F. (ed.), Ibn Isḥāq/Ibn Hishām, *Sīrat rasūl Allāh* (Göttingen: J. B. Metzler, 1859–60).

Wuthnow, Robert, *America and the Challenges of Religious Diversity* (Princeton: Princeton University Press, 2005).

Wyschogrod, E., *An Ethics of Remembering: History, Heterology, and the Nameless Others* (Chicago: University of Chicago Press, 1998).

Wyschogrod, M., 'Faith and the Holocaust', *Judaism*, 20 (1971), 286–94.

Yaḥyā, ʿUthmān Ibn ʿArabī (ed.), *Al-futūḥāt al-makkiyya* (Cairo: al-Hayʾa al-Miṣriyya al-ʿĀmma li-l-Kitāb, 1972–91).

Yang, Fenggang, and Helen Rose Ebaugh, 'Transformations in New Immigrant Religions and Their Global Implications', *American Sociological Review*, 66 (2001), 269–88.

Yates, G. (ed.), *In Spirit and in Truth: Aspects of Judaism and Christianity: A Symposium* (London: Hodder & Stoughton, 1934).

Young, R. F., and G. S. B. Senanayake, *The Carpenter Heretic: A Collection of Buddhist Stories about Christianity from 18th Century Sri Lanka* (Colombo: Karunaratne & Sons, 1998).

—— and G. P. V. Somaratne, *Vain Debates: The Buddhist–Christian Controversies in Nineteenth Century Ceylon* (Vienna: Publications of the De Nobili Research Library, 23, 1996).

Zartman, I. William, and J. Lewis Rasmussen (eds), *Peacemaking in International Conflict: Methods and Techniques* (Washington, DC: United States Institute of Peace Press, 1997).

Zevit, Ziony, *The Religions of Ancient Israel* (London and New York: Continuum, 2003).

Zwilling, Leonard (ed.) with Michael J. Sweet (tr.), *The Mission to Tibet: The Extraordinary Eighteenth Century Account of Father Ippolito Desideri, s.j.* (Boston: Wisdom Publications, 2010).

INDEX